PRINCETONIANS
1791–1794

PRINCETONIANS

=== 1791–1794 ===

A BIOGRAPHICAL
DICTIONARY

By J. JEFFERSON LOONEY AND

RUTH L. WOODWARD

PRINCETON UNIVERSITY PRESS
PRINCETON, NEW JERSEY
1991

Library of Congress Cataloging-in-Publication Data
(Revised for vol. 4-5)

Princetonians: a biographical dictionary

Includes bibliographical references and indexes.
Contents: [1st] 1748-1768 / by James McLachlan—[etc.]—[4th]
1784-1790 / by Ruth L. Woodward and Wesley Frank Craven—
[5th] 1791-1794 / by J. Jefferson Looney and Ruth L. Woodward.
1. Princeton University—Alumni—Biography—Dictionaries. I.
McLachlan, James, 1932- . II. Harrison, Richard A., 1945-
III. Title.
LD4601.P75 1976   378.749'67   81-47074
ISBN 0-691-04639-5 (v. 1: alk. paper)
ISBN 0-691-04772-3 (v. 5: alk. paper)

Publication of this book has been aided by grants from
the New Jersey Committee for the Humanities
the New Jersey Historical Commission
the National Endowment for the Humanities

This book has been composed in Baskerville

Princeton University Press books are printed on
acid-free paper, and meet the guidelines for permanence
and durability of the Committee on Production Guidelines for
Book Longevity of the Council on Library Resources

Printed in the United States of America
by Princeton University Press, Princeton, New Jersey

10 9 8 7 6 5 4 3 2 1

President John Witherspoon
BY CHARLES WILLSON PEALE

CONTENTS

LIST OF ILLUSTRATIONS

PREFACE

THIS volume, the last in the *Princetonians* series, contains brief biographies of the 164 students who attended the College of New Jersey with the classes of 1791 through 1794. An appendix adds four more that properly belong in earlier volumes, but proof that these men attended the College has only now come to light. Altogether the five volumes of *Princetonians* include 1,032 biographies.

Less than two months after commencement in 1794, John Witherspoon died quietly at "Tusculum," his mansion about a mile north of the campus. In 1791 he remarried at the age of 68, and undergraduates used the occasion to extort from him a three-day holiday from their studies. Apart from his ability to distinguish light from dark, Witherspoon was totally blind during the last two or three years of his life, but he engaged a distant relative, John Ramsey Witherspoon (A.B. 1794), to read and write for him. A man who had always refused to speak from notes, President Witherspoon continued to lecture to the seniors on moral philosophy, eloquence, and "chronology"—a recasting of ancient history that, in his version, put Israel, rather than Greece or Rome, at the center of the story. As America's most influential college president for his generation, he had shaped policy at Nassau Hall for a quarter of a century, signed the Declaration of Independence as a member of Congress, and helped to reorganize the Presbyterian Church after the war. He also turned loose upon the world a band of extremely influential alumni. In the two or three decades after his death, his successors could not easily sustain the dedication to Christian values and republican imperatives that had seemed a natural combination to the "old doctor," as students now called this extraordinary immigrant from Scotland. The end of the Witherspoon era is a fitting place to conclude this dictionary.

This volume was planned by the late Wesley Frank Craven on the same basis as its immediate predecessor. The two share a common introductory essay, and the staff owes debts of gratitude to the same people and institutions. The donors to the Wesley Frank Craven Memorial Fund, all of whom are listed on the dedication page of *Princetonians, 1784-1790*, also provided support for this volume. When completion of the dictionary ran beyond the three-year period originally calculated for it, the following benefactors provided enough financial support to see the project through: Presidents William G. Bowen and Harold T. Shapiro; Provosts Neil L. Rudenstine and Paul Benacerraf; Deans of the Faculty Aaron Lemonick and Robert C. Gunning; History Department Chairmen Cyril E. Black (now deceased), Robert L. Tignor, and Daniel T. Rodgers; and Lawrence Stone and Natalie Zemon Davis, directors of the Shelby Cullom Davis Center for Historical Studies. Generous subventions from the New Jersey Committee for the Humanities, the New Jersey Historical Commission, and the National Endowment for the Humanities have made it possible for Princeton University Press to publish this volume. We are particularly grateful to Paul A. Stellhorn, Richard L. Waldron, and Howard L. Green for their advice and encouragement in this process. The manuscript repositories to whom we are endebted are listed in the previous volume. Mary R. Murrin has carefully proofread the entire manuscript. At Princeton University Press, Gail Ullman, Julie Marvin, Bill Laznovsky, and Lynne Haggard have been wonderfully supportive. The individual authors wish to thank the editorial committee for saving them from numerous errors, but they accept responsibility for any that remain.

The main contrast between this volume and the fourth is in authorship. J. Jefferson Looney mastered his responsibilities as a research assistant very quickly and moved on to become a resourceful coauthor. He and Ruth L. Woodward have done nearly all of the writing for this volume. Their loyalty to the project and determination to complete it even when funding seemed precarious deserve the highest accolades. The editorial structure of this volume, however, has remained unchanged from the system set up for its predecessor. We also used the same typesetting technology and again wish to thank John Catanzariti, director and editor of the Papers of Thomas Jefferson, for his cooperation.

This volume includes several appendices not found in the previous four. Appendix A contains biographies of four men whose presence in pre-1784 classes has been demonstrated only after publication of the first three volumes. One inquirer urged us to add David Brearly to this group. A chief justice of New Jersey and member of the Constitutional Convention of 1787, Brearly was a distinguished man whom Princeton University would love to claim as an alumnus. Unfortunately, although several standard sources declare that he attended the College, we have found no contemporary verification of his presence. In Appendix B, J. Jefferson Looney has contributed a note on the connection between a master's degree and preparation for a learned profession. His findings, we suspect, may be relevant to other institutions besides the College of New Jersey. Appendix D is Ruth L. Woodward's list of additions and errata for the first three volumes that turned up while conducting research for the fourth and fifth.

Through the generosity of an anonymous donor, the University
retained Ruth L. Woodward from 1986 to 1990 to continue her study
of Princetonians, concentrating on the classes of 1795 through 1802.
Although no publication of this material is under contemplation, her
biographies of later students have helped to resolve some knotty
points about men included in the fourth and fifth volumes of this
series. Her lives of these men are being placed in the alumni files in
the University Archives where future researchers can consult them.

John M. Murrin
October 1990

Sketches are signed as follows:

WFC	Wesley Frank Craven
JJL	J. Jefferson Looney
JMM	John M. Murrin
LKS	Linda K. Salvucci
RLW	Ruth L. Woodward

INTRODUCTION

BY JOHN M. MURRIN

EVEN after the American War for Independence ended victoriously in 1783, the Revolution continued its profound impact upon the lives of Princetonians. It affected everything from the physical condition of the College to the size of the faculty, the regional balance of the student body, the career choices of alumni, and—most vividly—the memories and experiences that both students and faculty brought with them.

The significance of American independence saturated undergraduate oratory, especially when the French Revolution convinced many onlookers that what had started in Britain's distant colonies was about to sweep across the entire world. Liberty, declared Nathaniel Cabot Higginson (A.B. 1787) in an address which he prepared and John Henry Hobart (A.B. 1793) delivered at Nassau Hall on the Fourth of July in 1793, "will not do her work by halves. She will continue to knock at the doors of those sleeping tyrants of the East, 'till she rouses them from the delusive dream of security & breaks forever the spell of arbitrary power." On another occasion Hobart, a future Episcopal bishop, wondered at the "series of fortunate events, which ... fall little short of miraculous, [that] appeared to aid the cause of freedom" after the fighting began in 1775. For him the Federal Constitution inspired even greater awe. At a time when no public figure had yet formulated a coherent idea of an unbreakable American union, this college senior proclaimed that "The strength of [the Constitution's] pillars promises a perpetual duration." John Bradford Wallace (A.B. 1794) redefined "enthusiasm" as "that ardor of soul ... which fired the bosoms of our countrymen and blazed so high" at the outset of the Revolution. Most of his elders still reserved the word for popular delusions and madness. Wallace saw in the French Revolution "a scene perhaps the most astonishing that has been exhibited since the morning of the creation," a rather awkward position for a student to affirm at Nassau Hall, if only because he seemed willing to let events in France exceed even the Redemption in overall significance. As a high Federalist a few years later, he probably regretted some of these pronouncements.[1]

[1] An earlier version of this essay appeared as "Christianity, Enlightenment, and Revolution: Hard Choices at the College of New Jersey after Independence," *Princeton University Library Chronicle* (hereafter, *PUL Chron.*), 50 (1988-1989), 221-61 .

See Nathaniel Cabot Higginson, "The Cause of Freedom" (July 4, 1793), 1 (MS in

Wallace's exuberance was hardly confined to the campus. By 1793 both the College and the community of Princeton were awash in euphoria over the French Revolution, which was widely seen as in some way an extension and fulfillment of its American predecessor. In mid-January, reported a local informant, "a very respectable meeting of inhabitants of this town and neighbourhood" celebrated "the prosperity of the Republic of France" with fifteen toasts, no doubt one for every state in the Union, which by then included Kentucky and Vermont. "May the memory of every *little* and *great* despot from Nimrod down to the present day, be held in everlasting abhorrence," proclaimed one offering. "The colonies of South America: May they become happy and free as we are," proposed another. "The millenium of universal liberty, peace, and virtue" raised everyone's glasses once more. After also saluting the marquis de Lafayette (then in Hapsburg confinement) and the people and government of the United States, the gathering offered a final oblation to "THE COLLEGE of NEW-JERSEY, and the general interests of science and religion."[2]

July brought still greater excitement, beginning with a grand ball of collegians and young ladies on Independence Day and followed by an equally magnificent celebration of Bastille Day on July 14. "The illumination of the college was really beautiful," reported a Miss S. S. Gibson to her friend Elizabeth Meredith. "It is a long range of buildings & in every window was placed a great many lights. Over the door in the middle of this building was a fine transparency of the American & French colours in the form of arms. Round the French flag was the American stars throwing the first gleam of light on the nation & under it was written Liberty Throughout the World." In the evening forty-eight "gentlemen" (most of them undoubtedly students from the College), twenty-four young women from the area, and several musicians and other visitors from Philadelphia began dancing at a local tavern at 8 p.m. After three hours they moved upstairs for an elegant supper during which "two of the gentlemen sang us the Marseilles Hymn most enchantingly." A patriotic toast, according to Miss Gibson, almost brought "the room ... down with the stamping and clapping." At midnight the guests resumed their dancing, and

---

John Henry Hobart Papers, Archives of the Episcopal Church, U.S.A., Austin, Texas); Hobart, "Oration on the Past Blessings and Future Prospects of America" (1792), 4, 5 (MS in same); John Bradford Wallace, "Enthusiasm: An Oration Delivered at Princeton College, July 4, 1792," 1 (MS in Wallace Family Papers, Historical Society of Pennsylvania); Wallace, "Arbitrary Imprisonments: An Oration delivered at Princeton College, March 1792," 49 (MS in same). Cf., Kenneth M. Stampp, "The Concept of a Perpetual Union," in his *The Imperiled Union: Essays on the Background of the Civil War* (New York, 1980), 3-36.

[2] Philadelphia *National Gazette*, 26 Jan 1793.

they finally went home or back to their College rooms around 2:30 a.m.[3]

Perhaps the most remarkable feature about this celebration was when it happened. In 1793 Bastille Day fell on a Sunday when, according to College regulations, students were supposed to attend divine service and otherwise spend the day studying Scripture, a catechism, or other religious materials, perhaps broken only by a meditative stroll. With the full complicity of such staunch Presbyterians as President John Witherspoon, the French Revolution was quite actively undermining the Protestant sabbath in the very bowels of the College of New Jersey.

Of course, much like undergraduates of the twentieth century, those of the 1780s at typical moments worried less about the cosmic issues of the day than about examinations, which made them very nervous. "Our examination begins today, my heart already palpitates," confessed James Gibson (A.B. 1787) on September 18, 1786. "Euclid is wished into non existence by many." Students also complained endlessly about their meals and found frequent diversions. Some enjoyed the indoor game of battledores, mostly in winter months. Many tried the outdoor sport of "baste ball," probably some form of rounders or cricket, which John Rhea Smith (A.B. 1787) played "in the campus" (a new word first appearing in Princeton sources in 1775) but was beaten, "for I miss both catching and striking the Ball." An unamused faculty sourly prohibited the game in November 1787 as an exercise "unbecoming gentlemen & students" and "attended with great danger to the health by sudden and alternate heats and colds as it tends by accidents almost unavoidable in that play to disfiguring and maiming those who are engaged in it." Excitement took many other forms. "There was a rumour that the Devile was seen in college wrapt up in a white sheet," reported one diarist in 1786. "I did not see him."[4]

However, the Revolution overshadowed even these pressing teenage concerns. Members of the Class of 1784 were attending the summer term of 1783 when Congress, in flight from protesting soldiers in Philadelphia, moved to Princeton and established itself at

---

[3] S. S. Gibson to Elizabeth Meredith, 18 July 1793, in *Princeton Alumni Weekly* (3 Nov 1915), 133 (punctuation modernized).

[4] According to the *Oxford English Dictionary*, battledores was a game played with small racquets and a shuttlecock. James Gibson mentions it frequently in the opening pages of his diary for 1786 (Historical Society of Pennsylvania, microfilm at Princeton University Library); for the devil, see 9 Feb. For "baste ball," see Ruth L. Woodward, ed., "Journal at Nassau Hall: The Diary of John Rhea Smith, 1786," *PUL Chron.*, 46 (1985), 286-87. For the broad impact of the Revolution on the College, see Mark A. Noll, *Princeton and the Republic 1768-1822: The Search for a Christian Enlightenment* (Princeton, 1989).

the College from June 26 to November 4. As Charles Thomson, secretary to Congress since 1774, entered Nassau Hall for the first time, he "passed by the chambers of the students, from whence in the sultry heat of the day issued warm steams from the beds, foul linen & dirty lodgings of the boys." (Indeed, in 1786 one student recorded on July 17 that he "went to the Brook and Bathed for the first time this session," which had begun in early May.)[5] "I found the members [of Congress]," Thomson continued, "extremely out of humour and dissatisfied with their situation." But the sojourn of Congress at Princeton, which Thomson saw as an ominous threat to the Union, undoubtedly seemed much more exciting to the students. They watched respectfully as College Trustee Elias Boudinot, then the president of Congress, and half a dozen alumni, led by Virginia delegate James Madison (A.B. 1771), helped to decide the future of the young republic. The collegians celebrated July 4 with the leaders of the nation. Some of the students may even have heard Congressman David Howell (A.B. 1766) suggest that Princeton become the permanent capital of the United States. In September Gen. George Washington, already a legend, attended the most impressive commencement ceremony the College had yet held, and Nassau Hall soon received his portrait by Charles Willson Peale. The glorious news of the signing of the definitive Peace of Paris reached Congress at Princeton during fall intersession on October 31, thus confirming the independence of the United States. Recollections of these events remained alive at the College well into the 1780s, if only because some of the boys who witnessed them while attending the Nassau Hall grammar school did not complete their Princeton studies for many more years. Even later students who had no direct link to the events of 1783 could see and feel effects of the Revolution every day in the battle damage that still disfigured Nassau Hall.[6]

Above all, the Revolution remained a palpable experience in the lives of most members of the College community. Many associations were pleasant and heroic. Joseph Caldwell (A.B. 1791), who was only ten when the war ended, vividly remembered for the rest of his life his childhood encounters with the "marching of troops, a circumstance which I always hurried out to gaze on with sensations

---

[5] In the 1780s few Americans washed the entire body at a single time more than once a year, if that often. This student was probably going for a swim, but while not every bath involved swimming, virtually all swimming was also a bath. See Richard L. Bushman and Claudia L. Bushman, "The Early History of Cleanliness in America," *Journal of American History*, 74 (1987-1988), 1213-38.

[6] Eugene R. Sheridan and John M. Murrin, eds., *Congress at Princeton, Being the Letters of Charles Thomson and Hannah Thomson, June-October 1783* (Princeton, 1985), esp. 5-6, 14, 16, 45; Gibson Diary, 17 July 1786.

rising almost to transport; the fife's shrill and piercing notes, stirring into reckless activity emotions of which I had scarcely known myself capable; the drum rattling into madness every impetuous feeling that thrilled along the nerves or swelled in the heart."[7] Maturin Livingston (A.B. 1786), who saw part of the Battle of Princeton as a boy, enjoyed giving fellow students an expert tour of the site. No doubt anecdotes and tales of heroism and suffering flew fast over meals and at other times of relaxation. Students who heard John Witherspoon preach without notes on Sunday, or seniors who listened to his lectures on moral philosophy, saw not only America's most famous educator and the nation's most prestigious Presbyterian divine, but also a Signer of the Declaration of Independence who had served in Congress for most of the war. James Morris (A.B. 1784) and Henry Clymer (A.B. 1786) were sons of Signers. So were three graduates of the Class of 1787, which celebrated its commencement nine days after the Constitutional Convention finished its work forty miles away in Philadelphia—Meredith Clymer, John Read and Lucius Horatio Stockton. The father of George Willing (A.B. 1792), by contrast, had refused to sign.

Other memories could not easily be sentimentalized. Most of South Carolina's large student contingent had had to endure a period of exile and family dislocation after the British overran the state in 1780. William J. Lewis (Class of 1788) fought against Britain's toughest counterinsurgency commander, Banastre Tarleton. John Wells (A.B. 1788) endured a still greater horror when most of his family was massacred during the war. The mother of John P. Ryers (A.B. 1792) reportedly died of fright when she heard that the enemy had landed on Staten Island in 1776. Robert G. Johnson (A.B. 1790) was held captive as a small boy by a band notorious for slaughtering women and children. At age fifteen Nathaniel B. Boileau (A.B. 1789) saw the results of one of the most vicious atrocities of the war. Memory of it doubtless intensified his lifelong anglophobia. In an action that occurred partly on his father's Pennsylvania farm, British soldiers threw wounded American militiamen onto buckwheat straw in May 1778, set it ablaze, and burned them alive. Silas Wood (A.B. 1789) grew up on Long Island under British occupation, and forty years after the event he still recalled with bitterness how a famous loyalist officer had desecrated the Huntington cemetery. By contrast, the family of David and William A. Hosack (A.B. 1789 and 1792) was probably loyalist or neutralist, much like the family of the woman whom future Bishop Hobart married.

[7] Joseph Caldwell, "Autobiography," *North Carolina University Magazine*, 9 (1859), 9.

Only toward the end of the collegiate period covered in these biographies were students beginning to appear at Princeton who were too young to remember the war. Henry Knox Kollock (A.B. 1794) was only two years old when the British surrendered at Yorktown, and perhaps that is why his parents named him for a patriot general. James Gildersleeve Force of the Class of 1794 was probably the last revolutionary veteran to enter the College. By the late 1790s the Revolution would be a heritage, not a memory, for nearly all students.

The war's physical presence remained powerful. The British occupation, an American bombardment in January 1777, and the subsequent American garrisoning of the College severely damaged Nassau Hall. When Gov. William Livingston tried to help in 1779 by lending Witherspoon a group of prisoners of war to provide labor for repairs, several residents of Princeton found these outsiders so menacing that they petitioned the state to have them removed. Livingston finally instructed Witherspoon to send all but ten of the men back into conventional captivity, despite Witherspoon's assurance that they were no danger to anyone and that some even planned to remain in America after the war. Thus when Ashbel Green (A.B. 1783) entered as a junior, the two top floors of Nassau Hall were still unusable, and parts of the lower floors remained strewn with debris. The College library that Witherspoon had energetically collected had been scattered. The armies had nearly wrecked the marvelous orrery (the eighteenth-century predecessor of a modern planetarium) that David Rittenhouse had built and donated to the College, and they had destroyed fences and trees throughout the area. As late as 1784, students had to endure shortages of firewood and candles.[8]

Improvement came slowly. The third floor was again in use by 1784, but the trustees could not afford to repair the roof until 1791, fourteen years after the Battle of Princeton. Travelers in the mid-1790s still remarked on the building's deteriorated condition. A British visitor in July 1796 thought that Nassau Hall "better deserves the title of a grammar school than a college." He described the library as "most wretched, consisting, for the most part, of old theological books, not even arranged with any regularity." The orrery was again

[8] Larry Gerlach, ed., *New Jersey in the American Revolution, 1763-1783: A Documentary History* (Trenton, N.J., 1975), 299; William Livingston to Jacob Bergen, 19 Nov 1779; Livingston to John Witherspoon, 15 Dec 1779, in Carl E. Prince et al., eds., *The Papers of William Livingston* (Trenton and New Brunswick, N.J., 1979-1988), III, 224-25, 268-69; Ashbel Green, *The Life of the Revd John Witherspoon, D.D., LL.D., with a Brief Review of his Writings: and a Summary Estimate of his Character and Talents*, ed. Henry Lyttleton Savage (Princeton, 1973), 194-95n; Howard C. Rice, Jr., *The Rittenhouse Orrery: Princeton's Eighteenth-Century Planetarium, 1767-1954* (Princeton, 1954); "Princeton in 1784: The Diary of James W. Wilkin of the Class of 1785," *PUL Chron.*, 12 (1950-1951), 60-63.

"quite out of repair." The rest of the science collection consisted chiefly of "a couple of stuffed alligators, and a few singular fishes, in a miserable state of preservation, the skins of them being tattered in innumerable places from their being repeatedly tossed about." A French visitor agreed and also noted the sad condition of the campus's outer walls and objected to the animal dung in the yard. Not until the rebuilding after the fire of 1802 would Nassau Hall again return to its impressive prewar condition.[9]

One of the few things that the Revolution did not change was the Princeton curriculum, a rather surprising fact in light of what was happening elsewhere. From England came Richard Price's assurance that the creation of the American republic "makes a new opening in human affairs which may prove an introduction to times of more light and liberty and virtue than have yet been known." Benjamin Rush (A.B. 1760)—father of John Rush (Class of 1794), Richard Rush (A.B. 1797), and James Rush (A.B. 1805)—agreed and called for "a revolution in our principles, opinions, and manners, so as to accomodate them to the forms of government we have adopted." Proposals for educational reform proliferated everywhere and generated several calls for a national university at the seat of government, whose location was still to be determined.[10]

Most colleges got caught up in this ferment. In those tinged with loyalism—William and Mary, Philadelphia (the University of the State of Pennsylvania), King's (Columbia), and even Dartmouth—survival required adjustments to the revolutionary demands of the surrounding community. In this spirit William and Mary, for example, created a professorship of law and introduced modern languages and political economy as new subjects. Even when a college's allegiance to the republic was never in doubt, a new president such as Ezra Stiles (A.B. Yale 1746) at Yale could produce similar results. But Witherspoon provided continuity on both sides of the revolutionary divide. His graduates supported the Revolution in overwhelming numbers, and he faced no pressures to introduce dramatic changes. The result was by no means entirely positive, however. As deteriorating health took its toll on Witherspoon's energy and ability, the

[9] College of New Jersey, Minutes of the Trustees, 1778-1796 (typescript copy, Princeton University Archives), 30 Sept 1790, 28 Sept 1791, 27 Sept 1792 (hereafter, Min. Trustees); Isaac Weld, Jr., *Travels through the States of North America and the Provinces of Upper and Lower Canada during the Years 1795, 1796, and 1797* (London, 1799), quoted in *PUL Chron.*, 4 (1942-1943), 122; Varnum L. Collins, *President Witherspoon: A Biography* (Princeton, 1925), II, 175-76; Thomas Jefferson Wertenbaker, *Princeton, 1746-1896* (Princeton, 1946), 69-70.

[10] David Madsen, *The National University, Enduring Dream of the USA* (Detroit, Mich., 1966), 15-42. For the exchange between Rush and Price, see Lawrence A. Cremin, *American Education: The National Experience, 1783-1876* (New York, 1980), 1.

College slipped into routines less dynamic and exciting than the transformations that had preceded independence or that were now occurring elsewhere. Considering the heavy losses sustained by the College during the war, a return to the modest prosperity of 1773 was, perhaps, the loftiest ambition to which the Princeton faculty and trustees could reasonably aspire. Nevertheless, some College officials hoped for change. According to a Dutch traveler in 1784, the faculty was discussing modest curricular improvements during Witherspoon's absence abroad, but the course of study being prepared by the faculty for approval by the trustees differed hardly at all from the one laid out in *Laws of the College* ten years later and was, according to the 1784 visitor, "nearly followed already before." The main difference was that Witherspoon's lecture course on chronology—a history of the ancient world that subordinated classical Greece and Rome to events recorded in the Bible—moved from the junior to the senior year by 1794.[11]

Upon entrance a student was expected to be able to translate passages from Sallust, Caesar, and Virgil; convert a standard English text into grammatical Latin; and translate portions of the Greek Gospels into English, analyzing the Greek grammar. Freshmen concentrated on the same authors, along with Lucian and Cicero. Sophomores turned to Xenophon, Homer, and Horace but spent most of their time studying English texts that explored Roman antiquities, geography, English grammar and composition, and arithmetic. Continuing an innovation that Witherspoon had introduced before the war, juniors mainly emphasized mathematics and science—algebra, geometry, trigonometry, conic sections, and natural philosophy—in addition to learning more English grammar and composition. Seniors studied logic and more natural philosophy, but above all they attended Witherspoon's lectures on criticism, chronology, and moral philosophy. They were expected to take verbatim notes, and Witherspoon checked to see that they did it properly.[12]

Such a regimen would seem stultifying today, and most of it would be completed in high school, not college. Even granting that eighteenth-century Princetonians tended to be two or three years younger than their modern counterparts, it takes an act of historical imag-

[11] David W. Robson, *Educating Republicans: The College in the Era of the American Revolution, 1750-1800* (Westport, Conn., 1985), chaps. 4-5; Gijsbert Karel van Hogendorp, *The College at Princetown, May 1784*, ed. Howard C. Rice (Princeton, 1949), 3-5.

[12] See Francis L. Broderick, "Pulpit, Physics, and Politics: The Curriculum of the College of New Jersey, 1746-1794," *William and Mary Quarterly*, 3d ser., 6 (1949), 42-68; and *Laws of the College of New-Jersey Reviewed, Amended and Finally Adopted, by the Board of Trustees, in April 1794* ... (Trenton, N.J., 1794), 22, 25, 37, and passim.

ination to discover how any intellectual excitement was smuggled
into the students' daily routine. College regulations required them
to study in their rooms from after morning prayer until 8 A.M.,
from 9 A.M. to noon, and from 2 P.M. to 5 P.M. Recitations for
all students and lectures for upperclassmen were also scheduled during these hours. Tutors emphasized learning by rote, and those at
Princeton were probably similar to the ones who exasperated young
John Quincy Adams at Harvard in 1786: They "are so averse to
giving ideas different from those of the author they are supposed
to explain, that they always speak in his own words and never pre-
tend to add anything of their own." Likewise the content of lectures
changed little, if at all, from one year to the next.[13]

Nevertheless, the classical sources read by undergraduates strongly
reinforced the republican principles of the Revolution by emphasizing how corruption had undermined liberty in ancient Greece
and Rome. Witherspoon's moral philosophy lectures pulled together
personal and public morality in the challenging modern idiom of
the Scottish Enlightenment and were designed to serve as the cap-
stone of a Princeton education. Each evening after prayers the faculty required at least two students to give an oration, the text of
which was always approved in advance—to the undying annoyance of
John Randolph (Class of 1791), who later dazzled Congress with his
extemporized speeches. Finally, the American Whig Society and the
Cliosophic Society achieved vigor and energy during Witherspoon's
administration. Their libraries contained far more current materials than the College collection and were much more accessible to
undergraduates. Mainly through the debates promoted by these societies, students consciously applied ancient principles to public and
ethical issues of immediate concern.[14]

The College's biggest difficulties were, of course, financial. The war
was an economic disaster for the American people, who experienced
more than a 40 percent drop in per capita income—roughly compa-

[13] Henry Adams, "Harvard College, 1786-1787," in his *The Great Secession Winter
and Other Essays*, ed. George Hockfield (New York, 1958), 230-31.

[14] H. Trevor Colbourn, *The Lamp of Experience: Whig History and the Intellectual
Origins of the American Revolution* (Chapel Hill, N.C., 1965); *Laws of the College of New-
Jersey*, 25; and James McLachlan's two essays, "Classical Names, American Identities:
Some Notes on College Students and the Classical Traditions in the 1770s," in John
W. Edie, ed., *Classical Traditions in Early America* (Ann Arbor, Mich., 1976), 81-98,
and *"The Choice of Hercules*: American Student Societies in the Early 19th Century,"
in Lawrence Stone, ed., *The University in Society* (Princeton, 1974), ii, 449-94. For
outstanding introductions to the Scottish Enlightenment and the public issues that
it addressed, see Douglas Sloan, *The Scottish Enlightenment and the American College
Ideal* (New York, 1971) and, more generally, Istvan Hont and Michael Ignatieff,
eds., *Wealth and Virtue: The Shaping of Political Economy in the Scottish Enlightenment*
(Cambridge, England, 1983).

rable to the loss inflicted by the Great Depression after 1929.[15] Witherspoon, having accepted his salary for two years in paper money that had become almost worthless, demanded payment in specie in 1781. The trustees responded by launching a lottery to raise the cash, only to face another setback. When their effort failed to generate a sufficient amount even to pay off the winner, they had to sell enough of the College's dwindling resources to make up the difference. The salary problem still was not solved. In September 1782 the College treasurer reported a cash balance of only £14.[16]

Thus, with peace almost at hand by 1783, the trustees turned to Europe for help. Fearing that "the very existence of this benevolent and useful institution is become doubtful, unless some certain and effectual relief can be obtained from the friends of virtue and literature, who have not been exposed to such dreadful calamities," they dispatched Witherspoon and Joseph Reed (A.B. 1757) to Great Britain to raise money. By 1783 the investment of College funds in depreciating continental securities had dissipated the impressive endowment that Witherspoon had raised a decade earlier, and domestic donors were in no condition to give generously. Witherspoon considered the foreign appeal unwise, but he made the trip anyway between December 1783 and September 1784—only to learn that his reservations were justified. Dartmouth, the College of Rhode Island (now Brown University), Yale, Columbia, and Dickinson were all trying to raise money abroad. Two American diplomats in Europe, Benjamin Franklin and John Jay (A.B. King's 1764), were mortified by public appeals that seemed to acknowledge the new republic's inability to educate its own youth. Old World friends of Witherspoon, whatever their continuing regard for him, could not support charity to the "nursery of sedition" that had just helped the United States humiliate the British government.

On January 31, 1784, two days after landing at Dover, Witherspoon greeted loyalist exile William Smith of New York—the son of one of the College's founders—on the streets of London, but Smith did not recognize him "in his own Hair," that is, without a wig. Two weeks later another, very angry, loyalist publicly hectored Witherspoon at the New York Coffee House, "and spoke of him with a loud Voice, and the opprobrious Ephitets, of Villain, Rascal &c that had the Impudence to beg Money in this Country for the Jersey College,"

---

[15] John J. McCusker and Russell R. Menard, *The Economy of British America, 1607-1789* (Chapel Hill, N.C., 1985), 373-74 estimates a loss of 46 percent from 1774 to 1790, as against 48 percent from 1929 to 1933. The authors also caution against relying too much on the precision of these calculations.

[16] John F. Roche, *The Colonial Colleges in the War for American Independence* (Millwood, N.Y., 1986), 172.

reported Smith. "The Doctor made no Reply, but soon went to the Philadelphia Coffee House where this man followed him & treating him in the same Manner, the Doctor left that House very soon." Even a deeply orthodox Congregationalist minister, who had sympathized with the American cause until the issue became independence, could not understand how Witherspoon could have supported an alliance with popish France. He told Smith that the President "was come too early and that before the Americans asked Favors in this Country they should shew themselves friendly to Britain and her Friends."

The whole experience must have been deeply humiliating for Witherspoon. To complete the fiasco, he lost the vision in one eye as a result of a shipboard accident, and he also found that a cataract was slowly depriving him of the use of the other. He brought back a pitiful £5.14.0. Only the sale of valuable College woodlots for £1,200 and a desperate appeal to Presbyterian churches kept the College stumbling along into the late 1780s, when the books at last began to show a small surplus. Efforts to merge with nearby Queen's College (now Rutgers University) came to naught in 1793, as did repeated appeals to Congress to pay back rent for its use of Nassau Hall and to compensate the College for battle damage.[17]

Despite inadequate resources, the College began to recover. While Witherspoon was in Britain, the faculty was reduced to two tutors and one professor, Samuel Stanhope Smith (A.B. 1769), for the academic year 1783-1784. Some undergraduates, such as Robert Goodloe Harper and James W. Wilkin (both A.B. 1785), were even teaching in the grammar school to meet their own college expenses. Although William Churchill Houston (A.B. 1768) resigned as professor of mathematics and natural philosophy in 1783, the trustees did not replace him with Ashbel Green until 1785—and then only by reducing the number of tutors to one. After Green also resigned to accept a Philadelphia pulpit in 1787, Witherspoon filled the position with outstanding astronomer and mathematician Walter Minto, who had studied at Edinburgh with David Hume and at Pisa with the distinguished Guiseppe Slop, and who had received an honorary doctorate of laws from the University of Aberdeen in recognition of his scientific publications.[18] Beginning in the academic year 1787-

[17] Green, *Witherspoon*, 192-231 for the European fundraising trip ("the very existence," 197). See also L. F. S. Upton, ed., *The Diary and Selected Papers of Chief Justice William Smith, 1784-1793*, Publications of the Champlain Society, XLI-XLII (2 vols., 1963-65), I, 5, 19, 42 (Smith quotes); Min. Trustees, 30 Sept 1784, 20 Aug, 25 Sept & 19 Dec 1793; Wertenbaker, *Princeton*, 69; Collins, *Witherspoon*, II, 170; Roche, *Colonial Colleges*, 175-76; Gerald W. Breese, *Princeton University Land, 1752-1984* (Princeton, 1986), 233-34.

[18] Luther P. Eisenhart, "Walter Minto and the Earl of Buchan," *Proceedings of the American Philosophical Society*, 94 (1950), 282-94.

1788, the College finally had an adequate faculty—Witherspoon, two other professors, and two tutors—to educate a student body that had grown from approximately forty in November 1780 to about double that number for the rest of the period. By then Witherspoon's role was becoming less central, as his declining health and the reorganization of the American Presbyterian Church drew upon his limited energy. Late in the war he had moved to his new mansion, "Tusculum," located about a mile north of the campus off what is now Witherspoon Street. His son-in-law, Samuel Stanhope Smith, occupied the president's residence (now Maclean House), then the only building on campus other than Nassau Hall. Smith exercised round-the-clock supervision of the College.

As the recollections of Titus Hutchinson (A.B. 1794) indicate, Witherspoon could still awe a lad by the way he conducted the initial interview and oral examination that determined class placement. He still lectured to seniors, but day-to-day decisions fell increasingly to Smith, whom the trustees named vice president in 1786. After Witherspoon went completely blind around 1791, Smith actually ran the institution.[19]

The College's 246 A.B. degrees awarded between 1784 and 1794 demonstrate significant postwar recovery, as shown in Table A. From 1784 through 1790, Princeton's 136 graduates ranked fourth in the United States, a considerable distance behind Yale's 320, Harvard's 288, and—a newcomer to the scene—Dartmouth's 163. None of the other three colleges had suffered war damage comparable to Princeton's. Between 1791 and 1794, however, most of that gap closed. Nassau Hall's 110 graduates almost equaled Yale's 120 and Harvard's 131, but by then Dartmouth had captured the national lead with 160.

Tables B and C chart this progress in a somewhat broader context. The College's share of North American degrees had exceeded 18 percent by the eve of the Revolutionary War, but the conflict reduced it by nearly half, to 9.9 percent. For the postwar years of 1784 through 1794, Nassau Hall generated 12.2 percent of the republic's graduates, and from 1791 through 1794 the figure reached 13 percent, better than one-eighth of the total. Over the entire period from 1748 through 1794, Princeton produced 791 A.B. degrees, roughly half the amount of Harvard or Yale and not quite double that of the fourth largest contributor, Dartmouth.

The revolutionary crisis at Princeton was also part of a larger regional pattern. The Mid-Atlantic colleges had been gaining steadily on those in New England before the Battle of Lexington, but the war set them back the equivalent of nearly two decades. Not until

---

[19] Green, *Witherspoon*, 232-57; Wertenbaker, *Princeton*, 70-75; Collins, *Witherspoon*, II, 119-81; Min. Trustees, 27 Sept 1786.

the 1790s did the Mid-Atlantic states regain and then exceed the proportion of students they had claimed before 1775. Throughout the 1780s New England, with about a quarter of the nation's population, continued to graduate nearly three-fourths of the liberal arts students in the land. Within that region, the old quarrels of the Great Awakening no longer blazed so fiercely, and Dartmouth provided the evangelical environment that had once drawn Yankees to Nassau Hall. Sensing this pattern, the trustees and faculty of Princeton began to identify their own Mid-Atlantic region, the South, and eventually the West as the richest recruiting ground for new students. Tables D and E reveal the results of this policy.

The loss of the College's New England constituency forced it to look to the South. This trend had begun before 1768, gained momentum in Witherspoon's early years, and continued to increase after the war. By the early 1790s the College had already established the pattern that would characterize the institution in antebellum years (1820-1860), when Southerners composed about 40 percent of the student body and New Englanders just over 1 percent. If unknowns are excluded, Southerners reached 39 percent between 1791 and 1794, while New Englanders remained under 2 percent. Nevertheless, eleven of the thirteen original states sent young men to Nassau Hall between the end of the war and the death of Witherspoon, a very broad distribution.[20]

After leaving the College, Princetonians scattered across most of the republic. Very few chose to live in New England, and an equally small number settled north of the Ohio River, all of them in Ohio. Of other states in the Union, by the mid-1820s alumni lived in every one but Alabama and Missouri. The College performed this national service without slighting its home region. Throughout the entire period from 1748 through 1794, the percentage of students from Mid-Atlantic colonies or states reached a peak around independence and then began to decline. It grew from 61.2 percent in the classes of 1748 through 1768 to 67.1 percent for the classes of 1769 through 1775, after eliminating unknowns. It was still high at 65.1 percent for the next eight classes and then dropped to 56.3 percent for the classes of 1784 through 1790. It fell still further to 50.7 percent for the last four classes. Again if unknowns are subtracted, 54 percent of the new alumni from 1784 through 1794 found homes in the Mid-Atlantic region. (See Tables F and G.)[21]

[20] Ronald David Kerridge, "Answering 'the Trumpet to Discord': Southerners at the College of New Jersey, 1820-1860, and Their Careers" (Senior Thesis, Princeton University, 1984), 5 for the antebellum pattern. Kerridge's study is sophisticated and very useful.
[21] These distributions are recalculated from James McLachlan, *Princetonians, 1748-1768: A Biographical Dictionary* (Princeton, 1976), xx; Richard A. Harrison, *Princeton-*

TABLE A

A.B. DEGREES AWARDED BY AMERICAN COLLEGES, 1784-1794

Year	Harvard	Yale	CNJ	RI	Penn	Columbia	Dartmouth	Q's	Hamp-Syd	Dickinson	Other*	Totals
1784	44	52	24	0	8	0	17	0	—	—	4	149
1785	32	70	10	0	5	0	20	0	—	—	0	137
1786	44	51	25	15	9	8	25	0	8	—	0	185
1787	51	58	23	10	8	5	27	1	2	9	1	195
1788	28	35	19	20	7	4	19	4	6	13	3	158
1789	47	30	21	9	17	10	24	10	3	9	1+	181
1790	42	24	14	22	16	7	31	3	4	12	0	175
1784-90	288	320	136	76	70	34	163	18	23	43	9	1180
1791	27	27	25	16	15	21	49	5	8	0	1	194
1792	37	34	37	18	36	12	27	6	?	33	0	240
1793	38	37	21	12	21	25	39	6	0	0	2	201
1794	29	22	27	20	9	15	45	5	1	20	18**	211
1791-94	131	120	110	66	81	73	160	22	9	53	21	846
1784-94	419	440	246	142	151	107	323	40	32	96	30	2026

In this and subsequent tables and computations, the following students at the College of New Jersey are tabulated as nongraduates: John Parker (A.B. *honoris causa* 1784), Samuel Platt Broome (A.B. *ad eundem* 1786), and Peter Schuyler Livingston (A.B. *ad eundem* 1788). Broome and Livingston earned their conventional A.B. degrees from Yale and Columbia, respectively, and are tabulated under those colleges. Holloway Whitefield Hunt (A.B. 1794) is included with other degree recipients despite the trustees' reservations about what kind of diploma they were giving him. Finally, students who earned a conventional A.B. degree at the College of New Jersey and also another such degree at a different institution (usually Hampden-Sydney College) are included under both.

*Liberty Hall claims five A.B. degrees from 1790 through 1800. All have been arbitrarily assigned to this year.

SOURCES: *Quinquennial Catalogue of Officers and Graduates of Harvard University* (1925); F.B. Dexter, *Biographical Sketches of the Graduates of Yale College with Annals of the College History* (1885-1912), IV and V; *Historical Catalogue of Brown University, 1764-1934* (1936); *University of Pennsylvania, Biographical Catalogue of the Matriculates of the College 1749-1893* (1894); M.H. Thomas, *Columbia University Officers and Alumni, 1754-1857* (1936); *General Catalogue of Dartmouth College and the Associated Schools, 1769-1900* (1900); *Catalogue of the Officers and Alumni of Rutgers College (Originally Queen's College) in New Brunswick, N.J., From 1770 to 1871* (1872); *General Catalogue of the Officers and Students of Hampden-Sidney College, Virginia, 1776-1906* (1908);

*includes St. John's College and Washington College in Maryland, the College of William and Mary and Liberty Hall (later Washington College, now Washington and Lee University) in Virginia, and the College of Charleston in South Carolina. No degree data have been found for Mt. Sion College in South Carolina, which several students attended before transferring to the College of New Jersey.

+Liberty Hall claims one A.B. through 1789, which has arbitrarily been assigned to this year.

?Data not extant for this year.

G.L. Reed, Alumni Record: Dickinson College (1905); An Address of the Visitors and Governors of St. John's College to the State of Maryland (1794; Evans No. 27666); personal communication of Jean P. Bierman of the Clifton M. Miller Library, Washington College, Chestertown, MD, to John M. Murrin, Nov. 24, 1986; A Catalogue of the College of William and Mary in Virginia from its Foundation to the Present Time (1859); Catalogue of the Officers and Alumni of Washington and Lee University, 1749-1888 (1888); J.H. Easterby, A History of the College of Charleston, Founded 1770 (1935).

TABLE B

PERCENTAGE OF A.B. DEGREES GRANTED BY

Year	Harvard	Yale	CNJ	RI	Penn	Columbia	Dartmouth	Q's	Hamp-Syd	Dickinson	Others
1748-68	38.4	36.1	17.6	—	4.8	3.1	—	—	—	—	—
1769-75	37.1	22.7	18.1	5.3	6.0	5.3	3.7	1.8	—	—	—
1776-83	32.1	34.5	9.9	3.6	5.8	0.8	11.0	2.1	—	—	—
1784-90	24.4	27.1	11.5	6.4	5.9	2.9	13.8	1.5	1.9	3.6	0.8
1791-94	15.5	14.2	13.0	7.8	9.6	8.6	18.9	2.6	1.1	6.3	2.5
1748-94	30.7	28.5	14.5	4.0	6.1	3.9	8.1	1.3	0.6	1.8	0.5

TABLE C
REGIONAL DISTRIBUTION OF A.B. DEGREES BY GRANTING COLLEGE
PERCENTAGE AWARDED IN

Years	New England	Mid-Atlantic	South
1748-68	74.5	25.5	—
1769-75	68.8	31.2	—
1776-83	81.3	18.7	—
1784-90	71.8	25.5	2.7
1791-94	56.4	40.1	3.5

TABLE D
PRINCIPAL RESIDENCE OF CNJ STUDENTS BEFORE ENTRY

State, etc.	Number 1784-90	Percent 1784-90	Number 1791-94	Percent 1791-94	Number 1784-94	Percent 1784-94
Vermont	1	0.5	0	0.0	1	0.3
Massachusetts	2	1.0	2	1.2	4	1.1
Connecticut	0	0.0	1	0.6	1	0.3
New York	26	13.6	16	9.8	42	11.8
New Jersey	49	25.7	52	31.7	101	28.5
Pennsylvania	29	15.2	18	11.0	47	13.2
Delaware	7	3.7	1	0.6	8	2.3
Maryland	13	6.8	21	12.8	34	9.6
Virginia	12	6.3	21	12.8	33	9.3
North Carolina	10	5.2	7	4.3	17	4.8
South Carolina	22	11.5	14	8.5	36	10.1
Georgia	4	2.1	0	0.0	4	1.1
Bermuda & West Indies	4	2.1	3	1.8	7	2.0
Canada	0	0.0	1	0.6	1	0.3
Unknown	12	6.3	7	4.3	19	5.4

NOTE: Because the war disrupted the early lives of many students, deciding on a principal place of residence is no self-evident task. In several cases, room for disagreement remains.

TABLE E
REGIONAL ORIGINS OF CNJ STUDENTS
PERCENTAGE FROM

Classes of	New England	Mid-Atlantic	Upper South	Lower South	Other	Unknown
1748-68	24.6	54.5	7.9	2.1	—	10.9
1769-75	10.7	60.7	9.0	10.1	—	9.5
1776-83	4.4	61.4	17.1	5.7	—	11.4
1784-90	1.6	58.1	13.1	18.8	2.1	6.3
1791-94	1.8	53.0	25.6	12.8	2.4	4.3

NOTE: Delaware is classified as Mid-Atlantic, North Carolina as Lower South.

TABLE F
PRINCIPAL RESIDENCE OF CNJ STUDENTS AFTER COLLEGE

State, etc.	Number 1784-90	Percent 1784-90	Number 1791-94	Percent 1791-94	Number 1784-94	Percent 1784-94
Vermont	1	0.5	1	0.6	2	0.6
Massachusetts	1	0.5	1	0.6	2	0.6
New York	26	13.7	23	14.1	49	13.9
New Jersey	34	17.9	26	16.0	60	17.0
Pennsylvania	23	12.1	18	11.0	41	11.6
Delaware	6	3.2	1	0.6	7	2.0
Maryland	8	4.2	18	11.0	26	7.4
District of Columbia	2	1.1	1	0.6	3	0.8
Virginia	10	5.3	13	8.0	23	6.5
North Carolina	10	5.3	5	3.1	15	4.2
South Carolina	22	11.6	13	8.0	35	9.9
Georgia	6	3.2	2	1.2	8	2.3
Kentucky	1	0.5	2	1.2	3	0.8
Tennessee	2	1.1	2	1.2	4	1.1
Mississippi	2	1.1	0	0.0	2	0.6
Louisiana	0	0.0	3	1.8	3	0.8
Ohio	1	0.5	3	1.8	4	1.1
Bermuda	1	0.5	0	0.0	1	0.3
West Indies	1	0.5	2	1.2	3	0.8
France	1	0.5	0	0.0	1	0.3
Unknown	32	16.8	29	17.8	61	17.3

NOTE: Excludes John C. Vergereau (Class of 1786) and James R. Corbin (Class of 1794) who died as undergraduates.

TABLE G
REGIONAL DISTRIBUTION OF CNJ MEN'S PRINCIPAL RESIDENCE AFTER COLLEGE
PERCENTAGE GOING TO

Classes	New England	Mid-Atlantic	Upper South	Lower South	Old Southwest	Old Northwest	Other	Unknown
1784-90	1.1	47.4	10.5	20.0	2.6	0.5	1.6	16.3
1791-94	1.2	41.7	19.6	12.3	4.3	1.8	1.2	17.8
1784-94	1.1	44.8	14.7	16.4	3.4	1.1	1.4	17.0

NOTE: George Crow (A.B. 1787), listed as unknown in Table F, is here classified as Mid-Atlantic because he almost certainly lived in either Delaware or Pennsylvania.

Recovery came at a price. Witherspoon had taken charge of a Great Awakening college, an institution dedicated primarily to supplying the Mid-Atlantic and New England colonies with a committed band of evangelical clergy. More than any other individual, he also brought the Scottish Enlightenment with him to America, and for the rest of his life he labored to integrate what he undoubtedly considered the most exciting trends of his time—the outpouring of vital piety and the growth of scientific enlightenment. "It hath been generally a favourite point with me, to recommend the union of piety and litera- ture, and to guard young persons against the opposite extremes," he told the Class of 1787 on the Sunday before their commencement. "We see sometimes the pride of unsanctified knowledge, do great injury to religion," he warned; "and on the other hand, we find some persons of real piety, despising human learning, and disgracing the most glorious truths, by a meanness and indecency hardly suffer- able in their manner of handling them." Princeton men, especially Princeton-trained ministers, should be, he insisted, both pious and learned.[22]

Witherspoon urged balance and moderation upon his students— humility before God, a critical but respectful approach to learning, and a temperate indulgence of the appetites. Part of the message impressed James Gibson, whose diary for August 7, 1786 records his disgust when he first read about the drunken excesses of Alexander the Great. The "old doctor," as undergraduates now called Wither- spoon, had less success with Richard Hugg King (A.B. 1786), who eventually achieved the awesome weight of 404 pounds and could no longer sustain his ministerial functions.

An agreeable marriage between piety and the new learning was easier for Witherspoon to preach than for the children of the Revolu- tion to achieve in practice. The percentage of Princetonians choosing the ministry had fallen sharply during the war years. At Harvard and Yale, where the decline had begun earlier, the ratio rose or stabilized with the peace. At Nassau Hall it continued to drop.

Of the clergy graduated by these colleges, as Table H indicates,

ians, 1769-1775: A Biographical Dictionary (Princeton, 1980), xxiii; Harrison, *Princeton- ians, 1776-1783: A Biographical Dictionary* (Princeton, 1981), xxix; and Appendix A of *Princetonians, 1791-1794: A Biographical Dictionary.*

[22] Francis Allison also brought the Scottish Enlightenment to the College of Philadelphia, but that school remained a much smaller institution. See David F. Nor- ton, "Francis Hutcheson in America," *Studies on Voltaire and the Eighteenth Century*, 154 (1976), 1547-68. For the quotation, see John Witherspoon, *Address to the Senior Class of Students, Who Were to Receive the Degree of Bachelor of Arts and Leave the College, Sept 25, 1787* ... (Paisley, Scotland, 1788), 7. This address repeated almost verbatim his advice to the Class of 1775, published in his *Lectures on Moral Philosophy. Carefully Revised, and Freed from the Errors of Former Editions. To Which is Added, ... An Address to the Students of the Senior Class, and Lectures on Education and Marriage* (Philadelphia, Pa., 1822), 181.

New England produced 79.3 percent of the nation's total for the classes of 1784 through 1790 and 71.8 percent for the classes of 1791 through 1794, as opposed to 20.7 percent and 28.2 percent respectively for the Mid-Atlantic schools. (Perhaps some of the sixty-two graduates of Southern colleges also went on to hold pulpits, but no biographical dictionaries exist to permit us to enumerate them.) By contrast, Princeton alone between 1769 and 1775 had graduated 29.4 percent of all college-educated clergymen trained in North America, and Mid-Atlantic colleges had generated 33.5 percent. What began as wartime disruption at Nassau Hall was becoming permanent, and the drop appears even more dramatic if nongraduates are calculated in the total. Of the 164 students who entered the College in the classes of 1791 through 1794, only 9.8 percent studied divinity.

Instead, as Table I shows, Princeton men studied and practiced law in record numbers, although at least one lawyer—Nathaniel B. Boileau—hated the legal profession and did his best to tame its pretensions. Nevertheless, lawyers outnumbered ministers by three or four to one in most classes from 1784 through 1794, the approximate reverse of the ratio before Witherspoon took charge in 1768. Medicine, by contrast, held a fairly steady percentage of career choices from 1748 through 1794, varying from 10 percent to 13.5 percent. Overall the number of students entering the professions fell to 56.3 percent from the high of 74.5 percent recorded by the first twenty-one classes. Clearly, more students were settling into business or becoming planters. But for those who earned degrees, the College remained basically a preprofessional school. Fully 69.8 percent became ministers, lawyers or physicians, as against only 23.9 percent among the nongraduates.

The thirty-seven Princetonians who studied for the ministry represented a broader denominational constituency than their wartime predecessors, among whom seventeen of eighteen had been Presbyterians. Only nineteen (51.4 percent) served the Presbyterian Church exclusively. Another seven (18.9 percent) can be counted as Presbyterians for only part of their careers. Four of these seven affiliated at some point with the Dutch Reformed Church, two spent part of their lives as Methodists, and one as a Congregationalist. In addition, two Princetonians were exclusively Baptists, one a Congregationalist, four Dutch Reformed, and five were Episcopalians, the twelve comprising 32.4 percent of the whole. In effect, the classes of 1784 through 1794 returned to the multiple denominational pattern that had characterized graduates before the war when the College had produced 149 Presbyterians, 58 Congregationalists, 14 Anglicans or Episcopalians, 6 Dutch Reformed, 3 Baptists, and 1 Lutheran.

The percentage of educators, which had fallen to an all-time low

Table H
Ordained Clergymen among College Graduates

College	ABs 1791-94	Clergy 1791-94	ABs 1784-90	Clergy 1784-90	%Clergy 1791-94	%Clergy 1784-90	%Clergy 1776-83	%Clergy 1769-75
Harvard	131	32	288	67	24.4	23.3	15.5	18.8
Yale	120	29	320	82	24.2	25.6	22.1	36.2
CNJ	110	16	136	21	14.5	15.4	21.0	48.0
RI	66	14	76	22	21.2	28.9	26.7	31.8
Penn	81	5	70	10	6.2	14.3	14.6	12.0
Columbia	73	9	34	9	12.3	26.5	0.0	4.5
Dartmouth	160	47	163	71	29.4	43.6	40.6	74.0
Queen's	22	5	18	7	22.7	38.9	41.2	13.3
Dickinson	53	13	43	16	24.5	37.2	—	—

SOURCES: *Princetonians, 1776-1783*, p. xxxi, Table G; and same as for Table A, above, except for Harvard, for which see *Catalogus Senatus Academici Collegi Harvardiani, et Eorum Qui Muneribus et Officiis Praefuerunt, Quique Honoribus Academicis Donati Sunt in Universitate Quae est Cantabrigiae in Civitate Massachettensium* (1885). Data for southern colleges are not available.

Table I
Later Careers of CNJ Students

Classes	Clergymen N	%	Lawyers N	%	Medicine N	%	Education N	%	Business N	%	Farmers & Planters N	%
1748-68	159	46.6	49	14.4	46	13.5	17	5.0	—	—	—	—
1769-75	72	40.4	28	15.7	18	10.1	8	4.5	10	5.6	—	—
1776-83	18	11.4	31	19.6	18	11.4	3	1.9	17	10.8	—	—
1784-90	21	11.1	78	41.1	19	10.0	22	11.6	20	10.5	23	12.1
1791-94	16	9.8	49	30.1	20	12.3	9	5.5	30	18.4	23	14.1

NOTE: Percentage of clergymen varies from Table H because nongraduates are here included. Some individuals are counted under more than one profession if they actually pursued several.

during the war, reached a new peak of 11.6 percent in the classes of 1784 through 1790 before returning to 5.5 percent for the next four classes, slightly above the prewar norm. These men often came from the ranks of the clergy, many of whom taught small schools that met in their own homes or churches, but many others now pursued a much wider variety of careers. Some became full-time teachers and administrators, the most outstanding being Joseph Caldwell, president of the University of North Carolina. Robert Hett Chapman (A.B. 1789), who relieved Caldwell for a few years, much preferred preaching to teaching. Ira Condict (A.B. 1784) spent a good part of his professional career rescuing Queen's from collapse. However, the College had an even greater impact on education through its many lay graduates who became trustees of schools or academies, some of which were later expanded into colleges or universities. Princeton alumni were also active in founding library, literary, and historical societies in their various communities.

The careers of Princeton men continued to diverge significantly from those of their fathers, if only because they remained far more likely to enter one of the three learned professions: the ministry, law, and medicine. The sons of "Gentlemen"—an amorphous category of southern planters, wealthy northern landholders, and miscellaneous individuals of comfortable means who engaged in no visible profession—provided over a quarter of the total student population (and better than a third after unknowns are subtracted). By contrast, the percentage of fathers who were ordinary farmers plummeted from nearly a third for the classes of 1769 through 1775 to just 8.5 percent for the classes of 1791 through 1794. Fathers with miscellaneous urban occupations rose, but several of them were undoubtedly wealthy, particularly the iron manufacturers. Merchants also gained, but not dramatically. (See Table J.)

One conclusion seems inescapable. As the student body lost its evangelical character, it became a much more elite society. Paradoxically, the College had to learn to serve the affluent—not because it was rich, but because it was poor. The faculty could see what was happening and did not like it. When Benjamin Rush complained, as he often did, that American colleges wasted far too much time on classical languages and that they ought to concentrate on modern subjects, Samuel Stanhope Smith responded in an extraordinary letter of February 25, 1790.

Rush's concern, Smith insisted, was already very much out of date. "In speaking of the state of learning at Princeton," he wrote, "you seem to have in your mind what it was at the period when you were acquainted with the college, although it is in very many respects essentially changed." The "ignorance & confined ideas of American

TABLE J

STATUS OF FATHERS OF CNJ STUDENTS, 1784-1794, AS COMPARED WITH
FATHERS' STATUS, CLASSES OF 1769-1783

Fathers' Status	Number 1791-94	Number 1784-90	Percent 1791-94	Percent 1784-90	Percent 1776-83	Percent 1769-75
Farmer	14	26	8.5	13.6	15.2	32.0
Minister	8	12	4.9	6.3	8.2	14.1
Lawyer	9	6	5.5	3.2	3.8	3.4
Medicine	8	8	4.9	4.2	2.5	1.7
Military/ Naval	5	1	3.0	0.5	0.0	1.1
Gentlemen	38	55	23.2	28.9	22.2	10.1
Miscellaneous Urban	17	11	10.4	5.8	5.7	7.3
Merchants	29	28	17.7	14.7	16.5	13.0

parents," he insisted, prevent students from "obtaining even a smattering in the circle of public letters & sciences." Americans subordinate all education "to getting money. And they aim at no other scholarship than that that will *soonest* put them in a way of turning a penny." Foreigners were correct, he thought, in describing the United States as "a nation of little dealers, & shifty sharpers, without any dignity, without any enlargement of idea, without taste, without a sense of national honor, & intent only on profit." At Princeton, Smith pointed out, "the *science of calculation*" was already "an object of study from the beginning of the Freshman to the end of the Senior year." Nassau Hall, he believed, at least matched all rivals in this respect. "But it is an hundred to one that the son of a merchant will not learn this or any thing else *at a college*," he complained. "At home he has never seen any thing honoured but money—he has never heard one thing spoken of but freights & cargoes among men, or among women but fashion & equipage. He has not one idea of honor annexed to scholarship, nor one spark of ambition to improve."

Smith's tirade extended to portions of the curriculum taught in English. Although College regulations still described the sophomore year as dedicated mainly to the classics, that emphasis had already changed in practice. Unfortunately, no sophomore's diary has survived to provide a close look at the process. "Almost the whole of the last three years in the college is employed in the most *useful* branches of literature & science," which were all taught in English, Smith affirmed. He doubted that any college could "make good scholars" in four years, "the utmost now that [parents] will allow us. And since they have in great measure banished the learned languages, of which they might learn a little at country schools, & have substituted no other study in their place that might profitably, or even intently engage the minds of youth," he raged, students "often come forward here the most unmatriculated creatures in nature, without any previous habits of study, & without preparation, for the higher branches which they want to pursue, by reading of any kind." Many, he insisted, had not even been taught to write until age fourteen or fifteen, and yet parents expected the College to perfect this elementary skill as well. Because the typical student around 1790 was sixteen or seventeen at entry, this problem could be severe.[23]

The anger of a frustrated teacher blazes from the pages of this lengthy letter. Smith probably exaggerated what was happening or underrated his own skills, to judge only from the impressive record of public service amassed by his students. But clearly he was getting at something real, something that surviving faculty records disclose in greater detail. For the ten academic terms between November 1789 and May 1794, nine class lists survive, covering all but the summer semester of 1793. These lists make it possible to calculate the total size of the student body at several points in time, to track in detail the classes of 1790 to 1794 through their undergraduate years, and to speculate on what was happening to the official four-year program. (See Tables K, L, and M.)

Not surprisingly, the size of the senior class corresponded closely to the number who received degrees. For the classes of 1792 and 1794, the junior and senior years were stable, but the classes of 1791 and 1793 suffered considerable attrition from the junior to the senior year. The lists reveal even more significant facts about underclassmen. We know that in 1782 nine graduates of the Nassau Hall grammar school were admitted to the freshman class, but we have no evidence that three of them ever actually matriculated in the Class of 1786. However, not even this pace could be sustained. The College dramatically expanded the number of freshmen from 1785-86 through 1787-88. Nearly half (47.4 percent) of the students in the Classes of 1789 through 1791 entered the College as freshmen, but only about a third of them (35.2 percent) earned the degree, a sharp decline from earlier freshman performance standards. (See Table M). Thereafter only about a quarter of the College's students matriculated as freshmen, but those who did again became more likely to survive.

Overall 45 percent of the entire cohort from 1784 through 1794

<hr/>

[23] Samuel Stanhope Smith to Benjamin Rush, 25 Feb 1790, photocopy in Samuel Stanhope Smith Papers, Princeton University Library. For the strong sophomore emphasis on English as early as 1784, see Hogendorp, *The College at Princetown, May 1784*, 4.

TABLE K
STUDENTS AT THE COLLEGE, 1789-1794

Term	Date		Seniors	Juniors	Sophomores	Freshmen	Total
Winter	10 Nov.	1789	20	38	19	7	84
Summer		1790	16	31	20	5	72
Winter	29 Nov.	1790	24	36	10	9	79
Summer	May	1791	23	38	19	12	92
Winter	11 Nov.	1791	37	27	16	7	87
Summer		1792	36	28	19	6	89
Winter	10 Oct.*	1792	20	29	15	5	69
Summer	None						
Winter	11 Nov.	1793	30	31	11	4	76
Summer	10 May	1794	30	38	17	5	90
Average Size			26	33	16	7	82

SOURCE: Class lists, Minutes of the Faculty, 1789-1810, Princeton University Archives.
*Although this month is given on the class list and has been respected in the biographies, it is probably a slip of the pen for November.

TABLE L
STUDENTS PRESENT AS

Class of	A.B.s	Total Class Size	Freshmen		Sophomores		Juniors		Seniors	
			W	S	W	S	W	S	W	S
1790	14	30							20	16
1791	25	48					38	31	24	23
1792	37	43			19	20	36	38	37	36
1793	21	29	7	5	10	19	27	28	20	N/A
1794	27	44	9	12	16	19	29	N/A	30	31

NOTE: Total class size = A.B. degrees plus nongraduates.
W = Winter term; S = Summer term; N/A = Not available.
SOURCE: Class lists, Minutes of the Faculty, 1789-1810, Princeton University Archives.

entered as juniors or seniors. The later a student joined his class, the more likely he was to remain for his degree. The typical student entered as a junior, which became the minimum standard when in 1788 the trustees reaffirmed the two-year residence requirement for the A.B. degree, which had been relaxed during the war. George Crow (A.B. 1787) may have compelled the trustees to act, for after graduating in one year himself, he founded an academy at Morristown and boasted in a newspaper that there "The different branches

TABLE M
STUDENTS ENTERING AS

Class of	Class Size*	Freshmen A.B.	N.G.	Sophomores A.B.	N.G.	Juniors A.B.	N.G.	Seniors A.B.	N.G.
1784	21	4	1	2	0	13	0	0	1**
1785	11	0	1	1	0	8	1	0	0
1786	20	5	1	4	2	6	1	1	0
1787	30	5	1	3	2	11	4	4	0
1788	28	3	1	4	5	10	2	2	1**
1789	36	7	11	3	2	8	2	3	0
1790	30	6	9	1	5	7	2	0	0
1791	48	6	15	8	6	11	2	0	0
1792	43	7	2	10	2	18	2	2	0
1793	29	3	5	11	0	7	3	0	0
1794	44	4	9	8	4	11	4	4	0
Total		50	56	55	28	110	23	16	2**
Percent		47	53	66	34	83	17	89	11

NOTE: Excludes 5 from 1784, 1 from 1785, and 9 from 1786, all of whom received the degree, but their time of entry is unknown.
A.B. = received the degree.   N.G. = nongraduate
*In this table only, class size = A.B.s plus N.G.s minus those whose year of entry is completely unknown.
**The nongraduating seniors were John Parker (A.B. *honoris causa* 1784) and Peter Schuyler Livingston (A.B. *ad eundem* 1788). Livingston's earned A.B. degree was from Columbia College.
SOURCE: The 340 biographies remaining after 15 unknowns are excluded.

of literature and knowledge will be taught requisite to fit young gentlemen for the senior class in Princeton College." David Hosack (A.B. 1789) and George Washington Campbell (A.B. 1794) also received their degrees after spending a single year in residence, while Titus Hutchinson (A.B. 1794) entered the College nearly midway through the junior year. The trustees continued to make occasional exceptions for promising ministerial students as well.[24]

[24] College of New Jersey, Minutes of the Faculty, 10 Nov 1789–10 May 1794, *passim* (Princeton University Archives; hereafter Min. Faculty); Min. Trustees, 27 Sept 1788; Elizabethtown *New-Jersey Journal, and Political Intelligencer*, 31 Dec 1788. The class list for the summer term of 1790 is on a separate sheet folded into the opening pages of Min. Faculty, I, and it is hereafter described as Min. Faculty, summer 1790 class list.

Well into the nineteenth century, commencement occurred on the last Wednesday in September, and the new academic year began in November after a six-week vacation. The winter term ended in early April, and after a four-week vacation, the summer term began. Thus it can be proper to say that someone began a semester in the fall or spring, but the term itself fell predominantly in winter or summer. Contemporaries dated the change of seasons at 1 Dec, 1 Mar, 1 June, and 1 Sept, thus reinforcing for them the notion of winter and summer semesters.

Twenty-six Princeton students spent less time at the College because they apparently transferred from other institutions. At least ten came from two colleges founded or staffed largely by Princeton alumni, Hampden-Sydney and Mt. Sion (Zion). The seven from Hampden-Sydney in Virginia included five—David Meade (A.B. 1787), Henry Tate Callaway (A.B. 1791), Robert J. Callaway (A.B. 1791), George Minos Bibb (A.B. 1792), and William Morton Watkins (A.B. 1792)—who had already received their bachelor's degree there and simply pursued another at Princeton. Two others, Joseph Clay (A.B. 1784) and Walter Coles (Class of 1793), came to Princeton while still undergraduates. Likewise Mt. Sion (Zion) College in South Carolina sent three students to the College of New Jersey: John Taylor (A.B. 1790), Jesse Taylor (A.B. 1791), and James Chesnut (A.B. 1792). Two brothers from South Carolina, Lewis Ladson Gibbes and Thomas Stanyarne Gibbes (both Class of 1790), also entered the sophomore class as transfers from some other college, probably either Mt. Sion or the College of Charleston.[25]

In addition, Edward Graham (A.B. 1786), David Hosack (A.B. 1789), William Arden Hosack (A.B. 1792), and John Staples (Class of 1793) came from Columbia College; Henry Smalley (A.B. 1786) transferred from Queen's; Richard Randolph (Class of 1788) arrived from William and Mary, as may have Bennett Taylor (A.B. 1793); Nathaniel B. Boileau (A.B. 1789) probably came from Pennsylvania; John Henry Hobart (A.B. 1793) had first matriculated at the College of Philadelphia; and James Cresap (A.B. 1794) may have attended Cokesbury College, a short-lived Methodist institution, before coming to Princeton. Isaac Wayne (Class of 1791) transferred from Dickinson College and returned there after his junior year, where he finally received his A.B. in 1792. Three other students are identified as transfers—Ephraim McMillan (A.B. 1788), Isaac Watts Crane (A.B. 1789), and John Hollingsworth (Class of 1790)—but we do not know which college may have first enrolled them. Four Maryland graduates of the Class of 1789 are described in the faculty minutes as being admitted "from other Colleges"—John Collins, Thomas Donaldson, Thomas Pitt Irving, and Ephraim King Wilson. But they had probably attended, not a college, but Washington Academy in Somerset County on the lower Eastern Shore, which was near the homes of nearly all of them. In 1785 its Presbyterian principal was

---

[25] For Princeton's impact on southern colleges, see Donald Robert Come, "The Influence of Princeton on Higher Education in the South before 1825," *William and Mary Quarterly*, 3d ser., 2 (1945), 359-96. For the little that is known about Mt. Sion's brief career as a college, see J. H. Easterby, *A History of the College of Charleston, Founded 1770* (Charleston, S.C., 1935), 16-19; and George C. Rogers, Jr., "The College of Charleston and the Year 1785," *South Carolina Historical Magazine*, 86 (1985), 282-95.

replaced by an Episcopalian from Oxford University, a change that could have prompted the exodus to Princeton, which began in 1787. On the other hand, it remains at least possible that these boys—and Hollingsworth—had been attending Washington College in Chestertown, Maryland, a more distant institution but one that did grant degrees.[26]

Relations between the University of the State of Pennsylvania and the College of New Jersey raise some unique questions about transfer students. The university, as the College of Philadelphia in its prewar incarnation, had offered preparatory studies through its English and Latin schools. Its undergraduate curriculum had been organized as a philosophy school, an arrangement that was supposedly continued after 1779 when the state government reorganized the institution as a public university. Yet in the 1780s several students came to Princeton from the philosophy school who were clearly not treated as transfers. Daniel Bell (A.B. 1790) entered the Nassau Hall grammar school, not even the College. George Clarkson (A.B. 1788) matriculated as an advanced freshman after spending two years in the philosophy school. The only ambiguous case is that of James Gibson (A.B. 1787), who moved directly into the sophomore class from the philosophy school where he too had studied for at least two full years. But because most graduates of any academy entered the College as either sophomores or juniors, there is no need to assume that Gibson was transferring from one undergraduate program to another.[27]

Aside from Isaac Wayne at Dickinson, at least ten other Princeton men may have transferred out of the College. John and Theodorick Randolph (Class of 1791) switched to Columbia, and their brother Richard (Class of 1788) just may have accompanied them. John also later enrolled at William and Mary, but none of the three brothers ever received a degree. The other transfer students scattered broadly. Samuel Platt Broome (A.B. *ad eundem* 1786) earned his degree at Yale. Nathaniel Howe (Class of 1786) graduated from Harvard, Christian DeWint (Class of 1789) from Queen's, Gerard Clarkson (Class of 1790) from Pennsylvania, and James Witter Nicholson (Class of 1791) from Columbia. Henry Steele (Class of 1792) may have moved on to St. John's and Andrew Caldwell (Class of 1794) to Dickinson, but there is no record that they graduated. In addition to these eleven, if St. C. (Class of 1785) really was Daniel St. Clair, he spent at least a semester at Washington College in Maryland after leaving Nassau Hall.

[26] Raymond B. Clark, "Washington Academy, Somerset County, Maryland," *Maryland Historical Magazine*, 44 (1949), 200-10.

[27] Edward P. Cheyney, *History of the University of Pennsylvania 1740-1940* (Philadelphia, 1940), 71-73, 135.

Tables K and L rest exclusively on the class lists and thus capture only some of the students who joined their comrades after the semester had begun. Names added out of alphabetical order at the end of a list probably indicate late registrants, as perhaps do some of those squeezed into the proper niche on a roster. But they were not the only ones to arrive well into a semester. Still others are known only from their initial appearance in other sources, such as a student diary, a faculty minute, or quite often the records of the Cliosophic Society. For example, two freshmen and one sophomore joined the Class of 1791 in July or August, very near the end of the academic year. George Washington Morton (A.B. 1792) arrived in September of his sophomore year during the last few weeks of the second semester. Table M draws upon all of these sources to indicate the level at which most students (340 of 355) are believed to have entered the College. Although room for doubt remains about many of the 340, the table does indicate the latest year in which these students could have arrived. No doubt some were present earlier.

Tables K, L, and M reflect considerable fluctuation in the size of a class as it proceeded through the College. The most stable of the last five classes was 1792, which still had about 86 percent of its members present for both the junior and senior year. By contrast the Class of 1791 had lost over a third (35.4 percent) of its members by the second term of the junior year and graduated just over half (52.1 percent). In only one semester did it have as many as two-thirds of its young men in residence at the same time. The Class of 1793 had nearly everyone present in the junior year but lost a quarter of its men by commencement. The Class of 1794 reached the two-thirds plateau for its forty-four members only in the senior year, when four new men were admitted despite the two-year residency requirement. But then four other seniors failed to graduate.

In sum, the freshman year was becoming almost remedial, and some sophomores felt free to arrive quite late in the year, probably after most Latin and Greek instruction had been completed. Apparently most students did not take the classical curriculum very seriously, especially if Smith was correct in asserting that the bulk of sophomore instruction was in English. Even Harvard, an institution much better served by a supporting network of Latin grammar schools, faced similar discouragements. "It is very popular here to dislike the study of Greek and Latin," reported John Quincy Adams in 1786. Smith's bitterness becomes more comprehensible in light of the hard choices the faculty thus had to make to keep the College functioning. They and the trustees never approved a one-year A.B. program like that at Dickinson College (authorized for three years beginning in 1799), but in 1800 Princeton trustees would sanction a Bachelor of

Science certificate to students who met all requirements except those in the ancient languages.[28]

The continuing budget crisis was clearly affecting the curriculum. The College needed paying students, even if half or more could not be persuaded to stay longer than two years. From a student's perspective, a college education remained expensive even for that brief period. The father of Robert Gibbon Johnson (A.B. 1790) calculated that he spent over £680 on the Princeton education of his son, one of the few to reside four years at the College. This amount translates into about $225 per semester, which seems quite high and probably reflects not real costs, but the inflated currencies of the 1780s. Another student, possibly John Jordan (Class of 1793), spent $67.53½ from June 1 through September 29, 1792, a period nearly a month shy of a full term. Students with Presbyterian scholarship support were expected to get along on £40 per year, or about $107. The average cost was probably closer to $150 per year, enough to make a 50 percent down payment on 300 acres of prime western farmland in 1800.[29]

The College's revised "laws" of 1794 include a list of fees that permits us to calculate these expenses more closely. Each entering student paid a one-time only fee of $4.67. Tuition was $8 per term, room rent $5.33, and miscellaneous fees another $1.34. Board was set at $1.67 per week in an academic calendar that recognized a six-week vacation in the fall and a four-week break in the spring. A diligent entering student who spent forty-two weeks at the College would thus have to pay $102.66, or almost exactly the amount allocated for scholarships given to potential Presbyterian ministers. No doubt most students spent more on food than the steward's minimum, and this strict budget also made no allowance for the purchase of clothing, books, firewood, or anything else. (Affluent students spent far more, of course.) But because board (at $70 for forty-two weeks) accounted for more than two-thirds of an undergraduate's total min-

---

[28] Henry Adams, "Harvard College, 1786-1787," 228; Howard Miller, *The Revolutionary College: American Presbyterian Higher Education 1707-1837* (New York, 1976), 173, 184-85.

[29] See Holloway Whitefield Hunt (A.B. 1794); Walter Minto to unnamed student's mother, 29 Oct 1792, manuscript AM 12,826 (Princeton University Library); Ray Allen Billington, *Westward Expansion: A History of the American Frontier*, 4th ed. (New York, 1974), 255. Technically the minimum one could purchase was 320 acres for a down payment of $160. The minutes of the trustees contain much financial information for the 1780s, but fluctuating currencies make this data difficult to analyze, much less quantify. Hence the following discussion concentrates on the 1790s, although even then the faculty complained of the sharply rising cost of provisions. See, for example, Min. Trustees, 28 Sept 1785, 19 Apr & 27 Sept 1786, 18 Apr & 27 Sept 1787, 28 Sept 1791, 27 Sept 1792, 24-25 Sept 1794.

imum expenses, this item also possessed the greatest flexibility for economizing. By securing permission to stay home an extra four or five weeks per semester, some students were probably able to save $14 to $17 per year.

Combined with information from the class lists, this table of fees makes it possible to estimate the College's operating budget during the early 1790s, once Alexander Hamilton's fiscal reforms had stabilized the American dollar. Between 1790 and 1794 average attendance per academic year peaked at 88 in 1791-1792 and then bottomed at 69 in the winter of 1792-93. If we assume that a typical student spent no more than forty weeks in residence each year, then the College budget must have fluctuated between $6,600 and $8,500. If we further assume that board was provided at or near cost, the College's real income ranged between about $2,000 and $2,600 per year. In comparison, this amount equalled only about an eighth to a fifth of William and Mary's assured prewar income of £5,000 to £6,000 Sterling per year, at a time when the Virginia institution was the wealthiest college in the colonies.

Because all fees except board were fixed for an entire semester or year, the College benefited by increasing the number of students paying those charges. Given the flexibility of the board costs, students had an interest in reducing their stay in Princeton to the shortest period compatible with satisfactory academic progress—a choice that involved obvious risks. The combination of these two trends did little to improve the overall academic environment. In all probability the College lowered standards to attract more students, and it had to accept another surge in the percentage of nongraduates (Table N), at least until March 1790, when the faculty took sharp action to reduce absenteeism by requiring Witherspoon's permission for any departure longer than one day. Table O illustrates the nongraduate phenomenon by grouping classes in clusters suggested by the data.[30]

Between 1779 and 1786 the faculty nearly succeeded in making the A.B. degree the norm that it had been prior to 1774, and scattered evidence (best consulted in the biographies themselves) suggests a serious effort to sustain a four-year degree program. But class size also dropped to a new low. The average number of students enrolled in each class more than doubled for the period from 1787 through 1794, but so did the proportion of nongraduates, which exceeded a third of the total. To some extent this phenomenon may be a statis-

[30] For the academic calendar and list of fees, see *Laws of the College of New-Jersey*, 36, 37. For William and Mary before the war, see Roche, *The Colonial Colleges in the War for American Independence*, 174. See also Min. Faculty, 1787-1810, for Mar 1790 (Princeton University Archives).

TABLE N
GRADUATES AND NONGRADUATES OF CNJ, 1784-1794

Class	A.B.s	N.G.s	Total	Percent N.G.s
1784	24	2	26	7.7
1785	10	2	12	16.7
1786	25	4†	29	13.8
1787	23	7	30	23.3
1788	19	9	28	32.1
1789	21	15	36	41.7
1790	14	16	30	53.3
1791	25	23	48	47.9
1792	37	6	43	14.0
1793	21	8	29	27.6
1794	27	17†	44	38.6
Totals	246	109	355	30.7

† includes one who died in College

TABLE O
GRADUATES AND NONGRADUATES OF CNJ, 1748-1794

Classes	A.B.s	N.G.s	Percent N.G.s	Ave. students per class
1748-68 (pre-Witherspoon)	313	28	8.2	16
1769-73 (early Witherspoon)	103	10	8.8	23
1774-75 (onset of Revolution)	47	18	27.7	33
1776-78 (war crisis)	39	67	63.2	35
1779-86 (recovery)	102	18	15.0	15
1787-94 (transition to Smith)	187	101	35.1	36

tical mirage generated by the class lists compiled in the 1790s. Comparable evidence for earlier years would turn up more nongraduates, who no doubt did attend the College in the 1780s and left no trace in surviving records. However, the Cliosophic Society's membership lists are complete for the entire period. All three student diaries and much of the surviving undergraduate correspondence cluster between 1784 and 1786, and one class list for the 1786-1787 academic year and another for April 1789 are extant at the New Jersey State Library. A closer look at the pattern, class by class, indicates that the rise was substantial enough, even if it can never be measured with absolute precision.

Table N shows a rise in the percentage of nongraduates beginning in 1787 and increasing steadily through the peak year of 1790. Smith's angry letter and the faculty action against absentees both came at the height of this phenomenon. The figure remained high in 1791, then dropped impressively the next year. (Class size also fell dramatically in 1793 and climbed again in 1794, mostly by doubling the number of nongraduates.) Significantly, the records are much better for 1792 through 1794, when the percentage of nongraduates was somewhat lower than for the peak years from 1788 through 1791, whose students cannot be traced with the same exactitude. It is almost as if the faculty attempted to admit and retain nearly everybody it could until the roof was repaired and the top floor of Nassau Hall was made habitable in 1791—and then tried to raise standards again. The effort probably failed. Some students told to retake a year, such as John Jordan (Class of 1793) or Samuel Voorhees (Class of 1794), simply quit. The College averaged about twenty-eight A.B. degrees per year from 1791 through 1797, but the number fell to eighteen from 1798 through 1803 before shooting up again, a pattern that suggests dramatic but as yet unconfirmed growth in the percentage of nongraduates for the six classes beginning with 1798.[31]

Some but not all of the rise in nondegree students resulted from the recruitment of Southerners in place of New Englanders. Among students from the five South Atlantic states from Maryland to Georgia, 56.9 percent earned degrees, as compared with 81 percent from northern states. Because William and Mary seldom granted degrees and the College of Charleston issued no more in the eighteenth century after granting six in 1794, the distinct possibility exists that planters sent their sons to Nassau Hall with a strong expectation that they would earn a degree, as nearly three of five did. On the other hand, over 40 percent did not, a ratio more than twice as large as the percentage among northern students. But those southerners who remained through graduation won a disproportionate share of academic honors. In the Class of 1790, for example, the two highest-ranking graduates were both from South Carolina: William Johnson, Jr., and John Taylor.

Financial constraints also limited the College's ability to experiment. The 1780s marked the beginning of serious demands

---

[31] For the class lists, see Min. Faculty, 10 Nov 1789–10 May 1794, *passim*. See also the class lists for the 1786-1787 academic year and for 10 Apr 1789 in the Hancock House Manuscripts, New Jersey State Library, Trenton; and Cliosophic Society Records, Seeley G. Mudd Library, Princeton. Ruth L. Woodward's preliminary survey of the evidence for later classes suggests that, in addition to sixty students who received the A.B. between 1798 and 1801, at least sixty others attended the College with those classes, and almost certainly more, perhaps another five or ten.

to educate women. When Mahlon Dickerson (A.B. 1789) attended his first school, all of his original classmates were girls. The practice was more common in Connecticut, where President Ezra Stiles spent much of one Monday in December 1783 interviewing Lucinda Foot, the precocious twelve-year-old daughter of a nearby minister. Stiles was so impressed with her Latin and Greek that he gave her a Latin certificate affirming that, but for her gender, she was fully qualified to enter Yale. He also had his college students debate frequently whether women should vote, hold office, or seek higher education. One Princetonian, Isaac Van Doren (A.B. 1793), would later lead the nation in attempting to provide almost a full college education for young women. His efforts antedated the founding of Mount Holyoke College, which is usually credited with being the first in such an endeavor. Nathaniel Randolph Snowden (A.B. 1787) also founded a female academy. Although this ferment affected individual Princetonians, it had considerably less influence on the College itself, beyond providing an occasional topic for debate, as with James W. Wilkin (A.B. 1785), Turnor Wootton (A.B. 1788), and especially John Bradford Wallace, the admirer of "enthusiasm," who also championed the political liberation of women.[32]

In fact Princeton students deliberately avoided some of the most controversial questions of the day, as against those—such as the French Revolution—that had nearly everyone excited. Walter Minto, after spending a year on the faculty, evidently noticed this pattern and tried to do something to change it. With the trustees' approval in September 1788, he offered to relinquish £5 of his yearly salary to establish a medal or prize to be awarded at each commencement. He proposed to use this device to reward the best "dissertation" on either of two topics then dividing the larger community. The first was "The unlawfulness & impolicy of capital punishments, & the best methods of reforming criminals, & making them useful to society." The second was "The unlawfulness & impolicy of african slavery, & the best means of abolishing it in the United States; & of promoting the happiness of free negroes." Yet over the next six years hardly any undergraduates chose to address these themes. On such questions the faculty and trustees were more "enlightened" and controversial than the students, as some of the College's other decisions also indicate.[33]

---

[32] Edmund S. Morgan, *The Gentle Puritan: A Life of Ezra Stiles, 1727-1795* (New Haven, Conn., 1962), 344, 432; Franklin B. Dexter, ed., *The Literary Diary of Ezra Stiles, D.D., LL.D., President of Yale College* (New York, 1901), III, 102-03; John Bradford Wallace's portion of a 1793 debate on "Have Women a Right to Govern?" in Wallace Family Papers, Historical Society of Pennsylvania.

[33] Min. Trustees, 27 Sept 1788.

Before the Revolution the College had shown a serious interest in educating Indians and Africans, as part of an evangelical impulse prompted by the Great Awakening. This movement also inspired Eleazar Wheelock to found Dartmouth College originally as an Indian school, and it sent Jonathan Edwards (A.B. Yale 1720, president of the College of New Jersey, 1758) to do missionary work with the Stockbridge Indians for several years. Similar efforts brought two Delaware Indians to the College of New Jersey, Jacob Woolley (Class of 1762) and Bartholomew Scott Calvin, also known as Shawuskukhkung or Wilted Grass (Class of 1776). Although these attempts at education accomplished little, by 1774 Witherspoon was ready to try again, this time with two Rhode Island Africans.

The initiative came from Samuel Hopkins, a Newport minister and New Divinity theologian (i.e., a strict Calvinist disciple of Edwards), who had found two promising Christians among Newport's slave community and hoped that they could be trained as ministers and sent back to Africa. Ezra Stiles, a moderate Calvinist pastor of Newport's other Congregational church and a future president of Yale, discouraged Hopkins until early 1773, when divine providence seemed to intervene in a striking way. The two blacks won $300 in a Rhode Island lottery, enough to buy their freedom once Hopkins had contributed an extra $50. In a bid for broad ecumenical backing, both ministers tried to involve Charles Chauncy, a Boston Arminian or anti-Calvinist, who sourly told Stiles "that the Negroes had better continue in Paganism than embrace Mr. H[opkins]'s scheme," which Chauncy judged "far more blasphemous." Approaching mainly the New Light community thereafter, the two pastors built considerable support, distributed a public appeal for funds throughout the colonies and the British Isles, and negotiated with Wheelock about sending the ex-slaves to Dartmouth. When that effort failed, they turned to Witherspoon.

The two blacks whose religious development so impressed Hopkins were John Quamine (Quaumino) and Bristol Yamma, both of whom had experienced impressive conversions. Quamine's personal story was particularly moving. His prominent African father had sent him at age ten to Rhode Island to receive a Christian education, but instead the ship captain had sold him into slavery. In November 1774 the two blacks departed for Princeton, and Witherspoon wrote Hopkins about their progress three months later. "Bristol Yamma has received the money you sent him. He and his companion behave very well. They are becoming very good in reading and writing & likewise have a pretty good Notion of the Principles of the Christian faith." They remained under Witherspoon's private tutelage at least into April 1776, when Hopkins and Stiles launched a second public appeal to continue their support. The two ministers announced that Quamine had established contact by letter with his aging mother and indicated that two more Africans were now ready to undertake the same training. Instead the Revolutionary War shattered the whole effort, cut off North America from both Africa and Britain (the main source of donations), and closed the College. Quamine died aboard an American privateer in August 1779, but as late as 1791 Yamma was still awaiting an opportunity to return to Africa.

No account of these men appears in earlier volumes of *Princetonians* because, in all probability, they never entered the College. In April 1773 Stiles recorded his extensive examination of Quamine's skills. His account shows that the man was still learning to read English. Despite the progress reported by Witherspoon, the two could hardly have mastered enough Latin and Greek to enter the freshman class by 1776, though they may have been enrolled by that time in the Nassau Hall grammar school. By then Witherspoon had apparently decided against admitting the boys to the College, for a circular of April 1776 declared that they were already so well "qualified for the mission proposed, that they would enter upon it directly, were there opportunity to send them." The escalating war with Britain had probably compelled Witherspoon to try to find some way of getting them to West Africa quickly, armed with whatever spiritual and educational resources they had had time to acquire. This choice probably did not reflect his judgment of their abilities.[34]

In 1779 Witherspoon admitted three more Delaware Indians to preparatory studies in the grammar school, one of whom—George Morgan White Eyes—went on to matriculate in the College with the Class of 1789. The three received direct financial support from Congress, marking what was probably the first instance of federal aid to education, even though Congress expected the Delaware nation to reimburse the United States by ceding land at some later date. The congressional initiative was really blood money, given because White Eyes's father (uncle of the other two boys) had been murdered by the American force which he served as guide. Their family history is perhaps the most tragic one recorded in these volumes, but it evi-

---

[34] Stiles, *Literary Diary*, I, 363-66, 486, 489; II, 378. By far the best account of this incident is in Joseph A. Conforti, *Samuel Hopkins and the New Divinity Movement: Calvinism, the Congregational Ministry, and Reform in New England Between the Great Awakenings* (Grand Rapids, Mich., 1981), 143-47; see also Edwards A. Park, *Memoir of the Life and Character of Samuel Hopkins, D.D.*, 2d ed. (Boston, Mass., 1854), 129-37, esp. 134. See also the strong junior paper by Aims McGuinness (A.B. 1990), "Gospel, Grammar and the Revolution: The Education of two Africans in the Age of Revolution" (fall semster 1988), in "Blacks at Princeton" file, Princeton University Archives.

dently failed to move Witherspoon. By 1782 he had already decided that efforts to educate Indians were foolish. "On the whole it does not appear, that either by our people going among them, or by their being brought among us," he reported to a French inquirer, François Marbois, "that it is possible to give them a relish of civilized life. There have been some of them educated at this college, as well as in New England; but seldom or never did they prove either good or useful."[35] A college president with this attitude probably did not make things comfortable or easy for young White Eyes. It may be no accident that White Eyes left the College at the end of his junior year, just before he would have come under Witherspoon's close personal supervision.

Witherspoon did not indicate whether he had reached the same conclusion about blacks, nor do we know when he acquired the two slaves listed in the estate inventory taken after his death. But either he, Smith (who owned at least one slave), or the trustees took one more initiative in educating an African. On September 27, 1792 the trustees voted to use the Lesley Fund ("for the education of poor and pious youths with a view to the ministry of the Gospel in the Presbyterian Church") on behalf of John Chavis, a light-skinned free black and Revolutionary War veteran from Virginia. One of the most remarkable African-Americans of the antebellum era, Chavis became a noted Latinist and a tutor to prominent white boys, particularly in the Magnum family of North Carolina. His name appears on no Princeton class list, but strong family tradition insists that he attended. If so, he was the College's only black student before the mid-twentieth century, but he did not stay long. The one semester he would most likely have been at Princeton was the summer term of 1793, for which no class list survives. In other words, the family tradition may well be accurate and has been accepted by several generations of archivists at Princeton University. But unless Chavis entered with junior class standing, which seems highly improbable, he would necessarily have been assigned to the Class of 1795 or 1796. For this reason, his biography does not appear in these volumes.

[35] John Witherspoon, "A Description of the State of New Jersey," in *The Miscellaneous Works of the Rev. John Witherspoon, D.D., LL.D., Late President of the College of New Jersey* (Philadelphia, Pa., 1803), 312. This piece is undated, but Marbois's queries went out in late 1780 and early 1781. See Julian P. Boyd et al., eds., *The Papers of Thomas Jefferson* (Princeton, 1950-), IV, 167n for the dates. The most famous response was Thomas Jefferson, *Notes on the State of Virginia*, ed. William Peden (Chapel Hill, N.C., 1955). Witherspoon passed the queries on to Gov. William Livingston in December 1781 with the apparent expectation that Livingston would answer them. When the governor refused, Witherspoon evidently decided to respond himself. See Prince et al., eds., *Papers of William Livingston*, IV, 353-54. Thus Witherspoon's "Description" was almost certainly written in 1782.

Ironically, as Nassau Hall's evangelical impulse, which insisted that all men are equally sinners, yielded priority to the revolutionary belief that all men are equal in rights, the College for the first time became an institution for whites only.[36]

As with earlier classes, Princeton alumni continued to serve the young nation in many impressive ways. Above all, the College taught its men to speak in public. All examinations were oral. The two debating societies competed fiercely for honors and recognition at graduation, and the faculty cared far less about who wrote a speech than about how it was delivered. William Paterson (A.B. 1763), Benjamin Rush, and Witherspoon himself probably wrote or supplied orations for undergraduates to deliver by rote. Student notebooks also passed from hand to hand without ever raising questions of plagiarism. Witherspoon explained the logic of this system to the seniors. Eloquence "has been, I think, in all ages, one of the most envied and admired talents," he insisted. "Military skill and political wisdom have their Admirers; but far inferior in Number to those who admire, nay and would wish to imitate him who has the Power of Persuasion." As much as any one sentence could, that statement epitomizes Witherspoon's hopes for the College. In church or in commonwealth, Princetonians had a mission to persuade others.[37]

On balance, they did far more for commonwealth than for church. The classes of 1784 through 1794 produced two Supreme Court justices, one of whom, William Johnson, Jr., did more than anyone else to shape the Court's dissenting tradition. The College could also claim four cabinet members, four governors, ten senators, twenty-five congressmen (seven of whom also sat in the Senate), twenty-one

[36] Min. Trustees, 27 Sept 1792. The fullest account of Chavis is in Daniel L. Boyd, "Free-Born Negro: The Life of John Chavis" (Senior Thesis, Princeton University, 1947). See also the "Blacks at Princeton" file, Princeton University Archives; and Edgar W. Knight, "Notes on John Chavis," *North Carolina Historical Review*, 7 (1930), 326-45. For Smith as slaveholder, see Trenton *New-Jersey Gazette*, 30 Mar 1784.

[37] Witherspoon wrote the Latin address for one valedictorian who, though probably the third best student in his class, had enough trouble with it that he went to Ashbel Green for help. See J. H. Jones, ed., *The Life of Ashbel Green, V.D.M., Begun to be Written by Himself in his Eighty-Second Year and Continued to his Eighty-Fourth* (New York, 1849), 347. See also George Clarkson (A.B. 1788) for Rush, and Edward Graham (A.B. 1786) for Paterson. The notes on Witherspoon's lectures taken by John Dickinson (Class of 1791) and Samuel Sharp Dickinson (A.B. 1791) were written in the same manuscript volume now in the Princeton University Library. The variety of handwriting in this volume suggests that the two students engaged someone to copy their rough notes in a fair hand, the product of which they then inspected and usually signed. Other signatures also appear in this volume. See Lecture Notes on Moral Philosophy, Criticism, and Chronology, given by John Witherspoon, 1790-1791, taken by John Dickinson and Samuel Sharp Dickinson (Princeton University Library). For Witherspoon on eloquence, see his "Lectures on Eloquence, Moral Philosophy and Chronology," manuscript of Antonio Marvine (Princeton University Library), section entitled "Lectures on Composition and Oration," 1.

state legislators, and numerous other officeholders. Princeton men divided far more closely over the issues of the early republic than their predecessors had over the Revolution, when loyalists had been extremely rare. Of 110 Princetonians with reasonably clear political affiliations, 62 (56.4 percent) became Federalists, and 48 (43.6 percent) Jeffersonians. Because most of the country south and west of New England went heavily Jeffersonian by about 1800, Princeton's Federalists found themselves swamped in a hostile tide and had less impressive careers than the Republican minority from the College, some of whom remained active and important well into the Jacksonian period.

This alignment suggests another point. In the 1790s Samuel Stanhope Smith became as ardent a Federalist as Witherspoon had been a patriot by 1775. While Witherspoon had carried nearly the entire College with him, Smith could not. In the regions from which Princeton increasingly recruited, the Jeffersonian tide was too powerful for any college president to overcome.

The men that the faculty sent out into the world were quite young when they left Princeton, although a student's average age at the time his class graduated increased by almost a year over the decade—from 18.6 for the classes of 1784 through 1788, to 19.0 for the next two, and to 19.5 for the last four. Through the Class of 1789, two-thirds of the students were under the age of twenty at commencement. From 1790 through 1794 this percentage fell to 55.8.

Many Princetonians also died young, as Table P indicates. Hugh Ker, John Rush, and William Tennent Snowden—all nongraduat-

TABLE P

AGE AT DEATH, CNJ MEN, CLASSES OF 1784-1794

Class	Teens	20s	30s	40s	50s	60s	70s	80s	90s	Unknown
1784	0	3	1	7	1	2	5	2	0	5
1785	0	0	3	0	0	3	2	1	0	3
1786	1	2	2	6	2	6	5	1	0	4
1787	0	5	1	7	0	6	1	4	0	6
1788	0	3	4	5	2	3	1	3	0	7
1789	0	2	5	6	1	8	2	5	0	7
1790	0	6	6	3	1	4	4	2	0	4
1791	0	9	3	6	2	7	11	4	0	6
1792	1	4	6	6	5	5	5	2	3	6
1793	1	1	5	5	2	2	0	5	1	7
1794	1	3	4	5	3	4	8	5	1	10
Totals	4	38	40	56	19	50	44	34	5	65

ing members of the Class of 1794—suffered acute mental illness, William Gordon Forman (A.B. 1786) was murdered, and Samuel Platt Broome (A.B. *ad eundem* 1786) and James D. Ross (A.B. 1792) committed suicide. Confronting yellow fever and other perils, many others never had much of a chance to contribute significantly to American society. If unknowns are eliminated (and the chances are that many of these men also died young, if only because long lives leave traces), only the Class of 1784 had fewer than 20 percent dead by age forty, and the Class of 1790 lost 40 percent before their fortieth birthdays. Altogether 28 percent of the men in these eleven classes had died by that age, and another 19 percent succumbed in their forties. Median age at death for the entire cohort was about fifty-four. On the other hand, 29 percent also lived past seventy. The last man in this group to die was William Belford Ewing (A.B. 1794), who expired on April 23, 1866, in his eighty-ninth year, outlasting ninety-two year old James Chesnut (A.B. 1792) by two months.[38] Nonetheless, life expectancy had fallen sharply compared with the experience of earlier Princeton students and the graduates of other colleges in previous decades. For Princeton classes from 1748 through 1770, the median age at death was sixty-four or sixty-five, and the mean sixty-one. Only 16.5 percent died before the age of forty. Among the Harvard classes of 1751 through 1770, the median age at death was sixty-two, while the comparable figure for Yale graduates was sixty-one. Among classes from other schools it was sixty-four at King's, fifty-eight at Philadelphia, and fifty-six at William and Mary.[39]

The Revolution thus left a profoundly ambiguous heritage to the College, one that would become more troublesome as the demands of a republican society and the needs of the American Presbyterian Church increasingly seemed to conflict. The nation, whose population still doubled with every generation, had thousands more pulpits to fill than seats in Congress, where the number rose from fifty-nine representatives and twenty-two senators in 1789 to 213 representatives and forty-eight senators by the early 1820s. By sending twenty-eight legislators to the nation's capital and only thirty-seven

[38] Individuals were included if their age of death could be placed within a particular decade of their lives with reasonable certainty. In a few cases when, for example, death probably occurred between age 29 and 31, the person is classed as someone who died in his 30s, except for one person for whom the probability seems quite strong in the other direction.

[39] We are grateful to James McLachlan for providing these statistics. We have made no effort to explain the sharp decline among Princetonians, nor do we know how student cohorts at other colleges in the same decade fared. No doubt the replacement of New Englanders by students from the South accounts for part of the change.

students into the ministry, the classes of 1784 through 1794 made a proportionately far greater contribution to government than to the church.

This shift in emphasis may have created new difficulties in alumni relations. Although the pool of eligible teenage sons of alumni must have been larger than ever during this period, only twenty-six former Princetonians (including one stepfather) sent sons to the College during these years. Altogether, thirty alumni, trustees, and former College stewards accounted for just thirty-eight students (10.7 percent) of the total enrollment, five of whom were sons of Trustee Isaac Snowden. As numerous biographies show, the Princeton network was a broad and complex web that included mothers' kin, uncles, cousins, and local ministers or school teachers. The link to Princeton did not have to pass from father to son. Yet only thirteen ministers who were either alumni or trustees sent a total of fourteen sons to Princeton, a number that must seem small for an institution that had produced 231 clergymen through the Class of 1775.

Several ministers' sons in these classes were no credit to their fathers' profession. Andrew Stockton Hunter (Class of 1794) was expelled as incorrigible, while Henry Purcell (Class of 1791) was conspicuously irreverent and also failed to earn his degree. Likewise, two graduates who became ordained were later compromised in sexual scandals. Thomas Yardley How (A.B. 1794) was unfrocked by the Protestant Episcopal Church, while David Barclay (A.B. 1791) got into nearly as much trouble with his Presbyterian congregation. Matthias Cazier (A.B. 1785) managed to alienate quite a succession of congregations. Nathaniel Howe (Class of 1786, A.B. Harvard 1786) offended on other grounds, with his light-hearted punning and irrepressible humor. Richard Hugg King's obesity, as we have seen, forced him to retire early, while the intemperance of John Brown Slemons (A.B. 1794) eventually caused even graver embarrassments. Several other ministers, such as Nathaniel Randolph Snowden (A.B. 1787), had careers that were largely ineffective.

In sum, of Princeton's thirty-seven ministerial students, four had brilliant careers and thirteen others were quite successful, typically guiding the same congregation for several decades. But four others either died or quit before even accepting a pulpit, two more died a few years after ordination, and eight either moved too often to be effective for very long or could not hold a pulpit at all. The rest either left the profession early, resigned under scandalous circumstances, or entered the ministry late in life. At most only about twenty of the thirty-seven made solid to impressive public contributions to the religious life of the United States.

While Witherspoon lived, religious and secular demands remained in at least a symbolic balance. Most students appeared faithfully for their 5:00 A.M. and late afternoon prayers, and for Sunday worship. Even so, four freshmen and two sophomores admonished on September 10, 1788 for visiting "a house of ill fame" (the phrase may have meant no more than a boisterous tavern, but it could also have carried its twentieth-century connotation), were straining the limits of propriety. The eight who drank excessively on June 26, 1790, then overturned the outhouse and placed a calf in the pulpit of the College's main hall probably were making a pointed statement. At least so the faculty believed when they expelled all offenders who refused to apologize. A pseudonymous graduate of 1789 was more explicit in a poem he published in a Philadelphia newspaper. His description of "masters whip and pupils yell" depicted a regime of corporal punishment that the College did not practice, but mostly he tried to deflate Nassau Hall's religious pretensions.[40]

> Adieu ye reverend hypocrites, little wits!
> Subjected to you [sic] tyrant hands
> With tears in eyes I've cursed your bands;
> In terror mark'd your rolling eyes
> And meagre visage in disguise;
> Distorted with that rage and heat
> Which bade us tremble at your feet;
> Your cycic [sic] snarls and grins are o'er,
> Now flown, subsided, heard no more.
>
> — — — — — — — — — — — — — —
>
> Adieu thou hall! devotion's seat—
> Where righteous men and Satan meet,
> With aspect pale, on humble knees,
> Who weep and pray like Pharisees. . . .

When Witherspoon died on November 15, 1794, the transition to Smith's presidency was smooth and expected. Everything seemed to suggest continuity, rather than a major break. Yet the death of "the old doctor" was at least a minor watershed in the College's history. In a nation which would have more than two dozen colleges by 1802, Nassau Hall could not long expect to generate an eighth or more of the republic's A.B. degrees, certainly not when the number of graduates began another cycle of decline in 1798. Witherspoon's

---

[40] J. Bennett Nolan, ed., "Other Times, Other Manners: A Princeton Valedictory of 1789," *PUL Chron.*, 16 (1954-1955), 17-22, esp. 20, 21.

final decade may have been the last period in which the College significantly increased its share of American graduates.

Witherspoon's legacy as a famous patriot, innovative educator, and Presbyterian leader proved a heavy burden for Smith and his successor, Ashbel Green, if only because the two men eventually fought each other over its meaning. In 1795 Smith joined the growing alarm, stemming ultimately from the French Revolution, against religious infidelity on American campuses. After the massive Nassau Hall fire of 1802, the faculty suspected the students of arson, a judgment that no modern scholar has sustained but one that signaled a disastrous deterioration in relations between the two groups. When the widespread student rebellion of 1807 explicitly pitted revolutionary rights against Presbyterian discipline, Green concluded that Smith was the College's biggest problem, organized an alumni revolt against him, forced his resignation by 1812, and presided over the creation of Princeton Theological Seminary—founded in order to guarantee an adequate supply of ministers. Although cool toward the Second Great Awakening, Green did encourage vital piety on campus and presided over the first revival among the students since Independence. In the process the College became more denominational and parochial, less "enlightened" than it had been under Witherspoon. An anonymous traveler of 1823 casually observed the moral. He described Nassau Hall as "one of the oldest, and formerly, most reputed colleges in North America."[41]

The College had been founded as a citadel of the First Great Awakening and in the 1770s had become a "seminary of sedition," a school for republicanism. Under Smith it would avoid any close association with the Second Great Awakening, and it would find student affirmation of republican values increasingly threatening to faculty control. Even before Witherspoon died, these underlying trends had acquired a momentum that his successors could not easily deflect, much less reverse. Frightened by its own past and deeply troubled by an uncertain future, the College of New Jersey had entered upon less forgiving times.

---

[41] On the fire, see Wertenbaker, *Princeton*, 126-31. For a list of American colleges to 1820 with the dates of their founding and of the first granting of degrees, see Jurgen Herbst, *From Crisis to Crisis: American College Government, 1636-1819* (Cambridge, Mass., 1982), 244-53. See also, Gary B. Nash, "The American Clergy and the French Revolution," *William and Mary Quarterly*, 3d ser., 22 (1965), 392-412; Mark A. Noll, "The Response of Elias Boudinot to the Student Rebellion of 1807: Visions of Honor, Order, and Morality," *PUL Chron.*, 43 (1981-1982), 1-22; Noll, "The Founding of Princeton Seminary," *Westminster Theological Journal*, 42 (1979-1980), 72-110; Miller, *The Revolutionary College*, part 3, passim; Anonymous, Diary of a Journey through the U.S., 1821-1824, 3 vols. (New-York Historical Society), I, 421.

ABBREVIATIONS AND SHORT TITLES
FREQUENTLY USED

AASP *Proceedings of the American Antiquarian Society*

A/C U.S. Congress, *Debates and Proceedings in the Congress of the United States* (1st-18th Congress, 1789-1824, published 1834-56, 42 vols.). Also known as *Annals of Congress*

AHA American Historical Association

AHR *American Historical Review*

Albany city directories See city directories

Alexander, *Princeton* S. D. Alexander, *Princeton College during the Eighteenth Century* (1872)

als autograph letter signed

Balt. city directories See city directories

BDUSC *Biographical Directory of the United States Congress, 1774-1989: Bicentennial Edition* (1989)

Beam, *Whig Soc.* J. N. Beam, *American Whig Society* (1933)

Biog. Dict. Md. Leg. E. C. Papenfuse et al., *Biographical Dictionary of the Maryland Legislature, 1635-1789* (1979-85, 2 vols.)

Biog. Dir. S.C. House Rep. W. B. Edgar et al., eds., *Biographical Directory of the South Carolina House of Representatives* (1974- , 4 vols)

Boston city directories See city directories

Brooklyn city directories See city directories

Butterfield, *Rush Letters* L. H. Butterfield, ed., *Letters of Benjamin Rush* (1951, 2 vols.)

Cal. Va. St. Papers *Calendar of Virginia State Papers* (1875-93, 11 vols.)

Charleston city directories See city directories

Cincinnati city directories See city directories

city directories All directories cited thus are available in photo-facsimile in *City Directories of the United States Through 1860* (Research Publications, Inc., microfiche edition). Bibliographic information on individual items can be found in D. N. Spear, *Bibliography of American Directories Though 1860* (1961)

Clay Papers James F. Hopkins, Robert Seager et al., *Papers of Henry Clay* (1959- , 9 vols.)

Clio. lists two variant MS Cliosophic Society membership lists, 19th-century copies of lost originals, PUA

Clio. Min. MS Cliosophic Society Minutes, 2 July 1792 to 1810, PUA

CNJ College of New Jersey

DAB A. Johnson and D. Malone, eds., *Dictionary of American Biography* (1928-37, 21 vols.)

Dexter, *Yale Biographies* F. B. Dexter, *Biographical Sketches of the Graduates of Yale College ... 1701-1815* (1885-1912, 6 vols.)

DLC Library of Congress

DNA National Archives, Washington, D.C.

Dunlap & Claypoole's Amer. Daily Advt. Dunlap and Claypoole's *American Daily Advertiser*, Philadelphia

Dunlap's Amer. Daily Advt. Dunlap's *American Daily Advertiser*, Philadelphia

Elmer, *N.J. Bench & Bar* L. Q. C. Elmer, *Constitution & Government of the Province & State of N.J., with Biographical Sketches of the Governors from 1776 to 1845 and Reminiscences of the*

Bench & Bar, During More Than Half a Century (1872)

First Census U.S. Bureau of the Census, *Heads of Families at the first Census of the United States Taken in the year 1790* (1907-08, 12 vols.)

Foote, *Sketches, N.C.* W. H. Foote, *Sketches of North Carolina, Historical and Biographical* (1846 repr. 1966)

Foote, *Sketches, Va.* W. H. Foote, *Sketches of Virginia, Historical and Biographical* (ser. 1-2, 1850-55)

GHQ Georgia Historical Quarterly

Gibson Diary MS journal of James Gibson (A.B. 1787), 1786, PHi, microfilm at NjP

Giger, Memoirs G. M. Giger, MS Memoirs of the College of New Jersey, PUA

GMNJ Genealogical Magazine of New Jersey

Hageman, *History* J. F. Hageman, *History of Princeton and Its Institutions* (1879, 2 vols.)

Hamilton Papers H. C. Syrett et al., eds., *Papers of Alexander Hamilton* (1961-87, 27 vols.)

Hancock House MSS two CNJ class lists of uncertain provenance: undated list from 1786-87 academic year and another dated 10 April 1789, found at the Hancock House, Salem, New Jersey, now in possession of Nj. The 1789 list includes only the senior, junior, and sophomore classes.

Harper Papers B. E. Marks, ed., *Robert Goodloe Harper Family Papers* (1970 microfilm ed., 5 reels, MS 431 in MdHi)

Heitman F. B. Heitman, *Historical Register of Officers of the Continental Army ... 1775-83* (rev. ed. 1914)

Heitman, *U.S. Army* F. B. Heitman, *Historical Register & Dictionary of the United States Army* (1903, 2 vols.)

Heriot letters John Ouldfield Heriot (Class of 1789) to "Robert," probably Robert Goodloe Harper (A.B. 1785), four letters dated 9 January to 15 August 1786, transcripts on pages 126-27 of Caldwell Woodruff, "Family of Heriot ..." (1918 typescript in DLC)

Hobart, *Corres.* J. H. Hobart, *Correspondence of John Henry Hobart* (1911-12, vols. 1-6 of Protestant Episcopal Church in the U.S.A. General Convention. *Archives of the General Convention*)

Jefferson Papers J. P. Boyd et al., eds., *Papers of Thomas Jefferson*, 1st ser. (1950- , 24 vols.)

KSHS Reg. Register of the Kentucky State Historical Society

LCHSPA Lancaster County [Pa.] *Historical Society Papers and Addresses*

LMCC E. C. Burnett, ed., *Letters of Members of the Continental Congress* (1921-36, 8 vols.)

Maclean, *History* J. Maclean, *History of the College of New Jersey* (1877, 2 vols.)

MB Boston Public Library

Martin's Bench & Bar J. H. Martin, *Martin's Bench and Bar of Philadelphia* (1883)

MCCCNY Minutes of the Common Council of the City of New York, 1784-1831 (1917-30, 21 vols.)

MdHi Maryland Historical Society, Baltimore

Md. Leg. Hist. Proj. Legislative History Project, Maryland State Archives, Annapolis, Md.

MHi Massachusetts Historical Society, Boston

MHM Maryland Historical Magazine

MiD Detroit Public Library

Min. Fac. MS Minutes of the Faculty, College of New Jersey, 10 Nov. 1787 to 22 Feb. 1810, PUA

Min. Gen. Assem., 1789-1820 Minutes of the General Assembly of

the Presbyterian Church in the U.S.A., 1789-1820 (1847)

Min. Trustees MS Minutes of the Trustees, College of New Jersey, 1748 to date, PUA

N New York State Library, Albany

Nc North Carolina State Library/Archives, Raleigh

NCHR North Carolina Historical Review

NcD Duke University Library, Durham, North Carolina

NcU University of North Carolina Library, Chapel Hill

NEHGR New England Historical and Genealogical Register

New Brunswick Presby. Min. Presbytery of New Brunswick, Minutes, 1738-1910 (MS in PPPrHi, microfilm at Princeton Theological Seminary Library)

NHi New-York Historical Society, New York City

Nj New Jersey Library/Archives, Trenton

NJA Documents Relating to the Colonial, Revolutionary and Post-Revolutionary History of the State of New Jersey (also called New Jersey Archives) (first series unless otherwise indicated)

N.J. Gazette New-Jersey Gazette, Trenton

NjHi New Jersey Historical Society, Newark

NJHSP New Jersey Historical Society Proceedings; superseded in 1967 by New Jersey History

N.J. Jour. New-Jersey Journal, Elizabethtown

N.J. Jour., & Polit. Intelligencer New-Jersey Journal, and Political Intelligencer, Elizabethtown

NjP Princeton University Library

NjP-SSP Samuel Lewis Southard Papers, Princeton University Library

NjPHi Historical Society of Princeton

NjR Rutgers Library, State University, New Brunswick, New Jersey

N.J. Wills Calendar of New Jersey Wills, 1670-1817 (13 vols., in NJA, XXIII-XLI (1901-1949)

NN New York Public Library, New York City

N.Y. City directories See city directories

NYGBR New York Genealogical and Biographical Record

NYHS Coll. New-York Historical Society Collections

N.Y. Wills Abstracts of Wills, 17 vols. in NYHS Coll., 1893-1913

O'Neall, Bench & Bar S.C. J. B. O'Neall, Biographical Sketches of the Bench and Bar of South Carolina (2 vols., 1859)

OSAHQ Ohio State Archaeological and Historical Quarterly (earlier vols. were called Ohio Archaeological and Historical Publications and Ohio Archaeological and Historical Quarterly, but this abbreviation is used throughout).

Pa. Arch. Pennsylvania Archives (1852-1935, 9 series, 123 vols.)

Pa. Packet, & Daily Advt. Pennsylvania Packet, and Daily Advertiser, Philadelphia

PGM Pennsylvania Genealogical Magazine (called until 1948 Publications of the Genealogical Society of Pennsylvania, but this abbreviation is used throughout)

PHi Historical Society of Pennsylvania, Philadelphia

Phila. city directories See city directories

Pintard, Letters Letters From John Pintard to His Daughter Eliza Noel Pintard Davidson 1816-1833 (1940-41, 4 vols., NYHS Coll., 1937-40)

PMHB Pennsylvania Magazine of History and Biography

PPL Library Company of Philadelphia

PPPrHi Presbyterian Historical Society, Philadelphia

Princetonians, 1748-1768 J.

McLachlan, *Princetonians, 1748-1768: A Biographical Dictionary* (1976)

Princetonians, 1769-1775 R. A. Harrison, *Princetonians, 1769-1775: A Biographical Dictionary* (1980)

Princetonians, 1776-1783 R. A. Harrison, *Princetonians, 1776-1783: A Biographical Dictionary* (1981)

PUA Princeton University Archives

PUL Chron. Princeton University Library Chronicle

R-B C. Rinderknecht, S. Bruntjen, et al., comps., *Checklist of American Imprints, 1830-39* (1972-89, 13 vols.)

Riker W. Riker, *Rules of the Supreme Court of the State of New Jersey* (1901, lists attorneys admitted to New Jersey bar)

Rush, *Autobiography* G. W. Corner, ed., *Autobiography of Benjamin Rush* (1948)

ScCoAH South Carolina Department of Archives and History, Columbia,

SCHGM South Carolina Historical and Genealogical Magazine (name changed in 1959 to *South Carolina Historical Magazine*, but this abbreviation is used throughout)

ScHi South Carolina Historical Society, Charleston

ScU University of South Carolina Library, Columbia

Sh-C R. Shoemaker & M. F. Cooper, comps., *Checklist of American Imprints for 1820-1829* (1964-73, 12 vols.)

Sh-Sh R. R. Shaw & R. H. Shoemaker, comps., *American Bibliography ... Imprints, 1801-1819* (1958-66, 22 vols.)

Sibley's Harvard Graduates J. L. Sibley & C. K. Shipton, *Biographical Sketches of Those Who Attended Harvard College* (1873-1975, 17 vols.)

Smith Diary MS journal of John R.

Smith (A.B. 1787), 1786, DLC, photocopy at NjP

Som. Cnty. Hist. Quart. Somerset County [N.J.] *Historical Quarterly*

Sprague, *Annals* W. B. Sprague, *Annals of the American Pulpit* (1857-69, 9 vols.)

St. Rec. N.C. W. L. Saunders & W. Clark, eds., *State Records of North Carolina* (1886-1907, 26 vols.; vols. 1-10 were called *Colonial Records of North Carolina*, but this abbreviation is used throughout)

STE C. K. Shipton & J. E. Mooney, *National Index of American Imprints Through 1800: The Short Title Evans* (1969, 2 vols.)

Stryker, *Off. Reg.* William S. Stryker, *Official Register of the Officers and Men of New Jersey in the Revolutionary War* (1911 repr. 1967)

Susquehannah Papers J. P. Boyd & R. J. Taylor, eds., *Susquehannah Company Papers* (1930-71, 11 vols.)

T Tennessee State Library and Archives, Nashville

THi Tennessee Historical Society, Nashville

Thomas, *Columbia* M. H. Thomas, *Columbia University Officers & Alumni 1754-1857* (1936)

THQ Tennessee Historical Quarterly

TxAuCH Archives of the Episcopal Church, USA (formerly Church Historical Society), Austin, Texas

Tyler's Quart. Tyler's Quarterly Historical and Genealogical Magazine

UPenn-Ar University of Pennsylvania Archives, Philadelphia

VHi Virginia Historical Society, Richmond

Vi Virginia State Library, Richmond

ViU University of Virginia Library, Charlottesville

VMHB   *Virginia Magazine of History and Biography*

Wash. city directories   See city directories

Washington Writings   J. C. Fitzpatrick, ed., *Writings of George Washington ... 1745-1799* (1931-44, 39 vols.)

Wickes, *Hist. of Medicine N.J*   S. Wickes, *History of Medicine in New Jersey and the Medical Men from the Settlement of the Province to A.D. 1800* (1879)

Williams, *Academic Honors*   J. R. Williams, ed., *Academic Honors in Princeton University 1748-1902* (1902)

Wilmington city directories   See city directories

WMQ   *William and Mary Quarterly*

WPHM   *Western Pennsylvania Historical Magazine*

CLASS OF 1791

David Barclay, A.B.

John Rutger Bleecker, A.B.

William Bordley (Boardly)

Thomas Contee Bowie

Jacob Burnet, A.B.

Joseph Caldwell, A.B.

Henry Tate Callaway
(Calloway), A.B.

Robert J. Callaway
(Calloway), A.B.

James Campbell, A.B.

William Campbell

John Dennis

John Dickinson

Samuel Sharp Dickinson, A.B.

Allen Bowie Duckett, A.B.

John Edmondson

William Cattell Ferguson

Robert H. Gale, A.B.

Maltby Gelston, A.B.

Richard Hall Harwood, A.B.

Thomas Robins Hayward

George Henry

Samuel Henry III

Henry Hollyday, A.B.

Alexander Johnes

Stevens Johnes Lewis, A.B.

John McCrady
(McCready), A.B.

Peter Timothy Marchant
(Merchant)

Francis Markoe, A.B.

Peter Markoe

John Berrien Maxwell

Boyd Mercer

James Witter Nicholson

John Noble, A.B.

Ebenezer Howell Pierson, A.B.

Henry Purcell

John Randolph

Theodorick Bland Randolph

Ebenezer Rhea, A.B.

James Christopher Roosevelt,
A.B.

Charles Ross

Frederick A. Stone, A.B.

John Sullivan

Jesse Taylor, A.B.

Elias Van Arsdale
(Vanartsdalen), A.B.

Isaac Wayne

Stephen Wayne, A.B.

Peter Wikoff (Wickoff,
Wykoff, Wyckoff,
Wycoff), A.B.

Thomas Wright

(Commencement took place on Wednesday, September 28, 1791)

David Barclay

DAVID BARCLAY, A.B., A.M. 1800, Presbyterian clergyman, was born on May 9, 1770, the youngest of the three sons and two daughters of Charles and Catherine Gordon Barclay. The father operated a farm two miles from Cranbury, Middlesex County, New Jersey. He was the grandson of John Barclay, who emigrated from Scotland to Perth Amboy around 1682, and in 1687 was deeded a proprietorship of East Jersey by his brother Robert, the absentee governor and renowned Quaker apologist. Despite his Quaker heritage and his grandfather's Anglicanism, Charles Barclay was a leading member of the Presbyterian Church of Cranbury. His wife Catherine was one of five children of Peter Gordon of Freehold, Monmouth County, and his first wife Margaret Melvin.

In November 1789 Barclay entered the College as a junior. On December 23 of that year, he joined the Cliosophic Society, taking as his pseudonym Sylvester, possibly in honor of Joshua Sylvester (1563-1618), translator into English heroic couplets of the florid scriptural epic of Guillaume du Bartas. Barclay is also listed as a member of the American Whig Society. Given the date on which he joined the Cliosophic Society, he probably joined it first and then left it for some reason and entered Whig. At his commencement on September 28, 1791, he was respondent in a disputation on the question "Are not lotteries for public purposes, disadvantageous to the community?"

After graduation Barclay studied for the ministry under the guidance of John Woodhull (A.B. 1766), the Presbyterian minister at Freehold. On April 24, 1793 he was "admitted as probationer for the sacred office" by the Presbytery of New Brunswick. He was licensed to preach on June 10, 1794 and later that year was called to the pulpits of Basking Ridge and Bound Brook, both in Somerset County, New Jersey. He accepted the latter charge, replacing the deceased Israel Read (A.B. 1748), and was ordained there on December 3, 1794.

Barclay's pastorate at Bound Brook lasted ten years and five months. Around the time of his ordination he married Mary Dey (or Dye), the daughter of William Dey. At least three daughters and three sons were born to them. Barclay prospered sufficiently that he bought the parsonage from his church's trustees during his term of service and sold it back on his departure, which occurred after scandal erupted in 1804. On August 29 of that year the Presbytery of New Brunswick met at Bound Brook to try Barclay on charges of attempting to seduce Mary Perine Bush a year previously and of adultery with a Mrs. Cain. Evidence for the second charge was slight, indicating that the two had kept company alone on several occasions, which was indiscreet but not criminal. The first charge was more serious, for the woman testified that before her marriage to John Bush, Barclay waited until they were alone and "catched hold of me" twice. After she rebuffed him, "he said 'I was only trying your honesty to John.' " The presbytery apparently accepted Barclay's defense, which was that he had indeed not been in earnest, for he was exonerated and his chief accuser, Dr. Ambrose Cook, was censured. Despite this victory, Barclay apparently no longer found service at Bound Brook desirable, for on April 24, 1805, he accepted a call from Oxford and Knowlton in Sussex (now Warren) County, New Jersey, and from Lower Mount Bethel in Northampton County, Pennsylvania. Each of the three congregations agreed to pay him $200 a year for one-third of his time. Bound Brook, which had made a final effort to retain his services after he received this new call, discovered that Barclay apparently had removed or destroyed the minutes of sessions and trustees' records, thus eliminating one copy of his trial proceedings.

In his new home, Barclay was initially a success, enjoying "high standing" and preaching to crowded churches. But soon he began getting into "little troubles," both because he was "constitutionally imprudent" and because he loved to trade horses and to speculate in land, from which activities quarrels frequently arose. In 1811 the little troubles began to develop into a major crisis. Accusations were made against Barclay before the Presbytery of New Brunswick in October 1811, and a meeting was scheduled to investigate them. After some false starts and maneuverings by the pro- and anti-Barclay factions, the presbytery convened a trial at Oxford in October 1812. During this and a later, related trial, Barclay was accused either formally or in passing of attempting to seduce Catherine Adams, Rachel Stout, Nelly Lance, and his wife's niece, Mary Dey Cool; of the theft of a lease; of lying, perjury, suborning witnesses, impiety, profanity, defamation of character, and neglect of duty; of inhumanly beating his "negro wench" Chloe; of shady dealing in a horse trade; of baptizing a horse; and of paying less attention to a child of his than to a land speculation during the child's final illness.

Barclay was found not guilty, or at least not sufficiently guilty to convict, on six out of the seven formal charges. The accusation of attempted seductions was found to be not fully substantiated, but the presbytery nonetheless judged that "Mr. Barclay has been guilty of gross and criminal indelicacy, towards females, and that at different times." While the specific charge of lying was not confirmed, two other instances in which Barclay had prevaricated were held to have been established by the testimony. He was therefore admonished, his pastoral connection with the three congregations was dissolved, and he was advised not to preach in Oxford or Knowlton.

Assessing the evidence with certainty is difficult now, especially since the main source, a 400-page polemic by one of his parishioners, is biased against Barclay. However, even his defense does not show him in a very impressive light. Regarding the charge that he had attempted to violate his wife's niece's chastity, he was forced to admit that "I might probably in a jocose way have laid my hand on the outside of her breast before Mrs. Barclay." One of the two falsehoods of which he was found guilty involved a remonstrance to the presbytery by parishioners friendly to Barclay, which he had claimed was totally spontaneous. When it was established that he had had a larger role in its drafting than he had initially acknowledged, Barclay's defense amounted to a proof that he had not lied to the presbytery duly assembled, though in conversations with individual members he might have overstated the case. Regarding the second falsehood, Barclay was driven to trying to prove that in a complicated legal dispute about the sale of a raft he had been accused of assault rather than perjury. Even the most favorable reading of the trial record suggests that Barclay was given to overstatement and lacking in the prudence required to avoid raising eyebrows as minister in a small community.

Neither side was pleased with the trial's outcome and both appealed to the Synod of New York and New Jersey, which ordered the presbytery to reconsider its judgment, both because the sentence seemed too lenient and because Barclay had new evidence in his defense. The second trial was held in Hackettstown on January 11, 1814. The charges of misbehavior toward females and prevarication were again upheld, and he was prohibited from performing any ministerial duties in all three of his old congregations. Only a conclusion that the "unchristian warmth" of his accusers had hindered his defense saved him from deposition or suspension.

After his two trials, Barclay still managed to retain the support of the majority of the Knowlton and Lower Mount Bethel congregations, and he refused to concede defeat for five more years. The congregations locked their churches against the supplies provided by the presbytery in Barclay's stead, until in November 1814 the ban on his preaching was lifted at the price of another admonition. In 1813, 1814, twice in 1815, twice in 1816, and in 1817, attempts by one or both of these congregations to call Barclay as pastor or have him made their stated supply were vetoed by presbytery. In October 1818, apparently as a result of its inclusion a year previously in the new, possibly more receptive Presbytery of Newton, Lower Mount

Bethel finally succeeded in having him named their stated supply. But it was too late; Barclay had given up and was planning a move to western Pennsylvania.

After scouting the area the previous year, Barclay and his son-in-law Dr. John W. Jenks moved to Jefferson County, Pennsylvania, in the spring of 1819. In 1820 they laid out the town of Punxsutawney in eight squares, including the public square, which is now known as Barclay Square. Barclay soon presided over a congregation, which met at his house until 1822. It next shared a building with the school, until in 1826 the church moved into a log building of its own and from there graduated to one built of brick in 1833. On March 27 of the latter year the congregation was formally admitted to the Presbytery of Blairsville. A contemporary who met him during these years recalled that "Mr. Barclay was a man of decided ability; quick, earnest, and energetic in his motions and his speech; of stout, athletic frame, but impetuous temperament."

In addition to his pioneer activities in Punxsutawney, Barclay served several other congregations. He was stated supply of Harmony, Lower Plum Creek, and Glade Run, Armstrong County, for most of the period between 1820 and 1828. He served as pastor in 1825 at Indiana, Indiana County. From 1828 to 1830 he was stated supply to Jefferson, Jefferson County, and in 1830 he ministered for one year to the nondenominational church of Washington Township, Indiana County, contracting to preach there once a month. His work at the latter place may have influenced its decision to organize in 1831 as a Presbyterian congregation. In all of these positions he presumably commuted from Punxsutawney. In western Pennsylvania Barclay achieved a success he had previously lacked. His work led to revivals in 1821, 1822, and 1825.

In 1836 Barclay decided to step down at Punxsutawney in favor of his son Charles Ray (or Ried) Barclay (Class of 1816), who had just completed his theological training. The son agreed to take over only on condition that the congregation follow him in converting to the Cumberland Presbyterian Church, a breakaway frontier movement which held that there are no eternal reprobates and that Christ died for all rather than a part of mankind. The change in allegiance was agreed to, but whether Barclay as well as his son joined the Cumberland Presbyterians has not been discovered.

David Barclay died in Punxsutawney on April 26, 1846. In his will he left the College $50.

SOURCES: *NJHSP*, 58 (1940), 202-15, 254-66; R. B. Moffat, *Barclays of N.Y.* (1904), 17-37, 56-64; R. B. Walsh *Cranbury Past & Present* (1975), 179, 181, 546; *GMNJ*, 36 (1961), 61-63; 39 (1964), 106; J. G. Symmes, *Hist. Sketch of the First Pres. Church of*

Cranbury (1869), 11, 13, 30-31; *NJA*, xxii (1900), 158; alumni file, PUA; *N.J. Wills*, xii, 27-28; Min. Fac., 10 Nov. 1789, 9 July 1791; Clio. lists; Amer. Whig Soc., *Cat.* (1840), 6; *Dunlap's Amer. Daily Advt.*, 4 Oct. 1791 ("Are not"); Trenton *Federalist & N.J. State Gazette*, 14 Oct. 1800; als, David English to Charles D. Green, 15 Aug. 1793, 17 Nov. 1794, NjP; New Brunswick Presby. Min., 1793-1819, *passim* ("admitted as," 24 April 1793; "catched hold," "he said," 29 Aug. 1804); *Som. Cnty. Hist. Quart.*, 1 (1912), 305; J. H. Kler, *God's Happy Cluster: Hist. of the Bound Brook Pres. Church* (1963); 59-60; J. Kerr, *Several Trials of the Rev. David Barclay* (1814), passim ("little troubles," "constitutionally," 11; "negro wench," 64; "I might," 84; "Mr. Barclay has been," 130; "unchristian," 282); Northampton Cnty. Hist. & Geneal. Soc., *Scotch-Irish of Northampton Cnty., Pa.* (1926), i, 462-70; R. B. Foresman, *Memorial Discourse Delivered in the First Pres. Church, Lower Mount Bethel* (1876), 15-19; J. W. Fraser, *Hist. of the Presby. of Clarion* (n.d.), 155-58, 197; Presby. of Newton, *Proc. of the Convention at Washington, N.J., Nov. 20th, 1867* (1868), 33-34 ("Mr. Barclay was a man" [memoir by D. X. Junkin]); Presby. of Redstone, *Minutes ... 1781 to December, 1831* (1878), 307-11, 367-68, 382-84; Pres. Church of the U.S.A. General Assembly, *Minutes*: (1825), 320; (1828), 342; (1829), 472; (1830), 99; (1831), 260; D. H. Sloan, *Hist. of the Presby. of Kittaning* (1888), 203-04, 220, 239, 291, 354-55.

In 1943 a descendant reported owning a notebook by Barclay of Witherspoon's lectures on moral philosophy, dated April to July 1788, which could suggest that he was at the College by that time. However, other sources agree that he entered the College in November 1789. Witherspoon's course in moral philosophy was generally reserved for seniors and certainly not for the freshman Barclay would have been in the spring of 1788. Perhaps the date given is for someone else's lecture notes, which Barclay later copied. See the letter of A. E. Hall, 13 Sept. 1943, in Barclay's alumni file, PUA.

See Moffat, 28-32, for letters by DB and his father in March 1802 to their distant English cousins Robert and David Barclay, agreeing to a change in the entail of 1722 which governed inheritance of the family's large estate at Ury, near Aberdeen, Scotland. Under the entail the estate would pass to the descendants of John Barclay if several specified branches of British Barclays failed in the male line, and so the approval of a sizable group of American Barclays had to be obtained before the entail could be altered. The Americans consented cheerfully and with expressions of delight at hearing from their British cousins, with whom they had had no contact since 1774. The legal effect of the change, approved by a parliamentary act in 1805, was to void the entail and eliminate any hope of the descendants of John Barclay claiming the estate, which was sold out of the family in 1854. DB seems to have had the impression, carefully encouraged by his English correspondents, that he was agreeing to a minor change in the lands constituting the entailed estate in order to do a cousin a favor, rather than signing away his birthright. He probably never understood the consequences of his signature, and in any event the chances that he or his heirs would ever inherit were extremely remote. The male line in Britain continues to thrive, and even had it failed at least ten American Barclays were ahead of DB in the line of succession in 1802.

MANUSCRIPTS: NjP

JJL

John Rutger Bleecker

JOHN RUTGER BLEECKER, A.B., real estate developer, the son of Rutger Bleecker and Catherine Elmendorf Bleecker of Albany, New York, was named for his grandfather, Johannes Rutgerse Bleecker.

Born on December 20, 1771, he was baptized two days later in the Dutch Reformed church. The first member of the Bleecker family in America had come from Holland in 1658 as a trader. The family was noted for its business ability, and by the eighteenth century they had acquired a great deal of land. Bleecker's uncle, Peter Edmund Elmendorf (A.B. 1782), was his mother's brother, and Lucas Conrad Elmendorf (A.B. 1782) was her first cousin. Another of his mother's brothers, John, was the father of Edmund Elmendorf (A.B. 1794), James Bruyn Elmendorf (A.B. 1807), and William Crooke Elmendorf (A.B. 1807). Mrs. Bleecker's sister, Blandina, and Jacobus Severyn Bruyn (Class of 1775) were the parents of his Bruyn cousins, Edmund (A.B. 1801) and Severyn (A.B. 1803). His great-grandfather had married into the Abeel family, giving Bleecker a distant connection with John Nelson Abeel (A.B. 1787).

Bleecker entered the College as a sophomore in November 1788. He was accompanied on the journey from Albany to Princeton by his uncle, Peter Edmund Elmendorf, who had written to his mother the previous month to say that he would deliver "little Johnny" either to Princeton or New York College. Johnny obviously preferred Princeton. On December 4, 1788 he followed in his uncle's footsteps by becoming a member of the Cliosophic Society, where he adopted the name Lysimachus, the Macedonian general who founded the city of Lysimachia and declared himself king. Peter Elmendorf had apparently assumed financial responsibility for his nephew's education, since on April 10, 1789 Samuel Stanhope Smith (A.B. 1769) sent him two bills totaling £25 "specie proc.," which was "just the amount of Mr. Bleecker's board for the present session in College according to our agreement." The agreement may have been on how to value the bills as the rate of exchange fluctutated during the transition to the new federal government. Bleecker's father was well able to afford the cost of his son's education, and Elmendorf may have been acting only as his agent. Smith's letter adds in a postscript, "I have just to inform you that Mr. Bleecker merits all the praise since he has been here that he has received in other places. He is modest, ingenious, & fine Tempered. And has been generally at the head, or near the head of his Class." The following November Bleecker was joined at Princeton by his younger brother, Peter Edmund Bleecker (A.B. 1792). Apparently John Bleecker was not able to maintain his position at the head of his class, for he was assigned to deliver one of the intermediate orations at his graduation. The topic on which he spoke was the moral influence of polite literature.

Except for a vague reference to Bleecker as a "forwarding agent," nothing has been found to indicate that he either studied for or pursued a professional career. He owned an enormous amount of real estate in New York State, including both improved and unimproved properties. He had no financial need for a career and he probably was kept quite busy with the management of his real estate. He inherited a portion of the Bleecker and Otsquaga patents in the Mohawk Valley, which had been obtained by his great-grandfather in 1729. He also inherited some 5,000 acres in Oneida County, comprising part of the western portion of Cosby's Manor. Rutger Bleecker and three partners had purchased this land at a sheriff's sale in 1772 for fifteen pence an acre. Bleecker's portion of the acquisition contained the land on which the city of Utica developed, and as the town grew the family's wealth increased. Rutger Bleecker had also owned tracts of land in Montgomery County totalling 8,600 acres. When he died in 1789 his wife received support from the estate as long as she remained a widow, with the real estate divided among his children.

Bleecker and his sisters donated land to Utica Academy, with the condition that the building erected upon it should always be available for town meetings, as well as sessions of the town and county courts. The building was never constructed, and in 1851 the heirs consented to the sale of the property to the county as a site for a proposed courthouse and jail. In April 1823 Bleecker was one of the commissioners appointed to raise subscriptions for the construction of the Albany basin, at the terminus of the Erie and Champlain canals. The basin and the Albany pier were completed in 1825, but the basin had no free outlet and silt soon accumulated. The city undertook the task of dredging and improving the basin and then presented the canal commissioners with a bill for $12,462.63 plus interest for expenses incurred.

On November 26, 1799 Bleecker married Eliza Ten Eyck Atwood, daughter of Dr. Thomas Bridgen Atwood, in New York City. She died March 23, 1803. His second marriage took place in Albany on May 18, 1808, when he wed Esther Bailey Linn, daughter of Col. John Bailey and Aeltje VanWyck and widow of John Blair Linn of Philadelphia, who was the son of William Linn (A.B. 1772). Esther Bleecker's death came on May 14, 1823. One son and two daughters were born to each marriage, but both sons predeceased their father.

Bleecker's daughter Catherine became the fourth wife of Col. James Neilson of New Brunswick, brother of John Neilson (A.B. 1793). His daughter Mary married Horatio Seymour, future governor of New York. Bleecker was apparently in ill health for some time before his death at age seventy-seven, and Seymour was acting as his local land agent before becoming his son-in-law. Bleecker died on April 2, 1849 without leaving a will, and his four sons-in-law assumed

responsibility for the administration of his estate, which was valued
at more than $400,000.

SOURCES: Alumni files, PUA; G. A. Worth, *Random Recollections of Albany* (1850), 18; J.
Pearson, *Early Records of the City & Cnty. of Albany* (1869), 88; J. Munsell, *Collections on
the Hist. of Albany* (1865-71), IV, 98; *Princetonians, 1776-1783*, 356-63; als, S. S. Smith
to P. E. Elmendorf, 10 Apr. 1789, NjP; Hancock House MSS; Min. Fac., 10 Nov. 1789,
9 July 1791; Clio. lists; *Dunlap's Amer. Daily Advt.*, 4 Oct. 1791; G. R. Howell & J.
Tenney, *Hist. of the Cnty. of Albany, N.Y.* (1886), 500-01; M. M. Bagg, *The Pioneers
of Utica* (1877), 7-8, 649-50; R. T. Thompson, *Col. James Neilson* (1940), 91-100; S.
Mitchell, *Horatio Seymour of N.Y.* (1938), 36.

RLW

William Bordley (Boardly)

WILLIAM BORDLEY (BOARDLY) was admonished by the faculty on
September 10, 1788, along with three other freshmen and two sophomores, for frequenting a neighborhood spot "lying under a bad
reputation." Bordley was among the three judged least at fault in
the incident. This was his only appearance in the College records.

Despite the spelling of "Boardly" in the faculty minutes, the Princetonian was probably one of the Bordleys from the Eastern Shore
of Maryland, a region sending many students to the College at this
time. One candidate is William Hopper Bordley, a physician and
planter who was one of the three sons and three daughters of James
and Mary Anne Hopper Blake Bordley of Corsica Creek, Queen
Annes County. The father was a planter, justice of the peace, and
state legislator, who owned in excess of 1,000 acres in Queen Annes
County at his death around 1793. During his lifetime he manumitted
all his slaves, subject to various terms of service. He was an Anglican
vestryman who later probably converted to Methodism. By May 1769
he had married Mary Anne, the widow of Philemon Charles Blake
and the daughter of William and Mary Anne Wright Hopper, all of
Queen Annes County. Through her mother she was a first cousin
of William Bordley's classmate Thomas Wright. Bordley and Wright
both entered the College as freshmen and could well have traveled
there together.

In 1783 William H. Bordley's father contributed to a subscription to help change the Kent County School at Chestertown, Maryland, into Washington College, which suggests that the son may have
received his early education there. The record of his postcollegiate
career is sparse. Around 1801 he joined the Medical and Chirurgical
Faculty of the State of Maryland, the state medical society. In June
1807 he was fined in Centreville, Queen Annes County, because his
chimney caught fire. He was living near Centreville in May 1808 and

died there on January 9, 1813. His wife Maria had died on January 22, 1812, leaving "a disconsolate companion and helpless offspring." The names of their children have not come to light, although one was very likely the William H. Bordley who was married in Queen Annes County in 1826. Bordley died intestate and his estate was administered by a John W. Bordley, probably his brother John Wesley. The personal estate was valued at $6,505 and included eight slaves plus the remaining terms of service of three more who were to be freed, large quantities of wheat and corn, and a herd of livestock which included about sixty cattle, thirteen horses, and fifty sheep. Bordley also left about 700 acres of land located some three miles from Centreville, property which was sold by court order five years after his death.

At least one other William Bordley may have been the Princetonian. A William Clayton Bordley married Margaret Keener (or Keiner) in Baltimore on July 10, 1798. Given the middle name, he was probably the son of William and Sarah Clayton Bordley of Maryland. Through his mother, he too would have been related to Thomas Wright, who was probably his first cousin. William C. Bordley was resident in Queen Annes County at the time of the 1800 census and died there on October 12, 1803. He left a personal estate valued at $904, including six cows, a pair of oxen, and five horses. At the time of his death he owned no slaves.

SOURCES: Min. Fac., 10 Sept. 1788 ("lying under"); *Biog. Dict. Md. Leg.*, I, 144-48, 460-61; [Easton, Md.] *Republican Star*, 18 Oct. 1803 (death of WCB), 4 Feb. 1812 ("a disconsolate"), 9 Feb. 1813 (sale of WHB's personal property), 11 Aug. 1818 (sale of WHB's land); *MHM*, 6 (1911), 164, 168-69; E. F. Cordell, *Medical Annals of Md. 1799-1899* (1903), 328; F. Emory, *Queen Anne's Cnty., Md.* (1950), 67, 186, 276, 343, 422; R. B. Clark, *Queen Anne's Cnty. Md. Marriage Licenses 1817-58* (1963), 3; MS estate inv. of WHB, 6 Feb. 1813, recorded 15 Jan. 1814, & of WCB, dated 4 Nov. 1803, recorded 10 Apr. 1804, Md. Hall of Records, Annapolis (photocopies in PUA); R. Barnes, *Md. Marriages 1778-1800* (1979), 20; *MHM*, 57 (1962), 371-73; C. R. Teeples, *Md. 1800 Census* (1973), 49; R. V. Jackson, *Md. 1810 Census Index* (1976), 9; M. B. Emory, *Colonial Families & their Descendants* (1900), 6-7. Cordell seems to have confused William H. Bordley with an older Dr. William Bordley, possibly the father of William C., who was on the corresponding committee of Kent County in 1774. John Beale Bordley (1727-1804), the prominent Maryland and Pennsylvania politician and experimental agriculturalist, was at best related only distantly to the Princetonian. See E. B. Gibson, *Biog. Sketches of the Bordley Family of Md.* (1865), & *Biog. Dict. Md. Leg.* The latter asserts that WHB married Deborah, the daughter of John Fisher of Queen Annes County, and this seems confirmed by J. Bordley, *Hollyday & Related Families of the Eastern Shore of Md.* (1962), 231, which asserts that John Fisher bequeathed a plantation called "Corsica," on Corsica Creek to his daughter Deborah, wife of WHB. Both sources have apparently confused WHB with his brother John Wesley Bordley, who married Deborah on 6 October 1803. John and Deborah both seem to have survived WHB. See [Easton, Md.] *Republican Star*, 11 Oct. 1803, 18 Jan. 1814. Wanda S. Gunning kindly supplied references used in this sketch.

JJL

Thomas Contee Bowie

THOMAS CONTEE BOWIE, planter, was born in Nottingham, Prince Georges County, Maryland in 1771, the second son of Fielder and Elizabeth Clagett Eversfield Bowie. The mother was the daughter of Rev. John Eversfield, rector of St. Paul's Parish, Prince Georges County. Thomas John Claggett (A.B. 1764), the first Episcopal bishop of Maryland, was her first cousin. John Eversfield was a native of England and an outspoken loyalist who suffered confiscation of his property during the Revolution, though it was eventually returned to him and his wife. Capt. Fielder Bowie ran a large mercantile concern in Nottingham in partnership with Col. Thomas Contee and was a state legislator from 1785 to 1790. His financial affairs were so tangled that at his death in 1794 all of his personal property and some of his land were needed to satisfy his creditors. He was the half-brother of Priscilla Fraser Bowie Duckett, the mother of Thomas Contee Bowie's classmate Allen Bowie Duckett.

Bowie was admitted to the College on August 3, 1788. He was not on a class list dated April 10, 1789 but had returned to the College by August 5 of that year, when he joined the Cliosophic Society, taking the pseudonym Argyle. The best-known of that name was Archibald Campbell, eighth earl of Argyll (1607-1661), the great Scottish covenanter and foe of episcopacy during the British Civil War. The use of his name by the grandson of an Anglican minister seems odd. Bowie obtained an honorable dismission from the College on May 29, 1790 while in his junior year.

Bowie then returned to Maryland and took up the life of a landed gentleman on a farm his father gave him near Queen Anne, Prince Georges County. On February 7, 1801 he married his second cousin, Mary Mackall Bowie Wootton, widow of Turnor Wootton (A.B. 1788), and daughter of Robert Bowie, later governor of Maryland, and Priscilla Mackall Bowie. The wife's six siblings included 1st Lt. James John Bowie (Class of 1807). Thomas Bowie and his wife had four daughters and five sons, including Mary Mackall Bowie, Jr., the wife of Reverdy Johnson of Baltimore, who served as United States senator from 1845 to 1849 and from 1863 to 1868 in addition to brief stints as United States attorney general and envoy to Great Britain; and Thomas Fielder Bowie, a United States congressman and general in the militia, whose son was Thomas Fielder Bowie, Jr. (Class of 1856).

After his marriage Bowie moved into "Essington," also near Queen Anne, the estate of his wife's late husband. Bowie was entitled to live there during the minority of his stepson William Turnor Wootton, of whom he was appointed guardian. A family historian describes Bowie as handsome and of unusual physical strength. He was reputedly interested in politics and a frequent and powerful orator, though he seems never to have held elective office. Bowie died suddenly on April 28, 1812, leaving personal property worth $20,000 plus valuable real estate. He was buried at "Essington."

SOURCES: E. G. Bowie, *Across the Years in Prince George's Cnty.* (1947), 671-73, 677-81, 697-701; *Biog. Dict. Md. Leg.*, I, 150-52; Clio. lists; Min. Fac., 10 Nov. 1789; alumni file, PUA; H. W. Brown, *Index of Marriage Licenses, Prince George's Cnty., Md. 1777-1886* (1971), 26; J. D. Warfield, *Founders of Anne Arundel & Howard Cnties.* (1967), 128; R. Barnes, *Marriages & Deaths from Balt. Newspapers 1796-1816* (1978), 33. A portrait by Thomas Sully of Bowie's daughter Mary Mackall Bowie Johnson is in the Princeton University Art Museum. It is reproduced on the cover of *Antiques*, 92 no. 5 (Nov. 1967). Thomas Bowie (1767-1823), another Prince Georges County resident, the son of Allen Bowie Jr. and the husband of Margaret Belt, should not be confused with TCB. See E. G. Bowie, 690-91.

JJL

Jacob Burnet

JACOB BURNET, A.B., A.M. 1794, LL.D. 1848, LL.D. Transylvania 1823, lawyer, judge, elected official, banker and historian, was born in Newark, New Jersey, on February 22, 1770, the tenth of eleven children of the prominent physician William Burnet (A.B. 1749) by his first wife, Mary Camp Burnet. His six brothers included Ichabod (A.B. 1775) and George Whitefield Burnet (A.B. 1792). Daniel Thew (A.B. 1787) married his sister Elizabeth. His early tutelage at home by his father, who was expert in languages, was probably followed, as with his brother George, by education at the Newark academies kept by Alexander MacWhorter (A.B. 1757) until 1786 and thereafter by John Croes (A.M. 1797), later Episcopal bishop of New Jersey.

Burnet entered the College as a junior in November 1789. He joined the American Whig Society. At his commencement on September 28, 1791, he stood fourth in his class and gave "an oration on the mathematics," the College's first honorary mathematical oration. After taking his degree, Burnet spent a further year in Princeton as a "resident graduate, reviewing his collegiate studies [and] extending his reading in history, political economy, and metaphysics." In later years he acknowledged John Witherspoon's strong influence.

In 1792 Burnet returned to Newark as the apprenticed law clerk of Elisha Boudinot (College trustee, 1802-1819). He was sufficiently industrious in his studies to attract the comment of his friends. In a letter from Newark dated December 3, 1792, John Johnson Sayrs (A.B. 1792) told John Henry Hobart (A.B. 1793) that "your friend

Jacob Burnet, A.B. 1791
BY CHARLES B. J. FEVRET DE SAINT MEMIN

Jacob Burnet applies himself to Study I think as close as when he
was at Princeton." After its revival in Newark in June 1794 Burnet
joined the *Institutio legalis*, a moot court at which aspiring attorneys
supplemented their traditional clerkship training in the law. Possibly
in late 1794 and certainly by December 1795 he was back in Princeton, where he lived at Nassau Hall while studying law under Richard
Stockton (A.B. 1779). In April 1796 he was admitted to the bar by
the supreme court of New Jersey.

Even before graduating from the College, Burnet had decided to
move west after completing his professional training. His father, who
had died in 1791, had invested in the Miami Purchase, a million-
acre speculation at the fork of the Ohio and Greater Miami rivers
organized by Judge John Cleves Symmes. Since Jacob, along with
his nine surviving siblings and half-siblings, was willed an equal one-
tenth share in his father's estate, taking his share in the western lands
and moving there to develop them may have offered the best hope
of turning a fairly small legacy to account. By settling in the west he
could also profit from his contacts with New Jerseyans active in western speculation, a possibility fully realized in the years ahead when he

was the local agent of Jonathan Dayton (A.B. 1776), Elias Boudinot (College trustee, 1772-1821), and no doubt other speculators as well. He confirmed his decision to move to the Ohio valley and hit upon Cincinnati as his future home in 1795 when, obliged to suspend his legal studies and to travel for his health, he made his first visit to the region.

Burnet therefore lost no time in settling his affairs after being called to the bar and moved to Cincinnati, determined, as he put it, on "rising or falling with it." He spent the rest of his life there, during which its population rose from 600 people to well over 100,000. By September 1796 he was ensconced at Griffin Yeatman's hotel, suffering an attack of malaria. Neither this illness nor his generally frail health deterred him from following the territorial court on its circuit from Cincinnati to Marietta to Detroit, with less frequent visits to Vincennes and Kaskaskia. Although he later left a vivid account of the hardships of circuit riding at this time, he claimed not to have missed a term between 1796 and the formation of Ohio's state government in 1803. This strenuous regimen apparently cured his ailments and was remunerative as well: in his first term at Detroit he earned $1500.

In 1798 the Northwest Territory was admitted to the second grade of territorial government provided for in the Ordinance of 1787, which permitted the creation of a territorial legislature. Burnet was accordingly selected for a five-year term in the legislative council, the body's five-man upper house. As the ablest lawyer in attendance he was very active at the legislature's first session in September 1799. He drafted many of the bills passed in an effort to instill order in the chaotic legal code then in effect, prepared rules of procedure for the legislature, and wrote the council's address to the governor.

Burnet was a staunch Federalist and an influential supporter of Governor Arthur St. Clair in the latter's ultimately unsuccessful effort to defer indefinitely the granting of statehood to Ohio. The controversy over statehood had sectional and political components. The boundaries of Ohio set out in the Ordinance of 1787 left Cincinnati and Marietta on the edges of the state with no compelling claim as the future site of the state capital, and they gave centrally located Chillicothe the inside track in the quest for this prize. Hence Chillicothe interests championed Ohio statehood while those of Cincinnati and Marietta united in petitioning for a redrawing of the boundaries of Ohio and Indiana. Creating three territories instead of two would place Cincinnati and Marietta each comfortably in the middle of one of the new jurisdictions. By splitting existing population centers, this gerrymander would also defer hopes of statehood for years to come, a prospect pleasing to St. Clair and other Federalists in no hurry to see new Republican states sending representatives to Congress. As both a Federalist and an enthusiastic sponsor of Cincinnati's interests, Burnet had a double incentive to support the gerrymander and did so ardently. He probably wrote a petition supporting it and certainly guided the petition through the territorial legislature in December 1801. His priorities became clear next February, however, when Burnet came out in favor of immediately creating *two* states out of Ohio rather than the one his opponents sought, if only the lines could be drawn so that Cincinnati would dominate one of them. This eleventh-hour maneuver failed to salvage anything for his cause, and Ohio entered the Union in 1803.

With statehood came Republican domination and Burnet entered temporary political oblivion, since his opposition to statehood was ascribed to a distaste for the wider franchise and the popularly elected governors the change involved. He accordingly directed all his attentions to his legal practice. Almost from the beginning of his residence in Cincinnati, and indeed even in the long span between his retirement and death, Burnet was the acknowledged leader of the local bar. He was active in most of the important cases of the day. Harman Blennerhassett engaged him as defense counsel when it seemed possible that his acquittal in the Burr treason trial in Virginia would lead to a second trial in Ohio on lesser charges. Burnet also defended Justice George Tod of the Ohio Supreme Court when he was impeached by the lower house of the state legislature for nullifying a legislative act. Tod's acquittal by the upper house in January 1809 established the principle of judicial review in Ohio. Burnet was soon well on his way to becoming wealthy. As early as 1805 his half-brother Isaac observed that, thanks to being "concerned in every case that is tried," Jacob had amassed $50,000. In the list of landholdings compiled by Ohio in 1810, Burnet appears as one of the wealthiest men in the state. He owned 5,793 acres himself and shared ownership of another 17,138 acres, including one plot of 14,240 acres, the largest single tract listed, jointly owned by Burnet, James Findley and W. Corey.

Burnet remained a fiery Federalist. In March 1810 he wrote a letter to Elias Boudinot lamenting the "great and numerous ... evils which have flowed from the machiavellian reign of Mr. Jefferson" and concluding that "when he was raised to the head of the nation, he found it politically virtuous—at the end of eight years he left it corrupted and depraved." Despite his decided opinions, tempers from the statehood controversy had cooled by 1814, when Burnet was elected to the first of two successive terms in the state legislature.

During this service he wrote a report which unsuccessfully sought to establish Ohio's right to joint jurisdiction over the Ohio River on its border with Kentucky.

In 1816 Burnet declined to seek reelection to the legislature, and in the same year he retired from his legal practice. He used his new leisure to manage his growing portfolio of investments. Not long after its creation in 1803, he had bought stock in the Miami Exporting Company which, despite its name, was exclusively a bank after 1807. In the period from 1813 to 1818 Burnet became a shareholder in the Merino Sheep Company; the Wool and Cotton Manufacturing Company; the Cincinnati Bell, Brass and Iron Foundry; the Cincinnati Exporting and Importing Company; a sugar refinery; and a small cotton factory. None of these enterprises was long-lived; those which lasted until 1819 were swallowed up in the panic of that year.

Burnet himself played a leading role when financial disaster hit Cincinnati. In 1817 a branch of the Bank of the United States was opened in Cincinnati, and with the aid of some lobbying in Congress by William Henry Harrison, Burnet became its president. The branch had a short and troubled history. A period of inflation had begun nationwide around 1815, with the founding of many new banks and a massive increase in the amount of paper currency in circulation. For a year the Cincinnati branch encouraged the inflationary trend by a program of liberal loans.

In 1818 the directors of the parent bank concluded that the situation had become intolerable. Its assets were flowing west and south to be locked up in uncollectable debts secured by mortgages on over-valued land. They resolved to send their massive holdings of rapidly depreciating notes issued by local banks, which had been deposited in the national bank by the land office, to the nearest branch offices and require them to enforce immediate payment in specie. Fiscal sanity would be restored even though the certain outcome would be the collapse of most local banks, misery for many debtors, and the writing-off of a large loss by the parent bank.

The Cincinnati branch accordingly received an allotment of some $900,000 in local paper. Its directors immediately perceived that converting this money to specie was impossible and that an attempt to do so would be catastrophic to the local economy, but they were unaware or unwilling to admit that deflation at whatever cost was precisely what the bank's national directors had in mind. They concluded that the best way to retrieve the bank's investment in the local paper, "trash" whose value was lessening daily, was to loan it at par on good security, and they did so after notifying the bank's Philadelphia head-quarters of their intentions and hearing nothing for some time. This action did not endear them to the main office, which had initiated the program to increase its liquidity, not add to its long-term loans. In October 1820 the Cincinnati branch was discontinued and legal action was begun on all debts to the bank as they came due. As a result the bank wound up owning much of Cincinnati and 50,000 acres of good farmland in Ohio and Kentucky. Many of Cincinnati's leading citizens were impoverished. Burnet had built up a large debt to the bank and was obliged to sell the square at Third Avenue and Vine on which his house was situated, one of the finest properties in the city, for $25,000 in order to clear himself. However he managed to retain scattered properties on the outskirts of the city which became valuable enough to reestablish his wealth as Cincinnati expanded.

Burnet was understandably bitter at this inglorious end to his banking career, and in later years he blamed it on the rapacity and poor judgment of the national directors and their agent in Ohio, a Mr. Wilson. Burnet asserted that the Cincinnati branch had been prudently managed and that its discounts were less than "at any other office, in a place of the same population and business," at least until it received the fatal $900,000. The latter claim is certainly untrue. In May 1819 the branch had discounts exceeding those of every other branch except Baltimore, far in excess of what prudence would dictate in a frontier town, and most historians have agreed that its operations were reckless. The bank faced problems which the most prudent management could not have resolved, however, especially the negative balance of payments between East and West created by the huge debts owed the federal government for land purchases. Ultimately the bank's losses in liquidating its holdings in Cincinnati were surprisingly low, thanks to the city's growth, which justified the faith of Burnet and his associates in Cincinnati's future, whatever their business acumen.

The depression which began in 1819 highlighted the problems faced by purchasers of public lands. Most had bought large tracts on an installment plan and succeeded in making only one or two payments. Much of the population of the West was now hopelessly in debt to the national government and was in danger of losing its entire investment and the labor expended in clearing its land. Burnet claimed to have originated the solution to this problem and was certainly a key figure in the grassroots campaign which helped secure passage of the National Land Act of 1821. This law provided that a purchaser who had paid for a fraction of the cost of a tract be given title to the proportion of the land for which he had actually paid, thus clearing his debt while in most cases permitting him to retain his improvements.

In July 1821 Burnet was appointed to the Ohio supreme court to complete the remaining months of the term of a recently deceased judge. In December of that year the legislature elected him to a full seven year term. A contemporary recalled that Burnet and Peter Hitchcock were the most learned of the justices at this time and that, in contrast to the latter, Burnet commended himself to the members of the bar by his "amiable and courteous manners" and considerate treatment of young lawyers. On the other hand, another contemporary, while granting Burnet's acute intellect, observed that "he gave dissenting opinions, which manifested more of his own opinion than of law. No man ever questioned his integrity, but no man ever knew him swerve from his own side."

In November 1822 the Kentucky legislature chose Burnet to represent that state on a proposed commission to arbitrate its dispute with Virginia over the validity of certain land grants between the Green and Tennessee rivers. Burnet accordingly traveled to Washington early in 1823, only to learn that the Virginia legislature had declined to participate. During the 1824 presidential campaign he actively supported Henry Clay and apparently backed the bid of John C. Calhoun (A.B. Yale 1804) for the vice presidency as well. In November 1828 Burnet ruled that atheists could not give evidence as witnesses in Ohio courts. This decision was among his last judgments, for in December he was elected to fill out the remainder of the United States Senate term of William Henry Harrison, who had resigned to become ambassador to Colombia.

Burnet spoke very little on the floor of the Senate. An intriguing explanation was provided by a contemporary who noted that he had lost two front teeth and "could not endure to lisp the language" he had spoken so powerfully. He refused the partial remedy offered by false teeth. Burnet's main contribution as a senator was successful sponsorship in 1830 of an act which granted public lands on liberal terms to the state of Ohio to subsidize construction of a canal linking Cincinnati to Lake Erie via Dayton and Toledo. The canal opened in 1845. Burnet also steered a bill through the Senate permitting Ohio to charge a toll on its stretch of the National Road and use the funds for the road's upkeep, adroitly dodging claims that such an act had overtones in the continuing debate on the constitutionality of federal involvement in internal improvements.

In 1831 Burnet's term in the Senate expired and he kept his election promise by declining to seek a full term. The decision presumably was his own, since a fellow anti-Jacksonian was elected in his stead. He retired to private life but maintained his interest in politics. Although he continued calling himself a Federalist to his dying day, he was among the Ohio leaders of the Whig Party formed from the wreckage of the National Republican Party around 1834. In that year he was involved in efforts to promote the candidacy for president of John McLean, United States Supreme Court justice and an Ohio native son. Burnet, who was described by Henry Clay as McLean's "right hand man," wrote a friend in April that "you may be as certain as you can be of anything future that he will be the next president." In 1839-40 Burnet made a politically more astute choice by playing a prominent role in the log cabin campaign of his old friend William Henry Harrison. Burnet led the Ohio delegation to the Whig national convention in Harrisburg, Pennsylvania, where he gave a speech on December 7, 1839 depicting Harrison's character in glowing terms. During the ensuing election this speech was reprinted in English, German, and Welsh, and Burnet's slogan, "The Union of Whigs for the Sake of the Union," became one of the campaign's stock phrases. Burnet's triumph in the election's outcome was tempered by his disappointment at what he saw as Harrison's ungrateful reserve thereafter, which peaked when Burnet learned only by reading a newspaper account that Harrison had made two cabinet selections.

Burnet's activities encompassed most aspects of emerging Cincinnati society. As early as 1802 he subscribed to an abortive effort to begin a library. In 1815 he organized a joint stock company which founded a school based on the educational theories of Joseph Lancaster. By 1819 this institution was dormant and its building was used to house the second incarnation of Cincinnati College. Burnet contributed $5,000 in cash plus other property to the latter school and served as president of its first board of trustees. He probably had a hand in luring west Elijah Slack (A.B. 1808), who had resigned as vice president of the College in 1817 following the great student rebellion that year. Slack became head of the Cincinnati Lancaster Seminary, and following its demise he became president of Cincinnati College. Burnet became a trustee of the Medical College of Ohio under its new charter of 1825, and his long tenure on its board thereafter included service as president. In 1836 he was a vice president of the Western Education Society, an organization dedicated to preparing young men for the ministry.

Burnet participated in the founding of the Second Presbyterian Church of Cincinnati and served on its first board of trustees, although he held heterodox views on the Lord's Supper which kept him from entering its communion. The city's wealthiest Presbyterians belonged to this church, which was a stronghold of fairly liberal theology under the Reverend Lyman Beecher. Burnet also served as president of the Hamilton County Bible Society and first vice president of the Cincinnati Sunday School Society.

An enthusiastic advocate of the movement to send freed blacks to Africa, Burnet was an officer of the Cincinnati Colonization Society and a vice president of the national body. He subscribed $100 a year to the movement for ten years. His activities took an ugly turn when he was among those chosen by a public meeting in July 1836 to threaten James G. Birney with unpleasant consequences if he did not cease publication of an abolitionist newspaper (abolition being anathema to most colonizationists) called *The Philanthropist.*

Burnet served as president of the Historical and Philosophical Society of Ohio from 1838 until 1841 and again in 1844. In 1847 he published his *Notes on the Early Settlement of the North-Western Territory,* an expansion and revision of a series of letters published by the society in 1839. The work is a somewhat idiosyncratically arranged blend of history and memoir, still frequently cited for its reminiscences of life in frontier Cincinnati but not always a reliable source. The account of the Ohio statehood controversy, for example, ignores the sectional and political stakes involved in order to present Burnet's actions in a more favorable light. The book's most interesting and neglected feature is its sympathetic treatment of the Indians. The earlier version outspokenly asked "why should our black crimes, perpetrated on them, be forgotten by ourselves, or concealed from posterity? In my opinion, they should never be lost sight of." Burnet denied that there was any racial difference between Indians and whites, citing the successes of each culture in raising the other's children. He also attempted to explain the conquest of the Indians. All people hunt by preference, he argued, and engage in settled agriculture only when forced to do so by population pressures. The Indians were no exception, but the tragedy, he believed, was that the surge of white immigration which should have forced them to settle down actually prevented their doing so. Either the whites' fears led them to drive the Indians out, or the Indians contracted imported diseases and intemperance and became degraded. Since the Indians of the Northwest had farmed well before their first contact with Europeans, Burnet's analysis is quite romantic. He may have derived some of it from his undergraduate tutor, Silas Wood (A.B. 1789).

Burnet was also an amateur scientist. He showed an interest in the geological history of Cincinnati and reconciled the account of creation in Genesis with his own views by suggesting that the six days in the Biblical version need not be read literally and that the process of creation could have been governed by physical laws which were still in effect. When a lecture by the astronomer Ormsby Mitchel exposed Burnet to the Marquis Pierre Simon de Laplace's theory of a gradual creation of heavenly bodies in which gravity worked on vast quantities of nebulous matter, Burnet was thus able proudly to claim to have adopted similar theories "before they were publicly known." Mitchel was also the driving force behind the creation of the Cincinnati Astronomical Society in 1842, which Burnet served as first president. The society lost no time in bringing John Quincy Adams (LL.D. 1806) west to lay the cornerstone of its observatory which, when completed in 1845, contained a telescope which was the largest in the United States and the second largest in the world.

On January 1, 1800 Burnet married Rebecca Wallace, daughter of Robert Wallace of Marietta. She bore him three sons and four daughters, five of whom survived him. In appearance he was swarthy, slender, a bit above average height, and most notable for piercing black eyes with which he was expert at intimidating wayward witnesses. At the age of eighty he was still walking the streets of Cincinnati, wearing his hair in an old fashioned queue and displaying a reserved, dignified, somewhat forbidding demeanor. He died on May 10, 1853.

SOURCES: D. K. Este, *Discourse on the Life & Public Service of the late Jacob Burnet* (1853), *passim* ("resident graduate," 5-6); S. W. Fisher, *Occasional Sermons & Addresses* (1860), 413-53; J. Burnet, *Notes on the Early Settlement of the North-Western Territory* (1847), *passim* ("rising or falling," 22; "trash," "at any other," 408); J. Burnet, "Letters Relating to the Early Settlement of the North-Western Territory," *Trans. of the Hist. & Phil. Soc. of Ohio*, part 2 (1839): 9-180 ("why should," 97); letters from Transylvania Univ., 3 Aug. 1982, & Cincinnati Hist. Soc., 12 Aug. 1982; Amer. Whig Soc., *Cat.* (1840), 6; Min. Fac., 10 Nov. 1789, 9 July 1791, 7 & 14 Dec. 1795; *Dunlap's Amer. Daily Advt.*, 4 Oct. 1791 ("an oration"); Williams, *Academic Honors*, xii, 12-13; *Dunlap & Claypoole's Amer. Daily Advt.*, 7 Oct. 1794; *Newark Daily Advt.*, 29 June 1848; D. C. Skemer, "The *Institutio legalis* & Legal Education in N.J.: 1783-1817," *N.J. Hist.*, 97 (1979), 131, 134; Hobart, *Corres.*, I, 20, 98, 140 ("your friend"); Riker, 46; *N.J. Wills*, VIII, 59; R. C. Downes, *Frontier Ohio, 1788-1803* (1935), 200, 228-39; B. W. Bond, *Civilization of the Old Northwest* (1934), 112, 121, 146; B. W. Bond, *Foundations of Ohio* (1941), 437-49, 463; W. T. Utter, *Frontier State 1803-25* (1942), 4-5, 26, 50, 263-95; F. P. Weisenburger, *Passing of the Frontier 1825-40* (1941), 43, 150, 199, 236-37, 249-50, 284, 289 ("you may be"), 366, 396; A. B. Sears, *Thomas Worthington* (1958), 65, 78, 109-11; W. H. Safford, *Blennerhassett Papers* (1864 repr. 1971), 519; L. Henshaw, ed., "Burr-Blennerhassett Documents," *Quart. Pub. of the Hist. & Phil. Soc. of Ohio*, 9 (1914), 3, 68; als, Isaac G. Burnet to Garret D. Wall, 9 June 1805, NjP ("concerned in every"); G. M. Petty, *Ohio 1810 Tax Duplicate* (1976), 22; L. Soltow, "Inequality Amidst Abundance: Land Ownership in Early 19th Century Ohio," *Ohio Hist.*, 88 (1979), 140-45; als, JB to Elias Boudinot, 17 March 1810, NjP ("great and numerous"); E. O. Porter, "Boundary & Jurisdictional Problems on the Kentucky-Ohio Border," *OSAHQ*, 55 (1946), 155-64; R. Stevens, "Samuel Watts Davies & the Industrial Revolution in Cincinnati," *Ohio Hist. Quart.*, 70 (1961), 95-127; F. P. Goodwin, "Rise of Manufactures in the Miami Country," *AHR*, 12 (1906/7), 771-73; D. B. Goebel, *William Henry Harrison* (1926), 197, 303-04, 345; I. J. Cox, "Selections from the Torrence Papers," *Quart. Pub. of the Hist. & Phil. Soc. of Ohio*, 2 (1907), 105-06, 115-16; 6, no. 2 (1911), 13-16; R. C. Catterall, *Second Bank of the U.S.* (1903), 66-67, 79-80; E. D. Mansfield, *Personal Memories* (1879), 155-61 ("he gave"); G. I. Reed, *Bench & Bar of Ohio* (1897), 17, 62 ("amiable and courteous," reminiscence by H. B. Curtis); R. C. Buley, *Old Northwest: Pioneer Period 1815-40* (1950), II, 167, 344, 409-20, 488, 621; P. J. Treat, *National Land System 1785-1820* (1910), 140-51; *Clay Papers*, III, 288-89, 326-27, 389, 398, 513-14, 870-72; IV, 668; V, 7-9; VIII, 286-87, 769 ("right hand"); U.S. Cong., *Reg. of Debates in Cong.*, 21st Cong., 2d sess., 102, 209, 278-91; C. L. Martzolff,

ed., "Autobiog. of Thomas Ewing," *OSAHQ*, 22 (1913), 162 ("could not endure");
R. G. Gunderson, *Log-Cabin Campaign* (1957), 66, 73 ("The Union"); H. D. Moser,
ed., *Papers of Daniel Webster: Corres.*, V (1840-43) (1982), 74-75; D. V. Martin, "The
Truth about Cincinnati's First Library," *OSAHQ*, 53 (1944), 193-208; R. Walters,
Hist. Sketch of the Univ. of Cincinnati (n.d.), 13-14, 17-20, 45-47; J. P. Foote, *Schools
of Cincinnati & its Vicinity* (1855), 5-6, 188-89; O. Juettner, *Daniel Drake & his Followers*
(1909), 128; Cincinnati city directories: (1819), 39, 45, 72, 97; (1829), 178, 191, 194;
(1831), 184, 189; (1834), 257, 266; (1836/7), 210, 237; N. Wright, *Memorial Address
Delivered ... April 28, 1872* (1872), 11, 16; H. N. Sherwood, "Movement in Ohio to
Deport the Negro," *Quart. Pub. of the Hist. & Phil. Soc. of Ohio*, 7 (1912), 53-77; W. H.
Venable, *Beginnings of Literary Culture in the Ohio Valley* (1891 repr. 1949); J. Burnet,
Annual Address, Delivered Before the Cincinnati Astronomical Soc., June 3, 1844 (1844),
passim ("before they," 24); "Ormsby M. Mitchel," *DAB*; I. N. Burnet, *Dr. William Burnet
& his sons Jacob, Isaac and David* (1938), 2-3; H. Howe, "Some Recollections of Hist.
Travel ...," *OSAHQ*, 2 (1889), 463. See D. M. Reynolds, *Hiram Powers & His Ideal
Sculpture* (1977), 1055, & E. M. Clark, *Ohio Art & Artists* (1932), 134-35 (photo) for
Powers' marble bust of JB ca. 1837. The frequently encountered assertion that JB
was elected to the French Academy of Sciences on the nomination of the Marquis de
Lafayette (LL.D. 1790), who had befriended him in 1825 during his visit to Cincinnati,
seems to be without foundation. It may have originated in a confusion with JB's
election as an honorary member of the French Society of Universal Statistics. See JB's
als accepting the latter honor, 18 Nov. 1830, NjP.

PUBLICATIONS: See Sources, above. For JB's speech endorsing Harrison, see *Proceedings
of the Democratic Whig National Convention ... 4 Dec. 1839* (1839), 33-42.

MANUSCRIPTS: NjP; NjP-SSP; Cincinnati Hist. Soc.; Cincinnati Public Lib.; Ohio Hist.
Soc., Columbus; DLC; MB; MiD; Pierpont Morgan Lib., N.Y.

JJL

Joseph Caldwell

JOSEPH CALDWELL, A.B., A.M. 1794, D.D. 1816, A.M. University of
North Carolina 1799, Presbyterian minister, educator, mathematician, and president of the University of North Carolina, the third
child of Rachel Harker and Joseph Caldwell, was born April 21,
1773 in Lamington, New Jersey, two days after his father's death.
His father had been a physician of Irish descent, and his mother was
the daughter of a Presbyterian clergyman. Rachel Caldwell moved
her family frequently, both because of her straitened circumstances
and her desire to avoid the proximity of British troops. It is not certain whether the family had a home of its own or depended entirely
on the hospitality of relatives and friends. For at least part of his
childhood Joseph was cared for by his widowed grandmother Rachel
Lovel Harker, and he later remembered many instructive and uplift-
ing conversations with her. The Caldwells stayed at various times in
Amwell, Black River, Newton, and Trenton. Caldwell received his
first schooling when the family moved to Bristol on the Pennsylvania
side of the Delaware River. Here, also, his older brother Samuel rescued him from drowning after a forbidden swim on the Sabbath.

Joseph Caldwell, A.B. 1791

Caldwell later cited this incident as the intervention of providence in guiding his life.

He was eleven when the family moved to Princeton and his mother enrolled him in the Nassau Hall grammar school. In September 1784, as a member of the third class, he placed third in the school's competition for premiums. Shortly afterwards the family moved to Newark where he entered the school run by Alexander MacWhorter (A.B. 1757). Moving from Newark to Elizabethtown, Mrs. Caldwell decided to give up the financial struggle of educating her son and obtained a place for him in the office of a local printer. However, she hesitated to have him begin his apprenticeship, and during this interim President John Witherspoon, passing through by stage, paid a visit to the family, another incident which Caldwell credited to providential guidance. Witherspoon assured his mother that the boy's talents would be wasted as a printer and, promising financial assistance should it prove necessary, offered to act as patron if Caldwell matriculated at the College.

Caldwell's scholastic record fully justified Witherspoon's interest in him, despite an early setback. Returning to Princeton in the spring of 1787 Caldwell was examined by the president and, much to the teenager's disappointment, assigned to the first class in the grammar school. At the end of the school year in September he placed first in the examinations for Latin grammar, syntax, and vocabulary, and was admitted to the College as a freshman. At the end of his junior year he placed first in the English competitions for undergraduates, and at his commencement in 1791 he delivered the Latin salutatory address, but only because his classmate Robert Gale, who was the first choice of the faculty, declined the honor. As an undergraduate Caldwell joined the American Whig Society. In spite of being the recipient of Witherspoon's personal attention, he was one of a group of students reprimanded on June 22, 1791 for swimming in the evening and returning to the College "at a very unseasonable hour." He may have had this incident in mind when he later stated, "If there was any pleasure in the moments of clandestine acts of mischief, it was so mixed, in my bosom, with the agitation of apprehended discovery and dread of consequences, that I should be far from recommending it on the score of enjoyment." He also remembered an occasion when the entire student body participated in a strike protesting the unvarying supper of bread and milk served in the College dining hall, when they thought coffee should be served on alternate evenings. For several days they refused to eat, even when Vice President Samuel Stanhope Smith (A.B. 1769) joined them for supper. At this point classes were suspended until order and authority could be restored. Caldwell later claimed that the firmness and reasonableness employed by the faculty in breaking the strike served him as an example when he was called upon to handle more serious outbreaks at the University of North Carolina. No mention of this strike appears in the minutes of the faculty; perhaps it was regarded simply as a minor act of rebellion, easily quelled. On another occasion Caldwell praised the College diet, noting that the students were served buckwheat cakes for breakfast, "which being light, well made, and bespread liberally with butter, were counted by many of us at least among our luxuries."

After graduation Caldwell lived for a time with his mother and older brother Samuel on a farm in Black River, Morris County, New Jersey, that Samuel had inherited from their maternal grandfather. Here Caldwell opened a school for young children, but within a year he obtained a position as an assistant teacher in a school in Elizabethtown. Coming under the influence of the Reverend David Austin (A.B. Yale 1779), pastor of the Presbyterian church there, Caldwell began the study of theology with him. Austin was a popular, but erratic preacher, who became more and more obsessed with prophecy and the Second Coming, which he finally became convinced would occur on May 15, 1796. After waiting through the day with a church full of zealous followers, he finally decided that he had made a slight error in computation. He later proposed a "New Jerusalem Church" at nearby Springfield, inviting believers of all denominations to meet as the "American Israel." He also spent much of his personal funds in preparing and stocking a large storehouse for the benefit of American Jews, who were to meet at Springfield before traveling together to Jerusalem to await the coming of the Messiah. Before Caldwell could become too involved in this prophetic fervor, he was removed from Austin's influence by an invitation to become a tutor in the College. Although he did not begin his duties as a tutor until 1795, on April 4, 1794 the trustees of the College received him for six months under the Lesley Charitable Fund, which had been established for the benefit of poor and pious young men who wished to study for the ministry. His presence in Princeton during 1794 is confirmed by references to him in letters written that year by Joseph Warren Scott (A.B. 1795) to John Henry Hobart (A.B. 1793). Scott reported that Caldwell frequently gave him "sharp strokes" when he found him reading David Hume. Caldwell may have studied theology under both Witherspoon and Smith, but the elderly and blind Witherspoon probably had little time or energy to expend, even on a former protégé. Caldwell later remembered Smith's method of instruction: "There was a class of us, who were studying theology ... under Dr. Smith.... The business of the class occupied much ... time; and no small portion of it was given to the preparation of Dr. Smith's lectures, which we had to write and study closely. We had also to prepare experimental discourses, on such texts as we selected for ourselves." In September 1794 Smith gave a favorable report to the trustees on "the character and improvement" of the young men receiving assistance from the Leslie Fund, and it was resolved that they be supported for another six months. On December 2, 1794 Caldwell was admitted to the New Brunswick presbytery on trial as a candidate for the ministry, and on May 5, 1795, as anticipated, he was appointed a tutor at the College. In January 1796, upon the resignation of David English (A.B. 1789), Caldwell was assigned the extra duties of the clerk of the faculty. Still pursuing his theological studies, he was licensed by the presbytery in September 1796.

Meantime, a correspondence with Caldwell had been initiated by Charles Wilson Harris (A.B. 1792), professor of mathematics and natural philosophy at the University of North Carolina, which had opened in January 1795. Harris had already resigned his post in order to study law, and he hoped that Caldwell might be interested in replacing him at Chapel Hill. Caldwell expressed interest in the professorship, noted that he was studying for the ministry, but indicated that he might be persuaded to teach rather than preach. He felt "diffident" about teaching mathematics, he said, but expressed confidence that he could prepare himself "with assiduity and attention" and asked Harris to send him all information possible about the southern college. By the time Harris answered on July 24, 1796, he had been promoted to presiding president of the university and could assure Caldwell that the trustees would approve his appointment if he wished the position. He noted that, "We imitate Nassau Hall in the conduct of our affairs as much as our circumstances will admit." He considered the neighborhood healthy but the society uncultivated, the cost of living less than at Princeton and the food at the university commons better. The professorship would pay $500 a year, but Harris was confident that it would soon be raised to $600. Considering their college training in experimental philosophy to have been "shamefully & inexcusably deficient," he suggested that Caldwell stop in Philadelphia to learn the use of various pieces of scientific equipment available there. Sometime in August Caldwell wrote to Harris accepting the position.

Caldwell's letter presents an interesting picture of the state of affairs at the College of New Jersey after President Witherspoon's death. Upon hearing of the position offered to Caldwell, Stanhope Smith had expressed his dissatisfaction with his own situation at the College and his interest in a possible relocation to the North Carolina institution, "if the trustees or those in whose power it should be, would give up the disposition and direction of affairs into his hands, the ordering of the buildings in their structure and situation, of the environs of the University, the choice of the Library &c. &c." The college at Princeton, still struggling to repair the damages caused during the war years, was not in a very good financial position, and Smith was discovering that even after years of serving in the vice presidency under his father-in-law, the trustees were not willing to let him broaden the curriculum as he wished. Caldwell believed that Smith's position as president put him under a great deal of expense in entertaining visitors to the campus, who expected to be received with proper ceremony, and that "being on a road which is travelled more than any other in the U. States," such visitors were a frequent occurrence. His letter adds:

It is by no means necessary for me to inform you that the inhabitants of this place were never agreeable to him nor he to them. As to his health, he declares that he is seriously apprehensive of the effects of the next winter upon it. He has filled the office of the president with more mildness than he did that of vice president. The trustees of this place would certainly be very unwilling to part with him.

Smith's concern for his health in a New Jersey winter was not unfounded, since he had an arrested case of tuberculosis and was far from robust. On July 25 Caldwell wrote to William R. Davie (A.B. 1776), who seemed to be the de facto head of the trustees of the University of North Carolina, reiterating Smith's interest in receiving a proposal from the trustees. This letter was also written to advance the cause of John Maclean, professor of chemistry and natural history, who was interested in leaving the College because of his small salary and lack of future prospects. "I do not hesitate to say that so far as the reputation of this college depends upon its immediate professors, you have an opportunity of transferring it in a great measure to the University of your State," Caldwell wrote. Neither Smith nor Maclean received an offer from the trustees, who perhaps felt that they were not in a position to offer enough financial inducement to persuade anyone to leave an already established college. If they had responded, the exodus of Caldwell, Smith, and Maclean, along with the death that fall of Walter Minto, professor of mathematics and natural philosophy, would have left the College at Princeton in the hands of one inexperienced tutor.

Harris advised Caldwell to buy a horse and chair for the journey as a savings over traveling by stage, even suggested a used chair for the sake of economy, and recommended following the post road. He also thought it a good idea to bring enough clothing for a year because such items were more expensive in North Carolina. He estimated that the journey would take a month but that Caldwell would be able to learn a great deal about the geography of the country en route. Leaving Princeton sometime after the September 28 commencement, Caldwell made Philadelphia his first stop. Here the newly licensed ministerial candidate was invited to preach in the Arch Street Church where Ashbel Green (A.B. 1783) was pastor. Caldwell's sermon so impressed the visiting members of another Presbyterian congregation in the city that they called on him the next morning, offering him the vacancy that existed in their own pulpit. It seems doubtful that he had much chance even to consider the offer, for Green immediately dismissed the visitors by curtly observing, "He is on his way to Carolina and to Carolina he is certainly to go. To speak of other places will be in vain." Caldwell reached Chapel Hill on the last day of October, and after resting a day began his teaching duties on November 2, 1796.

The unfinished school and the realities of frontier life were apparently a great shock to him, and he expressed his dissatisfaction in letters to friends at Princeton. A particular cause of distress was the antireligious feeling prevalent in the state and the university.

> The State appears to be swarming with lawyers. It is almost the only profession for which parents educate their children. Religion is so little in vogue, that it affords no temptation to undertake its cause.... In North Carolina, and particularly in the part east of Chapel Hill, every one believes that the way of rising to respectability is to disavow as often and as publicly as possible the leading doctrines of the Scripture.... One reason why religion is so scouted from the most influential part of society, is that it is taught only by ranters, with whom it seems to consist only in the powers of their throats, and the wildness and madness of their gesticulations and distortions.

A letter from John Henry Hobart in Princeton, dated November 30, 1796, indicates that Caldwell had described both the countryside and the manners of the nearby planters as barren and gloomy. "I feel for your situation thus deprived of religious conversation and society, exposed to the insults of the profane and scoffs of the infidel." However, Hobart was happy to learn from Caldwell's latest letter that "your disagreeable feelings were wearing off, and that time and business were reconciling you to your situation." A letter from Thomas How (A.B. 1794) indicates that he and Caldwell had agreed to maintain a "literary correspondence" as two persons engaged in the pursuit of science.

When Harris's resignation took effect at the end of the year, Caldwell was reluctantly persuaded to take over the duties of presiding president, but by late June he had submitted his resignation, claiming that his constitution was too weak to stand the anxiety and fatigue of additional duties. The July 1797 minutes of the trustees show that one cause of dissatisfaction was a disagreement with the tutors in the preparatory school, where Caldwell instructed some twenty students in reading. The trustees authorized an assistant tutor to be hired and resolved that the preparatory school should be conducted according to Caldwell's representation. Correspondence between trustees Davie and James Hogg shows that both men were pleased with his accomplishments and hoped to be able to retain him, even if he was only willing to remain as professor of mathematics. By August Caldwell had decided that he would stay until the following July, since it would probably be difficult to find a replacement. Sometime in the fall of 1797 he made a trip to Charleston, where he had many College acquaintances, and he may have taken the time to investigate career opportunities in that city. Before the end of the year the trustees had offered the professorship of natural philosophy and the title of principal of the university to James Smiley Gillespie (Gillaspie), and Caldwell agreed to continue as professor of mathematics and to teach French in the preparatory school. Caldwell delivered the address when the cornerstone of South Building was laid on April 14, 1798 as part of the university's building program. In July the institution held its first commencement, and Caldwell had apparently decided to remain for at least another term.

Sometime in the latter part of 1797 or early in 1798 a controversial letter was addressed to the board of trustees, scaldingly denouncing Samuel Allen Holmes (possibly Allen S. Holmes, Class of 1788), professor of languages. The letter is presumed to have been the joint effort of the remaining members of the faculty, who accused Holmes of anarchy and atheism and of repeatedly presenting his beliefs to the students. The undated and unsigned version of this letter preserved in the University of North Carolina archives is in Caldwell's handwriting, evidently a copy made for his own records. The trustees' minutes contain no mention of the receipt of such a letter. One paragraph states that "the undersigned professor of mathematics" had tendered his resignation because he found Holmes intolerable to work with in view of his envy, unprincipled ambition, and secret treachery. Holmes was accused of announcing to students and strangers alike that the "undersigned professor of mathematics" was indolent and ignorant and was constantly attempting to introduce "tyrannical and unjust measures against the rights that students must always claim and defend even in the face of any authority." The opening sentence of the last paragraph contains the phrase, "Both the undersigned," and the paragraph continues the use of the plural. Holmes did not resign until July 8, 1799. Whether or not it was at his instigation, the 1798-99 academic year was marked by constant student insubordination and disorderly conduct. On October 28, 1799 Holmes died in Raleigh where he had gone to study law. On Sunday, December 15, 1799 Caldwell preached in that city, delivering a eulogy for his former colleague. It seems out of character for him to have been completely hypocritical in praising Holmes; it may have been done in a spirit of forgiveness, or perhaps differences were partially reconciled when they were no longer aggravated by daily contact.

A spirit of revolt against authority was certainly rife in the nascent university, and sometime in 1797 Ebenezer Pettigrew had been withdrawn by his father because of the "danger of having all fear of the Almighty eradicated from his mind." In the summer of 1798 young Pettigrew received a letter from a friend still at the school, describing the wholesale expulsions and suspensions that were taking place. Ebenezer wondered whether the great number was caused by an increase in the depravity of the students or in the strictness of the faculty. The latter were all young, relatively inexperienced, and obviously not in accord, and their ability to discipline was hampered by the interference of the trustees. Students were crowded into small quarters, in some cases as many as six to a room, in a rural area which offered little outside recreation, and they were presented with a strict code of rules forbidding any form of sport. By November 1799 the student body had dropped from 115 to 84, Gillespie had been beaten in a student riot and had tendered his resignation, and the trustees were looking for a new president, "a man skilled in the Sciences, of polished manners, with dignity in his Appearance, and an established Character."

Caldwell wrote to one of the trustees that some of the expelled students were threatening to return to seek vengeance and that he and William Edwards Webb, the only other member of the faculty, were not only armed but fully resolved to use their weapons if necessary. Both Stanhope Smith and Ashbel Green were approached in regard to the presidency but showed no interest. Even before Caldwell's formal resignation in December, the trustees were advertising to fill three vacant professorships, but he was somehow persuaded to remain as professor of mathematics and chairman of the faculty, a title which he held until 1804, when he was made president in name as well as function.

It is impossible to tell just when Caldwell's antipathy to his situation turned into a real dedication to the University of North Carolina. The trustees drew up a new set of rules in December 1799, and probably most of the remaining students were fearful of the complete demise of the university. With experience and more authority, Caldwell learned to be a strict but respected disciplinarian, later described as "strong of arm and swift of foot" in meting out punishments. He was able to make changes in the curriculum, and without the antagonistic attitude of Holmes the faculty could present a united front to the students. By the early 1800s Caldwell's letters show that he was a firm advocate of the university, quick to defend it from all criticisms. He explained that young men often found restraints irksome and tedious and that it was unjust to destroy an institution for "the disorders of a few wrongheaded young people." Trouble erupted again in 1805 over the appointment of student prefects to help keep order, but this insurrection was part of a general trend in colleges throughout the country that was blamed on the influence of the French Revolution and its antireligious principles. By 1807 most colleges had agreed to blacklist all students from other schools who did not have certificates of honorable dismission.

Caldwell became the object of much personal criticism in a strongly Republican state, where his Federalism was suspected of being too aristocratic. He was able to maintain a religious and moral atmosphere during his tenure, although he was criticized for loading the faculty with too many Presbyterian ministers for a nonsectarian institution. Nevertheless, he is universally credited with being the person who managed to keep the struggling institution from extinction and within a few years raising it to the level of a respected university. Another cause of public criticism of the institution was the effort of the trustees to collect funds under an act of 1794 by which the general assembly granted the trustees all unsold confiscated land. Even the assembly was so outraged by this attempt that it repealed the act of 1794 and tried unsuccessfully to repeal a 1789 act that granted escheated land.

In 1804 Caldwell married Susan Rowan, daughter of Robert Rowan of Fayetteville, North Carolina. She and an infant daughter died three years later. In 1809 Caldwell took a second wife, the widowed Helen Hogg Hooper of Hillsboro, daughter of university trustee James Hogg. She brought two stepsons to the marriage, William and Thomas Clark Hooper. Helen Caldwell taught a Sunday school class in the university chapel and was a graceful as well as forceful addition to social life at Chapel Hill in her role as the president's wife. However, she had at least one detractor in a visitor who claimed that she, not her henpecked husband, really ruled the university.

During the summer vacations of 1809 and 1811 Caldwell canvassed throughout the state "with heroic energy," traveling in a "stick-back gig" until he had raised enough money in subscriptions to complete the South Building, a great boost for the university's morale. He then asked to be relieved of his duties as president so that he could devote more time to teaching and mathematical studies. He also wished to complete a treatise on geometry. He had earlier experimented with writing an elementary geometry textbook and circulating it among the students in manuscript form, allowing them to make their own copies. This soon resulted in a multiplicity of errors, of which the students were quick to take advantage, always blaming any of their own mistakes on an incorrect version of Caldwell's book. To succeed himself as president he approached Robert Hett Chapman (A.B. 1789), a Presbyterian minister, whose experience at teaching had been a short stint as tutor at Queen's College in New Brunswick, New Jersey. Chapman, who took over the duties of president in September 1812, was not a successful administrator and much preferred preaching. He resigned in November 1816 and Caldwell again assumed the duties of president, a role which he filled for the rest of his life.

Caldwell was soon recognized throughout the state for his mastery of mathematics and his wide knowledge of science. In 1813 he served as North Carolina's expert when the boundary was run between that state and South Carolina and Georgia. The Georgia boundary was particularly controversial, since the thirty-fifth degree of latitude had not been properly surveyed and a twelve-mile-wide strip of land was claimed by both states. After the boundary was set, there were several skirmishes before Georgians accepted the fact that this area would henceforth be part of Buncombe County, North Carolina. In 1822 Caldwell and Elisha Mitchell, professor of mathematics and natural philosophy at the University of North Carolina, were commissioned by Davidson County to determine the exact geographic center of the county, upon which they then proposed to erect their courthouse. Caldwell located the central point in the county and then used his report as a means of advocating that the county seat be located "upon a spot recommended at once by the quality of the soil, the pleasantness of the site, the prospect of health, and the opportunities of business." This would enable country people visiting the town to return home with their minds enlarged, their information increased, and their business in markets and courts satisfactorily completed, thereby gratifying their public spirit. He probably made more than a few enemies when he went on to describe many of the existing county seats as places of "wildness and rudeness, intemperance, ferocity, gaming, licentiousness, and malicious litigation."

Caldwell did not avoid facing public issues head on. He was an early supporter of the American Colonization Society, not only by personal contributions, but as president of the Auxiliary Society of Chapel Hill. He was a member of the committee appointed in 1818 by the Presbytery of North Carolina, pledged "to employ his influence and personal exertions" toward promoting the establishment of further auxiliary societies and propagating the goals of the society. These were initially the abolition of the Atlantic slave trade and removal to Africa of free Negroes, but eventually came to include the emancipation of all slaves and their settlement in the society's colony in Liberia. In 1824 Caldwell began a series of newspaper articles under the pen name of Carlton, urging public transportation in North Carolina, in particular a railroad from Beaufort to the Tennessee line. He managed to arouse enough public interest so that the 1834 legislature chartered the Wilmington and Raleigh Railroad Company, although a line was not actually opened until 1840. This project, with his advocacy of improved roads, earned him the title of the "father of internal improvements" in the state. An early proponent of public schools, he published in 1832 a series of eleven *Letters on Popular Education Addressed to the People of North Carolina*, which were highly critical of the state's educational system. He presented a model of an ideal public school system, with provisions for the training of teachers and a plan for elementary, secondary, and higher education. In 1827 he was one of the founders of the North Carolina Institute for the Deaf and Dumb at Raleigh. Two years later he took the unpopular stand of advocating raising taxes for public schools and internal improvements. The state, he declared, was three centuries behind the times on both of these issues. He did not disguise his conviction that the state was parsimonious toward the university that bore its name. He also firmly opposed nullification.

Always interested in the latest developments in mathematics and science, Caldwell persuaded the trustees, during a period of unprecedented prosperity for the university in 1824, to allocate $6,000 with which to purchase scientific equipment and books. He paid his own expenses on a European trip in order to spend this money to the best advantage. It was well that he did, for the financial panic of 1825 resulted in a sharp drop in the number of students and consequently in income. For the remainder of Caldwell's life he worried about the university's indebtedness. In 1827 he had an observatory built on the campus at his own expense, although he was reimbursed for the cost of 430.29\frac{1}{2}$ shortly before his death. Apparatus that he had ordered in London—a meridian transit telescope, an altitude and azimuth telescope, a telescope for observations on the earth and sky, and an astronomical clock with a mercurial pendulum—were installed in the building. He later added a sextant, a portable reflecting circle, and a Hadley's quadrant, also manufactured by London firms. Caldwell is credited with establishing the first observatory at an educational institution in the United States and also with being the first in this country to make systematic observations of the skies. A few years after his death the instruments were removed because of a leaky roof in the observatory, and soon afterwards the building was destroyed by fire.

When he introduced the study of physics to the curriculum in 1829, Caldwell spent £153.4.6 to have a London firm construct what was said to be the first equipment used to teach about electricity in the United States. Its specifications describe a "three-feet plate electrical machine with large branch conductors, supported by two glass pillars, double collectors, mounted in strong mahogany varnished frame with six brass legs fitted into brass sockets and screw nuts, with negative brass conductor on claw feet ... with connecting tubes, brass bells and wires." Although Caldwell was a strong advocate of the classics who reinstated Latin and Greek into the required curriculum after they had been removed by Harris, mathematics and science were his real interests. By the time his students were juniors they were subjected to logarithms, plane trigonometry, mensuration of heights and distances, surveying, spherical trigonometry, navigation, conic sections (analytical geometry), and fluxions (calculus). As seniors they studied natural philosophy, the progress of the mathematical and physical sciences, astronomy, chronology, chemistry, mineralogy, geology, and the philosophy of natural history.

Caldwell died on January 27, 1835, after nine years of "bodily and mental suffering" from a "painful and lingering disease." He had become the acknowledged educational leader in the state and the leading mathematician and astronomer in the South. In 1841 the general assembly named a county for him in recognition of his services. At his death its executive committee resolved on a eulogy that was read at the next commencement of the university, declaring Caldwell "one of the noblest benefactors of the State." The students passed a resolution to wear a "suitable badge of mourning." Caldwell was buried in the village cemetery but was disinterred the following November so that the artist Alfred Waugh could make a cast of his features in order to produce a bust for the university. On October 31, 1846 the body was removed to be buried beside that of his wife and stepson near the university's Dialectic Hall. In 1858 a marble monument to his memory was erected on the campus.

SOURCES: *DAB*; alumni file, PUA; "Autobiog. of Rev. Joseph Caldwell, D.D.," *Univ. of N.C. Mag.*, 9 (1859), 1-25, 65-93; *N.J. Gazette*, 4 Oct. 1784; Min. Fac., 10 Nov. 1789, 22 June ("unseasonable hour") & 9 July 1791; Amer. Whig Soc., *Cat.* (1840), 6; Hancock House MSS; Williams, *Academic Honors*, 12-13; *Dunlap's Amer. Daily Advt.*, 4 Oct. 1791; *Dunlap & Claypoole's Amer. Daily Advt.*, 7 Oct. 1794; *Trenton Federalist*, 7 Oct. 1816; Min. Trustees, 4 Apr. 1794, Sept. 1794, May 1795, Apr. 1796; *Appleton's Cyclopædia of Amer. Biog.* (1888-89 repr. 1968), I, 497-98; Foote, *Sketches, N.C.*, 534-57; Dexter, *Yale Biographies*, IV, 93; E. R. Hatfield, *Hist. of Elizabeth, N.J.* (1868), 596-601, 605-06; J. McVickar, *Early Life & Professional Years of Bishop Hobart* (1838), 96-97, 155-56; New Brunswick Presby. Min., 2 Dec. 1794–22 Sept. 1796 *passim*; *Hobart Corres.*, I, cxii; II, 36; K. P. Battle, *Hist. of the Univ. of N.C.* (1908), *passim*; S. J. Novak, *The Rights of Youth* (1977), 19-24, 106-14; A. Henderson, *North Carolina* (1941), I, 444-45, 496, 501, 537-39, 614, 719-20; S. M. Lemmon, ed., *Pettigrew Papers, I, 1685-1818* (1971), 219-21; *Annual Reports of the Amer. Soc. for Colonizing the Free People of Colour of the U.S.*, vols. 1-10 (1818-27, repr. in 1 vol. 1969): 7th Annual Report, 165; 10th Annual Report, 70-71, 93; K. P. Battle, *Sketches of the Hist. of N.C.* (1889), *passim*; G. G. Johnson, *Ante-Bellum N.C.* (1937), 24, 116-17, 228, 263-64, 267, 294, 296, 331-32, 714; R. D. W. Connor, *Doc. Hist. of the Univ. of N.C., 1776-99* (1953), *passim*; H. M. Wagstaff, "The Harris Letters," *James Sprunt Hist. Pubs.*, 14 (1916), 1-91.

PUBLICATIONS: STE # 37081; Sh-Sh #s 1982, 28064, 40380; Sh-C #s 8239, 28361, 32549; R-B #s 11617, 23661; and "On the Perfection of the Divine Law," in Colin McIver, *Southern Preacher* (1824). See also the posthumously published autobiographical sketch cited above.

MANUSCRIPTS: Univ. of N.C. Archives; T; DLC

RLW

Henry Tate Callaway (Calloway)

HENRY TATE CALLAWAY (CALLOWAY), A.B., A.B. Hampden-Sidney 1788, attorney and public official, was born on April 24, 1769 in Bedford County, Virginia, the tenth child of Col. James Callaway and his first wife, Sarah Tate. In all, Callaway married three times and had twenty-two children, including Henry's brother and classmate Robert. John Callaway (Class of 1802) may have been a half-brother. The colonel was a leading citizen of southwestern Virginia. He sat for Bedford County in the house of burgesses from 1766 to 1769. During the Revolutionary War, he was detached from active service to make iron for the use of the American military at his Oxford iron works. He also owned working lead mines. When Campbell County was set off from Bedford County in 1782, he became its county lieutenant, a position he had also held in Bedford. In 1789 he transferred his civic activities back to Bedford. This flexibility is probably explained by extensive landholdings in both counties as well as by his residence near New London, on the border between the two counties.

Henry Callaway received an A.B. degree from Hampden-Sidney College in September 1788, but the absence of other records makes it impossible to say how long he had been a student there. Perhaps he received his preliminary education at the attached grammar school. After an unexplained gap of a year, Callaway ventured north and entered the junior class of the College. His name was added at the end of a class list dated November 10, 1789, suggesting that he was not yet in attendance when it was first compiled. Certainly he had become a student by March 31, 1790, when he joined the Cliosophic Society. He took as his pseudonym Tellomont, an apparent reference to Sebastien Le Nain de Tillemont (1637-1698), the French ecclesiastical historian praised by Edward Gibbon.

Callaway's placement in the junior class is rather puzzling in light of his previous baccalaureate degree from Hampden-Sidney. Others of its graduates who entered the College became seniors. He appears in the class list of November 29, 1790 as a senior, but not that of May 1791, and although he was awarded an A.B., he did not attend the commencement exercises. There is therefore some question whether

Callaway spent much more than a year at the College and whether his second degree was more than a courtesy bestowed on what was essentially a postgraduate student.

The history of Callaway's education is further complicated by his having also studied at the College of William and Mary for an indeterminate period "about 1790," perhaps during the academic year 1788-89. Alternatively, he could have attended law lectures there after leaving the College in 1791. The latter is, perhaps, the more satisfactory theory, given the next fix on his activities. On May 13, 1795 he was admitted as an attorney in the court of Botetourt County, Virginia.

Frontier lawyers generally qualified and practiced in a number of county courts, and there is no reason to assume that Callaway ever lived in Botetourt. He seems rather to have made his home at Rocky Mount in Franklin County, which was carved out of pieces of Bedford and Henry counties in 1786. On January 23, 1800 he was chosen to the Republican corresponding committee of Franklin County for the ensuing election, and he became one of three county commissioners to supervise the presidential election of that year. He represented Franklin in the state house of delegates from 1804 to 1806.

At his father's death in 1809 Callaway inherited a large estate on the Blackwater River in Franklin County, as well as a tract of 310 acres in Montgomery County. On July 5, 1812 he married Martha (or Elizabeth) Guerrant, a daughter of Col. Peter Guerrant, who came to Franklin from Buckingham County in 1805. She bore him five daughters and two sons.

Callaway was wealthy, as evidenced by his giving one daughter a dowry of 3,000 acres on the Blackwater and thirty slaves when she married in 1845. When a post office was established in July 1833 at Retreat in Franklin County, he was its first postmaster. He headed the list of members when the Piedmont Presbyterian Church was founded at Callaway (named for Henry and his brother James), also in Franklin County, in the years 1850 to 1851. Henry Tate Callaway died in 1852.

SOURCES: M. D. Ackerley & L. E. J. Parker, *"Our Kin": Genealogies of . . . the Early Families . . . of Bedford Cnty.* (1930), 295-305; L. Pecquet du Bellet, *Some Prominent Va. Families* (1907 repr. 1976, 4 vols. in 2), II, 720-24; R. H. Early, *Campbell Chronicles & Family Sketches* (1927), 359, 362-65; Heitman, 140; H. C. Bradshaw, *Hist. of Hampden-Sydney College* (1976), I, 74; letter from the librarian, Hampden-Sydney College, 8 Nov. 1982, PUA; Min. Fac., 10 Nov. 1789, 29 Nov. 1790; Clio. lists; *Dunlap's Amer. Daily Advt.,* 4 Oct. 1791; College of William & Mary, *Provisional List of Alumni, Grammar School Students, . . . 1693-1888* (1941), 11 ("about"); L. P. Summers, *Annals of Southwest Va. 1769-1800* (1929), 461; *Cal. Va. St. Papers,* IX, 78, 84, 124; M. Wingfield, *Marriage Bonds of Franklin Cnty., Va., 1786-1858* (1939), 52; M. Wingfield, *Franklin Cnty., Va.: A Hist.* (1964), 5-6, 118, 214, 228. Although the trustees' minutes of 27 Sept. 1791 do not list the Callaway brothers among the A.B. recipients, both the newspaper account of the commencement and the 1792 College catalogue credit them with the degree.

JJL

Robert J. Callaway (Calloway)

ROBERT J. CALLAWAY (CALLOWAY), A.B., A.B. Hampden-Sidney 1788, perennial student, was born in 1771, the eleventh of twelve children of James and Sarah Tate Callaway of Bedford County, Virginia, and the brother of his classmate Henry Callaway. John Callaway (Class of 1802) may have been a half-brother. The father served as a colonel in the Virginia militia from 1780 to 1781, but his main contribution to the war effort came through his operation of iron and lead mines. He lived near the border of Bedford and Campbell counties and was influential in both.

In every piece of evidence relating to Robert, he appears in the company of his brother Henry. They graduated from Hampden-Sidney in late September 1788, after a term of residence which could possibly have begun at its affiliated grammar school. They both attended the College of William and Mary for an indeterminate period "about 1790," which means that they were there either during the academic year 1788-89 or after leaving Princeton. They both were admitted to the College as juniors sometime after November 10, 1789 and before March 31, 1790, when they joined the Cliosophic Society. Robert took the pseudonym Cleamicus, the source of which is obscure, unless it simply means "friend of Clio." Although the brothers were both awarded A.B. degrees *in absentia*, they seem to have left the College sometime between the compilation of the class lists of November 29, 1790 and May 1791. Perhaps they were regarded as special students with their second degree awarded as a courtesy, rather like the contemporary practice of awarding masters' degrees *ad eundem* to qualified alumni from other colleges.

Robert died unmarried in 1794.

SOURCES: M. D. Ackerley & L. E. J. Parker, *"Our Kin": Genealogies of ... the Early Families ... of Bedford Cnty.* (1930), 295-305; L. Pecquet du Bellet, *Some Prominent Va. Families* (1907 repr. 1976, 4 vols. in 2), II, 720-24; R. H. Early, *Campbell Chronicles & Family Sketches* (1927), 359, 362-65; Heitman, 140; H. C. Bradshaw, *Hist. of Hampden-Sydney College* (1976), I, 74; letter from the librarian, Hampden-Sydney College, 8 Nov. 1982, PUA; Min. Fac., 10 Nov. 1789, 29 Nov. 1790; Clio. lists; *Dunlap's Amer. Daily Advt.*, 4 Oct. 1791; College of William & Mary, *Provisional List of Alumni, Grammar School Students, ... 1693-1888* (1941), 11 ("about").

JJL

James Campbell

JAMES CAMPBELL, A.B., of Virginia, was admitted to the College as a junior in November 1789. He did not join either literary society. He appears on the class lists for the start of the summer terms in 1790 and 1791, but not on the intervening list of November 29, 1790. The discrepancy is unexplained. Perhaps he was just late getting back from the vacation. How long he remained on campus after May 1791 has not been discovered. He was not assigned a part when the faculty was ordering the commencement exercises in July and did not attend his commencement in September.

Campbell has not been identified. The name is common in Virginia, with the 1820 census listing seventeen James Campbells from twelve counties. Perhaps James was related to his classmate William Campbell or the Mr. Campbell of the Class of 1795 who entered the College as a freshman in 1791, but these possibilities remain unsubstantiated.

SOURCES: Min. Fac., 10 Nov. 1789, 9 July 1791, & undated class lists ca. May 1790 & May 1791; *Dunlap's Amer. Daily Advt.*, 4 Oct. 1791; J. R. Felldin, *Index to the 1820 Census of Va.* (1976), 67. In no special order, James Campbells who are sufficiently contemporary to be reasonable prospects have been found in the town of Petersburg, (*WMQ*, 2d ser., 17 [1937], 29; *VMHB*, 77 [1969], 335; *Tyler's Quart.*, 19 [1937], 65, 77; B. H. Latrobe, *Va. Journals of Benjamin Henry Latrobe* [1977], 537), & the counties of Amherst (W. M. Sweeny, *Marriage Bonds & Other Marriage Records of Amherst Cnty., Va.* [1937], 15); Augusta (M. C. Pilcher, *Hist. Sketches of the Campbell, Pilcher & kindred Families* [1911], 210); Bedford (M. D. Ackerley & L. E. J. Parker, *"Our Kin"* [1930], 267, 277, 281); Berkeley, (J. E. Norris, *Hist. of the Lower Shenandoah Valley* [1890 repr. 1972], 294; *Cal. Va. St. Papers*, IX, 47); Botetourt (R. D. Stone, *Seed-Bed of the Republic* [2d ed., 1962], 341); Campbell (*VMHB*, 36 [1928], 258); Charles City (*Cal. Va. St. Papers*, VI, 83); Norfolk (*VMHB*, 23 [1915], 413); Prince William (Writers' Program, Va., *Prince William* [1941], 80); Rockbridge (*Cal. Va. St. Papers*, IX, 427; D. F. Wulfeck, *Marriages of Some Va. Residents 1607-1800*, 1st ser. [1961-67], II, 13; Pilcher, 205; R. B. Woodworth, *Hist. of the Presby. of Winchester* [1947], 453); Rockingham (Wulfeck, 1st ser., II, 13); & Wythe (*Cal. Va. St. Papers*, IX, 217, 297; W. C. Torrence, *Va. Wills & Administrations 1632-1800* [1965], 69).

JJL

William Campbell

WILLIAM CAMPBELL has not been positively identified. His only appearance in the College sources came in a manuscript class list dated April 10, 1789, when "William Campble" from "V." was listed as a sophomore. Assuming that "Campble" meant Campbell and that "V." stood for Virginia seems reasonable, but this does not sufficiently narrow the field, because the name was very common there. William Campbells were marriage grooms at least six times in Vir-

ginia between 1792 and 1800, and the 1820 census lists fully twenty-one of them, from seventeen counties. Perhaps James Campbell,
William's classmate and also a Virginian, and a Mr. Campbell (Class
of 1795) were related to him, but given the proliferation of the name,
and the fact that James did not arrive at the College until after
William left, even this conjecture is open to dispute.

SOURCES: Hancock House MSS; D. F. Wulfeck, *Marriages of Some Va. Residents 1607-
1800*, 1st ser. (1961-67), II, 16; R. T. Green, *Geneal. & Hist. Notes on Culpeper Cnty.,
Va.* (1900), 59; J. R. Felldin, *Index to the 1820 Census of Va.* (1976), 67. One possibility
is that William was the son of Col. Arthur Campbell of Washington County, Virginia,
a pioneer settler on the Holston River, soldier in various wars with the Cherokee, and
member of the house of burgesses, convention of 1776, and general assembly. His
eldest son William was an ensign who commanded a detachment of twenty militiamen
at Powell's Valley which was threatened by the Cherokee in summer 1792 and who
perhaps was also the man endorsed by Lee County as a suitable addition to its
commission of the peace in 1796. He married Sarah Adams, had at least two sons,
and was still alive in 1840. His birthdate has not been discovered, but his parents
were married on May 12, 1773, which would suggest that he was probably somewhat
young to be attending the College in 1789. See M. C. Pilcher, *Hist. Sketches of the
Campbell, Pilcher & kindred Families* (1911), 55-59, 104, 129; *Cal. Va. St. Papers*, V,
578, 635, 639, 653; VI, 96, 175; VIII, 396. Other at least potentially contemporary
William Campbells can be found in Bedford (*VMHB*, 80 [1972], 74; 7 [1900], 238);
Botetourt (R. D. Stoner, *Seed-Bed of the Republic* [2d ed., 1962], 157, 232); Campbell,
Princess Anne, Norfolk (Wulfeck, 1st ser., II, 16); Culpeper (Green, 59); & Rockbridge
counties (Pilcher, 205; Wulfeck, 1st ser., II, 16; *VMHB*, 6 [1898], 431); plus the city
of Richmond (*VMHB*, 7 [1900], 229-37). The Princetonian cannot have been the son
of Gen. William Campbell, commander of the American forces at the Battle of King's
Mountain, whose only son, Charles, died very young. See Pilcher, 82.

JJL

John Dennis

JOHN DENNIS, lawyer and public official, was born in 1771 at "Beverly," on the Pocomoke River, Worcester County, Maryland, a younger
son of Littleton and Susannah Upshur Dennis. The father was a
wealthy planter and attorney who possessed £10,000 in personal
estate and 5,000 acres in land at his death in 1774. John Dennis
was educated at home and then at the Washington Academy, near
Princess Anne, Somerset County, Maryland. He seems to have served
later as a trustee of that school.

In November 1788 Dennis entered the College as a sophomore.
He joined the Cliosophic Society on June 10, 1789, taking as his
debating name Horatio, the mythical hero of ancient Rome renowned
for his single-handed defense of a bridge against the entire Etruscan
army. On May 29, 1790 he obtained an honorable dismission from
the College.

Dennis must have spent the next few years reading law, for he was

John Dennis, Class of 1791
BY CHARLES B. J. FEVRET DE SAINT MEMIN

admitted to the bar in 1793 and then opened an office in Princess
Anne. He immediately embarked on a precocious political career.
In 1793, 1794, and 1795, he represented Worcester County in the
Maryland House of Delegates, and in 1797, the first year he was old
enough, he entered the United States House of Representatives for
the first of four consecutive terms. He represented a district comprising Dorchester, Somerset and Worcester counties. By January of
the next year he was sufficiently esteemed by his colleagues to be
one of the eleven managers chosen to present the House case to the
Senate in the impeachment trial of Senator William Blount of Tennessee. The first of its kind under the Constitution, the trial ended on
January 14, 1799 with dismissal of the charges due to lack of jurisdiction, thus establishing the principle that members of Congress are
not liable to impeachment.

Dennis was a Federalist who allied himself with the wing headed
by John Adams in its battles against both Republicans and supporters
of Alexander Hamilton (LL.D. 1791) within the Federalist party. He
was probably the author of a 1798 tract which supported Adams's
firmness toward the French and condemned the president's enemies

as "abandoned miscreants many of whom have recently fled from
the just vengeance of offended justice." A year later he pledged
his support to Adams if he would send a peace mission to France
and dismiss from the cabinet Timothy Pickering (LL.D. 1798) and
James McHenry, who supported Hamilton and a French war. Dennis
abstained in the final vote on the Sedition Act on July 10, 1798
and also steered a moderate course when the presidential election
of 1800 was decided in the House of Representatives. He was one
of those who voted for Aaron Burr (A.B. 1772) in order to deny
Thomas Jefferson (LL.D. 1791) the presidency. Ultimately, however,
he was one of six Federalists who decided against risking the collapse
of the Union to keep Jefferson out of office. They abstained, thus
permitting his election.

Dennis spoke regularly on the floor of the House, although his
voting record does not suggest extraordinary conscientiousness in
attendance. He participated in about half of the roll call votes conducted while he was in Congress. He spoke in favor of the bill by
which Congress established its jurisdiction over local government in
the District of Columbia in February 1801, and he opposed subsequent efforts to "retrocede" responsibility for its governance to
Maryland and Virginia. In January 1804 he locked horns with John
Randolph (Class of 1791) over the impeachment of Supreme Court
Justice Samuel Chase. Dennis framed his objections to the impeachment largely on procedural grounds, arguing that the motion cre
ating a committee of inquiry must state the specific grounds which
were thought to merit impeachment. Lack of specificity would permit
the creation of a politically motivated inquisitorial committee which
"might become an engine of oppression."

Dennis resided at "Beckford," near Princess Anne. He married
Elinor Wilson Jackson, the daughter of Henry Jackson of Working-
ton, in Somerset County. Among their four sons and three daughters were Littleton James Dennis (A.B. 1816), John Dennis, subsequently a congressman from 1837 to 1841, and Elizabeth, the first
wife of Abel Parker Upshur (Class of 1807). Upshur, while secretary
of state under President John Tyler, was killed in 1844 when a newly
designed cannon exploded on the decks of the *U.S.S. Princeton.*

No evidence on John Dennis's career subsequent to his leaving
Congress has been found, but he was in Philadelphia for some reason
on August 17, 1806, when he died suddenly.

SOURCES: *Biog. Dict. Md. Leg.,* I, 261-62; R. V. Truitt & M. G. Les Callette, *Worcester
Cnty.: Md.'s Arcadia* (1977), 178-79 (photograph of "Beverly"), 314-15, 532-33; *BDUSC,*
896; *MHM,* 21 (1926), 157; 41 (1946), 231; 44 (1949), 205; Clio. lists; Hancock House
MSS; Min. Fac., 10 Nov. 1789; letter from Md. Leg. Hist. Proj., 29 Jan. 1982, PUA;

F. Emory, *Queen Anne's Cnty., Md.* (1950), 368; L. M. Renzulli, Jr., *Md.: The Federalist Years* (1972), 187, 195, 207, 230; J. Dennis (supposed author), *An Address to the People of Md.* (1798, STE # 33626) ("abandoned miscreants," 49); N. K. Risjord, *Chesapeake Politics 1781-1800* (1978), 532; E. G. Roddy, "Md. & the Presidential Election of 1800," *MHM*, 56 (1961), 246, 263; T. H. Benton, *Abridgement of the Debates of Congress, from 1789 to 1856* (1857-61), II-III, *passim*, for sample of roll-calls ("might become," III, 111); *A/C*, 5th Cong., 2d sess., 957; MS will of John Dennis, 8 July 1800, proved 10 Sept. 1806, Somerset County Court House, Md. (photocopy in PUA); alumni file of Littleton James Dennis, (A.B. 1816), PUA; *Poulson's Amer. Daily Advt.*, 19 Aug. 1806. *BDUSC* asserts that Dennis attended Yale, but the archivist of Yale University has no record of his attendance (letter of 1 Mar. 1982, PUA). Through his son-in-law and possibly also through his mother, JD was connected to Jacob G. Parker (A.B. 1802) and Caleb Upshur, Jr. (A.B. 1802). Identification of the Princetonian Dennis with the congressman rests on the fact that the Cliosophic Society records give his native state as Maryland and list his occupation as "law," and on the connection of his son with the College. However another contemporary John Dennis, from Baltimore, cannot be completely ruled out. All that has been learned of this John Dennis is that he was born in 1770, married Ann Thomas of Cecil County, Maryland, in 1796, and died in 1818. See *MHM*, 34 (1939), 203.

PUBLICATION: See Sources.

JJL

John Dickinson

JOHN DICKINSON of Maryland appears among the sophomores on a manuscript list of students of the College dated April 10, 1789, now in the New Jersey State Archives. The only other evidence of his stay at the College is an undated set of notes on a series of lectures on "Chronology," or ancient history. He does not appear on the class list of November 10, 1789. A positive identification remains to be made, but he may have been the brother of his classmate Samuel Sharp Dickinson. Their stays at the College probably overlapped, and John's notes on chronology are bound with Samuel's notes on moral philosophy and criticism in the extant volume at the Princeton University Library. Perhaps Samuel was given John's notes when the latter withdrew from the College.

If John was Samuel Sharp Dickinson's brother, he may have been raised at the ancestral home of "Crosiadore" on the Choptank River in Talbot County, which Samuel eventually inherited. Samuel was the son of Samuel Dickinson, who in turn was probably the nephew of John Dickinson of Pennsylvania (LL.D. 1769), the Revolutionary statesman and political writer.

Unfortunately no direct evidence that Samuel had a brother John has been located. Another prospective identification of the Princetonian is the John Dickinson who was the son of an earlier John Dickinson (ca. 1726-1789), who was born in Talbot but had moved to Dorchester County by 1774. The elder John Dickinson held 1,500 acres in Caroline, Dorchester, and Talbot counties at his death. In 1758 he married Ann, the daughter of Henry and Elizabeth Trippe, by whom he had six sons and one daughter. Ann was the first cousin of Elizabeth Hindman Perry, the mother of William Perry (A.B. 1789). The date of birth of the younger John Dickinson has not been discovered, but he must have been of approximately the right age to be the one who attended the College, in which case his absence after 1789 might be explained by the death of his father in that year. He seems to have been related at best only very distantly to Samuel Sharp Dickinson. By 1810 he had died without progeny.

Choosing between these two hypotheses without further evidence is impossible. Fortunately the record of Dickinson's postcollegiate career is less tangled, albeit sparse. The 1800 Maryland census lists one John Dickinson, in Talbot County, where he had nineteen slaves and six whites in his household. He was married to Sarah Lloyd in Talbot County on April 25, 1801, by Mr. Bowie, an Episcopal minister. He does not appear in the 1810 census.

SOURCES: Hancock House MSS; MS vol. of Witherspoon lecture notes by JD & Samuel Sharp Dickinson, NjP; B. S. Ball & V. D. Bales, *Dickenson Families of England and Amer.* (1972), 16; P. P. Dickinson, *Dickinson Geneal.* (1970), 79-82; C. J. Stillé, *Life and Times of John Dickinson* (1891), 10, 12-14; G. N. MacKenzie, *Colonial Families of the U.S.A.* (1907-20 repr. 1966), I, 200, 533, 535; *MHM*, 36 (1941), 325; *Biog. Dict. Md. Leg.*, I, 269-70; II, 841; O. Tilghman, *Hist. of Talbot Cnty., Md. 1661-1861* (1915), I, 65-66, 524; Md. Geneal. Soc., *Bull.*, 14 no. 2 (1973), 20; R. B. Clark & S. S. Clark, *Talbot Cnty., Md. Marriage Licenses 1792-1824* (1965), 10. The will of Samuel Sharp Dickinson's father Samuel, dated 27 Oct. 1803, mentions no son John. Presumably either John was dead by 1803 or Samuel Sr. had no such son (MS will of Samuel Dickinson, 27 Oct. 1803, proved 19 June 1804, Md. Hall of Records, Annapolis [photocopy in PUA]).

JJL

Samuel Sharp Dickinson

SAMUEL SHARP DICKINSON, A.B., physician and planter, was born in 1771 near Trappe, Talbot County, Maryland, one of at least four sons and two daughters of Samuel Dickinson and his wife, whose maiden name was Sharp. The father was probably the son of Henry Dickinson, the half-brother of John Dickinson (LL.D. 1769), the author of *Letters of a Pennsylvania Farmer*. Samuel Dickinson, Sr., owned 1,314 acres and seventeen slaves in Talbot County in 1798, when his property valuation placed him seventeenth on the county tax lists. Quite likely his namesake was born and raised at "Crosiadore," the "splendid plantation" on the north bank of the Choptank River which belonged to the Dickinson family from the late 1600s to at least 1950. Dickinson was probably related to and possibly named for the Samuel Sharpe who was on the Talbot County committee of observation during the Revolutionary War. The Talbot County Sharps and Dickinsons were both traditionally Quaker, but by the later eighteenth century many had converted to Episcopalianism, including Samuel, Sr., and his son. Samuel S. Dickinson and classmate John Dickinson were probably brothers or cousins. Hard evidence is lacking, but a manuscript volume of notes on John Witherspoon's lectures now at the Princeton University Library is partly by Samuel and partly by John Dickinson, which suggests a close relationship.

Dickinson entered the College as a sophomore in November 1788. His absence from the class list of April 10, 1789 suggests that he returned late from the spring vacation. On August 5 of the same year he joined the Cliosophic Society, taking as his pseudonym Penn. The records of the Cliosophic Society list him as "dismissed" for unstated reasons in February 1790. The extant lecture notes cover Witherspoon's class on moral philosophy beginning in November of Dickinson's senior year, and a course in "Criticism." The notes for the latter are bound after but probably precede the former chronologically, since one page of the criticism notes is dated Easton, also in Talbot County, July 21, 1790. Why Dickinson was in Easton on this date is unclear, since school was in session. On November 29, 1790 Dickinson and five other students, four of whom were his classmates and three of whom were also Marylanders, were boarding out of the College, as evidenced by a complaint from the steward. At his commencement Dickinson was replicator in a debate with the topic "Are not lotteries for public purposes disadvantageous to the community?"

Dickinson then began medical studies in Philadelphia. He attended medical lectures at the University of Pennsylvania for the academic year 1792-93 but took no degree. He is described on the class list of Benjamin Rush (A.B. 1760) as a resident of Delaware, where his family possessed extensive landholdings. Subsequently he returned to Talbot County, where he seems to have concentrated on agricultural pursuits. He never practiced medicine, although he joined the Medical and Chirurgical Faculty of the State of Maryland, the state medical society.

Dickinson was living on a farm belonging to his father called "Howells Point" when the latter made his will on October 27, 1803. After the death of the elder Samuel sometime before June 19, 1804, Dickinson inherited "Crosiadore" with the stipulation that he pay any debts owing when his father died. "Howells Point" went to Samuel S.

Dickinson's brother Solomon. On December 16, 1806 J. McClaskey, a Methodist minister, married Dickinson to Mary (or May) Trippe Webb in Talbot County. She was the daughter of William and Mary Noel Trippe and the widow of Maj. Peter Webb. No information on whether the Dickinsons had children has been found.

One historian describes Dickinson as having been a Republican during the "First Party Era," when he was a member of Talbot County's levy and county courts. On May 29, 1798 President John Adams nominated Samuel Dickinson of Maryland a lieutenant in the Corps of Artillerists and Engineers, United States Army, and the Senate confirmed him three days later. If this was Samuel Sharp Dickinson the appointment was unusual, since most such posts were then reserved for Federalists. Apparently he declined the appointment or served only briefly, for he is not listed in Francis B. Heitman's comprehensive listing of U.S. Army officers. Dickinson subsequently became one of Talbot County's leading Jacksonians at a time when the party was in the minority there. He chaired several meetings and went as a delegate to party conventions between 1832 and 1834.

In the Talbot County tax list of 1832, Dickinson owned 500 acres and eight slaves. The total tax valuation of $3,693 was not among the county's fifty highest. He happened to be in Washington on June 2, 1838 when he visited Secretary of the Navy Mahlon Dickerson (A.B. 1789). Apparently the passage of fifty years worked no fundamental change in Dickinson's appearance, for Dickerson commented that "We were companions at College, & I had never seen him since we parted in September 1789—I knew him immediately & was much pleas'd with him. Walk'd with him at ev'g." Dickinson died in 1840 or 1841.

SOURCES: E. F. Cordell, *Med. Annals of Md. 1799-1899* (1903), 377 ("splendid"); B. S. Ball & V. D. Bales, *Dickenson Families of England & Amer.* (1972), 16; P. P. Dickinson, *Dickinson Geneal.* (1970), 79-82; C. J. Stillé, *Life & Times of John Dickinson* (1891), 10, 12-14; A. W. Burns, comp., *Md. Will Book* (1937-39), XXXI, 125-26; G. N. MacKenzie, *Colonial Families of the U.S.A.* (1907-20 repr. 1966), I, 200, 533, 535; *MHM*, 36 (1941), 325; 37 (1942), 324-25; C. B. Clark, *Eastern Shore of Md. & Va.* (1950), 3-4; D. J. Preston, *Talbot Cnty.: A Hist.* (1983), 24-25, 124 (photograph of "Crosiadore" before it was razed in 1976); W. H. Ridgway, *Community Leadership in Md., 1790-1840* (1979), 36, 38, 324, 328, 331 ("First Party"); *Biog. Dict. Md. Leg.*, I, 269-70; O. Tilghman, *Hist. of Talbot Cnty., Md. 1661-1861* (1915), I, 65-66, 524; Clio. lists; MS vol. of Witherspoon lecture notes by SSD and John Dickinson, NjP; Min. Fac., 10 Nov. 1789, 9 July 1791; *Dunlap's Amer. Daily Advt.*, 4 Oct. 1791 ("Are not"); MS class list of Benjamin Rush's medical students, UPenn-Ar; MS will of Samuel Dickinson, 27 Oct. 1803, proved 19 June 1804, Md. Hall of Records, Annapolis (photocopy in PUA); R. B. Clark & S. S. Clark, *Talbot Cnty. Md. Marriage Licenses 1792-1824* (1965), 10; U.S. Senate, *Journal of the Executive Proc.*, 1st to 19th Cong. (1828), I, 277; MS Mahlon Dickerson Diary, 2 June 1838, NjHi ("We were"); Alexander, 254. Alexander's assertion that Dickinson represented Talbot County in the state legislature is incorrect (letter from Md. Leg. Hist. Proj., 29 Jan. 1982, PUA). College catalogues began giving Dickinson's surname as "Dickerson" in 1851. This is in error; all other sources, including his own signature in the MS lecture notes, agree that it was Dickinson. The signature also justifies the preference of "Sharp" over "Sharpe," and so does SSD's father's will. The *Gen. Cat.* and Cordell both credit Dickinson with an M.D., but this has not been verified.

JJL

Allen Bowie Duckett

ALLEN BOWIE DUCKETT, A.B., A.M. 1794, lawyer and public servant, was one of the three sons and two daughters of Thomas Duckett of Queen Anne Parish, Prince Georges County, Maryland, by his first wife, Priscilla Fraser Bowie Duckett. Thomas Duckett was a merchant and planter who eventually served in both houses of the state legislature. At his death in 1806 he left 929 acres in Prince Georges County and personal property valued at £4,649. His wife Priscilla was the half-sister of Fielder Bowie, the father of Thomas Contee Bowie (Class of 1791).

No information on Duckett's earlier schooling has been found, but it was far enough advanced to get him into the junior class when he entered the College in November 1789. He joined the Cliosophic Society on November 25, 1789, taking the pseudonym Abelard, for Peter Abelard (1079-1142), the great French scholastic philosopher and lover of Heloise. Duckett was voted intermediate honors by the faculty at the time of his graduation. At his commencement he delivered "An oration on the public credit."

Duckett combined a legal career with an active political life. In 1793, 1794, and 1795, he served as assistant clerk of the house of delegates, the lower house of the Maryland legislature. He sat in the house of delegates himself from 1796 to 1800, representing Prince Georges County. From 1801 to 1806 he served on the executive council of the state of Maryland, which was chosen by the state legislature and designed to serve as a check on the governor's already limited powers; the council's advice and consent were required before the chief executive made any major decision. The council comprised five people, elected to one-year terms, and its members had to be able to prove that they owned £1,000 in freehold property.

Duckett was a Republican. He wrote a letter in 1804 lauding the "attachment to Republican principles and the present administration of the General Government" of a colleague seeking a federal office. Thomas Jefferson (LL.D. 1791) presumably was satisfied that Duckett himself was similarly attached, for on February 26, 1806, he appointed Duckett an associate justice of the circuit court of the District of Columbia. This tribunal, comprising a chief justice and two associates, was created by the congressional act of February 27, 1801, which set up a judicial system for the District. Its ten square miles were divided into two counties: Alexandria County for the portion across the Potomac River originally belonging to Virginia (and returned to that state in 1846), and Washington County for the area, originally part of Maryland, which now constitutes the District. Virginia law was to apply in the former and Maryland law in the latter, with the circuit court to hold quarterly sessions in each county.

The most important case considered by the court during Duckett's tenure came in January 1807, when it ruled on the sufficiency of the evidence for holding Dr. Justus Erich Bollmann and Samuel Swartwout in custody on charges of treason. Bollmann and Swartwout were messengers of Aaron Burr (A.B. 1772) who were arrested in New Orleans by Gen. James Wilkinson when the Burr Conspiracy hysteria was at its peak. Wilkinson suspended their right to sue for release via *habeas corpus* and sent them in irons directly to President Jefferson at Washington. After a hearing which attracted widespread attention, Duckett and fellow Republican Nicholas Fitzhugh voted down Chief Justice William Cranch, the sole Adams appointee, and ruled on January 30 that the pair be held without bail. One historian has called this decision "the first time in our history a National Court divided on political grounds." However within a month the Supreme Court ordered the release of Bollmann and Swartwout on a writ of *habeas corpus*.

Duckett's service as justice ended with his death on July 19, 1809. During his residence in Washington he lived on K Street, between 26th and 27th Streets. Duckett had married Margaret, the daughter of Joseph and Margaret Hall Howard, on October 17, 1799. Only one of their five children, Thomas Duckett (A.B. 1825), survived infancy.

SOURCES: *Biog. Dict. Md. Leg.*, I, 283-84; R. H. McIntire, *Annapolis Md. Families* (1980), 206, 343; E. G. Bowie, *Across the Years in Prince George's Cnty.* (1947), 647, 679, 709-10; G. M. Brumbaugh, *Md. Records* (1967), II, 432; alumni files, PUA; Clio. lists; Min. Fac., 10 Nov. 1789, 9 July 1791; "Annual Hists. of Amer. Whig Soc.," PUA; *Dunlap's Amer. Daily Advt.*, 4 Oct. 1791 ("An oration"); *Dunlap & Claypoole's Amer. Daily Advt.*, 7 Oct. 1794; *Votes & Proc. of the House of Delegates of the State of Md.*: (1793), 3; (1794), 2; (1795), 1-2; letter from Md. Leg. Hist. Proj., 29 Jan. 1982, PUA; F. M. Green, *Constitutional Development in the South Atlantic States, 1776-1860* (1930), 90-91 (executive council); als from Duckett, 28 Sept. 1804, supporting application of Lewis Duvall to be U.S. commissioner of loans for Md. & filed under the latter, DNA: Rec. Group 59, Letters of Application & Recommendation ("attachment to Republican"); W. B. Bryan, *Hist. of the National Capital* (1914), I, 455; C. M. Green, *Wash.: Village & Capital, 1800-78* (1962), 26-27, 173-74 (judicial structure of Wash., D.C.); A. J. Beveridge, *Life of John Marshall* (1929), III, 346 ("the first time"); P. S. Clarkson & R. S. Jett, *Luther Martin of Md.* (1970), 239-40; E. S. Brown, ed., *William Plumer's Memorandum of Proc. in the U.S. Senate, 1803-07* (1923), 596. McIntire and *Biog. Dict. Md. Leg.* assert that

Duckett was born around 1774 or 1775. If so, he was rather a young graduate of the College, state legislator, member of the executive council, and judge.

MANUSCRIPTS: See sources for letter in DNA

JJL

John Edmondson

JOHN EDMONDSON, planter and public official, was born around 1773 in Talbot County, Maryland, the son of Pollard Edmondson of Talbot County by his second wife, Rachel Birckhead McManus Edmondson. The mother was the widow of Philip McManus and the daughter of Christopher Birckhead. Although himself an Anglican vestryman, Pollard Edmondson was the scion of a long line of Talbot County Quakers, including the renowned John Edmondson at whose home George Fox stayed in 1672 and 1673 during his American tour. Pollard frequently represented Talbot County in the lower house of the colonial and state legislatures between 1751 and 1785. He had four sons and five daughters and left at least 2,051 acres on the Eastern Shore at his death in 1794.

John Edmondson joined the Cliosophic Society on June 11, 1788, taking the pseudonym McPherson, undoubtedly a reference to James MacPherson (1736-1796), the Scottish "translator" of the Ossianic poetry cycle. For some reason, however, a class list in the faculty minutes gives his date of admission to the College as November 1788. He left the College on October 1, 1789.

The 1798 tax list shows that Edmondson owned 536 acres and eight slaves in Talbot County. His total valuation of $2,670 was the forty-second-highest in the county. By 1832 he had risen to twenty-third, with 538 acres, thirty-two slaves, and a valuation of $7,295. On March 28, 1799 he married Susanna, daughter of Samuel Harvey Howard of Annapolis.

An Episcopalian like his father, Edmondson was also active politically. He represented Talbot County in the house of delegates as a Federalist from 1798 to 1800 and from 1808 to 1809. During an election campaign in August 1821 he was one of the Federalist leaders attacked in a broadside published in Easton, Talbot County, and in the same month he published one of his own in which he sought to refute allegations that he wanted to restrict the poor man's right to vote. He later became an Anti-Jacksonian and sat on Talbot's levy and county courts. Between 1834 and 1840 he served several one-year terms on the board of directors of the Eastern Shore branch of the Farmers' Bank of Maryland.

Edmondson died sometime before May 31, 1841, when his will was filed at the orphans' court. Apparently no issue from his marriage survived him, for he left the bulk of his estate to a niece, Charlotte Matilda Plater. He died while engaged in making the will, and legal squabbling between his widow and Mrs. Plater apparently ensued. One result seems to have been the taking of two separate, almost identical inventories of his personal estate in June and July 1841. The inventories valued his movables at $18,161 and $15,034 respectively, and agreed that he owned thirty-one slaves plus the terms of service of two more who were eventually due to be freed, standing crops of wheat, corn, and oats, a livestock herd of at least twenty horses, seventy-five cattle, one hundred sheep, and two hundred swine, some bank and turnpike stock, and a library of about thirty titles, mostly concerned with law and legal procedure.

SOURCES: *Biog. Dict. Md. Leg.*, I, 301-03; W. H. Ridgway, *Community Leadership in Md., 1790-1840* (1979), 324, 328, 330, 335, 337; Clio. lists; Hancock House MSS; Min. Fac., 10 Nov. 1789; R. Barnes, *Marriages & Deaths from Balt. Newspapers, 1796-1816* (1978), 101; *MHM*, 28 (1933), 230; R. Semmes, "Vignettes of Md. Hist.," *MHM*, 40 (1945), 38-39; letter from Md. Leg. Hist. Proj., 29 Jan. 1982, PUA; E. Buse, *150 Years of Banking on the Eastern Shore* (1955), 61, 162; MS will of JE, undated, exhibited for probate 27 Nov. 1841, & MS estate invs. of JE, June & July 1841, Md. Hall of Records, Annapolis (photocopies in PUA). For the 17th-century John Edmondson see F. B. Edmondson & E. B. Roberts, "John Edmondson—Large Merchant of Tred Haven Creek," *MHM*, 50 (1955), 219-33. The Clio. lists confirm that the Princetonian came from Maryland. The identification of him as Pollard's son is based on his age and status, on the fact that several Talbot County men were his classmates, and on the lack of other likely prospects. A Dorchester County John Edmondson married Sarah Mann on December 11, 1794, but his age as given in the 1800 census is wrong for a 1791 Princetonian. See R. Barnes, *Md. Marriages 1778-1800* (1979), 66; *Md. Geneal. Soc. Bull.*, 16 (1975), 153. For other possibly contemporary Marylanders of the same name, see M. G. Malloy, *Abstracts of Wills: Montgomery Cnty., Md.* (1977), 44; M. R. Hodges, *General Index of Wills of Anne Arundel Cnty., Md. 1777-1917* (1922), 41.

JJL

William Cattell Ferguson

WILLIAM CATTELL FERGUSON, attorney, was born in January 1774, the son of Thomas Ferguson of Charleston, South Carolina. The elder Ferguson was a partner in a sawmill on the Edisto River and had extensive landholdings throughout the colony. Politically, he was associated with the radical element led by Christopher Gadsden. He served in the royal assemblies and the state legislature continuously from 1762 until his death on May 12, 1786. His third wife, Martha Reilly (O'Reily), was the mother of William Cattell Ferguson. He was the youngest of her four sons, and she probably died at or soon after his birth, since her husband was married for the fourth time on August 4, 1774 to Elizabeth Gadsden Rutledge, widowed daughter of Christopher Gadsden. During the Revolution Thomas Ferguson supplied lumber to Gen. Francis Marion, and as a member of the privy council he strongly opposed the surrender of Charleston to the British. By 1777 he had married his fifth wife, Ann Wragg, and when he was exiled to St. Augustine she took the young Fergusons to Philadelphia, where their father was eventually able to join them. When the British evacuated Charleston they took forty-one of Ferguson's skilled slaves and left him heavily in debt. He planned to recoup his losses by exporting timber to the West Indies, but his death occurred before he had an opportunity to carry out this plan. In spite of his debts, he still owned 11,613 acres of land scattered throughout the state, and fourteen slaves staffed his Charleston home. William Cattell Ferguson was also one of the heirs of William Cattell, a wealthy rice planter of Berkeley County, who died childless in 1778 and after whom he was undoubtedly named.

William and his older brother John Horry Ferguson were sent to the grammar school at Nassau Hall where, in the fall of 1785, William placed third in the overall competition among the students. On August 3, 1787 John Witherspoon wrote to Thomas Fitzsimons, a Philadelphia merchant, regarding a shipment of rice which had been remitted to Fitzsimons by Charleston factor Thomas Gadsden, to be applied toward the account of "two Young Gentlemen John & William Ferguson." Witherspoon inquired about the likely profit from the sale of the rice and how soon he could expect to receive it. On May 12, 1788 Witherspoon again wrote to Fitzsimons, requesting him to secure a passage for John Ferguson on the first vessel bound for Charleston, since that young man apparently did not wish to enroll in the College. Since there is usually no surviving record of why a student may have left the College, nor of just how precipitously he may have made his decision, this letter throws an interesting light on Witherspoon's real concern for the boy's actions and the time and trouble spent in trying to dissuade him from an unwise choice. "After I had conferred fully with him about 10 Days ago," Witherspoon informed Fitzsimons, "he agreed that if he did not hear from Mr. Gadsden by the end of last week he would then proceed to Charlestown by the first opportunity. He dined with me today & having heard nothing he seems quite desirous to go & I think as discreet & humble in his Behavior & Designs as ever I saw him." The Mr. Gadsden mentioned may have been Thomas Gadsden, the factor, or Christopher Gadsden, a step-grandfather, a more likely person to have been appointed guardian of the boys. Witherspoon's letter expresses his concern for the younger brother:

I had told him that it was the Opinion of many People that he was hurting his younger Brother Billy by his Example. This seems to have deeply impressed him & I know he has been at much pains to advise his brother to be regular & stick to his Studies. Accordingly, as the Session of College began on Saturday Billy has gone into College & seems to be ambitious to apply to his Books.

After telling Fitzsimons that he would inform him more fully when next they met in Philadelphia, Witherspoon let his impatience show through in writing that "... in the mean time [I] shall not be wasting on young John my best advice as to his future Conduct."

Apparently Billy neglected his brother's counsel about sticking to his studies; on September 10, 1788 he was one of four freshmen and two sophomores called before the faculty and administered a "serious admonition" because they had "frequented a house of ill fame in the neighborhood." The two sophomores and Charles Ross of the freshman class were judged the most guilty, but all were cautioned against visiting "the same or any other place lying under a bad reputation." There is no hint of expulsion being considered for this misdemeanor, but Ferguson may have been looking for an excuse to leave; his name is not on lists of students drawn up in April and November 1789. None of the six students involved in this escapade remained at the College long enough to graduate; the names of several reappear in future disciplinary actions.

Ferguson returned to Charleston, where he became a member of the bar in 1800. This would have been an unusually long period of apprenticeship if he began his study of law in 1789, or even if he completed his college studies elsewhere before undertaking law. It seems reasonable to assume that his law studies did not begin until 1796 at the earliest. On November 6, 1792 Ferguson married Elizabeth (Eliza) Colcock, daughter of John Colcock and Millicent Jones Colcock, and sister of Charles Colcock (Class of 1790), who had attended the Nassau Hall grammar school with Ferguson and who was one of the leaders in the visit to the house of ill fame in 1788. On August 21, 1799 the Fergusons' only son William F. Ferguson died. Ferguson himself died on February 15, 1801 at age twenty-seven and was buried in St. Michael's Churchyard. He was survived by two daughters, Martha and Eliza; his nephew and namesake William Ferguson Colcock was born three years later.

Sources: *Biog. Dir. S.C. House Rep.*, II, 147-48, 248-50; *SCHGM*, 3 (1902), 218-21, 224; 21 (1920), 129; 25 (1924), 184; 31 (1930), 193; C. T. Moore, *Abstracts of Wills of ... S.C. 1760-84* (1969), 128, 271-72; *Md. Gazette: or, the Balt. Gen. Advt.*, 14 Oct. 1785; *N.J. Gazette*, 10 Oct. 1785; als, J. Witherspoon to T. Fitzsimons, 3 Aug. 1787, 12 May 1788,

NjP; Charleston & Phila. city directories; Min. Fac., 10 Sept. 1788; O'Neall, *Bench &
Bar S.C.*, II, 600; C. Jervey, *St. Michael's Church & Churchyard Charleston, S.C.* (1906),
96-97.

RLW

Robert H. Gale

ROBERT H. GALE, A.B., public official, was one of the four sons of
Levin and Leah Littleton Gale of Somerset County, Maryland. His
brothers George Gale (Class of 1774) and Littleton Gale both married
sisters of his classmate Henry Hollyday. Samuel Wilson (A.B. 1788)
was probably his second cousin. Levin Gale served in the provincial
legislature off and on from 1756 to 1774 and belonged to the Anglican church. He was a merchant, shipbuilder, attorney, and planter
who owned at least 3,412 acres in Somerset County at his death in
1791. One of his partners was John Stewart, the father of Alexander
Stewart (A.B. 1793). Leah Littleton Gale was Levin's first cousin, and
the daughter of Levin Gale (ca. 1704-1744).

In 1779 Levin Gale was a trustee of Washington Academy, Somerset County, where Robert probably received his early education.
Late in 1789 he entered the College as a junior. He joined the Cliosophic Society on December 23 of that year, taking Cliophilus as his
pseudonym. On November 29, 1790 the steward complained that
Gale, Alexander Stewart, and four other students were infringing
on his perquisites by boarding out of the College. When the faculty
arranged his commencement exercises in July 1791, Gale stood first
in his class and was "appointed to deliver the Latin salutatory, but
declined speaking."

Gale's subsequent career was brief. He attended a meeting of the
Cliosophic Society in July 1793. The reason for his visit to Princeton
at that time has not come to light. He married a woman named Jane,
whose last name has not been discovered. In 1794 he was elected to
represent Somerset County in the house of delegates but died while
in office and was buried at 4 p.m. on December 25, 1794. The house
voted to attend the funeral and wear mourning for ten days.

SOURCES: *Biog. Dict. Md. Leg.*, I, 334-38; II, 778-79, 900-01; J. B. Kerr, *Geneal. Notes
of the Chamberlaine Family of Md.* (1973), 38-40; letter from Md. Leg. Hist. Proj., 29
Jan. 1982, PUA; *MHM*, 44 (1949), 203; Min. Fac., 10 Nov. 1789, 29 Nov. 1790, 9
July 1791 ("appointed"); Min. Trustees, 27 Sept. 1791; *Dunlap's Amer. Daily Advt.*, 4
Oct. 1791; Clio. Min., 11 July 1793; Clio. lists; C. N. Everstine, *General Assembly of Md.
1776-1850* (1982), 223. Gale is referred to as Robert H. Gale in the accounts of his
graduation; no other verification for the middle initial has been found. Robert, the son
of Levin Gale, is identified as the Princetonian on the basis of his brother's Princeton
education and connection by marriage with the family of Robert's classmate Henry

Hollyday, his father's trading connection with the father of Alexander Stewart (A.B. 1793), the absence of other likely candidates, and the fact that the Princetonian, who was definitely from Maryland, is first listed as deceased in the 1797 College catalogue, the first one to appear after the death of Levin Gale's son Robert. Without Robert's date of birth, however, the identification cannot be regarded as absolutely certain.

JJL

Maltby Gelston

MALTBY GELSTON, A.B., lawyer and banker, was one of the four children of David and Mary Robins Gelston of Bridgehampton, Suffolk County, Long Island, New York. An ardent patriot, David Gelston was a delegate to the second, third, and fourth provincial congresses and a member of the 1777 state constitutional convention. He sat in the state assembly from 1777 to 1785, serving as its speaker during the last two years, and was a delegate to the last Confederation Congress. In 1786 the family moved from Long Island to New York City, where Gelston had mercantile interests. The following year he became surrogate of the city, a position that he held until 1801, when he was appointed to the lucrative federal post of collector of the port of New York, for which he was recommended by Aaron Burr (A.B. 1772). He was forced to retire by the provisions of the Tenure of Office Act of 1820, introduced in Congress by Senator Mahlon Dickerson (A.B. 1789), which established a four-year term for all federal officials whose duties involved financial responsibilities. In a letter to James Monroe (LL.D. 1822) dated June 12, 1820, Secretary of the Treasury William H. Crawford stated that in his opinion the bill was passed simply as a means of unseating the eighty-year old Gelston, who had become cranky and unreasonable with age. The elder Gelston was a Presbyterian and a "Burrite" Republican.

Maltby Gelston was admitted to the College as a sophomore in November 1788 and joined the American Whig Society. On July 2, 1790 he was one of the group of students accused by the faculty of eating and drinking to excess at David Hamilton's tavern and then capping the evening's festivities by placing a calf in the pulpit of Nassau Hall and overturning the college necessary. Gelston did not put in an appearance on that date but when the faculty reconvened he confessed to "the facts alleged against him," was admonished by the president of the College in the presence of the faculty, and was readmitted to his former standing. On November 29, 1790 he was one of the six students reported by the steward to be boarding out of the College. Vice President Samuel Stanhope Smith (A.B. 1769) was delegated to call on them and "cause them to perform what the law required," i.e., eating in the College dining hall unless they had medical certificates entitling them to special privileges. For his commencement exercises Gelston was assigned the role of opponent in a dispute on the question, "Is an hereditary nobility an advantage to a nation—does it tend to the improvement of the human character in social life, and is it consistent with civil liberty?"

Following graduation Gelston studied law, probably in New York City. In 1794 he joined the United States legation to France as the private secretary of James Monroe, the newly appointed minister to that country. When Monroe was recalled from Paris two years later, Gelston was one of a group of "fellow citizens now at Paris" who addressed a letter to him, praising his conduct in office, particularly his willingness to go beyond official requirements in protecting the private interests of the Americans residing in France. The letter ended with the hope that he would receive "just approbation" from his fellow citizens. The manuscript of Monroe's famous speech to the French National Convention on August 15, 1794 is written in a flowing penmanship quite unlike his own rather cramped style of writing; it may have been a fair copy made by Gelston.

Gelston returned to New York sometime before November 16, 1797, when Albert Gallatin conveyed this news to his brother-in-law James Nicholson (Class of 1791), who was residing in New Geneva, Pennsylvania. There was apparently a close relationship between the Gelston and Nicholson families, who resided in the same area of the city and shared political ideologies; Gelston's father was to serve as a pallbearer for Nicholson's father in 1804 when he was described as an "active, benevolent and valuable" friend who was "almost a member of the family." The two sons had matriculated in the College at the same time and been involved in the same escapade which preceded Nicholson's transfer to Columbia College. Further correspondence between Gallatin and Nicholson indicates that Gelston was considering joining Nicholson in western Pennsylvania, where the latter was supervising the affairs of a land speculation company in which he and Gallatin were partners. However, by March 9, 1798, Gallatin informed Nicholson that Gelston had joined George Clinton in the practice of law in New York.

Gelston's marriage to Mary, the daughter of Dr. Thomas Jones, a New York physician, gave him connections to two prominent New York families. Mary Gelston's mother was a member of the Livingston family, and her sister Catherine was the second wife of DeWitt Clinton. A watercolor by John Searle, now in the collection of the New-York Historical Society, depicts a performance of *Monsieur Tonson* at the Park Theatre on the evening of November 7, 1822, with

Gelston, his wife, and Catherine Clinton seated in the box closest to the stage on the left side of the theatre.

In 1802, the year after his father's appointment as collector of customs, Gelston became a notary at the custom house. Tax lists show that in 1815 his personal property was valued at $10,000; by 1820 it had increased to $15,000. In 1821 he was elected alderman of the third ward of the city. Though he served on other committees, the major portion of his time and efforts was devoted to the standing committee on wharves, piers, and slips. During this period the Fulton Market was being readied for opening on January 21, 1822, and preparations included licensing of butchers with stalls in the market, determining lamp lighters' wages, and dealing with the problem of disorderly boys who assembled at the market site after hours and on the Sabbath and conducted themselves in a "riotous and improper manner." Gelston's business and residential addresses are listed in the New York City directories until 1826-27 when his name appears with only the notation "Jamaica." Since he still had family connections on Long Island it seems likely that he moved there, rather than to the island of Jamaica. His name is absent from city directories until 1829-30.

In April 1799 state senator Aaron Burr was responsible for the passage of an act authorizing the chartering of the Manhattan Company in order to supply pure and wholesome water to the City of New York. Inserted within the terms of the act was a clause granting the company the right to use its surplus funds for any purpose not inconsistent with the state or federal constitution or laws. Within six weeks of the passage of this bill Burr had enough subscribers to raise the capital of $2,000,000 required to incorporate the company. One of the first acts of the directors was to purchase a house on Wall Street and open the Bank of the Manhattan Company, thereby giving the Republicans of the state their own bank and breaking the Federalist monopoly on bank funds. Burr's election to the vice presidency is attributed largely to his political coup in establishing the Manhattan bank. In 1802 Burr and his friend John Swartwout were ousted from the directorate of the company by the Clintons and Livingstons, resulting in a duel between Swartwout and DeWitt Clinton. Clinton continued to give full support to the bank and to use its funds as a political tool, gaining additional power in the state, as well as the animosity of the Federalists.

In 1831 Gelston was appointed president of the Manhattan Bank, a position which he held during the panic of 1837 when shortages forced banks to suspend payment in specie. The Bank of the United States tried to delay resumption of specie payments until January 1,

1839, but the New York banks resumed on May 10, 1838, forcing other banks to follow suit and precipitating the closing of the Bank of the United States the following year. Perhaps the turmoil of this period was hard on the aging bank president, for he retired in 1840. His years as a banker had been profitable, for a tax list of 1845 credits him with assets worth $300,000. He died on December 2, 1860. A son John M. Gelston was in the commission business in New York; a daughter Mary married Henry R. Winthrop.

SOURCES: Alumni file, PUA; *BDUSC*, 1051; B. F. Thompson, *Hist. of Long Island* (3d ed., 3 vols., 1918), II, 165-66, 647; H. Ammon, *James Monroe: The Quest for National Identity* (1971), 494-95; M. Lomask, *Aaron Burr: The Years from Princeton to Vice President, 1756-1805* (1979), 239, 299; Hancock House MSS; Min. Fac., 10 Nov. 1789, 2 July 1790, 29 Nov. 1790, 9 July 1791; Amer. Whig Soc., *Cat.* (1840), 6; *Dunlap's Amer. Daily Advt.*, 4 Oct. 1791; N.Y. City directories; James Monroe, *A View of the Conduct of the Executive in the Foreign Affairs Connected with the Mission to the French Republic* (1794), 401-02; P. Smith, *John Adams* (1962), II, 913; MS Monroe speech to French National Convention, 15 Aug. 1794, NjP; Alexander, 254; Microfilm Ed. of the Papers of Albert Gallatin (1970, C. E. Prince, ed.; originals in NHi), letters of Gallatin to J. W. Nicholson, 16 Nov. 1797, 12 Jan. & 9 March 1798, 5 Sept. 1804 ("almost a member"); J. G. Wilson, *Mem. Hist. of the City of N.Y.* (1893), III, 347, 352; H. W. Lanier, *Century of Banking in N.Y.* (1922), 102, 108; *MCCCNY*, VI, 299; XI & XII, *passim*; Manhattan Co., "*Manna-hatin*" *The Story of N. Y.* (1929), 128-29; *Princetonians, 1769-1775*, 192-204; *Legislative Hist. of Banking in the State of N.Y.* (1855), 19; D. Babbe, *DeWitt Clinton* (1933), 87-88, 105-05, 117, 131, 140-41; *Bank of the Manhattan Company* (undated booklet).

MANUSCRIPTS: David Gelston Papers, G. W. Blunt White Lib., Mystic Seaport Museum, Mystic, Conn., has papers relating to MG's efforts to obtain payment of claims his deceased father had on the United States government.

RLW

Richard Hall Harwood

RICHARD HALL HARWOOD, A.B., A.M. 1794, state legislator and judge, was born on October 23, 1771, the only son among three children of Richard and Margaret Hall Harwood of All Hallow's Parish, Anne Arundel County, Maryland. The father, Col. Richard Harwood (1737-1826), served in both houses of the state legislature in a career which began in 1785 and concluded with service as president of the state senate from 1801 to 1805. He was a planter, but in 1800 he was obliged to mortgage all his land to his brother to meet his debts, and he seems not to have regained control of it thereafter. Margaret Hall Harwood was the daughter of Henry and Elizabeth Lansdale Hall.

No information on Harwood's early education has been found. He entered the College on August 1, 1789 and was admitted to the junior class in November of that year. He joined the Cliosophic Society on the twenty-fifth of the same month, taking Gillies as his pseudonym. John Gillies, the Scottish classical scholar, had published his *History*

of Ancient Greece, its Colonies and Conquests, in 1786, and the choice
of Gillies's name is evidence of the immediate vogue the work, which
was antidemocratic in emphasis, enjoyed on both sides of the Atlantic.
At his commencement, Harwood was replicator in a debate on the
question "Is an hereditary nobility an advantage to a nation—does it
tend to the improvement of the human character in social life, and
is it consistent with civil liberty?"

Harwood's subsequent activities imply that he became a lawyer
upon his return to Maryland. He represented Anne Arundel County
in the Maryland House of Delegates for six consecutive terms starting in 1798. In January 1806 Governor Robert Bowie appointed
him an associate judge of Maryland's third judicial district, which
encompassed Calvert, Anne Aundel, and Montgomery counties. Presumably Harwood shared Bowie's Republican political loyalties. In
the 1816-17 legislative session a joint resolution calling on Governor
Charles Ridgely to remove Harwood passed the house by a 43 to
24 margin but failed in the senate. The framers of the resolution
charged of Harwood and another judge, Zebulon Hollingsworth, that
their

> intemperate habits ... are wholly incompatible with their official
> character and usefulness, and that they have severally failed to
> give that attendance on the courts which the nature of their
> appointment and the interest of the public absolutely require.

Testimony in the house showed that recently Harwood had attended
the court only nine out of fifty-six days it was in session. He had
attended only one day out of thirteen in Anne Arundel while missing
Calvert County altogether. The senate's failure to join in the call for
Harwood's removal left open less ignominious ways to leave office,
of which Harwood took advantage by resigning sometime before
August 11, 1817 when his successor was appointed.

On October 23, 1798 Harwood had married Ann C. Greene,
daughter of Frederick and Anne Saunders Greene. Frederick Greene
was a postmaster and the joint publisher of the *Maryland Gazette* of
Annapolis. Four daughters were born of the marriage. Richard Hall
Harwood died in Annapolis on May 21, 1819.

SOURCES: R. H. McIntire, *Annapolis Md. Families* (1980), 282, 312; *Biog. Dict. Md. Leg.*,
I, 384-85, 421-22; J. D. Warfield, *Founders of Anne Arundel & Howard Cnties. Md.* (1967),
96-99; Min. Fac., 10 Nov. 1789, 9 July 1791; Clio. lists; *Dunlap's Amer. Daily Advt.*, 4
Oct. 1791 ("Is an hereditary"); *Dunlap & Claypoole's Amer. Daily Advt.*, 7 Oct. 1794;
letter from Md. Leg. Hist. Proj., 4 June 1985, PUA; C. N. Everstine, *General Assembly
of Md. 1776-1850* (1982), 365-66 ("intemperate habits"); *MHM*, 28 (1933), 229; 42
(1947), 291 (citing the Annapolis *Md. Gazette*, 27 May 1819). Richard Harwood was a
common name in Maryland at this time. The identification of Richard Hall Harwood

as the 1791 A.B. rests largely on the trustees' minutes, September 27, 1791, and the newspaper account of his commencement. Both sources refer to him as "Richard H. Harwood." A Richard Harwood of Maryland held a commission as lieutenant in the United States Marine Corps, 10 July 1798–10 Nov. 1799. Given his other activities in 1798 this was probably not the Princetonian but another Richard Harwood, perhaps the son of Thomas Harwood of Annapolis who was born about 1774. See McIntire, 312-13; E. W. Callahan, *List of Officers of the Navy of the U.S. & of the Marine Corps from 1775 to 1900* (1901), 688.

JJL

Thomas Robins Hayward

THOMAS ROBINS HAYWARD, planter, was born on October 8 or 9, 1771, at "Locust Grove" in Bayley's Neck, Talbot County, Maryland, the son of William and Margaret Robins Hayward. William Hayward, an Anglican, was a planter and attorney who served Somerset County, Maryland, in the colonial assembly in the 1760s and sat on the governor's council from 1770 until 1776. Margaret Robins Hayward was the daughter of George Robins, a wealthy landowner who represented Talbot County in the lower house of the colonial legislature from 1727 to 1731, and Henrietta Maria Tilghman Robins. Through his mother's sisters, Thomas Hayward was first cousin to both his classmate Henry Hollyday and Robins Chamberlaine (Class of 1793). He had an older brother George; two sisters died in infancy. In 1782 their father transferred 1,915 acres in Talbot County to the two sons and a nephew. Yet he still owned at least 1,500 acres in Somerset and Talbot counties, plus £3,782 in personal property, when he died in 1791. Thomas's exact share of the inheritance has not been ascertained.

According to a class list in the faculty minutes, Hayward entered the College as a sophomore in November 1788. However, he was on campus by June 11 of that year when he joined the Cliosophic Society, taking as his pseudonym Ascanius, the son of Æneas. He obtained his dismission as a junior in August 1790.

After leaving the College, Hayward returned to Talbot County and the life of a wealthy farmer. In an Episcopalian ceremony on May 12, 1795, he married Mary Smythe (or Smith), the sister of his brother's wife Margaret and the daughter of Thomas and Margaret Smythe. Thomas Smythe was a merchant at Chestertown in Kent County, Maryland. Hayward's two sons and four daughters issued from this marriage. Mary died on June 13, 1811, and on September 21, 1813 he married Mary Bond, the widow of William S. Bond.

The 1832 Talbot County tax list named Hayward as owner of 471 acres of land and thirty-six slaves. His overall valuation of $9,118 was the county's eighteenth-highest. In his will, dated May 12, 1837, he described "the Farm or Plantation on which I now reside" as part of "the Tracts of Land called 'Marshy Point' & Canterbury alias 'Canterbury Manor.'" He died shortly before July 5, 1838, when "Mr. Thos. Hayward of Bayly's Neck" was buried in St. Michael's Parish, Talbot County.

Hayward left indeterminate but probably substantial lands and a personal estate valued at $13,411, including twenty-eight slaves, 228 ounces of silver, thirteen horses and forty-two cattle, wheat, corn, and oats in the barn, and a large crop of corn in the field. However, the will suggests that he was deeply in debt, and he set aside the bulk of his property for the satisfaction of his creditors. The estate inventory lists more than one hundred titles in Hayward's library, which had a strong literary bent and included works by David Hume, Adam Smith, Edward Gibbon, John Locke, John Milton, Joseph Addison, Richard Steele, Alexander Pope, Comte Georges Louis Leclerc de Buffon, Plutarch, Virgil, and Cicero.

SOURCES: *Biog. Dict. Md. Leg.*, I, 427-28; G. A. Hanson, *Old Kent: The Eastern Shore of Md.* (1967), 251, 295-96; J. B. Kerr, *Geneal. Notes of the Chamberlaine Family of Md.* (1973), 40, 45; J. Bordley, *Hollyday & Related Families of the Eastern Shore of Md.* (1962), 141-43; Min. Fac., 10 Nov. 1789; Clio. lists; Hancock House MSS; A. W. Burns, *St. Peter's Parish Reg., Talbot Cnty, Md.* (typescript, n.d.), I, 263, 296-97; R. Barnes, *Md. Marriages 1778-1800* (1979), 100; R. B. Clark & S. S. Clark, *Talbot Cnty. Md. Marriage Licenses 1794-1824* (1965), 17; W. H. Ridgway, *Community Leadership in Md. 1790-1840* (1979), 328, 338, A. W. Burns, *St. Michael's Parish Reg., Talbot Cnty., Md.* (typescript, 1939?), I, 55 ("Mr. Thos."); MS will of TRH, 12 May 1837, proved 25 July 1838 ("the Farm," "the Tracts"), & MS estate inv. of TRH, 9 Aug. 1838, recorded 24 Aug. 1838, Md. Hall of Records, Annapolis (photocopies in PUA). The 1837 catalog of the Cliosophic Society calls Hayward "Thomas K. Haymard." Both the middle initial "K" and the spelling of the surname seem to be typographical errors. The other College sources, including a manuscript Clio. membership list, spell the surname "Hayward" and give no middle initial.

JJL

George Henry

GEORGE HENRY was the son of Samuel Henry and Mary Oglebee of Trenton, New Jersey. He and his twin brother and classmate Samuel were born sometime in June or July 1770. Their grandfather, an Irish immigrant, had acquired large tracts of land in Trenton and established an iron foundry and steel works in the area east of Assunpink Creek.

Henry's father apparently still operated the iron foundry, for it was included among the properties left to his children at his death on May 10, 1784. His wife had apparently predeceased him, and a codicil to his will provided for the care of his children by Mary Yard, daughter of William Yard of Trenton. She was left a stone house and a lot, upon the condition that she live there and make a home for the Henry brothers and their sisters, Frances and Mary. In exchange for £15 per year per child she was expected to provide room, board, and clothing for the young Henrys "until Samuel and George be sent to Princeton Colledge for education and to receive them in at all vacancies [vacations], and other times when they may see fit to come." Although the executors of the father's will were appointed guardians of Samuel on July 22, 1785, it was not until May 18, 1789, when he was already enrolled at the College, that George Henry was taken under the guardianship of Bernard Hanlon, a Trenton merchant.

The Henry brothers probably received their early education at the Trenton Academy before entering the College as freshmen in November 1787. There is no evidence that they joined either of the debating societies on the campus, but since there are no records available for nongraduate members of the American Whig Society, they could have been members of that organization. On November 17, 1788 George Henry and his classmate Peter Marchant were found guilty by the faculty of "indecent conduct in the College" and sentenced to receive an admonition in the presence of their class. This rather light punishment, as opposed to an admonition or public confession before the entire College, indicates that their behavior was probably only mildly reprehensible. George Henry's name is included among the members of the junior class at the beginning of the winter session of 1789, but he is no longer listed at the start of the summer session of 1790.

Nothing has been found to indicate what profession Henry pursued, although he probably continued to operate the family iron foundry and to supervise his other properties. When his brother died early in 1795, George received the residue of the estate after personal bequests were distributed. He was probably the George Henry who was the grandson of Elizabeth Henry of Princeton, who in 1802 received a fourth of the residue of her estate, as well as a silver tankard, six silver teaspoons, a negro boy named Bob, and the bonds, bills, and notes in the possession of a Mrs. Mattison. In September 1802 when the Trenton Water Works was organized, Henry was among the stockholders, a group of men described as among the more prosperous of the town.

No date has been found for Henry's marriage to Mary Lowery, daughter of Esther and Col. Thomas Lowery of Alexandria (now Frenchtown), New Jersey, and younger sister of Grace Lowery, the wife of Aaron Woodruff (A.B. 1779). Thomas Lowery served with the Third Regiment of the Hunterdon County militia during the Revolution and was one of the commissioners who purchased the land for the New Jersey capitol. The three ladies of the family were among the "Virgins fair, and Matrons grave," who, on April 21, 1789, greeted George Washington as he entered the city of Trenton on the way to his inauguration in New York. Mary Henry died tragically on January 23, 1804. The victim of a convulsive attack while sitting near the hearth, she fell and her clothing caught fire. An elderly and ineffectual servant, the only person nearby, was of little help and Mary was severely burned. She died some hours later. George Henry died on October 23, 1846, aged seventy-six. Both are buried in the cemetery of St. Michael's Episcopal Church in Trenton.

SOURCES: W. Nelson, *N.J. Biog. & Geneal. Notes* (1916), 128-31; *N.J. Wills*, VI, 189; VII, 108; VIII, 173; X, 211; J. Hall, *Hist. of the Pres. Church in Trenton, N.J.* (1912) 155-56; Min. Fac., 17 Nov. 1788, 10 Nov. 1789; Hancock House MSS; Trenton Hist. Soc., *Hist. of Trenton* (1929), I, 200-02, 206; II, 370-71; E. F. Cooley, *Gen. of Early Settlers in Trenton & Ewing* (1883), 312; *Princetonians, 1776-1783*, 285-88. The conclusion that George and Samuel Henry were twins is based on the ages given at their dates of death and Samuel's age at the time his guardianship papers were signed.

RLW

Samuel Henry III

SAMUEL HENRY III was born in Trenton, New Jersey, about June or July 1770. He was the son of Samuel Henry, Jr., and Mary Oglebee, and the twin brother of George Henry (Class of 1791). The first Samuel Henry to settle in Trenton was a native of Ireland who operated an iron foundry and steel works at Assunpink Creek and also acquired extensive land holdings in Trenton.

Mary Oglebee Henry was already deceased at the time of her husband's demise on May 10, 1784. The tracts of land left to his children included "the old ironworks," as well as other property in Trenton, Nottingham Township, and Pennsylvania. A codicil to Henry's will left a house in Trenton to Mary Yard, daughter of William Yard, on the condition that she live in it and care for his children, the two boys and their sisters, Frances and Mary. She was instructed to "provide meat, drink, washing, lodging, mending and clothing until Samuel and George be sent to Princeton Colledge for education and to receive them in at all vacancies [vacations], and other times when they may see fit to come." For all of these services she was to receive £15 per year for each of the Henry children. The following July, Abraham Hunt and Charles Axford, executors of his father's will, were appointed as Samuel's guardians.

Quite likely the Henry boys were prepared for college at the Trenton Academy where Abraham Hunt was one of the original proprietors. This position gave him the right to send a boy to the school without the half-dollar charge for use of the building that most students paid in addition to tuition. The Henrys were admitted to the freshman class of the College in November 1787. Samuel Henry did not join the Cliosophic Society and no records are available for nongraduate members of the Whig Society during this period. On September 10, 1788, perhaps celebrating the end of his freshman year, Henry was among a group of students receiving a "serious admonishment" from the faculty for frequenting "a house of ill fame" in the neighborhood. On March 3, 1789 he was again called before the faculty, this time on the charge of assaulting Isaac Crane (A.B. 1789) and making a mess of his room. Of the eleven students accused, two were declared completely innocent, but Henry was among the three who were found most culpable as leaders in the assault and as having previously been censured and warned. Only their admission of guilt saved them from a more severe punishment than having their confession mentioned to the entire College at evening prayers. Henry enrolled for the winter session of his junior year on November 10, 1789, but by the summer session of 1790 his name was no longer included on the College lists.

Nothing more is known about Henry except his early death on January 9, 1795. His will freed his Negro man Peter and left the residue of his estate to his brother George, after the payment of legacies to his sisters and to the family of Dr. Nicholas Bellville. Dr. Bellville was a French physician who accompanied Count Casimir Pulaski on his trip to this country as the nobleman's personal surgeon. During a visit to Trenton, Bellville was persuaded by a resident doctor to set up practice in that city. The bequests to his wife and daughters in Henry's will suggest that Bellville may have been the doctor in attendance during the former's last illness. The September 6, 1794 date of the will, four months before he died, may be an indication of a lengthy illness. Henry was buried in St. Michael's Episcopal churchyard in Trenton.

SOURCES: W. Nelson, *N.J. Biog. & Geneal. Notes* (1916), 128-31; *N.J. Wills*, VI, 189; VIII, 173; J. Hall, *Hist. of the Pres. Church in Trenton, N.J.* (1912), 155-56, 260-62; Min. Fac., 10 Sept. 1788, 3 Mar. & 10 Nov. 1789; Hancock House MSS. No sources actually state that the Henry brothers were twins, but if the ages given for them at the dates of their deaths are correct this relationship must be assumed.

RLW

Henry Hollyday

HENRY HOLLYDAY, A.B., A.M. 1803, planter, lawyer, and public official, was born on September 11, 1771, at "Ratcliffe Manor," Talbot County, Maryland, one of the ten children of Henry and Anna Maria Robins Hollyday. His sister Anna Maria married George Gale (Class of 1774), the brother of Robert Gale (A.B. 1791). Through his mother he was first cousin to both his classmate Thomas Hayward and to Robins Chamberlaine (Class of 1793). Three of his elder brother James's sons, James Hollyday (Class of 1813), Henry Hollyday (Class of 1818) and George Steuart Hollyday (Class of 1818), also attended the College. The father was a planter who represented Talbot County in the house of delegates from 1765 to 1766. Although he engaged in no overtly pro-tory activity, he refused to take an oath of loyalty to the revolutionary government when independence was declared and thereby incurred confiscation of his livestock and triple taxation. These penalties kept his family in straitened circumstances for the duration of the war. At one point young Henry wrote a pathetic letter to his uncle, James Hollyday of "Readbourne," a patriot and prominent lawyer, complaining that he could not attend an upcoming ball at Talbot County Court House, now Easton, because his clothes were in rags. Uncle James did not fail him, and Henry went to the ball after all. In addition to pecuniary embarrassments, the peace of Henry's childhood must have been disturbed by the behavior of his mentally troubled and sometimes violent elder brother Thomas. Their father observed in 1783 that Thomas's outbursts had plunged the family into "a state of wretchedness not easily to be expressed."

Hollyday apparently entered the College after the compilation of class rosters on November 10, 1789, for his and Robert Gale's were among four names added to the bottom of the list of juniors, which was otherwise in alphabetical order. In February 1790 Hollyday joined the Cliosophic Society, taking as his pseudonym Regulus, for Marcus Atilius Regulus, an ancient Roman general renowned for his patriotism and inflexible adherence to his word. Hollyday did not speak at his commencement, being one of three seniors from Maryland who played no role "at their own solicitation."

In 1789 Hollyday's father died, leaving some 3,100 acres in Talbot, Queen Annes and Caroline counties. Henry's two surviving brothers received 1,600 acres of land between them, and so Henry's share must have been 1,500 acres, less whatever provision might have been made for his mother and sisters. Certainly Henry's share included "Ratcliffe Manor," at which he resided for the rest of his life. His mother also lived there until her death around 1805, but she resigned full control to him when he reached his majority in 1792. Hollyday prospered. In 1798 he was not among Talbot County's fifty most highly assessed taxpayers, but by 1832 he ranked ninth with an estate valued at $13,563, including 1,269 acres of land and fifty-eight slaves. He was an original stockholder in the Eastern Shore branch of the Farmers' Bank of Maryland, founded at Easton in 1805, and he served on its board of directors a number of times between 1811 and 1844.

Hollyday consistently manifested an interest in scientific farming. In 1805 he sat on the standing committee of the short-lived Society for the Promotion of Agriculture and Rural Economy for the Eastern Shore of Maryland. When the Maryland Agricultural Society was founded in 1822, he was one of the twelve trustees selected from the Eastern Shore.

Hollyday was also a lawyer, practicing in Easton. He served on the county's levy court, and from 1816 to 1821 he represented the Eastern Shore in the state senate, where he earned a reputation as a "high-toned" Federalist. He was a lieutenant in the Talbot County militia in 1799 and paymaster of the Eastern Shore militia in 1812. If a letter by "H.H." in the *Easton Gazette* of March 2, 1833, is correctly attributed to Hollyday, he supported the movement in that year to form a new state comprising Delaware and the Eastern Shore counties of Maryland and Virginia. An avid hunter and angler, Hollyday was also something of a scholar, for letters he wrote to his uncle and later to his brother looking forward to spending a day in the library of the estate at "Readbourne" are cited by the family historian.

In an Episcopalian ceremony on October 11, 1798, Hollyday married Ann Carmichael, the daughter of Katharine Murray and Richard Bennett Carmichael of "Bennet's Choice," Queen Annes County, Maryland. Seven daughters and four sons issued from this marriage, including Richard Carmichael Hollyday (A.B. 1829), Thomas Robins Hollyday (A.B. 1831) and William Murray Hollyday (A.B. 1838). Richard was longtime secretary of state of Maryland. Henry's daughter Elizabeth married her first cousin Richard Bennett Carmichael (A.B. 1828), who became a judge and a one-term United States congressman.

Hollyday died on March 20, 1850. He left extensive landholdings in Talbot and Queen Annes counties, including "Kinnersley" in the latter, which he willed to his daughters, and "Ratcliffe Manor" in the former, which was divided among his three surviving sons.

SOURCES: J. Bordley, *Hollyday & Related Families of the Eastern Shore of Md.* (1962), 106-25, 168-73, 177-78, 184-85; J. B. Kerr, *Gen. Notes of the Chamberlaine Family of Md.*

(1973), 38-40, 61, 63, 66; *Biog. Dict. Md. Leg.*, I, 192-93, 449-50; D. B. Smith, *Inside the Great House* (1980), 113-16, 254 ("a state"); alumni files, PUA; Min. Fac., 10 Nov. 1789, 9 July 1791 ("at their"); Clio. lists; *Dunlap's Amer. Daily Advt.*, 4 Oct. 1791; *Trenton Federalist*, 17 Oct. 1803; O. Tilghman, *Hist. of Talbot Cnty., Md.* (1967), I, 46-64, 393, 571; II, 24-25 ("high-toned"); W. H. Ridgway, *Community Leadership in Md., 1790-1840* (1979), 40, 330, 338; letter from Md. Leg. Hist. Proj., 29 Jan. 1982, PUA; E. Buse, *150 Years of Banking on the Eastern Shore* (1955), 160, 162; D. J. Preston, *Talbot Cnty.: A Hist.* (1983), 172, 187-88 ("H.H." letter in *Easton Gazette*), 189-90, 251; G. A. Hanson, *Old Kent: The Eastern Shore of Md.* (1967), 248-50; F. Emory, *Queen Anne's Cnty., Md.* (1950), 398, 504. See the cover of *MHM*, 41, no. 1 (March 1946), for a photograph of "Ratcliffe Manor."

JJL

Alexander Johnes

ALEXANDER JOHNES was admitted to the College as a junior in November 1789 and expelled the following July. He was one of nine students who were called before the faculty for getting drunk at Hamilton's tavern and subsequently placing a calf in the Nassau Hall pulpit and upsetting the College privy. Johnes was among the four who were found to be the worst offenders in the "enormities" committed, and ordered to leave the College immediately.

No other information about Johnes is available and it has been impossible to identify him.

SOURCES: Min. Fac., 10 Nov. 1789, 2 July 1790. Johnes was not, as his name may suggest, a member of the family of the Reverend Timothy Johnes, pastor of the Presbyterian church in Morristown and charter trustee of the College, whose son and several grandsons attended the College. Neither was Johnes the grandson of Grace FitzRandolph and Stephen Johnes of Maidenhead, brother of the Reverend Timothy Johnes. Johnes was a variant spelling of Jones and that family name was as common in the eighteenth century as it is today. See Johnes family folder, PUA; also genealogical information on Johnes family from *Hist. of the First Pres. Church, Morristown, N.J.* (1882?-85, 2 vols. in 1), II, 117-18, 134; R. S. Green & W. Durant, eds., *Record, First Pres. Church of Morristown, N.J.* (1880-85, 5 vols. in 1).

RLW

Stevens Johnes Lewis

STEVENS JOHNES LEWIS, A.B., physician, was born in Morristown, New Jersey, on May 27, 1773, the oldest son of Joseph Lewis and Anne Stevens Johnes. He was baptized on July 18 by his grandfather, the Reverend Timothy Johnes, pastor of the Morristown Presbyterian Church and a charter trustee of the College of New Jersey. His paternal grandparents were Edward Lewis of nearby Basking Ridge, who settled there after emigrating from Wales, and his wife

Sarah Morris. Joseph Lewis was a lawyer who served as clerk of the county from 1782 to 1787 and was a judge of the court of common pleas from 1800 to 1805. During the Revolution, as an aide to Gen. Nathanael Greene (A.M. 1781), he acted as quartermaster for the troops camped at Morristown and had the difficult task of providing housing, provisions, and firewood while still maintaining the good will of the local farmers. An active member of his father-in-law's congregation, Lewis, along with his wife, renewed his covenant with the church on July 18, 1773.

Joseph Lewis kept a diary or memorandum book which shows the many days he spent traveling the court circuits with trips to Trenton, New Brunswick, and Newark. The entry for May 9, 1785 states, "My son Stevens began to go to school to Doctr. Campfields." The school in Morristown met in the church, probably under Dr. Jabez Campfield (A.B. 1759). The following fall Ebenezer Pierson (A.B. 1791) and Mahlon Dickerson (A.B. 1789) came to board at the Lewis home which was conveniently close to the church, perhaps to insure that they would not miss school in inclement weather. On August 30, 1787 Joseph Lewis noted that the Latin scholars spoke on the stage, undoubtedly with his son among them. Stevens must have finished his preparatory education by the following spring, for on May 1, 1788 he accompanied his father to Princeton, where they called on President John Witherspoon, who examined young Lewis in Latin and Greek. Father and son lodged at the Sign of the College Tavern before returning home for a brief visit; Stevens Lewis enrolled at Nassau Hall on May 15. During his first term a brother Joseph was born who lived only fifty-eight days and was buried before Lewis's return on September 25. Lewis is not on a class list compiled on April 10, 1789, but he returned to the campus by June 10 of that year, when he joined the Cliosophic Society, using the name Patrocles, the Macedonian general and geographer. His father's diary records several occasions when the two traveled together between Princeton and Morristown. Because the diary ends on August 18, 1791, there is no record of Joseph Lewis's sentiments on the occasion of his son's commencement on September 27. The younger Lewis's part in the oratory of the day was to take the opposition side to the question, "Does the cultivation of science and the improvement of arts, tend to the improvement of morals and the encrease of happiness?"

Lewis pursued the study of medicine, probably in Morristown, where he could have studied with Dr. Campfield, or with his uncle, Timothy Johnes, Jr., both prominent physicians in the area. On September 26, 1792 he attended the annual meeting of the Cliosophic Society in Princeton. He enrolled as a medical student at

Columbia College during the academic year 1793-94 but did not obtain an M.D. degree.

On December 12, 1799 Lewis married Elizabeth Jones, daughter of Dr. Gardiner Jones of New York. The couple had three sons; the eldest died as an infant and the youngest was lost in a storm at sea at age thirteen. Their mother died on March 24, 1807. Lewis's name as a practicing physician first appears in New York City directories in 1796 and continues through 1802. Although there is no record of him in New York after this time, he must have remained in or near the city for at least another twenty years. He returned to Morristown by February 23, 1826 when the Presbyterian church of his boyhood accepted his transfer from the Reformed Dutch Church of Frankfort Street in New York.

At his father's death in 1814 Lewis inherited a sixth portion of his real and personal property. His mother's death on February 17, 1826 may have prompted his return to Morristown to look after family property. In his later life he became interested in the doctrine of Universalism, and after publishing some articles on his new beliefs he was excommunicated from the Presbyterian Church for heresy on November 27, 1837. He died in Morristown on June 23, 1855.

Lewis was a cousin of Timothy (A.B. 1783), Gabriel (A.B. 1784), and Jacob Ford (A.B. 1792), and of John Blanchard Johnes (A.B. 1804). William Johnes (Class of 1776) was an uncle.

SOURCES: Alumni file & Johnes family folder, PUA; T. Thayer, *Colonial & Rev. Morris Cnty.* (1975), 87, 163, 228, 232; "Diary or Memorandum Book Kept by Joseph Lewis of Morristown," *NJHSP*, 59-62 (1941-44), *passim*; *Hist. of the First Pres. Church, Morristown, N.J.* (1882?-85, 2 vols. in 1), II, 117, 134; *Hist. of Morris Cnty., N.J.* (1882), 31, 149-50, 321; R. S. Green & W. Durant, eds., *Record, First Pres. Church of Morristown, N.J.* (1880-85, 5 vols. in 1), I, 62; II, 102, 117, 150, 166, 174, 175, 177, 182, 184; *N.J. Wills*, XIII, 255; Min. Fac., 10 Nov. 1789, 9 July 1791; Clio. lists; Clio. Min., 26 Sept. 1792; *Dunlap's Amer. Daily Advt.*, 4 Oct. 1791; Thomas, *Columbia*, 182; N.Y. City directories.

RLW

John McCrady (McCready)

JOHN MCCRADY (MCCREADY), A.B., attorney, was born at Charleston, South Carolina, June 13, 1775, the only son of Edward and Elizabeth Campbell McCrady. The father had emigrated from Ireland and settled briefly in Philadelphia before moving to Charleston. An active whig during the Revolution, he was one of the citizens of Charleston sent as a prisoner to St. Augustine after the fall of the city.

Many of the wives and children of the St. Augustine prisoners journeyed to Philadelphia to wait out the war, and the families were eventually reunited in that city. A number of the Charlestonians enrolled their sons in one of the Princeton institutions before the families returned to the South. McCrady may have been quite young when he was sent to John Witherspoon for education. In 1785, probably before his tenth birthday, he was in residence at the Nassau Hall grammar school. In the fall of that year, as a member of the fourth class, he placed second in a contest on Latin grammar and syntax. On March 28, 1786 John Heriot (Class of 1789) noted in a letter that "Master John McGrady ... left this place yesterday at his Papa's desire." Whatever his reason for leaving, McCrady was back in Princeton in November 1787, when he entered the College as a freshman. During his four years there he joined neither campus debating society. On the afternoon of his commencement, he participated in the ceremonies as respondent to the question, "Does the cultivation of science and the improvement of arts, tend to the improvement of morals and the encrease of happiness?"

McCrady returned to Charleston to read law in the office of Charles Cotesworth Pinckney, was admitted to the bar on September 29, 1796, and presumably began a large and lucrative practice. Acquaintances praised his integrity, sense of humor, and vivacious disposition. His legal debates were described as "copious, without verbosity, logical without dryness, and eloquent, without the parade of metaphors, or the pomp of rhetorical flourish." On March 1, 1797 he married Jane Johnson, daughter of William and Sarah Nightingale Amory Johnson of Charleston, and sister of William Johnson, Jr. (A.B. 1790). They had three children, Eliza, Sara, and Edward, who were baptized in St. Philip's Parish Church in Charleston. McCrady died on June 12, 1803, twenty-eight years old. His son Edward (A.B. Yale 1820) became a Charleston lawyer and a prominent Unionist during the nullification controversy. His grandson, also Edward McCrady, wrote several histories of South Carolina and is often referred to as the historian of the state.

SOURCES: Alumni file, PUA; *N.J. Gazette*, 10 Oct. 1785; Heriot letters, 28 Mar. 1786 ("Master John"); Hancock House MSS; Min. Fac., 10 Nov. 1789; *Dunlap's Amer. Daily Advt.*, 4 Oct. 1791; O'Neall, *Bench & Bar S.C.*, II, 178-80 ("copious ..."); D. E. H. Smith & A. S. Salley, Jr., *Register of St. Philip's Parish, Charleston, S.C.* (1971), 16, 22, 29; *SCHGM*, 48 (1947), 186; 42 (1941) 126; W. S. Clemens, *N. & S. Carolina Marriage Record* (1927), 172.

RLW

Peter Timothy Marchant (Merchant)

PETER TIMOTHY MARCHANT (MERCHANT), printer, newspaper publisher, planter, and possibly artist, was the grandson of Ann Donovan Timothy and Peter Timothy, avid patriot and the leading printer and newspaper publisher in Charleston, South Carolina. In January 1769 their daughter Frances Claudia married Benjamin Lewis Marchant of Antigua. The name suggests that the groom had the same French Huguenot background as the Timothy family. The young couple must have remained in Charleston, since Marchant enlisted in the Fifth South Carolina Regiment on November 18, 1776. Their son Peter Timothy was born sometime in October 1773. Whatever Benjamin Marchant's reason for returning to Antigua, he died there on November 9, 1779 and was buried in St. Philip's Parish, described as "of Willoughby Bay."

As one of Charlston's leading patriots when the British occupied the city, Peter Timothy was among the group of Charleston men exiled to St. Augustine in 1780. Frances Marchant and her children accompanied her family to Philadelphia, where they awaited the father's release. When Peter Timothy joined them in the fall of 1782, he and his daughter Frances, along with her infant son and another of the Timothy daughters, set sail for Antigua, where Frances Marchant had inherited land from her husband, leaving young Peter in the care of his grandmother. The ship was not far off the coast of Delaware when it sank during a severe storm. Everyone aboard drowned.

Ann Timothy returned to Charleston to take over the management of the family printing business and the publication of the newspaper, whose name she changed from *The Gazette of the State of South Carolina* to *State Gazette of South-Carolina*. Before traveling south she enrolled her youngest son, Benjamin Franklin Timothy (Class of 1790), in the Nassau Hall grammar school. No lists are available to show whether or not her Marchant grandson entered the school at the same time.

Peter Marchant entered the College as a freshman in November 1787, a year after his uncle. No surviving evidence indicates that he joined either of the debating societies, but no records of nongraduate members of the American Whig Society are extant. On March 17, 1788 Marchant was one of a group of students convicted by the faculty of causing a riot in the College and sentenced to receive a public admonition, to read a confession in front of the assembled College, and to repair all damages. He was one of three who at first refused to accept this punishment and was immediately suspended.

He later recanted, asked the pardon of the faculty, accepted the punishment, and was readmitted to the College. On November 17, 1788 he and his classmate George Henry were convicted of indecent conduct and admonished in front of their class. Marchant left the College sometime in May 1790. Perhaps he found too restrictive a resolution passed by the faculty on March 21: "It appearing that leave of absence from College has in time past been too easily & sometimes improperly obtained by the Students. Resolved that no person absent himself from any of the duties of his Class except with permission from the teacher of it—or from College for more than one day except with permission from the President & his Teacher likewise." More likely, he decided to return home with his uncle because of the illness of Ann Timothy.

Benjamin Timothy took over the management of the Charleston newspaper with the issue of September 20, 1792. He subsequently brought Peter Marchant and William Mason, husband of his sister Sarah, into association with him on the paper. However, only Mason was taken into partnership. By January 1, 1794 the new publishers were able to bring out a daily edition and the name was changed to *South-Carolina State-Gazette & Timothy & Mason's Daily Advertiser*. The publication supported the Democratic-Republican party and was never loath to discuss political questions. Mason left the partnership in January 1798 to return to teaching, but there is no indication that Marchant was ever invited to buy into the business. During 1800 Timothy also published the weekly *Federal Carolina Gazette*, with two different partners. With the *South-Carolina Gazette* experiencing more and more financial problems, Timothy printed the last issue on September 20, 1802 and secured a position as a school principal.

Marchant's activities for the next several years are not known. His name first appears in Charleston directories in 1802, prior to which he had probably lived with the Timothy family. The daily *Charleston Courier* began publication in January 1803, no doubt to try to fill the gap created by the demise of the *Gazette*. On January 10, 1806 the *Courier* was purchased by the firm of Marchant, Willington & Co., which consisted of Peter T. Marchant, Aaron S. Willington, Stephen C. Carpenter, and Frederick Dalcho. The new partners adopted the motto, "The wreath or the rod," which was printed on the second page under the sub-title, *The Courier & Mercantile Daily Advertiser*. Carpenter withdrew from the partnership in July 1806. Beginning in November of that year the *Carolina Weekly Messenger* was also issued from the *Courier* office. In addition the firm did a variety of commercial printing. The 1806 Charleston directory lists Peter Merchant

[sic] as "book keeper, Courier office," and this function may have been his major responsibility. A subsequent issue says only "Courier office."

The partnership was dissolved in April 1809, and the paper continued publication under the firm of E. Morford, Willington & Co., consisting of Willington, Dalcho, and Edmund Morford (A.B. 1797). Marchant was the last member of the Timothy family to be associated with printing and publishing. His great grandfather Lewis Timothy and his grandfather Peter Timothy had established the first newspaper in South Carolina that had any degree of permanency and maintained a high standard of publishing integrity.

Another gap in our knowledge of Marchant's affairs ends with his reappearance in city directories from 1816 through 1824, now listed as a planter. Thereafter his name again disappears from the directories. However, he is mentioned briefly in the journal of the Reverend Abiel Abbot, who in 1827 traveled from New England to South Carolina for his health. On November 16 he dined at the home of Ebenezer Thayer, merchant and bookseller. When Miss Claudia Thayer played the piano after dinner, "A Mr. Merchant sang very well & a lady, I think Smith, with whom I joined in singing 'Strike the Cymbols' with the piano in fine time and spirit." The editor of the journal identifies Mr. Merchant as "Probably Peter Timothy Marchant, a Charleston newspaper man and artist of the early 1800s." Marchant died on October 29, 1834 of a "country fever," leaving a widow "advanced in years." John Timothy Trezevant (A.B. 1775) and Peter Timothy (A.B. 1813) were first cousins.

SOURCES: Nongraduate files, PUA; Min. Fac., 17 Mar. & 17 Nov. 1788, 10 Nov. 1789, 21 Mar. 1790; Hancock House MSS; C. Brigham, *Hist. & Bibl. of Amer. Newspapers 1690-1820* (1947), II, 1025, 1029, 1452; L. M. Hudak, *Early Amer. Printers & Publishers, 1639-1820* (1987), 146, 472-80; I. Thomas, *Hist. of Printing in Amer.* (1874), I, 342; II, 171; A. S. Salley, Jr., *Marriage Notices in Charleston Courier 1803-08* (1919), 3-5; A. S. Salley, Jr., *Marriage Notices in the S.C. Gazette & Country Jour. & The Charleston Gazette* (1904), 12; A. S. Salley, Jr., *Marriage Notices in the S.C. Gazette & Amer. General Gazette, & The Royal Gazette* (1914), 11; *SCHGM*, 44 (1943), 103; 68 (1967), 65 (quote from Abbot journal); B. G. Moss, *Roster of S.C. Patriots in the Amer. Revolution* (1985), 674; B. H. Holcomb, *Supplement to S.C. Marriages 1688-1820* (1984), 24; Charleston city directories; B. Holcomb, *Marriage & Death Notices from Charleston Observer 1827-45* (n.d.), 90.

Three different collections of newspaper notices variously cite Frances Claudia Timothy as married to "Mr. Benjamin Lewis Merchant, of the Island of Antigua," "Mr. Benjamin Merchant," and "Benjamin Lewis, merchant of West Indies." It therefore seems likely that the grandson given a bequest in the will of Ann Timothy in C. T. Moore, *Abstracts of Wills of Charleston District, S.C. 1783-1800* (1974), 279-80, as "Peter Timothy, merchant" was actually Peter Timothy Marchant, especially since no profession is listed for the other relatives mentioned. The abstract also states that her "grandsons are entitled to property in West Indies which was their late father's."

The Marchants of Antigua could trace their ancestry to the John Marchant who settled there in 1678 and had a son Benjamin. Not enough information is available to identify positively the parents of Benjamin Lewis Marchant, but his father was probably the Benjamin Marchant born June 12, 1732, of Willoughby Bay Harbor, who had two wives, (1) Sarah and (2) Anne. See V. L. Oliver, *Hist. of the Island of Antigua* (1894), I, 244; II, 235-39; III, 193.

RLW

Francis Markoe

FRANCIS MARKOE, A.B., merchant and speculator, was the fourth of the five children of Francis and Elizabeth Hartman Markoe of St. Croix, Danish West Indies. Born June 5, 1774, he was the younger brother of Peter Markoe (Class of 1791). His great-grandfather was the French Huguenot, Pierre Marcou, who fled from Montbeliard, France and settled on St. Croix in 1685. The family built up large sugar plantations and a flourishing trade with Europe and the northern British colonies. It was not unusual for sons to be sent to England or Philadelphia to be educated, and it was also a common family practice to have sons settle in different port cities to look after the family's mercantile interests at those locations. The spelling of their name was changed when they became Danish subjects, but the French pronunciation was retained.

The elder Francis Markoe died in 1779. When Elizabeth Markoe sent her two sons to Philadelphia for their education, they were entrusted to the care of their uncle Abraham Markoe. He had resided there since 1770 and was a respected and wealthy merchant whose grand house at 322 Market Street was the first in Philadelphia with marble lintels over the windows. Abraham Markoe was also well known as the founder and first captain of the First Troop Philadelphia City Cavalry. At the time that Philadelphia was being considered as the site of the national capital, he offered a parcel of land to the government to be used for the president's home. His two nephews from St. Croix were sent to the preparatory school of the University of the State of Pennsylvania, Peter on October 1, 1783, and nine-year-old Francis on January 1, 1784. They were promoted from the English school to the Latin school on July 1, 1784 and continued their studies there until the end of the winter term which began on December 16, 1785.

Perhaps in the interval before they enrolled at the College in November 1787 the Markoes visited their mother in St. Croix. They both joined the Cliosophic Society, Francis on November 26, 1788. Sometime in late 1788 or early 1789 Peter left the College. Francis continued with his studies and at the end of his junior year placed fourth in the English orations competition for undergraduates. In

June 1791 Markoe was one of a group of students called before the faculty for swimming late at night and returning "at a very unseasonable hour." They received a public admonition for this "great impropriety." At his commencement Markoe was opponent in a debate asking "Are not lotteries for public purposes, disadvantageous to the community?" Markoe also joined John Noble in a dialogue on luxury, a common theme in republican ideology. At about the time that Markoe was finishing college, his older sister Elizabeth married Benjamin Franklin Bache, radical Jeffersonian editor of the Philadelphia *Aurora*. Markoe's fairly frequent correspondence with Bache and his successor, Elizabeth's second husband William Duane, probably indicates Democratic-Republican loyalties in keeping with his commencement topic.

After graduation Markoe entered the counting house of James Yard of Philadelphia to learn the mercantile trade, in the course of which he made several voyages to the West Indies. On November 4, 1797 he married Sarah Caldwell, daughter of Martha Round and Samuel Caldwell, three weeks before her sixteenth birthday. They moved to St. Croix where they lived for about ten years before returning to Philadelphia. Apparently Markoe was a worldly man with an appreciation for the amusements wealth could provide. At a houseparty at St. Croix sometime "near the beginning of the century," Markoe found himself alone in his host's library where he picked up a compilation of tracts edited by William Jones, first published in 1795 and entitled *The Scholar armed against the errors of the time*. He read it and experienced an immediate religious conversion which changed the course of his life. Now abstaining from attending the theater and dancing, Markoe found that he had no companions to share his new spirituality and that none of the churches on the island satisfied his craving for evangelical preaching. While he prayed for an opportunity to move from St. Croix, "An opening presented itself to him in the country where he had received his education." The exact form of this opening is unknown, but he settled in Philadelphia. Before leaving the island Francis sold his share of the family estate to his brother and speculated with the proceeds. Misplaced trust in an agent, who was either fraudulent or unwise, resulted in the loss of his fortune after six or seven years. His experience in the West India trade helped him to find employment, but within a few years he moved to New York where he became a partner with a brother-in-law, Thomas Masters, in a shipping and commission business at 50 South Street, Masters, Markoe & Co.

Whatever the vicissitudes of the business world, Markoe's religious conversion was a serious and sustained one, and his faith remained unshaken. In Philadelphia he became a member of the First Presbyterian Church of the Northern Liberties, where the Reverend James Patterson was the pastor. Markoe, who taught a Sabbath Bible Class, and was "zealous in the instruction of the ignorant," prepared two or three hours each day for his class. With the spirit of revivalism sweeping Philadelphia, he found the congenial company he had lacked at St. Croix, and he joined several private prayer groups.

After moving to New York where he belonged to the Mercer Street Presbyterian Church, Markoe continued teaching a Sunday School class and served as an elder for ten years. His Christian principles were carried into his business life, where he was widely respected for his sincerity, tact, and courtesy, even by those who did not share his views. One can only wonder how he found time to conduct much business when he attended church meetings on Sunday morning, afternoon and evening, was always in attendance at mid-week meetings, and spent several hours each day in private study and prayer. Far from somber or condemning, his piety was good-spirited, generous, and kindly. He was tall and strongly built, erect in his carriage, with good features and a refined expression. Cheerful by nature, he enjoyed indulging in "innocent mirth."

Markoe died after several weeks of illness on February 16, 1848 at the age of seventy-three, of "perityphlitis." He was buried in the Marble Cemetery in New York City but was later reinterred in the Sleepy Hollow Cemetery beside his wife, who died in May 1862. They had ten children, one of whom was Thomas Masters Markoe (A.B. 1836, M.D. College of Physicians and Surgeons, New York City, 1841), who served as professor of anatomy at Castleton Medical College, Vermont; professor of pathological anatomy at New York University; and professor of surgery and of principles of surgery at Columbia. A grandson was Francis Hartman Markoe (A.B. 1876, A.M. 1901, M.D. Columbia 1879), who also became a professor at Columbia and a consulting surgeon at several New York hospitals. Edward F. Rivinus, Jr. (B.A. 1937) and J. Willis Martin Rivinus (B.A. 1950) are descendants.

SOURCES: Portions of a family history and genealogy kindly provided by F. Markoe Rivinus of Philadelphia. See also: alumni file, PUA; records of Univ. of the State of Pa., UPenn-Ar; F. Lewisohn, *St. Croix Under Seven Flags* (1970), 107, 113, 163-64, 172-73, 185-86; Clio. lists; Hancock House MSS; Min. Fac., 10 Nov. 1789, 22 June & 9 July 1791; Williams, *Academic Honors*, 12; *Dunlap's Amer. Daily Advt.*, 4 Oct. 1791; *DAB* (Abraham Markoe); Alexander, *Princeton*, 255; T. H. Skinner, *Religious Life of Francis Markoe, Esq.* (1849), *passim*.

MANUSCRIPTS: 22 letters in Bache Papers, Castle Collection, Amer. Phil. Soc., Phila. These letters became available too late for use above.

RLW

Peter Markoe

PETER MARKOE, planter and speculator, was born November 19, 1771 on the island of St. Croix in the Danish West Indies, the oldest son and third child of Francis and Elizabeth Hartman Markoe. The family traced their descent from the French Huguenot, Pierre Marcou, who left Montbeliard, France in 1685 after the revocation of the Edict of Nantes. One family tradition says that he was blown ashore at St. Croix during a storm. The Marcous prospered as sugar planters and traders. When they became Danish subjects they changed the spelling of their name, while retaining the French pronunciation. As their trading interests increased, family members settled in various important port cities as representatives of the clan's business interests.

When Peter and his younger brother Francis (A.B. 1791) were sent to Philadelphia to be educated, their father's older brother Abraham was there to welcome them into his home. The house was a spacious one at 322 Market Street, surrounded by ornamental gardens and noted for being the first house in Philadelphia with marble lintels over the windows. Abraham, a wealthy merchant, founded and served as the first captain of the First Troop Philadelphia City Cavalry. The banner he designed for the outfit may have been the earliest use of the device of the thirteen stripes. He enrolled his two nephews in the preparatory school conducted by the University of the State of Pennsylvania, Peter on October 1, 1783, and Francis at the beginning of the next quarter, January 1, 1784. Thereafter the two kept pace, moving up from the lower English school to the Latin school on July 1, 1784. Their attendance continued through the quarter term which began on December 16, 1785.

No further information has been found about the Markoes's activities until they matriculated as freshmen in November 1787. When Peter joined the Cliosophic Society on December 3, 1787, he adopted the pseudonym Cato, after one of the two ancient Roman statesmen and exemplars of republican virtue of that name. On March 17, 1788 Markoe was among a group of students found guilty by the faculty of rioting in the College. He and William Anderson (A.B. 1789) accepted a public admonition, read a confession aloud before the assembled College, and made restitution for damages. The others involved in this escapade refused the punishment and were suspended. Despite his submission to faculty discipline, Markoe may have become disenchanted with the College because of this episode. His name does not appear on a class list of April 10, 1789 preserved in the New Jersey State Archives, nor on one in the faculty minutes dated November 10, 1789.

Markoe returned to St. Croix, probably to manage the family plantations, since his father had died in 1779. Upon his mother's death in 1791 he inherited a large estate which was increased by his marriage to a wealthy second cousin, Mary Aletta Heyliger, in 1801. The couple had nine children, most of whom eventually settled in the United States. Apparently they were raised in great luxury, which meant living in a manorial style in one of the "Great Houses," filled with imported European furniture. Investing "to enlarge his income by various means such as the life of a West India planter permitted," Markoe eventually suffered serious financial losses. He may have overinvested in land or become involved in unprofitable trade agreements. The strain took a toll on his health, and he made a visit to the United States in the hope of regaining his strength. He died in 1841 at the New York home of his brother Francis. His wife survived him by nearly twenty years. He was described as a fairly good-looking man, with blue eyes and an amiable expression.

SOURCES: Family history provided by F. Markoe Rivinus of Phila.; *DAB* (sketch of Abraham Markoe); records of Univ. of the State of Pa., UPenn-Ar; Clio. lists; Min. Fac., 17 Mar. 1788; F. Lewisohn, *St. Croix Under Seven Flags* (1970), 107, 113, 163-64, 172-73, 185-86.

Peter Markoe should not be confused with his well-known cousin, Abraham's son Peter (1753-1792), often referred to as "Peter the poet."

MANUSCRIPTS: 14 letters in Bache Papers, Castle Collection, Amer. Phil. Soc., Phila. These letters became available too late for use above.

RLW

John Berrien Maxwell

JOHN BERRIEN MAXWELL is known only to have been from New Jersey and to have joined the Cliosophic Society on December 3, 1787, using Montgomery as his society name. Although no connection to the Berrien family has been found, Maxwell's name and the pseudonym he chose suggest that he may have been related to John Macpherson Berrien (A.B. 1796), son of Maj. John and Margaret Macpherson Berrien. The latter was the sister of John MacPherson (A.B. 1766), who was Gen. Richard Montgomery's aide-de-camp during the Revolution. The Berriens moved to Savannah, Georgia, shortly after the birth of their son, but they were originally from Rocky Hill, New Jersey, a few miles from Princeton. Major Berrien's sister, Mary Berrien Montgomery of Allentown, New Jersey, named her eldest son Alexander Maxwell Montgomery, which adds slightly to the probability of a Maxwell/Berrien family connection.

SOURCES: Alumni files & Berrien family file, PUA; Clio. lists; *NJHSP*, n.s., 5 (1920), 108; Berrien & Morris family files, NjPHi. George Clifford Maxwell (A.B. 1792) had a younger brother John, but nothing has been found to suggest that he was John Berrien Maxwell, and he was probably too young to have been the Princetonian. George Maxwell's uncle, Brig. Gen. William Maxwell, died unmarried. See H. D. Maxwell, *The Maxwell Family* (1895).

RLW

Boyd Mercer

BOYD MERCER, Presbyterian minister and justice, was born in 1766 in Frederick County, Virginia, near the town of Winchester. He may have spent his boyhood there, and no clue has been found as to when he moved to Pequea, Pennsylvania to study under the Reverend Robert Smith, father of Samuel Stanhope Smith (A.B. 1769). The recommendation to come to Princeton was surely made by Robert Smith. Mercer, as an overage student, probably received private instruction in theology from either Stanhope Smith or President John Witherspoon, while filling various gaps in his education as a matriculate at the College. His advanced age when admitted, and the fact that he came as a resident of Pennsylvania, suggest that his decision to study for the ministry was made as an adult and that he had already left the family home in Virginia. On a November 10, 1789 class list his name appears as "Boid Merser," with notations that he matriculated then and was dismissed from the College in May 1790. However, his name is included with the members of the senior class on the November 1790 list. Records of the Cliosophic Society show that he joined on December 19, 1789, using the name of Sarpedon, the Trojan War hero reputed to be a son of Zeus, and that the society dismissed him for unstated reasons in December 1791.

Mercer's name next appears in the June 26, 1792 minutes of the Presbytery of Redstone, where he was accepted on trial, examined in Latin and Greek, and assigned his exegesis topic. The Redstone presbytery was in existence from September 1781 to October 1793 and derived its name from Redstone Settlement, which covered most of Pennsylvania west of the mountains and also extended into Virginia. Many of the Presbyterians in the area had emigrated from Chester County, Pennsylvania, and the majority of the clergy in the presbytery came from the same county. The Princeton influence was strong, with John Clark (A.B. 1759), Thaddeus Dod (A.B. 1773), John McMillan (A.B. 1772), and Joseph Smith (A.B. 1764) among the presbytery members. McMillan, who had been serving since 1776 as pastor of both the Pigeon Creek and Chartiers congregations in what eventually became Washington County, Pennsylvania, appears to have taken Mercer under his care. Mercer's relationship with the presbytery proceeded through the various examinations and additional assignments required of a licentiate until April 16, 1793 when he became the last ministerial candidate to receive a license through that presbytery. This body held its final meeting on October 15, 1793, when all of the churches on the west side of the Monongahela became part of the new Presbytery of Ohio. Mercer was not present at this meeting. A call from the Mingo Creek and Horseshoe churches was transmitted to him through McMillan, with the minutes adding that "Mr. Mercer shall have his appointments made out by the Presbytery of Ohio if he thinks fit." He apparently declined the call to Mingo Creek and Horseshoe and chose instead to replace McMillan at the Pigeon Creek church. The latter was busy teaching and doing missionary work along with the care of his two congregations and was considered the most prominent Presbyterian in Washington County. Ordained by the Presbytery of Ohio on April 29, 1795, Mercer served the Pigeon Creek and Pine Run churches until the spring of 1799. He apparently never had another fulltime pastorate. From 1798 until 1802 he was a trustee of the Canonsburg Academy, an institution organized by the Presbyterian clergy of the area primarily for the training of future ministers. In 1802 it was granted a charter as Jefferson College.

On January 1, 1806 Mercer was commissioned an associate judge of the fifth district of Washington County, under presiding judge Samuel Robert. Disturbed by this association of church and state, the Ohio presbytery sought the advice of the general assembly, querying, "May a man hold the office of an Associate Judge and the office of the gospel ministry at the same time, or is it expedient for a Presbytery to continue a person in the office of the gospel ministry in such circumstances?" Mercer sent an accompanying letter to the assembly pleading physical infirmity as his reason for accepting the position, stating "that it is not his intention to decline the office of the holy ministry, and that he was led to devote himself for the present to the functions of an associate judge, by the state of health so infirm as to interrupt the regular discharge of his public duties as a minister of religion." The committee appointed to consider this question reported on May 23, 1806 that they found nothing in either the scriptures or the constitution of the Presbyterian Church prohibiting service in both the ministry and a civil office, and under the circumstances they advised the presbytery not to censure Mercer. However, they added a caution against covetousness, ambition, and worldly mindedness, suggesting that the clergy be reminded that the salvation of souls was their most important business and that they should, as much as possible, avoid temporal associations.

Whether because of poor health or worldly mindedness, Mercer held the office of judge for the remainder of his life. The fact that he lived until February 5, 1841, when he was seventy-five years old, and that he was able through the intervening years to travel to various churches as stated supply, suggests that he was not particularly infirm. He served as stated supply to churches in Charlestown (Wellsburg), Pitt Township, McKeesport, Muddy Creek, Jefferson, and New Providence. After McMillan's death he also preached occasionally at the Chartiers church. His longest association was with McKeesport, where he was given credit for "laying the foundations of organized Presbyterianism in this vicinity."

Mercer married Rebecca Blackstone of Fayette County, Pennsylvania, but no date has been found for the marriage. They settled on a farm near the Pigeon Creek church and in 1826 deeded ten acres of their land for the use of the church for the token sum of $1.00. At the time Mercer executed his will on March 6, 1840, he had two sons and three daughters. Apparently anticipating his death, he had already made gifts of cash and property to his children, $3,600 to each son, and lesser amounts to his married daughters. His legal books were divided between his sons, suggesting that law was their profession, while his religious books and his silver tablespoons were divided among his daughters. Some descendants probably remained on the family farm, while others settled further west. In a memorial written after his death, where one might expect to find lavish encomiums, Mercer is described merely as being under medium height, active in temperament, and a good preacher, although another source mentions that his sermons were instructive and evangelical, and yet another that he did not attain much distinction in the ministry.

SOURCES: Alumni file, PUA; Min. Fac., 10 Nov. 1789, 29 Nov. 1790; Clio. lists; D. M. Bennett, *Life & Work of Rev. John McMillan* (1935), 119-22; D. R. Guthrie, *John McMillan* (1952), 135; *Hist. of the Presby. of Redstone* (1889), 74, 103-04 ("laying the foundations"), 185; J. Smith, *Old Redstone* (1854), 128, 313, 436-38, 441-42, 446-50, 457; B. Crumrine, *Hist. of Washington Cnty., Pa.* (1882), 940; B. Crumrine, *Bench & Bar of Washington Cnty., Pa.* (1902), 49; W. F. Hamilton, *Hist. of the Presby. of Washington* (1889), 9, 12, 21, 25-26, 404-05; *Minutes of the General Assembly of the Pres. Church, 1789-1820* (1847), 359, 363-64 ("that it is not"); Boyd Mercer will, 6 Mar. 1840, proved 25 Feb. 1841, Wash. Cnty. Pa. Register of Wills.

RLW

James Witter Nicholson

JAMES WITTER NICHOLSON, A.B. Columbia 1792, merchant, manufacturer, and farmer, was born on April 20, 1773, probably at "Nicholson Manor," near Nicholson Gap, Maryland, the son of James and Frances Witter Nicholson. The mother was the only surviving child of Thomas Witter, a wealthy New York merchant born in Bermuda, and his wife Mary Lewis Witter. The elder James Nicholson was the senior officer of the American navy from early 1778 to the end of the Revolutionary War and was known thereafter as Commodore Nicholson. Born in Chestertown, Kent County, Maryland, he lived in New York City in the 1760s, was back in Kent County by the time of his son's birth, and returned to New York City after the Revolution. In the 1790s his house on William Street served as a gathering place of the Antifederalist movement. He was president of the Democratic Society of New York City in 1794, and during the ensuing year Alexander Hamilton (LL.D. 1791) challenged him to a duel following a political quarrel. After friends intervened, the duel was averted. Nicholson played a major role in the delicate negotiations in which Aaron Burr (A.B. 1772) was selected for the vice presidency in 1800. Nicholson and his wife had eight children, of whom James Witter and five daughters reached adulthood. Four of the girls married United States congressmen, including Hannah, the second daughter, whose husband Albert Gallatin, a Swiss immigrant then resident in Fayette County, Pennsylvania, later became secretary of the treasury under President Thomas Jefferson (LL.D. 1791).

James Witter Nicholson entered the College as a sophomore in November 1788. His career there was uneventful until the evening of June 26, 1790, when a boisterous group of students placed a calf in the pulpit of the College's prayer hall and knocked over an outhouse after drinking too much at a tavern. The faculty concluded that Nicholson was one of the culprits and expelled him on July 18 after he persisted in asserting his innocence. In August he finally confessed, apologized and was reinstated, but he did not return to the College in the fall. Instead he entered Columbia College. Either the transfer cost him a year or he was an indifferent student, for he graduated in 1792.

Nicholson's activities thereafter are obscure until July 31 and September 17, 1795, when he signed agreements by which he, his brother-in-law Albert Gallatin, John Badollet, Louis Bourdillon, and Charles Anthony Cazenove formed a partnership called Albert Gallatin and Co. Nicholson contributed $4,000, one-fifth of the company's total capital. The goal was to develop trade and exploit the natural resources of western Pennsylvania in the vicinity of "Friendship Hill," Gallatin's estate. The company bought a tract of several hundred acres at the confluence of the Monongahela River and Georges Creek in Fayette County, a spot from which Gallatin hoped a great deal of control over East-West trade could be exercised. The partners laid out and began selling lots at a town which they named New Geneva. This name reflected the Swiss background of the venture. All of the partners save Nicholson were Swiss, and Gallatin planned the community as a haven for Swiss refugees from the instability created in Europe by the French Revolution. Actual conditions in Switzerland never got bad enough to produce much emigration.

Nicholson and his partners moved to New Geneva in spring 1796 to supervise the company's concerns, and he wound up spending the rest of a long life there. In addition to selling real estate, the partners built and operated a retail store, a gristmill, a sawmill, and a ferry. In 1797 they attracted to New Geneva a group of German glass blowers headed by the brothers Christian and George Kramer, who had previously worked at Frederick, Maryland. Gallatin and Co. agreed to pay for construction of a glassworks in exchange for half the profits. The resulting concern was either the first or second glass factory west of the Alleghany mountains. The company diversified still further in February 1799 by obtaining a contract to manufacture and sell 2,000 muskets to Pennsylvania, part of the munitions the state decided to purchase when war with France seemed imminent.

The partnership was not very successful. Land sales were slow, and hopes that New Geneva might become a major entrepôt of East-West trade proved illusory. The initial expenses of the glassworks were very high and the profits never quite as large as anticipated, although the concern survived several changes of ownership and a move across the river to Greensboro, in Greene County, where it was still producing glass in 1833. The gun works lasted no longer than the state contract, the satisfaction of which was attended with much anxiety and many delays and probably yielded a modest profit at best. Although his duties in Congress and his family's inclinations kept him in the East most of the time, Gallatin was much the ablest of the partners and the only one in a position to raise more capital as the company encountered periodic fiscal crises. Those on the scene were soon bickering. Some became disheartened and left, and Gallatin bought out the rest. By about 1802 Gallatin and Co. had been dissolved, leaving Gallatin as sole or principal owner and Nicholson as the steward of his holdings in the West.

Nicholson married Ann Griffin, one of the ten children of Isaac and Mary Morris Griffin of Fayette County, on January 1, 1797.

Isaac Griffin was a native of Delaware who served as a captain in the Revolutionary War. Subsequent to his move to Fayette County he sat in the state legislature and, from 1813 to 1817, in the United States House of Representatives. Gallatin and Nicholson's family both regarded James as unprepared financially and therefore opposed the marriage as premature, although they were subsequently reconciled to it. That their assessment of the economics of the situation was right is suggested by Nicholson's eventual slippage from partnership with Gallatin to service as his agent. The marriage seems to have been happy, however, and lasted more than thirty-five years, during which at least seven children were born to the couple.

After his appointment as secretary of the treasury, Gallatin seldom visited New Geneva. Until his son Albert Rolaz Gallatin (Class of 1817) was old enough to do so, he trusted Nicholson to manage his interests there and often expressed his entire faith in him. In addition to his work on Gallatin's behalf, Nicholson kept a store in New Geneva and owned two farms encompassing 270 acres at nearby Jacobs Creek. From at least 1825 to around 1840 he also served as New Geneva's postmaster. Nicholson achieved modest success as a merchant. His finances were always tangled, and on several occasions he had to resort to help from relatives when his debts became too pressing. Only the receipt of a bequest upon the death of his mother in 1832 enabled him to retire. He could proudly boast, however, that he had maintained his credit unimpaired throughout his career and that only once, near the end of his life, had he been sued (and then unsuccessfully) for debt.

In 1803 Nicholson was complaining to his sister Adden of the loneliness of life at New Geneva, and he sometimes talked thereafter of moving. He came closest to doing so in July 1812, when President James Madison (A.B. 1771) appointed him one of the five deputy commissaries of purchases of the United States Army, with a salary of $2,000 a year. Gallatin congratulated him on this chance to fulfill his desire to return to New York. Nicholson was in that city in September, but he seems eventually to have declined the appointment. In 1833 Nicholson considered moving to Brownsville, Fayette County, but again thought better of it and instead retired to "Elk's Hill," his estate near New Geneva. His loyalty to the New Geneva area and status as a frontier settler were recognized in 1845 when the newly formed Nicholson Township, which includes New Geneva, was named after him.

Nicholson began suffering from rheumatism around 1832 and survived a severe attack of pleurisy in 1845. He died on October 6, 1851.

SOURCES: R. Walters, *Albert Gallatin: Jeffersonian Financier & Diplomat* (1957), 16-18, 21, 52-56, 124-25, 133-40, 219-21, 261, 315-17, 325-27, 346; F. Ellis, *Hist. of Fayette Cnty., Pa.* (1882), 695-96, 698-99, 701; *DAB* (James Nicholson [1736-1804]); W. P. Bacon, *Ancestry of Albert Gallatin ... & of Hannah Nicholson* (1916?), 36-39, 48; B. K. Stevens, *Geneal.-Biog. Hist. of the Families of Stevens, Gallatin & Nicholson* (1911), 32-35; *PMHB*, 63 (1939), 133n; Hancock House MSS; Min. Fac., 10 Nov. 1789, July-Aug. 1790; Thomas, *Columbia*, 113; letter from Columbia Univ. Columbiana curator, 21 June 1983, PUA; Microfilm Ed. of the Papers of Albert Gallatin (1970, C. E. Prince, ed.), letters to and from JWN, 21 Feb. 1792 to 22 Feb. 1847, *passim*, esp. Albert Gallatin to JWN, 14 Apr. & 9 Dec. 1796, 24 Nov. 1797, 2 Feb. & 9 Mar. 1798, 18 Jan., 1 Feb. & 13 Dec. 1799, 11 Sept. 1801, 22 Oct. 1802, 11 Jan. & 21 Dec. 1803, 26 Oct. 1804, 16 June 1806, 6 July 1812, 12 April & 4 May 1816, 22 July 1818, 28 Mar. 1821, 8 Nov. 1825, 13 Mar. & 3 Apr. 1826, 10 Oct. 1840, 12 July 1841; JWN to Albert Gallatin, 24 Apr. 1816, 6 Aug. 1817, 24 May 1818, 3 Nov. 1821, 15 Jan. 1846; JWN to Albert Rolaz Gallatin, 12 Jan. 1832, 13 Feb. & 18 June 1833, 29 Oct. 1834, 1 Apr. 1846; Adden Nicholson to JWN, 18 Jan. 1803; JWN to Frances Witter Nicholson, 8 May 1832; see also Albert Gallatin to Maria Nicholson, 1 Feb. 1797; G. S. McKearin & H. McKearin, *Amer. Glass* (1941), 117-24; J. D. Weeks, "Report on the Manufacture of Glass," in U.S. Census Office, *Report on the Manufactures of the U.S. at the Tenth Census* (1883), 1120-21; *Jour. Exec. Proc. U.S. Senate, 1st to 19th Cong.* (1828), II, 281, 284. Definitive evidence that James Witter Nicholson was the Princetonian has not been discovered. No College source gives his middle name. The identification is based on his age, a dearth of other likely prospects, and the known acquaintance between James Witter Nicholson and his classmate Maltby Gelston, also from New York. Gelston is mentioned as a friend of Nicholson in the Gallatin correspondence in 1797, and his father, David Gelston, was a close family friend of the Nicholsons. See Albert Gallatin to JWN, 16 Nov. 1797, 12 Jan. & 9 March 1798, 5 Sept. 1804, Gallatin Papers, microfilm ed. Gelston and Nicholson entered the College at the same time, and one can reasonably speculate that they did so together. Both were also involved in the incident which preceded Nicholson's departure from the College.

MANUSCRIPTS: The microfilm editions of the papers of Albert Gallatin include some 200 letters from or to JWN. Most belong to NHi. The James Witter Nicholson Collection at Columbia Univ. Lib. consists of 41 letters to JWN by his father and sisters.

JJL

John L. Noble

JOHN L. NOBLE, A.B., physician, was the son of Maj. Alexander Noble and his wife Catharine Calhoun. He was the brother of Patrick Noble (A.B. 1806), who served a term as governor of South Carolina. Patrick Noble was also a law partner of their cousin John Caldwell Calhoun (A.B. Yale 1804), with whom he became one of the leaders in the nullification movement. Ezekiel Pickens (A.B. 1790) was another first cousin of the Nobles, a relationship more firmly cemented by the marriages of Pickens's sister Rebecca to William Noble, brother of John and Patrick, and of Pickens's daughter Elizabeth to Patrick Noble. Although John Noble was born in North Carolina, probably in 1772, the family must have moved soon after to Abbeville, South Carolina. Patrick received his early education in Dr.

Moses Waddel's school at Willington, South Carolina, but nothing has been found to indicate whether John attended the same institution.

Noble matriculated at the College as a junior in November 1789 and joined the Cliosophic Society on December 19, assuming the name of Clarendon, the English royalist statesman and historian. At his graduation ceremonies his oration on the French Revolution, one of the intermediate honors, was delivered immediately after the Latin salutatory. Later in the day he joined his classmate Francis Markoe in a dialogue on luxury.

Noble next turned to the study of medicine, first in Philadelphia and later in France. Sometime in 1809 he opened an office on King Street in Charleston, where he maintained a successful practice until his death on February 4, 1819. Listings in the 1806 and 1807 Charleston directories for "doctor John Noble, apothecary and druggist," suggest that for those years he may have also operated an apothecary shop to fill the prescriptions of other doctors in the city. An obituary in the *Charleston City Gazette* gave the cause of his death as "apoplexy, connected with a paralytic affection," and his age as "about 47 years." It also noted his "professional talent, his urbanity of manners, and unblemished honor and integrity."

Nothing has been found to indicate that Noble ever married. His obituary mentioned five brothers and numerous relatives among his mourners. His will provided bequests only for his sisters, a sister-in-law, and a nephew. Four slaves were included in the list of individual bequests.

SOURCES: Alumni file, PUA; A. N. Waring, *Fighting Elder: Andrew Pickens (1739-1817)* (1962), 11, 203; E. B. Reynolds & J. R. Faunt, *Biog. Dir. of the Senate of the State of S.C.* (1964), 283 (brother); C. M. Wiltse, *John C. Calhoun* (1944), 43, 86; Clio. lists; Min. Fac., 10 Nov. 1789, 9 July 1791; *Dunlap's Amer. Daily Advt.*, 4 Oct. 1791; Charleston city directories; JLN Will, ScCoAH; *SCHGM*, 45 (1944), 196 (obit.).

RLW

Ebenezer Howell Pierson

EBENEZER HOWELL PIERSON, A.B., physician, was born in Morristown, New Jersey, on February 10, 1771, one of the two sons and three daughters of Aaron and Mary Howell Pierson. Israel Harris (A.B. 1790) was his third cousin, once removed. On October 23, 1786 Ebenezer was sent to board for seven shillings a week at the home of Joseph Lewis of Morristown, a lawyer and the father of Stevens J. Lewis (A.B. 1791). He was still there the following February. Pierson may have lived with the Lewises in order to join Stephen in attending the nearby school of a Dr. Campfield, probably Jabez Campfield (A.B. 1759).

Pierson entered the College as a junior in November 1789. On December 19 of that year he joined the Cliosophic Society, taking the pseudonym Eusebius, after the pioneer historian of early Christianity. At his commencement on September 28, 1791, he was replicator in a debate on the topic "Does the cultivation of science and the improvement of arts, tend to the improvement of morals and the encrease of happiness?"

After his graduation, Pierson studied medicine and then returned to the Morristown area to practice. No information on his training has been discovered. Perhaps he was apprenticed to Abraham Canfield (or Campfield), Jr., of Morristown, whose sister Phebe he married in 1794. When the younger Canfield's health broke down at an early age, Pierson succeeded to his brother-in-law's practice. In 1795 he bought forty-seven acres of land in nearby Rockaway Township. He received $250 at the death of his father in 1803 and half of the bulk of the estate when his mother died in 1810.

Pierson served as lieutenant colonel of the Third or Northern Regiment of Morris County militia from 1801 to 1804 and became a justice of the peace of the county in 1813. His first wife died in September 1804, and a year later he married Phebe, the daughter of Samuel Day. The two marriages produced a total of six children, all girls but one. On March 17, 1812 Pierson was one of the five commissioners who opened subscription books creating a local bank, and four years later he contributed $50 towards the purchase of Morristown Green and its preservation as a public park. In 1816 and 1817 the state medical society appointed Pierson one of Morris County's five censors, or examiners of the credentials of new entrants to the medical profession.

Sometime between July 1817 and October 1819, Pierson moved from New Jersey to Cincinnati, Ohio, where he continued to practice medicine. Both the 1819 and 1825 city directories gave a Sycamore Street address. On February 21, 1821 Pierson was among the eighteen physicians who founded the Cincinnati Medical Association and adopted a code of ethics. When the "First District Medical Society of Ohio," comprising Hamilton and Clermont counties, was founded in May 1824, he became its first treasurer. He also served on the Board of Visitors of the Cincinnati Female Academy and as president of the local board of health. He became a trustee of the Medical College of Ohio under its new charter of 1825. The 1828 appointment of his first cousin Charles Edwin Pierson (A.B. 1807) to the institution's *materia medica* chair is sometimes ascribed to his influence.

Ebenezer Howell Pierson died at 8 a.m. on October 14, 1828 and was buried in Spring Grove Cemetery, Cincinnati.

SOURCES: *Hist. of the First Pres. Church, Morristown, N.J.* (1882?-85, 2 vols. in 1), II, 181, 184; "Diary or Memorandum Book Kept by Joseph Lewis of Morristown," *NJHSP*, 61 (1943), 48, 56; Clio. lists; Min. Fac., 10 Nov. 1789, 18 Mar. 1790, 9 July 1791; alumni file, PUA; *Dunlap's Amer. Daily Advt.*, 4 Oct. 1791 ("Does the cultivation"); Wickes, *Hist. of Medicine N.J.*, 196, 363; *Hist. of Morris Cnty., N.J.* (1882), 75-76, 79, 159, 162, 337-38; *N.J. Wills*, x, 352; XII, 295; XIII, 31; *Rise, Minutes & Proc. of the N.J. Med. Soc.* (1875), 150, 152, 161; *Cincinnati Directory* (1819), 136; *Cincinnati Directory for 1825* (1825), 110, 123, 127; O. Juettner, *Daniel Drake & his Followers* (1909), 128, 131-32. The *Princeton Univ. Gen. Cat.* (1908) credits Pierson with an M.D., but this attribution seems to be merely a courtesy, since the *Cincinnati Directory for 1825*, p. 110, implies that Pierson was licensed to practice but lacked a medical degree.

JJL

Henry Purcell

HENRY PURCELL was born in Charleston, South Carolina, on April 23, 1770, the third of the five children of the Reverend Henry Purcell (D.D. 1785) and Sarah Wood Purcell, the first of their offspring to be born in the American colonies and their only son. The Purcells emigrated from Essex, England, and arrived in Charleston on June 4, 1769, where Purcell had an appointment as assistant to the rector of St. Philip's Church. He later became rector of St. Michael's Church, where he served for twenty years. From 1779 to 1781 he was chaplain to the South Carolina Brigade of the Continental Army. In 1785 St. Michael's proclaimed itself a member of the Protestant Episcopal Church in America by sending Purcell as a delegate to the first general convention, where he helped in the preparation of the new prayer book. Musically talented, he wrote several of the tunes in the choral book and organized a boys' choir at St. Michael's, but the vestry definitely thought he had gone too far when he invited the band of the St. Cecelia Society to perform selections of sacred music in the church on a Sunday.

The younger Henry seems to have been the archetypical minister's son, rebelling against parental restrictions by breaking the rules as soon as he was away from home. On August 17, 1788, as a member of the freshman class of the College, he was summoned before the faculty and found guilty of "profane swearing and other irregularities" and sentenced to receive an admonition in front of his class. On September 22, near the end of the semester, he was again convicted of disobedience and "opposition to the officers of the College" for refusing to open the door of his room when commanded to do so and then neglecting to appear before the faculty to explain his conduct.

This charge was considered serious enough to warrant immediate expulsion from the College. Shortly after the new term began, the minutes of November 17 state that after "making such concessions as were thought sufficient, as well as many promises of good behavior in future," Purcell was readmitted. His name is included as a member of the sophomore class in the manuscript list of students of the College, dated April 10, 1789, preserved in the New Jersey State Archives, but it is not on the list of students included with the faculty minutes of November 10, 1789. Nothing further has been found about Purcell, except that he died in Charleston sometime in April 1819 and was interred in St. Michael's Churchyard.

SOURCES: Nongraduate file, PUA; *SCHGM*, 19 (1918), 150; 21 (1920), 14; 64 (1963), 2; G. W. Williams, *St. Michael's, Charleston* (1951), 40, 45, 48-50, 205, 313; A. S. Thomas, *Protestant Episcopal Church in S.C.* (1957), 12; Min. Fac., 17 Aug., 22 Sept., & 17 Nov. 1788; Hancock House MSS.

RLW

John Randolph

JOHN RANDOLPH, planter, congressman, senator, and minister to Russia, the third son of John Randolph and Frances Bland Randolph, was born June 2, 1773, at "Cawsons," the Bland family estate near the confluence of the Appomattox and James Rivers in Prince George County, Virginia. Both parents came from old Virginia families, and the younger John was particularly proud of the Indian blood that he inherited through his maternal grandmother, who traced her ancestry to Pocahontas and John Rolfe. Because the father died several months after the son's second birthday, John had no recollection of him except through his mother, whom he revered all his life. "Only one human being ever knew me," he exclaimed years later. "*She* only knew me." "I slept in the same bed with my widowed mother," he recalled in 1815; "—each night before putting me to bed, I repeated on my knees before her the Lord's Prayer and the Apostle's Creed— each morning kneeling in the bed I put my little hands in the same form." With her help he memorized the catechism so well that he remembered much of it even after years of avowed skepticism. Her marriage to St. George Tucker when John was five did not seem to have upset him at the time, although later events suggest that it may have been a traumatic experience. All early correspondence indicates a warm relationship with his stepfather, and John appears to have been genuinely fond of his younger half-brothers and sisters. He grew up with a strong sense of family pride, faith in the land, and religious convictions to which he would return in middle age.

John Randolph of Roanoke, Class of 1791
BY CHESTER HARDING

Tucker had emigrated to Williamsburg from Bermuda around 1771 in order to study law. He later became professor of law at William and Mary, and during John's boyhood he fought in the Revolution, receiving a slight wound in the last battle of the war. Because the Tuckers owned no land in Virginia, the family lived at "Matoax," the Randolph estate which the elder John Randolph had left for his wife's use during her lifetime. In January 1781 when Benedict Arnold's troops invaded Virginia, Tucker feared for the safety of his family and sent them to "Bizarre," another of the Randolph properties, which included land on both sides of the Appomattox. With the exigencies of war, Tucker found it impossible to continue instructing the Randolph boys and difficult to keep a tutor at "Bizarre." Young John wrote to him on May 25, 1779, "I will try all I can to be a good Boy & a favorite of Mamas & when you come home I shall be one of yours."

In January 1782 John Randolph, along with his older brothers Richard (Class of 1788) and Theodorick (Class of 1791), was sent to study under Walker Maury, a former classmate of Tucker's at

William and Mary. Maury's school was situated in a rather primitive building in Orange County, and John was miserably unhappy there. In a letter written as an adult he still complained that he and his brothers had received "scarcely the necessaries of life without an opportunity to acquire anything more than as much Latin as sufficed to furnish out a bold translation of the ordinary school books." He thought his schoolmates a "vicious and profligate crew" and had neither affection nor respect for his schoolmaster. "I was tyrannized over and tortured by the most peevish and ill-tempered of pedagogues, Walker Maury. This wretch excommunicated me body and soul." He remained in Orange County less than a year; in October the school was closed when Maury was invited to open a grammar school in conjunction with the College of William and Mary. Soon after this new institution was established in Williamsburg, the three Randolph brothers rejoined Walker Maury. John and Theodorick entered in the fourth class, under the charge of the chief usher, but the group progressed so well that it soon became the third class and was placed under Maury's direct supervision. John continued to complain about both the school and its master, and Maury probably disliked him quite as intensely, since a classmate recalled that Randolph was flogged regularly every Monday morning and sometimes two or three times a week.

Mitigating Randolph's wretchedness was the presence of his brothers and his classmate Littleton Waller Tazewell, with whom he formed a lifelong friendship. As a boy Randolph was described as beautiful rather than handsome, and when the students were required to act out Latin plays he was always given the feminine parts. He was rescued from school in the spring of 1784 when, because of delicate health, he was sent to Bermuda, where he stayed at the home of the father of St. George Tucker. Here he had a fine library at his disposal and a tutor whom he complained would not take the trouble of teaching him Greek. A year later the whole family came to Bermuda for a visit, then returned to Virginia in the fall of 1785, when the boys were again sent to Maury's school in Williamsburg. Because of Maury's "shocking barbarity," first Theodorick and then John left the school and returned home.

After spending some months at home the two brothers came to Princeton in March 1787, where they were assigned to the first class in the grammar school. Richard, who had been studying at William and Mary, joined them in Princeton a few months later. Enjoying Nassau Hall no more than Williamsburg, John claimed that he and Theodorick were placed in the grammar school only so that John

Witherspoon could make more money from them, and that they were actually further advanced than any of the freshmen and most of the sophomores. In 1813, in a letter written to a nephew, Randolph recalled: "In this subterranean abode of noise and misrule, I was pent for five long months, and in September, was transferred to the college with habits acquired in that school by no means propitious to study." On another occasion he wrote: "At Princeton College ... the prize of elocution was borne away by mouthers and ranters. I never would speak if I could possibly avoid it, and when I could not, repeated without gesture, the shortest piece that I had committed to memory.... I was then as conscious of my superiority over my competitors in delivery and elocution, as I am now that they are sunk in oblivion; and I despised the award and the umpires in the bottom of my heart." Despite these bitter recriminations he must have done well on his examinations, for on September 27 he wrote to his mother, "I expect the watch you promised me." In June their stepfather had written to John and Richard, setting forth their obligation to achieve in proportion to their talents and to do everything possible to improve in both virtue and understanding. Frances Tucker may have decided that a bribe would be more effective than a goad. Randolph joined the Cliosophic Society on December 3, using the pseudonym Antonio.

John and Theodorick went to New York to spend the 1787 Christmas holidays, with John complaining that Dr. Witherspoon had embezzled part of their spending money. While in New York they learned that their mother was gravely ill, and they hurried to Virginia for a last visit before she expired on January 10, 1788. John, only fifteen, was greatly affected by Frances Tucker's death. The young Randolphs did not return to school until the following May. John had probably convinced his stepfather that they were learning nothing at the College of New Jersey, for this time they tried Columbia College, where they entered as freshmen members of the Class of 1792. Here Randolph finally found a teacher who challenged him, William Cochran, professor of Greek and Latin. He claimed to be thirsting for knowledge denied him at Nassau Hall, and he was so eager to study with Cochran that he paid $8.00 a month extra for private tutelage. In a few months Cochran left Columbia for an appointment at Nova Scotia College, ending Randolph's only interlude of serious and systematic study, although he continued to read voraciously all his life. Now John blamed Theodorick and his dissolute companions for luring him from his studies. However, he was in New York at the right time to receive his first lessons in politics. He witnessed the inauguration of George Washington and often attended meetings of the First Congress where several relatives and family connections sat as members.

In the summer of 1790 Randolph accompanied Theodorick, now seriously debilitated, back to Virginia. Here it was decided that John should study law under Edmund Randolph, a distant cousin and the newly appointed attorney general of the United States. Randolph arrived in Philadelphia in September 1790, along with the executive officers and congressmen who were gathering at the new capital. John complained that Edmund Randolph was too engrossed in politics and the social life of Philadelphia to spare any time for his students, John Randolph and Joseph Bryan. Edmund, said John, did little more than assign them books to read in their rooms. After getting through part of William Blackstone's *Commentaries*, the two young men decided that the legal profession was not for them and that they would rather enjoy the pleasures of Philadelphia. They indulged in these as whole-heartedly as John had accused Theodorick of doing in New York. Although John complained that St. George Tucker did not provide him with enough funds, on at least one occasion Tucker sent a sizeable remittance to Philadelphia to be applied to gambling debts. Still, Randolph continued to listen to debates in Congress and also to attend occasional medical lectures with student friends.

Despite Randolph's dissatisfaction with his various teachers, he acquired an impressive education in the classics and the literature of Augustan England. He embraced with real passion the political culture and satiric style of the age of Jonathan Swift, a commitment that probably made him the most uncompromising "country ideologue" in the early republic. In a corrupt world, he expected executive power to undermine legislative autonomy and public virtue. For patriotism and political independence he looked to families of lineage, wealth, and cultivation. The Virginia of his youth became a golden age to him, and he devoted much of his energy to preventing its decay, and much of his scathing wit to castigating anybody or anything that threatened to destroy it.

A series of personal crises in the early 1790s intensified these convictions and imparted a sense of urgency to his public life. While traveling from Philadelphia to Virginia in July 1792, Randolph contracted a severe case of scarlet fever which left him beardless, a soprano, and—in all probability—impotent. His brother Theodorick died the same year, and in the fall a scandal involving his brother Richard, whom he idolized, and Nancy Randolph, the sister of Richard's wife, led to a hearing for possible infanticide, followed by a decision not to press criminal charges. At loose ends, John again tried to secure a formal education by enrolling at William and Mary late that year. Several months later a fellow student, Robert B. Taylor of Norfolk, challenged him to a duel, very likely provoked by Randolph's sarcasm. On the second shot Randolph wounded Taylor in the hip, after which the two arranged a genteel reconciliation. The duel ended Randolph's association with William and Mary.

He visited Philadelphia in 1793 and Charleston and Savannah in 1796, where he witnessed the aftermath of the Yazoo land fraud, a formative event in his political consciousness. But for the most part he spent the next years idly at "Bizarre," where the only requirements on his time seemed to be attendance at as many horse races as possible. His return from the Deep South was interrupted by illness which forced him to remain at Petersburg for several weeks. When he reached home in July 1796, he learned that Richard had died suddenly and unexpectedly on June 14. Though barely twenty-three, John immediately assumed the duties as the head of Richard's household, which gave him responsibility for Richard's widow Judith, her two young sons Tudor and St. George, her sister Nancy, plus a widowed cousin, Anna Bland Dudley, and her two children. Randolph took quite seriously his role as substitute father to the four children of the household, and some years later he also accepted responsibility for rearing the two orphaned sons of Joseph Bryan. A collection of his letters to Theodore Bland Dudley was published posthumously by Dudley as *Letters to a Young Relative*. These epistles reflect Randolph's obvious devotion to Dudley. They are newsy and full of advice about books to read and people to call upon. Randolph often included gifts of money, for he was financing Dudley's medical education. But whenever Randolph had been without return letters for some time, his affection became a smothering possessiveness in which he alternated between hurt feelings and worry over Dudley's health. Even when he did receive mail, there was often a petty querulousness about his demands for more details than were contained in a "scant letter." The correspondence also reflects Randolph's preoccupation with his own health and his habit of ignoring the advice of doctors and prescribing his own medication. He frequently complained about gout, rheumatism, diarrhea, headaches, and insomnia, and yet he spent a great deal of time on horseback and remained a superb horseman throughout his life.

Between 1796 and 1799, Randolph put Richard's affairs in order. Their father's estate had been encumbered by a British debt. To clear the estate and put his nephews' finances in good order, he was forced to sell "Matoax." Richard's will had freed his slaves and given them land on which to settle, and John Randolph took care of all the legal details necessary to carry out his brother's wishes. He saw to it that both "Bizarre" and his own estate of "Roanoke," about thirty miles away, were productive plantations before he decided to run for Congress in 1799.

Randolph was not yet twenty-six when he became the Democratic-Republican candidate for Congress from the District of Charlotte, which was composed of Charlotte, Prince Edward, Cumberland, and Buckingham counties. Powhatan Bolling was his Federalist opponent, but at Charlotte Court House he debated Patrick Henry, the last such contest for the aging orator Henry and the first public encounter for the neophyte Randolph. Henry was elected to the Virginia senate but died before he could claim his seat. Randolph was elected to the House of Representatives, which was firmly under Federalist control, and took his seat in December 1799. Only a month later he gave Congress a hint of his oratorical style. He spoke in support of a resolution which would have reduced the standing army, one form of "arbitrary" power that he always opposed. He spoke vehemently and did not hesitate at name-calling, in this case referring to the country's professional soldiers as mercenaries and ragamuffins. When the news of his maiden speech spread, Randolph was insulted by two officers while at the theatre. Undaunted, he wrote to President John Adams, protesting this attack on the independence of the legislature. After much discussion and one resolution aimed at placating Adams, the speaker of the house ruled that all further action on the subject was out of order. But the affair was discussed enough to make Randolph's name and political views well known, and when Thomas Jefferson (LL.D. 1791), his second cousin, succeeded to the presidency and made his appointments and recommendations, John Randolph became chairman of the important Ways and Means Committee.

For the next several years Randolph led the House with great parliamentary skill, usually managing to be both moderate and tactful. His first step in the new Congress was to propose the repeal of the Judiciary Act of 1801 which had allowed Adams to make numerous lame duck appointments. Randolph helped to implement the Louisiana Purchase by pushing through a bill which created certificates of stock in favor of the French government. On many occasions his chief opposition in a debate came from Federalist James Ashton Bayard (A.B. 1784). One memorable evening they continued to air their differences at their Washington lodging house, until the infuriated Randolph tossed his wine in Bayard's face and then broke the glass over his head.

In 1804 Randolph was appointed a manager of the impeachment

trial of Justice Samuel Chase. His opening speech rose to such heights of vituperative oratory that it became a favorite schoolboy exercise. The basic question raised by the impeachment was whether behavior that the House and Senate considered inappropriate could also be found impeachable under the "high Crimes and Misdemeanors" provision in Article II, section 4 of the Constitution. Jefferson was eager to silence Chase's intemperate condemnations of his administration from the bench, but Luther Martin (A.B. 1766), acting for the defense and more experienced and skillful than Randolph, easily demolished the latter's arguments. Randolph, who took all opposition as personal attacks, was almost irrational in his closing speech, which was delivered with grimaces, groans, and tears. Although a majority of the senators voted for conviction, a two-thirds margin was necessary, and Chase was acquitted. Randolph angrily dashed from the Senate to the House and there proposed that the Constitution be amended to read, "The judges of the Supreme and all other courts of the United States shall be removed by the President on the joint address of both Houses of Congress."

In 1807, as foreman of the grand jury that indicted Aaron Burr (A.B. 1772) for treason, Randolph was again pitted against Martin, who acted as Burr's successful defense counsel at his subsequent Richmond trial. To Randolph's disgust he could not even secure an indictment against Gen. James Wilkinson, "the only man that I ever saw who was from the bark to the very core a villain." The general retained Jefferson's support throughout the trial, though Randolph thought him more culpable than Burr.

On the question of the Yazoo fraud, which the House first considered in January 1805, Randolph's implacable hostility to the settlement supported by the administration cost him his leadership in the party. In bitter, vituperative speeches he condemned Yazoo corruption which, in his judgment, threatened the integrity of the republic. He was politically naive in refusing all efforts to frame a compromise and in vocalizing his utter contempt for all who favored such a settlement, including members of his own party. The corruption so repelled him that he could not find compassion even for its innocent victims. He sought to intimidate opponents by towering over them and hissing in their faces the word, "Yazoo." To administration supporters Randolph and his small band of admirers became known as the "Quids" or "Tertium Quids."

During the Ninth Congress, despite losing his party leadership, Randolph was able to retain his chairmanship of the Ways and Means Committee. He finally broke completely with Jefferson over the question of the Florida Purchase and became an outspoken critic of the

administration. In letters he mocked Jefferson with the nickname of
"St. Thomas of Cantingbury." Opponents in the House were often
effectively silenced by their fear of becoming the butt of his bitter
and biting satire. He opposed the Embargo Act and any system of
restrictive commerce, the War of 1812 and all offensive war. In 1813,
because of his hostility to the war, his seat in the House was won by
John W. Eppes.

Randolph's first electoral defeat initiated a period of personal crisis
for him that left him alarmed for his own sanity, but also completed
his transition from Jeffersonian radical to self-conscious conservative and spokesman for southern interests. During the campaign,
"Bizarre" burned to the ground, destroying his personal library. The
two together were his most powerful links with the past he revered.
The next year he lost three-fourths of his crop, and the British
burned Washington, including the Capitol, where he had served for
most of his adult life. By then his birthplace "Cawsons" and his childhood home at "Matoax" had also been destroyed by fire. He felt that
his life was going up in flames.

Randolph endured other, equally terrible shocks. Maria Ward,
daughter of Mrs. Benjamin Ward of "Winterpock" and a childhood
friend, broke her engagement to him and later married Edmund
Randolph's son Peyton. John also failed to arrange a marriage for his
deaf mute nephew, St. George, with the latter's cousin, Jane Hackley.
When that young man's precarious emotional balance worsened to
undeniable insanity, Randolph typically blamed the woman, whom he
described as "destitute of every personal charm." His uncle arranged
institutional care for the remainder of St. George's life. In the midst
of these troubles, Nancy Randolph, now Mrs. Gouverneur Morris,
admitted to John Randolph that Theodorick, not Richard, had gotten her pregnant in 1792. Prodded to a degree by his nephew Tudor,
John denounced her savagely. He accused her of murdering her bas-
tard infant in 1793, of poisoning Richard in 1796, of retaining a
mulatto lover, and of various other indiscretions. When he sent this
indictment to her husband, the aging Gouverneur Morris, Nancy
wrote a dignified but angry response and distributed full copies of
the exchange among their numerous Virginia friends. Evidently she
had few doubts about which of them would be believed. Finally, his
nephew Tudor Randolph, a brilliant student, died unexpectedly in
1815, the last hope for perpetuating the line of John Randolph, Sr.
In a two-year period Randolph had lost his past and his future. "The
death of Tudor finished my humiliation," he admitted a decade later.

This series of blows precipitated a profound religious crisis. "I
had tried all things but the refuge of Christ," he explained, "and to

that, with parental stripes was I driven." He indulged in sentimental memories of his mother and broke publicly with his foster father, whose rational religion he now despised. He also resented Tucker's presumption that his descendants were John's only logical heirs. For the first time Randolph accused Tucker of plundering his estate, and that of his brothers, before they came of age.

Christianity did not come easily to Randolph's personality. For some time he could find no way to love his enemies and forgive those who had wronged him except by becoming almost a hermit at his "Roanoke" plantation, where he lived alone in a crude cabin served by hundreds of slaves and surrounded by thoroughbred horses. As early as 1810, he had begun to sign himself "John Randolph of Roanoke," mostly to distinguish himself from a cousin of the same name whom he loathed. That he sometimes saw through his own affectations is suggested by his signature to a business letter in 1819: "John St. George Randolph of Bizarre." By 1815 he feared for his own lucidity. "I have lived in dread of insanity," he later confided to his Washington messmate, Thomas Hart Benton. He probably suffered acute depression after Tudor's death, and he may have spent part of 1818 in a religious ecstasy. In the judgment of friends, he was again not responsible for his actions for a time in 1820 and in 1831-32.

Randolph coped with his demons in several ways. He visited the ruins where he had been born, reflected darkly on the decay of Virginia's first families, read Edmund Burke avidly, deplored the war with Britain, reprobated the social and economic changes sweeping across the republic, and explained these disasters as manifestations of God's wrath. He also drank far too much. He emerged from his ordeal an adamant conservative, opposed to the rule of "King Numbers" and determined to protect the South against Yankee encroachments. He showed more respect to some Federalists, cultivating friendships with Josiah Quincy (A.M. 1796) and John Marshall (LL.D. 1802), and even finding flattering things to say about Alexander Hamilton (LL.D. 1791) and Timothy Pickering (LL.D. 1798), his much feared opponents of the late 1790s. His fondness for England increased as his disenchantment with American democracy intensified. He began to refer to her as "home," exulted in her role as Virginia's mother country at the moment of his birth, became an ardent Episcopalian, and told listeners that the administration of James Madison (A.B. 1771) was far more tyrannical than Frederick Lord North's had ever been, even though North had brought on the American Revolution. He visited England in 1822, 1824, and 1826, where he was well received in high society, particularly among enemies of the slave trade, which he frequently denounced. Although

Virginia remained first in his affections, England may well have replaced the United States in second place by the 1820s.

Randolph returned to the House in 1815 where he bitterly opposed the Second Bank of the United States, the tariff, and any other measures to strengthen the national government. He refused to stand for reelection in 1817 but served continuously from 1819 to 1825, fighting against all measures, such as the Missouri Compromise, that he thought enlarged the sphere of the federal government and infringed upon the powers of the states. He spoke almost daily, and usually at great length, both entertaining and dismaying his colleagues. His speeches continued to be brilliant and eloquent, and his sharp wit delighted those whom he was not castigating at the moment. However, he often wandered from the subjects under discussion, and he came to be considered a hindrance, as well as someone to fear and dislike.

His youthful attractiveness had changed to a peculiarity of appearance that matched his odd behavior. "I have been an idiosyncracy all my life," he remarked on his deathbed. He was described as tall and thin, with arms and legs disproportionately long for his torso. People remembered the angular fingers that would point to an opponent and the eyes that would gleam brilliantly while he harangued. When drinking excessively he was profane and obscene, and drunk or sober he never hesitated to ridicule or rebuke his fellow congressmen, most of whom hesitated to reply to his attacks because they feared the reprisal of his withering sarcasm. One of his most frequently quoted rebuttals was in answer to an irate colleague who had rashly mentioned Randolph's impotence: "You pride yourself upon an animal faculty, in respect to which the negro is your equal and the jackass infinitely your superior." His career in the House included his caning of Willis Alston and near-duels with Daniel Webster (LL.D. 1818) and John Eppes. In 1825 he was elected to complete the unexpired term of James Barbour in the Senate, where he finally sat with those he had previously referred to as "Their High Mightinesses."

Randolph and Henry Clay had fought on opposite sides of the House, and upon Clay's appointment as secretary of state under John Quincy Adams (LL.D. 1806), the new Senator Randolph renewed his attacks upon him. The denunciations became more bitter and excoriating, and worst of all they grew more personal, until in a memorable speech Randolph referred to the correct and puritanical Adams and the hard-drinking gambler Clay as "Blifil and Black George," characters in Henry Fielding's *Tom Jones*. Challenged by Clay, Randolph met him on the bank of the Potomac on April 6, 1826. Both of their first shots went wild, with Randolph presumably aiming for the legs.

He had threatened to disable Clay and spoil his aim. On the second round Clay's bullet went through the skirt of Randolph's coat, close to the hip, while Randolph discharged his bullet in the air. As the two met and shook hands after the exchange, Randolph exclaimed, "You owe me a coat, Mr. Clay." Clay replied that he was glad the debt was no greater, and the whole affair was described by a witness as a high-toned duel.

In 1827 Randolph was defeated for reelection to the Senate, but his constituents returned him to his old seat in the House, where he became a leader of the opposition to Adams. Sensing that this would be his last term, he released his oratorical venom as he boasted, "I bore some humble part in putting down the dynasty of John the First, and by the grace of God, I hope to aid in putting down the dynasty of John the Second." On one occasion he described Madison, whom he also despised, as as mean a man for a Virginian as John Quincy Adams was for a Yankee.

After Andrew Jackson's victory in 1828 Randolph announced that he would not seek reelection. His greatest effort during his years in Congress after 1815 had been in calling upon the southern states to unite and in solidifying their antinorthern bias. His concern was always for Virginia first, and he was the most ardent of the states' rightists. He proudly declared that he never voted for the admission of any new state into the union. Because he hated abolitionists, he became identified with the slave party, even though he denounced the slave trade. Toward his own slaves he was generally compassionate. His letters often contained inquiries about particular slaves by name and mention of clothing being shipped for their use. But even his favorites were often the helpless victims of his erratic and capricious moods.

Randolph served as a delegate to the Virginia Constitutional Convention of 1829-30, an illustrious gathering that included Madison, James Monroe (LL.D. 1822), Marshall and other dignitaries. Randolph opposed every suggestion for change in the existing Virginia constitution and defended the entrenched eastern interests against those of the western section of the state. Due in part to Randolph's powerful oratory, the convention ignored years of pressure by aggrieved westerners who were pitted against the established aristocratic elitism of the old Virginia families. Social divisions were exacerbated rather than reconciled by the convention, and they became the dominant theme of Virginia politics for the remainder of the antebellum period. Some historians consider Randolph's role in the convention as his most significant public act.

Before the convention met, President Jackson offered to appoint

Randolph envoy extraordinary and minister plenipotentiary to Russia, probably a ploy to keep him occupied at a safe distance from Washington. He accepted and sailed from Norfolk on June 28, 1830 and reached St. Petersburg on August 10, after a voyage uneventful except for Randolph's claim that as minister he outranked the captain and should be allowed to take command of the ship. After being presented at court he began negotiations for a commercial treaty with Russia, but his health was adversely affected by the Russian climate, and he soon found it necessary to ask permission to leave St. Petersburg. He went to England, hoping to return to Russia when he had recovered. Instead, he grew steadily worse, and after hemorrhaging from the lungs, he gave up all idea of resuming his duties. The following spring he sailed for New York, where he landed with an advanced case of tuberculosis. His mind was seriously deranged by now and for a year he was cared for in seclusion at "Charlotte Court," the Virginia home of John Marshall, who remained a loyal friend in spite of political differences. Still Randolph managed to send out a spate of letters abusing various public officials. During this period he drank excessively and openly admitted his addiction to opium. In the late spring of 1832 when his balance returned, he insisted on touring his district. He even attempted to make some speeches to his former constituents.

Feeling for some reason that he might recover in England, he managed to get as far as Philadelphia, from whence he hoped to sail. Too ill to go on, he died there on May 24, 1833. His instructions were that he be buried in an unmarked grave at "Roanoke," under a tall pine tree which he had selected, facing west so that he might still keep an eye on Henry Clay. He was later reinterred at Richmond. During the latter part of his life he had often been pressed for cash, but he owned more than 8,000 acres of land, nearly 400 slaves and a valuable stud of blooded horses. He left a number of wills, one written in 1819, one undated, one drafted in 1821 to which four codicils had been added, and one dated January 1, 1832. The first two wills were not admitted to probate, and the last was set aside because the court ruled him not of sound mind when it was written. After a long legal contest, the will of 1821 was accepted. It used most of his estate to emancipate his 300 slaves and remove them to free territory. It also contained a last vindictive barb aimed at his stepfather:

> I have not included my mother's descendants in my will, because her husband, besides the whole profits of my father's estate during the minority of my brother and myself, has contrived to get to himself the slaves given by my grandfather Bland, as her marriage portion when my father married her, which slaves were

inventoried at my father's death as part of his estate, and were as much his as any that he had. One-half of them, now scattered from Maryland to Mississippi, were entitled to freedom at my brother Richard's death, as the other would have been at mine.

Randolph's career is difficult to summarize, but in many ways he provided a historical bridge between Jefferson and John C. Calhoun, or even between the revolutionary spirit of Monticello and the Confederate defeat at Appomattox. The radical republican of 1799 did not change his views drastically on many subjects other than religion. He was one of few Americans who opposed both the Quasi-War with France when he first took office and war with Britain in 1812, largely on the same grounds. But the American people changed around him until his republican values seemed even in his own eyes quite explicitly conservative by the 1820s. The man who shared the Founding Fathers' hatred of slavery and who acquired a trans-Atlantic, though somewhat exaggerated, reputation as a benevolent master became one of the earliest and most strident defenders of the slave interest in Virginia and American politics, and he was also one of the first to see congressional control over commerce as a huge threat to slavery. Yet he, not Jefferson, freed his slaves at his death. This admirer of eighteenth-century planters and their elegant homes lived the last two decades of his life in near squalor while he denounced the tobacco-spitting proclivities of his neighbors and mocked their vernacular expressions. His most telling response to all of this change was a studied eccentricity of dress and address that made him as much an entertainer as a prophet. He left behind no devoted band of followers.

Yet he fascinated contemporaries, and they could not forget him. Long after Randolph's death fellow congressmen and former neighbors—in fact almost anyone who had had even slight contact with him—apparently delighted in describing his eccentricities and in trying to outdo one another in recalling examples of his barbed wit. His name lives on in Randolph-Macon College, along with that of his longtime friend and fellow Quid, Nathaniel Macon (Class of 1778). Established in 1830, this Methodist institution chose to honor the most prominent men in Virginia and North Carolina because of its location close to the border between the two states. A more cynical point of view says that both these non-Methodists were affluent planters, and the college hoped to realize some advantage from their wealth. However, there is no record that either ever contributed to or had any connection with the institution that bears their names.

Few self-proclaimed political failures have left an equal legacy to popular culture or been more carefully studied than John Randolph.

SOURCES: *DAB*; *BDUSC*, 1691; Clio. lists; G. W. Johnson, *Randolph of Roanoke* (1929), *passim*; H. A. Garland, *Life of John Randolph of Roanoke* (1856), *passim*; J. C. Bruce, *John Randolph* (1922), esp. I, 303-04 (Wilkinson as "villain"); II, 38 ("an idiosyncracy"), 274-95 (exchange with Nancy Randolph Morris), 355 (periods of insanity), 436 (trips to England); M. H. Coleman, *St. George Tucker* (1938), *passim*; P. Bouldin, *Home Reminiscences of John Randolph of Roanoke* (1878), *passim*; R. Dawidoff, *Education of John Randolph* (1979), *passim*, esp. 213 (JR's mother & religion), 212 (conversion), 210 ("John St. George Randolph of Bizarre"), 200 (Lord North v. Madison); T. H. Benton, *Thirty Years' View* (1856), I, 473 (fear of insanity); H. A. Johnson et al., eds., *Papers of John Marshall* (1974-   ), II, 161-78; R. I. Randolph, *Randolphs of Va.* (privately printed), 222, 271; F. A. Virkus, *First Families of Amer.* (1925), 863-64; D. H. Gilpatrick, *Jeffersonian Democracy in N.C.* (1931), 112; B. Merrill, Jr., *Jefferson's Nephews* (1976), 81; H. Adams, *Hist. of the U.S.* (1909), II, 228-43; G. Bradford, *Damaged Souls* (1923), 122-56; D. B. Smith, *Inside the Great House* (1980), 87, 96-97, 112; *VMHB*, 3 (1896), 315-16; 4 (1897), 212, 426; 9 (1902), 63, 66; 22 (1914), 445-46; 24 (1926), 72-76; *Tyler's Quart.*, 2 (1921), 139-40; 5 (1923), 450-54; 10 (1929), 146; *WMQ*, 1st ser., 8 (1899), 119-20, 180, 183; 17 (1909), 267-68; 24 (1915), 1-10; Thomas, *Columbia*, 114; R. Irby, *Hist. of Randolph-Macon College* (n.d., ca. 1890s), 16-17; *Princetonians, 1776-1783*, 230-36.

PUBLICATIONS: Sh-Sh #s 10319, 11240-47, 16034, 18476, 23785-86, 26564-66, 32608, 50723; Sh-C #s 17752, 34957-59; *Letters of John Randolph to a Young Relative; Embracing a Series of Years, From Early Youth to Mature Manhood* (Philadelphia, 1834, R-C # 26470).

MANUSCRIPTS: Alderman Library, ViU, has many originals, and copies of documents in other collections.

                                                           RLW & JMM

Theodorick Bland Randolph

THEODORICK BLAND RANDOLPH was born January 22, 1771, the second son of John Randolph and Frances Bland Randolph of "Matoax," near Petersburg, Virginia. The parents were second cousins, both from old Virginia families who had intermarried with other Virginia families for generations. At his father's death on October 28, 1775, Theodorick, like his brothers, inherited a large plot of family land. Three years later his mother remarried. Theodorick's new stepfather, or father-in-law as he was termed at the time, was St. George Tucker, who had come to Williamsburg from Bermuda to study law. He served his adopted country during the Revolution, sustaining a slight wound at the Battle of Yorktown, and later became a professor of law at William and Mary.

Theodorick, along with his older brother Richard (Class of 1788) and his younger brother John (Class of 1791), spent the period of his mother's widowhood at her father's plantation, "Cawsons." The family returned to "Matoax" after her marriage to Tucker, but they were forced to flee in January 1781 when Benedict Arnold's troops invaded the area. They took refuge at "Bizarre," one of the Randolph properties which straddled the Appomattox River about ninety miles above Petersburg. Before his involvement in active duty Tucker had tutored his young stepsons. In a letter to their uncle Theodorick Bland, Jr., he wrote, "Two of them appear to be blessed with excellent capacities, but I confess I am afraid that the genius of your namesake, though possessed of great quickness and acuteness in many respects, does not lie in the literary line." In 1789 Bland was to leave to his nonliterary namesake the silver-hilted sword which he had used during Revolutionary battles. Tucker found it difficult to keep a tutor at "Bizarre" since most of the young men were involved with the militia, and in January 1782 the three boys were sent to the school of Walker Maury.

Maury had been at William and Mary with St. George Tucker, who apparently thought highly of his friend's school in Orange County. His stepsons, however, disliked both the school and its master. In October the school was closed when Maury was invited to open an academy in Williamsburg, to serve as a preparatory school for William and Mary College. After a few months' respite the young Randolphs were sent to Maury's new school. There Theodorick and John were assigned to the fourth class in charge of the chief usher. The class made such progress that it was soon renamed the third class and put under the direct supervision of Walker Maury. A family visit to Bermuda in 1785 gave Theodorick another several months away from Maury's school. Sometime after his return "the shocking barbarity of Maury towards my brother Theodorick drove him from the school," John Randolph later related. John soon followed his brother and after some months at home they were sent to Princeton in March 1787, where they were placed in the grammar school at Nassau Hall. In a letter to St. George Tucker written on September 13, Theodorick informed his stepfather that he and John expected to be examined in about a week, in order to qualify for entry into the College. He promised, "When we get Into College I shall study very hard not only to be the best scholar in the class but to give you and Mama all the pleasure in my power." And he mentioned that his class was then reading Virgil, John Mair's *Introduction to Latin Syntax*, and the New Testament in Greek.

That fall the brothers matriculated in the College as freshmen, and on December 3 they joined the Cliosophic Society, Theodorick using the name of the Greek general Philopoeman. During the Christmas break they went to New York where a letter from their stepfather reached them, summoning them back to Virginia because of their mother's serious illness. They reached home in time to see her before her death on January 10, 1788. Their abrupt departure left funds in

Witherspoon's hands which, for some reason, he delayed in settling. A letter from Theodorick Randolph to his stepfather, dated January 18, 1790, noted that he had seen Witherspoon and reminded him that Tucker wished a settlement of monies due to the Randolph estate which Tucker had several times requested. According to Theodorick, Witherspoon replied that he had not received Tucker's letters but that he did have a balance on hand that he was ready to pay to Tucker's account.

The Randolphs never returned to Princeton but in May 1788 enrolled at Columbia as freshman members of the Class of 1792. Certainly John despised the College of New Jersey enough to have objected to returning, but there is no evidence that Theodorick cared which school he attended. He had never shared his brothers' avid interest in reading, and after his unhappy experience with schooling under Maury he apparently decided that studies were not worth troubling himself about. This certainly seems to have been his attitude by the time he reached New York. Seventeen years old, he applied himself assiduously to the pleasures of the city rather than to scholarship. John complained that Theodorick and his "dissolute companions" often disturbed his studies by forcing open the door of his room and throwing his books onto the floor or out of the windows. In a letter written to his stepfather in October 1788, Theodorick expressed his disappointment that he and John were not to be allowed to come home for a three-week vacation but acknowledged that the restriction was probably made for their own good. By the following fall his stepfather had received word of his profligate mode of living, but Theodorick assured him that he was still interested in pursuing a medical education at Philadelphia, although Tucker seems to have considered sending him to the University of Edinburgh.

Sometime during the summer of 1790 the Randolph brothers left Columbia to return to Virginia. According to John's account, Theodorick was in poor health because of his excesses during the past two years. They joined the household of their brother Richard at "Bizarre," where Richard's young sister-in-law Ann Cary Randolph was a more or less permanent guest. Sometime during Theodorick's residency he became engaged to Ann (Nancy) Randolph, whose father strenuously objected because the Randolph property was encumbered by a British debt. Theodorick died on February 14, 1792 after a long illness which may have been consumption. He had lost a great deal of weight and was so incapacitated that he was unable to walk by himself. However, he managed to leave Nancy Randolph pregnant with a child that was either aborted or stillborn in October 1792. Rumors spread that Richard Randolph was the father of the child, and although he was brought before a magistrate's court for examination, accused of both incest and infanticide, he protected the name and reputation of his dead brother by maintaining silence on the subject.

SOURCES: G. W. Johnson, *Randolph of Roanoke* (1929), *passim*; W. C. Bruce, *John Randolph of Roanoke* (1922), *passim*; H. A. Garland, *Life of John Randolph of Roanoke* (1856), *passim*; H. A. Johnson et al., eds., *Papers of John Marshall* (1974-   ), II, 161-78; R. I. Randolph, *Randolphs of Va.* (privately printed), 222, 271; F. A. Virkus, *First Families of Amer.* (1925), 863-64; Clio. lists; als, TBR to Tucker, 13 Sept. 1787 & 12 Nov. 1789, VHi; Thomas, *Columbia*, 114; *VMHB*, 3 (1896), 315-16; 22 (1914), 445-46; *WMQ*, 1st ser., 16 (1909), 267-68.

RLW

Ebenezer Rhea

EBENEZER RHEA, A.B., medical student, was born in Philadelphia on November 15, 1773 and baptized in the Second Presbyterian Church of that city on January 1, 1774. He was the posthumous son of John Rhea, a prosperous merchant, and his wife Mary Smith. John Rhea (A.B. 1780) was an elder brother. On his father's side he was a cousin of Aaron Rhea (A.B. 1776), and a first cousin once removed of Nicholas G. R. Rhea (A.B. 1809). His mother's brother was Jonathan Bayard Smith (A.B. 1760), father of John Rhea Smith (A.B. 1787). The elder John Rhea seems to have been established in Philadelphia as early as the 1750s as a partner in "Wickoff & Rhea, Mrchts." In 1765 he was involved in the Philadelphia Company, which was organized to promote settlement of a land grant in Nova Scotia, and in 1770 he was a member of the group that formed a society for encouraging the culture of silk in Pennsylvania. The 1769 tax list for the North Ward of Philadelphia records him as possessing two servants and owning thirty-three acres, two horses, and one head of cattle, with a tax assessment of £21.13.4. He died on March 31, 1773.

College records describe Ebenezer Rhea as one of the freshmen admitted during November 1787 from another college. At this time the family was in straitened circumstances and his mother was operating a shop at 30 North Second Street in Philadelphia. Rhea joined the American Whig Society, and one of his closest friends seems to have been Alexander White (A.B. 1792) of Virginia, a fellow Whig. As a junior Rhea was fifth among undergraduate prizemen in English orations, and for his own commencement ceremonies he ranked fifth in his class and gave an oration "on the study of language."

Rhea studied medicine after graduation, but it is not known where or under whom. A letter of September 11, 1793 from Robert Smith, the Philadelphia merchant and banker who married Rhea's older sister Anna, mentions that Mrs. Rhea was in New York at that time and that she and Ebenezer were staying with the James Smiths of Green Street. It is impossible to determine from this letter whether Mrs. Rhea had journeyed to New York to visit her son, who might have been studying there, or whether they had traveled together from Philadelphia. However, a letter written two months later by John Henry Hobart (A.B. 1793) to Alexander White suggests that Rhea had absented himself from Philadelphia because of the yellow fever epidemic.

In 1794 Rhea accompanied his sister Sarah and her husband Nathaniel Higginson (A.B. 1787) to the Island of Dominica in the West Indies, where Higginson had been appointed United States agent in relation to spoliations. We can only speculate whether this was a vacation for Rhea or whether he went along with the idea of settling into a medical practice on the island. While at Dominica, Higginson contracted yellow fever and died in mid-July after an illness of ten days. Rhea and his sister left the Caribbean immediately, believing that they were leaving the source of the infection behind. However, Rhea was stricken while on the voyage and died before reaching home. The ship was held in quarantine at Reedy Island in the Delaware River, and news of the two deaths reached family and friends in early August. Mrs. Rhea had expected Ebenezer to begin practicing medicine soon, and she hoped that he would then be in a position to "enable her to get over her embarrassments." To the natural shock of a son and son-in-law both dying was added the loss of potential income as well.

On August 26 Hobart wrote from Princeton to White in Virginia about the death of their "common friend Rhea." White's reply of September 8 indicates the strong bond of friendship he felt for Rhea.

> To you who are acquainted with my attachment to our departed friend, I need not express the grief his death occasioned me. The time has been, when I thought I could scarcely live without him; but a long separation, though it did not lessen my affection, nevertheless diminished my dependence on his advice and example to direct my conduct; but I hasten from a subject on which my mind is but too inclined to dwell.

Sources: *Princetonians, 1776-1783*, 293-96; *PGM*, 7 (1920), 208; *PMHB*, 16 (1792), 304; *Pa. Arch.*, 3d ser., xvi, 188; Phila. city directories; alumni file, PUA; Min. Fac., 10 Nov. 1787, 9 July 1791 ("on the study"); Hancock House mss; Amer. Whig Soc., *Cat.* (1840), 6; Williams, *Academic Honors*, 12-13; *Dunlap's Amer. Daily Advt.*, 4 Oct. 1791; Hobart, *Corres.*, I, 34, 36, 40, 45, 59, 61, 345; als, Samuel Harrison Smith to Mary Ann Smith, 7 Aug. 1794, Peter Force Collection, DLC; H. L. Hodge, *Memoranda of*

Family Hist. (1903), 25, 27, 30; Boston Athenaeum, *Index of Obits. in Boston Newspapers 1704-95* (1968), II, 517; records of 2d Pres. Church of Phila., PHi; J. McVickar, *Early Life & Professional Years of Bishop Hobart* (1838), 43, 47-48 (quotes from Hobart and White letters).

The sketch of John Rhea (A.B. 1780) in *Princetonians, 1776-1783*, 293-96, and several other sources state that Ebenezer Rhea married the sister of Samuel Stanhope Smith (A.B. 1769), with no date ever mentioned. Smith's only sister was actually a half-sister, the only child of the second marriage of his father, the Reverend Robert Smith, to Sarah Seeley Ramsay. Born in 1780, Elizabeth Smith would have been only fourteen at the time of Rhea's death in 1794, and there is no indication that he was accompanied by a wife on his trip to the West Indies. The will of Sarah Smith, dated 8 Aug. 1801, names her daughter Elizabeth as beneficiary, with no married surname. The daughter signed an inventory on 2 Oct. 1801, and signed as executrix on 20 Oct. 1801, as "Eliza S. Smith" (will of Sarah Smith, Nj). Finally, four personal letters, two of which were written by relatives, tell of Rhea's untimely death with no mention of a wife or widow. See T. Cushing & C. E. Sheppard, *Hist. of the Cnties. of Gloucester, Salem & Cumberland, N.J.* (1883), 618; Sprague, *Annals*, III, 174; *N.J. Wills*, X, 415. These letters were written by Samuel Harrison Smith, Rhea's first cousin; Robert Smith, his brother-in-law; and John Henry Hobart and Alexander White, close college friends.

For more on John Rhea, see Appendix D: Errata and Additions.

RLW

James Christopher Roosevelt

JAMES CHRISTOPHER ROOSEVELT, A.B., the son of Christopher and Mary Duryea Roosevelt, was born November 10, 1770 in New York City and baptized in the Reformed Dutch Church the next day. He was a first cousin of James Roosevelt (A.B. 1780), who was the father of Isaac (A.B. 1808), the grandfather of Franklin Delano Roosevelt.

Roosevelt matriculated at the College in November 1788 as a sophomore. He joined the Cliosophic Society on December 10 of that year, assuming the name of Mentor. At the end of his junior year he took the second prize in English orations in the competition among the undergraduates, and at his commencement the following year he opened the afternoon session with the English salutatory oration. This address was normally delivered by the student with the second academic standing in the class, but since Robert Gale declined delivering the Latin salutatory, which was then assigned to Joseph Caldwell, Roosevelt must have ranked third. In spite of this fine record he appears not to have pursued any further studies.

Roosevelt inherited a considerable amount of real estate from his grandfather, Jacobus Roosevelt, and is said to have become a merchant. However, if he was involved in any of the Roosevelt mercantile establishments, it was probably only as an investor, since he is not listed as a merchant in any of the city directories, not even in the trade directories which list the inhabitants of the city by their professions or trades. Roosevelt relatives are listed as merchants, sometimes with specific designations of their wares. As the names of older members of the family disappear and those of the younger generation are added, it is easy to follow the gradual change from a family with mercantile interests to a family of attorneys. Roosevelt's frequent changes of address suggest that he may have been investing in real estate. From 1793 through 1814 he lived at nine different addresses in the city, and for two brief periods his name is missing from the directories, indicating that he may have resided outside the city for these intervals. In 1815 he settled at 17 Warren Street, where he lived for the remainder of his life.

On November 5, 1792 Roosevelt married Catharine, daughter of Evert and Mary Byvanck, at the Reformed Dutch Church of New York. Their children were Maria, born July 12, 1793; Catherine Louise, born March 9, 1796; and James Henry, born November 10, 1800. Aside from his trusteeship from 1823 to 1831 at Queen's College, which became Rutgers in 1825, Roosevelt seems to be remembered primarily as the father of James Henry. James Christopher died in New York City on June 12, 1840.

James Henry Roosevelt was a young man of great promise who had just been admitted to the bar when, like his more famous distant cousin, he was struck with polio. Able to walk only with crutches, he seldom left his home and is said to have renounced both the legal profession and marriage to his fiancée Julia Maria Boardman. He devoted most of his time to looking after his property, making shrewd investments which included real estate in New York City and Westchester County. At his death in 1863 he was worth more than a million dollars, most of which he left in trust for the establishment and permanent endowment of Roosevelt Hospital, which opened in 1871. At a time when many hospitals were denominational in origin and patronage, it accepted patients of every sect, nationality and color.

SOURCES: Alumni file, PUA; Clio. lists; Hancock House MSS; Min. Fac., 10 Nov. 1789, 9 July 1791; Williams, *Academic Honors*, 12; *Dunlap's Amer. Daily Adv.*, 4 Oct. 1791; N.Y. City directories, 1793-1842; K. Schriftgiesser, *Amazing Roosevelt Family* (1942), 107, 146-48; W. T. Cobb, *Strenuous Life* (1946), 41, 46; M. J. Lamb & B. Harrison, *Hist. of the City of N.Y.* (3 vols., 1877-96), III, 766; *Princetonians, 1776-1783*, 296-300; *Cat. of the Officers & Alumni of Rutgers College* (1909), 9.

In the vast amount of material available about the Roosevelt family, James Christopher, if he is mentioned at all, is usually awarded only a sentence or two.

RLW

Charles Ross

CHARLES ROSS, merchant, soldier, and sportsman, was born on October 5, 1772, the only son among the five children of John and Clementina Cruikshank Ross of Philadelphia. Both parents were immigrants from Scotland. The father was a merchant in Perth who arrived in Philadelphia shortly before his marriage in 1768 to Clementina, the daughter of British army captain Charles Cruikshank. A successful East India merchant, he spent much of the Revolution as a purchasing agent of the Continental Congress in Paris and Nantes. He advanced the Congress almost £20,000 in goods on his own credit and experienced financial hardships when his recompense proved slow in arriving. After the war, he was the agent of South Carolina in Philadelphia. His business prospered and he earned a reputation for the lavish hospitality he offered at "the Grange," an estate seven miles out of town which he bought from his father-in-law around 1783.

Charles Ross entered the College as a freshman in November 1787, one of four students who came from unnamed "other Colleges." He established a pattern as a disciplinary problem less than two months after his arrival when, on December 23, he was admonished both for insolence to a tutor and for damaging the College's outbuildings. His accomplices in the first offense were three juniors and in the second they were three sophomores, and so at least Ross seems to have been good at making friends with the upperclassmen. On September 10, 1788 he was among the three judged "most guilty" when six students were convicted of frequenting "a house of ill fame." On March 3, 1789 he was one of three students convicted as ringleaders of the seven students who had assaulted Isaac Crane (A.B. 1789) and committed a disorder in his room. Only the fact that they had come forward and confessed in order to spare some comrades who were under suspicion saved them from "any very pointed or severe punishment." Ross's college career finally ended abruptly as a result of the events of the night of June 26, 1790, when he and several other students were found guilty of drinking to excess, placing a calf in the pulpit at the College, and upsetting the latrine. He was first suspended and, when he remained unrepentant, was then expelled.

Ross subsequently returned to Philadelphia and became a merchant. He was a partner of John Simson at South Front Street from around 1796 to 1802. His father died suddenly in 1800 and left a tangled estate, which was still being settled seventeen years later and which left his family in much reduced circumstances. Charles thus became the sole support of his mother and unmarried sister.

In order to repair the family's fortunes he made several, reputedly six, trading voyages to Canton, China. He acted as supercargo on the *Active*, which left Philadelphia on August 13, 1806, and returned on March 7, 1808, and on the *Susquehanna*, whose voyage lasted from May 22, 1809, to April 12, 1810. On May 3, 1811 he sailed on the *Caledonia*, acting as supercargo and part-owner in a trip which ended on April 21, 1812.

Between 1803 and his death, Ross was listed only twice in city directories, in 1809 and 1810, as a merchant at 23 Dock Street. Presumably his travels account for his failure to maintain a city address. If his continuing acceptance among the social elite of the city is any indication, Ross's efforts to retrieve the family's financial position must have met with success.

Ross joined the First Troop Philadelphia City Cavalry as a private on May 12, 1794 and saw service in the expedition to put down the Whiskey Rebellion in the autumn of that year. He was elected cornet on November 2, 1796, first lieutenant on August 15, 1803, and captain on October 18, 1811, a post he held at his death. He therefore commanded the troop in the War of 1812. It saw little but ceremonial duty until the last half of 1814, when it was called into active service for three months in the wake of the burning of Washington and the attack on Baltimore. Ross and his men were stationed as vedettes at Mount Bull, a height commanding a good view of Chesapeake Bay, with the task of sending daily expresses reporting British movements to the forces defending Philadelphia. They returned on December 12 without having seen battle.

The First Troop was very much a creature of the Philadelphia elite, and it was closely allied socially with two other prominent bodies, the Schuylkill Fishing Company of the State in Schuylkill and the Gloucester Fox Hunting Club. The former, a convivial set of anglers organized in 1732, elected Ross on October 6, 1813. He was also a member of the hunting club, founded in 1766 and said to have been the earliest organized hunt in America. Indeed, a fellow member recalled later that Ross had been its "last master spirit," and that his demise had led the remaining members to dissolve the club. "One of the most ardent in the chase and liveliest at the banquet," Ross's amiable and agreeable nature, generosity, "manly athletic form, rough features and ... robust constitution" were all fondly remembered.

Ross invested in another Cantonese voyage of the *Caledonia* beginning on June 13, 1815. On June 3, 1816 he sailed for China himself, this time as supercargo on the *Natchez*. A sizable crowd of his friends saw him off, and his brother-in-law remarked in his diary that "perhaps no man is more beloved by his acquaintances, and very deservedly so, for he is a fine-tempered, noble-hearted fellow." The trip proved to be Ross's last. He returned home on May 10, 1817, ill with dysentery which one source blamed on his having had to drink impure water aboard ship. His convalescence proceeded only slowly, and while he was still weak an attack of what was diagnosed as typhus fever killed him. He died at 5 a.m. on October 8, 1817. Two days later, he was interred at the Pine Street Presbyterian Church graveyard. The service was well attended. The First Troop escorted the coffin in full uniform, and later erected an imposing tomb monument. The members of the Washington Benevolent Society, which was a Federalist fraternal club, and the Freemasons of Lodge 51 also turned out, which suggests that he belonged to these organizations as well.

Ross never married. He left his estate to his mother and unmarried sister. Nonetheless, he had good luck in perpetuating his name. He is recalled in the toast of the First Troop Philadelphia City Cavalry "To the Memory of Captains Ross, Butler, and James," still being given each November 17 at that body's annual banquet. On May 1, 1812 the Schuylkill Fishing Company received from Ross a nine-gallon china punch bowl decorated with pictures of fish, which the club had commissioned him to have made in Canton. It came to be known as the Ross Punch Bowl, and the club is still serving Fish House Punch from it on important occasions. The club also continues to cherish "two superb Mandarin hats" which Ross presented to it when he delivered the punch bowl.

SOURCES: J. G. Lee & P. C. F. Smith, *Philadelphians & the China Trade 1784-1844* (1984), 61-62 (photos of portrait of CR ca. 1786 & of the Ross Punch Bowl); *Hist of the First Troop Phila. City Cavalry* (1875), 34-36, 43-49, 145-47, 169; E. Mifflin, "Memoir of John Ross, Merchant of Phila.," *PMHB*, 23 (1899), 77-85; *PMHB*, 6 (1882), 109; Min. Fac., 10 Nov. ("other Colleges") & 23 Dec. 1787, 10 Sept. 1788 ("most guilty," "a house"), 3 Mar. 1789 ("any very"), 2 & 10 July 1790; Hancock House MSS; Hobart, *Corres.*, I, 220-21; Phila. city directories, 1797-1802, 1809-10; N. B. Wainwright, "Diary of Samuel Breck, 1814-22," *PMHB*, 102 (1978), 469-93, *passim* ("perhaps no man" & "To the Memory," 482); W. Milnor, *Memoirs of the Gloucester Fox Hunting Club near Phila.* (1830 repr. 1927), 10, 14-16, 24 ("last master," "one of the," "manly athletic"); First Troop Phila. City Cavalry, *By-Laws, Muster-Roll, & Papers* (1856), 56; *Hist. of the Schuylkill Fishing Company 1732-1888* (1889), 62 ("two superb"), 109, 377; *Hist. of the Schuylkill Fishing Company 1888-1932* (1932), 157, 189; *PGM*, 5 (1914), 279; D. H. Fischer, *Revolution of Amer. Conservatism* (1965), 110-28; letters, Curator, First Troop Phila. City Cavalry Museum, 29 Apr. 1985, N. B. Wainwright, 22 Nov. 1985, & P. C. F. Smith, 29 Nov. 1985, PUA.

JJL

Frederick A. Stone

FREDERICK A. STONE, A.B., law student, was born around 1769 in Frederick Town, Frederick County, Maryland, the only son of Thomas and Margaret Brown Stone. His paternal grandmother was the aunt of Daniel of St. Thomas Jenifer (Class of 1775) and Daniel Jenifer (Class of 1777). An Anglican, Thomas Stone was a lawyer and legislator who signed the Declaration of Independence, albeit reluctantly. His wife Margaret was the daughter of Dr. Gustavus Brown of Charles County, Maryland, and his second wife, Margaret Black Boyd. Stone used the £1,000 dowry from his marriage to purchase land near Port Tobacco in Charles County, to which he moved in 1771 and on which he built a house called "Habre-de-Venture" in the same year. Frederick, who seems to have been named for his father's brother, was orphaned in 1787. His mother died in June and his father, inconsolable at the loss, fell into a decline and died in October. He left an estate which consisted of 3,000 acres of land in Charles County, a house and several lots in Annapolis, and personal property valued at over £2,600, including at least twenty-five slaves.

Stone entered the College in July 1789. On August 5 of that year he joined the Cliosophic Society, taking as his pseudonym Newton, presumably a reference to the great English scientist. For unstated reasons the society later suspended him for four weeks. In a competition for undergraduates held the day before the commencement of 1790, Stone placed second in English grammar, syntax, and orthography. That November he was among six students, four of them Marylanders and five in the senior class, who were cited by the steward for boarding away from the College. He appeared before the faculty for a "gross breach of the laws" on two occasions during his senior year. He and George Washington Morton (A.B. 1792) were found guilty of being out of their rooms after curfew, throwing "the urns ... down from the college wall," and returning "in a disorderly manner" on the night of March 15, 1791. The faculty referred their punishment to the trustees; what ensued is not known. On August 25, just a month before his graduation, a faculty inquiry found that Stone had made "an assault" on his classmate Stephen Wayne. The affair must have been serious, for in addition to being required to sign a groveling confession and apology, Stone had to pay the expenses Wayne had already incurred from "proceedings begun in the case in the civil court" before Wayne would drop the matter. At his commencement, Stone was one of three Maryland students not participating at their own request.

Stone intended to become a lawyer and began legal studies in Philadelphia. There he apparently befriended John Randolph (Class of 1791). When the yellow fever epidemic of 1793 broke out, Stone sought to avoid it by removing to Princeton, where he attended a meeting of the Cliosophic Society on August 28. The effort to escape proved fruitless, however, for he died the morning of September 4. Initial concern that he might have infected other residents of Princeton proved unfounded. Two sisters survived Stone, who never married. Annis Boudinot Stockton commemorated his early demise with a poem, and the Clios noted his passing by agreeing to wear mourning and by having Henry Kollock (A.B. 1794) deliver an elegiac oration at their meeting on November 20.

SOURCES: *Biog. Dict. Md. Leg.*, II, 786-88; letters from John M. Wearmouth, 3 & 16 May 1984, PUA; John Sanderson, *Biography of the Signers to the Declaration of Independence* (1828), IV, 129-50; H. E. Hayden, *Va. Genealogies* (1891 repr. 1931), 175-77; Min. Fac., 10 Nov. 1789, 29 Nov. 1790, 18 Mar., 9 July & 5 Aug. 1791 (all quotes); Clio. lists; *Pa. Packet, & Daily Advt.*, 2 Oct. 1790; *Dunlap's Amer. Daily Advt.*, 4 Oct. 1791; Alexander, 559; *Federal Gazette & Phila. Daily Advt.*, 2 Oct. 1793; Clio. Min., 28 Aug., 4 Sept., 20 Nov. 1793; Annis B. Stockton, "Lines on a Young Gentleman," pp. 280-81 of her MS "Book of Verse" at NjHi. See Annapolis *Md. Gazette*, 26 Sept. 1793 for a laudatory obituary. Sanderson incorrectly asserts that Stone was "about twelve" when his father died. The *Pa. Packet*'s account of the 1790 commencement is the only source for Stone's middle initial, unless Stockton's poem, which gives his name as "Alexander Stone," is a reference to his middle name rather than an error. For a photograph of "Habre-de-Venture," see U.S. National Park Service, *Signers of the Declaration: Hist. Places Commemorating the Signing of the Declaration of Independence* (1973), 186-91. In 1977 fire gutted the interior of the building. The National Park Service acquired the property in 1980.

JJL

John Sullivan

JOHN SULLIVAN remains unidentified. He is on a list of matriculants dated April 10, 1789 when "John Solovon" of "M." was in the sophomore class. He appears in no other College source.

"Solovon" no doubt stood for Sullivan and the M. quite likely was short for Maryland, but the name was common there and no compelling prospect has emerged. The 1800 census lists John Sullivans in various spellings from Anne Arundel, Montgomery, Frederick, and Caroline counties. Men of the name were married in Cecil County in 1793, Anne Arundel County in 1797, and in Baltimore in 1799. Perhaps the Princetonian was one of them.

SOURCES: Hancock House MSS; C. R. Teeples, *Md. 1800 Census* (1973); D.A.R. Capt. Jeremiah Baker Chapter, *Cecil Cnty. Md. Marriage Licenses 1777-1840* (1974), 13; G. M. Brumbaugh, *Md. Records: Colonial, Revolutionary, County & Church* (1967), II, 474; R. Barnes, *Md. Marriages 1778-1800* (1979), 221. Searching for a John Solomon in the Maryland sources failed to produce any likely prospects. Given the paucity of Princetonians from New England at this time, coupled with the profusion of Marylanders, the M. is unlikely to have stood for Massachusetts. The branch of the Sullivan family to which belonged John Sullivan, Revolutionary War general and governor of New Hampshire, and his brother James, Republican governor of Massachusetts, seems to have produced no John Sullivan sufficiently contemporary to be the Princetonian. See *NEHGR*, 19 (1865), 302-05; C. P. Whittemore, *General of the Revolution: John Sullivan of N.H.* (1961), 6, 225.

JJL

Jesse Taylor

JESSE TAYLOR, A.B., was born October 2, 1774, the eldest son of James Taylor of Columbia, South Carolina, and his second wife Sarah Daniell Taylor. He was the cousin of John Taylor (A.B. 1790), Thomas Taylor (A.B. 1798), Jesse P. Taylor (Class of 1810), Benjamin Franklin Taylor (Class of 1810), and probably also of John Taylor (A.B. 1795). James Taylor and his brother Thomas were large landowners, whose holdings included the area that later became the city of Columbia. In 1787 his taxable property included 3,622 acres of land and 165 slaves. Serving as a captain in the Revolution, he was in Charleston during the siege of the city and took the oath of allegiance to Great Britain when the capital fell. After returning home he broke his parole, fighting under Gen. Thomas Sumter. He was captured by the British and tried on the charge of violating his oath but was acquitted through the false testimony of a friend.

In 1786 John Taylor transferred from John Reid's academy in Camden to Mount Sion College in Winnsboro, South Carolina, and several cousins are said to have transferred with him. Jesse is not specifically mentioned, but he was probably part of this family group, since he left South Carolina in June 1788, along with his cousin John and James Chesnut (A.B. 1792), to enroll in the College. The trio sailed from Charleston to Philadelphia. Taylor probably entered the College as a freshman before September. He joined the Cliosophic Society on November 26, 1788, taking as his pseudonym Vespasian, the Roman emperor. At his graduation exercises he took the part of respondent in debating the question, "Is an hereditary nobility an advantage to a nation—does it tend to the improvement of the human character in social life, and is it consistent with civil liberty?"

Taylor probably returned to Charleston to study law, as did the majority of the South Carolinians at Nassau Hall. One source says that he died in November 1793, another that his death came in the autumn of 1802.

SOURCES: Alumni files, PUA; *Biog. Dir. S.C. House Rep.*, III, 699-701; *SCHGM*, 8 (1907), 95-119; O'Neall, *Bench & Bar S.C.*, II, 168-70; Clio. lists; Hancock House MSS; Min. Fac., 10 Nov. 1789, 9 July 1791; *Dunlap's Amer. Daily Advt.*, 4 Oct. 1791.

There is confusion in the alumni records, where descendants of Robert Johnston Taylor (A.B. 1795), have identified Jesse Taylor as a brother of Robert. Robert Johnston Taylor was the son of Jesse Taylor of Alexandria, Virginia, who did have another son named Jesse, who in turn named his son Jesse. However, Jesse Taylor (A.B. 1791) is identified in both College and Cliosophic Society records as coming from South Carolina, and South Carolina records clearly identify him as the Jesse Taylor who matriculated at the College.

RLW

Elias Van Arsdale (Vanartsdalen)

ELIAS VAN ARSDALE (VANARTSDALEN), A.B., A.M. 1794, LL.D. 1845, attorney, was born near Freehold, Monmouth County, New Jersey on December 13, 1770, the only son in a family of three older sisters. His father was the Reverend Jacob Van Arsdale (A.B. 1765) who, while studying theology with the Reverend William Tennent of Freehold, married Mary Sutphin, daughter of Dirck Sutphin, a member of the Old Tennent Church. After being licensed to preach in 1768 Jacob remained in Freehold as supply pastor for churches in the surrounding area. Shortly after the birth of Elias the family moved to Kingston, Somerset County, where the father served the local Presbyterian church from June 18, 1771 through December 3, 1774. He next accepted a call to the Presbyterian church in Springfield, Essex County, where he served for the remainder of his life. A staunch whig, his church was burned by the British and rebuilt by the parishioners at the end of the war. He served the College as a trustee from 1793 to 1802.

Elias entered the College as a junior in November 1789, where most records use the older Dutch spelling of Vanartsdalen. He joined the Cliosophic Society on December 19, 1789, using the name of Palinurus, the helmsman in the *Æneid* who was cast overboard and killed by hostile natives as he tried to crawl ashore. At his commencement he was one of the intermediate honorary speakers, delivering an oration on commerce during the afternoon portion of the ceremonies.

Van Arsdale immediately began the study of law under Elisha Boudinot of Newark, a trustee of the College from 1802 to 1819. With his college classmate and fellow law clerk, Jacob Burnet, he became a member of the *Institutio legalis,* the moot court society where young lawyers practiced their skills. Admitted to the New Jersey bar as attorney in September 1795 and as counsellor in September 1798, he opened an office in Newark and practiced there for the rest of his life. He was an astute lawyer and a prominent member of the community. In November 1808 he became a sergeant-at-law. He served as a captain in the First Battalion, Third Regiment, of the

Essex militia. Although not interested in holding any political office, he sat in the state constitutional convention of 1844. On November 10, 1812 he was sworn in as the second president of the National State Bank of Newark. Van Arsdale served in this capacity during a period of rapid growth for the bank, until his death on March 19, 1846, without any interruption or diminution of his legal practice. In 1837 he was responsible for a revival of a moot court society patterned on the *Institutio legalis*, which had discontinued its meetings as law schools started establishing their own moot courts. The new group met in Van Arsdale's law offices but remained in existence for only a year or two. He is also credited with preserving the records of the original society.

On October 14, 1800 he married Margaret, daughter of Elizabeth Ogden and Robert Johnston of Dutchess County, New York. The Van Arsdales raised a family of two daughters and six sons, four of whom attended the College. Elias Jr. (A.B. 1819) read law in his father's office and suceeded him as president of the State Bank of Newark. Robert (A.B. 1826) also became a lawyer, but gave up his practice to devote himself to literary pursuits and his avocation of astronomy. He is credited with discovering five comets, one of which bears his name. Jacob (A.B. 1835), another lawyer, became a member of the common council of Newark and district attorney of Essex County. Henry (A.B. 1838) was a physician who practiced in New York City. Henry's grandson, the great-grandson of Elias, was Henry Van Arsdale (A.B. 1910), a patent attorney.

At Van Arsdale's death his colleagues in the bar passed a resolution memorializing him as "a most revered professional exemplar, whose variety and depth of learning, severe accuracy, untiring diligence, undeviating fidelity to his clients, intense and signal ability in the elucidation of difficulty, have greatly contributed at home and abroad, to enhance the reputation of the New Jersey bar."

Sources: Alumni files, PUA; *Princetonians, 1748-1768*, 533-34; E. V. Wright, *Hist. of the Kingston Pres. Church* (1952), 24; Min. Fac., 10 Nov. 1789, 9 July 1791; Clio. lists; *Dunlap's Amer. Daily Advt.*, 4 Oct. 1791; *Dunlap & Claypoole's Amer. Daily Advt.*, 7 Oct. 1794; D. C. Skemer, "The *Institutio legalis* & Legal Education in N.J.: 1783-1817," *N.J. Hist.*, 97 (1979), 131-34; Riker, 41, 76; Elmer, *N.J. Bench & Bar*, 177-78; W. H. Shaw, *Hist. of Essex & Hudson Cnties., N.J.*, (1884), I, 257, 260, 262, 265, 627; W. P. Stillman, *Story of a Bank & of the Community It Serves* (1937), 22-34; *Som. Cnty. Hist. Quart.*, 8 (1919), 106, 110, 115.

                                                                    RLW

Isaac Wayne

IsAAc WAYNE, A.B. Dickinson College 1792, lawyer and congressman, was the second child and only son of Gen. "Mad" Anthony
Wayne and Mary Penrose Wayne. Anthony Wayne's grandfather had emigrated from Ireland shortly before 1724, when he
bought a farm in Chester County, Pennsylvania, which he called
"Waynesborough." Mary Penrose was the daughter of a Philadelphia
merchant, Bartholomew Penrose. Their son was born in 1772 at
"Waynesborough," which is now in Paoli, Pennsylvania. Many boys
raised at this time suffered because of their fathers' absence during
the Revolution. Anthony Wayne never remained at home for more
than a few months at a time, and a steadily growing rift between
Wayne and his wife gradually led to their complete estrangement.
Still, Isaac seems to have been dominated by his father's exuberant
personality all through his life. Mary Wayne wrote to her husband
that when four-year-old Isaac saw her crying because of her husband's absence, he comforted her by saying, "my Daddy com a gayn
when he has run all the Sholders in and made them blead." In later
years, when Isaac was away at school, his mother would write him
long letters condemning his "earthly father" for his lack of morals
and praying that Isaac would become a better man.

On a visit home in 1777 Anthony found that his daughter Margaretta had been attending school in Philadelphia but that five-year-
old Isaac was thought too young by his mother. The father decided
that it was definitely time for his son to start school and learn to
be a man. "Let no mistaken fondness be a means of keeping them
from school," he wrote, "for that is the Rock that parents frequently
split upon." Two years later when Anthony was next at home, he
enjoyed seeing Isaac strut about the lawn with a sword and a gold-
laced hat which he had sent to him upon the occasion of his entering
school. The boy probably first attended a local school which had been
founded by Anthony's uncle, Gabriel Wayne. At age ten Isaac transferred to a Philadelphia school, probably the Philadelphia Academy.
During his first year or two at school he printed samples of his school-
work on the margins of his mother's letters so that his father could
monitor his progress. Although Anthony had not done well in school
himself, he urged that his son learn Latin and his daughter become
proficient in French. He wrote to his wife, "Nature has been bountiful
in giving them agreeable and pleasing features. I shall be much dis-
pleased if they do not move in the first circles." By 1782 he was opti-
mistically predicting that Isaac would be ready for college in another
year.

Isaac Wayne was actually admitted to the College on November 10, 1787, when the minutes of the faculty list him among freshmen entering from other colleges. Wayne is known to have attended both the College of New Jersey and Dickinson College in Carlisle, Pennsylvania, and it is probable that he attended Dickinson for a session or two before coming to Princeton. He joined the Cliosophic Society on December 12, 1787, using the pseudonym Augustus. For some reason his name is not on a class list compiled on April 10, 1789. When he was seventeen Wayne committed some youthful indiscretion that caused his father to cut his allowance to $10 monthly. Whatever his misdemeanor, it does not appear in the faculty minutes, which last place him at the College as a junior attending the summer session of 1790. The cut in his income probably made it difficult for Wayne to remain at the College. This decrease may have been as much for the father's benefit as the son's punishment. Anthony Wayne was deeply in debt because of sizeable expenditures during his military service and the mismanagement of "Waynesborough" during his absence. Bad planning and poor handling of a Georgia rice plantation, for which he had borrowed heavily, put him further in debt. A new Pennsylvania debt law had allowed his Pennsylvania property to be attached for the Georgia debt. In 1788 he wrote to his close friend Sharp Delany, customs collector for the port of Philadelphia, asking him to buy Isaac some clothing, pay his tuition fees, and advance him whatever spending money he might need. As early as July 1779, when Anthony Wayne had thought that he might die in the Battle of Stony Point, he had written to Delany saying, "I know that friendship will induce you to attend to the education of my little son and daughter."

Isaac probably returned to Dickinson College at this time. He is said to have begun a law course at Dickinson, which claims him as a 1792 graduate. However, there seems no doubt that he had not lived up to his father's early expectations. Anthony accused him of wasting six years at college without finishing his education and said that his slowness in acquiring polish had cost him a grand tour of Europe, since Anthony did not think him capable of profiting by travel. He suggested that Isaac, now twenty, be bound out to a lawyer but gave Delany carte blanche in determining his career. Delany followed Wayne's suggestion and made arrangements for Isaac to study law with William Lewis of Philadelphia. A year later, when Isaac wrote to his father asking for advice about continuing his law studies and mentioned his need for cash, he was told without any personal warmth that he should acquire a fluent speaking knowledge of French and German and apply himself diligently to the law. Isaac was described as a plodding law student, physically soft and plump, without any of his father's driving energy.

In spite of these handicaps Wayne completed his study of law and was admitted to the Philadelphia bar on June 2, 1795 and to the Chester County bar on August 21, 1795. He actually practiced less than eighteen months when, at the request of his father, he went to reside at "Waynesborough," with his aunt Margaret Penrose keeping house for him. There he devoted his time to the management of the family estate. He had been an undistinguished lawyer, but he was well trained in such matters as wills and mortgages, land law, and the rudiments of business methods, specialties of most use to his father, and he successfully and profitably managed the estate. Anthony Wayne died at Presque Isle, now Erie, Pennsylvania, on December 15, 1796 as commanding general of the American army, and for a time his son was free of his domination.

Isaac Wayne was a Federalist and in 1800 and again in 1801 he was elected to the state assembly. On August 25, 1802 he married Elizabeth Smith. Five children were born of the union, but his wife and all of the children predeceased him. In 1806 and 1810 Wayne was elected to the state senate but served only one year of his second term, possibly because of his activity in raising a regiment of cavalry, of which he was elected colonel. When war was declared against Britain he offered the services of his regiment to the government and spent the summer of 1814 at Camp Dupont in New Castle County, Delaware, when an attack on Philadelphia was thought imminent. However, the regiment never saw active service. In 1814 Wayne was nominated by the Federalists as candidate for governor of Pennsylvania and as candidate for Congress for the district composed of Chester and Montgomery counties. Though he ran ahead of his ticket, the Democrats won both contests. In 1822 he was elected to the Eighteenth Congress as one of the representatives from Chester, Lancaster, and Montgomery counties. He apparently did not participate in any debates or make any speeches during his term as a congressman. He declined renomination in 1824 and did not again enter political life.

By this time Wayne's wife and children were deceased and he was living alone at "Waynesborough." In these later years he gave more and more time to the memory of his father. His devotion came close to idolatry. He was described during this period as sentimental, neurotic, and "milk-sopish." In 1809, during Margaretta Wayne Atlee's last illness, she had begged her brother Isaac to travel to Erie to bring back their father's remains for interment in the family burial plot in

St. David's churchyard at Radnor, Pennsylvania. Wayne accordingly drove a one-horse sulky across the state and made arrangements for his father's body to be disinterred and his bones packed in boxes, which were to be strapped to the sulky. Dr. John Culbertson Wallace, who attended to the exhumation, found to his surprise that except for one leg, the general's body was in a very good state of preservation. Knowing that the coffin would be too large for the small sulky, he obeyed Wayne's orders literally by packing the bones in boxes for the journey to Radnor. He first followed a local Indian custom of dismembering the body and dropping the pieces in a large kettle of boiling water. As flesh dropped from the bones he scraped them clean and packed them. On July 4, 1809 Gen. Anthony Wayne's bones were buried in St. David's churchyard at Radnor, with the Society of the Cincinnati conducting the funeral rites for their past president and heading a procession more than a mile long. Dr. Wallace had quietly reburied the flesh, along with the instruments used in the dissection and cleaning, at the foot of the flagpole near the blockhouse at Erie. Isaac Wayne probably knew nothing of his father's other grave.

Before Anthony Wayne's death he had written to Isaac, ordering him to collect his trunks of documents at "Waynesborough," Philadelphia, Fort Washington, and Greenville. He admitted that his voluminous correspondence was not very well sorted and that there were many "miscellaneous, idle and juvenile letters" which he had intended to dispose of, and which he now commanded Isaac to destroy. Isaac spent a great deal of time sorting these letters and meticulously setting aside any that had any bearing on public affairs or his father's military activities. However, to the dismay of future historians, he burned all personal and family letters out of respect for his father's wishes. All correspondence which might add to his father's reputation as a womanizer and any references to his father's debts were reduced to ashes. In 1829 and 1830 Wayne published in *The Casket*, a Philadelphia magazine, a rather poorly written memoir of his father, including documents relating to his military career. The following year he presented a collection of his father's letters to the Chester County Athenaeum and his father's telescope to the Chester County Cabinet of Natural History.

On January 17, 1840 Wayne was elected a member of the American Philosophical Society. Although well off financially, he acquired the dread of many elderly people that he would be reduced to poverty before his death. He died October 25, 1852 and was interred in St. David's Episcopal Church Cemetery at Radnor. All of his real estate, including "Waynesborough," and most of his personal property, he left to his sister's grandson William Wayne Evans. Evans, who was Anthony Wayne's only lineal descendant of the third generation, then legally changed his surname to Wayne.

SOURCES: *BDUSC*, 2017-18; *DAB* (father); G. Tucker, *Mad Anthony Wayne & the New Nation* (1973), 18, 220, 222, 250, 257; J. H. Preston, *A Gentleman Rebel* (1930), 8-9, 35-36, 45; H. E. Wildes, *Anthony Wayne* (1941), 89-90, 112-13, 174-79, 293, 305, 332-34, 355, 370-71, 416-17, 449, 458-59, 461-63, 488 (all quotes from this source); C. J. Stillé, *Major-General Anthony Wayne & the Pa. Line* (1893), 370-73, 192-93; G. L. Reed, *Alumni Record, Dickinson College* (1905), 42; Min. Fac., 10 Nov. 1787, class list summer sess. 1790; Clio. lists; *Martin's Bench & Bar*, 322; A/C, 18th Cong.; G. M. Philips, *Hist. Letters from the Collection of the West Chester State Normal School* (1898), 3-4; J. T. Scharf & T. Westcott, *Hist. of Phila.* (1884), I, 577; E. J. Sellers, *Wayne Ancestry* (1927), 23-26, 28; T. Boyd, *Mad Anthony Wayne* (1929), 142, 197, 202, 217, 228, 308; E. C. Harrison, *Philadelphia Merchant* (1978), 399; Amer. Phil. Soc., *List of the Members* ... (1880?), 35. Information on the Wayne homestead from F. J. Dallett, historian for the Wayne Family Association, is gratefully acknowledged.

MANUSCRIPTS: Burton Hist. Collection, MiD; W. Darlington Collection, NHi; W. L. Clements Lib., Univ. of Mich., Ann Arbor; P. H. Ward Hist. Collection, Univ. of Pa. Lib.

RLW

Stephen Wayne

STEPHEN WAYNE, A.B., was the son of Richard and Elizabeth Clifford Wayne, who moved from Charleston, South Carolina, to Savannah, Georgia, in 1789. Richard Wayne, a Yorkshireman, had served as a major in the Royal Welsh Fusileers before settling in Charleston, and his sympathies remained with the British. The general assembly banished him from the state and declared his property confiscated. However, his wife's family connections kept the banishment from being enforced, and only a disqualification for public office remained. He prospered in Georgia, both as a rice planter with a plantation a few miles north of Savannah, and as head of a factorage and commission business which was deeply involved in the slave trade. A younger son James Moore Wayne, the twelfth of the thirteen Wayne children and a future Supreme Court justice, was sent to the College in 1804 and graduated in 1808.

James, growing up in Savannah, was educated at home by a private tutor, but it is not known whether the older brothers, who were raised in South Carolina, were educated in the same manner. Stephen Wayne entered the College as a sophomore on May 10, 1789. He joined the Cliosophic Society on June 10, 1789, where he was known as Adolphus, probably after Gustavus Adolphus, king of Sweden and brilliant soldier for the Protestant cause during the Thirty Years' War. When the faculty met on July 9, 1791 to make commencement assignments, Wayne was included among the group who were chosen to present intermediate orations. On August 25 the faculty met solely for the purpose of settling a dispute between Wayne and his classmate Frederick Stone. Stone was convicted of assaulting Wayne and was required to sign a statement acknowledging that his conduct had constituted an offence against the peace and law of the College and professing sorrow for his conduct. Both students then signed a joint statement declaring that they would forgive and forget their quarrel, that Wayne would halt the proceedings in civil court which he had instituted against Stone, and that Stone would defray the expenses that Wayne had incurred. Stone was also a Cliosophian, and the society records show that he was at some time suspended for four weeks, though there is nothing to indicate any connection to his attack on a society "brother." At the commencement ceremonies on September 28, 1791 Wayne delivered an oration on the influence of the fair sex in society. A newspaper account of the proceedings identifies him as a Georgian. All previous records list him as a South Carolinian.

Nothing has been found to indicate Wayne's future course. He drowned sometime before 1809. His father's will of that year does not include Stephen's name among his four surviving children. He is first listed as deceased in the 1818 catalogue of the College.

SOURCES: Alumni files, PUA; Clio. lists; Min. Fac., 10 Nov. 1789, 9 July & 25 Aug. 1791; A. A. Lawrence, *James Moore Wayne* (1943), 1-7, 9; *DAB* (sketch of James Moore Wayne); L. Friedman & F. L. Israel, *Justices of the U.S. Supreme Court* (1969), I, 601; W. J. Northen, *Men of Mark in Ga.* (1974), II, 426-28; M. F. LaFar & C. P. Wilson, *Abstracts of Wills, Chatham Cnty., Ga.* (1933), 168; *Dunlap's Amer. Daily Advt.*, 4 Oct. 1791; J. G. B. Bulloch, *Hist. & Gen. of the Families of Bellinger & DeVeaux* (1895), 85-86.

RLW

Peter Wikoff (Wickoff, Wykoff, Wyckoff, Wycoff)

PETER WIKOFF (WICKOFF, WYKOFF, WYCKOFF, WYCOFF), A.B., A.M. 1794, first appears in the College records in December 1788, when he joined the Cliosophic Society, taking the name of the orator Demosthenes. In February 1790 he was cited for boarding outside of the College without a certificate. Later the same year he took third prize in "reading English grammar, syntax and orthography" at the undergraduate competition held the day before commencement. His one serious infringement of College discipline came on the night of June 17, 1791 when he joined William Arden Hosack (A.B. 1792) and Robert Field (A.B. 1793) in riding without permission the horses pastured behind Nassau Hall. They then enticed three other students to join them in a swim, from which they returned very late. Wikoff was admonished "privately before the faculty" for this escapade. His punishment was lighter than that received by the other two instigators, suggesting either that his behavior hitherto had been better or that his culpability in the incident in question was not thought equal to theirs. Less than a month later the faculty ranked him sixth in his class and assigned him the valedictory oration at his commencement, which he duly delivered.

Wikoff attended the annual meeting of the Cliosophic Society in September 1792 and received his master's degree in 1794. Beyond that, he has not been positively traced. College sources refer to him as from East Jersey on one occasion and from Monmouth on another. Unfortunately, Peter Wikoff in various spellings was a very common name in New Jersey at this time, and two plausible prospects have been found.

Wikoff may have been the Peter Wikoff born on November 25, 1774, and baptized at Christ Church, Philadelphia, Pennsylvania, on February 16, 1775. He was one of six children of Isaac Wikoff, a merchant, and his wife Martha Cox. Ann Wikoff, who married Peter Wilson (A.B. 1778), and Elizabeth Forman, who married John Anderson Scudder (A.B. 1775), were his first cousins, and Manuel G. Wikoff (A.B. 1813) and George Wikoff (A.B. 1815) were probably his nephews. Peter was called "Jr." to distinguish him from his uncle Peter Wikoff, another merchant. Isaac had an unidentified son who fell sick in the yellow fever epidemic of 1793, and at the time John Henry Hobart (A.B. 1793) wrote to Alexander White (A.B. 1792) that "poor Wycoff" had fallen ill.

Peter Wikoff married Ann Sharp at Christ Church, Philadelphia, on September 27, 1798, and they had at least one son and three daughters. On July 24, 1800 Wikoff was admitted to the bar of the courts of Philadelphia. Actually he seems to have lived outside that city, perhaps near Glassboro in nearby Gloucester County, New Jersey. Around 1808 he purchased a half-interest in the large glassworks which gave Glassboro its name. His father died on October 29, 1814, and in that year Wikoff first appeared in a Philadelphia city directory, which listed him as a glass manufacturer, sharing premises at 34 Sansom Street with his brother, the merchant Isaac Cox Wikoff. Edward Carpenter, Peter's partner in the glassworks, died in 1814, and on March 22, 1816 Wikoff sold his own share to David Wolf. From 1817 to 1822 the Philadelphia directories identified Wikoff as a merchant at 146 South 10th Street. His name then disappeared from this source until 1835, after which he was consistently listed as a gentleman, first on North 10th Street and later at South 12th

Street. The single exception came in 1840, when he was described as a merchant with an office at 87 Chestnut Street in addition to his home address. Presumably he kept a house outside Philadelphia and maintained a business address within that city only erratically until he retired there around 1835. Wikoff's wife died on October 21, 1836 and he followed on September 27, 1848. They were both buried in the cemetery of St. Peter's Episcopal Church, Philadelphia.

No direct evidence has been found to show that Peter, the son of Isaac Wikoff, was the Princetonian. His age at graduation would have been unusually though not impossibly young. Furthermore, his father was a Philadelphia merchant, while the Princetonian came from Monmouth. However, William Wikoff, Isaac's father, was a Monmouth County farmer, and it is reasonable to suppose that his son the Philadelphian might have retained lands or resided there for a time. The family genealogy asserts that the Philadelphia lawyer who married Ann Sharp and died in 1848 was the Princetonian, although it identifies his parents incorrectly.

Alternatively, the Princetonian may have been the Peter Wikoff who was born on March 28, 1772, one of ten children of Peter and Alice Longstreet Wikoff. The mother was one of nine children of Derrick and Alice Longstreet of Shark River, Monmouth County. Peter Wikoff, Sr., a farmer in Upper Freehold Township, Monmouth County, served as a militia captain in the Revolutionary War and is said to have acted as one of Gen. George Washington's guides at the Battle of Monmouth, June 28, 1778. He died on April 1, 1821. His son Peter also was a farmer. He may have lived in Mt. Holly, Burlington County, New Jersey, but at the time of his death he was described as a resident of Millstone Township (carved from Upper Freehold and adjacent townships in 1844), Monmouth County. He married Mary Horsfall, by whom he had two sons, and he died intestate on March 21, 1847, leaving personal property with an assessed value of $786.70. Peter Imlay Wikoff (A.B. 1812) was his nephew.

Neither of these hypothetical identifications can be eliminated without further evidence.

Sources: Clio. lists; Hancock House mss (10 Apr. 1789 class list describes PW as resident of East Jersey); Min. Fac., 10 Nov. 1789, 19 Feb. 1790, 22 June ("privately before") & 9 July 1791; Pa. Packet, & Daily Advt., 7 Oct. 1790 (describes PW as from Monmouth); Dunlap's Amer. Daily Advt., 4 Oct. 1791; Clio. Min., 26 Sept. 1792; Dunlap & Claypoole's Amer. Daily Advt., 7 Oct. 1794; W. F. Wyckoff, Wyckoff Fam. in Amer. [1934], 445-50; W. F. Wyckoff, "Notes of the Wyckoff Fam.," Som. Cnty. Hist. Quart., 5 (1916), 289-90; 6 (1917), 50, 137-40; baptismal & marriage records, Christ Church, Phila.; Martin's Bench & Bar, 324; ms will of Peter Wikoff, 6 Nov. 1846, proved 13 Jan. 1849, Reg. of Wills, Phila. (photocopy in PUA); Pa. Archives, 2d ser., ii, 310-11; viii, 274-75; 6th ser., v, 509 ("Peter Wickoff, Junr.," a private in 1794 in First Company, Third Regiment, Philadelphia militia); N.J. Wills, x, 499; xi, 315; xii, 421,

437; XIII, 74; Butterfield, *Rush Letters*, II, 675-76; J. McVickar, *Early Years of the late Bishop Hobart* (2d ed., 1836), 76 ("poor Wycoff"); Phila. city directories, 1793-1849; R. D. Bole & E. H. Walton, *Glassboro Story 1779-1964* (1964), 55, 106-07; T. Cushing & C. E. Sheppard, *Hist. of the Cnties. of Gloucester, Salem, & Cumberland N.J.* (1883 repr. 1974), 229-30; *Poulson's Amer. Daily Advt.*, 19 Apr. 1834 (death of PW's son William Henry); W. W. Bronson, *Inscriptions in St. Peter's Church Yard, Phila.* (1879), 60-62; W. S. Hornor, *This Old Monmouth of Ours* (1932), 127-28, 180-81, 373-74; F. R. Symmes, *Hist. of the Old Tennent Church* (2d. ed., 1904), 176, 362, 420-24; Stryker, *Off. Reg.*, 418; MS estate invs. of Peter Wikoff, 9 Apr. 1821, recorded 10 Apr. 1821, & 8 Apr. 1847, recorded 12 Apr. 1847, Nj (photocopies in PUA). Perhaps the 1836 biographer of Hobart misread "Peter" as "Poor": the original of the letter from which he quoted has not come to light. W. F. Wyckoff asserts that the Princetonian was the son of William Wikoff, a Louisiana plantation owner, and grandson of Isaac Wikoff, the Philadelphia merchant who died in 1814. This is surely in error; the College sources all agree that Peter was from New Jersey, not Louisiana, and since Isaac Wikoff married in 1766, by this account Peter, as his grandson, could scarcely have been five years old when he graduated from the College. Presumably W. F. Wyckoff mistook Peter's brother for his father.

Several other Peter Wikoffs, some of whom may have been the right age, lived in Monmouth County around this time. Two Peter Wikoffs were born in Somerset County in 1774 and another in 1772. One could go even further afield and note that there were four Peter Wikoffs on Long Island in the 1800 census. See F. Ellis, *Hist. of Monmouth Cnty., N.J.* (1885), 139, 170, 178, 191, 231, 388, 508, 515-17, 621, 627-29; E. M. Woodward & J. F. Hageman, *Hist. of Burlington & Mercer Cnties.* (1883), 578; *GMNJ*, 33 (1958), 86, 88; 34 (1959), 26, 29, 66; 36 (1961), 43, 139-40; 37 (1962), 46; *Som. Cnty. Hist. Quart.*, 2 (1913), 188, to 6 (1917), 141, *passim*, esp. 3 (1914), 40-41, 204; 4 (1915), 221-25; *NYGBR*, 55 (1924), 24-25, 124, 129.

JJL

Thomas Wright

THOMAS WRIGHT, planter, was the son of Col. Thomas and Rachel Clayton Wright of "Reed's Creek," St. Paul's Parish, Queen Annes County, Maryland. He was the eldest son in a family of four boys and two girls. His brother Clayton (A.B. 1795) also attended the College, and William Bordley (Class of 1791) was probably a cousin. The mother was one of three children, all female, of William Clayton, a merchant of Queen Annes County, and his wife Sarah. The elder Thomas Wright amassed an estate which at the close of his life included 3,245 acres of land in Queen Annes, thirty-three slaves, and thirty-three horses. He represented his county in the lower house of the colonial legislature regularly between 1762 and 1771, and at all but one of the eight conventions which met between 1774 and 1776 as well. He also served as an Anglican vestryman and churchwarden, and in 1776 he was colonel of the Twentieth Battalion of Militia, Queen Annes County.

Thomas Wright, Sr., served as a visitor of Queen Annes School in 1775 and again for less than three years from 1781 to his death. Perhaps his sons attended this institution. In November 1787 young

Thomas entered the College as a freshman. He joined the Cliosophic Society on December 18, taking the pseudonym Polydore, probably a reference to Polydore Virgil (ca. 1470-1555), the English historian. He was not at Nassau Hall when a class list was compiled on April 10, 1789, but had returned by that November. He left the College in April 1790 but maintained an interest in the Cliosophic Society, attending its annual meeting in September 1792.

His father having died in or before January 1784, Wright apparently returned to "Reed's Creek" and settled in as a planter for the rest of his life. He married Margaret Lowrey on January 12, 1795. She was the daughter of Stephen Lowrey, a native of Ireland, and Sarah Spencer Lowrey, daughter of Elihu Spencer of New Jersey, Presbyterian clergyman and trustee of the College from 1752 to 1784. Margaret's dowry was a Queen Annes County plantation called "Church Farm." Among the Wrights' eight children were Thomas Wright (A.B. 1817) and Stephen Lowrey Wright (A.B. 1818). Wright had apparently encountered the educational theories of John Locke, for he did not believe in corporal punishment of his children, preferring instead to work on their feelings and appeal to their consciences. He apparently applied this viewpoint to his treatment of his slaves as well. If credence can be given to a 1900 family history, they were very fond of him. In his will Wright urged his descendants

> to treat my slaves with all possible kindness and humanity consistent with good order. Such a course will give its own reward, in the evening of life, it will throw a sunshine around the heart, that might otherwise be obscured by gloom.

An Episcopalian, Wright was involved in the repair or rebuilding in St. Paul's Parish of Chester Church, one mile from Centreville, Queen Annes County. A legislative act of January 15, 1799 authorized him and three others to use a lottery to raise money for this purpose. In the War of 1812 Wright was a lieutenant colonel commanding the Thirty-Eighth Regiment of Maryland militia. On August 13, 1813 his unit fought the only action of the war which took place in Queen Annes County, at Queenstown. Wright, however, was sick at home and missed it.

Wright may also have been the Thomas Wright chosen as vestryman of St. Paul's parish in 1796 and the one who represented Queen Annes in the lower house of the state legislature as a Jeffersonian in 1798 and 1799. Positive identification is hindered by the profusion of Wrights in general, and Thomas Wrights in particular, in Queen Annes County at this time. Thomas Wright's cousin shared the same name and was also active politically, and the subject of this sketch was the third in at least five successive generations in which this name went to the eldest son.

Wright died at "Reed's Creek" after March 21, 1835, when he wrote a codicil to his will, and before it was admitted to probate on September 1 of the same year. His personal estate had an appraised value of $18,073, including seventy-six slaves, a few books, four shares of stock in the American Fire Insurance Company of Philadelphia, large quantities of corn and wheat both growing and in the barn, and about fifty cattle and oxen, a dozen horses, six mules, and twenty-five sheep. He left substantial bequests to each of the four sons and two daughters who survived him, and counseled them "to cultivate the most friendly feelings one towards another" and "to avoid anything like legal disputation," referring any disputes over the division of his estate to the arbitration of friends and taking care not to fall much into debt to each other.

SOURCES: *Biog. Dict. Md. Leg.*, I, 144, 460-61; II, 925-26; alumni files of Thomas Wright (A.B. 1817) & Stephen Lowrey Wright (A.B. 1818), PUA; M. B. Emory, *Colonial Families & their Descendants* (1900), 6-7, 14, 20-21, 36-39, 72-73; *MHM*, 57 (1962), 371-73; F. Emory, *Queen Anne's Cnty., Md.* (1950), 179, 355, 375, 380-81, 426, 430; Min. Fac., 10 Nov. 1789 & 18 Mar. 1790; Clio. lists; Clio. Min., 26 Sept. 1792; letter from Md. Leg. Hist. Proj., 21 Jan. 1986, PUA; MS will of TW, 29 May 1834, codicil 21 Mar. 1835, proved 1 Sept. 1835 ("to treat," "to cultivate," "to avoid"), & MS estate inv. of TW, 24 Mar. 1836, recorded 3 May 1836, Md. Hall of Records, Annapolis (photocopy in PUA).

JJL

CLASS OF 1792

Joseph McKnitt Alexander, Jr., A.B.

Nicholas Bayard, A.B.

James P. Bayley (Bayly, Bailey), A.B.

George Minos Bibb, A.B.

Peter Edmund Bleecker, A.B.

George Whitefield Burnet, A.B.

James Chesnut, A.B.

William Chetwood, A.B.

Robert Deas

Peter Early, A.B.

Jacob Ford, A.B.

Charles Wilson Harris, A.B.

Robert Heriot (Harriott), A.B.

Benjamin Hodgdon, A.B.

William Arden Hosack, A.B.

Samuel Hughes

Edmund Jennings Lee, A.B.

George Merrick Leech (Leach)

Joseph Logan, A.B.

J. J. Long

David McRee, A.B.

George Clifford Maxwell, A.B.

Joseph Kirkbride Milnor II, A.B.

George Washington Morton, A.B.

John Conrad Otto, A.B.

Lewis Searle Pintard, A.B.

Joseph Reed, Jr., A.B.

James D. Ross, A.B.

William Ross, A.B.

James Ruan, A.B.

Robert Russel (Russell), A.B.

John Pelion Ryers, A.B.

John Johnson Sayrs (Sayres, Sayre, Sayers), A.B.

John Sloan, A.B.

William B. Sloan, A.B.

Henry Steele

Job Stockton

Jacob Ten Eyck, A.B.

Jacob Stern Thomson
(Thompson), A.B.

William Morton Watkins, A.B.

Alexander White, A.B.

George Willing, A.B.

Henry Veghte Wyckoff
(Wikoff, Wykoff,
Wickoff), A.B.

(Commencement took place on Wednesday, September 26, 1792. The account of the commencement in the *New-Jersey Journal* mistakenly gives the date as September 25, but the trustees' minutes confirm that it was held on the last Wednesday of the month, as custom had come to dictate.)

Joseph McKnitt Alexander, Jr.

JOSEPH MCKNITT ALEXANDER, JR., A.B., physician, was the son of Jane Bane and John McKnitt Alexander of Mecklenburg County, North Carolina. After serving an apprenticeship to a tailor, twenty-one year old John McKnitt Alexander migrated to Mecklenburg from Cecil County, Maryland, bringing with him some ready-made clothes and a supply of broadcloth. He prospered as a tailor, later becoming a surveyor and acquiring extensive land holdings. By 1790 he was the largest slave owner in his district of the county. His son Joseph was born April 28, 1774 at the family home, "Independence Hill," which was located near Clark's Creek, nine or ten miles north of Charlotte. The addition of "Jr." to his name was probably to distinguish him from his older cousin, Joseph Alexander (A.B. 1760). Their great-grandfather bore the same name.

John McKnitt Alexander was not only a signer of the Mecklenburg Declaration of Independence in 1775 but served as secretary of the convention that adopted it. All of the original papers of the convention were stored at his home and were lost when the house burned in April 1800. He attempted to reproduce the papers from memory, but the loss of the originals generated controversies about the declaration that are still being argued. Alexander was a member of the provincial congress of 1776 and later served in a number of local and county positions.

The most likely place for Joseph Alexander to have received his early education is Salisbury Academy in Charlotte, founded in 1784 to replace Liberty Hall Academy, which had been closed since Charles, Earl Cornwallis's invasion of the state, and which his father and other Alexander relatives had served as trustees. A devout Presbyterian, the father was an elder of the Hopewell Presbyterian Church and served as treasurer of the Synod of North and South Carolina. Perhaps following a family tradition, he selected one son to be educated at the College of New Jersey in order to devote his life to the church, as had his older brother Theophilus, whose son was Joseph Alexander (A.B. 1760); his cousin Abraham, father of Isaac Alexander (A.B. 1772); and his cousin Francis, father of Evan Shelby Alexander (A.B. 1787). Moses Alexander, a more distant family connection, also sent his son Nathaniel (A.B. 1776) to the College. However, only one of of these five, Isaac, actually became a clergyman.

Joseph Alexander appears to have entered the College in 1791 as a junior. He probably journeyed to and from Princeton on horseback, leaving his horse to be cared for in a nearby meadow when he was not using it. The catalogue of the combined American Whig-Cliosophic

Society, published in 1954, lists him as a member of the Cliosophic Society who joined in 1792. However, his name does not appear in either the manuscript society records or in an 1840 catalogue of the society. Neither does it appear on any available Whig records. However, in an April 23, 1793 letter to John Hobart (A.B. 1793), written while Hobart was still at the College, Alexander expressed a longing to hear from any of the present seniors and particularly from "our society." He closed as "your ever loving brother-friend." Hobart was a Whig and would only have been referred to as "brother" by a fellow Whig. At the commencement exercises on September 26, 1792, Alexander took the assigned role of opponent in a debate on the question, "Is not the belief of a revealed religion essential to the order and existence of civil society?" A contemporary source says that Alexander graduated "with eclat" and that he "early developed indications of not only genius and talents, but the highest attributes of intellect, sound judgment, and profound thinking." However, he was not chosen to deliver one of the honorary orations, which indicates that his undergraduate record was not outstanding.

Alexander's April 1793 letter to Hobart was written from Mt. Prospect, North Carolina, later to become Waynesville, the county seat of Haywood County. He expressed his nostalgia for college life, saying that he hoped for more frequent news from "that place which was once so agreeable to me." He chafed at the disappointment he felt in his current situation and remarked that "I am not yet a preacher.... I have spent this winter principly in reading, tho' not any particular branch," he added, suggesting that he was not yet ready to make a final choice of careers. He sent news of other college friends in North Carolina and indicated his hopes that the French Revolution would establish that "liberty in all the world which first dawned in America."

Alexander eventually decided to study medicine, probably because of both a natural inclination in this direction and a questioning of church dogma. He had not joined the church, and a nineteenth-century memorialist blamed his lack of spirituality on the influence of the French philosophes, though fortunately he was not "seduced from the paths of virtue." He was past middle age before he joined and became an active member of the Hopewell Presbyterian Church. Different sources credit him with studying medicine in North Carolina and at the University of Pennsylvania but without remaining long enough at either to receive a medical degree. One claims that he went to Philadelphia immediately after graduation and remained there until 1794. However, his letter of 1793 definitely places him in North Carolina the year after his graduation. He may well have spent some time at the University of Pennsylvania and later studied under a North Carolina physician. Whatever his training, he practiced successfully in Mecklenburg County, achieving both personal popularity and influence in local affairs. The success and esteem he earned as a physician would indicate that his interests and talents lay in this field. According to a contemporary who gives rather extravagant praise, Alexander was punctual and cheerful in his duties and was noted for his "integrity, public spirit and private virtue, practical judgment and common sense."

On August 3, 1797 Alexander married Dovie Wilson Winslow, said to be exceptionally beautiful, one of the daughters of Jean Osborne and Moses Winslow. Alexander's father gave him 1,250 acres of land on which he built a home, "Rosedale," for his bride. She died September 6, 1801, leaving one son, Moses Winslow Alexander, who eventually followed his father in the medical profession. When John McKnitt Alexander died in 1817 he left four tracts of land to his son Joseph, specifically including the one on which the latter lived, which suggests that this land had not been legally conveyed at the earlier date. John Alexander's will also left cash bequests of $2,400, one share to go to the families of each of his children, to be divided equally among the offspring in that family who were living at the time of his death. A codicil dated April 30, 1813 indicates that his children had expressed dissatisfaction with this distribution, since most had large families. "In order to cultivate peace and harmony among them and the world when I am dead," he left a specific bequest of $1,600 to Joseph's only child.

Alexander died November 17, 1841 at Alexandria, his father's former home, and was buried at the Hopewell Presbyterian Church. His son married Violet Wilson Winslow Graham, probably a relative on his mother's side, and had twelve children, one of whom was Joseph Hamilton Lafayette Alexander (A.B. 1852).

SOURCES: Alumni file, PUA (father's will); J. B. Alexander, *Hist. of Mecklenburg Cnty.* (1902), 80-83; W. S. Ray, *Mecklenburg Signers & Their Neighbors* (1946), 323, 335, 352, 371, 377, 415, 424, 533; Writer's Program, N.C., *Charlotte, A Guide to the Queen City of N.C.* (1939), 13, 19; S. A. Ashe, *Hist. of N.C.* (1908), II, 271; E. W. Caruthers, *Sketch of the Life & Character of the Rev. David Caldwell* (1842), 193; Min. Fac., class list ca. May 1791, 13 July 1792; *N.J. Jour.*, 10 Oct. 1792; D. L. Corbitt, *Formation of the N.C. Cnties.* (1950), 117; W. S. Powell, *N.C. Gazetteer* (1968), 522; Hobart, *Corres.*, I, 23-25 (quotes from JMA's letter to J. H. Hobart); Alexander, *Princeton*, 257; Foote, *Sketches, N.C.*, 203, 206, 209-10 (quotations re Alexander's character and personality).

RLW

Nicholas Bayard

NICHOLAS BAYARD, A.B., physician, was the youngest and fourth son of Col. John and Margaret Hodge Bayard to graduate from the College. He had been preceded by James Ashton (A.B. 1777), Andrew (A.B. 1779), and Samuel (A.B. 1784). James Ashton Bayard (A.B. 1784) was a first cousin. Col. John Bayard, merchant and patriot, served as a trustee of the College from 1778 to 1807. His wife was a sister of Andrew Hodge (A.B. 1772) and Hugh Hodge (A.B. 1773).

Born on October 18, 1774 at Philadelphia, Bayard was one of four students admitted to the freshman class "from other colleges" on November 10, 1787, but apparently he dropped back to the grammar school for a year, since faculty minutes have him entering again as a freshman in November 1788. As a sophomore on March 18, 1790 he was in arrears in payment for his "diet" in the College. On August 14, 1791 he was convicted of insolence toward an officer of the College and admonished before the junior class. Just several months before his graduation, he joined the Cliosophic Society on June 6, 1792, using the pseudonym Anacreon. At his commencement on September 26 he was respondent in a dispute on the question: "Is the emancipation of slaves, without preparing them by a proper education to be good citizens, consistent with humanity and sound policy?" Colonel Bayard had moved to New Brunswick after the Revolution, and so his son was described in newspaper accounts of the exercises as "of New Jersey."

What Bayard did right after graduation is unknown, but he studied medicine at Columbia College in New York City from 1793 to 1795. In the records of Columbia he is listed as Nicholas S. Bayard, the "S" standing apparently for the middle name of Serl, which he does not seem to have used at Princeton. Bayard received no M.D. degree, nor did he bother to pick up the M.A. at Princeton, although at times he has been credited with both degrees.

Bayard may have continued his studies after 1795 through an apprenticeship with a physician, or he may have entered the drug business he later combined, as did other doctors at the time, with the practice of medicine. Nothing definite is known until 1798 when, according to a city directory, he was practicing medicine at 85 Liberty Street in New York City. On March 10, 1798 in a local Presbyterian church, Dr. Nicholas Bayard married his cousin, Ann Livingston Bayard, daughter of Nicholas Bayard (A.B. 1757), a wealthy merchant and influential alderman of the city. Bayard's New York practice was destined to be short-lived. Nicholas Bayard, M.D., is listed at 193 Pearl Street in a directory for 1801, but not thereafter.

Perhaps the death of his wife in 1802 persuaded him to quit the city for a practice in Savannah, Georgia, which has been dated from 1803. The Savannah climate and the diseases of the coastal low country probably made the area an attractive professional challenge to younger doctors. On December 12, 1804 Bayard became one of the charter members of the Georgia Medical Society, founded for "the purpose of lessening the fatality induced by climate and incidental causes, and improving the science of medicine." Actually, the society failed to develop as a statewide organization and remained essentially a Savannah institution. Among its early efforts it tried to secure a prohibition against the cultivation of rice within a mile of the city on the ground that, "with our semi-tropical climate, there could be no worse nor more malignant incidental cause of disease than the stagnant water which remains on the rice fields exposed to an ardent summer sun and the subsequent exposure of the saturated soil when the water is drained off." This goal required several years to accomplish.

Bayard was married a second time on September 5, 1804 to Esther (Hetty) Ward, the well-connected widow of John Peter Ward. Sources reveal some differences as to the date of Bayard's death, but there seems to be no room for doubt that he died or was buried on October 28, 1821, when he had just attained the age of forty-seven. He was survived by three children, two daughters and a son named Nicholas James Bayard, who was born in New York City in January 1799 and who attended the College at Princeton from 1813 to 1815 without graduating.

SOURCES: Alumni file, PUA; J. G. Wilson, "Col. John Bayard ... & the Bayard Family of Amer.," *NYGBR*, 16 (1885), 49-72; Min. Fac., 10 Nov. 1787 ("from other"), 10 Nov. 1789, 18 Mar. 1790, 14 Aug. 1791, 13 July 1792; Clio. lists; *N.J. Jour.*, 10 Oct. 1792; Thomas, *Columbia*, 181; *NYGBR*, 13 (1882), 90; C. C. Jones, *Hist. of Savannah, Ga.* (1890), 437-38, 455-57 (quote); F. D. Lee & J. L. Agnew, *Hist. Record of the City of Savannah* (1869), 186 (quote); C. P. Wilson, *Annals of Ga.* (1928-33), III, 177.

                                                                                    WFC

James P. Bayley (Bayly, Bailey)

JAMES P. BAYLEY (BAYLY, BAILEY), A.B., entered the College as a junior in November 1790. In the same year he joined the Cliosophic Society, taking the name of Belisarius (c. 505-565 A.D.), one of the finest generals of the early Byzantine empire. Bayley was suspended on July 18, 1792 "for divulging the transactions of the Society." On August 16 the suspension was lifted, but the incident was not forgotten. In an unusual move, the membership turned down Bayley's request for a diploma on August 29. At the College commencement on September 26, Bayley received his degree but took no part in the exercises at his own request.

Bayley matriculated from Maryland. The name was not unusual there, and no further information on his family background has been discovered. Perhaps he was related to Thomas Bayley (A.B. 1797), later a United States congressman, who came from near Quantico in Somerset (now Wicomico) County. Thomas Bayley's parents were Esme and Sinah Polk Bayley.

James P. Bayley died young, in April 1795.

SOURCES: Min. Fac., 29 Nov. 1790, 13 July 1792; Clio. lists (date of death); Clio. Min., 18 July, 16 & 29 August 1792 ("for divulging"); *N.J. Journal*, 10 Oct. 1792; alumni file of Thomas Bayley, PUA; *BDUSC*, 592.

JJL

George Minos Bibb

GEORGE MINOS BIBB, A.B., A.B. Hampden-Sidney 1791, LL.D. Transylvania 1826, lawyer, judge, and public official, was born on October 30, 1776, in Prince Edward County, Virginia, the eldest child of Richard Bibb (Class of 1777) and his first wife Lucy Booker Bibb. The father was a planter, businessman, and public official who moved to Kentucky in 1797 and later became a Methodist preacher. George's first cousins, William Wyatt Bibb and Thomas Bibb, successively became governors of Alabama, and his brother John Booker Bibb achieved some renown by developing Bibb lettuce.

Bibb's father was a trustee of Hampden-Sidney College, and so it is not surprising that Bibb was sent to that school, graduating in 1791. He then came to Princeton and entered the senior class of the College. The practice of sending Hampden-Sidney graduates north for another year of education was common at the time. On December 27, 1791 Bibb joined the Cliosophic Society, taking as his pseudonym "Minos," after the ancient king of Crete. He gave the oration commemorating the anniversary of the society's revival on July 4, 1792, an honor reserved for its better speakers, served a monthly term as its president, and received its diploma. His subsequent adoption of Minos as his middle name suggests that he remembered the society fondly, although he invariably used the initial only, and may simply have felt that "George Bibb" by itself did not sound sufficiently distinguished. The faculty minutes show that Bibb was exempted from participating in the commencement exercises at his own request, but eventually he replaced Jacob Ten Eyck and acted as replicator in a debate on the question:

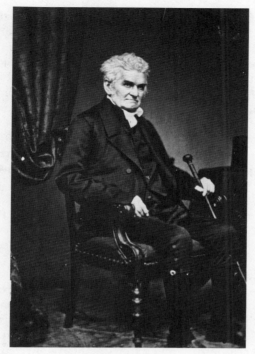

George Minos Bibb, A.B. 1792
PHOTOGRAPH BY MATTHEW BRADY

Considering the present state of human nature, does not the existence of war among nations seem necessary? In effect, do not wars contribute more to the elevation of the human character, to the improvement of the arts, and even to the happiness of mankind, than a state of universal peace, abused as the degeneracy of man always abuses the long continuance of prosperity?

The substitution is unexplained. Perhaps Ten Eyck was called away unexpectedly and Bibb agreed to fill in for him.

After graduating, Bibb returned to Virginia and began reading law in the office of Richard N. Venable (A.B. 1782) of Prince Edward County. He also attended the law lectures of St. George Tucker at the College of William and Mary for three years. In April 1796 he obtained his law license. For a year he practiced in Virginia, but in the spring of 1797, "with my parents & at their request," he moved to Kentucky. He soon attained eminence at that state's bar. A man who came to Kentucky in 1798 later recalled that Bibb, Jesse Bledsoe, and Henry Clay all began their careers around that time and that "they were all three great favorites with the people & considered very promising," although Clay soon took and kept the lead. Initially Bibb lived in Nelson County, not far from his father in adjoining Bullitt County. He may have resided in or near Bardstown, for it was near this town that he served as second to John Rowan on February 3, 1801, when Rowan killed Dr. James Chambers in a duel sparked by a disagreement as to whose classical education was superior. By 1804 Bibb had moved to Lexington in Fayette County. In that year he served as Worshipful Master of the Lexington Masonic Lodge, and from 1804 through 1807 he was Grand Master of the Grand Lodge of Kentucky. He had become Fayette County circuit judge by late 1806, for that is how he was described when he and Henry Clay ran for the United States Senate seat left vacant by the resignation of John Adair. Clay trounced Bibb, 64 to 10, but Bibb obtained some consolation on November 26, 1806 by winning the election to fill Clay's seat in the state house of representatives.

The legislature soon found itself pondering rumors of the treasonable designs of Aaron Burr (A.B. 1772). On December 5 Bibb moved "more effectually to secure the peace of this commonwealth" by granting the governor special military powers during the crisis. His legislative service terminated abruptly after only a few days, when he resigned because of "the sickness of his family." Bibb soon had to deal with the Burr conspiracy again. He had recently become the United States district attorney for Kentucky, and on July 20, 1807, he successfully represented the government at the extradition hearing which sent Harman Blennerhassett from Lexington to Richmond to stand trial with Burr for treason.

On January 30, 1808 Bibb was appointed to the court of appeals, Kentucky's highest court, and on May 30, 1809 Governor Charles Scott named him chief justice. Scott was another transplanted Virginian who, in addition to being a Revolutionary War general, was Bibb's father-in-law. Bibb had married Martha Tabb Scott on May 19, 1799. She bore him twelve children.

Bibb served only briefly as chief justice. He resigned in March 1810, a move possibly related to his decision to make another bid for the United States Senate. Later that year he won election to the state legislature from Logan County, where he may then have been living or where he may simply have owned enough property to run for the seat. Bibb's father, who then lived at Russellville, Logan County, probably helped look after his son's political interests.

Bibb won his Senate election and was in Washington when Congress convened on November 4, 1811. A Republican and close ally of the War Hawks, he lodged with like-minded Congressmen William Lowndes, Langdon Cheves, and John C. Calhoun of South Carolina, Felix Grundy of Tennessee, and Kentuckian Henry Clay in what became known as the "War Mess." On February 23, 1812 he argued in a letter intended for public consumption that negotiations with Britain then in progress were likely to fail, and that the only alternatives were "war or a most base and disgraceful submission." This attitude had not kept the War Mess from attending the British ambassador's ball the month before. Lowndes wrote his wife that he and Bibb, "who is I think as lazy as myself," had arrived by design too late for the dancing but in time for supper and after careful study concluded that the ladies present were "inferior to those of Carolina and Kentucky."

Bibb earned a reputation as a loyal administration man who helped lead its Senate supporters during his term, which ended with his resignation on August 23, 1814. Whether the resignation had political significance or was simply motivated by a desire to concentrate on his private concerns is unclear.

During the next fifteen years Bibb was intimately involved in the periodic crises which racked Kentucky's political life. By October 1815 he had moved to Frankfort, in Franklin County, the state capital, and in 1817 he represented the county in the state legislature. At this time he helped lead an effort to oust Gabriel Slaughter as governor. Governor George Madison had died in office in October 1816. Slaughter, the lieutenant governor, replaced him and quickly made himself unpopular by appointing to office two men who were thought by many to be too conservative, perhaps even Federalists. Since Madison was the first Kentucky governor to die in office, Slaughter's opponents argued that the lieutenant governor should succeed only until a special election could be ordered, not for the remainder of the term. Despite much popular support for a special election, the legislature sided with Slaughter.

Bibb once again became United States district attorney for Kentucky in 1819. Early in 1822 he and Henry Clay were sent East by the state to argue its case in the "occupying claimant" controversy. The land laws in Kentucky were very confused, with many tracts being claimed by several people simultaneously. Land patented at least once by Virginia before Kentucky became a state was often granted again by Kentucky. The oldest valid claim had legal precedence but could lead to Virginia absentees dispossessing settlers who had invested years of their lives in developing land they considered their own. The situation became highly charged. The Kentucky legislature passed laws in 1797 and 1812 affording the claimant actually on the land some protection from those with prior claims, but the United States Supreme Court struck down the laws in 1821. Bibb and Clay journeyed first to Richmond, in an effort to negotiate an agreement which would otherwise compensate those holding the older, Virginia claims, and then to Washington to argue that the Supreme Court should reconsider its earlier ruling. Both efforts failed, engendering much bitterness in Kentucky; not until 1831 was a successful settlement reached.

For much of the 1820s Bibb was enmeshed in the controversy over debtor relief laws which dominated state politics for years. The panic of 1819 left a large group of debtors at the mercy of their creditors. Specie and sound paper money were unavailable, and during a depression the creditors quite naturally refused to accept anything else. On June 4, 1819 Bibb attended a public meeting which passed the controversial "Frankfort Resolutions" calling for legislation permitting banks which had suspended specie payments to remain open and issue paper money nonetheless. The legislature responded to the debtors' grievances by passing a replevin law in 1820, which granted a two-year stay of execution to debtors, unless their creditors agreed to accept the paper of a newly chartered and financially precarious land bank, the Bank of the Commonwealth, in which case the stay was reduced to three months. Bibb quickly became a leader of the relief party. He himself had lost an indeterminate but probably large sum in the panic; one hostile observer asserted that Bibb's being "irredeemably Insolvent" explained his advocacy of relief. He is credited with writing the 1820 replevin law, also known as the "Christmas Act" for the day it passed. The law was ruled unconstitutional by a lower court judge in 1822 and by the court of appeals in 1823.

The ensuing outcry against the judges quickly shifted the focus of the struggle from relief *per se* to the judicial structure of Kentucky. Efforts to remove the judges fell short of the two-thirds majority required, and an attempt to call a constitutional convention in order to institute elective judgeships also failed. Finally, on December 24, 1824 the legislature passed the "Reorganization Act," also thought to have been drafted by Bibb. The law abolished the existing court of appeals (and thus the positions of those sitting on it) and created a new one, different only in having four members instead of three. A transparent subterfuge to evade the two-thirds majority required to remove judges, the law was regarded as invalid by the old court. For a time both courts sat and heard cases, with the relief and anti-relief supporters now known as the New Court and Old Court parties. Bibb's law may have been too clever for its own good. It provoked a reaction from the electorate which in the next two elections returned Old Court men who ultimately succeeded in destroying the New Court, the replevin laws, and the Bank of the Commonwealth.

On January 5, 1827 Bibb once again was made chief justice of the court of appeals. The appointment of a supporter of the recently defunct New Court has sometimes been depicted as a conciliatory gesture by the victorious Old Court party. This interpretation is implausible. New Court supporter Governor Joseph Desha nominated Bibb, and after a bitter debate he was only narrowly confirmed in a vote which split largely along New Court/Old Court lines. Bibb served for less than two years. His tenure was marked by a heated quarrel with Desha's successor, Old Court backer Thomas Metcalfe. The complex dispute centered on Bibb's contention that his two colleagues had resigned just prior to Metcalfe's election, and Bibb ultimately refused to hold meetings of the court until they were replaced. The argument ended and the final victory of the Old Court anti-relief supporters came only with Bibb's resignation on December 23, 1828 to accept election to a six-year term in the United States Senate.

During the relief and court struggle, state and national politics came to overlap significantly. Although Clay sought to stay above the struggle, his supporters became identified with the Old Court anti-relief party, while Andrew Jackson's followers were more likely to favor the New Court and relief. Political differences probably explain Clay's rupture with Bibb, who wrote a friend just prior to the 1824 presidential election that Clay "has broken the cords of friendship which bound me to him; they can never again be tied." The 1824 election confirmed the division. When it became clear that Clay could not win, Bibb led the Jacksonians in Kentucky in successfully urging the legislature, which had just passed his Reorganization Act, to instruct the state's congressional delegation, which paid no heed, to support Jackson rather than John Quincy Adams (LL.D. 1806).

During his second Senate term and indeed throughout his career, Bibb consistently sought to limit the role played by the federal government, a course of action which derived from his strict construction of the Constitution and from traditional republican perceptions of the threat to liberty posed by a strong central government. By favoring low prices for public lands and by opposing protective tariffs and federal sponsorship of internal improvements, Bibb hoped to keep the government's income and expenses as small as possible. On February 14, 1835 he identified three groups in the Senate; Jackson's Democrats, Clay's National Republicans, and "another party, to which he belonged, and which he was sorry to say did not meet with much favor now-a-days, denominating themselves the State-rights party, but who were stigmatized with the mad-dog name of nullifiers."

Bibb came to Washington in 1829 as a Jacksonian. On May 15, 1830 he ignored instructions from his legislature by voting against the famous "Maysville Road bill" which would have helped fund a turnpike, one in his own state no less. As a result, Bibb was soon being burned in effigy all over Kentucky. The subsequent presidential veto of this bill established Jackson's position that federal support of purely local internal improvements was both unconstitutional and a threat to his ultimately successful effort to pay off the national debt and reduce taxes.

Bibb's ardor for Jackson soon cooled. Deep divisions within the party could not long be papered over, and he increasingly identified himself with John C. Calhoun's followers. In March 1830 a meeting was held at Bibb's rooms in Washington at which Congressman Charles A. Wickliffe probably urged several colleagues from Tennessee, including James K. Polk, to join in urging the president to oust Secretary of War John H. Eaton from the Cabinet. This overt effort to limit Martin Van Buren's influence failed when the Tennesseans refused to go along. On April 13 of the same year Bibb was among the organizers of the celebrated Jefferson Day Dinner, an abortive effort to forge an alliance between South and West on a platform of low tariffs, cheap public lands, and strict construction. During this gathering Jackson offered his immediately famous toast to the preservation of the Union, which some contemporaries asserted was lifted almost verbatim from Bibb's speech at the banquet. The point is disputed; and, even if true, Jackson's ideas on how to preserve the Union obviously differed from those of Bibb, whose speech emphasized the crucial role states' rights played in defending liberty. When the Senate considered the nomination of Van Buren as minister to Great Britain in January 1831, Bibb seems to have missed the vote intentionally in order to set up the tie which enabled Vice President Calhoun to cast the deciding vote against Van Buren, his arch-enemy.

The nullification crisis sparked Bibb's final break with Jackson. He led off for the backers of South Carolina in the Senate debate on the Force Bill with a three-day speech which began on January 30, 1833. Later he sided against Jackson in the Bank War. Bibb despised all banks as the source of his own financial woes, and some of his earlier actions suggested hostility to the Bank of the United States. Nonetheless, Bibb said of Jackson's justification for removing government money from that institution and of dismissing Treasury Secretary

William J. Duane for failing to go along with this action, that "More alarming doctrines, or greater heresies, have never been preached from high places in the United States." Early in 1835 Bibb served on Calhoun's special Senate committee to investigate and deplore what Calhoun saw as the growing size, influence, and potential for corruption of the federal bureaucracy under Jackson.

Bibb was an active senator and spoke frequently on the floor. He sought reductions in the price of public lands several times. Having served as chairman of the post office committee from 1829-30, he took a special interest in the department thereafter, emphasizing that the mail should be carried at a profit but that all newspapers should be sent post-free, a backhanded swipe at the unofficial practice of permitting Jacksonian papers to pass through the mails at no charge. He decried corruption within the post office while defending the integrity of the postmaster general, fellow-Kentuckian William T. Barry.

Not having sought re-election, Bibb returned to Kentucky after his term expired in 1835. Since Clay had regained control of the state legislature, the decision not to run again probably made a virtue of necessity. Alternatively, Bibb could have already been offered, and preferred, his next position. From 1835 to 1844, he was chancellor of the newly created Louisville chancery court. The judgeship came at an opportune time. Bibb wrote his brother John in 1839 that thanks to the "banking system," and "my own confiding temper" which had "stript me of my own acquisitions," he was obliged even "at my time of life" to devote "the most intense application to the duties [of] an office which does not afford any surplus at year's end above the expense of my family." The family expenses were not decreasing. Bibb's first wife had died in April 1829, and in 1832 he entered into the first of two subsequent marriages which produced at least five children. His new wife was Rebecca Latham Ashton, daughter of Henry and Celia Brown Key Ashton of the District of Columbia. She was followed by Mrs. Mary R. Dyer. In 1838 Bibb was the featured speaker at the laying of the cornerstone of the Louisville Medical Institute, which ultimately became part of the University of Louisville. In the same year, he became first vice president of the newly chartered Kentucky Historical Society. He served briefly as its acting president in 1843 before his final return to Washington the ensuing year.

John C. Spencer, the United States Secretary of the Treasury, had resigned on May 2, 1844, after a disagreement with President John Tyler, and Tyler chose Bibb as his replacement. The president had presumably become friendly with Bibb when they were both fighting the Force Bill in the Senate in 1833, and Bibb's appointment was the final step in the process by which Tyler packed his Cabinet with states rights, strict-constructionist, southern Democrats who supported his desire to reduce the tariff, annex Texas, and resist abolitionists. During his brief tenure at the Treasury, which lasted from July 4, 1844 until Tyler's term ended on March 3, 1845, Bibb tried unsuccessfully to have the tariff lowered on a wide range of articles. His service was otherwise uneventful, but on June 6, 1845, in the last letter he wrote before he died, Andrew Jackson told President James K. Polk that:

> I am informed thro' a channel in which I have a right to confide, and is a man of much truth himself, That the late ex-Secretary of the Treasury, for the short time he was at the head of it, made ninety thousand dollars, by arrangements with the two brokers Banks, of New-york where large sums of the Public mony was deposited, and other deposite Banks in N. York. Enquire cautiously amonghst the clerk's in the city of Washington, by which you will find a key that may unlock the door to a proper enquiry.

Nothing seems to have come of the accusation, and since Jackson was, perhaps, unlikely to give charges against Bibb a fair hearing, the allegation of corruption must be regarded as unsubstantiated.

After Polk's inauguration Bibb stayed on in Washington as a practicing attorney, arguing before the district and supreme courts. Around 1850 Attorney General John J. Crittenden, one of Bibb's old law students, appointed him chief clerk, a post which made him Crittenden's second-in-command, and he was retained by Caleb Cushing in Franklin Pierce's administration. He resigned around 1855, thinking he could live off his profits as counsel to John C. Frémont in the latter's Mariposa land claim suit, but such hopes proved illusory and Bibb resumed his legal practice. He kept an office in Georgetown and lived with his family at a farm in nearby Rockville, Montgomery County, Maryland. In his last years "Chancellor Bibb" became a beloved figure in Washington. His courtly manners were a by-word; the graceful air with which he proffered snuff to all takers was much admired, and a little girl who befriended his young daughter recalled many years later that "the old Judge's only recreation was an occasional minstrel show to which he delightedly took us two little girls, and entertained us, as charmingly as he would have done the British Ambassador's wife." Actually his favorite hobby was not minstrelry but fishing, from which he gained "his reputation as the most patient and unsuccessful angler in the District." He refused to give up his knee breeches and buckled shoes and was the last man in the city to wear either. When he died on April 14, 1859 a widespread sense prevailed that Washington had lost its last "gentleman of the Old

School." President James Buchanan headed the large crowd attending his funeral at Oak Hill Cemetery in Washington. Later he was reinterred at the Kentucky State Cemetery in Frankfort.

SOURCES: *DAB*; als, GMB to J. H. [Casten?], 30 Dec. 1855, NjP ("with my"); *Princetonians, 1776-1783*, 149-51; Hampden-Sidney College, *Gen. Cat.* (1908), 14-15, 47; R. Peter & J. Peter, *Transylvania Univ.* (1896), 126; J. S. Goff, "The Last Leaf: George Mortimer Bibb," *KSHS Reg.*, 59 (1961), 331-42 ("banking system"); F. R. Stewart, *Bibb Family of Amer.* (1979), I, 23; *KSHS Reg.*, 1 (1903), 43-44; *Filson Club Hist. Quart.*, 46 (1972), 182; Min. Fac., 13 July 1792 & class lists ca. 11 Nov. 1791 & 5 May 1792; Clio. lists; Clio. Min., 4 July–22 Aug. 1792 *passim*; *N.J. Journal*, 10 Oct. 1792 ("Considering the"); College of William & Mary, *Provisional List of Alumni ... 1693 to 1888* (1941), 7; "Memoirs of Micah Taul," *KSHS Reg.*, 27 (1929), 353, 356 ("they were all"); G. G. Clift, *"Second Census" of Ky. 1800* (1954), 22; G. G. Clift, *"Corn Stalk Militia" of Ky., 1792-1811* (1957), 134; J. W. Coleman, *Famous Ky. Duels* (1969), 5-14; J. W. Coleman, *Hist. of Lexington Lodge No. 1, F. & A. M.* (1951), 26; L. Collins & R. H. Collins, *Hist. of Ky.* (1878), I, 30, 34-36, 497-98, 525; II, 241, 277-78, 488, 775-76; B. Mayo, *Henry Clay, Spokesman of the New West* (1937), 244, 402, 478; letter from William T. Barry to John Barry, 2 Jan. 1807, printed in *AHR*, 16 (1910/11), 329 ("the sickness"); *Clay Papers*, I, 298-99, 338, 343 ("more effectually"), 871; II, 82, 732, 770; III, 5-6, 151, 159-61, 171, 176-77, 207-09, 415; IV, 41, 265-66; VI, 16-17, 28-29, 53, 73; VII, 607-08; *KSHS Reg.*, 26 (1928), 158-61; *Filson Club Hist. Quart.*, 31 (1957), 40, 45; R. H. Brown, *Republic in Peril: 1812* (1964), 47 ("war or"), 111, 117-20; H. H. R. Ravenel, *Life and Times of William Lowndes of S.C. 1782-1822* (1901), 100 ("who is I think," "inferior"); U.S. Library of Cong., Division of MSS, *Calendar of the Papers of John Jordan Crittenden* (1913), 13-16, 22, 28-29, 33, 42-43, 96; *A/C*, 12th Cong., 1st sess., 215-16; U.S. Cong., *Reg. of Debates in Cong.*, 21st Cong., 2d sess., 81-82; 22d Cong., 1st sess., 154, 625, 629, 830-31, 875-77, 902, 907, 996-1000, 1022, 1032, 1177-78, 1186, 1398; 22d Cong., 2d sess., 46, 79, 178-79, 264-311, 600-01, 701; 23d Cong., 1st sess., 533-35, 605-06, 1247-49, 1309-10, 1488-1526 ("More alarming," 1507), 1538, 1732-33, 1813-14, 1954-56; 23d Cong., 2d sess., 179-95, 319-20, 344, 447-50 ("another party," 450); *BDUSC*, 617; A. D. Kirwan, *John J. Crittenden: The Struggle for the Union* (1962 repr. 1974), 9-10, 31-32, 94, 97-98; C. Kerr, *Hist. of Ky.* (1922), II, 587, 622, 637, 646-47, 659-73, 676, 696-97, 712-13, 1088; A. M. Stickles, *Critical Court Struggle in Ky. 1819-29* (1929), 25-26, 38-40, 49, 51, 108-09, 113-14; M. N. Rothbard, *Panic of 1819* (1962), 98-99; F. F. Mathias, "Relief and Court Struggle: Half-Way House to Populism," *KSHS Reg.*, 71 (1973), 154-76; E. G. Swem, *Letters on the Condition of Ky. in 1825* (1916), 10, 29-30 ("irredeemably"); T. S. Arthur & W. H. Carpenter, *Hist. of Ky.* (1852), 301-02; G. G. Van Deusen, *Life of Henry Clay* (1937), 158-59, 187; A. M. B. C. Coleman, *Life of John J. Crittenden* (1871), I, 14-16, 32-33, 60-62 ("has broken"); W. C. Barrickman, "Political Nominating Convention," *Filson Club Hist. Quart.*, 18 (1944), 37-51; H. Weaver, ed., *Corres. of James K. Polk* (1969), I, 430-33; C. G. Sellers, *James K. Polk: Jacksonian, 1795-1843* (1957), 146-48; C. M. Wiltse, *John C. Calhoun: Nullifier, 1829-39* (1949), 69, 72, 187-88, 255-57; R. L. Meriwether, W. E. Hemphill, C. N. Wilson, et al., eds., *Papers of John C. Calhoun* (1959– , 18 vols.), IV, 66-67, 92; IX, 179-80; XII, 4, 37, 88-89, 380, 447, 486; XIV, 559-60; W. O. Lynch, *Fifty Years of Party Warfare (1789-1837)* (1931), 405; M. Van Buren, *Autobiog.*, *AHA Rept. for 1918* (1920), II, 454, 533, 751; *KSHS Reg.*, 78 (1980), 132-33; *WMQ*, 1st ser., 7 (1899), 116; Washington city directories, 1846-60; *Filson Club Hist. Quart.*, 7 (1933), 142-44; *KSHS Reg.*, 41 (1943), 180-83, 190, 218-19; O. D. Lambert, *Presidential Politics in the U.S. 1841-44* (1936), 98-99; O. P. Chitwood, *John Tyler: Champion of the Old South* (1939), 298-99; R. J. Morgan, *Whig Embattled: The Presidency Under John Tyler* (1954 repr. 1974), 169, 173-75; J. S. Bassett, ed., *Corres. of Andrew Jackson* (1926-35 repr. 1969), VI, 356, 414 ("I am informed"); *Harper's Weekly*, 30 April 1859 ("most patient," "gentleman of"); C. Warren, *Supreme Court in U.S. Hist.* (1923), III, 73; J. B. Larner, ed., "Some Reminiscences of Mrs. John M. Binckley of Early Days in Wash.," *Records of the Columbia Hist. Soc.*, 29/30 (1928), 343-44, 349 ("The old Judge's"). Great confusion about Bibb's middle name exists. Mortimer, Motier, Martin, Marshall, and the initial M. signifying no name at all have each been suggested. Fortunately, a letter from Bibb himself in 1855 (the second source cited above) settles the issue; he responded to a correspondent curious on that very point: "My middle name is, Minos, after the King of Crete."

PUBLICATIONS: *Reports of cases at Common Law and in Chancery argued and decided in the Court of Appeals of the Commonwealth of Kentucky* (4 vols., 1815-17, covering the years 1808-17); *Exposition of the Meaning of the Clause* ... (ca. 1823); *Speech of the Hon. GMB ... delivered in the Senate of the U.S. April 28, 1834. On the President's Protest* (1834); *An Oration, Commemorative of Laying the Corner Stone of the College Edifice of the Louisville Medical Institute, on the 22nd of February, 1838* (1838); Bibb et al., *Petition to the Congress of the U.S....* (1824). See *National Union Catalog: Pre-1956 Imprints* for several legal briefs and opinions by Bibb. For an 1825 political broadside, see *KSHS Reg.*, 58 (1960), 344.

MANUSCRIPTS: NjP; NjP-SSP; Filson Club, Louisville, Ky; Univ. of Ky. Lib., Lexington; Ky. Hist. Soc., Frankfort; Western Ky. Univ., Bowling Green; DLC; MB; Pierpont Morgan Lib., N.Y.; Albert Gallatin Papers, NHi; NcU

JJL

Peter Edmund Bleecker

PETER EDMUND BLEECKER, A.B., was born at Albany, New York, on September 8, 1774, the son of Rutger Bleecker and Catherine Elmendorf Bleecker of that city. On September 11 he was baptized in the local Dutch Reformed church. The Bleeckers were members of a Dutch family who had been in the Kingston and Albany area since the middle of the seventeenth century. Rutger Bleecker had inherited a great deal of land, and in 1772 he and three partners bought at sheriff's sale a portion of Cosby's Manor in the Mohawk Valley. The southern half of this tract of over 43,000 acres was the area where the city of Utica was later developed. Peter Bleecker was preceded at the College by his brother John Rutger Bleecker (A.B. 1791). Peter Edmund Elmendorf (A.B. 1782) was their mother's brother, and Lucas Conrad Elmendorf (A.B. 1782) was her first cousin. Her brother John was the father of Edmund Elmendorf (A.B. 1794), James Bruyn Elmendorf (A.B. 1807), and William Crooke Elmendorf (A.B. 1807). Her sister Blandina married Jacobus Severyn Bruyn (Class of 1775), and they were the parents of Edmund Bruyn (A.B. 1801) and Severyn Bruyn (A.B. 1803).

Bleecker entered the College as a sophomore in November 1789 and on December 23, 1789 joined the Cliosophic Society, to which his brother already belonged. Here he took the name Chilo, a form of Chilon, the Spartan whose great wisdom ranked him among the Seven Sages of Greece. At his commencement Bleecker was one of the intermediate orators speaking, according to a contemporary newspaper account, on the effects of party spirit, although a printed program of the order of commencement had him scheduled to deliver an oration "On Benevolence." He died ten days after his nineteenth birthday on September 18, 1793.

SOURCES: Alumni files, PUA; Alexander, 259; Min. Fac., 10 Nov. 1789, 13 July 1792; Clio. lists; *N.J. Jour.*, 10 Oct. 1792; broadside 1792 "Order of Commencement," PUA; *Princetonians, 1776-1783*, 356-63.

RLW

George Whitefield Burnet

GEORGE WHITEFIELD BURNET, A.B., A.M. 1795, lawyer, was born in the autumn of 1772, in Newark, New Jersey, the youngest of the eleven children of William Burnet (A.B. 1749), the eminent medical practitioner, and his first wife Mary Camp Burnet. George's six elder brothers included Ichabod (A.B. 1775) and Jacob Burnet (A.B. 1791), and his sister Elizabeth married Daniel Thew (A.B. 1787). William Burnet, who was proficient in languages, tutored his son initially. Subsequently George attended two Newark academies: that kept until 1786 by Alexander MacWhorter (A.B. 1757), and then the school of John Croes (A.M. 1797), later Episcopal bishop of New Jersey.

Burnet entered the College as a junior in November 1790 and joined the American Whig Society. A classmate later remembered that George Burnet and his brother Jacob had been part of a closely knit circle of friends from that society which also included John Henry Hobart (A.B. 1793) and George's classmates William Chetwood, Charles W. Harris, David McRee, George C. Maxwell, John C. Otto and Alexander White. In a letter to Hobart in 1798 Burnet recalled his college years: "The bare mention of 'Nassau Hall' gives me pleasing and grateful sensations. I shall ever feel a thankful attachment to that seminary, which I view as the parent of the chief happiness I expect to enjoy." Burnet lamented that "through a blind but benevolent zeal" his father had sent him to the College at least two years too young, "so that I finished my classical education just as it was time to commence it." Even so, it had "given me, if no more, at least a relish for knowledge, which I trust will never be satiated while I am on this side the grave." Burnet graduated with intermediate honors; at his commencement on September 26, 1792, he gave "an oration on society."

Burnet then returned to Newark. John Johnson Sayrs (A.B. 1792) observed in a letter to a friend in December 1792 that while Jacob

Burnet was studying diligently, "George is going to Study Law, when I do not know, & I doubt whether he does himself." Eventually he entered the law office of Alexander Cumming McWhorter (A.B. 1784). He supplemented his legal training by joining the local moot court, called the *Institutio legalis*, sometime after its reconstitution in June 1794. Burnet, who was a "uniform and decided Federalist of the Washington school," displayed so great an interest in public affairs that in January 1796 Otto referred to him as "our political brother" in a letter to Hobart. In September 1796 the Supreme Court of New Jersey called Burnet to the bar.

Almost immediately after completing his legal training, Burnet moved to Cincinnati in the Northwest Territory. This move, like that of his brother Jacob to the same place, may have been prompted by a decision to claim an inheritance. His one-tenth share of his father's estate included land in the Miami Company's tract at the Ohio and Greater Miami rivers. He was quickly admitted to the territorial bar and followed the court to Detroit in spring 1797 and subsequently on its circuit from Detroit to Marietta, Cincinnati, and, less frequently, Vincennes and Kaskaskia. He wrote a series of articles around 1798 in *Freeman's Journal*, Cincinnati's weekly newspaper, discussing the proposed shift to the second stage of territorial government. In May 1799 he married Sophia Greene of Marietta, the daughter of the merchant Charles Greene. She bore him one child.

Burnet attended services at the Presbyterian church and contributed to its support, even though he did not enter its communion. He was an enthusiastic Mason. His brother William had been involved in the creation of Cincinnati's first lodge, although their father's death had forced him to return home before the lodge's organization in 1794. George delivered St. John's Day orations in 1798 and 1799 which were sufficiently well received to be published by the lodge.

In spring 1800 tuberculosis broke Burnet's health. His physician advised him to travel, and so in May his family set out for Marietta. He died on July 13, "under the shade of a tree by the side of the road on the banks of Paint creek, a few miles from Chillicothe."

George Whitefield Burnet's character seems to have impressed deeply those who knew him. A contemporary, Judge John Wilson Campbell, wrote a biographical memoir some thirty years after Burnet's death, which recalled his studiousness, diligence, orderliness, temperance and eloquence.

SOURCES: J. W. Campbell, *Biog. Sketches* (1838), 92-98 ("uniform and decided"); T. Alden, *Collection of Amer. Epitaphs & Inscriptions* (1814), IV, 272; Min. Fac., 29 Nov. 1790, 13 July 1792; J. McVickar, *Early Years of the late Bishop Hobart* (2d. ed., 1836), 203-04 ("The bare," "through a," "so that"); Amer. Whig Soc., *Cat.* (1840), 6; *N.J.*

Journal, 10 Oct. 1792 ("an oration"); *Dunlap & Claypoole's Amer. Daily Advt.*, 8 Oct. 1795; Hobart, *Corres.*, I, 20, 22, 140, 151 ("George is going," "our political"); D. C. Skemer, "The *Institutio legalis* and Legal Education in N.J.: 1783-1817," *N.J. Hist.*, 97 (1979), 127, 134; Riker, 46; *N.J. Wills*, VIII, 59; *OSAHQ*, 48 (1939), 237; J. Burnet, *Notes on the Early Settlement of the North-Western Territory* (1847), 37 ("under the shade"); [Newark, N.J.] *Centinel of Freedom*, 5 Aug. 1800. Campbell's assertion that George Whitefield was present at the birth of his namesake and requested that the infant be trained for the ministry is apocryphal. Whitefield died in 1770.

PUBLICATIONS: STE #s 35258 & 37069

JJL

James Chesnut

JAMES CHESNUT, A.B., A.M. 1795, planter and public official, was born February 19, 1773 at "Knight's Hill" plantation, Camden, South Carolina, the oldest son of Capt. John Chesnut and Sarah Cantey Chesnut. James's sister Sarah later married John Taylor (A.B. 1790), and his sister Margaret Rebecca married James Sutherland Deas, brother of David Deas (A.B. 1789), Henry Deas (Class of 1789), and Robert Deas (Class of 1792). The father was a wealthy merchant and planter, a partner in the Kershaw stores with his brother-in-law Ely Kershaw. At the beginning of the Revolution he was attached briefly to the Third South Carolina Regiment but resigned when an attack of rheumatism kept him in bed for six months. After his recovery he served in the Georgia campaign and later at Charleston, where he was taken prisoner at the evacuation of the city. He was on parole at his plantation in August 1780 when Francis Rawdon-Hastings, Lord Rawdon, ordered the inhabitants to take up arms against the approaching American army. John Chesnut was one of those who refused and, as a prisoner, was chained to the floor. He never lost the marks of the irons on his ankles or his resentment of the British for this treatment. He served in both houses of the South Carolina legislature and held a number of other public appointments, including that of presidential elector for Thomas Jefferson (LL.D. 1791) in 1796. At his death his estate included a town lot in Camden, 9,907 acres of land and approximately 205 slaves.

James Chesnut may have received some early schooling in Camden at the academy run by Capt. John Reid. He spent at least a year at the Mount Sion College in Winnsboro, South Carolina, rooming in the same boarding house as John Taylor. In June 1788 he set sail from Charleston with the two Taylor cousins, John and Jesse (A.B. 1791), bound for Philadelphia and Princeton, where he spent the next four years. A newspaper account of the Nassau Hall grammar school competitions the following fall places Chesnut third in the graduating class; presumably the faculty felt he needed additional preparation during the summer months before admitting him to the freshman class of the College. On June 10, 1789 he joined the Cliosophic Society, where he used the name of Hume, for David Hume, the Scottish philosopher, historian, and religious skeptic. On July 25, 1792 he was "deemed culpable and that thought a sufficient punishment for improper language concerning the Society when out of the same." Nonetheless, the society awarded him its diploma. At a meeting in July 1792 to make commencement assignments, the faculty selected Chesnut to deliver one of the intermediate orations. For some reason Chesnut did not participate in the ceremonies.

Chesnut returned to South Carolina and devoted his time to the management of his estates and to public affairs and civic duties. After inheriting three large plots of land from his father in 1818, he kept adding acreage until he owned five square miles of real estate south of Camden, all valuable land extending along the Wateree River. On September 20, 1796 he married Mary Cox, daughter of Esther and John Cox of Philadelphia, who had earlier owned a country seat on the Delaware River, not far from Trenton, New Jersey. When George Washington passed through Trenton in 1789 on his way to his inauguration as president, Mary Cox and her sister were among the thirteen young ladies who represented the various states in the welcoming celebration. As a student Chesnut may have traveled from Princeton to Trenton to observe these festivities. The couple had thirteen children, seven of whom survived to adulthood.

In 1797 Chesnut became an incorporator of the Pine Tree Navigation Company and also served as a commissioner for laying out the limits of the town of Camden, South Carolina. He apparently declined nomination to the South Carolina House of Representatives in 1802, but the following year he was elected and sat for Kershaw District from 1804 to 1806, 1808 to 1810, and 1814 to 1816. From 1806 to 1807 he was the intendant, or mayor, of Camden, and from 1810 to 1812 he sat in the South Carolina Senate. In 1832 he was again elected to the state senate as a unionist, after a bitterly fought campaign in which he defeated his brother-in-law John S. Deas of the nullifiers. He served in the senate until 1836. Chesnut was a colonel in the local militia, and at various times he was also commissioner of roads, commissioner to superintend repairs to the Kershaw District courthouse, and commissioner of public buildings. In 1808 he was an incorporator of the Camden Episcopal Church. He served as director of the Camden branch of the state bank from 1822 to 1833 and as a trustee of South Carolina College from 1853 to 1857.

Chesnut lived in Camden until 1820, when he built a home on

"Mulberry Plantation," two miles south of the town. It was a two and one-half story brick and stone house, severely plain, with a broad piazza and a ground floor basement, approached through a grove of oaks and laurels. Four dormers broke the lines of the slate roof to provide the extra half story. A long brick outbuilding was the domain of Mary Chesnut, where she taught her slaves spinning, weaving and other household crafts. Chesnut also built a second home at "Sandy Hill," three miles east of "Mulberry" on higher ground, where the family summered. A road, apparently kept in perfect order, was laid out between the two residences in a long straight line. Tradition claims that whenever Chesnut's coach traveled this road or the road to Camden, outriders were sent ahead to see that the way was perfectly clear.

The Reverend Robert Wilson, reminiscing about a trip to Camden in 1861, remembered that the Chesnuts were staying at the same hotel. He recalled James Chesnut as a courtly old gentleman who always rose when his wife entered the room, lit her candle at night, accompanied her to the stairway, and bowed as she went off to her room. Both died at "Bloomsbury," a home that Chesnut had built for their daughter Sarah, and were buried in the Chesnut family cemetery near Camden. Chesnut died February 17, 1866, aged ninety-three, less than two years after his wife's death.

A son John Chesnut entered the College as a sophomore in 1815 but was one of the fourteen students dismissed for taking part in the riot of January 1817, when rebellion over the length of reading assignments reached its peak. A letter of February 6 from his sister Serena conveyed family sympathy. Their father, she said, would like John to be readmitted, even if he later transferred to another college. James Chesnut had already written to President Ashbel Green (A.B. 1783) on the subject of his son's readmission, but his petition was apparently denied. John graduated from Union College in 1819 and became a state senator.

James Chesnut, Jr. (A.B. 1835), the youngest of the thirteen children, was reputedly one of the most popular southerners in the College. He served in both houses of the South Carolina legislature, where he was a firm opponent of the attempt to reopen the African slave trade. Elected to the United States Senate in 1858, he tendered his resignation on November 10, 1860. The resignation was not accepted, but he was formally expelled on July 11, 1861. He served as a military aide to Jefferson Davis with the rank of colonel and was promoted to brigadier general in the field for gallantry. His wife Mary Boykin Miller Chesnut became well known for her posthumously published Civil War memoir, first published as *Diary from*

Dixie, now available in a critical edition as *Mary Chesnut's Civil War* (1981). Charles H. Chesnut (A.B. 1958) is a direct descendant.

SOURCES: Alumni files, PUA; *Biog. Dir. S.C. House Rep.*, III, 138-40; *N.J. Jour., & Polit. Intelligencer*, 29 Oct. 1788; Min. Fac., 10 Nov. 1789, 29 Nov. 1791, 13 July 1792; Clio. lists; Clio. Min., 25 July & 16 Aug. 1792; *N.J. Jour.*, 10 Oct. 1792; *Dunlap & Claypoole's Amer. Daily Advt.*, 8 Oct. 1795; *SCHGM*, 11 (1910), 243-45; 61 (1960), 19; 62 (1961), 247-48; 66 (1965), 47, 52; Writers' Program, S.C., *S.C.: Guide to the Palmetto State* (1941), 312; T. J. Kirkland & R. M. Kennedy, *Historic Camden* (1905), I, 35, 367, 369; D. R. Roller & R. W. Twyman, *Encyc. of Southern Hist.* (1979); E. B. Reynolds & J. R. Faunt, *Biog. Dir. of the Senate of S.C.* (1964), 196-67.

MANUSCRIPTS: South Caroliniana Lib., ScU, has family letters and papers of three generations of the Chesnut family, including papers and letters of JC dated 1801-56 and the Clio. Soc. diplomas of John Chesnut (Class of 1818) and James Chesnut, Jr. (A.B. 1835)

RLW

William Chetwood

WILLIAM CHETWOOD, A.B., A.M. 1795, lawyer, soldier, banker, and public official, was born on June 17, 1771 in Elizabethtown, Essex (now Union) County, New Jersey, the son of John and Mary Emott Chetwood. The mother was the daughter of John and Marie Boudinot Emott and a first cousin of longtime College trustees Elias and Elisha Boudinot. John Chetwood was an early supporter of the American Revolution, serving on the Essex County committee of correspondence and representing the county as a delegate to the 1775 provincial congress. Apparently he was a lawyer, for he served as an associate justice of the state's supreme court from 1788 until 1797. A member of the state convention which ratified the Federal Constitution in 1787, he became a Federalist. The Chetwood family hailed originally from Salem County, New Jersey, where they were Quakers, but John was an Anglican, serving as one of the first vestrymen of St. John's Church in Elizabethtown, where he had William baptized on July 21, 1771. William's siblings included Elizabeth, who married Aaron Ogden (A.B. 1773), later governor of New Jersey, and John, who fathered John Joseph Chetwood (A.B. 1818). James C. Williamson and William R. Williamson (both A.B. 1794) were his first cousins once removed. His first cousin Jane Chandler married John Henry Hobart (A.B. 1793), third Episcopal bishop of New York.

The location of Chetwood's preliminary education has not been discovered. His father was a trustee of the Elizabethtown Academy, which reopened in June 1789 after a ten-year hiatus, and so he could have spent a year there. In November 1790 he entered the College as a junior. He joined the American Whig Society, and his

William Chetwood, A.B. 1792

classmate John Conrad Otto nostalgically recalled a few years after they graduated that Chetwood had been one of a large group of classmates from that society who were "much attached to each other." In June 1791 Chetwood was one of nine students reproved by the faculty for swimming at night without permission, but his years at the College seem to have been otherwise uneventful. When he graduated he was assigned an intermediate honors oration and spoke "On the condition of an old bachelor lately married."

Chetwood began reading law under his father. In 1794, however, he took a break from his studies to join the army being raised to put down the Whiskey Rebellion. On September 9, 1794 he enlisted for three months as a corporal in a troop of light dragoons, and only nine days later he obtained a commission as assistant brigade major, part of the general staff of the New Jersey Brigade. Here he somehow caught the eye of Gen. Henry Lee (A.B. 1773), commander of the army being sent to quell the insurrection, and became one of his aides-de-camp on October 20. The army returned from western Pennsylvania without having seen combat, and Chetwood and the rest of the New Jersey contingent were discharged in Trenton on December 25. For the rest of his life he was referred to as Major Chetwood.

Back in Elizabethtown, he resumed his legal studies. Sometime after it was revived in June 1794, he joined the *Institutio legalis*, a moot court consisting mainly of law clerks apprenticed to Newark or Elizabethtown attorneys. In September 1796 he was called to the bar of New Jersey as attorney, and on September 6, 1799 he became a counsellor-at-law. On August 16, 1804 he obtained an appointment as a master-in-chancery, and he became a sergeant-at-law in February 1816. He opened an office in Elizabethtown and practiced there successfully for many years. He also regularly attended the sittings of the supreme court at Trenton. A contemporary later recalled Chetwood as "one of those indefatigable workers who, by persistent industry, are pretty sure to succeed." From 1812 to 1829 he was Essex County's deputy attorney general, a post later called prosecutor of the pleas.

Chetwood married Mary Barber, one of three children of Francis Barber (A.B. 1767) and his second wife Anne Ogden Barber, on March 24, 1800, Rev. Henry Kollock (A.B. 1794) officiating. Francis Barber was a schoolmaster and Revolutionary War officer who died in 1783 while serving at Newburgh, New York. Mary Barber's brother was George Clinton Barber (A.B. 1796). Chetwood and his wife, who survived him, lived at 20 East Jersey Street in Elizabethtown and proceeded to raise a family of nine daughters and three sons, including Francis Barber Chetwood, the father of Robert Edes Chetwood (A.B. 1858) and Francis Barber Chetwood, Jr. (A.B. 1863).

In 1818 Aaron Ogden, Chetwood's brother-in-law, resigned the presidency of the State Bank at Elizabeth, which had been founded in 1812. Chetwood, who was already a director, took over as president and served until the end of 1821. He remained a director until 1828. His salary as president was $100 a year, and since the bookkeeper received $400 and the clerk $150, his responsibilities must have been fairly light. The discovery that Ogden had borrowed $30,000 of the bank's capital while president as part of his unsuccessful efforts to avoid bankruptcy, however, complicated Chetwood's tenure. The bank's subsequent efforts to retrieve the money continued long after Chetwood relinquished the presidency, but it contrived to weather the crisis. Although he remained a stockholder for the rest of his life, by 1837 Chetwood's connections with the bank may have loosened somewhat, for in that year he was one of twelve incorporators of the Citizens and Mechanics Bank of Elizabeth.

Chetwood was involved in a number of ventures designed to improve transportation. In June 1814 he and eleven associates started a steamboat and teamboat company, headed by John N. Simpson (A.B. 1794), which sought to compete with the company founded by Robert Fulton and Robert R. Livingston (A.M. 1780) in the passenger trade between New York and New Jersey. The legal monopoly on steamboat travel in New York state enjoyed by the Fulton group eventually proved too strong to contend with, and Simpson's company disbanded in March 1815. On February 9, 1831 Chetwood was named an incorporator of the Elizabethtown and Somerville Rail Road Company. It was the first railroad chartered in the state, but delays in construction prevented it from being the first built. At his death Chetwood owned stocks and bonds of several railroad companies, as well as a ferry company and a turnpike.

From his various activities Chetwood reportedly "accumulated a very handsome estate, a considerable part of which ... was invested in New York insurance company stocks, and was lost by the great fire which occurred in 1835, leaving him, however, a competent support." When he died the inventory of his personal estate came to almost $100,000, the bulk of which consisted of stocks, bonds, and obligations.

Politically William Chetwood began as a Federalist, as his father had been. In 1824, however, he supported Andrew Jackson. Many Federalists at this time abandoned John Quincy Adams (LL.D. 1806), whom they regarded as a renegade for having joined the cabinet of James Monroe (LL.D. 1822). In January 1828 Chetwood served as a delegate to the New Jersey Jackson convention, and later that year he participated in a mass meeting in favor of Jackson at Elizabethtown. His efforts notwithstanding, Adams carried the town by a two-to-one margin. In 1829 Chetwood received two votes in the balloting for governor in the state legislature. Perhaps his experience in banking motivated his subsequent defection to the Whigs, which seems to have been triggered by Jackson's attack on the Bank of the United States in 1832-33.

Chetwood's political career reached its zenith in 1836, when he was chosen to complete the term in the United States House of Representatives of Philemon Dickerson, brother of Mahlon Dickerson (A.B. 1789), who had resigned upon his election as governor of New Jersey. Chetwood was present when the second session opened on December 5, 1836 and was assigned to the committee on public expenditures. He participated in about three-fourths of the roll-call votes but did not speak on the floor of the House. He seems to have opposed abolition, for he voted to kill a bill to abolish slavery in the District of Columbia. After his term ended on March 3, 1837 Chetwood did not sit in Congress again. His officeholding concluded with service as mayor of Elizabethtown from 1839 to 1842 and with terms in the upper house of the New Jersey legislature in 1841 and 1842.

A contemporary later recalled that by February 1852 Chetwood had already "retired from active business." He continued to participate in community affairs as a member of the Elizabethtown Temperance Society and an active parishioner of St. John's Episcopal Church. In 1857 its rector, Samuel Adams Clark, published a history of the church which he dedicated "To the venerable senior warden of Saint John's Parish, the honorable William Chetwood." The recognition came just in time. Chetwood died on December 18, 1857 and was buried in Elizabeth's Evergreen Cemetery.

SOURCES: W. O. Wheeler, *Ogden Family in Amer.* (1907), 141, 259; J. J. Boudinot, *Life, Public Services, Addresses & Letters of Elias Boudinot* (1896), II, 391; *NYGBR*, 62 (1931), 22, 129-30; E. F. Hatfield, *Hist. of Elizabeth, N.J.* (1868), 320-21, 410-11, 418, 520, 542, 559-60, 650, 664; Elmer, *N.J. Bench & Bar*, 180-81, 279, 459-61 ("one of those," "accumulated," "had retired"); W. H. Shaw, *Hist. of Essex & Hudson Cnties., N.J.* (1884), I, 215-16, 244; R. P. McCormick, *Experiment in Independence: N.J. in the Critical Period 1781-89* (1950), 268, 294; *GMNJ*, 3 (1927/28), 14, 151; 6 (1930/31), 37, 39, 115; 7 (1931/32), 59; alumni file, PUA; Amer. Whig Soc., *Cat.* (1840), 6; Hobart, *Corres.*, I, 140 ("much attached"); Min. Fac., 29 Nov. 1790, 22 June 1791, 13 July 1792; broadside 1792 "Order of Commencement," PUA ("On the condition"); *Dunlap & Claypoole's Amer. Daily Advt.*, 8 Oct. 1795; N.J. Adjutant General's Office, *Records of Officers & Men of N.J. in Wars 1791-1815* (1909), separately paginated section on 1794 Pa. insurrection, 3-6, 10, 23; D. C. Skemer, "The *Institutio legalis* & Legal Education in N.J., 1783-1817," *N.J. Hist.*, 97 (1979), 127, 134; Riker, 35, 37-38, 41; P. L. Kleinhans, *Down Through the Years: The Story of the National State Bank of Elizabeth, N.J.* (1937), 28, 54-56, 61, 63, 68, 162; T. Thayer, *As We Were: The Story of Old Elizabethtown* (1964), 153, 217, 226-27, 243-48, 252; R. T. Thompson, *Col. James Neilson ... 1784-1862* (1940), 120, 124-25; WC's will, 3 Dec. 1850, proved 4 Jan. 1858, & estate inv., 16 Apr. 1859, proved 4 May 1859, MSS in Nj (photocopies in PUA); N.J. History Symposium, 9th, Trenton, 1977, *Jacksonian N.J.* (1979), 60, 81; *NJHSP*, n.s., 8 (1923), 170, 177; 9 (1924), 217; 14 (1929), 463-65; 16 (1931), 210; *NJHSP*, 56 (1938), 280-81; 57 (1939), 72; 77 (1959), 232;. R. Fee, *Transition From Aristocracy to Democracy in N.J. 1789-1829* (1933), 263; U.S. Cong., *Cong. Globe*, 24th Cong., 2d sess., 2, 18, 101; U.S. Cong., *Reg. of Debates in Cong.*, 24th Cong., 2d sess., 1156-57; letter from Ray Urbanik, Deputy City Clerk of Elizabeth, 1 May 1985, PUA; S. A. Clark, *Hist. of St. John's Church, Elizabethtown, N.J.* (1857), dedication page ("To the venerable"), 174-75.

PUBLICATION: The memoir of Chetwood's father-in-law Francis Barber by "W.C." in J. Herring & J. B. Longacre, *National Portrait Gallery of Distinguished Americans* (1834-39, 4 vols.), II, unpaginated, 4 pp. (not in later eds.), is attributed to Chetwood in *NYGBR*, 62 (1931), 21.

MANUSCRIPTS: NjP; NjP-SSP; MB

JJL

Robert Deas

ROBERT DEAS, physician, was the younger brother of David Deas (A.B. 1789) and Henry Deas (Class of 1789). He was one of the ten children of Elizabeth Allen Deas and John Deas of Charleston,

South Carolina, and "Thoroughgood Plantation" at Goose Creek, about whom Charleston wits liked to say, "he had nine sons and each had a sister." John Deas was a prominent and wealthy Charlestonian, active in community life, who was a partner with his brother in a slave trading firm.

The older Deas brothers had been trained at the College's grammar school, and Robert probably went to the same school, especially since his two brothers were then in residence at the College. He was admitted as a freshman in November 1788. Deas joined the Cliosophic Society on June 17, 1792 but its records incorrectly identify him as a resident of Virginia. The 1837 and 1840 Cliosophic catalogues list him as an honorary member. However, as Brother Cimon, he was an active member on July 5, 1792 when, as first-assistant, he chaired a society meeting in the absence of the president. He was required to repeat his junior year, for the faculty minutes list him as a junior in November 1790 and again for the winter session of 1791. The faculty minutes for July 20, 1792 show that Deas was called before the faculty because he had been "for some time quite irregular in his behavior and had not attended the examination [the quarterly examination at the end of the spring term] upon being reprimanded for his misconduct Deas treated the Faculty with such insolence and manifested so great a disposition for disorder that it was thought proper to remove him from the college resolved that he be dismissed from the college."

Deas became a physician in Charleston, practicing at 57 Queen Street. In 1799 he married Margaret Philp Campbell, daughter of Margaret Philp and Lt. Archibald Campbell. A stone in St. Michael's churchyard in Charleston notes the death of two of their children, Elizabeth Allan Deas, who died September 19, 1802, aged eleven months and twelve days, and Mary Philp Deas, who died July 10, 1810, aged nineteen months and six days. Deas himself died in January 1839 at Stoney Creek, South Carolina.

SOURCES: *Biog. Dir. S.C. House Rep.*, III, 178-80; H. K. Leiding, *Charleston, Historic & Romantic* (1931), 171; Min. Fac., 10 Nov. 1789, 20 July 1792 ("for some time"); Clio. lists; Clio. Soc., *Cats.*: (1837), 7; (1840), 29; D. E. H. Smith & A. S. Salley, Jr., *Reg. of St. Philip's Parish* (1971), 9; *SCHGM*, 57 (1956), 105; C. Jervey, *St. Michael's Church & Churchyard, Charleston, S.C.* (1906), 87; Charleston city directories.

RLW

Peter Early

PETER EARLY, A.B., lawyer, judge, and public official, was born on June 20, 1773 in the part of Culpeper County, Virginia, that became Madison County in 1792. He was the eldest son of Joel and Lucy Smith Early. Clement Early (A.B. 1799) was one of his four brothers and three sisters. Their mother was probably from Orange County, Virginia, since that is where she married. Joel Early was a planter who migrated to Georgia in 1791. There he resided in Wilkes County initially but eventually established himself at a plantation called "Early's Manor," at Scull Shoals on the west bank of the Oconee River in Greene County. A political supporter of Thomas Jefferson (LL.D. 1791), Joel Early was wealthy and affected to live in the style of an English baron in his mansion, which was reckoned to be one of the finest in his part of the state. In his will he attempted to extend his authority beyond the grave by placing his property in the hands of trustees until his sons were forty-five years old, disinheriting two younger sons, and giving directions on how to prune his orchards and rest his fields. Jubal Early, Peter's first cousin, was the grandfather of Jubal A. Early, lieutenant-general in the army of the Confederate States of America.

While "quite a young man," Peter Early joined a Baptist church in Virginia, although he later came to doubt that his conversion experience had been genuine and seldom attended services. He received his preliminary education at the grammar school in Lexington, Rockbridge County, Virginia. The repeated assertion that he went on to attend Liberty Hall Academy, the forerunner of Washington and Lee University, seems to be without foundation. He entered the College as a junior in November 1790. In the same year he joined the Cliosophic Society, taking as his name Addison, a reference to the English essayist and playwright. Early was active in the society, delivering several of its more important orations and receiving its diploma. At his commencement he delivered the English salutatory oration, an honor reserved for the student standing second in his class. The topic of his speech was "Sympathy."

For three years after his graduation Early pursued legal studies, dividing his time between Princeton and Philadelphia. He remained unusually active in the Cliosophic Society, serving one-month terms as president while staying in Princeton in December 1792 and June 1794. In Philadelphia he studied under the younger Jared Ingersoll (LL.D. 1821, A.B. Yale 1766), father of Charles Jared Ingersoll (Class of 1799) and Joseph Reed Ingersoll (A.B. 1804). Early was admitted to the Philadelphia bar on April 21, 1795.

Peter Early, A.B. 1792
BY BRYANT BAKER

Shortly after completing his education in the law, Early joined his father in Wilkes County, Georgia, and began a practice there. In 1797 he married Anne Adams Smith, the fourteen-year-old daughter of Francis and Lucy Wilkinson Smith, who had moved to Wilkes County from Bedford County, Virginia. She bore him three daughters and three sons. Early rapidly built up an extensive law practice and was soon acknowledged to be one of the leading attorneys in the up-country of Georgia. About 1801 he moved to Greene County and a residence near his father's later called "Fontenoy."

After John Milledge resigned from the United States House of Representatives in 1802 to become governor, Early won the subsequent election and took his seat on January 10, 1803. He was elected to the next two congresses as well. While he was in Washington he left his law practice in the care of William Harris Crawford, who later became a United States senator, cabinet member, and, in 1824, presidential candidate.

Early's election caused misgivings in some circles. In a letter to Governor Milledge, George M. Troup (A.B. 1797) declared that the "Western People" had sacrificed "political principle to personal attachment" in choosing Early, whom he classed with "sanctified Demagogues." Troup maintained that Early's "politics if not decidedly Federal are at least on that doubtful complexion with our Party." Senator James Jackson observed two weeks after Early arrived in Washington that Early "has hitherto given republican votes and behaved well," but hinted darkly that "the Yazoo lads depend greatly on him," a reference to Early's contention that however corrupt the transaction had been, Georgia could not violate its word by retracting its land grants in the celebrated controversy over the Yazoo land fraud of 1794-1796.

Actually Early turned out to be a good Jeffersonian on most issues and did not make himself obnoxious about the Yazoo claims. He spoke frequently and well. Jackson observed of his maiden speech on January 26, 1803, in favor of an unsuccessful bid to permit foreigners to take out patents, that it was made "very handsomely, & is much praised." On another occasion a few weeks later he said that Early "spoke well, and as a speaker is admired." Early's initial activities in Congress centered on unsuccessful efforts to obtain federal payment of wages owed to militiamen who had served on the Georgia frontier during Indian troubles from 1793 to 1794. Jackson blamed the bill's failure on a tactical error he ascribed to Early, but his maneuvers mattered less than the general conviction that Georgia had exceeded its authority in calling out the militia and had waived whatever claims were valid as part of the settlement by which it ceded its western lands to the federal government in exchange for a cash payment.

On January 2, 1804 the House chose Early one of eleven managers to conduct the Senate trial of United States District Judge John Pickering of New Hampshire, whose alcoholism and possible insanity led to his impeachment and subsequent removal from office. Early opened the case before the Senate on March 7, 1804, and was thus the first man to present formal articles of impeachment to that body. Early placed second in the balloting for the managers, ahead even of John Randolph (Class of 1791), suggesting the speed with which he gained the esteem of his House colleagues. That December Early's newly acquired expertise in impeachment law was again called on, when he was chosen one of seven House managers, along with Randolph and George Washington Campbell (A.B. 1794), in the unsuccessful Senate trial of Supreme Court Justice Samuel Chase, following Chase's impeachment by the House for misconduct in office. After the examination of witnesses was concluded, Early officially opened the case for the managers on February 20, 1805 by speaking for ninety minutes. The speech was generally conceded to have been eloquently delivered, but Senator John Quincy Adams (LL.D. 1806) observed that it cited no authorities and added little new to Randolph's remarks at the commencement of the trial. Senator William Plumer dismissed the address as "much declamation & little argument."

During his second full term in Congress, Early played a major role in the debates on banning the slave trade. On January 21, 1806 he spoke against a bill to impose a tax of $10 on each imported slave. He argued that since South Carolina was the only state which permitted the practice, such legislation would both wound its feelings and place a fiscal burden unfairly on just one state. Furthermore, if slavery was as wicked as its opponents said, the nation should not support itself by taxing it. In any event, every time slavery was discussed in the House, bad feelings and unruly passion ensued, and Early concluded that the subject "ought never to be introduced."

Later in the year Early's opposition even to discussing legislation on slavery must have altered, for he drafted the original bill reported by a select committee appointed to consider prohibiting the slave trade when the constitutional ban on such a measure ended in 1808. Presumably he was chosen to this committee by virtue of his position as chairman of the House committee of commerce and manufactures. The bill as written by Early immediately ran into opposition from opponents of slavery. It proposed treating slaves as contraband like brandy, to be condemned and sold, with part of the proceeds going to the informer. His opponents insisted that the slaves be freed, a move Early asserted would render the bill ineffectual by removing the informer's incentive. "Do the United States," he indelicately asked, "instead of selling it [smuggled brandy] as a forfeited article scatter it about the streets?" The analogy did not impress his foes, who hoped that a slave trader's fears could be as powerful a motive as an informer's greed. They proposed that violators of the slave importation ban be put to death. Early found this approach impractical on two counts. Southerners would never provide evidence if death were the penalty, since they "do not believe it immoral to hold human flesh in bondage." Many regarded slavery as a "political evil" likely to lead to grave problems in the future, but not a crime. Furthermore they would oppose the bill because it left freed slaves in their midst, and playing host to numbers of free blacks, ever "the instruments of murder, theft and conflagration," was more to be avoided even than slavery itself. If shiploads of blacks were freed on southern shores, the whites would act in their own defense: "Not one of them would be left alive in a year." Surely the opponents of slavery did not want this result, Early argued.

In the event, the bill which became law specified a prison term rather than death for importers and turned illegally imported slaves over to the jurisdiction of the state in which they were found. Early had originally proposed the latter as a compromise which would permit the slaves to be sold without implicating the federal government in the practice, but he voted against the bill in its final form. Either his original stance was disingenuous, or he could not approve of the imposition of prison terms in addition to fines, since they implied a moral judgment against slavery and set the treatment of slave importers apart from that accorded to other smugglers.

Other episodes in Early's congressional career suggest that he was a loyal Jeffersonian. He supported an unsuccessful bid to return jurisdiction over the parts of the District of Columbia not in the city of Washington to Maryland and Virginia, thus providing residents with representation and ending the "disgraceful" spectacle of "a country where the principles of freedom extend to the remotest extremity, whilst there is a despotism at the heart." He backed Jefferson's prosecution of the supporters of the Miranda Expedition in 1806 and opposed a motion criticizing Gen. James Wilkinson, and through him Jefferson, for their handling of the Burr conspiracy. Early fiercely opposed Congressman Andrew Gregg's proposal that imports of British goods be banned but voted for the much weaker measure which became law in the Non-Importation Act of 1806. Early did oppose Jefferson's defense policy. He showed a healthy skepticism about initial estimates of the cost of an ambitious fortification program and asked awkward questions about the relative cost and efficacy of Jefferson's program of building gunboats while neglecting the blue-water navy.

Early chose not to run for reelection and left Congress in 1807. The death of his father around this time may have prompted this move, or he may have become aware that a judgeship could be his and preferred the latter office. From December 1807 to November 1813 he was a judge of the Georgia superior court on the Ocmulgee circuit. The circuit was a new one comprising nine counties, some of them on the frontier and created so recently that Early presided over their first county courts. In order to obtain Early's services, his home county of Greene was transferred to the new circuit. At this time Georgia lacked a supreme court, so that the superior court justices were the highest judiciary in the state. Contemporaries later recalled Early as a model judge. Certainly he looked the part. Described as having a "natural dignity of manner," he appeared decisive, sad, reflective, and "severe and haughty" but not affected. One acquaintance could not remember having seen him smile.

For most of his adult years Early was active in efforts to promote education. He served on the board of trustees of the fledgling University of Georgia from October 1797 until 1808, and in November 1801 he became a commissioner of the Greene County Academy. In 1811 he again became a trustee of the University of Georgia as part of a reorganization which reduced the number of trustees to five. On August 9 of that year Josiah Meigs, the only faculty member who had been there for any length of time, was dismissed for calling all of the trustees except Early "a damned pack or band of Tories and speculators," bent on looting the school's land endowment. Eventually Rev. John Brown was found to replace Meigs, but when he resigned in May 1816 the school seemed to be on its last legs, and later that year classes were suspended briefly. Early, the senior trustee, was a key figure in keeping the university alive at this juncture. He probably influenced the successful tender of the presidency to Rev. Robert Finley (A.B. 1787) of New Jersey. The school reopened in January 1817 with Early himself serving as president pro tem until Finley's arrival in Athens on May 31. Under Finley, the prospects of the institution seemed to be improving, but he died in office within a year, shortly after Early's own death.

Early resigned his judgeship in 1813 to accept election to a term as Georgia's governor which began on November 5. The War of 1812 was the principal concern of his term, and Early is said to have been an energetic war governor, although hampered by his legislature's frugality. He maintained that the federal government must be permitted to run the war effort and was generally receptive to its needs, meeting its demands for levies of troops and seeking to have the militia laws revised to facilitate this task. On several occasions he took the risky step of advancing state money to local detachments of federal troops without waiting for legislative approval of the loans, but his trust both in state endorsement of his action and subsequent federal repayment seems to have been justified. The main problem Georgia faced throughout the war was holding in check the Creeks on its frontier, but the crisis of Early's tenure came in January 1815 when he learned that the British under Adm. George Cockburn had landed on Georgia's coast. On his own authority he ordered a contingent of militia commanded by Gen. David Blackshear to march to the threatened spot immediately. Blackshear's army had been placed under national authority and was under orders to proceed to Mobile, so that Early's order, which Blackshear obeyed, could have led to recriminations later. Instead both sides learned that the war had ended, keeping the damage the British inflicted and any criticism of Early to a minimum.

On November 11, 1814 Early vetoed the Alleviating Bill, a measure to extend the workings of a law preventing foreclosure on debtors first passed during the depression of 1808. He argued that the law was unconstitutional because it impaired the obligation of private contracts, that in addition it made *"fraud familiar"* by accustoming men to think that contracts imposed "no moral obligation," and that it was in any event no longer expedient, the depression being over. An initial attempt to override his veto failed. Although the measure passed in a modified form later in the session, Early's veto signaled a shift in public opinion away from the stay law, which emboldened the state's judiciary to strike the law down within a year. However, Early's action is credited with arousing enough enmity to ensure his defeat when he ran for reelection in November 1815.

Early must have realized that his veto would be unpopular, but he is said to have gone home disgusted and vowing to retire from public life. If so, his friends in Greene County talked him out of it a year later, when they sent him to the state senate. He died in office on August 15, 1817 and was buried on the west bank of the Oconee river near his plantation. A century later, Early was reinterred in a cemetery in Greenesboro, Greene County's seat. In 1818 the state legislature named Early County in his memory.

SOURCES: K. Coleman & C. S. Gurr, eds., *Dict. of Ga. Biog.* (1983), I, 281-82; S. F. Miller, *Bench & Bar of Ga.* (1858), I, 345-50 (memoirs supplied by Joel Crawford & John G. Slappey: "natural dignity," 347; "severe," 349; *"fraud,"* "no moral," 350), 415-60; *WMQ*, 1st ser., 4 (1895/6), 59; G. G. Smith, *Story of Ga. & Ga. People* (1901 repr. 1966), 165; L. L. Knight, *Ga.'s Bicentennial Memoirs & Memories* (1933), IV, 375-77; T. B. Rice & C. W. Williams, *Hist. of Greene Cnty., Ga. 1786-1886* (1961), 288-91; als, Joel Early to James Madison, 7 Dec. 1802, James Madison Papers, DLC (microfilm ed.); A. Sherwood, *Gazetteer of the State of Ga.* (3d. ed., 1837), 272-74 ("quite a young"); S. S. Early, *Hist. of the Family of Early in Amer.* (1896), 14-21; R. H. Early, *Family of Early* (1920), 107-08, 116, 293-98, 302, 314-17; letter from Special Collections Librarian, Washington & Lee Univ., 1 June 1983, PUA; Min. Fac., 29 Nov. 1790, 13 July 1792; Clio. lists; Clio. Min., 6 July 1792–9 July 1794, *passim*; broadside 1792 "Order of Commencement," PUA ("Sympathy"); Hobart, *Corres.*, I, 29-30; J. McVickar, *Early Years of the late Bishop Hobart* (2d ed., 1836), 76; *Martin's Bench & Bar*, 265; *WMQ*, 1st ser., 6 (1897/8), 48-49; H. M. Thomason, "Gov. Peter Early & the Creek Indian Frontier, 1813-15," *GHQ*, 45 (1961), 223-37; *BDUSC*, 945; C. C. Mooney, *William H. Crawford 1772-1834* (1974), 8-9; H. M. Salley, *Corres. of John Milledge, Gov. of Ga.* (1949), 70-71, 75, 89-90 ("has hitherto," "very handsomely"), 92 ("Western People"), 94-98 ("spoke well," 95), 110, 161; B. McCullar, *This is Your Ga.* (1972), 314-16; A/C, 7th Cong., 2d sess., 343, 424, 535-43; 8th Cong., 1st sess., 796, 968-75; 8th Cong., 2d sess., 312-29, 762, 887-91 ("disgraceful," "a country"); 9th Cong., 1st sess., 363-65 ("ought never"), 371-72, 381, 391-95, 514-15, 530-31, 623-28 ("the destruction," "the height"), 748-49, 877, 1090; 9th Cong., 2d sess., 113-14, 151, 167-69 ("Do the United"), 173-75 ("the instruments," "not one"), 182, 185, 188-89, 237-39 ("do not believe," "political evil"), 321, 461, 464, 477-78, 517-20, 627, 1266-70; P. C. Hoffer & N. E. Hull, *Impeachment in Amer. 1635-1805* (1984), 208, 215-16, 236, 242-45, 255; W. P. Cutler & J. P. Cutler, *Life, Journals & Corres. of Rev. Manasseh Cutler* (1888), II, 183; "Letters of Samuel Taggart, Representative in Congress, 1803-14,"

AASP, n.s., 33 (1923), 162; C. F. Adams, ed., *Memoirs of John Quincy Adams* (1874), I, 355; W. Plumer, *William Plumer's Memorandum of Proc. in the U.S. Senate 1803-07* (1923), 104-05, 295, 300, 533 ("much declamation"); *Jour. of the House of Rep. of the U.S.* (1826), V, 182, 465, 470; letters, Albert Gallatin to PE, 6, 22, 25 Jan. & 3 Feb. 1807, Gallatin letterbook, DNA, & on microfilm Gallatin Papers (for PE chairman of Comm. of Commerce & Manufactures); T. O. Brooke, *In the Name of God, Amen: Ga. Wills 1733-1860* (1976), 59; F. M. Chalker, *Pioneer Days Along the Ocmulgee* (1970), 35, 37-38; E. C. Hynds, *Antebellum Athens & Clarke Cnty. Ga.* (1974), 71-73, 149; E. M. Coulter, *College Life in the Old South* (1951), 20 ("a damned"), 23, 30; typescript of Trustees' Min., Univ. of Ga., photocopy of selected dates, 1810-17, supplied by its archivist, 8 Apr. 1985, PUA; E. W. G. Boogher, *Secondary Education in Ga., 1732-1858* (1933), 140; I. V. Brown, *Memoirs of the Rev. Robert Finley* (2d ed., 1857), 156-63, 174, 188; *Journal of the Senate of the State of Ga.*: (1813), 19, 34-36; (1814), 5-7, 33, 36-38, 40-41; (1815), 5-6; G. White, *Statutes of the State of Ga.* (1849), 220-22; R. W. Patrick, *Florida Fiasco* (1954), 99-100, 281, 287-90, 300; F. L. Owsley, *Struggle for the Gulf Borderlands* (1981), 51; J. C. A. Stagg, *Mr. Madison's War* (1983), 357-58; M. S. Heath, *Constructive Liberalism: The Role of the State in Econ. Development in Ga. to 1860* (1954), 168-69; A. Johnson, *Ga. as Colony & State* (1938), 202; *Niles' Weekly Reg.*, 11 Oct. 1817. The antecedents upon which were based the twentieth-century sculpture of PE depicted here have not been identified.

MANUSCRIPTS: Georgia Dept. of Archives & Hist., Atlanta; Thomas Jefferson Papers, DLC

JJL

Jacob Ford

JACOB FORD, A.B., lawyer, was born in Morristown, Morris County, New Jersey, on March 15, 1772, the youngest of the six children of Jacob Ford, Jr., and Theodosia Johnes Ford. He was preceeded at the College by two elder brothers, Timothy (A.B. 1783) and Gabriel (A.B. 1784). His maternal grandfather the Reverend Timothy Johnes, who baptized him on April 12, 1772, was a trustee of the College from 1748 until 1788, William Johnes (Class of 1776) was an uncle, and Stevens Johnes Lewis (A.B. 1791) was a first cousin.

The Ford family, originally from Duxbury, Massachusetts, settled in New Jersey around 1701. Ford's grandfather Jacob Ford, Sr., was a tavern owner, an iron manufacturer, and a county judge. He served as a representative to the New Jersey assembly in 1772 and was later active on the local committee of correspondence. Ford's father Jacob Ford, Jr., joined his father in the iron manufacturing business. In 1762 he married Theodosia Johnes, whose father was pastor of the Presbyterian church of Morristown. An ardent patriot, Jacob Ford, Jr., built a powder mill which supplied shot and shell for George Washington's army. He became a colonel of the local militia in 1775 and was involved in a number of skirmishes with the British. During one of these encounters he caught a severe chill which resulted in the pneumonia from which he died on January 11, 1777. Jacob was not yet five when his father died, but the father's will expressed his wish that his sons be provided with a "liberal education." In the winter of 1779-80, when the spacious Ford home was used to house General Washington's staff, Jacob, his mother, and siblings lived in two rooms in the side wing of the house.

Ford entered the College as a sophomore in November 1788 and joined the Cliosophic Society on the 26th of that month, taking the name of Cymbeline. He was evidently a poor student and repeated his junior year during the academic year 1790-91. It would be interesting to know just how he spent the summer of his senior year, since a note signed by John Witherspoon, dated June 9, 1792, states: "These testify that the Bearer Mr. Jacob Ford, a Member of the Senior Class in the College Now is in full Standing in his Class & without Reproach either as to his Study or Behavior so that whatever Reports may have been raised to his Prejudice at a Distance are without foundation."

Even though his study habits were above reproach, Ford was recommended for graduation only after being reexamined on the Monday before commencement. At his graduation exercises on September 26, 1792, Ford spoke as opponent to the question, "Is there any evidence from the radical resemblance of the languages of different nations, that mankind sprung from one source?" Attached to Witherspoon's testimonial of June 1792 is a list of the debts unpaid by Ford at the time of his graduation. Included are the accounts of the College steward and several local merchants for a total of £64.14.5 or $176.66, with a note "all paid since." A month before graduation Ford was dismissed from the Cliosophic Society as "deemed unworthy a seat in this Hall."

Jacob soon joined his older brother Timothy in Charleston, South Carolina, and probably received his law training there, for he was admitted to the South Carolina bar in 1796. He joined the law firm of Timothy Ford and Timothy's brother-in-law Henry William DeSaussure. Both of these men served in public offices and were also active in civic and religious organizations, but Jacob Ford does not seem to have achieved the same degree of prominence in the community.

On January 21, 1797 he married Ann Motte Peronneau, the daughter of Mary Hutson Peronneau and the deceased Arthur Peronneau, both members of prominent Charleston families. The father had been a well-known and wealthy merchant in the city. The Fords attended the Independent Congregational Church in Charleston, where Timothy Ford was an active member and where Mrs. Ford's family had worshiped for several generations. There are church records of the baptism of seven children born to Jacob and Ann Ford: Mary Hutson, Elizabeth DeSaussure, William Hutson, Henry William, Emma Theodosia, Arthur Peronneau, and Charles Edward. Timothy Ford's will, written July 25, 1827 and proved January 27, 1831, bequeathed the Ford family revolutionary sword, which both he and his father had carried, "to my nephew Frederick Ford, the Son of my brother Jacob." There is no baptismal record for Frederick, but he is probably the Frederick A. Ford who joined the South Carolina bar in 1826. Jacob Ford died in Charleston on April 22, 1834.

Sources: Alumni file, PUA; *DAB* (sketch of father); T. Thayer, *Colonial & Revolutionary Morris Cnty.* (1975), 109; R. S. Green & W. Durant, eds., *Record, First Pres. Church of Morristown, N.J.* (1880-85, 5 vols. in 1), I-II, 134; E. Lindsley, *A Certain Splendid House* (1974), 23-24; Clio. lists; Clio. Min., 22 Aug. 1792; MS testimonial of John Witherspoon, 9 June 1792, John Witherspoon Collection, NjP; Min. Fac., 10 Nov. 1789, summer sess. class list & 29 Nov. 1790, 13 July, 14 Aug., 25 Sept. 1792; *N.J. Jour.*, 10 Oct. 1792; O'Neall, *Bench & Bar S.C.*, II, 600; *SCHGM*, 5 (1904), 218-20; 12 (1911), 57; 13 (1912), 132-33; 23 (1922), 212; 33 (1932), 173, 310; 34 (1933), 96, 100, 102, 162, 164, 216; 59 (1958), 115.

RLW

Charles Wilson Harris

CHARLES WILSON HARRIS, A.B., A.M. 1796, A.M. University of North Carolina 1799, educator and lawyer, was born in 1771 at "Mill Grove," the family home on Rocky River in the Poplar Tent section of present Cabarrus County, North Carolina, which was once part of Anson and later of Mecklenburg County. His mother was Mary Wilson Harris, daughter of Zaccheus Wilson, a signer of the Mecklenburg Declaration of Independence. His father was Robert Harris, also a signer of the famous document, a planter and revolutionary veteran who lost an arm in the skirmish at Clapp's Mill, a preliminary to the battle of Guilford Courthouse. Robert Harris was the elder brother of Samuel Harris (A.B. 1787) and of Jane Harris Reese, mother of Edwin Tasker Reese (A.B. 1794). His daughter Jane Wilson Harris married Nathaniel Alexander, brother of Joseph McKnitt Alexander, Jr. (A.B. 1792).

Charles Harris was raised in what was a center of Scots-Irish Presbyterianism, where his father was a ruling elder of the Poplar Tent Church, and he received his early education in the Poplar Tent Academy. His name first appears on College records as a junior. He may have been a late matriculate in the summer session of 1791, for his name was added at the end of an otherwise alphabetical list of juniors. He joined the American Whig Society and at his commencement ranked third in his class and delivered the mathematical oration.

Harris next accepted a teaching position in a Virginia school, perhaps Hampden-Sidney. Wherever he was teaching during this period, he considered it only a temporary occupation and planned instead to study medicine with his uncle, Dr. Charles Harris. In a letter to his uncle dated April 28, 1793 Harris wrote that a teaching colleague had recommended the study of divinity, a suggestion that he firmly declined. He then discussed his intentions in regard to the study of medicine.

> The great Blackstone says a knowledge of law is necessary to a physician, that he may be useful to families upon sudden emergencies, in drawing up the formal part of last wills and testaments. Great encouragement indeed for one who has scarcely time to perfect the study of medicine, to set into the perusal of endless commentaries, reports, statutes, etc. But without so much preparation I have almost determined to go at once to physic. When I first undertook my present business I expected it and my professional study would agree, but it is otherwise. Next winter is the time appointed in my own mind for beginning on this new study. I shall acknowledge with a great deal of gratitude any directions you may transmit me. What are made the rudiments of this art and what branches are generally entered upon first? I may at a leisure hour look over some of them.

Harris studied medicine with his uncle, who was a half-brother of his father, and whose home estate "Favoni" adjoined that of Robert Harris. The aspiring doctor soon decided, however, that medicine was not his life's calling, and by the spring of 1795 he was installed as professor of mathematics at the University of North Carolina, which had opened in January with the Reverend David Ker (Kerr) as presiding professor, yet with no additional faculty members over whom he could preside. Harris's presence on the campus is first mentioned in a letter of April 5, 1795 to the Reverend Charles Pettigrew from his sons John and Ebenezer, who claimed that they liked Mr. Ker and "Mr. Harras" very well.

In spite of Harris's decision to abandon medicine, he maintained a warm relationship with his uncle, and on April 10 he wrote to him extolling the liberal constitution of the college. It is plain that Harris had absorbed some radical ideas from reading Mary Wollstonecraft, namely, that the natural weakness of a woman's body does not extend to her mind, and that "overloading the memory with words of a dead language" should not be a requirement for a college degree. He described Ker as a violent Republican and Samuel Stanhope Smith (A.B. 1769), vice president of the College, as an aristocrat, whose published sermon *The Divine Goodness to the United States,* "smells strong of British seasoning." A later historian of the University of North Carolina thought Harris was "tinctured with the prevailing Voltaireism of the day." Harris's letter suggests that his father may have refused to send Charles's younger brother, Robert Wilson Harris, to the institution because of a distrust of his elder son's ideas and principles; however, Robert did enter the University of North Carolina the following summer. By this time Harris had decided on law as a career and had started studying Blackstone on his own.

By June 1795 he had organized a group on the Chapel Hill campus known simply as the Debating Society, but with the name later Hellenized to the Dialectic Society. An early decision that the group should divide produced The Concord Society, and the two enjoyed the rivalry in oratorical contests with which Harris was familiar as a member of Nassau Hall's American Whig Society. In July he wrote to his uncle of plans to start a university museum and asked his assistance in donating worthwhile specimens and also in contacting friends and relatives who might be interested in helping. At the time of Harris's letter the sole acquisition of the new museum was an ostrich egg; in 1803 he was able to contribute a "Bezoar stone from the stomach of a deer." With the demands of these extra interests on his time, his progress in the study of law was slow, but he declared himself to be firm and determined in his course. A letter to his uncle written November 12, 1795, says of the trustees of the university, "The more I know of their affairs and of my own disposition and qualifications, the more I am determined against engaging in their business for life."

In spite of Harris's disinclination toward teaching and his habit of riding to nearby Hillsboro as often as possible to enjoy "refined society," he seems to have maintained a good rapport with Ker, and he probably roomed in the president's home. By the time of Ker's resignation in the summer of 1796, the Reverend Samuel McCorkle (A.B. 1772) had been added to the faculty as professor of moral and political philosophy and history, and Samuel Allen Holmes, possibly Allen S. Holmes (Class of 1788), and Nicholas Delveaux were tutors in the preparatory school. McCorkle had apparently accepted the professorship with the understanding that he would take over the duties of presiding professor. Presumably because of the opposition of trustee William R. Davie (A.B. 1776), who doubted McCorkle's

executive ability and distrusted the clergy in general, the board chose
to consider McCorkle's conditions of acceptance unreasonable and
therefore regarded them as a refusal of the position. Harris was
reluctantly persuaded to assume the responsibilities of the head of
the university, but at the same time he gave notice that he would
resign at the end of the term in December so that he could devote
his full attention to his long-delayed law studies.

Harris apparently acquitted himself well during his six-month
tenure as presiding professor; when the trustee members of the committee of visitation examined the students in December, the young
men showed more than satisfactory improvement and were accorded
the approbation of the committee. Meanwhile, Harris lost no time in
trying to procure a successor. On June 1, 1796 he wrote to his classmate John Conrad Otto, requesting the address of Joseph Caldwell
(A.B. 1791). Not realizing that Caldwell was a tutor at Nassau Hall,
Harris knew only that he had been engaged in teaching and hoped
that if not permanently settled he might be persuaded to accept his
own position as professor of mathematics and natural philosophy
at a salary of $500 per year, which "in time to come will be more
valuable." Caldwell answered within the month, indicating that he
had been preparing for the ministry and had been planning to apply
for his license the following spring but that he could be persuaded to
change that decision. He asked for full information about the North
Carolina institution, its faculty, students, buildings, and funds, and
whether Harris considered teaching there fatiguing and oppressive.
At the same time he cautioned that even if he considered the position, he would not be able to leave Princeton until after the College
commencement the following fall.

On July 24, after conferring with the trustees, Harris wrote a
lengthy letter in which he answered all of Caldwell's questions in great
detail and indicated that the trustees had authorized him to inform
Caldwell that he could be certain of the appointment if he decided to
accept the terms that Harris had outlined. Harris did not believe that
his duties had been oppressive. "I received my reward," he explained,
"in finding myself useful to an institution which was zealously patron-
ized by the whole state." He found Chapel Hill to be a healthy spot
but warned that because it was situated so far in the interior, clothing would be more expensive than at Princeton. He mentioned the
"uncultured & uninviting" society of the neighborhood and warned
that in such a rural location Caldwell would "generally be confined to
the company of teachers, students or books." However, there were
visits from some of "the most respectable gentlemen in the state."
Harris promised any assistance which might be needed and sent his

respects to members of the Princeton faculty, adding, "I would willingly receive the degree of A. M. if I should be thought worthy of it & it could be procured in my absence. I suppose there is some expense attending it, which if you defray I will remit by some opportunity." Caldwell apparently took care of this request and, to Harris's great satisfaction, accepted the professorship. When sending him traveling advice, Harris mentioned that he would be ordering about $100 worth of books "in the city," undoubtedly Philadelphia, and asked Caldwell to make arrangements to have them shipped along with his own trunks.

Harris relinquished his post of presiding professor at the end of the year in accordance with his previously tendered resignation, and by early April 1797 he was settled in the court town of Halifax, studying under the auspices of William R. Davie, who was elected governor of the state in the fall. Harris was licensed to practice in 1798, and the next year when Davie traveled to France as one of President John Adams's peace commissioners, he left his practice in his protégé's care. Harris's lively correspondence with his uncle and his brother Robert gives hints that he was already suffering from tuberculosis. He described Halifax as "sickly country," a place to leave during the "sickly months" whenever possible for travel to the higher areas of the state that he considered more healthy. In February 1799 he wrote of his recovery since the past October, through "a regular course of the Rushonion ... practice of physic," i.e., the massive bloodletting recommended by Benjamin Rush (A.B. 1760). Harris claimed to have regained his "former complexion and strength" by letting blood every other day and drinking salts continually. The copious amount of liquids that he drank may have helped him survive the regimen of bloodletting. In June he wrote of going through another period of the same treatment.

In spite of his ill health, Harris's legal abilities were respected enough that he was urged by fellow Federalists to submit his name to the general assembly for a judgeship, but he declined. However, his letters show a keen interest in politics and a strong Federalist bias. He maintained an active interest in the University of North Carolina, and in 1800 he was elected a trustee and appointed to the visiting committee which conducted the examinations of the students. Harris was generous with advice to his younger brother, but when the latter suggested that Charles move from Halifax to some more healthful spot, he answered on March 15, 1800:

It is possible I might recover my health by a removal and find business in my profession in other parts of the state, but I have not relinquished all hopes of a perfect recovery even here. I am now engaged in a practice about to become valuable, I have in a great measure overcome the embarrassments of a young prac- titioner, am employed in cases of great moment to my friends, their confidence in me has been personal. It would be a poor return for me to make them for their attention, either to with- draw myself from their suits or to place them in the hands of another Attorney....

In July he spent several weeks at Shockoe Springs in Warren County, where he hoped that the change of climate, regular exercise, and par- taking of the local mineral springs would bring about some improve- ment in his physical condition. His hopeful attitude toward the future never wavered as he began the study of French with the Marquis de Clugny, a French refugee who was staying in nearby Warrenton. He returned to Halifax feeling slightly better. In October he wrote of still being troubled by fever, but he kept busy clearing and planting a field for pasture and building a kitchen. "It is right," he insisted, "and the only way to make life comfortable, always to be engaged in some plans." A letter of 1802 expressed his pride in his new nephew and namesake, Charles Wilson Harris (A.B. 1823). Although he had earlier rejected an ocean voyage as taking too much time from his practice, by May 1803 he was making preparations for a passage to either Bermuda or the Bahamas, depending on which he could obtain. Still outwardly cheerful and hopeful of improvement, he now set his affairs in order, leaving a will appointing his brother execu- tor, arranging for a fellow attorney to collect his debts, and selling a young Negro girl to the owner of her father. He reached Nassau in the Bahamas on July 14, but the desired salubrious effect on his health did not materialize and late in the year he returned to North Carolina. He died at his brother's home at Sneedsboro on January 12, 1804.

SOURCES: Alumni file, PUA; Min. Fac., class list ca. May 1791, 13 July 1792; Amer. Whig Soc., *Cat.* (1840), 6; *N.J. Jour.*, 10 Oct. 1792; *Greenleaf's N.Y. Jour., & Patriotic Reg.*, 7 Oct. 1796; *Hobart Corres.*, I, 25; *Princetonians, 1769-1775*, 245-49; *Prince- tonians, 1776-1783*, 25-31; H. M. Wagstaff, "The Harris Letters," *James Sprunt Hist. Publications*, 14 (1916), 1-91 (quotes from letters). See K. P. Battle, *Sketches of the Hist. of the Univ. of N.C.* (1889), R. D. W. Connor, *Doc. Hist. of the Univ. of N.C. 1776-99* (1953), & K. P. Battle, *Hist. of the Univ. of N.C.* (1908), for background information on the University of North Carolina and biographical material on Harris and his colleagues.

Several sources speculate that upon his return to the South, immediately after his 1792 commencement, Harris taught for a time at Hampden-Sidney College in Prince Edward County, Virginia. That claim probably rests on the opening sentence in a letter dated July 30, 1793, to his uncle, Dr. Charles Harris, "I have just come from P. Edward which place I left in tip-top spirits, expecting on my return to find at least three or four letters in Petersburg." A letter of July 24, 1796 from Harris to Joseph Caldwell at the time Caldwell was considering a teaching position at the University of North Carolina, advised him to make a stop in Philadelphia and receive instructions in the use of various mechanical apparatus, since their exposure to "experimental Philosophy" at Princeton had been "inexcusably deficient." Harris then added, "I should have appeared often very ridiculous in my own eyes had I not gotten a smattering of experimental Philosophy by visiting Williamsburg in Virginia." This could indicate that Harris was actually living at Williamsburg in 1793 and had made a visit to Prince Edward County, stopping at Petersburg, the regular stage stop, on his return to Williamsburg. His letter to his uncle mentions the refugees from St. Domingo who had come to Virginia, news that would more likely be heard by someone residing in a coastal city. An earlier letter to his uncle dated April 28, 1793, refers to a Reverend Robinson, "a partner in teaching." Neither the catalogues of the College of William and Mary nor those of Hampden-Sidney College, both admittedly incomplete, lists Harris or Robinson as members of the faculty, although either or both could have been teaching in a preparatory grammar school near either institution.

RLW

Robert Heriot (Harriott)

ROBERT HERIOT (HARRIOTT), A.B., lawyer, was born May 1, 1773 in All Saints Parish, Georgetown, South Carolina, the son of Robert and Mary Ouldfield Heriot. His father was a Scottish immigrant who married a wealthy heiress of the Georgetown area in July 1761. Mary Ouldfield, the only child of John and Anne LaRoche Ouldfield, was orphaned in 1751 and inherited several large plantations and seventy-three slaves. Col. Thomas Middleton, under whom Robert Heriot, Sr., fought in a 1759 expedition against the Cherokees, was her guardian. By the 1790 census Robert Heriot, planter and merchant, listed holdings of 3,888 acres in Georgetown District and 128 slaves. His partner in the trading firm of Heriot and Tucker was Daniel Tucker.

The Revolutionary years were eventful ones for the family. Heriot fought on the side of his adopted country, while his wife took over the management of their plantation and that of her brother-in-law William Heriot. Even during the vicissitudes of the war she maintained a school for the children on the plantation. Lieutenant Colonel Heriot fought at the battle of Fort Moultrie and was captured after the fall of Charleston. Granted a parole stipulating that he proceed to one of the sea islands instead of returning to Georgetown, he was given special permission to visit his home because of serious illness in his family. His leave was extended on August 8, 1780 by Maj. James Wemyss because Heriot's wife and son were very ill and his daughter Janet had died the day before. The ailing son could have been either Robert or his older brother John (Class of 1789). In May 1781 when Francis Marion took Georgetown from the occupying British, a departing British ship fired a last defiant shot which passed through the Heriot house.

Sometime in 1784 young Robert sailed north to enter the Nassau Hall grammar school, stopping in Philadelphia where he was warmly received by the prominent merchant Tench Coxe. Coxe reported the arrival in a letter of July 28 that reached Georgetown two months later, but Robert Sr. had no opportunity to respond before October 24 because of "the distressed & calamitous situation of my family, particularly, one of my children having lain at the point of death, for above twenty days." Presumably that child was not John, who should also have been in the grammar school at that time and had probably traveled to Princeton with his younger brother. The father thanked Coxe "for your kind reception of my little Son," presumably eleven-year-old Robert and not John, who by then was about sixteen. He assured Coxe that "I shall consider it peculiar happiness, your taking him under your patronage, & a favor your supplying what money may be wanting for his use, which shall be thankfully & punctually reimbursed you, in what ever way you are pleased to direct." Coxe had already invited young Robert to spend his fall vacation with his own family in Philadelphia. The proud father could not resist describing the boy as a lad "of a most amiable natural disposition; & utterly free from vice." He "has not been wanting in improving to the best advantage, the little opportunity he has had of education, which has been no other for these some years past, than the little tuition he received from myself, & that, but too often, interrupted by the duties of a public active station, & a long exile. I beg he may want for nothing you think proper in his situation, & that he may have what pocket money you judge sufficient."

Robert Heriot entered the College as a sophomore in November 1789, shortly after his brother had left without taking a degree. Sometime during his three years at Nassau Hall he joined the American Whig Society. Just weeks before his graduation, he probably learned from a Philadelphia newspaper, the August 20, 1792 issue of *Dunlap's American Daily Advertiser*, that his father had died on July 22 in a tragic accident. While dining in Georgetown with other gentlemen, Robert Sr. heard a disturbance in the street, stepped out upon a second-story gallery to see what was happening, and tumbled to the ground with sixteen or seventeen others when the rotting structure gave way. "Col. Heriot had one of his legs broke and the foot of the other leg badly cut, which mortified in a few days and carried him off." Yet Robert Jr. remained in Princeton through graduation. At his commencement he was the opponent in the first dispute on the program: "Considering the present state of human nature, does not the existence of war among nations seem necessary? In effect, do not wars contribute more to the elevation of the human character, to the improvement of the arts, and even to the happiness of mankind, than a state of universal peace, abused as the degeneracy of man always abuses the long continuance of prosperity?"

Heriot returned to South Carolina to study law and won admission to the bar in 1797. Two years later he and his brother John became joint trustees for the property of their sister Susanna Mann Heriot in a prenuptial agreement drafted when she married Robert Brownfield, a Georgetown physician. On June 3, 1804 Heriot married his second cousin Maria (Marie) Elizabeth Heriot. He practiced in Georgetown and on at least one occasion engaged Daniel Webster (LL.D. 1818) to handle a complex, out-of-state, maritime case. Apparently Heriot avoided politics except to serve one term as mayor in 1819. However, he was an active participant in other community affairs. He belonged to the local fire company and on March 8, 1801 was elected one of its engine masters. In 1827 he headed a group that organized the local Bible society as an auxiliary of the American Bible Society, and that same year he helped draft the constitution of the Winyaw Anti-Duelling Association, which he then joined. Maria Heriot was responsible for organizing the Georgetown Ladies Benevolent Society. The couple had five sons and four daughters. Heriot died on March 12, 1846 and was interred in the burial ground of St. Luke and St. Paul's Church, Charleston.

SOURCES: Alumni file, PUA (geneal. information from descendant Wm. H. Harrington); R. Heriot, Sr., to T. Coxe, 24 Oct. 1784 ("distressed & calamitous"), Papers of Tench Coxe, Coxe Family Papers, PHi (microfilm ed., reel 46); Heriot letters, 15 Aug. 1786; Min. Fac., 10 Nov. 1789, 13 July 1792; Amer. Whig Soc., *Cat.* (1840), 6; *Dunlap's Amer. Daily Advt.*, 20 Aug. 1792 ("Col. Heriot"); *N.J. Jour.*, 10 Oct. 1792; *Biog. Dir. S.C. House Rep.*, III, 100-01, 331-32; A. S. Salley, *Marriage Notices in the S.C. Gazette & its Successors (1732-1801)* (1902), 22; *SCHGM*, 13 (1912), 113; 32 (1931), 197-98; 43 (1942), 181; G. C. Rogers, *Hist. of Georgetown Cnty., S.C.* (1970), 61, 118, 124, 133-34, 142, 165, 262, 309, 363, 528; O'Neall, *Bench & Bar S.C.*, II, 601; RH to D. Webster, 28 Nov. 1820, C. M. Wiltse, ed., *Microfilm Ed. of the Papers of Daniel Webster* (1971), reel 3, frame 2932; B. H. Holcomb, comp., *S.C. Marriages, 1688-1799* (1980), 29 (trustee for S. M. Heriot); T. E. Wilson & Janice L. Grimes, *Marriage & Death Notices from the Southern Patriot, 1831-48* (1986), II, 46.

MANUSCRIPTS: Daniel Webster Papers, Dartmouth College, Hanover, N.H.

RLW

Benjamin Hodgdon

BENJAMIN HODGDON, A.B., merchant, was the son of Samuel Hodgdon of Massachusetts (probably Boston) and Philadelphia, and his first wife Mary Ranger (Rainger), whom he married in Boston on July 19, 1768 when he was twenty-two. During the Revolutionary

War Samuel joined the patriot cause as a captain of artillery in 1776, served at Ticonderoga in 1776-77, then at White Plains and various places in Connecticut and New York at least into 1779. By then he was deputy commissary-general of military stores, and in July 1781 he was promoted to commissary-general, a position he held officially until 1784 and continued less formally after that. Probably about 1781 he moved his family to Philadelphia where, as the war ended, he and Timothy Pickering (LL.D. 1798), a future secretary of state, entered into a mercantile partnership in 1783. The firm did not prosper and dissolved after two years, but the two men and Tench Coxe, another Philadelphia merchant, also invested together in frontier lands in Pennsylvania and other states. From March 1791 to April 1792 Samuel, a Federalist, served as quartermaster general of the United States Army, an office that gave him the principal responsibility for supplying the disastrous expedition of Gen. Arthur St. Clair (father of Daniel St. Clair, possibly "St. C.," Class of 1785) against the Indians of the Northwest Territory. When the Indians routed St. Clair in November 1791, Hodgdon was for a time believed dead, a rumor that probably reached his son as he began his senior year at the College. In November 1790 in the Second Presbyterian Church of Philadelphia with Ashbel Green (A.B. 1783) presiding, Samuel had married his second wife Mary Hodge, daughter of Andrew and Jane McCulloch Hodge and sister of Andrew Hodge, Jr. (A.B. 1772), and Hugh Hodge (A.B. 1773). Thus Benjamin Hodgdon was a stepcousin to Hugh Lenox Hodge (A.B. 1814) and Charles Hodge (A.B. 1815).

Hodgdon matriculated at the College as a freshman. He joined the Cliosophic Society on March 10, 1790, using the name Septimus, probably for the Roman Emperor Septimus Severus. Society minutes for the annual commencement day meeting on September 26, 1792 record that "Brother Septimus" was granted a society diploma and that he delivered the valedictory address for the meeting. At his graduation ceremony he was replicator of the dispute on the question, "Is the policy of India and ancient Egypt, of dividing the people into different classes, and confining children to the profession of their fathers, preferable to that universal freedom of enterprize that prevails in Europe?"

By 1797 Hodgdon had settled in Boston where according to the federal direct tax records of 1798 he rented a shop at No. 67 Long-Wharf that measured twenty feet by thirty-five and was valued at $2,000. He acted as an agent for his father's firm and also tended to other family matters. For example, on December 29, 1797 he signed a receipt acknowledging the acceptance by Henry Knox of Samuel Hodgdon's draft for $2,500 due on January 13, "which sum is on account of a certain bond due by said Knox to Winthrop Sargent Esq. in possession of my father Samuel Hodgdon and accepted by George Meade for $1500" and of Knox's acceptance "of my father's bill payable the 19th of Jany. next for $800, on account of the above acceptance of George Meade." When his uncle Alexander Hodgden, Esq., a former state treasurer of Massachusetts, died in 1797, Benjamin joined the widow Nancy Lewis Hodgdon in trying to let the fine new Dedham home that Alexander had purchased a few years before. Benjamin Hodgdon, sometimes described as "junior" in Boston records probably to distinguish him from some older relative, was listed in the Boston directories of 1798 and 1800. He served the town as a clerk of the market in 1798-99.

In a strangely cold reference to Hodgdon, his father wrote Winthrop Sargent from Philadelphia on June 14, 1802 that "my family is well," but "Poor Benjamins health has obliged him to take a voyage to the West Indies. I doubt much of his return." Benjamin was probably suffering from a wasting disease, such as tuberculosis, and he may indeed have failed to survive the excursion. The Cliosophic Society recorded his death in 1803. No obituary has been found in Boston newspapers.

SOURCES: Daughters of the Amer. Rev., *D.A.R. Patriot Index* (1966), 334; Samuel Hodgdon pension records, Revolutionary War Pension Applications, File W3720, DNA; Heitman, 293; R. K. Showman et al., eds., *Papers of Gen. Nathanael Greene* (5 vols. to date, 1976-   ), IV, 15, 188, 196, 222; G. H. Clarfield, *Timothy Pickering & Amer. Diplomacy, 1795-1800* (1969), 11; J. E. Cooke, *Tench Coxe & the Early Republic* (1978), 81; E. Risch, *Quartermaster Support of the Army: A History of the Corps, 1775-1939* (1962), 77-110; Registry Dept., Boston, *Boston Marriages* (1903), 52; H. L. Hodge, *Memoranda of Family Hist.* (1903), 21, 121; MS Records of the Second Pres. Church of Phila., PHi; MS Summaries of Wills, Book 2, p. 54, PHi; Timothy Pickering Papers, MHi, microfilm ed., reel XXXV, 149; J. T. Scharf & T. Westcott, *Hist. of Phila.* (1884), I, 588; A. Ritter, *Phila. & Her Merchants* (1860), 83; *Hamilton Papers*, XXII, 129; O. Pickering & C. W. Upham, *Life of Timothy Pickering* (4 vols., 1867-73), II, 141; III, 22-24; Min. Fac., 10 Nov. 1789, 13 July 1792; Clio lists; Clio. Min., 26 Sept. 1792; *N.J. Jour.*, 10 Oct. 1792 ("Is the policy"); *Susquehannah Papers*, XI, *passim* Henry Knox Papers, MHi, microfilm ed., XLI, 52 ("which sum"); Boston city directories, 1798, 1800; W. H. Whitmore et al., eds., *Report of the Record Commissioners of the City of Boston* (39 vols., 1876-1909), XXII, 62; XXXV, 30; O. A. Roberts, *Hist. of the Military Company of the Mass. now Called the Ancient & Honorable Artillery Company of Mass., 1637-1888* (4 vols., 1895-1901), II, 207-08; Boston *Columbian Centinel*, 7 Mar. 1798; S. Hodgdon to W. Sargent, 14 June 1802 ("poor Benjamin"), Winthrop Sargent Papers, MHi (microfilm ed., reel 6).

The Benjamin Hodgdon, sea captain, listed in Philadelphia directories for 1797 and again from 1802 through 1808, when apparently he died at age 55, was not the Princetonian. He was probably the brother of Samuel Hodgdon.

RLW

William Arden Hosack

WILLIAM ARDEN HOSACK, A.B., attorney, soldier, and adventurer, was born on June 11, 1772, in New York City, the third son of Alexander and Jane Arden Hosack. His eldest brother was David Hosack (A.B. 1789), the eminent physician. Their father, a native of Scotland, served in the British army, with which he came to America during the French and Indian War. He chose to remain and set himself up in New York City as a merchant, first in liquor, then in woolen and linen drapery. In 1768 he married Jane, the daughter of a butcher, Francis, and Jane Jennings Arden. The Hosack family remained in New York City during the British occupation and apparently succeeded in maintaining a politic neutrality which kept them from being branded as tories thereafter. William received his early education at a boarding school, although which one is unclear. Perhaps like his brother he attended the academy Alexander MacWhorter (A.B. 1757) kept in Newark or the Hackensack academy of Peter Wilson. In 1788 he entered Columbia College and remained there for one year.

Hosack transferred to the College of New Jersey as a sophomore in November 1789 and joined the American Whig Society. His college career was a troubled one. On November 29, 1790 Hosack was convicted of lying, swearing and "acting in direct opposition to lawful authority to the number of eight different times in the course of a single week." For these "enormities" he was admonished in the presence of his class and required to read a confession to John Wright Vancleve (A.B. 1786), the tutor he had especially offended. Hosack experienced difficulty again on June 22, 1791 when the faculty identified him as the ringleader in two escapades on the night of June 17. First he and two other students rode the horses at pasture behind the campus. Then they rounded up five more students and went swimming, returning "at a very unseasonable hour." Hosack's offense was further compounded by "gross profanity." Accordingly he was suspended and readmitted a week later only after reading a confession and apology. Despite these misadventures, Hosack graduated on September 26, 1792. At his commencement he took part as opponent in a disputation on the topic "Is the emancipation of slaves, without preparing them by a proper education to be good citizens, consistent with humanity and sound policy?"

Hosack's whereabouts for the next five years have not been ascertained, but presumably he read law for at least part of the time, since a 1797 New York City directory listed him as an attorney at 2 Pine Street. By 1798 he had moved to 45 Vesey Street, his father's house. The return to his father's address may hint that his legal practice was not prospering, for the next year Hosack gave it up to take a commission in the United States Army. He may also have acquired a taste for the military in New York City's brigade of militia, where he served as ensign in 1794, lieutenant in 1797, and captain in 1798. Whatever the motivation, Hosack was lieutenant in the Second Regiment of Artillerists and Engineers, United States Army, from September 9, 1799 to May 8, 1801. His brother David was by this time a friend and the family physician of Alexander Hamilton (LL.D. 1791), and this relationship may explain Hosack's appointment. Presumably he was a Federalist, for almost all appointments to the officer corps at this time went to those sympathetic to that party. No reason for his resignation has been discovered, unless he regarded his prospects for advancement as blighted by the succession of Thomas Jefferson (LL.D. 1791) to the presidency. In 1802 he was once again listed as an attorney in a New York City directory, this time at 7 Nassau Street. He was at 62 William Street in 1803 and back again at his father's address in Vesey Street in 1804.

His frequent changes of address and failure to escape reliance on his father may once again point to an unsuccessful legal career, or perhaps boredom was just setting in when, on February 2, 1806, Hosack sailed away on the *Leander*, bound for South America with the Miranda Expedition. This venture, headed by Francisco de Miranda, was an attempt to free Colombia and Venezuela, and ultimately all of South America, from Spanish rule. Some 200 New Yorkers were recruited by Miranda and his agents under a variety of pretexts, with many not knowing the expedition's precise destination and objectives until the ship was under sail. On February 14 Hosack received his commission as a first lieutenant of artillery in the "army of Columbia." Before the year was out the expedition had dissolved in chaos. Two descents on the coast of Venezuela proved conclusively that the natives were not prepared to flock to Miranda's banner and resulted only in the capture of sixty of the American volunteers, of whom ten were ultimately executed. Hosack was not among those captured and was probably with the *Leander* when it limped into Grenada on October 21, 1806. Here the expedition disbanded. Some of its members were impressed into the British Navy while trying to make their way home to New York. It is tempting to place Hosack in this category, for he next surfaced in London as a companion of Aaron Burr (A.B. 1772).

Burr arrived in England in July 1808 and first mentioned Hosack in his journal in March 1809. From then until December they were on intimate terms, often sharing lodgings and traveling together during moves from London to Stockholm, where they stayed from May until

October. From there they went to Hamburg and finally to Brunswick, where Burr left Hosack to go to Paris. Burr was seeking European backing for his schemes against Spanish possessions in America while he waited for the furor over his trial for treason and for pressure from his creditors to die down in the United States. The nature of his connection with Hosack at this time is obscure because the only source, Burr's journal, mentions Burr's objectives only rarely and in the most veiled language, but it seems likely that Burr had enlisted Hosack as an aide in his latest attempt at empire. He would have known of Hosack through his brother David, a friend and the family physician of Burr. Hosack's demonstrated, albeit unfortunate, experience as a soldier and filibuster would in any event have commended him to Burr.

Certainly the British government believed that Hosack was Burr's man, for when it arrested Burr and seized his papers on April 4, Hosack was taken into custody later the same day. Both were soon released, Burr with an apology. The motivation for the incident is unclear, although it reflects the government's embarrassment at and disapproval of Burr's activities at this time. While they were in Stockholm, Burr was angling for Russian support; he mentioned sending a letter to "Count Romanyoff" via a Russian courier on August 2. He also said Hosack "ought to write by this Russian messenger a letter on which his very existence depends; have been urging him a fortnight; it could be done in fifteen minutes, but will not be done." Sure enough, the Russian messenger left without Hosack's letter.

If Hosack was indeed Burr's right-hand man at this time, Burr soon found that he was not a flawless one. He constantly complained of Hosack's lack of punctuality, his laziness and forgetfulness, and his delicate constitution. Several time Hosack failed to keep appointments when he had arranged to meet Burr. While in Stockholm Burr wrote that "Hosack came in at 9 to *breakfast*, as engaged; no other way to make him punctual." On another occasion Burr walked several miles out of Stockholm to attend a "musical party" to which he had been invited only to find no one at home. The next day he learned that Hosack had been charged with telling him that the party had been postponed but had neglected to do so. Despite these shortcomings, Burr was evidently fond of Hosack, with whom he enjoyed playing chess. He must also have trusted him, for in Hamburg, after a long spell of tight finances, Burr contrived to cash two large bills of exchange the same day "so I am at this moment rich. Left the sacks [of money] at Hosack's and walked home."

For his part Hosack must quickly have found that attendance on an emperor-in-waiting was more exciting in theory than practice. The tasks Burr assigned him ranged from the mundane to the menial. At one time or another Burr had Hosack change his currency, carry messages, help him pack, copy a French translation of the Swedish constitution, and help him get into formal dress for the coronation of a new Swedish king. Furthermore, Burr seems to have regarded him patronizingly; at one point he commented that Hosack "came in at 10, and amused me with the news of the day and his little incidents." On the whole their parting on December 24, 1809 must have been mutually bearable, if not agreeable.

In Stockholm, Hosack befriended another New Yorker, Thomas Robinson, whom Burr described as "an amiable, intelligent, well-behaved young man." From September until Burr parted from them in December, Hosack and Robinson are described as being together, and after Burr left for Paris they stayed on in Brunswick. They shared a taste for music; twice Burr referred to their having been out at concerts. Burr last mentioned Hosack in his journal a year later, when he recorded a mutual acquaintance's report that from Brunswick, Hosack and Robinson had proceeded to Blakenburg, which the journal's editor identifies as a town fifty miles southeast of Brunswick. There Hosack "went shooting and in shooting at a hare shot a man; not dead, but wounded badly, which cost him money and gave him much trouble. When he got rid of that affair he left the place, but whither gone is not known."

Nothing further of Hosack's European adventures has been found. One mystery associated with this period is the source of his money. He was neither well-off nor thrifty. Burr noted in July that Hosack had "changed his *last eight*" guineas into Swedish currency, and in November he commented that recently Hosack had been gambling and been "unfortunate." On December 8, when Robinson and Hosack visited there was "great distress about the finances of the latter," but by the 19th "Hosack had got out of his trouble." Perhaps Hosack's father was sending him money. Alexander Hosack's will, made in 1822, divided his estate equally among his three surviving sons and one daughter, but only after deducting advances made to his sons. In William's case the advance had amounted to $7,000.

Sometime between 1810 and 1815 Hosack returned to America. Early in the latter year he seems to have been in Albany, New York. He wrote then of his efforts to enlist Burr's support for a bill benefiting David Hosack. Despite David's low opinion of Burr's influence, William wrote confidently that Burr "can get any thing, through the house above & below, that he wishes, & that without appearing or having his name mentioned." In the same letter he described himself as a physician and told of a patient he had advised, although he may

have been being facetious. No other source hints at his having practiced medicine. Later in 1815 a New York City directory listed him
as an attorney and notary at 33 Cedar Street. He was still there in
1816, but was then absent from the directories until 1822, when he
was at Grand Street, near its intersection with Laurens Street. He last
appeared in a city directory in 1823, this time giving 138 Reed Street
as his address.

Hosack had apparently become an embarrassment to his family.
In 1805 he had handled an action for debt in which, the defendant
having became insolvent, he could not pursue the matter further.
While Hosack was abroad the plaintiff had gone to Hosack's brother, the physician, and claimed that William had in fact collected the
money owed and simply pocketed it. Hosack's family thought so little
of him that they immediately paid the claim without troubling to ver-
ify its accuracy. Around 1815 both Hosack's strained family relations
and his pretensions as a beau manifested themselves in a letter he
wrote to his brother David's close friend and fellow physician, John
W. Francis:

> I never was in better case in my life for I've got in the handsomest
> suit I ever had, & indeed when I look in the glass I hardly
> know it's me, I look so much like a gemman—i'm in whacking
> spirits for I've been confined to my room the last s'ennight in
> consequence—When I return to the old nest I shall drop down
> below zero if my *par nobile fratrum* give me the go by as they've
> done the last 2 or 3 years; they are not perhaps aware of the
> crooked reflections & surmises which must naturally occur to the
> minds of their friends & visitors when they *see* a poor wight like
> me kept *out of their sight* at my dear brother'ss [sic].

After 1823 Hosack apparently gave up any pretense of trying
to earn a living, relying instead on the charity of his brothers and
friends, including Burr. He seems never to have married. On October 12, 1831 he died of inflammation of the lungs. According to Dr.
Francis, Hosack had a "wretched end." He was "in the lowest state of
poverty & Bush the Irish anatomist wished to seize the body." George
Bushe had been professor of anatomy at David Hosack's Rutgers
Medical College when it disbanded in 1830, and his readiness to dis-
sect the brother of his former colleague can be seen as a final proof
that the brothers were known to be cool to each other. However, the
Hosack family put the best possible face on things. Hosack was given
a respectable funeral service at the home of his younger brother Dr.
Alexander Hosack, Jr., and buried in New York Marble Cemetery.

SOURCES: C. C. Robbins, *David Hosack: Citizen of N.Y.* (1964), 9-12; Thomas, *Columbia*, 114; Min. Fac., 10 Nov. 1789, 29 Nov. 1790 ("acting in direct"), Dec. 1790, 22-29 June 1791 ("very unseasonable," "gross profanity"), 13 July 1792; Amer. Whig. Soc., *Cat.* (1840), 6; *N.J. Journal*, 10 Oct. 1792 ("Is the emancipation"); *Longworth's Amer. Almanac, N.Y. Reg., & City Directory* for 1797, 1798, 1802, 1803, 1815, 1822, & 1823/4; *John Langdon & Son's N.Y. City Directory* (1804/5); Heitman, *U.S. Army*, I, 543; als, WAH to Alexander Hamilton, 16 Sept. 1799 (DLC microfilm of Alexander Hamilton Papers, original in DLC); N.Y. (State) Council of Appointment, *Military Minutes 1783-1821* (1901), I, 287, 368, 465, 509; J. A. Scoville, *Old Merchants of N.Y. City*, 2d ser., (1864), 124, 205-06 ("army of Columbia"); A. Burr, *Private Journal* (1903), I, *passim* ("came in at 10," 90; "musical party," 130; "Hosack came in," 169; "changed his *last*," 181; "ought to write," 192; "amiable, intelligent," 225; "unfortunate," 267; "so I am," 277; "great distress," 300; "Hosack had got," 322); II, 53 ("went shooting"); als, WAH to John W. Francis, undated but ca. early 1815 ("can get," "I never was"), N (photocopy at PUA); als, WAH to Burr, 18 June 1818, NHi (also on reel 8 of microfilm *Papers of Aaron Burr*); J. Parton, *Life & Times of Aaron Burr* (1858), 606; *Diary of William Dunlap* (1929-31), III, 830 ("wretched end"). For Miranda's Expedition, see W. S. Robertson, *Life of Miranda* (1929), I, 293-320; J. H. Sherman, *General Account of Miranda's Expedition* (1808). The 1903 edition of Burr's *Private Journal*, which lacked an index, is indexed in M. Kline, *Guide & Index to the Microfilm Edition of the Papers of Aaron Burr* (1978), 91-100. Use of the journal is rendered more difficult by the presence of a "W. E. Hosack," a fellow passenger on Burr's passage across the Atlantic. This is not a misprint for W. A. Hosack, for Longworth's 1808 New York directory lists "W. E. Hossack," a merchant at 22 Duane Street. Fortunately, W. E. Hosack makes his last appearance some months before Burr begins referring to the subject of this sketch. The index is in error in classing the entries from March 7 to May 15, 1809 (*Private Journal*, I, 89-109), under William E. rather than William A. Hosack.

MANUSCRIPTS: John W. Francis Papers, N; Alexander Hamilton Papers, DLC; Aaron Burr Collection, NHi

JJL

Samuel Hughes

SAMUEL HUGHES, lawyer, was born in July 1773, one of the twelve children of Daniel Hughes of that part of Frederick County, Maryland which became Washington County three years later. Daniel Hughes and his brother Samuel were ironmasters whose three furnaces in the Antietam Valley, Washington County, produced cannon for the Continental Army in the Revolutionary War. The Hughes brothers also attested their patriot sympathies in the Revolution by joining the local committee of observation. Daniel's first wife, Rebecca Lux of Baltimore, was the mother of Samuel and his brother Robert (A.B. 1787). She was a Lutheran and Daniel was an Episcopalian; in which church their children were raised is unclear. Daniel's younger brother John married Margaret, the sister of Robins Chamberlaine (Class of 1793).

Hughes appears as a junior on the College class list of November 29, 1790, although his name is one of two at the end of an otherwise alphabetical sequence. Either he arrived at Nassau Hall after the winter term began or his name was accidentally omitted when the list was first compiled. In the same year he joined the Cliosophic Society, using as his pseudonym Chatham, for the great English statesman. Hughes is also on the class list compiled around May 1791, but he did not return for his senior year.

Subsequently Hughes became an attorney in Hagerstown, Washington County. He and his half-brother Daniel, another Hagerstown attorney, seem also to have helped manage the family's industrial interests, for they joined their father in constructing a furnace at Mount Alto, Franklin County, Pennsylvania. Hughes's household consisted of seven whites, a free black, and two slaves at the time of the 1800 census. He had become a justice of Washington County by 1805, for his court docket from that year survives. On May 15, 1810 he gave a speech supporting the establishment of a secondary school in Hagerstown at a public meeting called to promote this goal. The state legislature incorporated the Hagerstown Academy that December, with Hughes as one of the trustees. In 1813 the new school opened its doors with Thomas Pitt Irving (A.B. 1789) as the first headmaster.

Hughes married a Miss Holker and they had five sons and four daughters. The parents seem to have had a taste for European royalty, for they named a son Napoleon B. and a daughter Marie Antoinette Hughes.

Samuel Hughes probably died around 1825.

SOURCES: J. T. Scharf, *Hist. of Western Md.* (1882 repr. 1968), II, 1011-12, 1156-57; *MHM*, 12 (1917), 142, 338; J. B. Kerr, *Geneal. Notes of the Chamberlaine Family of Md.* (1880 repr. 1973), 40, 46; Clio. lists; Min. Fac., 29 Nov. 1790, class list ca. May 1791; T. J. C. Williams, *Hist. of Wash. Cnty., Md.* (1906 repr. 1968), I, 555; J. W. Thomas & T. J. C. Williams, *Hist. of Allegany Cnty., Md.* (1923 repr. 1969), I, 670; *MHM*, 66 (1971), 466; R. B. Clark, Jr., *Wash. Cnty. Md.: 1800 Census* (1964), 21; R. V. Jackson, *Md. 1810 Census Index* (1976), 46; R. V. Jackson, *Md. 1820 Census Index* (1977), 55; D. W. Morton & D. S. Jensen, *Wills of Wash. Cnty., Md.: An Index 1776-1890* (1977), 17. Identification of Hughes is complicated because extant Cliosophic Society sources call him Samuel "Huger" or "Hugher." The published Clio. catalogs of 1837 and 1840 call him a native of New Jersey, but this is evidently a transcription error involving Hughes and Alexander Stewart (A.B. 1793), who MS membership lists clearly say were both from Maryland. The original Clio. register does not survive, and later copies probably perpetuate a misreading of "Huges," a variant spelling of Hughes sometimes encountered in contemporary sources. Huger is a very rare name in Maryland at this time, not appearing at all in the first four federal censuses. The two class lists clearly say "Hughes," but because they give no first name, identification of Samuel Hughes as the Princetonian is not quite ironclad.

JJL

Edmund Jennings Lee

EDMUND JENNINGS LEE, A.B., A.M. 1795, attorney and public official, was born on May 20, 1772, the youngest of the five sons of Henry and Lucy Grymes Lee of "Leesylvania," Prince William County, Virginia. He was presumably named for his great-grandfather Edmund Jennings, acting governor of Virginia from 1706 to 1710. Henry Lee, a planter, was among the one hundred wealthiest men in Virginia in the late 1780s. Edmund's brothers included Henry (A.B. 1773), Charles (A.B. 1775) and Richard Bland Lee (Class of 1779). William Ludwell Lee (Class of 1794) was his first cousin once removed, and Cassius Lee (Class of 1798) was his second cousin and later his brother-in-law. Alice Lee, his first cousin once removed, married William Shippen, Jr. (A.B. 1754).

Like his elder brothers Charles and Richard, Lee may have come to Princeton as a student of the grammar school. He entered the College as a freshman in November 1788. On June 10, 1789 he joined the Cliosophic Society, taking as his pseudonym Cowley, the seventeenth-century English poet and essayist. Twice during his stay at the College he was called before the faculty on disciplinary grounds. He and his classmate James Ross were admonished in June 1791, following a dispute in which they made an "improper use" of their sword canes. In April 1792 another classmate, George Washington Morton, took issue with something Lee had said and "assaulted him in his own room." Morton was found chiefly to blame, since Lee had spoken "more thro imprudence than malice."

Lee was a good student. He took third prize in English oration at the competition of underclassmen held at the commencement of 1790. A year later, he took second prize in the same category and third in "reading grammar, and orthography of the English language." At his commencement he stood sixth in his class, was assigned the second of two "honorary orations one to begin the other to close the morning exercises," and he spoke "on sympathy." He also received a Cliosophic Society diploma.

Lee then read law, though where he did so is unclear. Around 1796 he married his second cousin Sarah, the daughter of Richard Henry Lee and his second wife Anne Gaskins Pinckard Lee. Sarah Lee's nephew was Francis Lightfoot Lee (Class of 1820). The couple was living in Alexandria, then in the District of Columbia, by 1797, for in that year Lee was one of twenty-nine Alexandrians who subscribed $200 each toward construction of a theatre, a rather puzzling move in light of his strong and somewhat humorless evangelical principles. Lee bought a property at 428 North Washington Street from his

Edmund Jennings Lee, A.B. 1792

brother Charles for $5,000 in 1801 and resided there the rest of his life. Edmund seems actually to have lived there for some years previously, and whether it was he or his brother who constructed the fine house, which dates from the 1790s and is still standing, is open to dispute. By 1835 he also owned a farm named "Ellerslie," near Leesburg, Loudoun County, Virginia. The marriage of Edmund and Sarah Lee produced five sons and four daughters, including Edmund Jennings Lee, Jr. (A.B. 1817).

An 1800 directory lists Lee as qualified to practice before both the high court of chancery, Richmond, and the Virginia court of appeals. In April 1801 he was one of eight attorneys who took their oaths in Alexandria at the inaugural session of the District of Columbia's United States Circuit Court. This tribunal alternately sat in the District's two counties, Alexandria and Washington. Virginia law applied in the former, which comprised the section of the District originally part of Virginia (and reclaimed by it in 1846), and Maryland law in the latter. Lee eventually became the clerk of this court and held the office for many years. At his death, he was the last surviving charter member of its bar.

Lee's main avocation was promotion of the interests of the Protestant Episcopal Church. He was a warden and vestryman of Christ

Church, Alexandria, a member of the diocese of Virginia's standing committee, and a frequent delegate to the diocesan and general conventions. In June 1818 he helped found the Society for the Education of Pious Young Men for the Ministry of the Protestant Episcopal Church, which served the dioceses of Virginia and Maryland, and he sat on its board of managers for the rest of his life. Several letters from Lee to John H. Hobart (A.B. 1793) from late 1809 and early 1810 survive, and they show Lee, acting on behalf of the rest of the vestry of Christ Church, asking Hobart, by this time an eminent Episcopal clergyman in New York, to recommend a man to fill their vacant parish and help them persuade him to come south. In time an offer was tendered, but on his way to Virginia the man in question was snapped up by a congregation in Baltimore and never reached Alexandria. Lee swallowed his irritation at the man's "extraordinary conduct" and asked Hobart for another nominee, but a month later was able to write smugly that Hobart's assistance was no longer required; a man had been found and inducted. Unfortunately a year later the new rector, Francis Barclay, was obliged to resign when his wife, whom he had deserted a decade previously in the West Indies, inconveniently turned up. Lee and his fellow trustees finally found a pastor to their taste when they replaced him with William Meade (A.B. 1808), later bishop of Virginia.

Lee and Meade were among the young Turks who attempted to revive their church by promoting evangelical zeal, and in 1814 they secured a victory for their faction by successfully advocating the election of Richard Channing Moore as bishop of Virginia. A letter from Moore suggests that he sometimes found Lee's enthusiasm impolitic; while agreeing with him that "we may, with equal propriety, attempt to serve God and mammon, as to reconcile an indulgence in fashionable amusements with the divine life," too sudden an attack on "balls, the theatre and card table" might "produce a commotion overwhelming in its effects and desolating to our interest." Whatever his reaction to this letter, Lee in general was not one to temporize; as Meade said, "there was no compromise at all in him." During a term as mayor of Alexandria, he initiated a drive against gambling which led to fines for some of the town's principal citizens. He also took pains to enforce a strict sabbatarianism, in the town as a whole as well as his own home, and was a stickler for the rules at his church's conventions. He helped found the American Colonization Society in December 1816 and was elected to its first board of managers.

Lee's vocation and avocation combined in his protracted and ultimately successful defense of Christ Church's 566-acre glebe. Under an act of 1802 the Virginia legislature appropriated the glebes of the state's Episcopalians to each county's respective overseers of the poor. In 1811 Lee led the vestry in challenging this statute and personally argued the parish's case in a protracted legal struggle which reached the United States Supreme Court twice and was not finally resolved until 1828, with the complete vindication of Christ Church's title to the land. Although the Supreme Court's ruling in favor of Christ Church in 1815 declared the Virginia act of 1802 unconstitutional, it seems to have established no precedent, and all the other glebes were successfully seized by the overseers. On another occasion Lee successfully blocked an effort by the town council to widen Cameron Street at the expense of the churchyard of Christ Church.

Lee was one of Alexandria's leading men for several decades. From March 1815 to March 1818 he was the town's mayor, and he also served several terms as president of its common council. In August 1814 he was among the town leaders who negotiated its surrender to the British after Fort Washington was abandoned and the town rendered defenseless. Since capitulation saved the town from being pillaged and resistance would have been futile, this decision seems eminently sensible. Love of the town coupled with his authoritarian temperament could also have its amusing side; upon seeing people sitting on their doorsteps on a summer night, he is said to have exclaimed "Neighbors, neighbors, this will never do! You will get chills and fevers, and give our neighborhood a bad name."

Lee's wife Sarah, who "for more than thirty years ... was gradually dying of consumption," finally succumbed on May 8, 1837. Edmund Jennings Lee died on May 30, 1843.

SOURCES: C. H. Lee, "An Old Va. Churchman," *Va. Seminary Mag.*, (July 1888), 334-40 ("we may"); E. J. Lee, *Lee of Va.* (1895), 208, 291-301, 374-82, 468-82; J. T. Main, "The One Hundred," *WMQ*, 3d ser., 11 (1954), 377; *Princetonians, 1769-1775*, 301; Min. Fac., 10 Nov. 1789, 10 June 1791 ("improper use"), 6 Apr. ("assaulted," "more thro") & 13 July 1792 ("honorary orations"); Clio. lists; Clio. Min., 15 Aug. & 5 Sept. 1792; *Pa. Packet, & Daily Advt.*, 7 Oct. 1790; *Dunlap's Amer. Daily Advt.*, 4 Oct. 1791 ("reading"); *N.J. Journal*, 10 Oct. 1792 ("on sympathy"); *Dunlap & Claypoole's Amer. Daily Advt.*, 8 Oct. 1795; G. M. Moore, *Seaport in Va.* (1949), 28, 225-29; M. Lindsey, *Hist. Homes & Landmarks of Alexandria* (1962), 10; als, EJL to Samuel L. Southard, 16 Feb. 1835, NjP-SSP ("Ellerslie"); "Extracts from the Annual Register & Va. Repository for the year 1800," *Tyler's Quart.*, 17 (1936), 89; C. M. Green, *Wash.: Village & Capital, 1800-78* (1962), 26-27, 173-74 (judicial structure of Wash., D.C.); *Records of the Columbia Hist. Soc.*, 5 (1902), 297; W. Plumer, *William Plumer's Memorandum of Proc. in the U.S. Senate 1803-07* (1923), 291 (EJL a defense witness at Samuel Chase's impeachment trial, 1805); Alexander, *Princeton*, 261-62; W. Meade, *Old Churches, Ministers & Families of Va.* (1857 repr. 1900), II, 143, 268-69 ("there was no," "for more"); D. L. Holmes, "William Meade & the Church of Va., 1789-1829" (Ph.D. diss., Princeton, 1971), 193, 221, 267; J. P. K. Henshaw, *Memoir of the Life of ... Richard Channing Moore* (1843), 118, 121-38, 142-47; W. A. R. Goodwin, *Hist. of the Theological Seminary in Va.* (1923), I, 105, 124-26; II, 617-46, *passim*; Hobart, *Corres.*, VI, 325-26, 350, 365-68, 379-80 ("extraordinary"); J. Packard, *Recollections of a Long Life* (1902), 159-60; P. J. Staudenraus, *African Colonization Movement 1816-65* (1961),

27, 30, 258; M. N. Stanard, *Richmond* (1923), 107; C. O. Paullin, "Virginia's Glebe near Wash.," *Records of the Columbia Hist. Soc.*, 42-43 (1940/1), 225-32; G. M. Brydon, *Va.'s Mother Church* (1952), 504-05, 516-17, 525-31; letter from A. W. Robbins of the Alexandria Library, 21 Aug. 1985, PUA; M. G. Powell, *Hist. of Old Alexandria* (1928), 176-77, 253-57, 300 ("Neighbors"). For photographs of a miniature of EJL upon which the engraving depicted above was probably based and for a matching likeness of his wife, see Alexandria Association, *Our Town: 1749-1865* (1956), plate XVIII. See Moore, 228, and Lindsey, 10, for photographs of Lee's house in Alexandria.

MANUSCRIPTS: VHi; Vi; College of William and Mary; PHi; MiD; John Henry Hobart Papers, TxAuCH; James Madison Papers, DLC; NjP-SSP

JJL

George Merrick Leech (Leach)

GEORGE MERRICK LEECH (LEACH) was the only son of Joseph and Molsy Vail Leech of Change and East Front Streets, New Bern, Craven County, North Carolina. Molsy was one of six daughters of Jeremiah Vail of Craven County. Joseph Leech was a wealthy merchant and tanner who in 1798 owned 44,181 acres in eight counties, including 30,780 in Craven, and ten slaves. A leading member of the local Episcopal church and of the masonic lodge, the elder Leech was also active politically. He served in the lower house of the provincial assembly before independence and as state treasurer and a member of the six-man council of state afterwards. He led the Craven County militia in the campaign against the Regulators in 1771 and served as a delegate to the state conventions which in 1788 and 1789 first rejected and then ratified the United States Constitution.

George Leech made his only appearance in extant College records in 1790, when he joined the Cliosophic Society, taking the pseudonym Menander, in honor of the ancient Greek writer of comic drama. Leech must have stayed at the College only briefly, for he appears in none of the class lists recorded twice a year in the faculty minutes at that time. He is placed with the class of 1792 because his name is sandwiched between known members of that class on both surviving manuscript copies of the lost original Cliosophic Society membership roll.

Leech attained nothing like his father's eminence. He inherited a one-third interest in 550 acres of Craven County land from his mother before July 5, 1796, when he deeded it to his sister Frances. The 1800 census indicated that he lived in Craven County, but he was not listed in 1810. He presumably inherited a substantial estate upon the death of his father in 1803. The only fact to surface concerning his subsequent activities is that in 1804 he owned a swampy island in central Craven County formed by the Neuse River on the east and Bachelor Creek and The Gut on the west, which was known as Leaches Island. Even if one assumes that it was named for him rather than his father, this modest form of immortality was denied him. Sometime after the United States Coast Survey map of 1865 appeared, the island's name changed to Hog Island.

SOURCES: E. Moore, *Records of Craven Cnty., N.C.* (1960), I, 135-36; W. S. Powell et al., *Regulators in N.C.: A Documentary Hist. 1759-76* (1971), 586; G. S. Carraway, *Years of Light: Hist. of St. John's Lodge, no. 3 A. F. & A. M. New Bern, N.C.* (1944), 17, 21, 30, 128; A. T. Dill, *Gov. Tryon & His Palace* (1955), 68, 164, 227; *NCHR*, 1 (1924), 96, 108; 12 (1935), 167-68; 23 (1946), 344, 520; Clio. Soc., *Cat.* (1840), 7; Clio. lists; E. P. Bentley, *Index to the 1800 Census of N.C.* (1977), 142; W. S. Powell, *N.C. Gazetteer* (1968), 230-31. The 1840 Cliosophic Society catalogue gives Leech's middle initial as "W," but this is contradicted by the manuscript lists, which say "M." See H. B. Taylor, ed., *Guide to Hist. New Bern, N.C.* (1974), 54, for a photograph of the "Leech House," 209 Change Street, apparently still standing. The building dates from approximately the year of Joseph Leech's death and thus could have been built either by him or by the Princetonian. Wanda S. Gunning kindly supplied references used in this sketch.

JJL

Joseph Logan

JOSEPH LOGAN, A.B., was born on June 15, 1772, one of six sons and four daughters of William and Rebecca Gaston Logan of Peapack, Bedminster Township, Somerset County, New Jersey. He was a second cousin of Joseph Gaston Chambers (Class of 1778, see appendix). William Logan was a captain in the Somerset County militia in the Revolutionary War and fought at the battles of Trenton and Princeton. A blacksmith, his moveable property was valued at $1,615 plus about $800 in bad debts when he died intestate in 1814. His wife Rebecca was the daughter of Hugh and Jennet Gaston.

Logan entered the College as a junior in November 1790, as did his classmates John and William B. Sloan, and since both their fathers were elders of the Lamington Presbyterian Church, one can reasonably speculate that the trio came to the College together. Logan joined the American Whig Society. When planning his class's graduation exercises in July 1792, the faculty assigned him the task of responding to the question "Are capital punishments just or politic?" However the schedule was later changed to accommodate an additional oration, Logan's disputation was canceled, and he did not speak at commencement.

Little has been discovered of Logan's subsequent activities. He married a Sarah Chambers. They had at least one child, a daughter Mary Ann. She lived in Jefferson County, Indiana, at the time of the 1830 census, which listed a Joseph Logan in the same county.

Whether this was her father or a brother has not been determined. The Princetonian died in 1833. His wife survived him by a quarter century. In 1940 the University received a letter from his great-great-granddaughter, who revealed that at that time his diploma remained in the family's possession.

SOURCES: *NJHSP*, n.s., 8 (1923), 57-58; *Som. Cnty. Hist. Quart.*, 3 (1914), 133; 4 (1915), 40-41; 5 (1916), 34-37, 40-43; 6 (1917), 180, 247, 270; J. P. Snell, *Hist. of Hunterdon & Somerset Cnties., N.J.* (1881), 710, 714; *N.J. Wills*, XIII, 259; Min. Fac., 29 Nov. 1790, 13 July 1792 ("Are capital"); Amer. Whig Soc., *Cat.* (1840), 6; *N.J. Journal*, 10 Oct. 1792; National Soc. of the Daughters of the Amer. Rev., *Lineage Book*, 157 (1937), 228 (lineage # 156727); R. V. Jackson & G. R. Teeples, *Indiana 1830 Index Census* (1976), 63, 74; letter of Mrs. M. A. Bridges, 3 Apr. 1940, PUA. Wanda S. Gunning kindly supplied references used in this sketch.

JJL

J. J. Long

J. J. LONG, lawyer, may have been John Joseph Long, one of at least eight children of Nicholas Long of "Quanky," an estate on Quanky Creek, Halifax County, in northeastern North Carolina, and his second wife Mary McKinney Long, the daughter of John McKinney. William Amis Lunsford Long (Class of 1841) was the nephew of John Joseph Long. A wealthy planter, Nicholas Long was a colonel of the Halifax militia and state commissary-general during the Revolution. He served in the provincial assembly, the first two provincial congresses, and the state senate.

Nicholas Long was a trustee of the Warrenton Academy, Warren County, North Carolina, at the time of its incorporation in 1786. Perhaps he sent his son there. The younger Long entered the junior class of the College in November 1790. The same year he joined the Cliosophic Society, taking as his pseudonym Lysander, for the Spartan warrior and diplomat who lived around 400 B.C. and spent most of his time scheming to increase his own influence in Sparta and Sparta's in Greece. On June 22, 1791 the faculty suspended Long, who had been "represented as one of the most active in the disorders of the dining room & also particularly guilty of insolent treatment to one of the officers of the college." A week later they readmitted him after he made "such concessions as the faculty deemed satisfactory." He did not return for his senior year.

The Cliosophic Society's records indicate that Long subsequently became a lawyer and was a "distinguished pract." When his father died on February 12, 1798 John Joseph Long inherited 200 acres of land and some slaves. He married Frances Quintard and they had several children. At the time of the 1800 census he lived in Halifax County. Subsequently he moved to Maury County, Tennessee, where he apparently belonged to the Zion Presbyterian Church. He died around 1816. His will provided that the portion of his estate "belonging to my children be put out at interest for the use of the children being educated."

SOURCES: *NEHGR*, 77 (1923), 250-51; M. M. Hofmann, *Geneal. Abstracts of Wills 1758-1824 Halifax Cnty. N.C.* [1970], 107, 176; W. C. Allen, *Hist. of Halifax Cnty.* (1918), 170-71; J. H. Wheeler, *Hist. Sketches of N.C.* (1851), II, 186; *NCHR*, 9 (1932), 203; 30 (1953), 53; C. L. Coon, *N.C. Schools & Academies 1790-1840* (1915), 574; Min. Fac., 29 Nov. 1790, 18 Mar., 22 & 29 June 1791 ("represented," "such concessions"); Clio. lists ("distinguished"); E. P. Bentley, *Index to the 1800 Census of N.C.* (1977), 146; M. W. Highsaw, "Hist. of Zion Community in Maury Cnty., 1806-60," *THQ*, 5 (1946), 111 ("belonging to"); W. B. Turner, *Hist. of Maury Cnty. Tenn.* (1955), 42. The Clio. membership lists confirm that Long was from North Carolina, but because all extant College sources give only the initials of his first and middle names, identification remains doubtful. John Joseph Long's parents were married in 1761, which means he was at least approximately the right age to be the Princetonian, and they were surely wealthy enough to send him to the College. The 1800 census lists thirty-eight individuals in North Carolina named Long with a first initial "J," from a wide range of counties, but only two of them include middle names, John Joseph Long and Joseph John Long, both of Halifax County. The D.A.R. Lineage Book calls Nicholas Long's son John a physician, but it also gives his middle name as Jackson and is otherwise unreliable (National Soc. of the Daughters of the Amer. Rev., *Lineage Book*, 54 [1919], 224-25 [lineage # 53506]). The Princetonian should not be confused with the John Long of Randolph County who served in the U.S. Congress from 1821-29, for the latter was born in 1785 (J. G. D. Hamilton, *Papers of Thomas Ruffin* [1918 repr. 1973], I, 297; II, 565). See National Soc. of the Colonial Dames of Amer, in ... N.C., *N.C. Portrait Index 1700-1860* (1963), 143-45, for John Joseph Long (1814-77) of Longwood in Northampton County, which adjoined Halifax County. He seems to have been the nephew of John Joseph Long, son of Nicholas. Wanda S. Gunning kindly supplied references used in this sketch.

JJL

David McRee

DAVID MCREE, A.B., lawyer, can be identified as coming from North Carolina. He was probably the son of William McRea of Mecklenburg County, whose parents were Robert and Margaret Polk McRee. McRees, with variations in spelling as McCrea, McRea, and McRae, were concentrated in the Steele Creek settlement in the southwestern section of the county. McRee's early schooling would most likely have been at Salisbury Academy in nearby Charlotte.

For some reason McRee's name does not appear on any of the 1792 class lists in any of its various phonetic spellings. However, an indecipherable name that could be "Mcrea" is included as a junior in November 1791. If this was David McRee he must have accelerated and joined the senior class sometime during the academic year. That

McRee was indeed on the campus is attested to by the fact that he not only became a member of the American Whig Society, where his name appears as "David M'Crea," but was apparently one of a group of Whig "brothers" who spent a good deal of time together. John C. Otto (A.B. 1792), in a letter to John H. Hobart (A.B. 1793), dated October 25, 1795, recalls their "happy circle in conversation." McRee's name is mentioned among the group who were wont to assemble for "happy converse." "Was there ever a more pleasing society?" Otto asked rhetorically. "I am sure college never knew so large an one so much attached to each other." When the faculty met on July 13, 1792 to make commencement assignments, McRee's name was again omitted, even from among the list of students who were excused from participating at their own request. However, the *New-Jersey Journal* of October 10, 1792 listed "David McKee [sic] of North Carolina" as a degree recipient. College catalogues include him as McCree.

A variant spelling of the name as McKee occurred again when a letter from Joseph McKnitt Alexander (A.B. 1792) to John Henry Hobart was printed in a collection of Hobart's correspondence. This was obviously an error in transcription because Alexander was not only a college classmate but probably had known McRee throughout his boyhood, and he would not have been likely to misspell his name in the original letter. Written from Mt. Prospect, North Carolina, on April 23, 1793, Alexander's letter expressed concern for McRee. "David McKee had this winter some alarming symptoms of a consumption—spat blood two week & frequently discharged large quantities—pain in his breast & he was much alarmed,—has now perfectly recovered. Tho is yet so lean that you would odds by all the trigers & flints in the french army & by all the rabits in Carolina that he was in love." A lighthearted postscript adds, "As David is studying law I will send a habeas corpus for Terhune [John Terhune (A.B. 1793)] provided he does not write & I know McKee will endeavor to indict him." This letter was delivered to Hobart by a "Mr. Cruiser," who was undoubtedly a relative of Rachel Cruser McRee, whose family resided in Mapleton, New Jersey, not far from Princeton. Her husband, the Reverend James McRee (A.B. 1775), was pastor of the Steele Creek Presbyterian Church and probably a relative of David McRee.

McRee's tuberculosis evidently did not prove fatal, and he may have gone on to complete his law studies. He may have been the David Polk McRee who acted as bondsman at the wedding of David Hartt and Diana McRee on August 16, 1797. He remained in North Carolina, at least until March 3, 1798, when Hobart wrote to Joseph

Caldwell (A.B. 1791), president of the University of North Carolina, and inquired about McCrea [sic], Alexander, and [George Washington] Campbell (A.B. 1794), all native North Carolinians. McRee is first listed as deceased in the 1824 issue of the College catalogue.

SOURCES: Min. Fac., class list ca. Nov. 1791 & 13 July 1792; Foote, *Sketches, N.C.*, 434-37; *Princetonians, 1769-1775*, 504-05; Amer. Whig Soc., *Cat.* (1840), 6; *N.J. Jour.*, 10 Oct. 1792; Hobart, *Corres.*, I, 23-25, 139-41 ("happy circle," "David McKee had"); R. D. W. Connor, *Documentary Hist. of the Univ. of N.C. 1776-99* (1953), II, 305; W. S. Ray, *Mecklenburg Signers & Their Neighbors* (1946), 355, 397, 399, 505-09; B. H. Holcomb, *Marriages of Mecklenburg Cnty., N.C.* (1981), 79.

                                                                    RLW

George Clifford Maxwell

GEORGE CLIFFORD MAXWELL, A.B., A.M. 1795, lawyer, justice, and congressman, was born May 31, 1774 in Greenwich Township, Sussex County, New Jersey, the third child and eldest son of John and Mary Ann Clifford Maxwell. Capt. John Maxwell, brother of Brigadier General William Maxwell, raised his own company of Sussex and Hunterdon County volunteers and fought in the battles of Trenton, Assunpink, Princeton, Brandywine, Germantown, Monmouth and Springfield.

Maxwell entered the College as a junior in November 1790, where he joined the American Whig Society. At his commencement his humorous oration on the marks of genius in young persons must have been a welcome diversion among the weightier topics being debated and orated.

He next studied law, apparently under the chief justice of the state, James Kinsey (LL.D. 1790) of Burlington, and was admitted to the bar as an attorney during the 1797 May term. Maxwell rose to counsellor in the 1800 May term and was appointed sergeant-at-law in February 1816. Residing in Flemington and practicing in the Hunterdon County courts, he was recognized as one of the ablest lawyers in the largely rural county. President Thomas Jefferson (LL.D. 1791) appointed him United States district attorney for New Jersey in January 1802. Maxwell resigned from this post on November 11, 1803. He supervised the legal training of his brother William after the latter graduated from the College in 1804.

Maxwell was nominated for Congress by the state Republican convention of 1810. His candidacy could have been accomplished only with the approval of James J. Wilson, the acknowledged Republican leader in Hunterdon County. The inclusion of three first-time candidates on the ticket while dropping long-time incumbents was justified by the convention as a means of providing rotation in office and selecting men "who have the confidence of the districts in which they reside and where they are best known." As a member of the Twelfth Congress, Maxwell was "non-partisan," voting according to party affiliation only about 40 percent of the time. Raising additional troops for the army was the only war measure that he supported. During his term in Congress he made only one short speech on the floor of the House. On January 1812 he was among the majority favoring a bill to raise an additional military force. When the Senate returned the bill three days later after greatly increasing the number of commissioned officers, Maxwell announced that he could not vote for the measure with the Senate's amendments. This version, he contended, could conceivably lead to an army of officers without soldiers to command. After a long harangue in favor of postponement by John Randolph (Class of 1791), Maxwell joined the majority in voting against postponement. He seems to have been as as much disturbed about the non-cooperation of the Senate as he was about whether or not the bill would pass. At the end of his term he returned to his legal practice in Flemington.

On September 28, 1803 Maxwell married Rachel Bryan, the daughter of Judge John Patterson Bryan and Mary Ann (or Marian) Sloan Bryan of Peapack, New Jersey, with the Reverend William Sloan (A.B. 1792), the bride's cousin, officiating. Two years later Rachel's sister Elizabeth became the second wife of Thomas Grant (A.B. 1786), pastor of the Flemington Presbyterian Church where the Maxwells were members. A trustee of this church in 1806 and 1809, Maxwell was elected president of the congregation on April 3, 1811. The Maxwells had two children. John Patterson Bryan Maxwell (A.B. 1823) was a lawyer, a Whig member of both the Twenty-fifth and the Twenty-seventh Congress, a trustee of the College from 1842 to 1845, and editor of the *Belvidere Apollo*, the Whig newspaper of Warren County. His sister, Anna Maria Maxwell, was the mother of George Maxwell Robeson (A.B. 1847), a Republican member of Congress from 1878 to 1892.

Maxwell died on March 16, 1816 and was buried in Pleasant Ridge Cemetery, Raritan Township, Hunterdon County, New Jersey. An inventory of his estate totaled $57,637.44, including a "long list of names in accounts," which probably indicates that he was still actively practicing at the time of his death.

SOURCES: Alumni file, PUA; Min. Fac., 29 Nov. 1790, 13 July 1792; Amer. Whig Soc., *Cat.* (1840), 6; *N.J. Jour.*, 10 Oct. 1792; broadside 1792 "Order of Commencement," PUA; Riker, 41, 63; H. D. Maxwell, *Maxwell Family* (1895), 1, 2, 75, 77; W. Nelson, *N.J. Biog. & Gen. Notes* (1916), 164; Thomas Jefferson's "Summary Journal of Letters,"

11 Nov. 1803, MS in Jefferson Papers, DLC; J. P. Snell, *Hist. of Hunterdon & Somerset Cnties.* (1881), 206, 300; C. E. Prince, *N.J.'s Jeffersonian Republicans* (1964), 168-69 ("who have the confidence"); R. L. Hatzenbuehler, "The War Hawks & the Question of Congressional Leadership in 1812," *Pacific Hist. Review*, 45 (1976), 4-5, 12; *A/C*, 12th Cong., 1st sess., 703; Alexander, *Princeton*, 262; G. S. Mott, *Hist. of the Pres. Church of Flemington, N.J.* (1876), 27; *BDUSC*, 1440; *N.J. Wills*, XIII, 280; *Trenton Federalist*, 17 Oct. 1803 (marriage notice), 1 Apr. 1816 (obit., where date of death is incorrectly given as 28 Mar. 1816).

RLW

Joseph Kirkbride Milnor II

JOSEPH KIRKBRIDE MILNOR II, A.B., A.M. 1795, merchant, was born on March 15, 1775 in Trenton, New Jersey, the eldest of the five children of Joseph Kirkbride Milnor and his wife Sarah Higbee. The father belonged to a family of Friends from Falls Township, Bucks County, Pennsylvania, who moved to Trenton in 1773, where he became a prominent merchant. He was read out of the Society of Friends for marrying a non-Quaker and for drilling with the local militia. Milnor then joined the Trenton Presbyterian Church. He was also a charter member of the Union Fire Company, one of the founders of the Trenton Water Works, and one of the members of the association which established the Trenton Academy on February 10, 1781. According to the 1779 rateables list he was one of the wealthiest men in Trenton, and he established his family in an imposing brick house on the northwest corner of Queen and Second streets, which later became Broad and State streets, the busiest intersection in the city. Sarah Milnor was one of the Trenton matrons selected to welcome George Washington on his passage through the city in April 1789, an indication of the family's social prominence. Daughter Elizabeth, who later married Lucius Horatio Stockton (A.B. 1787), was one of the young flower girls on this occasion, strewing petals in Washington's path.

Milnor probably received his early education at the Trenton Academy, entering the College as a junior in November 1790. Sometime during his residence at Nassau Hall he joined the American Whig Society; however, his name has not been found among the correspondence of a group of Whigs who maintained a close friendship during and after their college years. At his commencement ceremonies he was the respondent in a debate on the lengthy question, "Considering the present state of human nature, does not the existence of war among nations seem necessary? In effect, do not wars contribute more to the elevation of the human character, to the improvement

Joseph Kirkbride Milnor II, A.B. 1792
BY EDWARD GREEN MALBONE

of the arts, and even to the happiness of mankind, than a state of universal peace, abused as the degeneracy of man always abuses the long continuance of prosperity?"

Sometime around 1800, probably during the summer of 1798, Milnor sat for a portrait by the miniaturist Edward Greene Malbone, who had a reputation for reproducing excellent likenesses of his subjects. Milnor is depicted as a handsome young man with powdered hair, brown eyes and a very fair complexion. His most likely occupation at this time would have been some assignment in his father's mercantile firm.

The elder Joseph Milnor died intestate on February 28, 1806, leaving an estate valued at $22,056.77, which included a large inventory from his mercantile establishment and three slaves. On March 5, 1806 the younger Milnor, with his sisters Maria and Elizabeth and the latter's husband, Lucius Horatio Stockton, petitioned for permission to sell parts of the estate and divide the proceeds. Milnor probably used his share to finance a voyage to Canton, China, where he formed a partnership with William Bull and established the trading firm of Milnor and Bull. Milnor returned to the United States in 1810 to set up a branch of Milnor and Bull in New York City. When the threatened war with England forced the closing of the Canton establishment, Bull joined Milnor in New York.

On June 8, 1812 Milnor married Frances Coles, daughter of Gen. Nathaniel Coles and his wife Elizabeth Townsend of Dosoris (Oyster Bay), New York. A newspaper account of the event listed the groom as being "of Trenton." The following year his name appeared in a New York City directory with a Pearl Street address. By 1815 Milnor & Bull, merchants, were listed at the same address. Both Milnor as an individual and the mercantile company continued at this address until 1823, when Milnor & Bull moved to 31 Pine Street. The success of the business can be judged by the fact that Milnor's name is on a list of "Rich Men of 1822," referred to as a "financial Four Hundred," which included New York residents with assets of more than $30,000.

Sometime during 1827 Milnor moved to 32 Fourth Street, an address that his widow retained for a time after his death on April 16, 1828. The firm of Milnor & Bull was apparently immediately dissolved, and William G. Bull, merchant, soon advertised at 29 Pine Street. By 1831 Mrs. Milnor was living in a boarding house on Broadway. She had borne ten children, three daughters and seven sons, during her sixteen-year marriage. The miniature of her late husband is currently in the possession of Joseph Kirkbride Milnor VI, a member of the Class of 1946.

SOURCES: Alumni file, PUA; S. S. Toothman, *Trenton, N.J.* (1977), 182, 192, 382; Joseph Milnor's estate inv., filed 22 June 1807, Nj; Trenton Hist. Soc., *Hist. of Trenton 1679-1929* (1929), I, 20, 110, 200-02, 317, 370-71; A. H. Wharton, *Heirlooms in Miniature* (1898), 64; R. P. Tolman, *Life & Works of Edward Greene Malbone* (1958), 3-23, 213; Min. Fac., 29 Nov. 1790, 13 July 1792; Amer. Whig Soc., *Cat.* (1840), 6; *N.J. Jour.*, 10 Oct. 1792 (commencement); JKM et al., MS petition of heirs of Joseph Milnor, 5 Mar. 1806, Nj; Morristown *Genius of Liberty*, 20 Mar. 1806 (father's obit.); *Trenton Federalist*, 15 June 1812 (marriage), 21 Apr. 1828 (obit.); H. W. Lanier, *Century of Banking in N.Y., 1822-1922* (1922), 122; N.Y. City directories, 1812-32; entries from Milnor family Bible, courtesy of Joseph K. Milnor VI.

RLW

George Washington Morton

GEORGE WASHINGTON MORTON, A.B., lawyer and pedestrian, was born in 1775 in Elizabethtown, Essex County, New Jersey, one of the five sons and three daughters of John and Maria Sophia Kemper Morton. His brothers included Jacob Morton (A.B. 1778), John Morton (A.B. 1782), and George Clarke Morton (A.B. 1795). The father was a Scots-Irish Presbyterian who immigrated to America as a British army commissary but soon left the army and became a thriv-

George Washington Morton, A.B. 1792
BY CHARLES B. J. FEVRET DE SAINT MEMIN

ing merchant at Water Street, New York City. A committed whig, in 1775 he liquidated much of his capital and loaned it to the war effort, and his descendants later proudly claimed that he was "certainly the first" to name a child after George Washington. His wife Maria, the daughter of Jacob and Maria Regina Ernest Kemper, was born in Kaub on the Rhine in the Prussian province of Hesse-Nassau but immigrated with her parents to America at age two. They settled first on the frontier in New York and then moved to New Brunswick, New Jersey, before coming to New York City, where Jacob Kemper was a merchant.

When a British invasion seemed imminent, the Mortons prudently decided to move from New York to Elizabethtown. After a near approach by British troops caused a panic at Elizabethtown, the Mortons concluded that this location was also too exposed and departed for Basking Ridge, Somerset County, New Jersey. Soon Washington established his headquarters at nearby Morristown, and the Continental Army located its hospital on the Mortons' farm. More than once the smaller Morton children were sent to cottages in the hills when the British army was rumored to be on its way.

During the turmoil of the Revolution, Basking Ridge had no suitable schools. Washington Morton, as he was almost invariably referred to throughout his life, and his sister Eliza Susan were therefore sent to Germantown, Pennsylvania, to stay with their grandparents, the Kempers, who had moved there when the British took New York. In Germantown they attended the school of a "Master Leslie." Eliza later remembered Leslie as a good man but a boring teacher and a severe disciplinarian. Probably he was James Lesley (A.B. 1759), a schoolmaster who seems to have left New York during that city's occupation by the British.

Morton cannot have stayed long at Leslie's school. In the spring of 1782 his father died, and the Kempers moved from Germantown to Basking Ridge, presumably bringing their grandchildren with them. Late in 1783 the Mortons moved back to New York City, and Washington was "sent to school," but this time his sister's memoir neglects to say where.

In September 1790 Morton entered the College, and in the same year he joined the Cliosophic Society, with Alexander as his pseudonym. On September 27, 1791 he took second place in a competition in English grammar, reading, and spelling held for underclassmen the day before commencement. He was, however, a spirited lad known to the faculty less for scholarship than for regular breaches of discipline. On the night of March 15, 1791 he and Frederick Stone (A.B. 1791) were out of their rooms after hours and returned "in a disorderly manner," shortly after "the urns were thrown down from the college wall," a coincidence regarded as highly suspicious by the faculty, who referred the matter to the trustees. The minutes of the latter do not show what action they took. The Cliosophic Society dismissed Morton for unknown reasons on December 20, 1791. Then on April 6, 1792 "in consequence of something Mr. [Edmund Jennings] Lee [A.B. 1792] had said Mr. Morton ... called upon him for an explanation and after some words assaulted him in his own room." The faculty concluded that Lee had spoken "more thro' imprudence than malice" and that Morton, who was "chiefly in fault," should be privately censured. A scant eleven days later Morton was in trouble again, even though vacation had begun and the student body was, presumably, largely absent. The faculty minutes do not go into specifics but say that Morton committed "an act of the highest imprudence," "a flagrant breach of the order & rules of the house" compounded of such "indecency & enormity" that President John Witherspoon could not wait for the faculty to convene but "ordered him instantly to leave the college." Morton was readmitted only after reading a public acknowledgment of sorrow and repentence. He managed to avoid further misadventures, and at his commencement he was respondent to the disputation question: "Is the policy of India and ancient Egypt, of dividing the people into different classes, and confining children to the professions of their fathers, preferable to that universal freedom of enterprize that prevails in Europe?"

Morton then began to read law. One source suggests that he studied under one of the Stocktons, possibly Richard Stockton (A.B. 1779). He may also have received training from his eldest brother Jacob, an attorney of some eminence at whose address in 1796 he made his first appearance as an attorney in the New York City directories. By 1798 he had an office of his own, and in 1800 he called himself "attorney and counsellor-at-law." From 1800 to about 1805 he lived at Beaver Street and then moved to Greenwich Village, which was still distinct from the city. In 1804 he entered into a partnership with Stephen Price, with an office at Wall Street. The partnership lasted until within a year of Morton's death. Like his brother Jacob, Washington Morton was active in the New York militia, rising from the rank of lieutenant in 1793 to lieutenant colonel commanding a regiment in 1806.

A nephew Edmund Quincy described Morton as having had "extraordinary powers of mind" which enabled him to win "an honorable place at the bar of New York" even though "perhaps more time was given [by him] to the pleasures of the world than to its affairs." More than six feet tall and "splendidly handsome," he possessed "great bodily strength and athletic skills." Quincy reported that on one occasion Morton walked

> for a wager from New York to Philadelphia in one day, then an unprecedented feat. His walk finished and his wager won, after a bath and toilet, as he told the story to my mother, he spent the night with his friends who had accompanied him on horseback, and a party of Philadelphia choice spirits, over a supper-table spread in his honor.

This ninety-mile walk, which "made a great noise at the time," was remarkable but within the range of the best pedestrians of Morton's day, as evidenced by the examples of the Englishmen Foster Powell and Robert Barclay Allardice.

Morton's brother-in-law Josiah Quincy (A.M. 1796, Harvard A.B. 1790) described him as "a young man of strong passions." Morton demonstrated the characterization's validity in 1797 when he fell in love with Cornelia Schuyler, one of the eleven children of Gen. Philip and Catherine Van Rensselaer Schuyler of Albany. Her father, regarding the match as imprudent or at least premature, refused his consent and ordered his daughter not to communicate further with Morton. Nothing daunted, Morton carried through a midnight elopement from the Schuyler home in Albany, followed by an all-night ride to Stockbridge, Massachusetts. There, on October 8, 1797, Judge Theodore Sedgwick, a friend of both families, arranged to have them married. Eventually General Schuyler was persuaded to forgive the couple and left Cornelia a full share of his estate when he died in 1804.

By his marriage Morton became a brother-in-law of Alexander Hamilton (LL.D. 1791), thus adding a personal link to the strong Federalist bent held by all the Morton brothers. He named his eldest son after Hamilton, subscribed $1,000 to a fund to pay Hamilton's debts after his death in 1804 in a duel with Aaron Burr (A.B. 1772), and was outspoken in his opinion that Rufus King had acted improperly by leaving town before the duel but after Hamilton had been challenged and had asked King for advice. Later Morton himself played a part in another political duel. The paper war between William Coleman, editor of the Federalist *Evening Post*, and James Cheetham, editor of the *American Citizen*, organ of the Clintonian Republicans, blossomed into a challenge, with a duel prevented only after state supreme court judge Henry Brockholst Livingston (A.B. 1774) had both parties arrested and bound over to keep the peace. The matter could have ended there, but David Thompson, New York City harbormaster, began stating publicly that Coleman had refused to fight. Morton and other friends of Coleman then met and advised him to challenge Thompson. Morton conveyed the challenge to Thompson and may also have acted as Coleman's second at the duel on January 18, 1807, in which Thompson was fatally wounded.

Morton's wife Cornelia died in 1807. Two sons and three daughters were born of the marriage. Morton is said to have been so afflicted by her loss that he went traveling in Europe in an attempt to assuage his grief. The New York City directories, however, continued to list him there until 1810. In any event, he died in Paris on May 3, 1810. Soon rumors were flying that he had gone to Europe to seek out and challenge Aaron Burr, in order to avenge his brother-in-law's death, and that Burr had killed him in the ensuing duel. Unfortunately this romantic addition to the growing Burr mythology is contradicted by the facts. Morton's family had the testimony of John Armstrong, Jr. (Class of 1776), then minister to France, and of other Americans then at Paris, that Morton had died "very suddenly of some disease of the throat." Besides, as his nephew later observed, had he felt called on to avenge Hamilton, "Washington Morton was not the man to let the suns of six years go down upon his wrath before entering upon the office."

SOURCES: E. S. M. Quincy, *Memoir of the Life of Eliza S. M. Quincy* (1861), 1-71 *passim* ("certainly the first," 18; "Master Leslie," 29; "sent to school," 42), 191, 265-66; *NJA*, 2d ser., v (1917), 244; Clio. lists; *Dunlap's Amer. Daily Advt.*, 4 Oct. 1791; Min. Fac., 29 Nov. 1790, 18 Mar. 1791 ("in a disorderly," "the urns"), 6 Apr. ("in consequence," "more thro' imprudence"), 17 Apr. ("a flagrant," "ordered him"), 6 May, 12 June ("an act," "indecency"), 13 July 1792; *N.J. Journal*, 10 Oct. 1792 ("Is the policy"); Giger, Memoirs; N.Y. City directories, 1795-1811; *Military Minutes of the Council of Appointment of the State of New York, 1783-1821* (1901-02), I, 278, 369, 848; E. Quincy, *Life of Josiah Quincy of Mass.* (1868), 76-81 ("extraordinary," "an honorable," "perhaps more," "splendidly," "great bodily," "for a wager," "made a great," "a young man," "Washington Morton was not"); T. F. Gordon, *Gazetteer of the State of N.J.* (1834), 221; G. W. Schuyler, *Colonial N.Y.: Philip Schuyler & his Family* (1885), II, 242-43, 274; M. J. Lamb & B. Harrison, *Hist. of the City of N.Y.* (3 vols., 1877-96), III, 444-45, 478-80; *Hamilton Papers*, XXIII, 56-57, 65, 370-73; XXIV, 343; XXV, 85; XXVI, 137-38; *N.Y. Hist.*, 18 (1937), 378-85; F. Hudson, *Journalism in the U.S. from 1690 to 1872* (1873), 217-18; *N.Y. Spy*, 20 Jan. 1807, & *N.Y. Weekly Museum*, 24 Jan. 1807 (for correct date of Coleman/Thompson duel, given by Hudson as 1803); D. S. Alexander, *Political Hist. of the State of N.Y.* (1906), I, 128; *NYGBR*, 113 (1982), 211. The will of GWM's father John Morton apparently gives his son's name as "James Washington" (see *N.J. Wills*, VI, 284; *N.Y. Wills*, XII, 307-08), but this is contradicted by his sister's memoir, which asserts he was named after George Washington. The College records all call him George or George Washington. A MS volume in NjP of notes on Witherspoon's lectures taken by John and Samuel S. Dickinson of the Class of 1791 was apparently passed on to Morton after they left the College, and his signature as "George Washington Morton, New York," appears on it in two places. After his graduation he was invariably referred to simply as Washington Morton. He should not be confused with his brother Jacob's sons George W. Morton and Washington Q. Morton, who also became lawyers. See *NYGBR*, 71 (1940), 125-28, 259. For Powell and Allardice, see *Dictionary of National Biography* (1885-1901) and W. Thom, *Pedestrianism* (1813). The assertion in Alexander, *Princeton*, 262, that Morton practiced law only briefly before giving it up to become "a leading merchant in the St. Domingo trade" appears to be without foundation. No other source confirms it, and the city directories refer to him as an attorney and counsellor until his death.

JJL

John Conrad Otto

JOHN CONRAD OTTO, A.B., A.M. 1795, M.D. University of Pennsylvania 1796, physician, was born March 15, 1774, near Woodbury, Gloucester County, New Jersey, in the small town of Raccoon, now Swedesborough. The son of Dr. Bodo Otto, Jr., and Catharina Schwerghauser Otto, he was the elder brother of Jacob Schwerghauser Otto (A.B. 1797) and Daniel Bodo Otto (Class of 1799). The family also included an older sister Catharine. Bodo Otto, Jr., had emigrated from Germany with his physician father, who eventually set up practice among the German residents of Reading, Pennsylvania. Both served as surgeons during the Revolution, even though the elder Otto was sixty-seven when he volunteered. Otto Jr. joined the First Battalion of Gloucester County with the rank of colonel on September 16, 1777. Sometime during his military duty the family home was burned by the tories in the neighborhood. Otto died in

January 1782, leaving an estate valued at £1,987.5.0. Real estate in Pennsylvania was left to his wife, to be divided among the four children after her death; his New Jersey property was to be divided among the children when the youngest reached his majority. Catharina Otto died February 21, 1788, and her sons were taken under the guardianship of John Wilkins, their father's friend and executor, while Catharine was made a ward of the Reverend Andrew Hunter (A.B. 1772).

At least part of John Otto's early education was received at Andrew Hunter's academy in Bridgeton, New Jersey. Admitted to the College as a sophomore on November 10, 1789, Otto joined the American Whig Society. Later correspondence with John Henry Hobart (A.B. 1793), Otto's roommate during part of his residency at Nassau Hall, clearly shows the close fellowship that existed among the Whigs during their college years and how many later memories of those years focused on Whig gatherings. The faculty's choice of Otto to give one of two "honorary orations" at his commencement indicates that he ranked fifth in his class. He selected the topic of poetry and spoke immediately after the Latin salutatorian at the morning exercises.

Otto had barely begun his medical studies under the guidance of Benjamin Rush (A.B. 1760) of Philadelphia in the spring of 1793 when the yellow fever epidemic swept through the city. Of no practical use as a novice, Otto was persuaded to spend the summer out of the city, returning to his medical studies in the fall. As was the custom, he attended lectures at the University of Pennsylvania and made hospital rounds and other calls with Rush. Said to be attentive and assiduous in his studies, he became one of Rush's favorite pupils and later a close friend. Otto was already a member of the medical and chemical societies of Philadelphia by the time he submitted his thesis on May 17, 1796. Dedicated to Rush, "as a tribute of gratitude and esteem by his sincere friend and affectionate pupil," the essay was on the subject of epilepsy. The following week Rush wrote to Dr. John Redman Coxe that Otto was about to settle in Philadelphia, suggesting that he may have considered some other locations before coming to a final decision.

Less fortunate during the yellow fever epidemic of 1798, Otto contracted the disease while on his way to visit a sick friend at Woodbury. He remained there until his recovery, which was slow and difficult. On August 29 Rush wrote to his wife Julia, "Dr. Otto is ill at Woodbury. He sent for me yesterday to visit him. My present engagements forbade it. I sent him a good nurse, for his physician. Dr. Campbell informed me that he was deserted and shunned by the whole village, and that not a creature but himself would hand him even a dish of water." Otto must have at least tacitly agreed with Rush's controversial method of treating yellow fever by massive blood letting and purging, since he joined the short-lived medical society, the Academy of Medicine, on January 8, 1798. Organized by Rush and a group of his supporters, the society was chiefly interested in supporting Rush's views on yellow fever in opposition to those of the College of Physicians. Nothing has been found to indicate how Otto felt after personally undergoing the rigorous cure.

Otto's letters to Hobart during the period he was studying medicine are full of nostalgia for his Whig friends. He wrote on June 29, 1793, "Although absent from you [the Whigs], I have a bosom that glories in your success and sympathizes with your superiority over your rivals." Letters were sometimes delivered to Princeton by his classmate Peter Early, whom he saw frequently while the latter was studying law in Philadelphia, even though Early happened to be a Clio. Hobart appears to have been eager for the latest political news from Philadelphia, but Otto declared himself far removed from the worlds of both politics and business as he "glides down a medical stream." His loyalty to his alma mater was expressed in a letter of October 25, 1795: "A lapse of three years has had no influence in abating the warmth of my feelings for a place from which I have received so much pleasure, and I will add improvement."

By this time Otto's two younger brothers were enrolled at the College. Jacob was apparently doing well; he delivered one of the honorary orations at his commencement two years later. But by mid-January 1796 Otto was writing to Hobart about freshman Daniel's aversion to the study of Greek. Only because of his older brother's persuasion would Daniel remain at the College, and by June they had worked out a compromise whereby Daniel lived at Nassau Hall with Jacob without formal matriculation and received instruction in English grammar, geography and "figures" from Hobart. In his correspondence with the latter, Otto sadly commented, "it is impossible to describe my solicitude for his welfare." Nothing further has been found about Daniel who probably soon followed his inclination to go to sea.

In 1798 Otto was elected one of the physicians of the Philadelphia Dispensary, where he served for five years while also establishing a private practice from an office on Mulberry Street. During the summer of 1802 he made a short visit to New England, which may have been partially for professional reasons, for he carried a letter of introduction from Rush to Dr. John Warren of Boston.

On December 18, 1802 Otto married Eliza Tod, daughter of Alexander Tod, a justice of the court of common pleas of

Philadelphia. The marriage produced nine children, seven of whom survived their father. The best known was William Tod Otto (A.B. University of Pennsylvania 1833), a distinguished jurist and Abraham Lincoln's secretary of the interior, whose volumes on the United States Supreme Court became standard works on that institution. Otto is said to have led a quiet personal life, rarely attending social functions, retiring at ten and rising before six each morning for an hour of meditation and study before facing the responsibilities of the day. A Presbyterian, he still favored Thomas à Kempis's *The Imitation of Christ* for his morning meditations.

At Rush's death in 1813, Otto succeeded him as one of the physicians of the Pennsylvania Hospital, a position which he held until his resignation in 1835. Never considered an exceptionally brilliant doctor, and apparently very diffident about his own abilities, he was known for his deep sense of responsibility and devotion to his patients. Said to have little imagination for experimentation in diagnosis, his practice was therefore considered "safe." In charge of the medical wards at the hospital, Otto was known to stop by each patient's bed and courteously inquire about his condition. Eschewing any teaching responsibilities, Otto, like other physicians, was followed on his hospital rounds by students attending lectures at the medical school. His clinical remarks to them were noted for their clarity and conciseness. He limited himself to the practice of medicine, avoiding the usually more lucrative fields of surgery and obstetrics.

For twenty years Otto gratuitously attended patients at the Philadelphia Orphan Asylum, and he was also a physician to the Magdalen Asylum. Elected a member of the American Philosophical Society on January 17, 1817, he regularly attended and actively participated at meetings. In March 1819 he was elected a fellow of the College of Physicians. In this capacity he was one of three members appointed to form a committee with members of the Philadelphia College of Pharmacy. As a result of their deliberations the College of Physicians endorsed a uniform standard for the preparation of medicines and recommended the "Pharmacopoeia" prepared by the National Medical Convention of 1820. Otto served as a censor of the college for a number of years, considering the office not only as an opportunity for advancing medical knowledge, but also as an instrument by which professional ethics could be established and preserved. In his capacity as censor he took an active part in revising the by-laws and rules for professional conduct. When the cholera epidemic of 1832 reached Philadelphia, Otto was chosen head of the group of physicians appointed by the city to adopt whatever measures they felt necessary to check the spread of the epidemic. This group worked without remuneration throughout the summer, and the following spring a grateful city presented each with an inscribed silver pitcher. In 1834 Otto served for a year on the College of Physicians' committee on theory and practice of medicine and the following year on the committee on public hygiene. He was appointed vice president of the College of Physicians on July 7, 1840, a position which he held until his death.

Although Otto was one of a group of four physicians who edited *The Eclectic Repertory and Analytical Review, Medical and Philosophical,* he seldom wrote for medical journals. Probably his greatest contribution to medical knowledge was his short article, "An Account of a Hemorrhagic Disposition Existing in Certain Families," which appeared in New York's *Medical Repository* in 1803 and described the characteristics of hemophiliac patients, especially the hereditary transmission of the disease through the female members of a family to male descendants. Two years later he published a second article in John R. Coxe's *Philadelphia Medical Museum,* in which he detailed the history of a Maryland family that had sustained four fatal cases of hemorrhage and among whom the disease could be traced back for almost a century. Otto's "cure" by administering sulphate soda "in ordinary purging dose" two or three days in succession seems simply a variation of Rush's theory of curing most ailments by purging, but Otto's articles were the first published on the subject, and the interest they generated soon led to others and to the recognition of hemophilia as an hereditary disease. Similarly, his paper on "Congenital Incontinence of Urine," read before the College of Physicians in 1830, suggested no effective cure but did establish incontinence as a disease or organic disorder, rather than simply a bad habit. His dosage of pulverized sage, ginger, and unbruised mustard seed was also undoubtedly ineffective in curing epilepsy, but the calomel and opium which he prescribed for chronic rheumatism probably quickly masked the pain of this condition and was considered quite efficacious.

For several years before his death Otto suffered from frequent attacks of gout, and by late 1843 or early 1844 he was visibly failing. He apparently planned to leave Philadelphia in the hope of gaining relief in a different climate and sold his medical books to the College of Physicians for $200, thus providing the nucleus of its future library. He died, still in Philadelphia, at 6 p.m. on June 26, 1844 of "extreme organic disease of the heart." He was described as slender, with a slightly stooped figure in his later years. His memoir, read before the College of Physicians on March 4, 1845, in which one might expect extravagant praise, described him as kind and useful, rather than brilliant, a man who had been sustained throughout his practice by the belief that a physician is a minister of good to his fellows.

SOURCES: *DAB* ("extreme organic"); I. Parrish, *Biog. Memoir of John C. Otto* (1845), *passim*; alumni file, PUA; Andrew Hunter Account Book, p. 12, Stockton Family Papers, NjPHi; T. Cushing & C. E. Sheppard, *Hist. of Cnties. of Gloucester, Salem & Cumberland, N.J.* (1883), 40-41; *PMHB*, 58 (1934), 312, 337-38; *N.J. Wills*, IV, 295-96; VII, 173; Min. Fac., 10 Nov. 1789, 23 July 1792 ("honorary orations"); Amer. Whig Soc., *Cat.* (1840), 6; Williams, *Academic Honors*, 13; *N.J. Jour.*, 10 Oct. 1792; J. F. Schroeder, *Memorial of Bishop Hobart* (1831), xx-xxi; Hobart, *Corres.*, I, 28-33, 139-42, 150-52, 194-96, 214-15 (all quotes from letters); Alexander, *Princeton*, 262-64; J. C. Otto, *Essay on Epilepsy* (1796); Butterfield, *Rush Letters*, I, 260; II, 775, 778, 797, 804, 850-51; F. P. Henry, *Hist. of the Medical Profession of Phila.* (1897), 119, 141, 150, 455, 495; J. T. Scharf & T. Westcott, *Hist. of Phila.* (1884), I, 633; II, 1610; C. E. Rosenberg, *Cholera Years* (1962), 6, 13-98; Amer. Phil. Soc., *List of the Members ...* (1880?), 25; W. S. W. Ruschenberger, *Acct. of the Inst. & Progress of the College of Physicians of Phila.* (1887), 87-88, 129, 163, 192-93, 198, 254.

PUBLICATION: STE # 30934

RLW

Lewis Searle Pintard

LEWIS SEARLE PINTARD, A.B., A.M. 1795, was the only son of Abigail Stockton and Capt. Samuel Pintard of New Rochelle, New York. Pintard's French Huguenot great-grandfather Antoine Pintard had immigrated to what was then called La Rochelle, and later moved to Shrewsbury, Monmouth County, New Jersey. Samuel Pintard worked his way up from ensign to captain in the Twenty-Fifth British Regiment of Foot, was badly wounded on a German battlefield, and returned home "full of honors and wounds." Family tradition claims that he was offered both a commission as a brigadier general by the American Army and as major by the British. He neatly straddled the fence by refusing both offers on the grounds that he would fight neither against his king nor his country. He married Abigail Stockton of Princeton in 1770, which made him the brother-in-law of Richard Stockton (A.B. 1748) and Elias Boudinot, trustee of the College, whose French ancestors had also settled in La Rochelle. Thus, Lewis was a first cousin of Richard Stockton (A.B. 1779) and Lucius Horatio Stockton (A.B. 1787), as well as of John Pintard (A.B. 1776), son of his father's brother John. Two of his Stockton cousins were married to Benjamin Rush (A.B. 1760) and Andrew Hunter (A.B. 1772), and while Lewis was a sophomore at the College his cousin Martha (Patty) Pintard, daughter of his father's brother Lewis and his mother's sister Susannah Stockton, married Samuel Bayard (A.B. 1784). There were more distant relationships with other Stocktons connected with the College, as well as with Thomas Hutchins (A.B. 1789), whose maternal grandmother had been a Pintard.

Pintard's aunt Catherine Pintard married the Reverend Leonard Cutting, who supervised the college preparation of John Pintard at the classical school that he operated at Hempstead, Long Island. Lewis Pintard may also have attended the school at Hempstead until Cutting's retirement in 1784, but nothing positive is known about his early education. Pintard entered the College as a freshman and joined the American Whig Society. He progressed with his class until his senior examination, when he and his classmate Jacob Ford performed so poorly that the faculty did not recommend them to the trustees for the A.B. degree. Reexamined just prior to commencement, they were given favorable reports and joined their classmates in receiving their degrees. In spite of the last minute nature of this decision, they were prepared to participate in the debate on the question, "Is there any evidence from the radical resemblance of the languages of different nations, that mankind have sprung from one source?"

Nothing has been discovered about Pintard's involvement with any profession or trade, either as a student or a practitioner. His father and uncles had mercantile interests in New York City, and he probably assumed some responsibilities connected with the family businesses. He settled in New Rochelle, but whether immediately after his graduation from the College or after his father's death in April 1805 is not known. He was in Princeton on November 9, 1794, either as a resident or a visitor, when he was among the family members gathered to say goodbye to his cousin Martha Pintard Bayard and her husband Samuel Bayard before their departure for England. Martha recorded in her journal, "I behaved very well till Lewis Pintard, who I believe loves me like a Sister, burst into tears and left the table; this was too much, I was obliged to rise and go upstairs." The "Lewis Pentard" who was one of the commissioners of schools in New Rochelle in 1797 could have been either the Princetonian or his uncle Lewis. By 1812 it was "Lewis S. Pintard" who received permission from the annual town meeting to remove rocks and stones from the road adjoining his property, provided that he fill the holes from which the stones were removed.

What little else is known about Lewis Pintard can be gleaned from the family letters of his cousin John Pintard, an extremely biased source. Lewis is depicted as an intemperate wastrel who was involved in an unfortunate marriage to an extravagant wife, whom John was persuaded was "the principal cause of his degeneracy." Lewis had married Ann T. Burling Bennett, "the wild daughter of a very respectable Quaker Ebenezer Burling," and John remarked after his cousin's death that, "he had led a miserable life ever since his imprudent marriage with a low minded vulgar artful widow, who drew him into her toils & abused his confidence." She may have been the

Ann Burling who was "disowned for marriage out" by the New York Friends' Meeting on January 5, 1814. Lewis's mother was staying with relatives in Burlington, New Jersey at the time of her last illness, whether from choice or because her daughter-in-law refused to care for her in New Rochelle is not known.

In April 1817 Lewis Pintard suffered a violent attack of typhus, from which both his family and his doctor feared that he would not recover. However, he managed "to struggle yet a while," even though "His stamina is completely burnt up & he is feeble as a child." Although Lewis was partially recovered by May, John felt he could only look forward to "linger[ing] out a wretched existence." During this period Lewis's seventy-nine-year-old mother was approaching her demise in a chronically feeble condition at Burlington. When John visited her shortly before her death on October 11 he noted: "She spoke but little when I took her by the hand & told her that I had heard from her son who has been a source of affliction to her & literally brought her grey hairs with sorrow to the grave." Shortly after Abigail Pintard's death, John Pintard's wife Elizabeth traveled to New Rochelle to advise Lewis to go to Burlington if possible "& implicitly to follow his Uncle Boudinot's advice." Lewis was now the sole heir of his father's estate, which John Pintard estimated might yield an annuity of $750 a year and which, with an unencumbered home, farm, and woodland at New Rochelle, John felt should be enough to provide Lewis a comfortable living, although he added: "His poor father & mother submitted to many privations that their only son might go gallant & gay. He has spent in shameful riotous living the chief of his subsistence."

Lewis Pintard died at 3 p.m. on Wednesday, August 12, 1818. His cousin John made the arrangements for his interment in the family vault at St. Esprit, the French Protestant church in New York City that had been built by Huguenot refugees. Elizabeth Pintard visited Lewis's widow the following month to retrieve some borrowed books and to try to purchase some of the Pintard family silver in Ann's possession. However, Samuel Bayard was planning to contest Pintard's will in court, making it impossible to sell any part of the estate and not unnaturally arousing the resentment of the widow. John Pintard had earlier remarked that because of Lewis's wife's "riotous profusion," Lewis had not left a cent to any of his family. However the courts agreed that rights of the widow did take precedence over those of cousins, and by October 1819 "Mrs. Pintard had succeeded in establishing the will & to act as sole Executrix." As soon as John and Elizabeth learned that she was selling personal effects, they decided that "no time was to be lost," and Elizabeth set off for New Rochelle in a near hurricane. However, she found the widow "at present quite flush of money and ... very fond of *her* family plate," and Elizabeth returned empty handed, with only a promise of first refusal should it prove necessary to sell the silver. Ann Pintard died of a stroke on January 19, 1828, when she was only forty-four.

John Pintard performed one last service for his cousin when St. Esprit was razed in 1831 and he superintended the removal of all of the family remains to a new vault in St. Clement's churchyard on Amity Street (West Third Street). When this building was demolished in 1910, all of the Pintard remains were removed to St. Michael's Cemetery in Queen's County, Long Island. The 1831 transfer was difficult for John Pintard since, for some reason, all of the coffins had to be opened and inspected. John had at one time thought of Lewis as his "dear brother," and all references to him after his death were to "poor Lewis." Because of the family's experience with Lewis he could say: "Of all curses, that of intemperance is among the most bitter." He mentioned in his correspondence the deaths of John G. Bogert and a Mr. Duff, a wine merchant, both of whom had been noted for their intemperance; both had been "boon companions" of Lewis.

SOURCES: Alumni file, PUA; Min. Fac., 10 Nov. 1789, 23 July, 17 Aug., 25 Sept. 1792; Amer. Whig Soc., *Cat.* (1840), 6; Min. Trustees, 25 Sept. 1792; R. Bolton, *Hist. of Westchester Cnty.* (1881), I, 679; S. B. Dod, ed., *Jour. of Martha Pintard Bayard* (1894), 13 ("I behaved"); Pintard, *Letters*, I, x-xi, 59, 64, 81, 83, 84, 86, 88, 99, 112, 138, 142-43, 148; III, 6, 51, 164, 234-35, 241 (all additional quotes); J. A. Forbes, *Records of the Town of New Rochelle* (1916), 385-86, 406; W. W. Hinshaw, *Encyc. of Amer. Quaker Gen.* (1940), III, 54; D. L. Sterling, "New York Patriarch: A Life of John Pintard" (Ph.D. diss., NYU, 1958); Stockton Family Papers, NjPHi; MS Records of Princeton Chapter D.A.R, NjPHi.

RLW

Joseph Reed, Jr.

JOSEPH REED, JR., A.B., lawyer and public official, was born in Philadelphia on July 11, 1772, the second child and oldest son of Joseph Reed (A.B. 1757), the Revolutionary statesman who served as military secretary to George Washington and adjutant-general of the Continental Army, and in a succession of high offices culminating in a term as president of the supreme executive council of Pennsylvania. Elected to the board of trustees of the College in 1780, he was also president of the board of the University of the State of Pennsylvania. Reed's English bride was Esther, the only daughter of Dennys DeBerdt, London merchant and the colonial agent for Massachusetts.

Joseph Reed, Jr., A.B. 1792
BY CHARLES B. J. FEVRET DE SAINT MEMIN

The couple's two younger sons were Dennis DeBerdt Reed (A.B. 1797) and George Washington Reed (A.B. 1798).

Young Joseph's childhood was marked by repeated family upheavals. The summer of 1776 was spent in two locations in New Jersey, with the necessity of further flight a constant threat. The Reeds returned to Philadelphia, but when British occupation again seemed likely they moved on to Norristown, Pennsylvania, then to Burlington, and finally Flemington, New Jersey. The father rarely spent time with his family, since his presence was deemed an additional danger. In 1778, when he was elected president of Pennsylvania, he moved his wife and children to the official residence on Market Street in Philadelphia. They also enjoyed the summer residence provided for the president on the east bank of the Schuylkill River.

After the strains of the war, the year 1780 finally wore out Esther Reed. She delivered her youngest son in May shortly after recovering from smallpox. She expended energy on entertaining Martha Washington as a houseguest in late June and on her duties as head of the Philadelphia women who were raising funds to provide clothing for the American soldiers. On September 18, 1780, shortly after the family's return to the city, she succumbed to acute dysentery and was buried at the Second Presbyterian Church on Arch Street. The children were cared for by their maternal grandmother, who was visiting in Philadelphia, and by their father's sister Mary.

When Reed retired from the supreme executive council the following year the family moved again, this time to a leased house on Third Street. For a short period the children saw more of their father, but in the winter of 1783-84 he sailed for England with his mother-in-law and with the hope that the sea voyage would improve his failing health. He also agreed to join President John Witherspoon, at his own expense, in soliciting funds to help repair wartime damage to Nassau Hall and to replace books and equipment. While Witherspoon traveled to his native Scotland, Reed contacted acquaintances in England, but they found that American causes were not popular and decided to make no appeals on the continent. After Witherspoon's expenses were deducted, the College lost money from their efforts.

During their father's seven-month absence, the children were cared for by family friends, Joseph and Dennis staying with Jared Ingersoll, Jr. (LL.D. 1821, A.B. Yale 1766), Reed's legal protégé, and his wife Elizabeth Pettit, parents of Charles Jared Ingersoll (Class of 1799) and Joseph Reed Ingersoll (A.B. 1804). Sometime during this period Joseph was sent to the Moravian School in Bethlehem, Pennsylvania to study German. On May 2, 1784 his father wrote to him from England,

> Remember my dear Boy that to be a great Man, or what is better a good Man, you must mind your Book when you are young, be obliging and kind to all your Companions, avoid all bad Language and above all never tell a Lye on any account nor take anything which is not your own. Think what pleasure it will be to me to find when I come Home that every Body loves and praises you, what an example it will be to your Brothers who will mind what you do. It will not be long now before I see you if I am well, and I shall not leave you again very soon.

The father returned to Philadelphia in September 1784 and died the following March, leaving his children under the combined guardianship of Ingersoll, his law partner and friend Charles Pettit, and a third close friend, William Bradford, Jr. (A.B. 1772). The three were also co-executors of the will in which Reed made the following provisions for the education of his children:

> As my sentiments of education differ widely from the common mode, I desire that my boys be taught writing, arithmetic, mathematics, and the German and French languages, in preference

to all other learning, and on no account to meddle with the dead languages till they arrive at the age of fifteen, nor then unless they discover remarkable genius. My present intentions are that Joseph be bred to trade, but not sent abroad till he has served his apprenticeship to the age of twenty; Dennis to be bred to the law; under the care of my good friends Mr. Ingersoll or Mr. Bradford; Washington is of too tender an age yet to say anything of him, but that I would have the same mode of education as to him, and that they go to Bethlehem at proper ages to learn the German—to Canada to learn French, if practicable, but none to go out of America till twenty.

This assessment of his sons' abilities proved wrong, for Dennis turned to trade, while Joseph became an attorney. Reed, "considering the education of my children of more importance than giving them fortunes, & being unable to do both," directed his executors to sell his property, invest the money, and use the interest for the education of his children, adding that even the principal should be used for that purpose if necessary.

Joseph Reed, Jr., entered the College as a freshman and joined the American Whig Society. At the end of his sophomore year he was declared first in English orations in the competitions held among the underclassmen each year. As a junior he was first in both English grammar and English orations, and as a senior he was ranked fourth in his class and selected to deliver the valedictory oration at his commencement. In 1781, during a period of acute financial need for the College, the trustees had borrowed £39 from Reed's father, and on April 15, 1791 the board voted that this amount, plus interest, should be credited toward the son's college expenses.

J. H. Martin's *Bench and Bar of Philadelphia* gives the date of Reed's admission to the Philadelphia bar as March 10, 1792, more than six months prior to his graduation from college, and another source credits him with the study of law "while at college." No law courses were available at the College. Reed, a bright young man, was brought up among lawyers, whose households usually included law clerks studying under them. Unlike other college students, he probably started reading law as an extracurricular study. Possibly Richard Stockton (A.B. 1779) took an interest in him and oversaw his law studies during the period he was in residence at the College, since Reed's father had studied law under Stockton's father. Reed's name as an attorney is not found in Philadelphia city directories until 1800, but his commission as clerk of the court of quarter sessions on January 22, 1800 indicates that he must have been practicing prior to that date.

Reed lost one of his legal mentors when William Bradford died in 1795. In a will drawn in 1788, Bradford, "In grateful remembrance of the friendship and patronage I experienced from Joseph Reed, Esquire," left £1,150 to each of Reed's children, along with a tract of 1,005 acres in Northumberland County to be divided among them. However, in the famous case of *Boudinot v. Bradford*, this will was judged invalid, and Thomas Bradford was declared the heir at law of his brother. By May 1796 Reed was acting as substitute parent for his brother Dennis, who had expressed a desire to leave the College. Notified of his brother's intentions, Reed informed him that he strongly disapproved of such a measure, and he then checked with John Henry Hobart (A.B. 1793), a tutor at the College, to be sure that Dennis had actually returned to his classes.

Reed was considered both a skillful and a precise lawyer. He maintained an extensive practice while continuously holding important public offices, but he never achieved the degree of fame and recognition accorded to his father. For at least part of his legal career he was associated with Thomas Barton Zantzinger, another prominent Philadelphia lawyer. On January 2, 1806 Reed succeeded Edward Burd as prothonotary of the supreme court of Pennsylvania, Burd having resigned to run for the state senate only after being assured that Reed would accept the position. Appointed by the mayor to act as city solicitor for Philadelphia for the year 1810, Reed was also attorney general of the commonwealth for the brief period from October 2, 1810 until January 26, 1811, when he was succeeded by Richard Rush (A.B. 1797). In October 1810, Reed was also appointed by the governor as recorder of the City of Philadelphia, a position which he held until August 1829. The recorder, considered second in importance only to the mayor, acted as an assistant to the mayor and could hold court both as a justice of the peace and a justice of oyer and terminer.

When the Pennsylvania Republican party split during the virulent gubernatorial campaign of 1817, Reed was one of the leaders of the group variously called Old School Democrats and Independent Republicans, which supported Joseph Hiester, father of John Hiester (A.B. 1794), for governor. Hiester lost by a narrow vote to William Findlay, New School Democrat, but succeeded him as governor in 1820. Reed's name as an attorney last appears in the Philadelphia directory for 1829, when he presumably discontinued his private practice at the same time that he gave up his position as city recorder. In 1822, with the authorization of the legislature, he had edited the sixth and seventh volumes of *The Laws of the Commonwealth of Pennsylvania*, which started with the statutes of 1812-13. Part of Reed's retirement years were spent in editing the next three volumes, which took the laws up to the legislative session of 1829-30.

Prominent in affairs of the city, Reed was elected to membership in the prestigious First Troop Philadelphia City Cavalry as early as May 1789. He resigned in 1810, perhaps feeling it a conflict of interest with his position as city solicitor. Reelected to membership on August 27, 1814, he again resigned on August 4, 1815. During this period he was among the Philadelphia citizens who organized a committee of defense when an invasion by the British was thought imminent, serving as temporary secretary for the group. He was elected to membership in the American Philosophical Society on January 19, 1816, and in the summer of 1818 he was among the federal and state officials selected to make arrangements for the visit of President James Monroe (LL.D. 1822) to Philadelphia. The same year he also became a member of the first board of control of the public schools of the city.

On June 15, 1805 Reed married Maria Ellis Watmough, daughter of Anna Christine and James Horatio Watmough. The Reeds' second daughter Margaretta married John Sergeant (A.B. 1795), the 1832 Whig candidate for vice president on the ticket with Henry Clay. The Watmough estate, located on the Bethlehem Pike at Whitemarsh, about fourteen miles from Philadelphia, was called "Hope Lodge" in honor of Colonel Watmough's guardian, Henry Hope. Both the Reeds and Sergeants often resided there, and it became their home away from the city.

Reed died in Philadelphia on March 4, 1846, with his widow surviving him by more than twenty years. Their eldest son William Bradford Reed (A.B. University of Pennsylvania 1822), who served as district attorney of Philadelphia and attorney general of Pennsylvania, also received diplomatic appointments to Mexico and China. He is best remembered for his defense of his grandfather in *Life and Correspondence of Joseph Reed*, published in 1847 in response to an attack on the latter's integrity in George Bancroft's *History of the United States*. Henry Hope Reed (A.B. University of Pennsylvania 1825) was also trained as a lawyer, but preferred to teach English history and English literature at the University of Pennsylvania. He edited various standard works of English literature and initiated a long correspondence with William Wordsworth, becoming the special interpreter of the poet's works to the American public.

SOURCES: Alumni file, PUA; *DAB*; *Princetonians, 1748-1768*, 200-04; H. Simpson, *Lives of Eminent Philadelphians* (1859), 837: E. F. Ellet, *Women of the Amer. Revolution* (1900), I, 47-70; J. F. Roche, *Joseph Reed* (1957), *passim*; Min. Fac., 10 Nov. 1789, 13 July 1792; Min. Trustees, 15 Apr. 1791; Hobart, *Corres.*, I, 206-07; Amer. Whig Soc., *Cat.* (1840),

6; *N.J. Jour.*, 10 Oct. 1792; Phila. city directories, 1800-30; *Martin's Bench & Bar*, 25-27, 82-83, 88, 97, 124, 305; L. B. Walker, *Burd Papers* (1899), 109-10; J. Jackson, *Encyc. of Phila.* (1933), IV, 1043; J. Jackson, *Market Street, Phila.* (1918), 115; P. S. Klien, *Pa. Politics 1817-32* (1974), 79-96; H. D. Eberlein & C. V. Hubbard, *Portrait of a Colonial City* (1939), 164-66, 296, 493-95; H. D. Eberlein & H. M. Lippincott, *Colonial Homes of Phila.* (1912), 279-80; *Hist. of the First Troop Phila. City Cavalry* (1875), 181; *Autobiography of Charles Biddle* (1883), 351-52; E. P. Cheney, *Hist. of the Univ. of Pa.* (1940), 129-30, 223, 230-31, 242-43; Univ. of Pa., *Biog. Cat. of the Matriculates ... 1749-1893* (1894), 66, 73; *PMHB*, 62 (1938), 123, 358, 529; Amer. Phil. Soc., *List of the Members ...* (1880?), 24.

PUBLICATION: See *Martin's Bench & Bar*, 188-89, for *Laws of the Commonwealth of Pa.*, vols. 6-10 (1822-44)

RLW

James D. Ross

JAMES D. ROSS of Virginia, A.B., planter, was probably the son of David Ross and the brother of his classmate William Ross. As measured by tax records, in the late 1780s David Ross was Virginia's richest man, possessing 100,000 acres from Fluvanna to Mecklenburg counties, with large holdings in the Shenandoah Valley. His assessment for horses was highest and for cattle the second highest in the state, and he owned 400 slaves. A native Scot, he is variously described as a resident of Fluvanna County, of Richmond, and of Petersburg. He was a merchant, flour miller, shipowner, and the proprietor of coal and iron mines and the Oxford Iron Works in Campbell County. From 1780 to 1782 he served as the commercial agent of Virginia, and in 1786 he was in the state's delegation to the Annapolis Convention.

James Ross first appears in the College sources as a junior in November 1790. He did not join either literary society. The faculty minutes record several infractions by Ross. On June 10, 1791 he and his classmate Edmund J. Lee were admonished privately for having made an "improper use" of their sword canes. A week later he joined eight other students in taking a late-night swim, for which he earned a public reproof. Near the end of June 1792 James and William Ross became involved in a violent quarrel with Isaac Gibbs (Class of 1794). The faculty minutes provide little detail, but the language used suggests that the affair was serious. The trio had "grossly violated the laws of the institution & deserved severe reprehension" and were required to apologize, "lay aside all animosity against each other & solemnly promise never to renew this quarrel in college or anywhere else." Ross graduated three months later but at his own request did not participate in the exercises.

Ross became a tobacco planter in Fluvanna County and died intestate sometime before July 11, 1801, when his estate was inventoried. Probably he was the "Mr. James Ross, son of David Ross, Esq.," who died in September 1800 near the Warm Springs, Bath County, Virginia. According to a newspaper account, one day Ross departed alone from that place bound for Red Springs in present-day Monroe County, West Virgina. His horse returned without him and his body was found two days later. It was "supposed from there being no appearance of a mangled state, that Mr. Ross has made use of laudanum to put an end to his existence."

At his death Ross's personal property was assessed at more than $3,000, including ten slaves, seven horses, and a "Book Case with contents" which, estimated at $150, was among his most valuable possessions. His marital status has not been discovered, unless he was the James Ross who in 1795 married Elizabeth, daughter of William Griffin, in Bath County.

SOURCES: J. T. Main, "The One Hundred," WMQ, 3d ser., 11 (1954), 363, 381; VMHB, 77 (1969), 180-84; 78 (1970), 393-95; WMQ, 3d ser., 31 (1974), 189-224; K. Bruce, Va. Iron Manufacture in the Slave Era (1931), 64; W. T. Hutchinson, W. M. E. Rachal, et al., eds., Papers of James Madison (1962-   ), 1st ser., III, 60; letter from R. F. George, Fluvanna County Circuit Court, 19 Jan. 1983, PUA; Min. Fac., 29 Nov. 1790, 10 & 22 June 1791, 25 & 27 June, 13 July 1792 ("an improper," "grossly," "lay aside"); N.J. Journal, 10 Oct. 1792 (JDR a Virginian); Claypoole's Amer. Daily Advt., 27 Sept. 1800 ("Mr. James," "supposed from"); estate inv. of James D. Ross, dated 11 July & recorded 27 July 1801, MS will book I, Fluvanna County Circuit Court ("Book Case"); O. F. Morton, Annals of Bath Cnty., Va. (1917), 131. The identification of James as David's son rests on the connection of both with Fluvanna County and on James's middle initial, which could have stood for David. On the other hand, the middle initial is also a problem, since a contemporary source refers to David and his son "James N. Ross" discussing the prospects for investment in Georgia on a visit to Prince Edward County, Virginia on October 8, 1792. See Tyler's Quart., 2 (1920), 138; VMHB, 20 (1912), 313-15. David Ross had a brother James, but the latter seems to have left no issue. Wanda S. Gunning kindly supplied references used in this sketch.

JJL

William Ross

WILLIAM ROSS, A.B., was the son of David Ross of Virginia, and probably the brother of his classmate James D. Ross. David Ross was a Scots immigrant who had amassed one of the largest fortunes in Virginia by the late 1780s, although his wealth diminished somewhat in his old age. His holdings of land were scattered over much of Virginia, and different sources refer to him as a resident of Richmond, Petersburg, and Fluvanna County. He owned plantations, iron and coal mines, extensive iron works, ships, a mercantile concern, and flour mills, and he was a director of the James River Canal Company. In 1786 he represented Virginia at the Annapolis Convention.

William Ross made his first appearance on a College class list as a junior in November 1790. He joined the Cliosophic Society in the same year, taking as his pseudonym Chimenes, possibly a reference to Cardinal Francisco Ximenéz de Cisneros, the early sixteenth-century primate of Spain. Since he was inquisitor general of Castile, Cardinal Ximenéz seems an odd role model for a Princetonian of 1790, but his founding of a university and sponsorship of the Complutensian Polyglot Bible could explain the choice. For unknown reasons Ross was dismissed from the society on May 31, 1792. Less than a month later, on June 25, 1792, Ross found himself in trouble with the faculty as well. He and James Ross and Isaac Gibbs (Class of 1794) were found to have been "guilty of very indecent violence against each other" and were obliged to express "sorrow for the outrage," listen to a public admonition before their respective classes, and promise "not to renew the quarrel at college or in any other place." Ross chose not to participate in the exercises at his commencement.

Little has been found about Ross's subsequent career. When he died at "Cobbham," his father's seat, on September 18, 1804, he was referred to as William Ross "of Mount Ida." A newspaper obituary observed that "his illness was long, and marked by that inveterate obstinacy peculiar to his disease." It asserted that he had been a model husband, son, and brother but said nothing of his being a father. His wife, whose name has not been discovered, survived him.

SOURCES: J. T. Main, "The One Hundred," *WMQ*, 3d ser., 11 (1954), 363, 381; *VMHB*, 77 (1969), 180-84; 78 (1970), 393-95; *WMQ*, 3d ser., 31 (1974), 189-224; K. Bruce, *Va. Iron Manufacture in the Slave Era* (1931), 64; W. T. Hutchinson, W. M. E. Rachal, et al., eds., *Papers of James Madison* (1962-), 1st ser., III, 60; letter from R. F. George, Fluvanna County Circuit Court, 19 Jan. 1983, PUA; Min. Fac., 29 Nov. 1790, 25-27 June & 13 July 1792 ("guilty," "sorrow," "not to"); Clio. lists; *N.J. Journal*, 10 Oct. 1792; *Richmond Enquirer*, 26 Sept. 1804 ("of Mount," "his illness"). Alexander, *Princeton*, 264, and Princeton Univ., *Gen. Cat.* (1908) assert that William Ross served in the New York legislature for a period of years starting in 1812, but this is certainly an error. All contemporary sources agree that the Princetonian was from Virginia, while the New York legislator was born and bred in Orange County, New York. See E. M. Ruttenber & L. H. Clark, *Hist. of Orange Cnty., N.Y.* (1881), 144.

JJL

James Ruan

JAMES RUAN, A.B., A.M. 1810, was the son of John Ruan, a planter of St. Croix in the Danish West Indies, and the brother of John Ruan (A.B. 1790). The boys' mother was already deceased when their father died in 1782. Their guardians no doubt felt that James, probably still less than ten years old, was too young to accompany

John and an older brother when they were sent north to further their education. Whether or not James later joined them at the Trenton Academy, he did follow in John's footsteps by entering the College as a junior. Enrolling in the fall of 1790, he again emulated his brother by joining the American Whig Society. At his commencement he was the opponent in the second dispute, "Is the policy of India and ancient Egypt, of dividing the people into different classes and confining children to the profession of their fathers, preferable to that universal freedom of enterprize that prevails in Europe?"

Nothing has been found to show whether Ruan pursued any profession. Since John Ruan had two brothers living in St. Croix in 1821, it is possible that James Ruan returned to the island to look after a family plantation. College catalogues first list him as deceased in 1839.

SOURCES: Alumni file, PUA; Min. Fac., 29 Nov. 1790, 13 July 1792; Amer. Whig Soc., Cat. (1840), 6; N.J. Jour., 10 Oct. 1792. Nothing on the Ruan family has been found in available St. Croix sources. John Ruan appears in most Pa. census records through 1840 as the head of a household; he also appears in the Philadelphia city directories from 1823 through 1844. There is no census record of James, and the only James Ruan in the Philadelphia directories is a carter, whose name does not appear until 1840. A notebook containing "Burial Records of the Board of Health of Philadelphia" at PHi contains a death certificate, signed by Dr. John Ruan, for a Thomas Ruan, son of James Ruan, dated 3 Feb. 1840.

RLW

Robert Russel (Russell)

ROBERT RUSSEL (RUSSELL), A.B., Presbyterian minister, was born in Fagg's Manor or New Londonderry, Chester County, Pennsylvania, around 1757. The 1790 census shows that several families of Russels and Russells in that area had sons over sixteen. None of them was a slave owner. A lack of funds may have been the reason for Russel's advanced age at the time he entered the College.

Russel matriculated as a member of the junior class in November 1790. He approached graduation still owing £11.2.0 for tuition and £39.2.0 to the College steward. The trustees, meeting on September 25, 1792, decided: "Inasmuch as Mr. Russell has uniformly borne the Character of a prudent and pious young Man who has in View the Ministry of the Gospel *Resolved* that Mr. Russel is a proper object of the Charity of the Board and that out of funds appropriated for the Education of poor & pious Youth the Treasurers Account shall be defrayed except £7.10.0 paid by Jonathan Bayard Smith [A.B. 1760] & the Rev. James Boyd [A.B. 1763] out of Funds in their hands for a similar purpose—also the Account of the Steward for the last

Summer Session amounting to £7.0.0." At his own request, Russel was exempted from taking part in his commencement exercises.

For the next year he studied somewhere within the bounds of the Presbytery of New Castle. In order to return to Princeton to study under Samuel Stanhope Smith (A.B. 1769), Russel applied to the Presbytery of New Brunswick for support. On September 17, 1793 that body voted to undertake his support while he studied divinity at Princeton, since inquiry had shown that he was "a person who bears an unblemished moral character, has long been in the communion of the Church, and was estimated truly pious, & may prove useful to the cause of Christ." The following day he was examined to the satisfaction of the presbytery and admitted as a probationer under the care of Dr. Smith, who was allocated funds for the purpose. Smith was also asked to request from the trustees of the College whatever financial assistance their funds would permit, to go toward the support of Russel and Holloway Hunt (A.B. 1794). On December 18 the trustees voted that the two ministerial candidates would be among those receiving support, not to exceed £40 per year, from the funds left by James Lesley (A.B. 1759) of New York "for the education of poor and pious Youth, with a View to the Ministry of the Gospel in the Presbyterian Church." The funds were to be used at the discretion of the trustees of the College, under the superintendance of the General Assembly of the Presbyterian Church. The College trustees required a semiannual report from the faculty on the progress of those receiving help from the fund.

The following April Smith gave a favorable report. The board then discussed the appropriateness of defraying the expenses of maintenance and clothing, as well as of instruction, from Lesley's fund and determined that they had the right to do so. Accordingly the stipend was increased to £50 per year for the next six months. For the April meeting of the presbytery Russel produced an extract from the minutes of the New Castle presbytery attesting to his good moral character and his full communion with the church and granting him permission to transfer to the New Brunswick presbytery. He continued to receive favorable reports on his character and improvement, and at the meetings of the presbytery he delivered assigned orations and sermons and was tested on various aspects of Presbyterian theology and church history, fulfilling the last of the requirements for being licensed as a probationer on April 29, 1795.

Russel's epitaph was later to credit him with receiving the A.M. degree from the College, which would have been the usual course upon the completion of his theological studies. However, neither College records nor newspaper lists of degree recipients include Russel among those receiving the higher degree. He joined the Cliosophic Society on November 26, 1794, two years after his graduation, taking the pseudonym Laurin. A manuscript membership list, which includes the year of graduation of most of the members, has the unusual designation "1795(2)" by Russel's name, perhaps indicating that he expected to receive a second degree at that time.

For over a year Russel served as a supply minister for the New Brunswick presbytery, preaching in various churches under its jurisdiction. The majority of his Sundays were spent at New Brunswick and Allentown, New Jersey, and in April 1796 the latter congregation requested as much of his time as possible. In September he requested and was granted dismission from the New Brunswick presbytery in order to unite with the Presbytery of New Castle.

During the remainder of 1796 and through 1797 Russel continued to serve as a supply, frequently preaching for the English Presbyterian congregation of Allen Township in Northampton County, Pennsylvania. This congregation had been served by Francis Peppard (A.B. 1762) until disagreements due to Peppard's opposition to a new religious academy in the community and his rigidity in interpretation of church discipline caused him to ask for release from his pastoral duties. Russel and Uriah Dubois were the two candidates considered by the congregation to replace Peppard, with the younger members favoring Dubois and the older ones preferring Russel. The latter group prevailed and Russel became the sixth pastor of the Allen Township church, his first and only pastorate. He was required to go through a trial period by the Presbytery of Philadelphia, which he joined on December 2, 1797. For this purpose he preached several sermons and was examined on experimental religion, systematic divinity, ecclesiastical history, church government, and the arts and sciences. On April 18, 1798 he was ordained and formally installed as pastor of the Allen Township church, with the Reverend Ashbel Green (A.B. 1783) of Philadelphia preaching the ordination sermon and the Reverend William Tennent (A.B. 1763) of Abington and the Reverend Nathaniel Irwin (A.B. 1770) of Neshaminy delivering the charges.

It was probably not long afterward that Russel married Margaret Armstrong, daughter of Thomas Armstrong, an elder in his congregation, who had been commissioned county coroner in 1755. Early in the nineteenth century the Allen Township church was weakened by the westward migration of a number of families. However, the membership must have increased substantially by 1813, when it was decided that two houses of worship were needed, with services alternating between the two. A new building was erected near the site of the old church in the section of the township known as Weaversville. The academy, about three miles away in the Borough of Bath, was renovated so that it could also be used for divine worship. The academy was abandoned in 1826 but is considered the forerunner of Lafayette College. Its closing may have been caused by the same financial problems that plagued the church, since 1825 saw another period of depletion in the community, and only Russel's voluntary cut in salary enabled the congregation to fulfill its obligations. In 1827 the failure of the Northampton Bank, in which the church owned stock, led to real financial difficulties, and Russel's salary was paid only through August 5. On November 7 the trustees passed a motion that Russel serve only half time, presumably with half pay. It was, in any case, probably time for him to lighten his work load, for he was in his seventieth year. He died on December 16, 1827. His wife had predeceased him on April 10, 1824 and his eldest son died on February 5, 1827. There were three other children, none of whom left descendants.

Russel was interred in the old churchyard at Weaversville with a plain marble stone marking his grave. His epitaph read in part: "He was a man full of the Holy Ghost. How well he taught them many a one will feel unto their dying day, and when they lie on the grave's brink unfearing and composed, their speechless souls will bless the holy man whose voice exhorted and whose footsteps led unto the path of life."

The one secular activity in which Russel seems to have participated was a Polemic Society, organized in December 1807, which sometime later changed its name to the Franklin Society. Russel was chosen chairman of the group, whose members debated various political and philosophical subjects. In a lighter vein, the topic assigned for discussion at their second meeting was, "Which has the greatest influence over men, Women or Wine?"

SOURCES: Alumni file; Min. Fac., 29 Nov. 1790, 13 July 1792; Clio. Min., 22 & 26 Nov. 1794; Clio. lists; Min. Trustees, 25 Sept. 1792, 18 Dec. 1793, 8 Apr., 24 Sept. 1794, 5 May 1795; Alexander, *Princeton*, 264; *First Census, Pa.*, 67; New Brunswick Presby. Min.; J. C. Clyde, *Hist. of the Allen Township Pres. Church* (1876), 57-101 (epitaph); J. C. Clyde, *Genealogies, necrology & rem. of the Irish Settlement in Northampton Cnty., Pa.* (1879), 16, 29-30, 276, 288-89, 292; A. Nevin, "Roll of Ministers & Licentiates," *Hist. of the Presby. of Phila.* (1888), 10.

LKS & RLW

John Pelion Ryers

JOHN PELION RYERS, A.B., A.M. 1795, public official, was the only son of Gozen Ryerss (Ryerse) of Richmond County, Staten Island, New York, who sat for Richmond County in the state assembly from 1791 to 1794 and was the first judge of the Richmond County court of common pleas from 1793 until his death in 1802. He also served as a member of the state constitutional convention of 1801. His wife Jutegh (Judith) Dissoway is said to have died of fright when the British landed on Staten Island. The Ryerss family claimed as their ancestor Wilhelmus Reyerszoon, burgomaster of Amsterdam, Holland in 1390. Gozen Ryerss was an exceptionally wealthy man, with real estate in various parts of Richmond County. He was also an extremely obese man, needing two ordinary chairs in order to sit comfortably. One source notes that his wife "was in the same condition." The reference was probably to his second wife Cornelia Duffee, daughter of his neighbor Jacob Corsen, whom he married in 1780. The family lived at Port Richmond in a house large enough to be known as the "St. James Hotel," presumably furnished with sufficient chairs.

By a deed of July 7, 1786 the elder Ryerss acquired a large piece of "Land Farm and plantation" on the northern shore of Long Island from Alexander McDonald of the Island of Jamaica. McDonald appointed "the Reverend Doctor John Witherspoon, president of the College of New Jersey, and John Rutherford [A.B. 1776], Esq., Attorney at Law, New York, his true and lawful Attornies," to act on his behalf in the land transfer. This contact with Witherspoon may have influenced Ryerss's decision to send his son to the College.

John Ryers matriculated as a junior in the fall of 1790 and joined the Cliosophic Society before the end of the calendar year, using the pseudonym of Archimedes. He received the society's diploma in August 1792. At his commencement he delivered the last oration of the afternoon on "the progress of freedom in the European states." Although no confirmation has been found that Ryers next pursued the study of law, he may have done so, if only to prepare himself for managing the family properties.

In 1791 Gozen Ryerss took title to a tract of 300 acres of land in eastern New York. When the boundary between New York and Massachusetts was finally decided, this acreage fell on the Massachusetts side. As compensation, the state of New York in 1800 patented to Gozen Ryerss a tract of 1,800 acres lying in the center of Wilmington Township in Essex County. John Ryers may have been involved in the management of this land. He had returned to Port Richmond at least by 1800 when he was elected to the state assembly as a representative of Richmond County. When in Albany for sessions of the assembly, he resided at Mrs. Skinner's Coffee House on Green Street.

Sometime prior to 1800 Ryers married Hannah Waln, daughter of Richard and Elizabeth (Betsy) Waln, Philadelphians who had a country seat, "Walnford," in Monmouth County, New Jersey. The Waln family had mercantile interests in the city and were prominent members of the Society of Friends. John and Hannah Ryers's first child, Gozen Adrian, was born some time before October 21, 1800, when he was mentioned in his grandfather Ryerss's will. When Gozen Ryerss died early in 1802, he divided his property among his son, his daughter Margaret, and his two grandsons Gozen Adrian Ryers and Ryerss DeHart, as well as any other grandchildren "that may be born hereafter." John Ryers inherited the family home; a ferry which may have been the predecessor of the Staten Island Ferry, including all of the buildings, wharfs, and boats, as well as the exclusive franchise for operating the ferry; and a two-thirds share of the residue of the estate. He and his uncle Lewis Ryers were made executors of the estate.

John and Hannah Ryers had three more children: Eliza, who died as a child; Elizabeth Waln Ryers; and Joseph Waln Ryers. Robert Waln Ryers (A.B. University of Pennsylvania 1851), who was admitted to the Philadelphia bar on December 11, 1856, was a son of Joseph. Gozen Adrian Ryers died before reaching maturity.

Hannah Waln Ryers must have been separated from her husband before June 23, 1808, when her father's will left his home on Conduit Street in Philadelphia and the sum of $1,000 a year in trust "for the Uses of my Daughters Elizabeth & Hannah & for the maintenance of Hannah's children—if they continue as they now are under their Mother's *sole* care, or their Aunt Elizabeth's care in case of their Mother's decease." Waln's will was proved June 7, 1809.

On October 27, 1812, "at the request of John P. Ryers, Esq.," the Richmond County clerk recorded an earlier transfer of land to Gozen Ryers. No further trace of John Ryers has been discovered in either Richmond County or Philadelphia records. He is first listed as deceased in the 1869 catalogue of the College, an indication that the College authorities had no information about the date of his death.

SOURCES: Alumni file, PUA; A. W. Ryerson, *Ryerson Genealogy* (1916), 316; Clio. lists; Clio. Min., 7 [i.e., 8] Aug. 1792; Min. Fac., 29 Nov. 1790, 13 July 1792; *N.J. Jour.*, 10 Oct. 1792; E. C. Hoagland, *Twigs from Family Trees* (1940), 105; R. M. Bayles, *Hist. of Richmond Cnty., Staten Island, N.Y.* (1887), 328, 330, 569; I. K. Morris, *Mem. Hist. of Staten Island, N.Y.* (1900), II, 102; W. C. Watson, *Hist. of Essex Cnty., N.Y.* (1869), 310-11; J. J. Clute, *Annals of Staten Island* (1877), 141-42, 147, 419-20; *N.Y. Evening Post*, 7 Jan. 1802 (father's obit.), 24 Feb. 1802; H. Simpson, *Lives of Eminent Philadelphians*

(1859), 932-37; J. W. Jordon, *Colonial Families of Phila.* (1911), I, 209-12; broadside "Members of the House of Assembly," 3 Feb. 1800, microfilm at NjP; MS will of Gozen Ryerss, Book E, 103, Richmond Cnty., N.Y., Surrogate's Office; Deed Books G, 27 & E, 103, Richmond Cnty. Court House; *Martin's Bench & Bar*, 308; Univ. of Pa., *Biog. Cat. of the Matriculates ... 1749-1893* (1894), 177; MS will of Richard Waln, Book 2, 505, Reg. of Wills, City Hall, Phila. "Burholme," the Ryers villa near Fox Chase in the Philadelphia suburbs, was built by John Ryers's son and is now on the National Register of Historic Places. See *PMHB*, 67 (1943), 238; S. F. Hotchkin, *York Road Old & New* (1892), 422, 424-25.

RLW

John Johnson Sayrs (Sayres, Sayre, Sayers)

JOHN JOHNSON SAYRS (SAYRES, SAYRE, SAYERS), A.B., A.M. 1795, Episcopal clergyman and teacher, was born around 1774 in Newark, New Jersey, one of two children, and the only son, of Caleb Sayre, and his wife, a daughter of Jonathan Johnson. The father was "a man of considerable property" but his occupation has not been discovered. He served for many years as a vestryman of Trinity Episcopal Church, Newark. Stephen Sayre (A.B. 1757) was Caleb's second cousin.

The younger Sayrs entered the College as a sophomore in May 1790. He joined the American Whig Society. At his commencement, he was respondent in a debate on the question "Is not the belief of a revealed religion essential to the order and existence of civil society?"

In December 1792 Sayrs was back in Newark, where he wrote a friend that he was suffering post-graduate depression: "I thought that when I left Princeton, I should be far more happy than when confined there, but I am much deceived; I am now unsettled, undetermined what Study to undertake, & doubtful whether I shall come to princeton this Winter, as I expected to do." The mood did not last; Sayrs was soon studying for the Episcopal ministry. On June 5, 1794 he was admitted as a candidate for holy orders by the Diocese of New Jersey, and late in 1795 he was ordained a deacon by Bishop Samuel Provoost. From December 25, 1795 to February 14, 1798 he ministered to Christ Church, Poughkeepsie, and Trinity Church, Fishkill, New York.

The vestry of Christ Church started by paying Sayrs £120 a year for officiating three Sundays out of four; they later raised his salary to £140. Presumably Trinity Church contracted separately for Sayrs's fourth Sunday. During Sayrs's ministry, a subscription to build a steeple at Christ Church was opened, although construction did not begin until after his departure. The register of baptisms, marriages and burials he kept there was still extant as of 1911. The parish historian suggests that owing to his comparative youth and the vestry's being accustomed to running things, Sayrs was seldom consulted in the ordering of the "material concerns" of the parish, a premise which may help explain his decision not to remain at the church after February 1798. An alternate explanation is provided by the comparative poverty of the parish, which owned neither a glebe nor a parsonage.

Sayrs then spent almost a year without a charge. He was in Newark in October 1798, preparing to travel south. He was also contemplating residing in Pennsylvania, but instead he accepted the rectorship of Durham Parish, Port Tobacco, Charles County, Maryland, on January 14, 1799. During his tenure there he married Sophia Sprake, a granddaughter of the Reverend Lee Massey, one of his predecessors at Durham Parish. She bore him two sons. Sayrs supplemented his income by opening a "flourishing school." In 1801 he was ordained priest by Bishop Thomas John Claggett (A.B. 1764).

After about five years Sayrs moved to Georgetown, District of Columbia, becoming the first rector of St. John's Episcopal Church in spring 1804. Here he also kept a school, although he was in feeble health. A call upon pewholders to contribute toward completing the church was made during his ministry. St. John's apparently prospered at this time and included in its congregation some of the city's most prominent residents. On December 3, 1806 the United States Senate elected Sayrs a congressional chaplain. He received twelve of eighteen votes cast. The custom at this time was "that two chaplains, of different denominations, be appointed to Congress" each session, "one by each House, who shall interchange weekly." The session ended on March 3, 1807.

Several letters written by Sayrs to John Henry Hobart (A.B. 1793) during the 1790s survive. On one occasion Sayrs observed that "the interest of religion ... has suffered more from the moroseness & gloominess of some of its professors than any other cause, or perhaps every other combined." On another he advanced the theory that, although punishment in the afterlife for sin would be proportioned to the crime, it would also be eternal. "The infinite majesty of an offended God adds I think an infinite evil to sin, & therefore exposes the sinner to infinite punishment, but as the limited nature of the creature can only bear a finite Degree of misery, the Duration must be infinite, & the Creature be ever paying a Debt which he will never discharge." After he got his charge at Poughkeepsie, Sayrs complained that his imagination was becoming barren from writing "so many sermons" and asked Hobart to send some of his; "it would afford me great satisfaction to see them, as well as enable me to be lazy a little." In the same letter, dated March 17, 1796, Sayrs asserted that the *Minerva*, a Federalist newspaper, was "the only one worth reading, or that deserves to be credited. I beleive our present government a good one & well administered, & I wish we had a botany bay to transport every upstart who either through ignorance or misanthropy condemns it."

John Johnson Sayrs died on January 6, 1809. Francis Scott Key, who was one of the church's vestrymen, wrote an epitaph which is on a memorial tablet on the side wall of St. John's Church. Sayrs is buried under the altar. The Reverend William Lewis Gibson of Alexandria preached the funeral sermon. Some three months later, David English (A.B. 1789) wrote asking Hobart to intercede with Sayrs's father on behalf of his daughter-in-law and grandsons, who had been left "unprovided for" by Sayrs's death. It is unclear whether Caleb Sayre's failure to help his son's family was caused simply by bad communication or by a rift between father and son, but English's hint, that "the advice of some friends might induce him to do what he would not if left to himself" seems to point to the latter. On the other hand, Caleb left property to both grandsons when he died in 1830.

SOURCES: T. M. Banta, *Sayre Family* (1901), 106, 196-97; Min. Fac., 10 Nov. 1789, 13 July 1792; Amer. Whig Soc., *Cat.* (1840), 6; broadside 1792 "Order of Commencement," PUA ("Is not"); *Dunlap & Claypoole's Amer. Daily Advt.*, 8 Oct. 1795; Hobart, *Corres.*, I, 19-22 ("I thought," "flourishing school"), 122 ("the interest"), 143-45 ("the infinite"), 172 ("so many," "it would," "the only one"); II, 118; VI, 204-06 ("unprovided for," "the advice"); H. W. Reynolds, *Records of Christ Church, Poughkeepsie, N.Y.* (1911), 92, 94-95, 105, 276-79 ("material concerns"); Hist. Records Survey, *Inventory of Church Archives in the Dist. of Columbia* (1940), I, 114, 161-63; R. P. Jackson, *Chronicles of Georgetown, D.C, from 1751 to 1878* (1878), 169-71; Sprague, *Annals*, V, 407; *Jour. of the Senate of the U.S.* (1821), IV, 106, 110 ("that two").

JJL

John Sloan

JOHN SLOAN, A.B., physician, was one of five sons of Henry and Elizabeth Kirkpatrick Sloan of Lamington, Bedminster Township, Somerset County, New Jersey. William B. Sloan (A.B. 1792) was his brother, and William H. Sloan (A.B. 1816) and John H. and William B. Sloan (both A.B. 1830) were his nephews. Both parents were of Scots-Irish descent. Henry Sloan operated a 370 acre farm near Greater Cross Roads and served as an elder of the Lamington Presbyterian Church. His wife was the daughter of David and Mary McEowen (or McEwen) Kirkpatrick of Minebrook, Somerset County, and the sister of Andrew Kirkpatrick (A.B. 1775), later chief justice of the New Jersey Supreme Court. John Sloan's first cousins included Jacob Kirkpatrick (A.B. 1804), Walter Kirkpatrick (A.B. 1813), and Littleton and Hugh Kirkpatrick (both A.B. 1815). His first cousin Elizabeth Bryan was the second wife of Thomas Grant (A.B. 1786), and her sister Rachel married George Clifford Maxwell (A.B. 1792).

No information on Sloan's early education has come to light, although he and his brother William may well have attended the classical school of Rev. Samuel Kennedy (A.B. 1754) at nearby Basking Ridge. Both John and William entered the College as juniors in November 1790, and both joined the American Whig Society. On July 3, 1792 the faculty assigned John Sloan the task of opposing the question "Are capital punishments just or politic?" at his commencement, but the newspaper account shows that the dispute did not take place. Numerous orations were scheduled in addition to six disputations. Sloan's was the last debate scheduled, and the faculty may simply have decided that it was expendable. He accordingly received his degree at commencement but did not speak.

Sloan turned next to medicine and attended medical lectures at Columbia College from 1794 to 1796. He may also have received training from Hugh McEowen, a physician who seems to have been Sloan's mother's first cousin and who lived at Millington, Somerset County, which was near Sloan's parents' home. Evidence to prove that McEowen taught Sloan is lacking, but the fact that Henry Sloan specified in his will in 1801 that John's brother David was to study medicine with McEowen is suggestive.

Sloan's subsequent career was brief. He moved to North Carolina. The one piece of evidence on his final years is a tombstone on a plantation near Holly Grove in northeast Gates County on the edge of the Great Dismal Swamp, which reads:

> Here lies the body of Dr. John Sloan
> Who was greatly worth [sic] of Prince Town College
> Who departed this life Dec. the 3rd 1799.

Sloan is not known to have married.

SOURCES: Alumni files of JS ("Here lies") & other Sloans & Kirkpatricks, PUA; letter from William H. Sloan, 15 June 1921, Sloan family folder, PUA; *Som. Cnty. Hist. Quart.*, 3 (1914), 268-74; 6 (1917), 180; 7 (1918), 276-80; D. Murray, *Hist. of Education in N.J.* (1899), 93-94; *N.J. Wills*, x, 61, 407; Min. Fac., 29 Nov. 1790, 13 July 1792; Amer. Whig Soc., *Cat.* (1840), 6; *N.J. Journal*, 10 Oct. 1792; Thomas, *Columbia*, 182; Wickes, *Hist. of Medicine N.J.*, 325.

JJL

William B. Sloan

WILLIAM B. SLOAN, A.B., Presbyterian clergyman, was born on December 13, 1771, near Lamington, Bedminster Township, Somerset County, New Jersey, one of eight children of Henry and Elizabeth Kirkpatrick Sloan. John Sloan (A.B. 1792) was one of his brothers, and Andrew Kirkpatrick (A.B. 1775), chief justice of the New Jersey Supreme Court from 1803 to 1824 and a trustee of the College, was his uncle. Several cousins and nephews were also alumni. The father was a farmer and an elder of the Lamington Presbyterian Church.

Sloan and his brother John may have attended the academy of Rev. Samuel Kennedy (A.B. 1754) at nearby Basking Ridge. They entered the College as juniors in November 1790, and both joined the American Whig Society. At their commencement on September 26, 1792, William was respondent in a dispute on the question: "Is there any evidence from the radical resemblance of the languages of different nations, that mankind have sprung from one source?"

Sloan then began to study for the ministry under the guidance of John Woodhull (A.B. 1766), the pastor of Old Tennent Church near Freehold, Monmouth County, New Jersey. While living there he met and, on June 7, 1796, married Mary, one of eight children of Henry and Abigail LaRue Perrine (or Perine) of Freehold. Mary's siblings included Sarah, who married Ira Condict (A.B. 1784), and Matthew LaRue Perrine (A.B. 1797). Sloan apparently outlived his first wife and remarried, for in his will he gave his wife's name as Nancy. By these marriages he had two daughters and three sons, including William Henry Sloan (A.B. 1816).

On April 27, 1796 the Presbytery of New Brunswick accepted Sloan as a "candidate for the office of the holy ministry," and on May 31, 1797 he was licensed to preach. The presbytery forwarded him a call on September 20, 1797 from the congregations of Greenwich and Mansfield Woodhouse in the part of Sussex County, New Jersey, which became Warren County in 1824, each congregation contracting for half of his time. Sloan accepted on November 14, 1797 and was ordained and installed on February 13-14, 1798. He lived on a farm near Bloomsbury in Greenwich Township on what was then the border between Sussex and Hunterdon counties. Greenwich paid him £90 a year in 1799, and presumably he received a comparable sum from Mansfield Woodhouse.

Sloan served both congregations until April 27, 1815 when the presbytery sanctioned Greenwich's call for all of his time and dissolved his pastoral tie to Mansfield Woodhouse. The growth of the two congregations and Sloan's ill health probably explain the change.

William B. Sloan, A.B. 1792

The number of communicants in Greenwich doubled between 1812 and 1834, and Sloan was ill enough in 1812 and 1817 that the presbytery had to send supply ministers to attend to his congregation while he recovered. In the latter year poor health prevented him from attending the organizational meeting of the Presbytery of Newton, newly set off from that of New Brunswick.

Sloan continued as minister at Greenwich until late 1834. On September 27 of that year the congregation voted to concur in his request to "lay down his duties as pastor due to increasing infirmities and weakness of voice as well as difficulties in covering this large and extensive field." A contemporary recalled that "a weakness of the lungs made it difficult for him [Sloan] to speak loud," and the condition had apparently worsened. The Presbytery of Newton agreed to accept the resignation and dissolved the pastoral tie in October.

Sloan's long ministry seems to have been a success. In 1830-31 and 1833 revivals occurred in Greenwich, with thirty-three new members attending communion on one occasion in 1831. When he resigned in 1834 the congregation used the occasion "to express our veneration and affection" for "our venerable and beloved pastor," then concluding "the labours of his office which he has exercised so long

and faithfully in our midst." His successor at Greenwich, Rev. David
X. Junkin, came to know Sloan during the latter's retirement and
recalled that:

> Mr. Sloan was one of the finest-looking men I ever beheld—
> above medium height, straight, erect, slender but well formed,
> his features finely chiselled, yet manly and dignified in expres-
> sion; his eye a clear expressive blue, his gait and bearing stately
> yet unconstrained—his manners those of a gentleman of the
> old school; his was an impressive presence. Some esteemed him
> haughty, but it was because they did not know him; for a more
> kindly heart never throbbed. He was a man of warm affections,
> and easily moved to tears. His talents were very respectable,
> though not great; his scholarship respectable; his style simple
> and unaffected; his sermons rather of the admonitory and prac-
> tical, than argumentative or doctrinal. He was not a very vigorous
> thinker, but was an earnest and affectionate preacher of practi-
> cal truth. His delivery, before the failure of his voice, was clear,
> correct, and impressive, though not rising to the higher range
> of elocution.

After his resignation Sloan continued to live at his Greenwich
Township farm. On July 3, 1839 while visiting a brother at his Lamington birthplace, he died and was buried at Greenwich two days
later. A congregational history published in 1962 shows that at that
date his thirty-six years of service in Greenwich was still a record.

SOURCES: Alumni files of WBS & other Sloans & Kirkpatricks, PUA; letter from
William H. Sloan, 15 June 1921, Sloan family folder, PUA; Presby. of Newton, *Proc.
of the Convention at Washington, N.J., Nov. 20, 1867* ... (1868), 42-44 ("a weakness,"
"Mr. Sloan"); J. E. Rush, *Our Greenwich Heritage: The Hist. of the First Pres. Church of
Greenwich* (1962), 34-45, 73-74 ("lay down," "to express"); *Som. Cnty. Hist. Quart.*, 3
(1914), 268-74; 6 (1917), 180; 7 (1918), 276-80; *N.J. Wills*, x, 61, 407; Min. Fac., 29
Nov. 1790, 13 July 1792; Amer. Whig Soc., *Cat.* (1840), 6; *N.J. Journal*, 10 Oct. 1792
("Is there"); *NJHSP*, n.s., 10 (1925), 73; F. R. Symmes, *Hist. of the Old Tennent Church*
(2d ed., 1904), 237, 396-97; J. P. Snell, *Hist. of Hunterdon & Somerset Cnties.* (1881),
207-08; New Brunswick Presby. Min., 1796-98, *passim* ("candidate," 27 Apr. 1796), &
27 Apr. 1815; als, WBS to Rev. Jacob Kirkpatrick, 22 Feb. 1812, NjP; Presby. of Newton, *1817-1917: Centennial* (1917), 44-45, 70-72, 76; J. P. Snell, *Hist. of Sussex & Warren Cnties.* (1881), 566-68, 597-99; Hist. Records Survey, N.J., *Inventory of the Church
Archives of N.J.: Presbyterians* (1940), 89-92; MS will of WBS, 22 June 1839, recorded
17 July 1839, Nj. The Mansfield Woodhouse church became the First Presbyterian
Church of Washington, Warren County, in 1877, and the Greenwich congregation is
now called Old Greenwich Presbyterian Church. William B. Sloan's middle name may
have been Bryan, perhaps in honor of his aunt Marian Sloan Bryan or her in-laws.
He named a son John Bryan Sloan. See *N.J. Wills*, x, 61.

MANUSCRIPTS: NjP; NjP-SSP

JJL

Henry Steele

HENRY STEELE was probably the youngest son Henry born in 1772 to Henry and Anne Billings Steele of "Weston," near Vienna, Dorchester County, on Maryland's Eastern Shore. His brother Isaac may have been Isaac Steele (Class of 1790), who entered the College around the same time he did. Anne Billings Steele was the daughter of Anne Rider Billings Lookerman and her first husband, James Billings of Oxford, Talbot County, Maryland. The elder Henry Steele emigrated from Whitehaven, England, in 1740 and prospered as a merchant and planter. He served several terms in the lower house of the colonial legislature and died in 1782. His eldest son James apparently inherited the bulk of his property, consisting of 6,470 acres of Dorchester County land and a personal estate valued at £4,789, including eighty-six slaves. The size of Henry's share has not been discovered.

The minutes of the faculty indicate that Steele entered the College in November 1788, but he was already on campus on June 11 of that year, when he joined the Cliosophic Society, taking the pseudonym Akenside. Mark Akenside (1721-1770) was an English poet and physician best known for his poem on the *Pleasures of the Imagination*. Steele last appears in the College records on a class list compiled during the 1790 summer session. He is identified as "Harry Steel" from Maryland in a manuscript list of the students of the College dated April 10, 1789.

A source which refers to the younger Henry Steele of Dorchester County as "Harry" also asserts that he died before reaching adulthood. His death as a young man could explain his failure to graduate from the College. Alternatively he may have withdrawn from the College and been the Henry Steele who belonged to the charter class of 1793 of Saint John's College, Annapolis, Maryland. He attended that institution sometime between 1790 and 1792 but did not graduate.

Nothing of Steele's subsequent career has been discovered. His name does not appear in the 1800 or 1810 Maryland censuses.

SOURCES: *Biog. Dict. Md. Leg.*, II, 769-70; E. Jones, *New Rev. Hist. of Dorchester Cnty. Md.* (1966), 458-60; Colonial Dames of America, Chapter 1, Balt., *Ancestral Records & Portraits* (1910), II, 676-77; C. W. Mowbray & M. I. Mowbray, *Early Settlers of Dorchester Cnty. & Their Lands* (1981), I, 79; Clio. lists; Min. Fac., 10 Nov. 1789 & class list for 1790 summer sess.; Hancock House MSS; *MHM*, 29 (1934), 306; 44 (1949), 92; St. John's College, *Alumni Reg. ... 1793-1960* (1961), 1. The class list of 10 April 1789 identifies Steele as a sophomore by this date. If so he repeated his sophomore year, for he was still in that class in summer 1790. The Dorchester County Steele is identified as the Princetonian on the basis of his birthdate, the possibility that his brother attended the College at the same time, the wealth of his family, and the absence of other candidates. Without evidence that he was still alive in 1790, the finding cannot be called conclusive.

JJL

Job Stockton

JOB STOCKTON, soldier and farmer, was the second son of Helen McComb and Robert Stockton of "Constitution Hill," Princeton, New Jersey. The father was a quartermaster for the Continental Army and later earned the rank of major in the local militia. George Washington is reputed to have enjoyed his hospitality at "Constitution Hill" during the first week of December 1776 while his troops rested in Princeton on their retreat from New Brunswick. Robert Stockton was a first cousin of Richard Stockton (A.B. 1748), Samuel Witham Stockton (A.B. 1767) and Philip Stockton (Class of 1769). Job was therefore a second cousin of Richard (A.B. 1779) and Lucius Horatio Stockton (A.B. 1787). He was also preceded at the College by his brother Ebenezer (A.B. 1780). His sister Nancy married Francis Jefferson James (A.B. 1781), and his sister Elizabeth married Ashbel Green (A.B. 1783).

The only record of Stockton's presence at the College is in the trustees' minutes of September 29, 1790, at which time an indignant letter from Robert Stockton was read, in which he complained of the faculty and particularly Samuel Stanhope Smith (A.B. 1769), vice president of the College. Stockton's letter claimed:

His son Job Stockton had received personal violence and abuse from Dr. Smith in a cruel and illegal manner. His son had been sent from the institution in an arbitrary and unprecedented manner. The faculty had yielded their right to the judgment of an individual, to pronounce sentence without the concurring voice of the faculty, and that individual one who, as he conceived had no right to sit as a member of the faculty.

Smith defended his position, and when the board reconvened the following morning Robert Stockton was invited to be heard and both parties to present proof of their testimonies. The board concluded that the charges against Smith were not substantiated but noted that the faculty, upon hearing informal charges against Job Stockton, should have "exerted the authority vested in them with that regularity and decision which so high an office merited." Because the faculty minutes contain no mention of any misdemeanor on Stockton's part, Smith evidently acted alone in reprimanding Stockton. In spite of this altercation, the account book of Job's physician brother Ebenezer shows that Samuel Stanhope Smith was his patient between 1804 and 1810. Job Stockton's name does not appear on any of the class lists, and so it has been assumed that the incident referred to took place during the summer session of 1790. Since the majority of the students at that time entered as sophomores or juniors, Stockton has been arbitrarily assigned to the Class of 1792. He may have joined the American Whig Society as a number of Stockton relatives did, but no records of nongraduate members are available.

Except for a brief period of service in the army Stockton remained in Princeton, where he supported the local Presbyterian church and was a member of the Princeton Volunteer Fire Company. His name was on the list of candidates for army appointments which Alexander Hamilton (LL.D. 1791) sent to James McHenry on August 21, 1798. His cousin Richard Stockton recommended him as a "young Gentleman of liberal education moral and political principles correct," which meant that he was a Federalist. Hamilton noted that he preferred the cavalry and that he was a strong candidate. In spite of his preference, Stockton was commissioned a captain in the Eleventh Infantry of the United States Army on January 8, 1799. He was honorably discharged on June 15, 1800 when the twelve regiments of the "Additional Army," recruited when war with France seemed imminent, were disbanded. On December 9, 1801 he married Sarah Beckman of Hunterdon County, New Jersey. At the death of his father in 1805, Stockton was left the front portion of the homestead farm adjoining Richard Stockton's land. He was also entrusted with the care of his mother and instructed to provide her with a horse and chair and a cow; he shared the executor's duties with his brother Ebenezer. Their brother James received the rear portion of the farm. Apparently Job alone managed the family plantation and probably also looked after James's share of the property.

Stockton died on January 9, 1820 and was buried beside his father at the Friends' burial ground near their Stony Brook meeting house. He was described as "a fine-looking and genial man, but ... never married." However, another stone in the Friends' cemetery is that of Sarah Stockton, "Wife of Job Stockton," who died October 21, 1818. The existence of his wife is confirmed by the inventory of Job Stockton's personal estate, where the wearing apparel of Mrs. Stockton is listed, as well as that of the deceased. Also included in the inventory is a "Legacy from Jno. Harrison to Mrs. Stockton wife of the deceased $1200." This was a bequest of John Harrison of the Township of West Windsor, Middlesex County, New Jersey, in his will dated June 17, 1815, to his niece "Sally Stockton." The inventory of Stockton's estate shows that he was the owner of seven slaves, whose worth varied from $5 to $300, and of a pew valued at $100 in the Princeton Presbyterian Church.

SOURCES: *Princetonians, 1776-1783*, 303-04; W. F. Cregar, *Stockton Family in Eng. & the U.S.* (1888), 96, 98; Min. Trustees, 29 & 30 Sept. 1790; Hageman, *History*, I, 77-78 ("fine looking"); II, 19, 83, 99; *N.J. Wills*, X, 427-28 (father's will); XIII, 191 (John Harrison will); *Hamilton Papers*, XXII, 127-28, 131, 383-88; Heitman, *U.S. Army*, I, 927; *NJHSP*, 51 (1933), 144; N.J. Soc. of Colonial Dames, *Letters of Moore Furman* (1912), 31-32; H. E. Deats, *Marriage Records of Hunterdon, Cnty., N.J.* (1986), 273; MS estate inv. of Job Stockton, Nj.

RLW

Jacob Ten Eyck

JACOB TEN EYCK, A.B., lawyer and justice, the son of Abraham Ten Eyck and Annatje Lansing, was born in Albany, New York on February 17, 1772. His grandfather Jacob C. Ten Eyck was a judge of the court of common pleas and mayor of Albany from 1748 to 1750. By profession he was a goldsmith and silversmith, and examples of his silverware are preserved in the Metropolitan Museum of Art. Abraham Ten Eyck was a member of the Albany committee of correspondence and a paymaster of the First Albany Regiment with the rank of lieutenant. In 1792 he became a partner in a glass works in Coeymans, six miles outside of Albany.

Ten Eyck entered the College as a sophomore in November 1789, and on December 23 he was received into the Cliosophic Society as Brother Alcibiades, after the Athenian warrior and friend of Socrates. He served for a time as president of the society, with the meeting of July 12, 1792 being his last evening in office, and received its diploma. When the faculty met on July 13 to make commencement assignments, Ten Eyck was given the role of replicator for the first dispute, but George Bibb took over this responsibility on commencement day. The fact that Ten Eyck's name is omitted altogether from a newspaper account of the proceedings suggests that he was not present. Minutes of the trustees confirm that he was among those awarded a degree.

It is not known where Ten Eyck pursued his legal studies, but presumably he returned to Albany where, on March 6, 1795, he married Magdalena Gansevoort, daughter of Leonard and Hester Cuyler Gansevoort. They had nine children, six of whom lived to adulthood. In 1800 the Ten Eycks moved to "Whitehall," the family homestead just outside of Albany in the Township of Bethlehem, where Jacob lived for the rest of his life. The same year he won election to the state assembly, where he represented Albany County until 1803. On June 8, 1807 he was appointed one of the presiding judges of the Albany county court, where he sat until 1812. Nothing else has been discovered about what must have been a long career. Ten Eyck died at "Whitehall" on July 26, 1862, aged ninety years, five months and nine days. His wife died the following year aged eighty-six.

SOURCES: Alumni file, PUA; Clio. lists; Clio. Min., 12 July & 7 [i.e., 8] Aug. 1792; Min. Fac., 10 Nov. 1789, 13 July 1792; Min. Trustees, 25 Sept. 1792; J. Pearson, *Genealogies of First Settlers of Albany Cnty., N.Y.* (1976), 110; *NYGBR*, 63 (1932), 164, 277, 321; G. R. Howell & J. Tenney, *Hist. of the Cnty. of Albany* (1886), 129, 155, 261, 354, 661, 780. The Ten Eycks were a large family with Jacobs in every generation who were related by various degrees of cousinship. The Jacob H. Ten Eyck who was a prominent merchant in Albany should not be confused with the Princetonian. Ten Eycks intermarried with Bleeckers, but no close connection with John R. Bleecker (A.B. 1791) and Peter Bleecker (A.B. 1792) has been found.

RLW

Jacob Stern Thomson (Thompson)

JACOB STERN THOMSON (THOMPSON), A.B., A.M. 1795, lawyer, farmer, and public official, was born in 1772, one of three sons and five daughters of Mark and Ann Breckenridge Thomson of Changewater, Sussex County, New Jersey. The family later moved to Marksborough which, like Changewater, was in the part of Sussex County which became Warren County in 1824. The father was a miller and iron manufacturer with extensive landholdings. Marksborough is said to have been named for him. He left in excess of $17,000 in moveable property alone at his death in 1803. In 1776 he commanded the Sussex County militia and led the battalion of detached New Jersey militia which was with George Washington when he moved his army from Massachusetts to New York in that year. Colonel Thomson was wounded at the Battle of Princeton. He sat in both houses of the New Jersey legislature and served in the United States House of Representatives as a Federalist from 1795 to 1799.

Jacob Stern Thomson was named for Jacob Starn, an ironmaster of nearby Mansfield Woodhouse, in Hunterdon County. The nature of the relationship does not appear, but Starn left his namesake £300 in his will when he died around the end of 1773. Thomson entered the College as a sophomore in November 1789. He joined the American Whig Society. When ordering the commencement exercises in July 1792, the faculty assigned him a role in a disputation, but a month later, after the final examination, they decided to award intermediate honors to Thomson, "whose general conduct has been very laudable

& whose examination was approved." He accordingly delivered "an oration on the happy deliverance of Europe from the tyranny of superstition."

Thomson proceeded to study law and was admitted to the New Jersey bar as an attorney in November 1796 and as a counsellor in May 1804. He lived and practiced in the vicinity of Marksborough. In February 1800 Governor Richard Howell made him his interim appointment as clerk of Sussex County, and that October the state legislature in joint session elected him to a full five-year term. He sought reelection in October 1805 but received only seven votes to John Johnson's thirty-four.

Thomson's political views probably sparked this rebuff. A Federalist like his father, he was elected in 1806 to Sussex County's seat on the council, the New Jersey legislature's upper house, thanks to a split in the ranks of the Republicans. He did not hold political office thereafter until 1823, when he was elected to four consecutive one-year terms on the council, the latter two from newly formed Warren County. From 1812 to 1817 he was paymaster of the Sussex County brigade of militia.

The diary of William Johnson, a merchant of Newton, Sussex County, mentions Thomson a few times between 1802 and 1807. They traveled together on several occasions, attended balls, parties, and a wedding and once joined three other men in playing flutes and violins at an impromptu concert. Thomson became part-owner of an island in the Delaware River near Philadelphia in December 1820, apparently in connection with a plan by the Pennsylvania and New Jersey Communication Company to build a bridge. When the scheme came to nothing, he disposed of this property in 1827. Thomson seems never to have married. At his death in 1831 his personal estate was valued at almost $16,000, most of it in stock in the Easton Bank and in notes, bonds, and mortages. The inventory shows that he owned and operated a farm. He grew wheat, rye, and corn, and kept fourteen cows, two oxen, five horses, and ten swine. Presumably he remained a Federalist at heart, for when he died he still owned a portrait of Alexander Hamilton (LL.D. 1791).

SOURCES: F. B. Lee, *Geneal. & Memorial Hist. of the State of N.J.* (1910), I, 345; *NJHSP*, n.s., 8 (1923), 59; D. C. Skemer & R. C. Morris, *Guide to the* MS *Collections of the N.J. Hist. Soc.* (1979), 60, 84, 115-16; *BDUSC*, 1936; A. Pepper, *Tours of Hist. N.J.* (1965), 161; E. S. Miers, *Crossroads of Freedom: The Amer. Revolution & The Rise of a New Nation* (1971), 12; R. P. McCormick, *Experiment in Independence: N.J. in the Critical Period 1781-89* (1950), 130; *N.J. Wills*, v, 494; x, 445; Min. Fac., 10 Nov. 1789, 13 July & 17 Aug. 1792 ("whose general"); Amer. Whig Soc., *Cats.*: (1837), 5; (1840), 6; *N.J. Journal*, 10 Oct. 1792 ("an oration"); *Dunlap & Claypoole's Amer. Daily Advt.*, 8 Oct. 1795; Riker, 75; Alexander, *Princeton*, 265; J. P. Snell & W. W. Clayton, *Hist. of Sussex & Warren Cnties., N.J.* (1881), 159-60, 162, 480; W. Johnson, "A Young Man's Jour. of 1800-

13," *NJHSP*, n.s., 7 (1922), 49, 212, 215-16, 305-06, 310-12; 8 (1923), 153, 224; C. E. Prince, *N.J.'s Jeffersonian Republicans: The Genesis of an Early Party Machine 1789-1817* (1967), 80-83; *NJHSP*, 78 (1960), 286; *PMHB*, 22 (1898), 423, 433-34; MS estate inv. of JST, 10 Jan. 1832, proved 12 Jan. 1832, Nj (photocopy in PUA). See *GMNJ*, 40 (1965), 105 for the Warren County tombstone of Jane Read Drake Thompson, who died aged 52 in 1837, the wife or widow of "Elder J. S. Thompson." The possibility that she was the Princetonian's wife seems ruled out by the assertion in *NJHSP*, n.s., 8 (1923), 59, that Thomson "never married."

MANUSCRIPTS: Jacob Stern Thomson Papers, Anderson Family Papers, & Frelinghuysen Family Papers, NjHi; NjP-SSP; Newark [N.J.] Public Lib. See Skemer & Morris, 60, for a description of the Jacob Stern Thomson Papers, NjHi

JJL

William Morton Watkins

WILLIAM MORTON WATKINS, A.B., A.B. Hampden-Sidney College 1791, lawyer, planter, and public official, was born April 22, 1773, the son of Col. Joel Watkins and Agnes Morton Watkins. The father had come from Cumberland County, Virginia, to Charlotte County in 1764. When he married Agnes Morton, his father-in-law Joseph Morton gave him a tract of land near the Staunton River. Here he built the family home, "Woodfork," a modest frame dwelling where his son William was born.

Watkins matriculated at Hampden-Sidney College in 1789 and received the A.B. degree there in 1791. His father was a charter trustee of Hampden-Sidney, serving from 1783 until his death in 1820; his uncle Francis Watkins was a charter trustee of both Hampden-Sidney and its predecessor, Prince Edward Academy; and William Morton, the uncle for whom he was named, served as a trustee of both institutions from 1782 to 1812. Following a fairly common pattern among Hampden-Sidney men, Watkins decided to spend an additional year at the College of New Jersey in order to earn a degree from the latter institution. On October 15, 1791 he left Prince Edward County, Virginia, traveling north with Abraham Venable (A.B. 1780), who was on his way to Philadelphia to attend a session of Congress, and Walter Coles (Class of 1793), who was also planning to enroll at the College. During his year at Nassau Hall Watkins joined the American Whig Society, but the following July, when commencement assignments were made, he asked to be exempted from participation in the exercises.

Watkins returned to Virginia, where he studied law under Judge Creed Taylor of Cumberland County. In a letter of August 26, 1794 to Alexander White (A.B. 1792), John Henry Hobart (A.B. 1793) passed on news from their fellow Whig: "I got a letter the other day from Watkins. In the southern states they are for tarring & feathering everyone who does not approve of every violent measure which hot-headed demagogues may advocate. Freedom of opinion, that very essence of liberty is destroyed among them, & yet they wish to make a monopoly of republicanism." If Hobart was correctly relaying Watkins's views, William was already a Jeffersonian Republican.

On December 5, 1799 Watkins married Elizabeth Woodson Venable at her family home, "Springfield," in Prince Edward County. She was the eldest daughter of Col. Samuel Woodson Venable (A.B. 1780) and Mary Carrington Venable. Abraham B. Venable (A.B. 1780), Richard N. Venable (A.B. 1782), and Nathaniel E. Venable (A.B. 1796) were Elizabeth Venable's uncles, and Joseph Venable (A.B. 1783) was her father's cousin. The marriage served to strengthen Watkins's ties with Hampden-Sidney. The older Venables, before receiving their degrees from the College, had first attended Prince Edward Academy, which, until its incorporation as Hampden-Sidney in 1783, did not grant degrees. Nathaniel E. Venable, like Watkins himself, had obtained a degree at Hampden-Sidney prior to enrolling at the College. Samuel Woodson Venable was appointed a trustee of Prince Edward Academy by the Presbytery of Hanover only two years after his graduation from the College, and he remained a trustee of the academy and its successor, Hampden-Sidney, until his death in 1825. Elizabeth Venable's grandfathers, Nathaniel Venable and Paul Carrington, were charter trustees of both institutions.

Watkins built a brick dwelling called "Do Well," whose name was later elided to "Dowell," which gained the reputation of being one of the handsomest estates in Charlotte County. Here his eleven children were born, the seven sons who survived infancy all becoming graduates of Hampden-Sidney. In 1803 Watkins's sister Susannah, the widow of William Pitt Hunt (A.B. 1786), married the Reverend Moses Hoge (D.D. 1810), who was the president of Hampden-Sidney from 1807 to 1820. Although qualified to practice law, Watkins apparently preferred the life of a planter and was wealthy enough to feel no pressure to practice. When his father-in-law died his wife received half interest in a tract of land of about 800 acres on Difficult Creek, a third interest in a lot in Richmond, £400, a negro boy named George, and a share in the residue of the estate. When her mother died in 1837 Elizabeth Watkins received $500 and a copy of the painting, "The Last Supper."

Watkins not only eschewed the practice of law but usually did his best to shun public life. Nevertheless, he was commissioned a justice of the peace in 1809 and was elected to the Virginia House of Delegates as a representative from Charlotte County from 1812 to

1815 and again from 1830 to 1831. He served as a trustee of Hampden-Sidney from 1803 to 1835, soon being joined on the board by his brother Henry A. Watkins (A.B. Hampden-Sidney 1793) and his cousin Henry E. Watkins (A.B. 1801), the latter of whom became treasurer of the board of Union Theological Seminary, which was established on the Hampden-Sidney campus in 1823. Watkins is said to have contributed generously to both institutions. He was a Presbyterian and, in spite of his avoidance of public life, was considered to be very patriotic. He died at "Do Well" on February 5, 1865, aged almost ninety-two.

SOURCES: Alumni file, PUA; R. A. Lancaster, Jr., *Historic Va. Homes & Churches* (1915), 432; Hampden-Sidney College, *Gen. Cat.* (1908), 47-48; "Diary of Richard N. Venable 1791-92," *Tyler's Quart.*, 2 (1921), 137; *VMHB*, 6 (1898), 175-77, 180-82; 7 (1900), 32, 34; *WMQ*, 2d ser., 21 (1941), 179; Min. Fac., class list ca. Nov. 1791, 13 July 1792; Amer. Whig Soc., *Cat.* (1840), 6; *Trenton Federalist*, 8 Oct. 1810; A. J. Morrison, *College of Hampden-Sidney* (1912), 172, 174, 176; *Princetonians, 1776-1783*, 310-13; V. Dabney, *America's Bicentennial '76 College* (1973), 13-14; G. E. Hopkins, *Col. Carrington of Cumberland* (1942), 76-77; E. M. Venable, *Venables of Va.* (1925), 45-46, 51-53, 63; Foote, *Sketches, Va.*, 1st ser., 404, 562; J. McVickar, *Early Life & Professional Years of Bishop Hobart* (1838), 48.

RLW

Alexander White

ALEXANDER WHITE, A.B., A.M. 1795, lawyer and public official, was born around 1773. He was the son of either John or Robert White, two of the three sons of Dr. Robert and Margaret Hoge White of Frederick County, Virginia. Margaret Hoge White, grandmother of Alexander, was the aunt of John Hoge (A.B. 1749).

White entered the College as a sophomore in November 1789. He joined the American Whig Society. His correspondence with John Henry Hobart (A.B. 1793) after White's graduation shows him to have been a zealous supporter of the Whigs, frequently asking about the society's prospects of earning academic honors, rejoicing that "our fraternity still stands forth as the school of virtue and useful knowledge," and nostalgically recalling his days both as a member of the society and of the College. His particular friends included his classmate John Conrad Otto and Ebenezer Rhea (A.B. 1791), as well as Hobart. When Rhea died in 1794, White observed that "the time has been, when I thought I could scarcely live without him," although time spent apart since graduation had "diminished my dependence on his advice and example to direct my conduct." White was ranked first in his class when he graduated and accordingly gave the Latin salutatory, an oration "on the advantages of mental cultivation."

White then returned to Virginia to read law at "Woodville," near Winchester in Frederick County. "Woodville" was the estate of his uncle, also named Alexander White, who was a noted lawyer, a Federalist United States congressman from 1789 to 1793, and a commissioner of the city of Washington from 1795 to 1802. As a congressman he is best known for a compromise he and fellow Virginian Richard Bland Lee (Class of 1779), hammered out over the supper table of Thomas Jefferson (LL.D. 1791). They agreed to vote for the federal assumption of state debts incurred in the Revolution, in return for which Alexander Hamilton (LL.D. 1791) undertook to marshal northern votes for moving the national capital south to the Potomac. The first letter from his nephew to Hobart shows that he was at "Woodville" by December 3, 1792. White observed that he had stayed up past midnight writing to friends from College and that "you ought to consider that as a great mark of my friendship for you all, as you know very well it is not a trifle that could induce me to do such a thing." In March 1794 he reported that while he was making progress in his legal studies, they were taking longer than he expected. "It is impossible, I find, to apply to them with *Nassovian* diligence." He announced that he intended to begin "a regular course of reading, intermixing history, &c., with the law, and will take the Bible as the first and most important history." Earlier that year, when Hobart was thinking of going into trade, White playfully proposed "that when we become men of business, I should send our backwoods' merchants to deal with you, and you in return should empower me to collect from those who might prove delinquent."

In 1795 White was admitted to the bar of Frederick County. Otto reported in June 1796 that White "is well & very much engaged in business. He expects to be married soon." Unfortunately, the name of the woman in question has not been discovered.

White settled in the area of Berkeley County which became Jefferson County in present-day West Virginia. He may have been there by August 1795, when either he or his uncle was chosen as a trustee at the organizational meeting of the Charles Town Academy, which was incorporated in 1797. By 1801, when Jefferson County was created, the younger White had amassed enough property and reputation to be one of the thirteen justices of the peace who comprised the first county court when it met at Charles Town in November. His was the pivotal vote in the election of the first county clerk, a race which aroused sufficient interest that the elder Alexander White was lobbied in an effort to influence his nephew to vote for George Hite, the eventual winner.

Nothing of White's subsequent career has been discovered. He is first listed as deceased in the 1818 College catalogue.

SOURCES: *VMHB*, 23 (1915), 195-96; J. H. Tyler, *Family of Hoge* (1927), 20-23; K. G. Greene, *Winchester, Va. & its Beginnings 1743-1814* (1926), 265, 353, 356; J. McVickar, *Early Years of the late Bishop Hobart* (2d ed., 1836), 72-86 ("our fraternity," "the time," "you ought," "it is impossible," "that when"); Min. Fac., 10 Nov. 1789, 13 July 1792; Amer. Whig Soc., *Cat.* (1840), 6; broadside 1792 "Order of Commencement," PUA ("on the advantages"); Min. Trustees, 29 Sept. 1795; W. G. Russell, *What I Know about Winchester* (1953), 26, 179; "Alexander White (1738-1804)," *DAB* (states that the elder AW, not the Princetonian, represented Berkeley Cnty. in the Va. House of Delegates, 1799-1801); C. M. Green, *Wash.: Village & Capital, 1800-78* (1962), 8; Foote, *Sketches, Va.*, 2d ser., 23; J. E. Norris, *Hist. of the Lower Shenandoah Valley Cnties.* (1890), 193; Hobart, *Corres.*, I, 140-41, 216 ("is well"); M. K. Bushong, *Hist. Jefferson Cnty.* (1972), 94, 102-03. There seems to be no relationship between the subject of this sketch and Rev. Alexander White of King William County who was involved in the Parson's Cause controversy of 1763-64. See E. H. Ryland, *King William Cnty., Va.* (1955), 32; *WMQ*, 1st ser., 19 (1910/11), 21-22.

MANUSCRIPTS: A copy of White's 1792 Latin salutatory oration is in the John Henry Hobart Papers, TxAuCH (photocopy in PUA). It appears to be the earliest extant CNJ Latin salutatory.

JJL

George Willing

GEORGE WILLING, A.B., merchant and agriculturalist, was the ninth of the thirteen children of Anne McCall and Thomas Willing of Philadelphia. Born April 14, 1774, he was an older brother of Richard Willing (Class of 1793) and William Shippen Willing (Class of 1796). Their father, as a partner with Robert Morris in the firm of Willing and Morris, was one of the leading merchants in Philadelphia and probably in all of the colonies. Trained in England as a lawyer, Thomas Willing was mayor of Philadelphia in 1763 and also served as a justice in the city court, the court of common pleas, and the supreme court of Pennsylvania. He was one of the first Philadelphia merchants to sign the non-importation resolutions of 1765; however, as a member of the Continental Congress he voted against the Declaration of Independence, arguing that the Pennsylvania delegates were not authorized to join the majority vote and that the colonies were ill-prepared for war and not yet ready for independence. Nevertheless, he contributed large sums toward provisioning the Continental Army. He and Morris were instrumental in founding the Bank of North America in 1781. Willing became its first president and continued in that capacity until 1791 when he became president of the new Bank of the United States. He was also a trustee of the College of Philadelphia and the University of the State of Pennsylvania and a vestryman of Christ Church. The family lived in a large house on the southwest corner of Third Street and Willing's Alley and enjoyed a country estate called "Willington" on present North Broad Street.

The four eldest Willing brothers were all sent to the preparatory school at the University of the State of Pennsylvania for their early education. George entered the mathematics school on January 10, 1781 at the age of seven, but by spring he had been transferred to the lower level English school. Except for one term spent in the Latin school he remained in the English school through the term that began on October 1, 1783. Sometime after that he transferred to the grammar school at Nassau Hall, where in September 1787 he ranked second in the second class, and the following September ranked second in the first class. He entered the College as a freshman that November, and on December 19, 1789 he joined the Cliosophic Society, using the name of Thales, the Greek philosopher. Later he left that organization and became a member of the American Whig Society. The faculty chose him to give one of the intermediate orations at his commencement, and on that occasion he delivered a eulogium on Christopher Columbus.

After graduation Willing became associated with his father's mercantile interests, specifically with the firm of Willing and Francis. This was a family business, since the elder Willing's sister Anne had married Tench Francis, and George Willing's sister Dorothy married her cousin Thomas Willing Francis. Willing made at least one voyage to India for the firm, which carried on a large import trade with that country. Apparently wealthy enough to be able to retire early from commercial pursuits which did not particularly interest him, he occupied himself with "elegant agriculture" at his country estate of "Richland," just outside of Philadelphia, and he was a member of the Society for the Promotion of Agriculture. His sister Anne Willing Bingham was the acknowledged leader of Philadelphia society, and no doubt Willing was sometimes involved in the rounds of visits and parties that went with such a position. His sister Mary married Henry Clymer (A.B. 1786).

Willing apparently had some impetuous moments as a young man. Elected to membership in the socially prestigious First Troop Philadelphia City Cavalry on May 31, 1798, he had resigned by January 1799. Presumably he preferred to see action as a second lieutenant in the Sixth City Troop of Light Dragoons which offered its services to the president, if and when needed. On February 9, 1799 he was one of several angry Federalists arrested for rioting on the grounds of St. Mary's Catholic Church as a result of the high feelings generated by William Duane's attempt to secure the repeal of the Alien and Sedition Acts. Tried and convicted of assault, he was ordered to pay court costs and a nominal fine. On October 1, 1814 he was reelected to the First Troop so that he could join the members who had left on August 28, under the command of Capt. Charles Ross (Class of 1791), for Mount Bull, overlooking Chesapeake Bay. Here they were stationed as vedettes, apprising the militia defending Philadelphia of the movements of British troops. Discharged by the adjutant general's office on December 11, 1814, the First Troop marched into Philadelphia for dismissal the following day. Willing was elected an honorary member the following September.

Willing was first married on October 1, 1795 to Maria Benezet, daughter of Maria Bingham and John Benezet. Benezet, like his son-in-law a Philadelphia merchant, was the brother of Anthony Benezet, the Quaker antislavery advocate. Maria Benezet Willing died childless. On November 26, 1800 Willing married Rebecca Harrison Blackwell, daughter of the Anglican clergyman Robert Blackwell (A.B. 1768) and his first wife Rebecca Harrison. She was Blackwell's only child, and he built a large townhouse for the couple. Among the nine children of this marriage were Rebecca Harrison, who married George Henry Thompson (A.B. 1826), and Dorothea Francis, who married John William Wallace, son of John Bradford Wallace (A.B. 1794).

At his father's death in January 1821 Willing received, among other bequests, a share of the money realized from the sale of western lands, seventy shares in the Farmers and Mechanics Bank, and an annual annuity. His own death came on December 22, 1827, and he was buried in the grounds of Christ Episcopal Church.

SOURCES: Alumni file and nongraduate alumni card catalogue, PUA; A. DuBin, *Willing Family & Collateral Lines* (1941), 3-11; *PMHB*, 5 (1881), 452-55; 46 (1922), 265; 47 (1923), 366; MS tuition books, Univ. of the State of Pa., UPenn-Ar; *N.J. Jour., & Polit. Intelligencer*, 10 Oct. 1787, 29 Oct. 1788; Min. Fac., 10 Nov. 1789, 13 July 1792; Clio. lists; Amer. Whig Soc., *Cat.* (1840), 6; *N.J. Jour.*, 10 Oct. 1792; C. R. Keith, *Provincial Councillors of Pa.* (1883), 89-93, 101-03; Alexander, *Princeton*, 266; *Princetonians, 1748-1768*, 631-34; *Hist. First Troop Phila. City Cavalry* (1875), 181; First Troop Phila. City Cavalry, *By-Laws, Muster-Roll & Papers* (1840), 26-27, 59; B. A. Konkle, *Thomas Willing* (1937), 120-21, 137, 162; T. W. Balch, *Willing Letters & Papers* (1922), ix, x, xv, xxxiv-xxxviii, xlix, lvi, 173-214; J. W. Jordan, *Colonial Families of Phila.* (1911), I, 127-28; W. B. Bronson, *Inscriptions in St. Peter's Church Yard* (1879), 2, 546; E. L. Clark, *Record of Inscriptions on the Tablets & Grave-Stones in the Burial Ground of Christ Church* (1864), 84.

RLW

Henry Veghte Wyckoff (Wikoff, Wykoff, Wickoff)

HENRY VEGHTE WYCKOFF (WIKOFF, WYKOFF, WICKOFF), A.B., A.M. 1797, Dutch Reformed clergyman, was born on February 15, 1770, one of eight sons and four daughters of Peter Wyckoff, owner of a large farm near Hillsborough, Somerset County, New Jersey, and his second wife Jemima (or Jacomientye) Veghte, the daughter of Hendrick and Nelly Veghte of Sowerland, Somerset County.

Wyckoff first appears in the College sources as a junior in a class list taken at the start of the 1791 summer session. On the evening of June 17, 1791 he was one of six students who went "a swiming & returned at a very unseasonable hour," as a result of which the faculty reproved him "publicly in the Hall." He belonged to both the American Whig and the Cliosophic societies. Possibly he joined the Whigs first and then transferred. He took the pseudonym Aristophanes when he was admitted to the Cliosophic Society on July 6, 1791, received its diploma on August 16, 1792, and attended its annual meeting on September 3, 1794. At his commencement he spoke as replicator in a debate on the topic: "Is not the belief of a revealed religion essential to the order and existence of civil society?"

After graduation Wyckoff studied for the ministry of the Dutch Reformed Church under Rev. John Henry Livingston, who taught theology at his New York City residence until 1796 and thereafter conducted his divinity school at Flatbush, Long Island. Wyckoff was licensed by the Classis of New York in 1798 and ordained by the Classis of Albany in 1799. In the latter year he became the pastor of a congregation in Charleston, Montgomery County, in east central New York, where he continued his ministry for the whole of his career. Eventually he concluded that the Dutch Reformed Church had become overly liberal and lax and insufficiently Calvinist in doctrine. On October 22, 1822 he led his flock in seceding and joining six other congregations in organizing the True Reformed Dutch Church in the United States of America, under Dr. Solomon Froeligh's leadership. The new sect had thirty congregations by 1830, but three decades later the figure had dropped to sixteen, and in 1890 the church merged with a later (1857) secessionist movement, the Christian Reformed Church in North America.

Wyckoff married Nellie Schenk on April 20, 1797 and had at least two children, a son and a daughter. He seems to have retired in 1830. He was living at Glen, Montgomery County, when he died on March 6, 1835, and is buried there.

SOURCES: W. F. Wyckoff, "Notes on the Wyckoff Family," *Som. Cnty. Hist. Quart.*, 2 (1913), 193; 3 (1914), 40-41, 204; *N.J. Wills*, IV, 457; XII, 437; XIII, 452; Min. Fac., class list ca. May 1791, 22 June 1791 ("a swiming"), 13 July 1792; Amer. Whig Soc., *Cats.*: (1837), 5; (1840), 6; Clio. Min., 16 Aug. 1792, 3 Sept. 1794; Clio. lists; broadside 1792 "Order of Commencement," PUA ("Is not"); Trenton *State Gazette & N.J. Advt.*, 17 Oct. 1797; J. H. Raven, *Biog. Record: Theol. Sem. New Brunswick 1784-1911* (1912), 30, 60; P. N. Vandenberge, *Hist. Directory of the Reformed Church in Amer. 1628-1978* (1978), 211; C. E. Corwin, *Manual of the Reformed Church in Amer.* (5th ed., 1922), 601; W. C. Kiessel, "Dr. Solomon Froeligh," *NJHSP*, 73 (1955), 28-40; *NYGBR*, 14 (1883), 102; 58 (1927), 165; 60 (1929), 288. Identification of the New York clergyman as the Princetonian rests on his date and place of birth and subsequent occupation. College sources do not give a middle name or initial, and sources for the career of the Dutch Reformed clergyman do not confirm his attendance at the College. W. F. Wyckoff, the family historian, mistakenly identifies the Princetonian as the son of Peter and Althea Cox Wikoff of Philadelphia. Their son Henry (1770-1826) was a Philadelphia attorney. He cannot have been the 1792 College graduate because he graduated from the University of the State of Pennsylvania in 1787 and was called to the Philadelphia bar in March 1791. Furthermore, College sources agree that the Princetonian came from New Jersey and became a clergyman. See Wyckoff, *Som. Cnty. Hist. Quart.*, 6 (1917), 137-40; W. F. Wyckoff, *Wyckoff Fam. in Amer.* [1934], 448; Univ. of Pa., *Biographical Cat. of the Matriculates of the College ... 1749-1893* (1894), 27; *Martin's Bench & Bar*, 323.

PUBLICATION: Wyckoff is credited with authorship of *Reasons for Withdrawing from the Reformed Dutch Church* (1820) by J. P. Snell & F. Ellis in their *Hist. of Hunterdon & Somerset Cnties., N.J.* (1881), 630, and later historians have repeated this assertion (e.g., see Raven & Corwin, above). No evidence that such a work was published has been found: it is listed neither in Sh-C nor in Sh-Sh nor in the *National Union Catalog Pre-1956 Imprints*. Perhaps Snell & Ellis were alluding to HVW's share in the 1822 work entitled *Reasons Assigned by a Number of Ministers, Elders, & Deacons, for Declaring Themselves the True Reformed Dutch Church in the U.S.A.* (Sh-C #s 10487, 10488).

JJL

CLASS OF 1793

—— Archer
Joseph Bonney, A.B.
Robins Chamberlaine
Walter Coles
Edward F. Conrad, A.B.
Dow Ditmars, A.B.
Manuel Eyre, A.B.
Robert Field IV, A.B.
John Gibson, A.B.
John Henry Hobart, A.B.
Jacob Motte Huger
Nathaniel Hunt, A.B.
Robert Hunt, A.B.
John Jordan
Stephen Maxwell

John Neilson, A.B.
Robert Ogden IV, A.B.
William Roat, A.B.
Abraham Skinner, A.B.
Enoch Smith
John Staples, A.B.
James T. Stelle (Still), A.B.
Alexander Stewart, A.B.
Bennett Taylor, A.B.
Charles Tennent, A.B.
John Terhune, A.B.
Isaac Van Doren, A.B.
Joshua Maddox Wallace, Jr., A.B.
Richard Willing

(The 1793 commencement was canceled due to a yellow fever epidemic)

—— Archer

ARCHER makes his only appearance in the College sources on a class list for the summer session of 1792, when he was a junior. Without his first name or an address, no positive identification has been possible, but if a relationship to other Princetonians with the surname is assumed, then several strong candidates from Virginia and Maryland emerge. Making a positive identification seems unjustified in the absence of further evidence.

SOURCES: Min. Fac., class list ca. May 1792.

An Edward Archer from Virginia received his A.B. from the College in 1795. Edward has not been positively identified, but a likely candidate is the man of that name who on May 27, 1797 married Mary Jefferson Bolling, the daughter of John Bolling and his wife Mary, the sister of Thomas Jefferson (LL.D. 1791). Edward Archer was the son of Edward and Mary Archer and had two brothers, William and Field Archer. On February 20, 1794 Field married Martha Bolling, the sister of his brother's future wife. This marriage produced five sons and five daughters. Perhaps, then, the subject of this sketch was William or Field Archer. See letter from James S. Patton, 20 Mar. 1986, PUA; W. Randolph, *George Archer I of the Umberslade Archers* (1965), 53-55. Edward Archer may have resided in Norfolk; see *WMQ*, 2d ser., 8 (1928), 103; *Cal. Va. St. Papers*, IV, 629-33; IX, 302; T. J. Wertenbaker, *Norfolk* (1962), 92.

Edward Archer and the unidentified Archer may even be one and the same. Edward first appears on a class list in October 1792, which is the list next after the one on which the unidentifed Archer makes his sole appearance. To retrogress from being a junior to a sophomore at the start of a new academic year would have been unusual, but perhaps not impossible if the initial class assignment was unduly optimistic.

Archer could also have been either Robert Harris Archer or John Archer, both of whom were sons of John (A.B. 1760) and Catharine Harris Archer, brothers of Stevenson Archer (A.B. 1805), and nephews of Robert Harris (A.B. 1753). The elder John Archer was a prominent physician and a United States representative from Harford County, Maryland.

His son Robert was born on August 28, 1775 and spent some time around 1790 studying at Rev. John Ireland's Sion Hall Academy, near Havre de Grace in Harford County. He later received training at the medical school his father conducted out of his home, which he had named "Medical Hall" for the purpose. Robert then became a physician, practicing in Baltimore from 1798 to 1805, in Lancaster, Pennsylvania, from 1805 to 1809, in Cecil County, Maryland, from 1809 to 1822, and in Harford County from 1822 until his death on May 19, 1857. He spent some time as physician to the Baltimore City Hospital and twice served as surgeon to regiments of Maryland militia. He represented Cecil County in the Maryland House of Delegates in 1820 and 1821, and was elected three times to the governor's council, serving from December 1823 to January 1827. Later he served as a judge of the orphans' court. In 1826 he became an elder of the Churchville Presbyterian Church in Harford County. He married Mary Stump in Cecil County on April 1, 1805, and they had at least one child.

Robert's brother John Archer, Jr., who was born on October 9, 1777, also became a physician. He received his initial education at "Medical Hall" and went on to earn an M.D. at the University of Pennsylvania in 1798. Perhaps he was the John Archer who married Elizabeth Kittleman in Baltimore on November 21, 1797. If so, she was dead by November 16, 1802 when he married Ann, the daughter of John and Cassandra Wilson Stump of Stafford, Harford County. John Stump was one of Maryland's most prominent merchants and manufacturers. John and Ann had eleven children, including James J. Archer (A.B. 1835). In the War of 1812 John Archer served as a surgeon in the Maryland militia. He attended a state convention of the National Republicans at Baltimore in July 1827. He died in Baltimore on May 21, 1830.

Of the two, Robert H. Archer's age is more appropriate for membership in the Class of 1793. He would have been eighteen at graduation. However, John, though young, was not too young to be in the same class, and it may be significant that one of his sons attended the College. Without more data none of the possibilities advanced here can be ruled out. For the Maryland Archers see *Princetonians, 1748-1768*, 300-02; E. F. Cordell, *Medical Annals of Md. 1799-1899* (1903), 304-05, 749-50; C. M. Wright, *Our Harford Heritage: A Hist. of Harford Cnty. Md.* (1967), 175, 231, 374, 399-401, 404; D.A.R. Capt. Jeremiah Baker Chapter, *Cecil Cnty. Md. Marriage Licenses 1777-1840* (1974), 25; W. W. Preston, *Hist. of Harford Cnty., Md.* (1901), 181-82, 216-18, 245; letter from Md. Leg. Hist. Proj., 4 June 1985, PUA; R. T. Obert, *Balt. Md. City & Cnty. Marriage Licenses 1777-99* (1975), 3; R. Barnes, *Marriages & Deaths from Balt. Newspapers 1796-1816* (1978), 8; R. Walsh & W. L. Fox, *Md.: A Hist. 1632-1974* (1974), 267; *MHM*, 54 (1959), 408, 410, 417, 420; 39 (1944), 104; 66 (1971), 196; A. J. M. Pedley, *Manuscript Collections of the Md. Hist. Soc.* (1968), 20; R. V. Jackson, *Md. 1820 Census Index* (1977).

JJL

Joseph Bonney

JOSEPH BONNEY, A.B., physician, was the son of James and Anna Bonney of Woodbridge Township, Middlesex County, New Jersey. James was appointed one of the town surveyors of Woodbridge Township in 1776. References in his will to the "home plantation" and to a cider mill and presses suggest that his main occupation was farming.

Born in 1769, Bonney was several years older than any of his classmates. His name first appears on College records as a sophomore in the spring of 1791, and there is no indication that he joined either of the debating societies on the campus. On March 14, 1793 he was among the group of students called before the faculty for "having neglected recitation & resorted to the public tavern & created unlawful & unnecessary disturbance." All signed the rather abject apology required of them, but the next day several of those involved presented a petition to the faculty which claimed that their characters had been stigmatized by the allegations in the faculty-prepared apology and that they were therefore requesting dismission from the College. Again called before the faculty, the petitioners, with the exception of Bonney and James Cresap (A.B. 1794), withdrew their names. The two holdouts were promptly expelled. The following day they laid a second petition before the faculty, requesting readmission. "As the object of the punishment seemed to be answered they were reenstated in their former standing." It may have been Bonney's relative maturity that caused him to rebel at what he probably considered a childish reprimand. For his commencement he was assigned the part of the respondent to the proposition, "Ceteris paribus. Does the world pay more respect to one born of honorable and reputable parents or to the son of a rascal." However, the commencement ceremonies were canceled because of the yellow fever epidemic in nearby Philadelphia.

Bonney went on to the study of medicine, but it is doubtful whether he actually earned the M.D. with which he is credited in the general catalogue of the University. He is not listed among Columbia or University of Pennsylvania medical students. Although his home remained in Woodbridge Township, he is said to have practiced in Bound Brook and Middlebrook, now a part of Bound Brook, in Somerset County, and he may have done so for a time, but he is also said to have practiced in Rahway. When Bonney's father died in 1802 he bequeathed Joseph the "wearing apparel & books he had at college." Joseph also inherited the family home, with the provision that his mother have the use of it during her lifetime. She died in the fall of 1805, leaving her estate to be divided among her five daughters.

Bonney married Polly Davison of Basking Ridge, who died on May 3, 1806. Buried beside her were three infants who had died between November 1804 and December 1805. When Bonney himself died late in 1807 he had one surviving daughter, Ann Caroline. In the event of her death before the age of twenty-five, his estate was to revert to the trustees of the Presbyterian Church of Metuchen. With so many family deaths within a few years time, Bonney's rather grim epitaph seems quite appropriate.

> Our days alas our mortal days
> Are short and wretched too
> Evil and few the Patriarch says
> And well the Patriarch knew.

SOURCES: Alumni file, PUA; Min. Fac., class list ca. May 1791, 14-16 Mar. & 15 July 1793; R. Wolk, *Hist. of Woodbridge, N.J.* (1970), 35; Wickes, *Hist. of Medicine N.J.*, 161-62 (epitaph); J. W. Dalby, *Woodbridge & Vicinity* (1976), 286; *N.J. Wills*, x, 46-47; xi, 39.

A confusing number of place names are associated with Bonney's abbreviated career. Bound Brook, though considered to be within Bridgewater Township in Somerset County, spilled over into Piscataway Township in Middlesex County. The major area of the city of Rahway was north of Woodbridge Township, just across the border in Essex County; however a portion of Rahway was actually within the limits of Woodbridge Township. Metuchen was completely within the Woodbridge Township limits. In 1793 the Woodbridge Presbyterians separated to form a second church in Metuchen. It was to the latter that Bonney made a bequest, but he was buried in the family plot in Rahway.

RLW

Robins Chamberlaine

ROBINS CHAMBERLAINE, planter and soldier, was born in 1773 at "Peach Blossom" in Talbot County, Maryland, the son of Henrietta Maria Robins and James Lloyd Chamberlaine. Through his mother he was a first cousin to both Henry Hollyday (A.B. 1791) and Thomas Robins Hayward (Class of 1791). His sister Margaret married an uncle of Robert (A.B. 1787) and Samuel Hughes (Class of 1792). James Chamberlaine was a merchant and planter who amassed a fortune in trade, sat in the lower house of the colonial and state legislatures off and on from 1771 to 1781, owned a privateer during the Revolution, and served briefly as brigadier general of militia for the Upper District of the Eastern Shore in 1776. His marriage to the daughter of George and Henrietta Maria Tilghman Robins may not have had the entire approval of his parents, for he later wrote in the family Bible:

> My father having omitted to record my marriage with those of my elder and younger brothers, be it known to all the world, that on May 16th, 1757, James Lloyd Chamberlaine was married to miss Henrietta Maria Robins of "Peach Blossom," and hope to spend their days in as much honor and credit as any of the family.

Robins Chamberlaine had two sisters, but of three brothers only he reached adulthood. He entered the College as a freshman on November 10, 1789. On December 23 of the same year he joined the Cliosophic Society, taking as his pseudonym Porus, for a native prince whose valor greatly impressed Alexander the Great at the time of the latter's invasion of India. In the class list for the winter session of 1791, Chamberlaine appeared among the juniors, but he was no longer listed in the summer of 1792. Perhaps Chamberlaine's withdrawal was prompted by the death of his mother in 1791. Since his father was already dead, Robins's presence may have been required at home to look after his interests. On the other hand, he may have left under a cloud, since on August 22, 1792 the Cliosophic Society moved to expel him for his "infamous conduct." The minutes fail to say what this behavior was.

Chamberlaine's subsequent career was unfortunate. His father had left his children a large estate, including 4,010 acres in Talbot and Caroline counties and personal property valued in excess of £3,500. In 1798 Chamberlaine was assessed for 736 acres and nine slaves in the Talbot County tax list. His overall valuation of $9,346 was the sixth-highest in the county. He dissipated his fortune with such alacrity and success that he was insolvent by 1804. A lover of music and an accomplished violinist, he evinced his expensive tastes by purchasing a Cremona violin for $1,000. The instrument was later sold by his executors to his first cousin James Lloyd Chamberlaine (A.B. 1806) of "Bonfield," near Oxford, Talbot County. Unfortunately, the cousin sent it for repair to Baltimore, where the workman either ruined it or, as the family suspected, appreciated its quality and substituted an inferior instrument, for the one returned was never the same.

From May 27, 1800 to June 1, 1802 Chamberlaine served as a lieutenant in the First Regiment of Artillerists and Engineers, United States Army. Since army appointments usually went to party loyalists, Chamberlaine was probably a Federalist. His military service can be viewed either as a brief interlude on his road to ruin or a desperate effort to recoup his finances by obtaining a job suitable for a gentleman. Possibly his honorable discharge after two years was connected to the merger of the two regiments of artillerists and engineers into a single regiment of artillerists on April 1, 1802. At some point he also served as brigade major in the Talbot County militia.

Chamberlaine married twice. On January 30, 1794 he wed Mary Crookshanks (or Cruickshanks), daughter of Charles Crookshanks, a Baltimore merchant. Two sons and a daughter were born of the marriage, including a son who moved to Cincinatti and became a merchant there. According to the family historian, this was the first Chamberlaine to leave the Eastern Shore since the family's arrival in Maryland in 1714. Second, he married Catharine Blake of Queen Annes County, Maryland. No evidence of issue from that union has been found. Chamberlaine died in 1807 or 1808 and was buried at "Peach Blossom."

SOURCES: J. B. Kerr, *Gen. Notes of the Chamberlaine Family of Md.* (1880 repr. 1973), 14, 36-40, 57-58, 86 ("My father"); *Biog. Dict. Md. Leg.*, I, 206-07; J. T. Scharf, *Hist. of Western Md.* (1882 repr. 1968), 1011-12; J. Bordley, *Hollyday & Related Families of the Eastern Shore of Md.* (1962), 143-44; O. Tilghman, *Hist. of Talbot Cnty., Md.* (1915 repr. 1967), I, 545-46; Min. Fac., 10 Nov. 1789, 11 Nov. 1791; Clio. lists; Clio. Min., 22 Aug. 1792 ("infamous"); W. H. Ridgway, *Community Leadership in Md. 1790-1840* (1979), 328; Heitman, *U.S. Army*, I, 50-51, 293; R. Barnes, *Md. Marriages, 1778-1800* (1978 repr. 1979), 36. The extant portrait of Mrs. William Goldsborough and her grandson Robins Chamberlaine attributed to John Hesselius and reproduced in Kerr, plate V, should not be confused with the subject of this sketch. It depicts Robins Chamberlaine's elder brother and namesake, whose death at age five prompted his parents to give their new son the same name.

JJL

Walter Coles

WALTER COLES, planter, county official, and horse breeder, was born in 1772, the second of the thirteen children of Col. John Coles and Rebecca Elizabeth Tucker of Albemarle County, Virginia. The family was prominent in Virginia from the time that John Coles's father became one of the first settlers in Richmond early in the century. John Coles's mother was a sister of the mother of Patrick Henry, and there was a more distant cousinship with Dolley Madison. Coles was a colonel in the militia during the Revolution, and after the surrender of Burgoyne he was one of the officers in charge of the English prisoners held at Charlottesville.

At the death of his father, John Coles inherited the family summer residence, "Enniscorthy," ten miles south of "Monticello." Thomas Jefferson (LL.D. 1791) was a close friend, and he and his family found refuge at "Enniscorthy" in June 1781 when Banastre Tarleton sought to surprise and capture him at Charlottesville. Coles improved the house at "Enniscorthy" by adding wings and large piazzas until he had one of the largest homes in the state. Walter Coles was raised here, where fine horses were an important part of the way of life and southern hospitality included a constant stream of visitors, many of them prominent men of the state. In 1782 the personal property tax of John Coles was £39.1.6. There were only three higher tax assessments in the county, those for Thomas Jefferson and for two members of the wealthy Carter family.

The younger sons of the Coles family were privately tutored at home, and presumably the same was done for Walter. He enrolled in Hampden-Sidney in 1790, where he was a member of the Union Society, a campus literary society. On October 15, 1791 he set out from Prince Edward County with Abraham Venable (A.B. 1780), who was en route to Philadelphia to attend a session of Congress. The diary of Richard Venable (A.B. 1782) noted that his brother was accompanied by Walter Coles and William Watkins (A.B. 1792), "who are now going to finish their education at Princeton." Coles is listed among the juniors at the College for the winter sesion of 1791 and the summer session of 1792, after which his name disappears from the College records. He is not known to have joined either of the debating societies on the campus. At least three of his younger brothers received their educations first at Hampden-Sidney, later transferring to William and Mary. Walter was probably in the category of the one son selected by many southern families to receive an education in the north.

Coles returned to Albemarle County where in 1796, on land that was part of one of the crown grants to the Coles family, John Coles built the house called "Woodville" for his eldest son, stocking it with slaves, horses, cattle, and sheep. On November 11, 1797 Coles married Eliza (Betsy) Fox Cocke, daughter of Bowler Cocke of Turkey Island. The marriage produced three sons and two daughters; their son Walter later inherited "Woodville." Eliza died on August 4, 1811; her father's will of March 1, 1812 left bequests to the children of his deceased daughter. Coles's second marriage, on February 28, 1813, was to Sally Thompson Swann Craig of Powhatan County, widow of Robert Craig and daughter of John Swann and Jane Selliway. A daughter and three sons were added to the family by this marriage.

For a member of such a prominent family, surprisingly little information is available about Coles. His brother Isaac served as private secretary to Thomas Jefferson during his second administration, and another brother, Edward, performed the same service for James Madison (A.B. 1771) for six years. Later emigrating to Illinois in order legally to emancipate his slaves, Edward Coles became the second governor of that state. Walter Coles served as a county magistrate for a time, but he soon resigned this office. Perhaps, as the eldest son, he avoided political involvement in order to manage the family estates. Apparently someone with good managerial and business skills looked after the interests of the family. One county historian has observed that "the Coles family which emerges in the nineteenth century as the county's greatest concentration of wealth, is an example of shrewd management and careful attention to detail sometimes absent in other local families." Prior to the Civil War the members of the various branches of the Coles family in the county were worth more than $800,000 in real and personal property.

Coles was noted for his passion for horses and hunting. His sister Sallie had married Andrew Stevenson, who served as Speaker of the House of Representatives, and later as Andrew Jackson's minister to the Court of St. James from 1836 to 1841. Sallie Stevenson's letters to her family, written from England, mentioned "brother Walter" whenever she had the occasion to see some particularly fine horses. After a visit to Fonthill, in Wiltshire, in September 1836, she wrote, "I often think of brother Walter when I see the fox hunters with their red coats mounted on their beautiful hunters and surrounded by their dogs." In November 1838, on a visit to Raby Castle in Durham, the Stevensons were taken on a tour of the stables, and Sallie wished her dear brother could be along. She added that her husband remarked to his host, "My wife has a brother that would be delighted with all this." In a letter written by Coles himself on April 20, 1833, to David Higginbotham, he discussed the scheduling of one of his stud horses at various nearby farms, giving his assurance that he would try to accommodate Higginbotham without inconveniencing others on the horse's circuit.

Coles died at "Woodville" in 1854 at the age of eighty-two and was buried in the Coles cemetery on Green Mountain in Albemarle County. He had been an active member of the Episcopal church for many years. His will shows that he had invested in lands in Missouri as well as in Virginia.

SOURCES: R. A. Lancaster, *Historic Va. Homes & Churches* (1915), 413-15; W. B. Coles, *Coles Family of Va.* (1931), 51-57, 86-88; I. Brant, *James Madison: The President* (1956), 12, 31; I. Brant, *James Madison: Father of the Constitution* (1950), 401; *Gen. Cat. of Officers & Students of Hampden-Sidney College, Va.* (1908), 48; "Diary of Richard N. Venable 1791-92," *Tyler's Quart.*, 2 (1921), 137; Min. Fac., class lists 11 Nov. 1791 & ca. May 1792; R. Sobel & J. Raimo, *Biog. Dir. of the Governors of the U.S., 1789-1978* (1978), I, 366; E. B. Washburne, *Sketch of Edward Coles* (1882), 16; *Albemarle Cnty. Hist. Soc. Papers*, 5 (1944-45), 67; *VMHB*, 4 (1897), 447; 7 (1900), 101-02, 326-28; 35 (1927), 28; H. Moore, *Albemarle: Jefferson's Cnty.* (1976), 75 ("the Coles family"), 88, 151-53, 216; E. Boykin, *Victoria, Albert, & Mrs. Stevenson* (1957), 31, 189, 231; E. Woods, *Albemarle Cnty. in Va.* (1901), 172; als, Coles to Higginbotham, VHi; L. G. Tyler, *Encyc. of Va. Biog.* (1915), V, 901. Walter Coles, the Virginia congressman, was a nephew of Walter Coles, the Princetonian, the son of the latter's brother Isaac.

RLW

Edward F. Conrad

EDWARD F. CONRAD, A.B., physician and army officer, was born around 1772, one of the four sons and two daughters of Frederick and Maria Clara Leigh Conrad (or Conrod) of Winchester, Frederick County, Virginia. The father was a native of Baumholder in the German duchy of Zweibrücken who emigrated to Virginia around 1750 in the company of his wife-to-be and her father Stephen Leigh (or Ley). The couple settled in Winchester and were married there in 1757. Conrad came from a wealthy family and increased his estate by operating a tannery and a hop yard. He earned a reputation for hospitality, both to elite friends like Thomas, sixth Baron Fairfax, and to the poor. His open-handedness crossed political lines during the Revolution, for although a whig he opened his house to the Philadelphia Quakers who were banished to Winchester after refusing on religious grounds to take an oath of allegiance. He belonged to the German Reformed Church.

Edward Conrad first appears in lists of College students as a sophomore at the start of the summer 1791 term. He joined the American Whig Society. He was assigned a role in one of the disputations set for his commencement, but the outbreak of yellow fever in Philadelphia caused the ceremony to be canceled, with degrees awarded privately instead.

Frederick Conrad died late in 1793 and left legacies to all his sons. However, Frederick Jr., the eldest as well as the executor and residuary legatee, squandered the entire estate and then moved to Louisiana. Protracted litigation eventually ensued, but all efforts to retrieve Edward's inheritance seem to have failed. Edward began to read medicine at Winchester under his brother Daniel, who had studied in Edinburgh and London. He also attended the University of Pennsylvania Medical School for one year from 1795 to 1796 but did not take a degree. He seems then to have begun a practice in Winchester.

Conrad obtained a commission dated July 5, 1799 as a surgeon in the Eighth Regiment of Infantry, United States Army. The Eighth was one of twelve infantry regiments in the so-called "New Army" authorized by Congress in July 1798 when the possibility of war with France was at its height. Since strong Federalist leanings were one of the prime criteria used in selecting officers for the new units, Conrad was probably a Federalist. The expansion of the army was short-lived. The new regiments were paid off and disbanded by June 15, 1800, thus ending Conrad's military career.

During his brief period of service, the Eighth Regiment was one of several stationed at Harper's Ferry, in present-day West Virginia. The encampment's commander Charles Cotesworth Pinckney noted that sickness was rampant and solicited an opinion from his medical men. Conrad and two other physicians responded by diagnosing the problem as a "bilious inflammatory fever" caused, among other reasons, by the camp's "low and damp situation." Pinckney followed their recommendation that the camp be moved to higher ground and was rewarded by a drop in the incidence of illness.

After his discharge Conrad returned to Winchester and spent the rest of his life there. On February 16, 1809 he married Heriot Roberdeau, who was fifteen years his junior. She was the last child of Daniel Roberdeau by his second wife Jane Milligan. Roberdeau was a Philadelphia merchant and Revolutionary War general who moved to Alexandria, Virginia in 1784 and to Winchester in 1794, where he died a year later. His house in Winchester was Heriot's dowry, or part of it. Two sons were born of this marriage, both of whom also became physicians. Edward F. Conrad died December 25, 1821, at midnight. He was buried in Winchester.

SOURCES: "A Sketch by Mrs. Walls (of Winchester) of her Ancestors for her Children," *Annual Papers of the Winchester Va. Hist. Soc.* (1931), 157-60, 164-67; J. E. Norris, *Hist. of the Lower Shenandoah Valley* (1890 repr. 1972), 571; J. E. S. King, *Abstracts of Wills,*

Inventories, & Administrative Accounts of Frederick Cnty., Va., 1742-1800 (1961), 82, 96, 117; Min. Fac., class list ca. May 1791, 15 July 1793; Amer. Whig Soc., *Cat.* (1840), 7; Min. Trustees, 25 Sept. 1793; MS class list of Benjamin Rush's medical students, UPenn-Ar; Heitman, *U.S. Army*, I, 322; R. H. Kohn, *Eagle & Sword* (1975), 229, 243-44; *Hamilton Papers*, XXII, 383-88; XXIII, 229; XXIV, 429-31 ("bilious," "low"); R. Buchanan, *Geneal. of the Roberdeau Family* (1876), 101-02, 129, 151; W. G. Russell, *What I Know about Winchester* (1953), 93, 111. The *Princeton Univ. Gen. Cat.* of 1908 credits Conrad with an M.D., but this has not been confirmed. College catalogues, starting with the earliest relevant one in 1797, and the Whig Society catalogue are the only sources for Conrad's middle initial.

MANUSCRIPTS: Alexander Hamilton Papers, DLC

JJL

Dow Ditmars

DOW DITMARS, A.B., teacher, physician and farmer, was born on the family farm just outside the village of Jamaica, Long Island, New York, on June 12, 1771, the youngest child of Abraham Ditmars, Jr., and his wife Elizabeth Johnson. The father, a captain of militia during the Revolution, became known as the "rebel captain" to the British soldiers quartered at Jamaica, and his crops and provisions were constantly raided. On one occasion the British threatened to burn the farmhouse. After the family had been forced to evacuate their home, the soldiers left without matching bluster with action. The Ditmars were members of the Reformed Dutch Church of Jamaica, where Abraham was elected an elder in 1791.

Ditmars entered the College as a sophomore sometime during the 1790-1791 academic year and joined the American Whig Society. For the aborted commencement exercises of 1793 he was assigned the part of replicator in the third dispute: "Are Liberty and political Equality calculated to promote the happiness and improvement of mankind?"

Ditmars returned to Jamaica to a position as assistant tutor in Union Hall Academy at a salary of £40 per year. The academy, which had opened in the spring of 1792, derived its name from the fact that it was created through the united efforts of citizens of Jamaica, Flushing, Newtown, and New York City. Both Ditmars's father and grandfather were contributors to the building fund and charter trustees of the institution. Presumably Ditmars taught at Union Hall until he entered the Medical School of Columbia College in 1800, although he may also have studied with a local physician during that period. He was a nongraduate of Columbia and did not receive the M.D. degree with which he is credited in early Whig Society catalogues.

Upon completing his medical studies Ditmars traveled to Demerara, a Dutch settlement in British Guyana, South America, where he established a lucrative practice and remained for fourteen years. Upon his return he bought a farm at Hell Gate, now Astoria, Long Island, and apparently lived quietly there, without any resumption of his medical practice. He married Anna Elvira Riker, daughter of Samuel and Ann Lawrence Riker of Newtown, Long Island, and the couple had four children. Ditmars died at Hell Gate in 1860.

SOURCES: Alumni file, PUA; Min. Fac., class list ca. May 1791, 15 July 1793; Amer. Whig Soc., *Cat.* (1840), 7; P. Ross, *Hist. of Long Island* (1905), I, 275, 706; B. F. Thompson, *Hist. of Long Island* (3d ed., 3 vols., 1918), III, 539-40; H. Onderdonk, *Hist. of the 1st Reformed Dutch Church of Jamaica, L.I.* (1884), 73, 186; Hobart, *Corres.*, I, 48, 50, 68; Thomas, *Columbia*, 184.

RLW

Manuel Eyre

MANUEL EYRE, A.B., A.M. 1824, shipping merchant and banker, was born on February 1, 1777, the son of Manuel (Emmanuel) Eyre and his wife Mary Wright of Philadelphia. The father had come to Philadelphia from Burlington, New Jersey, to work at the shipyard of Richard Wright of Kensington. He acquired a complete knowledge of shipbuilding, married his employer's daughter, inherited the business, and brought in two of his brothers as partners. Active in public affairs, the elder Eyre was a justice of the court of common pleas, a sachem of the Society of the Sons of St. Tammany, a founder of the Society of the Sons of St. George, a vestryman of Christ Church, and in 1775 a delegate to the provincial congress and a member of the Philadelphia committee of correspondence. The Eyre shipyard was commissioned by the Philadelphia committee of safety to build the gunboat *Bull Dog*, which was completed so expeditiously that the Eyres were then commissioned to build the *Franklin*, the *Congress*, and the *Randolph*. By 1777 Eyre was a captain in John Cadwalader's brigade of Pennsylvania militia, and the following year he joined the Patriotic Association formed to mete out justice to the tories after the British evacuated the city. On January 9, 1794 his daughter Lydia married Ralph Hunt (A.B. 1786) in Philadelphia's Christ Church

The younger Manuel Eyre entered the College as a sophomore in November 1790 and joined the American Whig Society. Faculty minutes show two occasions when he received public admonitions for disregarding College rules: on June 22, 1791 for returning at a late hour after an evening swim, and on September 10, 1792 for playing cards on the Sabbath. When the faculty made assignments for the 1793 commencement exercises that were later canceled, Eyre was listed as opponent in the fourth dispute, "Ceteris paribus. Does the world pay more respect to one born of honorable and reputable parents or to the son of a rascal."

After graduation Eyre apprenticed in the countinghouse of Henry Pratt, partner in the Philadelphia firm of Pratt and Kintzing. In 1803 he formed a partnership with Charles Massey, formerly with the firm of Masseys and Shoemaker. Eyre and Massey operated for over forty years from 23 South Water Street and 28 South Wharves, becoming one of the largest mercantile houses in Philadelphia. They eventually owned more than twenty vessels and could list almost seventy ports of call in the United States, Europe, South America, and the East and West Indies. The company boasted that it never lost a ship and suffered only a few partial losses of cargo. The partners also became underwriters, insuring the vessels of other companies.

On December 5, 1802 Eyre married Juliet Phillips, daughter of Ralph and Ruth Phillips of Maidenhead (later Lawrenceville), New Jersey, and sister of William R. Phillips (Class of 1799) and Lewis W. R. Phillips (A.B. 1808). The bride was not yet seventeen when she died the following July. Her tombstone reads, "... the violence of her disease brought on the premature birth of her son who lies entomb'd with her." On July 10, 1806 Eyre married seventeen-year-old Anne Louisa Connelly of Philadelphia, daughter of John and Anne Little Connelly. The wedding took place at the bride's home on Front Street, with the Reverend James Wilson of the First Presbyterian Church officiating. John Connelly, a captain during the Revolution and an original member of the Hibernian Society, was the official auctioneer of the city of Philadelphia and in 1823 became the first president of the Columbia Railroad Company, forerunner of the Pennsylvania Railroad Company. He was the first railroad president in the United States. Eyre's second marriage produced twelve children, two of whom were Manuel (Class of 1838) and Mahlon Dickerson Eyre (A.B. 1838). In spite of her large family, Anne Eyre kept busy with charitable organizations and was one of the managers of the Orphan Society of Philadelphia. Her husband was involved in public affairs as well as the concerns of his mercantile firm.

The Manuel Eyre who was active in Republican politics in the 1790s was no doubt the father. One of Philadelphia County's "Anti-Treaty" men elected to the lower house of Pennsylvania in 1795, he was part of the coalition that repudiated Jay's Treaty by their votes in February 1796 against several proposed amendments to the Constitution. It was probably the father rather than the son who was a member of the committee in 1801 that planned the public demonstration held on the day of the inauguration of Thomas Jefferson (LL.D. 1791) to celebrate "the success of Democratic principles." The father was evidently a moderate Jeffersonian. Long active in politics, he was probably the Manuel Eyre who clashed openly in 1803 with the radical Michael Leib over county control of the Democratic-Republican party. The elder Eyre's last political act seems to have been the organization of the Society of Constitutional Republicans in March 1805. He died on November 1, 1805.

The younger Manuel Eyre, continuing the moderate politics of his father, was a member of the 1806 committee which sent a memorial to the president and Congress protesting British interference with American ships. When war with Britain was declared he became a member of the General Committee of Superintendence for the Protection of the River Delaware and the City of Philadelphia. He also served on the city council, on the board of directors of the Schuylkill Navigation Company, and on the board of both the Second Bank of the United States and the United States Bank of Pennsylvania which succeeded it. In 1819 Eyre was a member of a committee chosen to prepare a protest against the extension of slavery to new states being admitted into the Union. A Democrat, he was anti-Jacksonian and actively campaigned for Secretary of the Treasury William H. Crawford in 1824. It would be interesting to be able to determine whether Eyre and his father-in-law serendipitously enjoyed complete unanimity, or whether Eyre followed the lead of the latter's strong personality. John Connelly was a member of the Philadelphia Committee of Public Defense, a director of the Second Bank of the United States, a member of the committee of correspondence to aid in preventing the spread of slavery, and in 1824 a candidate for presidential elector in the interests of William H. Crawford.

In 1825 Eyre was a member of the committee of seventeen Philadelphia city and county residents who favored the prompt construction of a Pennsylvania canal which would be controlled by the state. Eyre was one of the twelve representatives from Philadelphia sent to the canal convention that met in Harrisburg that August. There was some opposition to his appointment because his position as a director of the Schuylkill Navigation Company appeared to be a conflict of interest. However, Eyre and John Sergeant (A.B. 1795), future president of the canal board, submitted one of the resolutions adopted by the convention:

> *Resolved,* That in our opinion, the people of Pennsylvania will fully sustain the Legislature in all such measures as may be necessary for effectuating this highly important and interesting object, as we believe them to be fully sensible to its political and social value, and they have never refused to support, to the utmost

of their ability, what their enlightened and patriotic judgment approved as fit to be done for the common good.

Sergeant later stated that it was largely through the perseverance of the Philadelphians that the law creating the Pennsylvania Canal was enacted.

In 1838 Eyre clashed with Nicholas Biddle (A.B. 1801), president of the floundering United States Bank of Pennsylvania, formerly the Second Bank of the United States. Eyre, as a director, was part of a small group who convinced the remaining directors that the officers of the bank had been permitted by the exchange commission to borrow large amounts for private speculation and that the loss of these assets endangered the bank. Biddle in return accused Eyre of being resentful of the aid given by the bank to the Reading Railroad, a competitor of the Schuylkill Navigation Company, in which Eyre was a principal stockholder.

Despite these two accusations of conflict of interest, both Eyre and the firm of Eyre and Massey maintained reputations for integrity and reliability. An easily recognizable figure as he walked through the city, Eyre was six feet tall and well proportioned in spite of being rather stocky. His strong facial features included a prominent nose and he was said to have an "independent" carriage. In 1816 he purchased "The Grange," a country estate in Haverford Township, Delaware County, Pennsylvania, the boyhood home of Charles Ross (Class of 1791). Here the Eyre family spent the summer months. Eyre eventually acquired another farm near the city and three in Delaware and spent a large portion of his time during the last twenty years of his life pursuing his interest in agriculture. In 1824, thirty-one years after his graduation, Eyre was awarded the A.M. degree by the College. His wife died on April 19, 1832, and Eyre died in Philadelphia on February 9, 1845. After his death the firm of Eyre and Massey was dissolved.

SOURCES: Alumni file, PUA; Min. Fac., 29 Nov. 1790, 22 June 1791, 10 Sept. 1792, 15 July 1793; Amer. Whig Soc., *Cat.* (1840), 7; G. L. O. Mershon, *Gravestone Inscriptions in Two Cemeteries at Lawrenceville, N.J.* (1943) 12; *GMNJ*, 31 (1956), 5; *PMHB*, 45 (1901), 587; 49 (1925), 502; 62 (1938), 175-204; J. T. Scharf & T. Westcott, *Hist. of Phila.* (1884), I, 571-72; III, 212; A. Ritter, *Phila. & Her Merchants* (1860), 60-63, 175; S. N. Winslow, *Biographies of Successful Phila. Merchants* (1864), 227-30; T. P. Gowan, *Nicholas Biddle* (1959), 326-27, 376-78; B. L. Daniels, *Pa.: Birthplace of Banking in America* (1976), 157-73; G. Dangerfield, *Era of Good Feelings* (1952), 99, 103, 167-69; H. M. Tinkcom, *Republicans & Federalists in Pa.* (1950), 142, 200, 300; S. W. Higginbotham, *Keystone in the Dem. Arch* (1952), 61; H. D. Eberlein, *Col. Homes of Phila. & Its Neighborhood* (1912), 54; "Eyre Family of Phila.," undated compilation of newspaper clippings at N (microfilm at Nj).

                                                                                RLW

Robert Field IV

ROBERT FIELD IV, A.B., A.M. 1797, agronomist, was the posthumous son of Robert Field III by his widow Mary Peale Field of "White Hill," Fieldsboro, Burlington County, New Jersey. The younger Robert Field was born on April 5, 1775, three months after his father was drowned in the Delaware River when a yawl in which he was sailing capsized. The family plantation, on a high bluff overlooking the Delaware, encompassed the small village of Fieldsboro, which included orchards, cider presses, a distillery, and a tanyard. The estate received its name from the appearance of the hillside when the apple and cherry orchards were in spring bloom. Robert Field left his pregnant wife with a son and four daughters to care for. His will contained a proviso that the funds she inherited would be forfeited at the time of any future marriage, but she was left real estate specifically to enable her to educate her children. In 1779 Mary Field married Commodore Thomas Read, uncle of John Read (A.B. 1787). She was widowed for the second time in October 1788. Robert Field IV was a cousin of Thomas Yardley How (A.B. 1794), whose mother Sarah Field How was a sister of the elder Robert Field.

Field entered the College as a freshman in May 1789 and progressed with his class until November 1790, the start of the junior year. Sometime between then and March 1791 he was put back into the sophomore class. In June 1791 he and two other students were called before the faculty for leaving Nassau Hall late at night and riding horses that were pastured behind the College. They were later joined by six companions for a swim and returned to the campus at "a very unseasonable hour." William Hosack (A.B. 1792), who already had a record of insubordination, was suspended, while Peter Wikoff (A.B. 1791) was admonished privately before the faculty. Field's punishment of a public admonition suggests that his behavior was more flagrant than Wikoff's. Field was again admitted to the junior class in the fall of 1791. Sometime during his senior year he found it necessary to withdraw because of illness. The August 20, 1793 trustees minutes read: "Mr. Robert Field, formerly a member of this class, but obliged to discontinue his studies through indisposition, was recommended to the board to receive his degree with the class. The board, considering his circumstances, and the necessity that obliged him to quit his studies, resolved that he be admitted [to the degree of Bachelor of Arts]." During his stay at Nassau Hall, Field joined the American Whig Society.

On January 10, 1796 Field married Abigail (Abby) Stockton, youngest daughter of Richard (A.B. 1748) and Annis Boudinot

Stockton of "Morven" at Princeton. Abigail was a sister of Richard (A.B. 1779), who had married Field's sister Mary in 1788, and of Lucius Horatio Stockton (A.B. 1787). She was also a sister of Julia Stockton, who married Benjamin Rush (A.B. 1760), and Mary Stockton, who married Andrew Hunter (A.B. 1772). Field's sister Lydia Field Hubley married James Stelle (A.B. 1793) in 1799. The Fields lived in the large brick house at "White Hill," where Annis Stockton joined them until her death in 1801. As far as is known Field had no career other than the management of the family estate, and he appears to have been ill-suited for this responsibility, requiring frequent loans from his brother-in-law Richard. As early as November 1798 Field was in debt to Stockton for £622, with the bond that he signed bearing a postscript containing his promise to repay Stockton $40 which he had borrowed two or three years earlier. Presumably Esther Reed, sister of Joseph Reed (A.B. 1792), was thinking of the financial difficulties of the Fields when, in a letter of February 15, 1804, she wondered what would become of them, adding, "I am thankful that I am in a state of single blessedness rather than matrimony upon such terms." When Field's nephew Richard Stockton III (A.B. 1810), son of Richard and Mary Field Stockton, died as a result of a duel in 1827, John Pintard (A.B. 1776) attributed the catastrophe to the traits that Stockton inherited from his mother's side of the family. "Her brother Field was wild, & dissipated a comfortable estate."

Field died at "White Hill" on April 4, 1810, leaving five children. Benjamin Rush wrote to his son James (A.B. 1805) that Field, as death approached, had been "resigned, penitent, and we hope in peace with his God." Abigail Field returned to Princeton, where her brother Richard gave her a small house across the road from "Morven," which was later known to the community as "Rose Cottage." Her eldest son Robert Field, who had shipped before the mast on a man-of-war at an early age, became a midshipman in the United States Navy in September 1811. On October 4, 1822 he resigned with the rank of lieutenant and settled in Natchez, Mississippi. Richard Stockton Field (A.B. 1821) studied law with his uncle Richard Stockton and had a career which included service as attorney general for New Jersey, as a member of the New Jersey constitutional convention of 1844, United States senator, and judge of the United States district court under President Abraham Lincoln. He was a professor of constitutional law and jurisprudence at the College from 1847 to 1855. The Field daughters Annis Stockton and Mary were successively married to William Dunbar (A.B. 1813), and Mary Field Dunbar was the mother of Field Dunbar (A.B. 1846). The youngest daughter Hannah Field Olmstead was the mother of George Tyler Olmstead, Jr. (A.B. 1860, and U.S. Military Academy 1865), and William Dunbar Olmstead (A.B. 1867).

SOURCES: Alumni files, PUA; Min. Fac., 10 Nov. 1789, 29 Nov. 1790, 18 Mar. & 22 June 1791; Amer. Whig Soc., *Cat.* (1840), 7; Min. Trustees, 20 Aug. 1793; Hageman, *Princeton*, I, 345; T. C. Stockton, *Stockton Family* (1911), 81; H. H. Bisbee, *Sign Posts* (1971), 85; J. D. Magee, *Bordentown 1682-1932* (1932), 61; H. H. Stockton, "Some Families Who Lived in Princeton 100 Years Ago," 3 (n.d., unpublished), NjPHi; F. B. Lee, *Mercer Cnty., N.J.* (1907), 471; will of Robert Field, proved 6 Mar. 1775, Nj; Field Family file, NjPHi; H. C. Conrad, *Hist. of the State of Del.* (1908), III, 859-60 (Thomas Read); *N.J. Wills*, v, 174; als, Esther Reed to Elias Boudinot, 15 Feb. 1804, NjP; Pintard, *Letters*, I, 31; II, 332 (quote re death of Richard Stockton III); A. H. Bill, *House Called Morven* (1954), 80, 122; bond, RF to Richard Stockton, 12 Nov. 1798, Stockton Papers, NjPHi; Butterfield, *Rush Letters*, II, 895, 1044 (quote re RF death); T. H. S. Hamersly, *Gen. Reg. of the U.S. Navy & Marine Corps* (1882), 249.

RLW

John Gibson

JOHN GIBSON, A.B., merchant, was the son of Anna Maria and John Gibson, a Philadelphia merchant who served as mayor of the city in 1771 and 1772. Born on September 20, 1775, John was the younger brother of James Gibson (A.B. 1787). Their father died in April 1782 and was interred in the churchyard of Christ Church, Philadelphia.

Gibson was sent to the grammar school at Nassau Hall and was among a group of eight students from the school who were admitted to the College in the fall of 1790. Although he was not one of those who excelled in the Latin competition, or one who was chosen to give an honorary oration, he received "great approbation" for his speech on the evening before the college commencement, when the grammar school scholars delivered their orations. Probably more indicative of his academic aptitude and preparation was the fact that he entered the College as a sophomore. He soon joined the Cliosophic Society as Brother Sully, named for a minister to Henry IV of France, and became an active member. Because of the society's monthly turnover of officers, he served in several capacities, twice as president. On several occasions he came unprepared to deliver his assigned oration at society meetings, a fairly common lapse among the members. A letter to his mother, dated May 24, 1792, shows that Gibson already knew what his future career was to be: "I have subscribed to Mr. Secard's dancing school, as there are a number of the cleverest students going & they pressed me to go to make up the number. I think I can derive as much improvement from him here if not more than at Philadelphia for when I go an apprentice I shall

be employed all the day time in the store & at night have to study
French so that it would be impossible for me to learn how to dance
then." Gibson's scholastic ability was recognized by his fellow students
as well as by the faculty, for John Conrad Otto (A.B. 1792), in a letter
of June 29, 1793 to John Henry Hobart (A.B. 1793), predicted the
honors that would be assigned by the faculty and chose Gibson for
the mathematical oration. Otto guessed right and Gibson was ranked
fourth in his class, but the oration was never delivered because the
yellow fever epidemic in Philadelphia forced a cancellation of the
commencement exercises. Gibson may have been ill during the last
weeks of the term, since he missed several Cliosophic Society meetings during this period. Despite his absence the society awarded him
its diploma on July 17, 1793.

Where Gibson filled his apprenticeship is not known, but he eventually became a prominent merchant in Philadelphia. Directories for
that city show that from 1805 through 1816 he shared quarters at 78
Walnut and 60 South Fourth with his brother James, whose dwelling
was at the Walnut address and whose legal office was on Fourth
Street, just below Walnut. In 1805 and 1806 John, as well as James,
is listed as an attorney, but since no other evidence that he became a
lawyer has been found, this attribution was probably erroneous. From
1807 on John is listed as a merchant. His departure from James's
address may have been due to the latter's marriage in 1817. John is
again listed as a merchant in the 1819 directory, with 331 Arch Street
as his address. Thereafter his name disappears from the directories.

John Gibson died on June 12, 1823, never having married, and
was buried beside his parents in the churchyard of Christ Episcopal
Church. John Gibson McCall (A.B. 1823) and Peter McCall, Jr. (A.B.
1826) were sons of his sister Sarah Stamper McCall.

SOURCES: Alumni files of John Gibson & James Gibson (which includes typescript of
letter from John to his mother), PUA; Clio. lists; Clio. Min., 6 July 1792–7 Aug. 1793
passim; Min. Fac., class list ca. May 1791, 15 July 1793; Williams, *Academic Honors*,
13; *Pa. Packet, & Daily Advt.*, 7 Oct. 1790 ("great approbation"); Alexander, *Princeton*,
267; Hobart, *Corrres*, I, 28, 30; *PMHB*, 6 (1882), 212; Phila. city directories, 1799-
1819; E. L. Clark, *Inscriptions in Burial Grounds of Christ Church* (1864), 36-37. The
Princetonian should not be confused with John Bannister Gibson, who was admitted
to the Philadelphia bar in Sept. 1805.

                                                                    RLW

John Henry Hobart

JOHN HENRY HOBART, A.B., A.M. 1796, D.D. Union 1806, teacher and Episcopal clergyman, was born in Philadelphia on September 14, 1775, the youngest of nine children of Enoch and Hannah Pratt Hobart. Hannah was the daughter of the gold- and silversmith Henry Pratt and his wife Rebecca Claypoole. The father was a West India merchant and sea captain. He died on October 27, 1776, leaving his widow just enough property to support their family respectably.

John Henry Hobart received his earliest education in or near Philadelphia at the school of a Mr. Leslie, possibly James Lesley (A.B. 1759), who seems to have taught at Germantown towards the end of the Revolution. Early in 1784 Rev. Dr. John Andrews founded his Episcopal Academy in Philadelphia, with Hobart among his first students. Hobart is said to have stood first in his class throughout his attendance. In 1785 he belonged to and apparently organized a schoolboy "Society for the Advancement of its Members in Useful Literature." When the College of Philadelphia was reestablished in 1789, Andrews became its vice-provost, and Hobart was one of many students who followed him there from the Episcopal Academy. He enrolled in the senior class of the Latin School, the preparatory division, in May 1789 and entered the College of Philadelphia proper that October. Here too he was active in student clubs. He may have had a hand in the foundation of a short-lived organization called the Philomathean Society. Next he joined the Ciceronian Society but resigned on November 28, 1789. He had renewed his membership by July 28, 1790, when as the secretary he began a revolt which successfully displaced the society's president, Aquila M. Bolton, on charges of high-handedness. Hobart was elected president in his stead on October 2, 1790.

Hobart left the College of Philadelphia on January 1, 1791. His whereabouts and activities for the ensuing ten months have not been discovered. He entered the junior class of the College in November 1791. His roommates upon his arrival were Alexander White and John Conrad Otto (both A.B. 1792). During Hobart's senior year Thomas Yardley How (A.B. 1794) was his roommate. Otto later recalled that Hobart had a good voice and used to entertain his companions with "a song or two early in the morning before we arose." Hobart's room on the north side of Nassau Hall was hard to keep warm during the bitter winter of 1791-92. He wrote his mother that even indoors he was wearing his greatcoat. Extant receipts show that he paid £5.12.0 for "Tuition, Room-rent, Library and Damage Money" and £10.0.0 "Diet" for the summer semester, May-September 1792.

John Henry Hobart, A.B. 1793
BY JOHN PARADISE

In the competitions for underclassmen at commencement, September 1792, Hobart was among three victors in "English Grammar reading & orthography" but did not place in "pronouncing
English Orations." His speech was "On the Past Blessings and Future
Prospects of America." In addition he and his classmate and close
friend Abraham Skinner presented a dramatic dialogue portraying
an incident from ancient Roman history. Hobart played Narva, the
venerable counsellor who persuades young king Massinissa (Skinner)
to abandon a romantic attachment in order more singlemindedly to
pursue virtue and glory.

Hobart had joined the American Whig Society shortly after matric-
ulating and remained an enthusiastic and active member even after
graduation. He would later urge his fellow Columbia College trustees
to sanction and encourage similar literary societies. Hobart represented the Whigs at the public competition held July 4, 1793, with a
speech on the "Cause of Freedom." The oration had been written for
him by Nathaniel C. Higginson (A.B. 1787), just as his Independence
Day oration of the preceding year had been written by his brother,

Robert Enoch Hobart. In later years John repaid such favors by writing orations for a number of younger Whigs. The practice of using speeches written by others, even for commencement, was very common at this time. The faculty knew about and apparently accepted the custom, although they drew the line in 1800 when James Carnahan, later president of the College, attempted to use an address supplied by Hobart for the English salutatory oration. On July 15, 1793 the faculty met to plan the commencement and concluded that Hobart and Bennett Taylor were tied for top honors. Hobart's backers won the coin toss which broke the deadlock. He was accordingly assigned the Latin salutatory, but the outbreak of yellow fever in Philadelphia forced cancellation of the exercises, and the degrees were awarded privately.

After graduation Hobart returned to Philadelphia and entered the countinghouse of his brother-in-law Robert Smith, a dry-goods merchant. After a few months his performance obliged his family to recognize that his heart was not in trade, and they abandoned the experiment. Around the beginning of July 1794 Hobart returned to Princeton to begin preparing for a professional career. Despite the urging of many of his friends that he study law, he soon decided to read for the ministry. In November 1794 he was sharing a room in Nassau Hall with his friends Joseph Warren Scott (A.B. 1795) and Robert Marshall Forsyth (A.B. 1796), and taking his meals off campus at Mrs. Knox's boarding house. He still resided in Nassau Hall in December 1795. Several previous efforts to obtain him a tutorship had proved abortive, but on January 16, 1796 he was chosen to succeed David English (A.B. 1789). On September 26, 1796 he also became clerk of the faculty.

The tutors were responsible for teaching the freshman and sophomore classes and for enforcing discipline in the College. Hobart began by instructing the freshmen, but in March 1796 the illness of Walter Minto also obliged Hobart to take over the mathematics class of the juniors. Minto soon died, and at the beginning of the academic year 1796-97 President Samuel Stanhope Smith (A.B. 1769) offered to give Hobart overall responsibility for teaching the juniors, whose curriculum consisted mainly of mathematics and natural philosophy. Hobart declined the offer and instead taught the sophomore class, which emphasized English and classical languages. He was a conscientious and, by several accounts, a popular teacher. Thomas Miller (A.B. 1799) later recalled that Hobart had given him individual lessons which he needed in order to keep up with the sophomore class, and that Hobart had refused his offers of compensation.

During his years as graduate student and tutor, Hobart attended the meetings of the American Whig Society infrequently but remained a force when controversy arose. In December 1796 he gave what one member called "the most eloquent speech that I have ever heard in the Whig Hall" supporting a bitterly contested and barely victorious effort to suspend the leader of an opposing faction. When an effort was made in 1798 to relax a rule by which any Whig cited for bad scholarship in a public examination was automatically suspended from the society, Hobart successfully opposed it in what Miller called "one of the most argumentative and eloquent speeches that I have ever heard from that day to this." With such exceptions, Hobart's energies as a debater were now reserved for the Belles Lettres Society, sometimes called the Graduate Society of Nassau Hall, which functioned somewhat like the undergraduate societies but consisted of "the members of the college faculty and of the resident graduates." On one occasion Hobart and his friend Henry Kollock (A.B. 1794) aired their opposing views on episcopacy at the society and the discussion was continued at several ensuing meetings.

As a devoted Episcopalian preparing for that faith's ministry, Hobart's position at the College was somewhat anomalous. He appears to have been the first College faculty member without either a Presbyterian or a Congregationalist background. Joseph Caldwell (A.B. 1791) later remembered that Hobart was the only Arminian and Episcopalian in a graduate class in theology taught by President Smith, and that he always spoke up to defend his position. Nonetheless "we were in habits of the utmost forbearance and good feeling." Hobart attended Presbyterian services and took the lead in organizing prayer meetings, both in College and the town, at which, as Caldwell recalled, "we prayed in turn, always extemporaneously, and then read some discourse." Hobart later was to conclude that he had erred both by his ecumenical activities and by his participation in extemporaneous prayer, and he became very much opposed to both. His letters from this period show that in politics he strongly supported the Federalists.

At the end of the spring semester in late March 1798, Hobart resigned his tutorship and returned to Philadelphia to spend a few weeks under Bishop William White's direct supervision, completing his studies for the ministry. White ordained him deacon on June 3, 1798, and he was installed at Trinity, in Oxford, and All Saints', in Lower Dublin Township, two rural parishes about ten miles from Philadelphia. The congregation of St. Paul's in Philadelphia soon offered to make him their assistant minister. Instead he accepted a call from Christ Church, New Brunswick, New Jersey, for one year starting May 4, 1799. He received $267 for officiating three out of every four Sundays. Hobart's main reason for accepting the position was his desire to continue his studies at nearby Princeton, where he seems to have lived during that year.

On May 6, 1800 Hobart married Mary Goodin (or Goodwin) Chandler in Elizabethtown, New Jersey. She was the youngest of six children of Jane Emott and her husband, Thomas Bradbury Chandler, an Anglican clergyman and Loyalist. William Chetwood (A.B. 1792) was her first cousin, Elias and Elisha Boudinot, longtime College trustees, were first cousins once removed, and Thomas B. C. Dayton (A.B. 1806) and Aaron Ogden Dayton (A.B. 1813) were nephews. Four daughters and three sons resulted from Hobart's marriage. His wife and all their children survived him.

Hobart accepted the rectorship of St. George's, Hempstead, Long Island, and moved there in June 1800. The salary was £150 per annum, plus a parsonage and firewood. He always had trouble living within his means and his mother's letters from this period show that he still relied on her for financial assistance. His stay on Long Island was brief. He was offered the rectorship of St. Mary's, the Bowery, New York City, on August 27, 1800. He declined and instead accepted a post as assistant minister at Trinity parish, New York City, with a salary of £500 a year, and moved there in December. Bishop Samuel Provoost (A.B. King's 1758) ordained him priest April 5, 1801. The move to Trinity ended Hobart's parish-hopping, for he remained in its service the rest of his life. His preference for Trinity is easily understood. Its size, antiquity, and extensive New York City landholdings made it the richest and perhaps the most prestigious parish in the Episcopal church, with a parish church and two chapels served by four ministers, headed by the bishop of New York. Almost immediately after his arrival Hobart became a dominant force in New York Episcopalianism. From 1801 to 1811 he was annually elected secretary of the diocesan convention and a member of the diocese's standing committee. In 1801, 1804, and 1808 he was a delegate to the General Convention, the latter two years as secretary of the House of Clerical and Lay Deputies. In 1801 he was also elected a trustee of Columbia College and led the Episcopal forces on its board during the rest of his life. He reinvigorated existing church organizations and took the lead in founding a host of new ones.

Hobart's success was based partly on the fact that he was enormously energetic, and eloquent in committees as well as the pulpit. He was quickly recognized as the most efficient and capable administrator in the diocese. More important still, perhaps, he united conservatism on matters relating to doctrine and church government, reverence for his faith's liturgy, and an ardent and demonstrative piety which the orthodox had been accustomed to condemn as improper. A contemporary recalled that initially Hobart puzzled his parishioners, who could not decide "whether to call him 'High Churchman' or 'Methodist.'" He was among the earliest and ablest of a new generation of Episcopal clergy bent on attacking their church's problems with a new vigor which, they hoped, would rescue it from the doldrums created by the rise of Methodism, associations with Loyalism during the Revolution, and disestablishment in the South.

Between 1804 and 1807 Hobart made a name for himself as author of a series of tracts and newspaper essays defending episcopal church government, culminating in his *Apology for Apostolic Order and its Advocates*, addressed to his Presbyterian foe John Mitchell Mason (A.M. 1794). Hobart maintained that only episcopal ordinations could be regarded as valid, a position which led to many attacks on him as an intolerant bigot. In the *Apology* he declared his support for "Evangelical Truth and Apostolic Order," a phrase he and his supporters repeated until it became their slogan. Hobart continued to publish prolifically throughout his career. He was not a deep or scholarly thinker and his works were mostly practical. In addition to periodicals and controversial and polemical pieces, he issued a catechism and a series of devotional tracts which enjoyed quite a vogue in his day. Often he adapted, rearranged, and enlarged the work of other authors, as in his most ambitious writing job, an American edition produced between 1818 and 1823 of the *Family Bible* of the English Society for Promoting Christian Knowledge.

In 1811 Benjamin Moore (A.B. King's 1768), who was both the bishop of New York and the rector of Trinity, suffered an attack of paralysis, and on May 29 of that year Hobart was consecrated assistant bishop. Bishop Moore remained disabled for the rest of his life, and so Hobart was acting diocesan until Moore's death on February 27, 1816 made Hobart bishop of New York and rector of Trinity in name as well as deed. The choice of Hobart in 1811 to lead the diocese aroused controversy on several counts. Thirty-five years in age, he was so young that he found it politic to sprinkle his hair with powder to make himself appear older. Even at Trinity he was not the senior assistant minister. Many perceived him as self-serving and unscrupulously ambitious. A colleague, Rev. Cave Jones, published an attack on Hobart's character in an unsuccessful bid to prevent his election by the diocesan convention. Jones's polemic offered evidence of little more than that Hobart was quick-tempered and irritable at times, given to sudden outbursts usually followed by gracious apologies. Public opinion dismissed the attack as petty, and it was ignored until Hobart's partisans celebrated his election with a campaign to drive Jones out of the diocese, a vindictive action which succeeded only after a bitter pamphlet war and some legal wrangling. Some critics thought Hobart insufficiently dignified. Although his eloquence was universally conceded, he spoke rapidly and read the church service too quickly. Small in stature, he walked so fast "that you might have supposed he was walking for a wager," and his widely remarked sincerity and candor were not conducive to tact or stately reserve.

Hobart quickly weathered these initial misgivings and set about to make his diocese over in his own image. His was a new vision of the role of bishop, hitherto frequently seen as little more than a decorous automaton dispensing consecrations, ordinations, and confirmations. Hobart was determined to lead every aspect of the religious life of his diocese. The diversity of his interests is reflected in the network of church-sponsored societies he organized, always with the bishop as ex-officio president. He founded or helped found the Protestant Episcopal Society for Promoting Religion and Learning (1802), the Committee for Propagating the Gospel in the State of New-York (1804), the Protestant Episcopal Theological Society (1806), the New-York Bible and Common Prayer-Book Society (1809), the New-York Protestant Episcopal Tract Society (1810), the New-York Auxiliary Bible and Common Prayer-Book Society (1816), the New-York Protestant Episcopal Sunday School Society (1817), the New-York Protestant Episcopal Theological Education Society (1820), the New-York Protestant Episcopal Public School (1826 reorganization of Trinity Charity School), the Protestant Episcopal General Sunday School Union (1827), and the Protestant Episcopal Press (1829).

Hobart interested himself in every aspect of parochial affairs, down to expediting personally the delivery of needed parts for a church organ in one of his country parishes. He issued pastoral letters to his clergy and laity, and in 1815 he began issuing charges to his clergy, a first in his diocese and probably in America. Each year he adhered to a grueling schedule of travel on visitations, frequently covering more than 2,000 miles and visiting from thirty to forty parishes. Until the consecration of John Croes (A.M. 1797) as bishop of New Jersey in 1815, Hobart performed many of the diocesan duties in that state as well, and he served as acting bishop of Connecticut during a vacancy from June 1816 to October 1819. During his nineteen-year episcopate he ordained one hundred deacons and ninety priests, consecrated seventy churches, took part in the consecration of nine bishops, and confirmed more than 12,000 people.

In 1815 Hobart spoke out against ecumenical Bible societies, and the next year he urged his flock not to join the newly formed American Bible Society. A bitter paper war followed. Hobart maintained specifically that the Bible should be distributed only with the Book of Common Prayer, and more generally that the fashionable liberality of the day, in which the differences dividing Protestants were regarded as involving only non-essentials, was specious and masked indifference about religion. He argued that far from being unimportant, his church's government and liturgy were as important as its doctrine and hence that Episcopalians should not unite with other sects in any organized religious activity. "Christian truth and Christian harmony are best preserved," he argued, "when Christians of different religious communions endeavour to advance the interest of religion in their own way," although this separatism "should never interrupt the harmony of social and domestic intercourse" among Christians. Hobart's emphasis on the distinctiveness of his church probably aided it as it sought to carve out a niche for itself in the still-fluid religious scene in western New York and the Old Northwest.

Hobart's anxiety to retain Episcopal money and energies within his church sprang as much from practical considerations as from his opposition to ecumenicism. As he traveled in visitations which took him as far west as Detroit, his inability to provide congregations with resources and ministers constantly frustrated him. He steadfastly opposed missionary efforts directed to foreign lands, arguing that the American church had more than enough to do at home. His biggest problem was a shortage of clergy, and he early and consistently sought to provide better ways of training them than the customary system of reading under an individual clergyman's supervision. In 1806 he organized the Protestant Episcopal Theological Society as an informal weekly class for divinity students in New York City. He offered in 1814 to contribute land at "Short Hills," his country estate in Summit, Essex (now Union) County, New Jersey, for a theological seminary, over which he would preside and at which he would also teach as time permitted, but the plan came to nothing. In the same year the founding of a general seminary was proposed at the General Convention. Hobart initially opposed this plan for a national Episcopal seminary, preferring a diocesan or private school which he could be sure of controlling.

By 1817 Hobart had followed public opinion in shifting to support of a general seminary, provided it was located in New York City, and he solicited contributions for the new school when that year's General Convention founded it. However, when the General Theological Seminary opened in New York in 1819, he found the number of trustees accorded his diocese too small and the faculty not to his liking, and he led his followers in turning such a cold shoulder toward the seminary that in 1820 it was moved to New Haven, Connecticut. Hobart then returned to his plan for a diocesan seminary and obtained enough backing for one to be opened in New York City in 1821. The specter of two nearby seminaries competing for resources was averted by the death in 1821 of Jacob Sherred, who left $60,000 in his will to an Episcopal seminary under terms sufficiently vague that both institutions claimed it. The diocesan seminary appeared to have the better case legally, but Hobart agreed to a compromise by which the two schools were merged as the General Theological Seminary, with the New Haven establishment moved back to New York and the diocese of New York given a much increased representation on the board of trustees. Hobart served the General Theological Seminary without salary as Professor of Pastoral Theology and Pulpit Eloquence from the merger until his death.

Overall, Hobart was not a model of consistency as he flipped back and forth between support of a general and a diocesan seminary. In 1823 he bitterly opposed Bishop Philander Chase's ultimately successful effort to found a seminary in Ohio. Hobart's assertion that such a seminary must be under the control of the General Convention, perhaps as a branch school of the General Theological Seminary, would have read better had he not made directly contrary arguments a few years previously favoring each diocese's right to educate its own clergy. The sincerity of his desire to improve the quality and above all to expand the numbers of Episcopal clergy is indisputable, and he is recognized as a key figure in founding and charting the early course of the General Theological Seminary, but his determination that the candidates be educated under his control and in ways fitting his ideological concerns is equally evident.

Episcopal colleges as well as seminaries preoccupied Hobart. He consistently led efforts to preserve and expand Columbia College's Episcopal identity, with such success that in 1824 John Pintard (A.B. 1776) remarked that "Bp. Hobart has so episcopalized it, as to have alienated" New Yorkers of other faiths. Hobart sent his sons to Columbia, although he retained enough interest in his *alma mater* to serve as one of the vice presidents of the Alumni Association of Nassau Hall from its founding in 1826 until his death. He also dreamed of starting an Episcopal college in western New York and thus became the most important figure in the founding there of Geneva College, which received a provisional charter in 1822 and a permanent one in 1825. However his plan to found a branch school of the seminary in Geneva failed. Geneva College was renamed Hobart College in his honor in 1852.

From early childhood Hobart had suffered from dyspepsia. In fall

1822 he suffered the first of a series of attacks of "bilious intermittent fever" which eventually wore him down and killed him. The next summer he took a vacation trip to Quebec and Montreal and suffered another attack on the way back. His doctors advised a trip to Europe to regain his health, and he sailed for England on September 24, 1823. During the next two years he traveled in England, Wales, Scotland, France, Switzerland, and Italy. He visited Robert Southey and William Wordsworth in the English Lakes District, studied the antiquities at Rome, and went on long hikes in the Alps.

Hobart arrived back in New York on October 12, 1825 in such improved health that in 1826 he was able to travel almost 4,000 miles on visitation. Shortly after his return he expressed his joy at being home in a sermon called *The United States of America Compared With Some European Countries, Particularly England* ..., in which he asserted that America's "physical, literary, civil and religious" blessings were superior. The most controversial section was his delineation of the flaws of the Church of England, most of which he blamed on its union with the state. He argued that even persecution by the civil government was to be preferred to its institutionalized favor. On other occasions he demonstrated his determination to keep his church out of politics by refusing to attend dinners with covert political messages like that in 1828 commemorating the Battle of New Orleans, and even by turning down a request by the city's corporation that he eulogize Governor DeWitt Clinton in his pulpit after Clinton's death in the same year. In his homecoming sermon Hobart also stressed the republican nature of Episcopal church government and pointed to similarities between it and the structure of the federal government. Although he was attacked in England for delivering what some saw as an exercise in chauvinism which ill repaid the abundant hospitality he had received there, the work served the useful purpose of reiterating Episcopal commitment to republican government and rejection of any lingering desire to regain government support.

In the same month that Hobart returned to New York the diocesan convention met. A series of resolutions welcoming him home was passed, but in order to obtain a unanimous vote they were watered down by failing to mention Hobart's policies, as opposed to affection for him personally. Hobart promptly gave a speech indignantly rejecting the resolutions and asking that they be expunged from the minutes. The policies he stood for were his "glory and pride" and without them he would rather not be honored at all. The convention hastily passed resolutions endorsing "the rectitude of his [Hobart's] principles, ... the purity of his motives, ... the soundness of his policy, and the correctness of his proceedings." The episode illustrates Hobart's dominance within his diocese, his abundant lack of timidity or humility, and his determination to identify himself among both his friends and enemies with a High Church emphasis on the distinctiveness and correctness of his church's doctrine, liturgy, and government.

In 1829 Hobart sparked his last major controversy with a pastoral letter attacking the Protestant Episcopal Clerical Association of the City of New-York, a small group that met in its members' homes for tea, prayer, and discussion. Hobart objected to the group because it met informally, beyond the control of the church. He consistently maintained that the prescribed services, following the approved liturgy and held inside church edifices, provided a perfectly adequate outlet for public devotion, and that any other communal religious meeting ran the risk of degenerating into a frenzied emotional effusion. Although the association used set prayers, Hobart feared that "the heats of enthusiasm will soon inflame religious conversation, and extempore prayers, stirring up the animal passions, [will] displace the dull routine of prescribed formularies." He also envisioned the association becoming a creature of faction. The members of the association tried to defend themselves but soon gave up and disbanded in the face of Hobart's public displeasure. Hobart's aversion to anything smacking of "enthusiasm" provides a counterpoise to his condemnation of "liberality" as manifested in the Bible societies.

Hobart fell ill while on visitation on September 2, 1830 and died at 4 a.m. ten days later at the parsonage house of St. Peter's, Auburn, New York. He was buried under the chancel of Trinity Church and commemorated by an elaborate monument sculptured by Ball Hughes. Hobart had presided over a period of massive expansion and institutional development in his church. During his episcopate the number of clergy in his diocese almost tripled, and the number of missionaries laboring there increased from two to fifty. He had helped set the course of his church on almost every level. The American supporters of the Oxford Movement later claimed him as a predecessor. He was arguably the single most influential man in the history of American Episcopalianism.

SOURCES: W. Berrian, "A Memoir of his Life," vol. I of Hobart's *Posthumous Works* (1833), *passim* ("Christian truth," "should never," 169-70; "bilious," 254; "glory and pride," 362; "the heats," 389); J. F. Schroeder, *Memorial of Bishop Hobart* (1831), *passim* ("a song," xxi; "the members," xxvi, quoting John Maclean [A.B. 1816]; "we prayed," xxvi; "we were in habits," xxviii); J. McVickar, *Early Years of the late Bishop Hobart* (2d ed., 1836), *passim* ("Society for the Advancement," 24); J. McVickar, *Professional Years of John Henry Hobart* (1836), *passim* ("whether to call," 66; "Evangelical Truth," 134-35); M. Dix, *Hist. of the Parish of Trinity Church in N.Y. City* (1901-06), II, 167-69,

197-336; III, *passim* ("the rectitude," 423; see frontispiece to this vol. for a different portrait of JHH than that depicted here); IV, 1-120; J. H. Hobart, *Correspondence* (1911-12), I-VI (in the series: Protestant Episcopal Church in the U.S.A., General Convention, *Archives of the General Convention*), *passim*; Sprague, IV, 440-53 ("that you might," quoting James M. Mathews); MS Tuition Money Book, Academy & College of Phila., 1789-91, UPenn-Ar; MS letters between JHH and mother, 1791-96, NjP; Min. Fac., Nov. 1791, 26 Sept. 1792 ("English Grammar"), 15 July 1793, 14 Dec. 1795, 16 Jan. & 26 Sept. 1796; Amer. Whig Soc., *Cat.* (1840), 7; MS undergraduate orations & receipts, Hobart Papers, TxAuCH ("Tuition, Room-rent," "On the Past," "Cause of Freedom"); Min. Trustees, 25 Sept. 1793; *Greenleaf's N.Y. Jour., & Patriotic Reg.*, 7 Oct. 1796; Union College, Schenectady, N.Y., *Centennial Cat.* (1895), 5; Beam, *Whig Soc.*, 69-72, 102 ("one of the most"); R. D. W. Connor, *Doc. Hist. of the Univ. of N.C., 1776-99* (1953), II, 78-81, 114-16 ("the most eloquent"), 303-06; Maclean, *History*, II, 55, 357-59, 384-85; *PMHB*, 27 (1903), 293-94; E. F. Hatfield, *Hist. of Elizabeth, N.J.* (1868), 538, 540, 550-51; *NEHGR*, 27 (1873), 236; *GMNJ*, 3 (1927), 17, 19; Thomas, *Columbia*, 14; Pintard, *Letters*, I-IV, *passim* ("Bp. Hobart has so," II, 143); alumni file, PUA; S. H. Turner, *Autobiog.* (1863), 86-168, *passim*; P. S. Dawley, *Story of the General Theol. Seminary ... 1817-1967* (1969), 1-110, *passim*; G. F. Smythe, *Kenyon College: Its First Cent.* (1924), 22, 29; R. M. Spielmann, *Bexley Hall: 150 Years* (1974), 10; W. H. Smith, *Hobart & William Smith: The Hist. of Two Colleges* (1972), 13-14, 27, 31-37, 43, 49, 57, 60, 66, 100; Hobart College, *Gen. Cat. ... 1825-97* (1897), 1-2, 13; *N.Y. Hist.*, 23 (1942), 14-23; C. C. Robbins, *David Hosack: Citizen of N.Y.* (1964), 81, 124, 127; J. A. Scoville, *Old Merchants of N.Y. City*, 1st ser. (1862), 213; 3d ser. (1865), 67-68, 79-80; 4th ser. (1866), 116-17; J. W. Francis, *Old N.Y.* (1866), 85, 168-71; R. W. G. Vail, *Knickerbocker Birthday* (1954), 30; J. H. Hobart, *The U.S.A. Compared With Some European Countries, Particularly England* (1825), *passim* ("physical, literary," 9).

PUBLICATIONS: For a complete bibliography of Hobart's output see Hobart, *Corres.*, I, ccv-ccix. His most important works include *Companion for the Altar* (1804); *Companion for the Festivals and Fasts* (1805); *Companion to the Book of Common Prayer* (1805); *Clergyman's Companion* (1806); *Collection of Essays on the Subject of Episcopacy* (1806); *Apology for Apostolic Order and its Advocates* (1807); *Christian's Manual of Faith and Devotion* (1814); *Candidate for Confirmation Instructed* (1816); *Mant and D'Oyley's Bible* (1818-23); *Sermons on the Principal Events and Truths of Redemption* (2 vols., 1824); and *Posthumous Works* (3 vols., 1832-33).

MANUSCRIPTS: TxAuCH owns the largest collection of Hobart papers, comprising 3,000 loose letters and papers and as many more mounted in blank books, the bulk of them letters to Hobart. In the *Correspondence* published in six volumes, 1911-12, the holdings up to February 1811 were published. A good selection of the rest is given in Dix, *Hist. of the Parish of Trinity Church*, III-IV. Dix, III, 487-96 indexes the loose letters and papers. TxAuCH's holdings include Hobart's speeches at the 24 Sept. 1792 and 4 July 1793 undergraduate competitions, and his dialogue with Skinner at the former (photocopies in PUA). Other Hobart MSS are in NjP; Gen. Theol. Sem. Lib.; DLC; Archives, Parish of Trinity Church, N.Y. City; and the Philander Chase Papers, Kenyon College Lib., Gambier, Ohio.

JJL

Jacob Motte Huger

JACOB MOTTE HUGER, United States Marine officer, the son of John Huger and Charlotte Motte Huger of Charleston, South Carolina, and "The Hagan" plantation on the Cooper River in St. Thomas and St. Dennis Parish, was the namesake of his maternal grandfather

Jacob Motte. The second of five siblings, Jacob was probably born in 1776. The eldest brother Daniel died as a young child. The Hugers belonged to a wealthy and prominent South Carolina family. John Huger saw service as an ensign in the Cherokee War and on the colonial council of safety at the outbreak of the Revolution. He was a member of the provincial congress of 1775-76, served as South Carolina's first secretary of state in 1776, and earned the rank of captain in the state militia.

John Huger inherited "The Hagan" from his father, along with a town house in Charleston and a plantation of more than 3,000 acres in Craven County. He increased his acreage so that at the time of his death "The Hagan" included almost 5,000 acres manned by over 200 slaves. Most of the postwar years were spent in the Charleston home, which was staffed by nine slaves. Huger was known as a compassionate master who impressed this principle on his children. He represented St. Thomas and St. Dennis from 1787 to 1790 in the South Carolina senate, was a delegate to the state ratifying convention of 1788, and served as intendant of Charleston from 1793 to 1795. He was an active member of the South Carolina Society and of St. Michael's Episcopal Church. His marriage to his second wife Ann Broun Cusack, widow of James Cusack, took place on January 11, 1785 and added four more children to the family.

Jacob Huger was sent to the Nassau Hall grammar school where, in 1787, he ranked highest in the second class. The following September he earned the same distinction in the graduating class and was admitted to the freshman class of the College. Huger's name appears on surviving College records only on a list of students compiled on November 10, 1789, which notes that he entered the College on November 10, 1788, but describes him as a freshman. It is very unlikely that a student with such an excellent record in the grammar school would have been retained in the freshman class for anything but a prolonged absence. On this list Richard Willing's name is directly above that of Huger's, with a notation that Willing left the College on April 10, 1790. This information is not correct, since Willing remained at the College until the summer session of 1792. His name is included on the list for the summer session of 1790 while Huger's is not, and it seems safe to assume that it was actually Huger who left in the spring of 1790, with the entry made on the wrong line.

No trace of Huger has been found for the years immediately following. He was in Charleston as one of the witnesses to the will of his stepmother's sister Jane Saunders, who died in February 1798. Huger joined the United States Marine Corps as a second lieutenant on May 1, 1799. He died in Philadelphia on November 8, 1799 and was buried the next day in the cemetery of Christ Church. The hasty burial suggests that he could have been a victim of the yellow fever epidemic of that year. Daniel Lionel Huger (Class of 1789) and Daniel Elliott Huger (A.B. 1798) were first cousins, and Benjamin J. Huger (A.B. 1850) was a second cousin.

SOURCES: Min. Fac., 10 Nov. 1789; C. T. Moore, *Abstracts of Wills of Charleston District, S.C., 1783-1800* (1974), 389; E. B. Reynolds & J. R. Faunt, *Biog. Dir. of the Senate of S.C.* (1964), 243 (father); *Biog. Dir. S.C. House Rep.*, II, 343-45 (father); D. E. H. Smith & A. S. Salley, Jr., *Reg. of St. Philip's Parish* (1971), 90, 94, 95; *Trans. of the Huguenot Society of S.C.*, 4 (1897), foldout chart "Pedigree of Huger of South Carolina"; *N.J. Jour. & Pol. Intelligencer*, 10 Oct. 1787, 29 Oct. 1788; T. H. S. Hamersly, *Gen. Reg. of the U.S. Navy & Marine Corps* (1882), 883; "Records of Christ Church, Phila., 1785-1900," PHi; *SCHGM*, 43 (1942), 151-53; G. C. Rogers, *Charleston in the Age of the Pinckneys* (1969), 24.

The Huger Pedigree in *Transactions of the Huguenot Society* and E. L. Clark, *Inscriptions in the Burial Grounds of Christ Church, Phila.* (1864), 175, both state that Huger died on October 8, 1798 at the age of 23. However, Hamersley gives November 8, 1799 as the date of death and the "Records of Christ Church" cite November 9, 1799 as the burial date. Huger could not have been 23 in 1798, since his brother Daniel was baptized on September 27, 1775 and was probably born a few weeks earlier. A 1776 birthdate would make Huger the average age for a member of the Class of 1793.

RLW

Nathaniel Hunt

NATHANIEL HUNT, A.B., farmer and teacher, was the son of Nathaniel Hunt of Cranbury, New Jersey, who served as a colonel in the second regiment of Hunterdon County militia during the Revolution. He also served as a county justice sometime during the war years, but his main occupation was farming, and he apparently sold produce to the College steward. Several sources list Keziah Phillips as the mother of Nathaniel Jr. However, a tombstone in the Cranbury Presbyterian churchyard shows that the elder Nathaniel had a first wife Hannah who died in 1785 and who would certainly have been the mother of the 1793 graduate, who was born sometime around 1770. Hunt's marriage to the widowed Keziah Phillips Lott probably took place in 1787 or 1788, since she sold her house in Princeton on January 10 of the latter year. The younger Nathaniel's classmate Robert Hunt was a cousin, the son of his father's brother Abraham, and Ralph Phillips Lott (Class of 1790) became his stepbrother.

Hunt entered the College as a sophomore in November 1790 and joined the American Whig Society. The faculty assigned him the part of the opponent in the first dispute scheduled for the subsequently canceled 1793 commencement exercises, "Can the fine arts more than philosophy flourish under arbitrary governments."

Nothing is known about where Hunt spent the years immediately after graduation, but in 1797 he entered the Litchfield (Connecticut) Law School of Tapping Reeve (A.B. 1763). He apparently did not remain long enough to complete his preparation for the bar, for he became a farmer in Amwell Township, Hunterdon County, while also teaching in a small country school nearby. He died January 23, 1807 and was buried in the Harbourton churchyard in Hopewell Township. An inventory of his estate, filed a week after his death, shows it to have been worth only $605.08.

SOURCES: Alumni file, PUA; E. F. Cooley, *Gen. of Early Settlers in Trenton & Ewing* (1883), 143, 184; R. B. Walsh, *Cranbury Past & Present* (1975), 557; Min. Fac., 29 Nov. 1790, 15 July 1793 ("Can the fine arts"); Amer. Whig Soc., *Cat.* (1840), 7; S. H. Fisher, *Litchfield Law School 1774-1833* (1946), 67; Alexander, *Princeton*, 269; Stryker, *Off. Reg.*, 353; Works Progress Admin., *Tombstone Inscriptions, Mercer Cnty.* (n.d.); *N.J. Wills*, IX, 188. Nathaniel was a popular name in New Jersey Hunt families and the many branches of that family make it difficult to be positive that identifications are not overlapping. Many references to Nathaniel Hunt have been eliminated as alluding to someone either too young or too old to have been a member of the Class of 1793.

RLW

Robert Hunt

ROBERT HUNT, A.B., A.M. 1797, lawyer and army officer, the fourth son of Abraham Hunt of Trenton, New Jersey, and his first wife Theodosia Pearson, was born in 1778. The father was a prosperous merchant who for many years was in partnership with Moore Furman, father of Moore Furman, Jr., and John White Furman, both members of the Class of 1794. In 1774 Hunt was a member of the New Jersey provincial assembly's standing committee of correspondence and the following year was appointed commissioner for the western division, authorized to purchase military necessities for the province. In 1776 he became a lieutenant colonel in the First Regiment of Hunterdon County. It was he who so hospitably entertained the Hessian Col. Johann Rall (Rahl) on Christmas night 1776, with the drinking and cardplaying extending into the early morning. Rall's befuddled state and incoherent orders at the Battle of Trenton, and the consequent bewilderment and eventual disorderly retreat of his men, were a result of the all-night partying at the Hunt home. Opinions have been divided as to whether Abraham Hunt was really a tory sympathizer or whether he deliberately determined to get Rall drunk; however, the 1777 order of the Continental Congress giving Hunt the responsibility of removing the papers and monies of the

Congress from Philadelphia upon the approach of the British indicates that he maintained the confidence of Congress. After the war he served as postmaster of Trenton for several years and was an alderman of the city in 1792. From 1805 to 1821 he was a director of the Trenton Banking Company, and he served as a trustee of the First Presbyterian Church for fifty-seven years.

As one of the founders of the Trenton Academy, Hunt would certainly have sent his son there for his early education. Robert Hunt entered the College as a junior in November 1791. On December 27 he joined the Cliosophic Society under the pseudonym of Cleomenes, which had been the name of three Spartan kings. At various times Hunt served the society as president, second assistant, censor, and corrector of composition. In the spring of 1793 he was selected to deliver the Fourth of July oration celebrating the revival of the society, and later that year he received its diploma. At the end of his junior year, in the annual competitions held among the underclassmen, he was one of the three prizemen in the competition on English grammar, reading, and orthography, and one of four in the competition on pronouncing English orations. The faculty ranked him third in his class and chose him to deliver the belles lettres oration at his commencement, an honor which would have been an innovation, but cancellation of the public ceremonies because of a yellow fever epidemic denied him the opportunity.

Hunt next studied law, probably in Trenton, and was admitted as an attorney of the supreme court of New Jersey during the 1799 February term. In August 1798 when he applied for a lieutenant's commission in the United States Army, Richard Stockton (A.B. 1779) recommended him for his liberal education and unblemished character. Philemon Dickinson of Trenton noted that he was a "decided federalist," and Timothy Pickering (LL.D. 1798) praised him as having "promising abilities great modesty good understandn [sic]." Alexander Hamilton (LL.D. 1791) considered him a strong enough candidate to recommend for a captaincy, which Hunt received in the Eleventh Regiment, United States Infantry, where he served from January 8, 1799 until his resignation on April 20, 1800, probably because of poor health. He practiced law in Trenton for a time and then "removed south."

Hunt's next older brother Abraham Jr. died sometime in the spring or early summer of 1799, leaving his watch and silver-hilted sword to Robert. Perhaps Abraham's early death may have prompted Robert's move to a less rigorous climate in an effort to improve his own health. However, according to an obituary in the *Trenton Federalist*, Hunt was again residing in that city when he died on October 11, 1802.

Apparently he suffered from a "pulmonary complaint" for several years, but in spite of his medical history, his death was sudden and unexpected: "About ten in the evening, a fit of coughing caused so profuse a discharge of blood from the lungs that before the family could be collected around him, he expired. Thus died, in the prime of his days, a youth of the most amiable manners, fine accomplishments, cultivated talents, and promising expectations."

Hunt's younger brother Philemon (A.B. 1800) also died young. Nathaniel Hunt (A.B. 1793) was their first cousin.

SOURCES: Alumni file, PUA; N.J. Soc. of Col. Dames of Amer., *Letters of Moore Furman* (1912), 122-23; Trenton Hist. Soc., *Hist. of Trenton* (1929), I, 113, 132-34; E. F. Cooley, *Gen. of Early Settlers in Trenton & Ewing* (1883), 142-43; Clio. lists; Clio. Min., 7 [i.e., 8] Aug. 1792–17 July 1793 *passim*; Min. Fac., Nov. 1791, 15 July 1793; Williams, *Academic Honors*, xii, 13; Alexander, *Princeton*, 269; Riker, 59; *Trenton Federalist*, 18 Oct. 1802; *Hamilton Papers*, xxii, 120, 131; U.S. Senate, *Jour. of the Executive Proceedings, 1st to 19th Cong.* (1828), I, 299, 303; Heitman, *U.S. Army*, I, 556; *N.J. Wills*, IX, 192.

RLW

John Jordan

JOHN JORDAN of Montreal, Canada, was the first matriculate of the College who is known to have been a native of that country. He was one of the ten children of Ann (Nancy) Livingston and Jacob Jordan of Montreal, who were married in that city on November 21, 1767. Ann Livingston Jordan was one of the nine children of Catherine Ten Broeck and John Livingston who settled in Montreal, where the father became a fur trader. Jacob Jordan immigrated to Canada sometime before 1761. He became an agent for the London Company, which provided supplies for the British army in America. With the ready access to cash that his position assured him, Jordan was able to become a successful merchant and trader. By 1788 his Terrebonne mills were the second most productive in Canada. However, in later years, without the easy availability of cash, he suffered a number of financial reverses, and several of his businesses failed.

Jacob Jordan was probably the Monsieur Jordan who contributed $100 toward the maintenance of a private school in 1774. In 1786 he was a member of a committee appointed to survey the political and economic situations in Montreal and suggest means of reform. From 1792 until 1796 he sat in the House of Assembly, representing Effingham County, Lower Canada. His second marriage, to Marie-Ann Raby, took place on February 23, 1793.

John Jordan was sent to Princeton in 1785 at the age of ten to attend the Nassau Hall grammar school. It was arranged that he live at the home of a Mrs. Livingston who was a distant connection of his mother's, most likely Susanna Smith Livingston, mother of William Smith Livingston (A.B. 1772), Peter Robert Livingston (A.B. 1784), and Maturin Livingston (A.B. 1786), who had run a boarding house in Princeton since the death of her husband. John may have been the brother of the unfortunate youngster about whom James Gibson (A.B. 1787) wrote to his mother on December 28, 1785:

> The Boys in general here are very fond of skating and a little fellow in the Grammar School went a few days ago with his Classmates to enjoy himself on the ice, but it not being very hard he got his feet wet, and caught a Pleurisy which terminated his existence last Sunday, he was buried on Tuesday, what renders it the more affecting is, he was eight hundred miles from home, his parents living at Montreal, he was eleven years old and has left a Brother younger than he.

At the close of the academic year in September 1787, Jordan was in the second class of the Nassau Hall school, ranking third in Latin grammar, syntax, and vocabulary. In spite of this quite respectable performance his father was apparently concerned about whether it would be worthwhile to continue his son's education at the College the next year. On October 26, 1787 he wrote to William Livingston, governor of New Jersey, requesting him to see what progress John had made and where his academic gifts lay. The father thought his son "rather dull when young" and did not wish him to waste time studying dead languages if his talents were in "more useful accomplishments." The two men had never met, but Governor Livingston was undoubtedly asked to do this favor because of his family connection with Mrs. Jordan. He commended the father highly for his interest in his son's education and first suggested that he might ask Dr. John Beatty (A.B. 1769), a close friend who resided in Princeton, to arrange an appointment with the boy. In this way neither President Witherspoon nor Vice President Samuel Stanhope Smith (A.B. 1769) would be likely to feel that an outsider was interfering in the affars of the College. Either Beatty declined or Livingston simply changed his mind, for on January 12, 1788 he wrote a very tactful letter to Witherspoon, praising the father's concern for his son, suggesting that he would like an appointment to examine the boy in Latin, and adding he had forgotten too much of his Greek to be a proper judge of that language. He also solicited Witherspoon's opinion on Jordan's progress.

Unfortunately, the results of this examination are not available, but they must have been satisfactory for Jordan entered the College as a freshman on November 10, 1788 upon his graduation from the grammar school. Illness, a trip home, or bad scholarship then intervened, for he remained a freshman on class lists compiled in November 1789 and the summer of 1790. No list of nongraduate members of the American Whig Society is available, but Jordan probably joined this group. Both Maturin and Peter Robert Livingston were Whigs, and as a youngster he had undoubtedly heard them extol the society to which they belonged. It may also have been recommended by Governor Livingston, who used "The American Whig" as a pseudonym, and for whom the College society was said to be named.

Jordan's sophomore and junior years were without recorded incidents until September 10, 1792, when the faculty met to investigate the report that a group of students had been guilty of playing cards on the Sabbath. Jordan, along with the other culprits, was required to read a public confession at evening prayers. However, as a first time offender, he was allowed to read from his seat rather than on the stage. He admitted being guilty of "a flagrant breach of the rules of the college, of the laws of this state & of christian morality." Whether frequent card playing interfered with his studies or the public disgrace kept him from concentrating is unknown, but on September 22 the minutes of the faculty recorded that Jordan and James Broom (A.B. 1794), also a Sabbath card player, were not to pass ahead with their class but to be reexamined "on particular branches of their studies" at the beginning of the next session. Jordan, however, did not return to the College. Nothing further about him has been found.

SOURCES: *N.J. Jour., & Polit. Intelligencer,* 10 Oct. 1787; James Gibson alumni file (copy of letter to mother), PUA; Min. Fac., 10 Nov. 1789, 10, 11 & 22 Sept. 1792; C. Bertrand, *Histoire de Montréal* (1942), 59, 219; *Dict. of Canadian Biog.*; F. Van Rensselaer, *Livingston Family in Amer.* (1949), 302-06; C. E. Prince et al., eds., *Papers of Wm. Livingston* (1979-88), v, 317-19, 328-29.

RLW

Stephen Maxwell

STEPHEN MAXWELL entered the College as a freshman on November 10, 1788 but did not move ahead to the sophomore class on schedule. He was still listed as a freshman at the start of the next academic year. He left the College on April 10, 1790, and nothing further is known about him. Jacob Huger (Class of 1793) apparently also left the College on that date, raising the question of whether the two simply decided to leave together, or were asked to leave because of some violation of the College rules in which both participated.

SOURCES: Min. Fac., 10 Nov. 1789.

George Clifford Maxwell (A.B. 1792) had only two brothers, John and William. A more distant relationship is possible, but Stephen's name is not found in a Maxwell genealogy that includes George Maxwell's family. A relationship with John Berrien Maxwell (Class of 1791) is also possible but cannot be confirmed.

The February 24, 1816 will of Richard Wistar of Philadelphia bequeathed real estate in the Northern Liberties which he had purchased from a Stephan Maxwell (see Phila. Wills, Bk. 7, p. 314, PHi). The 1800 census shows that a Stephen Maxwell was living in Newton Township, Delaware Cnty., Pa. Whether or not these two Maxwells were the same individual and whether either or both were the Princetonian has been impossible to confirm.

RLW

John Neilson

JOHN NEILSON, A.B., A.M. 1797, hon. M.D. Allegheny College 1825, physician, was born April 3, 1775 in New Brunswick, New Jersey. The first members of the family to settle in New Brunswick were the brothers James and John Neilson, who emigrated from Ireland. John, a physician, married Johanna Coeyman and became the father of Gertrude, who married Col. James Abeel and was the mother of John Nelson Abeel (A.B. 1787). The first John Neilson also had a posthumous son named John, who became the foster son of the childless James Neilson. James was a successful merchant and for five years a trustee of the College. His nephew was a nongraduate member of the Class of 1761 of the College of Philadelphia. This John Neilson, under the guidance of his uncle, became a prosperous shipping merchant. He served in the Continental Congress, in the New Jersey ratification convention of December 1787, and in the New Jersey assembly from 1800 to 1801. He attained the rank of colonel in the Revolution, fought in the Battle of Monmouth, and served as deputy quartermaster general for New Jersey from 1780 to 1783. He was on the board of trustees of Queen's College and of the New Brunswick Presbyterian Church; a member of the board of directors of the Princeton Theological Seminary from 1812 to 1816; and one of the founders, as well as the treasurer, of the New Jersey Bible Society. His marriage to Catherine Schuyler Voorhees, daughter of John Voorhees of New Brunswick, produced eleven children. The eldest son, the subject of this sketch, was named John after his grandfather and guided toward the medical profession to follow in his footsteps. The second son was named James after his great uncle and received a practical education directed toward joining the family mercantile business. A daughter Gertrude married George Spafford Woodhull (A.B. 1790).

John Neilson first appears on the College records as a sophomore

John Neilson, A.B. 1793

in the fall of 1790. The following spring he was joined at Nassau Hall by his cousin John Nelson Abeel, who was hired as a tutor, and by another cousin James Hude Neilson (A.B. 1794). The latter was the son of William Neilson of New York City, a nephew of the first John and James Neilson. John Neilson became a member of the American Whig Society, and when the faculty met on July 15, 1793 he was assigned to be the opponent in the third dispute planned for the commencement ceremonies, "Are liberty and political equality calculated to promote the happiness and improvement of mankind?" However, the exercises were canceled that year because of the yellow fever epidemic raging in Philadelphia.

After graduation Neilson moved to New York, where he studied medicine under Dr. Kearney Rodgers. He also took a number of courses at the medical school at Columbia College, being enrolled as a matriculate from 1794 to 1797, again from 1798 to 1799, from 1801 to 1802, and from 1807 to 1809. He never received a medical degree, but in 1820 he was elected a fellow of the College of Physicians and Surgeons. In 1803 he left Dr. Rodgers to begin his own practice.

Considering Neilson's long years of professional eminence in New York, surprisingly little information is available about his medical career. He is said to have prospered and to have been one of the leading New York physicians of his time, respected and honored throughout the city. In October 1819 John Pintard (A.B. 1776), writing to his daughter, mentioned Neilson as the physician attending his mother. Some other well known New York names among his patients were John Jacob Astor, Col. Nicholas Fish (Class of 1777), and the members of the Bleecker family, to whom he was related by marriage. He also treated many of the clergy of the city, but he never sent bills to them or to their widows. He practiced for over sixty years, through epidemics of smallpox, influenza, yellow fever and cholera. He was apparently well liked and admired by his patients and, according to one acquaintance, "retained his vigor of mind, his fine erect physique and elastic step" even in his later years.

On February 19, 1798 Neilson married Abigail Bleecker, daughter of Mary Noel Bleecker and Anthony Lispenard Bleecker, the heir to one of New York's oldest estates. Their home was on the northwest corner of Greenwich and Liberty Streets, where they raised six sons and six daughters. The eldest, John Jr., also became a physician, practicing with his father for a short period before giving up medicine in favor of a business career. The family attended the Collegiate Reformed Dutch Church, where Neilson was an elder.

Neilson served as an army surgeon for the Forty-First Regiment of Infantry, United States Army, during the War of 1812. A letter of August 11, 1814, written to his son John who was staying with relatives in New Brunswick, makes it sound a bit like a comic opera war. Still in New York, Neilson mentioned that fortifications were going up rapidly on Brooklyn Heights but that the expected visit of the British would probably be delayed because the weather was much too warm. In the midst of wartime conditions he was able to send a canary, along with proper food for it, for "Grandmama" and some "Nicknacks" for his daughter Mary to distribute to her cousins. Neilson was honorably discharged on June 15, 1815.

He was among the subscribers when the Bloomingdale Asylum for the Insane was first proposed. The building was completed in 1820 on land now occupied by Columbia University and was opened for patients the following year. Neilson was appointed the physician in charge, a position he held for a number of years, and contemporaries noted that he was able to exert a calming influence on the patients. In July 1822 Neilson was the first physician to report the incidence of yellow fever in the city to the health commissioners. His diagnosis of the "bilious malignant fever" was confirmed by David Hosack (A.B. 1789) on August 1, but the health commissioners of the city still did not respond. Neilson wrote a letter to the *Evening Post* soundly criticizing the commission. The editor of the *Post*, who had been publishing warnings of another yellow fever epidemic, followed up with editorials accusing the board of health of risking the lives of the citizens of the city. On August 5 the resident physician of the board finally confirmed the diagnosis of yellow fever and started quarantine procedures. This was the first time that the fever spread beyond the crowded poor sections of the city to the homes of the wealthy overlooking the Hudson River. Between July 10 and October 26 of that year 415 cases were reported, with 230 deaths. Both Neilson and his wife were affected, but he remained in the city and continued to care for his patients.

He had recovered by November 7, when he was in the audience at the Park Theater. The evening was memorialized in a drawing of the stage and audience by John Searle for William Bayard, which is in the possession of the New-York Historical Society. Many of the prominent New Yorkers in the audience, including Neilson, can be easily identified. A letter from his daughter Helena, written in August 1826 to her brother John who was traveling in France, reflects the family's affluent life style. In describing some of the changes that had taken place among the family's servants she mentions, among others, "Irish Sara the cook" and a "yellow boy" who rode in the gig with his master to swish the flies away. She also noted that some members of the family were vacationing at Saratoga, the most fashionable spa of the time. On May 30, 1832 Neilson was among the guests at a dinner at the City Hotel given in honor of Washington Irving. He was still active enough that year to accompany his daughter Kate on a trip to New Brunswick and return by horseback. When his father died the following March, the family members traveled to New Brunswick by sleigh and returned to New York via the Camden railroad and steamboat.

With the outbreak of the cholera epidemic in 1832, Neilson was appointed to the committee set up to make emergency arrangements for the city. When he died on June 19, 1857 he was the oldest medical practitioner in the metropolis. Two of his children married offspring of William Neilson, Jr., the elder brother of James H. Neilson (A.B. 1794). John Neilson, Jr., married Margaret Fish, daughter of Col. Nicholas Fish and Elizabeth Stuyvesant Fish, and a daughter Cornelia married the Reverend Orlando Harriman, an ancestor of Averill Harriman, twentieth-century governor of New York.

Neilson's youngest child, Henry, was involved in what has come to be known as "the Neilson affair" in Hawaiian history. In 1859 Henry Neilson was shot by his patron and friend, King Kamehameha IV, after a bout of heavy drinking. The king's jealousy was inflamed

by tales that Neilson was showing more than polite attention toward
Queen Emma. Kamehameha's own physician tended the wound, but
the victim never completely recovered. He died in 1862. Kamehameha's self-reproach and remorse when sober resulted in threats of
suicide or abdication. He emerged from the crisis with a changed
personality, becoming ardently pious but also remaining restless and
melancholy.

SOURCES: Alumni file, PUA; Univ. of Pa., *Biog. Cat. of Matriculates of the College* (1894);
Hageman, *History*, I, 230; II, 333; W. H. Benedict, *New Brunswick in Hist.* (1925), 285;
Min. Fac., 29 Nov. 1790, 15 July 1793; Amer. Whig Soc., *Cat.* (1840), 7; N.Y. City
directories; Heitman, *U.S. Army*, I, 742; R. W. G. Vail, *Knickerbocker Birthday* (1954),
17; J. W. Francis, *Old N.Y.* (1865), 308-09; J. A. Scoville, *Old Merchants of N.Y. City*,
3d ser. (1865), 36, 259; Pintard, *Letters*, I, 241; III, 193; J. Duffy, *Hist. of Public Health
in N.Y. City 1625-1866* (1968), 118; H. S. Mott, *N.Y. of Yesterday* (1908), 24-25; M.
J. Lamb & B. Harrison, *Hist. of the City of N.Y.* (3 vols., 1877-96), III, 684-86; R. T.
Thompson, *Col. James Neilson* (1940), *passim*; B. F. Thompson, *Hist. of Long Island* (3d
ed., 3 vols., 1918), II, 522-23; M. Armstrong, *Five Generations: Life & Letters of an Amer.
Family* (1930), 143-44, 146-48 (Neilson's letter to son John), 157-58 (letter from Helena
Neilson to John Neilson, Jr.), 161, 202, 208, 213; F. B. Lee, *Gen. & Mem. Hist. of the
State of N.J.* (1910), IV, 1651-57; Thomas, *Columbia*, 39, 76, 182, 385; W. H. Benedict,
Neilsons of the 18th Century (1924), 24-25; A. L. Korn, *Victorian Visitors* (1958), 129-36.

RLW

Robert Ogden IV

ROBERT OGDEN IV, A.B., lawyer and justice, was born in Elizabethtown, New Jersey, on September 15, 1775. Robert Ogden III (A.B.
1765) was practicing law in Elizabethtown and also serving as a commissary for the American troops at the time of his son's birth. Sometime during the next year or so, both because of the father's failing
health and the numerous British raids on Elizabethtown, the family
moved to Morristown in the northern part of the state. They seem
to have moved several times during the war, and the family's instability was increased by the death of the mother Sarah Platt Ogden
when Robert was six years old. In 1786 the father married his sister-in-law Hannah Platt of Huntington, Long Island. At this time
he exchanged his lucrative Elizabethtown law practice for property
in Sparta, Sussex County, owned by his brother Aaron. Here the
family finally settled permanently. Robert Ogden IV was one of a
group of first cousins of his generation who matriculated at the College, including George M. Ogden (A.B. 1795) and Henry W. Ogden
(A.B. 1796), sons of Matthias and Hannah Dayton Ogden; George
Clinton Barber (A.B. 1796), son of Mary Ogden and Francis Barber
(A.B. 1767); and Matthias Ogden (A.B. 1810) and Elias Ogden (A.B.
1819), sons of Aaron Ogden (A.B. 1773) and Elizabeth Chetwood

Ogden. Timothy Edwards (A.B. 1757), uncle of Aaron Burr (A.B. 1772) was an uncle to Ogden through marriage to his father's sister Rhoda Ogden. Robert Ogden's younger half-sisters Hannah and Phebe were to become successive wives of Thomas Coxe Ryerson (A.B. 1809).

Ogden entered the College as a junior in November 1790. Either he was originally promoted to the senior class in 1791 or his name was included there by the clerk's error. Whatever the reason, he apparently had to repeat his junior year during the 1791-92 terms. He joined the Cliosophic Society in 1790 and became one of its more active members, serving at least two monthly terms as president and receiving its diploma. He chose the name of Putnam in honor of the American Revolutionary general who had died the previous May. In August 1792 he was one of six speakers selected by the Clios to deliver addresses at the competition held on the evening before commencement, and on November 21 he gave the "exhortatory oration" with which Clio customarily began its semesters. Members of the society were often fined small amounts for infractions of rules such as arriving late, leaving early, or whispering during a meeting. On January 23, 1793 Ogden was fined nine pence for laughing while the society was in session. His oratorical skills were recognized by his choice as one of the society's representatives to speak at the Fourth of July celebration, and his additional assignment to speak on June 8 at the commemoration of the "first institution of the Society." If the minutes are correct he actually delivered the anniversary address on June 10, "to the general satisfaction of the society." On July 15 the faculty ranked him sixth in his class and chose him as one of the intermediate honorary orators at his commencement exercises—ceremonies which never took place because of the yellow fever epidemic raging in Philadelphia.

Ogden next studied law in the office of his uncle Aaron Ogden, who had an extensive practice in Elizabethtown. There Robert joined the *Institutio legalis*, the moot court society that numbered his father and uncle among its founders. Family tradition says that he also studied under Tapping Reeve (A.B. 1763), brother-in-law of his uncle Timothy Edwards, but the catalogue of Reeve's Litchfield Law School does not record his attendance. Ogden was admitted as an attorney of the supreme court of New Jersey in September 1797. If he practiced at all in New Jersey it was only for a short time, for at least as early as 1803 he was living in New Bern, North Carolina, where by a license issued May 7, 1803, he married Eliza Spaight Nash, sister of Frederick Nash (A.B. 1799) and daughter of Abner Nash, who had served as governor under the provincial constitution of 1776 and also as a member of the Continental Congress. Forming a partnership with Francis Xavier Martin, who had studied under Nash, Ogden practiced for a time in New Bern and then moved on to Charleston, where he was licensed to practice in 1810. Whether his moves were occasioned by restlessness or by an inability to attract clients, he certainly would have found many former college connections living in or near Charleston. By 1821 he had moved again, this time to New Orleans. A family history notes that many young Ogdens went to Louisiana after 1800. In 1825 Governor Henry Johnson appointed Ogden judge of the Parish of Concordia, located across the Mississippi River from Natchez. Here he finally settled until his death at Greenville on February 5, 1857. His responsibilities as judge included all "civil, criminal and police jurisdiction, to decide all cases which may arise within the limits of said parish and shall be brought before his tribunal."

Ogden's eight children included Frederick Nash Ogden, who became a physician; Robert Nash Ogden and Octavius Nash Ogden, both of whom became district court judges in Louisiana; and Abner Nash Ogden, who became a justice of the supreme court of Louisiana. The latter's son Abner Nash Ogden, Jr. (A.B. 1852), served in the Confederate Army, as did a number of other Ogden grandchildren.

SOURCES: Alumni file & Ogden family file, PUA; *Princetonians, 1748-1768*, 182-85, 509-12, 608-11; *Princetonians, 1769-1775*, 328-34; Clio. lists; Clio. Min., 1 Aug. 1792–25 Sept. 1793 *passim*; Min. Fac., 15 July 1793 & class lists of 29 Nov. 1790, ca. May & Nov. 1791, ca. May & 10 Oct. 1792; W. O. Wheeler, *Ogden Family in Amer.* (1907), 132, 248-49, 360, 363, 447; *N.J. Hist.*, 97 (1979), 123-34 (*Institutio legalis*); O'Neall, *Bench & Bar S.C.*, II, 602; *DAB* (sketch of Abner Nash); *La. Hist. Quart.*, 8 (1935), 88. While information about Ogden descendants is available in Louisiana sources, nothing further has been located about Robert Ogden IV while he resided in that state.

RLW

William Roat

WILLIAM ROAT, A.B., was a native of New Jersey for whom positive identification has not been possible. The family name has been found only in Hunterdon County records, where a William who lived in Kingwood was probably the son of John and Ann Roat of that community. John died on December 14, 1814, and the inventory of his personal estate made on January 25, 1815 indicates that he may have been a farmer. Both he and his wife, who died in 1825, are buried in the Kingwood Presbyterian Cemetery. The Kingwood church was one of the Hunterdon County churches served for over forty years by John Hanna (A.B. 1755), who could well have encouraged a young man in his congregation to study at Nassau Hall.

William Roat matriculated at the College as a junior in November 1791. On June 3, 1792 he joined the Cliosophic Society, using the name of Themistocles, the Athenian statesman. He served one monthly term as second assistant and two terms as first assistant and received its diploma; he was also suspended from the society for an unknown period of time and an undetermined reason. Society records show that he was a procrastinator. On two occasions he was unprepared to deliver an address, on another he was fined a shilling "for not performing his exercise," and he was once absent when scheduled to give an address. For the public commencement exercises that were canceled in 1793, Roat had been chosen by the faculty to act as respondent to the question, "Whether are mankind in general in their intercourse with each other more defective in the Virtue of Beneficence or Gratitude."

William Roat of Kingwood is included in the 1850 census as eighty years old, living alone, with no occupation, and owning real estate valued at $1,000. He died on October 18, 1850 and was buried in the Kingwood Presbyterian Cemetery, with his tombstone stating that he was in his eighty-second year. This means that his eighty-first birthday occurred between the gathering of the census data and his death in October. Roat's age would therefore have been a little above average, but not at all unreasonable, for a 1793 college graduate. An inventory of Roat's personal estate totalled $4,621.92, including rent due from a tenant, three bonds with interest, and seven notes with interest, which suggest that he may have engaged in some land speculation.

SOURCES: Alumni file, PUA; Min. Fac., Nov. 1791 class list, 15 July 1793; Clio. lists; Clio. Min., 6 July 1792–17 July 1793 *passim*; J. P. Snell, *Hist. of Hunterdon & Somerset Cnties. N.J.* (1881), 400; MS estate inventories of John & William Roat, Nj; microfilm copy, 1850 census, Hunterdon County, 147; Hunterdon Cnty. Hist. Soc., *Hunterdon Hist. Newsletter*, 11 no. 1 (1973).

Snell, p. 421, lists John Roat as a vestryman and warden of St. Thomas's Church in Alexandria, probably in the 1760s. Roat may have changed his affiliation to the Kingwood Presbyterian Church as a result of his move to the neighboring community, or perhaps because of the anti-Anglican feelings prevalent during the Revolution.

RLW

Abraham Skinner

ABRAHAM SKINNER, A.B., law student, was born in 1775 or 1776, the son of Abraham and Catherine Foster Skinner of Jamaica, Long Island, New York. The mother was one of Henry and Gloriana Cornell Foster's twelve children. The elder Abraham Skinner, an attorney, was a whig and later a Federalist. He served as commissary general of prisoners in the American army from 1780 to the end of the Revolutionary War, represented Queens County in the state assembly, 1784-85, and served as Queens County clerk from 1784 to 1796. In 1793 he became a vestryman of Grace Episcopal Church, Jamaica.

The younger Abraham Skinner received his preliminary education at Clinton Academy, East Hampton, Long Island, a school founded in 1784. He entered the College as a freshman on November 10, 1789. At the competitions for undergraduates held the evening before the 1790 commencement, he was the only freshman among six students whose performance in pronouncing orations earned commendation from the audience. A total of fourteen students took part. Skinner joined the American Whig Society and became particularly friendly with Alexander White (A.B. 1792) and John Henry Hobart (A.B. 1793), later Episcopal bishop of New York. White described Skinner in 1793 as "one of the few I have found among mankind who merit all the esteem of the purest heart."

At some point during his College years Skinner fell in with bad company, upon which Hobart stepped in, befriended Skinner, and "reclaimed" him "from idleness, and a threatening habit of dissipation." Thereafter they were very close. On September 25, 1792 Skinner and Hobart presented a dialogue at the precommencement competitions. Skinner played young King Massinissa, a vassal of Rome and friend of Scipio Africanus, who is successfully urged by his prudent old adviser Narva (Hobart) to resist the blandishments of a former lover recently come into his power and instead to seek only virtue and glory.

Skinner stood fifth in his class when he graduated. He was assigned the valedictory oration for the commencement exercises, which were canceled because of the Philadelphia yellow fever epidemic of 1793. Subsequently he returned to Jamaica. Inconclusive evidence suggests that he became an assistant tutor at that community's Union Hall Academy in 1794. His father, who was one of the trustees of the school and made a speech when it first opened in 1792, certainly could have influenced such an appointment.

If Skinner did teach at Union Hall, he was not there long. By August 1794 he had decided to follow his father's wishes and read law in his office, even though the younger Skinner feared he would not find the profession enjoyable. In the same month the Skinners moved to 60 Cherry Street, New York City. Abraham Jr. wrote Hobart in September that he was pursuing his legal studies to the exclusion of any other, although he hoped to attend Joseph Priestley's scientific lectures that winter. He also joined the Calliopean Society, apparently a literary or debating club.

Hobart and Skinner corresponded frequently after graduation separated them. In the 1830s Hobart's biographers had access to more than sixty letters Hobart wrote Skinner between 1793 and 1795. Surviving epistles are couched in very affectionate terms. Skinner addresses Hobart as "My Dearest John," asserts he is "as dear to me as any Relation I have in the world" and, when the letters begin arriving less frequently, exhorts Hobart: "Continue then my Love, to promote my happiness by writing to me, and let us revive with ardor a languishing correspondence." Such language from one young man to another may now come across as excessively passionate, but such a reading is probably anachronistic. Hobart gave as good as he got, in letters both to Skinner and to other close friends, and his biographers quoted from such letters extensively and approvingly. In a memoir of Hobart written in 1833, William Berrian described the Hobart-Skinner friendship as "of the most romantic character: in intensity and fervour it resembled that of Jonathan for David, *whose 'love was wonderful, passing the love of women.'* "

Skinner fell ill of yellow fever during the night of September 1, 1795, and died at 4 a.m. on September 6. He remained lucid almost to the last and, as his afflicted father reported to Hobart the same day, gave "strong proofs of his Resignation to the Will of heaven and a firm reliance on his God thro' the merits of a blessed Redeemer." In a later letter the elder Skinner glowingly remembered his departed son as "Affectionate, Dutiful, Striving to please. Conversing with his beloved Parents Striving to please *them*, soothing *their* Cares, advising his Sisters & his Brothers, benevolent to the Domestics, and possessing his Wonted Philanthropy." The Calliopean Society responded to his death by listening both to a eulogy by its president and a "monody" on the same theme. More than thirty years later a surviving member, James Swords, a publisher of religious works, recalled that Skinner's "warmth of friendship was equalled only by his love of literature, and his ardent desire to acquire knowledge."

Skinner was buried in New York City. Many years later, after his friend Hobart had become the leading Episcopal clergyman in that place, a macabre turn of events brought Skinner once more to his recollection. Berrian recalled that at a funeral Hobart found "the remains of his friend [Skinner, which] had been disinterred, and laid strewn before him, around the grave. Notwithstanding the lapse of time, it was an affecting and painful sight."

SOURCES: P. Irving, "Address on the Death of Mr. Abraham Skinner, Jr., delivered at the Calliopean Soc., 8 Sept. 1795," *N.Y. Magazine*, 6 (1795), 557-58; P. Ross & W. S. Pelletreau, *Hist. of Long Island* (1905), I, 275-76; II, 193-94, 365-67; *NYGBR*, 76 (1945), 92; Heitman, 499; *Civil List & Const. Hist. of ... N.Y.* (1880), 282, 389; *N.Y. Marriages Previous to 1784* (1860), 353; H. Onderdonk, *Antiquities of the Parish Church, Jamaica ...* (1880), 77, 79-80; Min. Fac., 10 Nov. 1789, 15 July 1793; MS dialogue between

Massinissa & Narva, 1792, John Henry Hobart Papers, TxAuCH; *Pa. Packet, & Daily Advt.*, 7 Oct. 1790; Amer. Whig Soc., *Cat.* (1840), 7; J. McVickar, *Early Years of the late Bishop Hobart* (2d ed., 1836), 54-57, 58 ("reclaimed from idleness," quoting Jacob Burnet [A.B. 1791]), 75, 77-78 ("one of the"), 86-104 ("monody," "warmth"), 130-31, 136-37, 159-60; Min. Trustees, 25 Sept. 1793; Hobart, *Corres.*, I, 28, 31, 46-50 ("as dear"), 66-69 ("My Dearest," "Continue then"), 80-82, 127-29 ("strong proofs"), 133-34 ("Affectionate"); W. Berrian, "Memoir of the Life of ... John Henry Hobart," vol. I of Hobart's *Posthumous Works* (1833), 17-32 ("of the most," "in attending"); *N.Y. Directory & Reg.* (1795), 196.

MANUSCRIPTS: The John Henry Hobart Papers at TxAuCH include three Skinner letters which are reprinted in Hobart, *Corres.* (cited above). The dialogue between Massinissa and Narva is in the same collection (photocopy in PUA). See McVickar for some of Hobart's letters to Skinner.

JJL

Enoch Smith

ENOCH SMITH, attorney, was the son of Jasper Smith and Jemima Lanning of Maidenhead (now Lawrenceville), New Jersey, and a brother of Daniel Smith (A.B. 1787). One source gives Enoch's birth date as "about 1763," while a second states that he was born in 1765, which could make him a twin of Daniel. In either case he would have been well beyond the average age of the students attending the College. Smith's late matriculation at the College may have been occasioned by his brother urging him to take advantage of the opportunities available to lawyers in Northumberland County, Pennsylvania, where the latter had recently settled.

Enoch is probably the Smith, listed only by last name in faculty records, who was a junior during the 1791-92 academic year, making him a member of the Class of 1793. Two separate manuscript records of the American Whig Society, which list degree recipients along with their society affiliations, include Enoch Smith, Whig, as a graduate member of the Class of 1794. In both cases the name has been added at the end of an otherwise alphabetical list, and in one instance it has clearly been added in a different ink, although in the same handwriting. No records of the College include any Smith as having received a degree in either 1793 or 1794.

After joining his brother Daniel in Sunbury, Northumberland County, Pennsylvania, Enoch was admitted to the bar in August 1798. He may have studied law under his brother's tutelage, and he was later associated with Daniel in his practice, although he never acquired a local reputation for being equal to the latter in professional ability. When Daniel died in 1810 he bequeathed to Enoch a little bay mare called Fan. He also made his brother coexecutor of his estate, with another Sunbury lawyer Ebenezer Greenough, and empowered them to care for his unfinished legal business.

Enoch Smith married Gayner Wallis, daughter of Joseph Jacob Wallis, one of the early settlers in the area. According to Sunbury's 1808 assessment, Smith owned and occupied a log house with stable on Front Street. Sometime later he moved to nearby Milton. An active member of the local Masonic lodge from his initiation on October 24, 1798, Smith held various offices in that organization during the remainder of his life. He was elected the worshipful master on December 5, 1805 and again on June 2, 1806. He died in Milton on February 9, 1817. When Jasper Smith died in 1820 he left bequests to his son Enoch's children but did not list them by name nor indicate how many there were.

SOURCES: Min. Fac., class lists ca. Nov. 1791 & May 1792 (two Smiths were members of the Class of 1795. One entered as a freshman in Nov. 1790 and repeated his sophomore year. The other entered as a sophomore in October 1792. The Smith entries for this period are quite confusing); *GMNJ*, 46 (1971), 59-61 (1763 birthdate); Pub. Comm. of Sunbury Bicentennial, Inc., *Sunbury, Pa.: Two Hundred Years* (1972), 77 (1765 birthdate); H. C. Bell, *Hist. of Northumberland Cnty., Pa.* (1891), 246, 455-58; L. C. Gedney, *Church Records of the Pres. Church of Lawrenceville, N.J.* (1941), 11, 14; will of Daniel Smith, Bk. 2, p. 122, file 109, Court House, Sunbury, Pa.; F. A. Godcharles, *Freemasonry in Northumberland & Snyder Cnties., Pa.* (1911), I, 49; II, 567. MS Whig Soc. "College Honors 1769-1810" & "College Honors 1769-1832" in PUA list Enoch Smith as a graduate member, as does Amer. Whig Soc., *Cat.* (1840), 7. Because the only extant list of Whig nongraduate members begins in 1802, it must be assumed that for some reason the clerk of the Whig Society at the time of Smith's active membership assumed that he would be awarded a degree.

RLW

John Staples

JOHN STAPLES, A.B., studied at Columbia College from 1788 to 1790 and then entered the College as a sophomore in November 1790. Before the end of the calendar year he joined the Cliosophic Society, assuming the name of Franklin. The society's records list him as being from New York, but College catalogues include him as a New Jersey resident. On March 23, 1791 he was dismissed from the society, but no reason for this action has been preserved. For the 1793 commencement exercises, canceled because of the yellow fever epidemic, Staples was to have taken the role of replicator on the question: "Ceteris paribus, Does the world pay more respect to one born of honorable parents or to the son of a rascal."

Except for the geographical identifications, there is strong circumstantial evidence that Staples was the eldest son of Susannah Perkins Staples and the Reverend John Staples (A.B. 1765), pastor of the Second Congregational Church of Canterbury, Connecticut. Their son John was born April 23, 1773, the oldest of eleven siblings. Three younger Staples sons attended Yale, which would have been more convenient for Connecticut residents. However, the Nassau Hall connection extends to two of Susannah Staples's brothers, Nathan Perkins (A.B. 1770) and Matthew Perkins (Class of 1777), and their cousin Eliphaz Perkins (Class of 1776). Nathan Perkins, pastor of the Congregational church in West Hartford, Connecticut, also conducted a school where he is said to have trained over 150 young men for college. While a student himself Perkins was one of the group instrumental in reviving the Cliosophic Society, the one which the younger Staples joined while at Nassau Hall.

Nothing further has been discovered about Staples or his future career. Columbia College records show him as deceased in 1809, but the catalogues of the College of New Jersey first list him as deceased in 1869.

SOURCES: Alumni file, PUA (where Staples is said to have come from New York); Thomas, *Columbia*, 114; Min. Fac., 29 Nov. 1790, 15 July 1793; Clio. lists; *Princetonians, 1748-1768*, 530-31; *Princetonians, 1769-1775*, 97-101; *Princetonians, 1776-1783*, 85-87, 199; *NEHGR*, 14 (1860), 115, 118. The John I. Staples who was a merchant in New York City could not have been the father, since he was joined in business by his son John I., Jr., when John Staples was still attending classes at the College. See N.Y. City directories. A John Staples died in Byram, Sussex County, New Jersey, in 1817 leaving a personal estate worth only $200.47. See estate inv. of John Staples, Nj.

RLW

James T. Stelle (Still)

JAMES T. STELLE (STILL), A.B., A.M. 1797, lawyer, soldier, planter, and public official, was born on June 25, 1773, one of six children of Thompson and Sally Langstaff Stelle of Piscataway Township, Middlesex County, New Jersey. He was a first cousin once removed of Benjamin Stelle (A.B. 1766), possibly a second cousin of Isaac Steele (Class of 1790), and probably also related to Stelle Fitz Randolph (A.B. 1802). The Stelles were an old Huguenot family founded by Poncet Stelle, who emigrated to America sometime before 1681. Thompson Stelle served as captain and paymaster of the First Middlesex Regiment of New Jersey militia during the Revolutionary War, and later as a justice of the peace and sheriff of Middlesex County.

By May 1791 Stelle was a sophomore at the College. He joined the Cliosophic Society on June 25, 1791, taking Galileo as his pseudonym. An active member, he saw service as president and as first assistant and represented the society more than once in public competitions. The faculty assigned him a role in a disputation at the aborted 1793 commencement. Afterwards Stelle's connection to Clio was broken. Society minutes refer to efforts to get Stelle to "discharge his arrears" on December 18, 1793 and January 22, 1794, and on the latter occasion Stelle was given two weeks to pay up before facing suspension. Perhaps he did not like his erstwhile companions' tone, for on March 26 Stelle, "who had been suspended having settled his arrears with the society was readmitted this evening & upon application was granted a dismission." He then joined the American Whig Society and attended its meetings as late as December 1796.

During these years Stelle was reading law with one of the Stocktons, most likely Richard (A.B. 1779), and was admitted to the New Jersey bar in November 1797. During his pursuit of a legal career he evidently came to enjoy "the confidence and esteem of Judge Paterson" (United States Supreme Court Justice William Paterson [A.B. 1763]), as a later letter put it. However if he went so far as to establish a practice, he did not persist in it for long.

On June 1, 1798 Stelle was commissioned a captain in the Second Regiment of Artillerists and Engineers, United States Army, and he retained that rank when the first and second regiments were merged into a single regiment of artillerists in April 1802. Stelle seems to have been stationed at Fort Jay on Governors Island in the harbor of New York City in October 1799. At that time he and Maj. Adam Hoops (Class of 1777) of the same regiment were sent to Fort Niagara by Alexander Hamilton (LL.D. 1791) to fill out the court-martial convened to hear charges made by Capt. James Bruff against the commander, Maj. John J. U. Rivardi. Hamilton later characterized Stelle and Hoops as "two intelligent & respectable officers" in partial explanation of his decision not to use officers stationed closer to Niagara.

On August 18, 1799 Stelle married Lydia Field Hubley, the daughter of Robert and Mary Peale Field of Mansfield Township, Burlington County, New Jersey. Stelle's classmate Robert Field IV and Mary Field, the wife of Richard Stockton (A.B. 1779), were siblings of Lydia, who was seven years older than Stelle. Her first marriage, to Adam Hubley, one of three contemporaries of that name from Lancaster County, Pennsylvania, ended with his death in 1798. She bore Hubley three daughters.

Stelle was back at Fort Jay on March 8, 1800, for on that day he conveyed a challenge to a duel by United States Navy Lt. John Rush (Class of 1794) to the English journalist William Cobbett. Cobbett, who was later to earn fame in England as a political journalist and radical leader and as the author of *Rural Rides*, was nearing the end of a virulent pamphlet war against Benjamin Rush (A.B. 1760) and his adherents. Cobbett had just published the first number of *Rush-Light*, a savage attack on Benjamin Rush's theories and the character

of both him and his son John. The result was Stelle's delivery of the
challenge. According to Stelle and Rush, Cobbett refused to fight and
invited them to "post him for a coward" if they pleased, which they
immediately did. Cobbett's own account differs mainly in depicting
Stelle, who visited his shop carrying a bludgeon cane, as a blustering
ruffian who was only deterred from violence by the iron poker with
which Cobbett was armed.

A scant month later Stelle took command of the garrison at West
Point, and soon found himself in hot water. On July 4, 1800 a patrol
checking up on a nearby alehouse which Stelle had declared off-limits
to his men was "insulted," disarmed, and its members "inhumanly
beat" by "a collection of low fellows" "from the mountains etc. that
had there assembled" to celebrate Independence Day. When Stelle
went to the barracks to muster his forces against this threat he found
that his men had already armed and sallied out to their brethren's
defense. Stelle caught up with them and attempted to bring them to
order, but they ignored him and at the inn a further brawl ensued in
which several of his men were wounded. At length Stelle reduced
his men to discipline and obtained the surrender of the civilians
barricaded at the alehouse. He put several of them in the stockade
and released them only after being advised to do so by his superiors.
The alehouse keeper, Thomas North, then had Stelle and several
of his men arrested for theft and riot and thrown in the county jail
when no one would stand bail for them. Eventually a writ of *habeas
corpus* was issued, and Stelle and his men were freed on "easy bail." In
1802 and 1803 Stelle unsuccessfully petitioned Congress to indemnify
him for "the costs and damages" resulting from North's lawsuit. His
petition of December 11, 1802, indicated that at that time he no
longer commanded the garrison at West Point.

Stelle was one of the soldiers sent to garrison Louisiana after the
territory was purchased from France in 1803. He may have been
in the original contingent which arrived in December of that year;
certainly he was in New Orleans by September 1, 1804, for his
name appeared on a petition of that place and date recommending
a man for an office. In 1804 and 1805 Stelle undertook at least two
reconnaissance trips to the borderland area of western Louisiana.
His objective apparently was to get a feel for that portion of the
territory claimed by both countries and to detect any Spanish movements in the disputed areas. In his report he described Spanish plans
to put a settlement on the Trinity (or Occockasaw) River. A somewhat melodramatic account by a contemporary French traveler, C. C.
Robin, described Stelle's journey as "a secret inspection of the internal provinces of Spain bordering on Louisiana." Although the atten-

dant risk of incurring "condemnation to the mines" caused his French guide to abandon him, Stelle was not deterred and went off alone, returning in about two months. According to Robin the government rewarded Stelle with a lucrative post for his intrepid conduct.

What office Robin had in mind is not clear; he said only that Stelle had been given a position "paying more than 10 thousand francs." Perhaps Stelle was the Mr. Still who served as clerk to the "Board of Commissioners on claims to lands lying within the Eastern District of the Territory of Orleans" for an unspecified amount of time prior to 1810. In August 1805 Stelle was angling, apparently without success, for a judgeship in Orleans Territory. A letter to President Thomas Jefferson (LL.D. 1791) from Judge D. A. Hall referred in glowing terms to his legal training, his "elegance of manners" and "pleasing deportment" which had endeared him to both American and Creole, and his rapid progress in learning French. Hall also noted that Stelle was planning to resign from the army, which he did on December 31, 1805.

Stelle's decision to leave the service was most likely linked to his concurrent changes in marital status. His marriage with Lydia Field Hubley failed totally, and she seems not to have accompanied him to Louisiana. The Stelles were granted a divorce in an act passed by the legislative council of Orleans Territory on January 23, 1805. The petition for the divorce asserted vaguely that "in consequence of an unhappy disappointment, resulting from circumstances of an afflicting nature, the said parties have been prevented from enjoying that harmony and domestic happiness which the conjugal state was designed to produce, and were induced shortly after said marriage to resolve upon and stipulate for a complete and perpetual separation." On December 1, 1805 Stelle married Margaret Cyrilla Watts Gayoso de Lemos, the widow of don Manuel Gayoso de Lemos, the astute Spanish governor of Louisiana who had died in 1799.

To her marriage with Stelle, Margaret brought an estate valued at more than $30,000. Her parents were Stephen and Frances Assheton Watts, Pennsylvanians who had moved to "Belmont" plantation in the Natchez District. Her sister Susan married William Wikoff, who probably fathered Manuel G. Wikoff (A.B. 1813) and George Wikoff (A.B. 1815) and who may have been the brother of Peter Wikoff (A.B. 1791). Stephen Watts was a planter and attorney who argued before American, English and Spanish courts during his career. Although the Watts family had a Baptist background, Margaret was baptized a Roman Catholic. She bore Gayoso de Lemos one son, who was presumably raised in the Stelle household along with the three sons and three daughters produced by the second marriage.

In January 1806 Stelle accepted commissions as captain in the Volunteer Blues and adjutant major of the Orleans Volunteers, two units in the local militia, but by May of that year the former had disbanded and Stelle was no longer listed as an officer of the latter. In February 1806 he and Joseph Saul were seeking a contract to carry the mail between New Orleans and Loftus Heights, Adams County, Mississippi Territory, but whether they obtained it has not come to light. Stelle was appointed sheriff of the Fifth Superior Court District of Orleans Territory on June 30, 1807. This district, newly created in that year, encompassed much of present-day western Louisiana. The court met in the town of Opelousas, the seat of government of St. Landry Parish. The appointment prompted or grew out of Stelle's move to this region, which he had explored during his travels for the army.

Stelle became a planter and amassed a large estate. He lived near Opelousas on a 1,217 acre farm in Bellevue quarter, St. Landry Parish, and also owned 340 acres on Bayou Teche in St. Martin Parish and 918 acres on Bayou Plaquemine in Iberville Parish. In the War of 1812 he served as paymaster of the Louisiana militia's Fourth Brigade, which included the contingent supplied by Opelousas. A legislative act of 1816 named him and four other residents of St. Landry Parish as commissioners of a lottery to fund improvements in the navigation of the Atchafalaya River and Bayou Cortableu. Stelle died on September 6, 1820 and was interred at the Crepe Myrtle Grove Cemetery in Opelousas. At his death his personalty, which included seventy-three slaves, and his real estate were valued at $79,068. His wife and six children survived him. Stelle's daughter Frances was the first wife of Joshua Baker, who served as governor of Louisiana in 1868.

SOURCES: Letters of O. B. Leonard, 20 Mar. 1915, & D. Dorr, 2 Aug. & 19 Nov. 1982, 26 Dec. 1985, 22 Jan. 1986, Alumni file, PUA; MS indenture, 7 July 1804, sale of property by James Stelle to Micajah Hart, NjPHi; *NYGBR*, 44 (1913), 64-65; O. E. Monnette, *First Settlers of Ye Plantations of Piscataway & Woodbridge* (1930-35), pt. 2, 238; pt. 5, 869; pt. 6, 1217; O. B. Leonard, *Outline Sketches of the Pioneer Progenitors of the Piscataway Planters* (1890), 14, 16-17; Stryker, *Off. Reg.*, 412; W. W. Clayton, *Hist. of Union & Middlesex Cnties., N.J.* (1882), 532-35; Min. Fac., class list ca. May 1791, 15 July 1793; Clio. lists; Clio. Min., 6 July 1792-26 Mar. 1794 *passim* ("discharge," "who had been"); Min. Trustees, 25 Sept. 1793, 26 Sept. 1797; Amer. Whig Soc., *Cat.* (1840), 7; R. D. W. Connor, *Doc. Hist. of the Univ. of N.C., 1776-99* (1953), II, 116; als, D. A. Hall to Thomas Jefferson, 6 Aug. 1805, filed under "James Still," DNA: Record Group 59, Letters of Application & Recommendation ("confidence and esteem," "elegance of manners"); Riker, 73; Heitman, *U.S. Army*, I, 919; *Hamilton Papers*, XXII, 520, 604-05; XXIII, 76, 286, 349-50, 488, 538; XXIV, 187-88 ("two intelligent"), 331-32; XXV, 10-15 ("insulted," "inhumanly beat," "from the mountains"), 44-45 ("easy bail"), 331-32; [William Cobbett], *Rush-Light*, I, no. 1 (15 Feb. 1800), *passim*; no. 2 (28 Feb. 1800), 111; N.Y. *Commercial Advt.*, 11 Mar. & 9 July 1800 ("collection of low"); M. E. Clark, *Peter Porcupine in Amer.: The Career of William Cobbett* (1937 repr. 1974), 163-65; *Jour. of the House of Rep. of the U.S.* (1826), IV, 246, 468, 503 ("the costs"); C. E. Carter, ed., *Territorial Papers of the U.S.* (26 vols., 1934-62), IX (*Territory of Orleans 1803-12*), 290, 581-82, 595, 640, 751, 938 ("Board of Commissioners"); XIII (*Territory of La.-Mo., 1803-06*), 166, 240; S. O. Landry, Jr., ed., *Voyage to La. by C. C. Robin 1803-05* (1966 trans. of 1807 Paris ed.), 222-23 ("secret inspection," "condemnation"); *NEHGR*, 113 (1959), 286; *PMHB*, 33 (1909), 129-31; *LCHSPA*, 40 (1936), 59-60, 65-66; *Acts Passed at the First Session of the Legislative Council of the Territory of Orleans* (1805), 454-56 ("in consequence"); *N.J. Wills*, VI, 209; D. Dorr, "The Devall Town Boom," La. Geneal. & Hist. Soc., *La. Geneal. Reg.*, 31 (Mar. 1984), 66-70; J. D. L. Holmes, *Gayoso* (1965), 124-27, 278; S. C. Arthur & G. C. Huchet de Kernian, *Old Families of La.* (1931), 307-11; P. A. Casey, *La. in the War of 1812* (1963), 39, appendix, v; *Acts Passed at the Second Session of the First Legislature of the Territory of Orleans* (1807), 4-8; MS estate inv. of JTS, 19 Feb. 1821, Clerk's Office, St. Landry Parish (photocopy in PUA); *La. Hist. Quart.*, 28 (1945), 841; *Acts Passed at the Second Session of the Second Legislature of the State of La.* (1816), 72-74. The spelling of Stelle's name seems to have confused his contemporaries, and the following variations have been encountered: Steel, Steele, Still, Stille, and Stella. Still or Stille were usually used in his postcollegiate career. The trustees' minutes are the authority for the decision to give "Stelle" priority. Stelle could possibly have been the James Stelle who served as a private from October 10 to December 23, 1794 in Capt. Jonathan F. Morris's detachment of infantry volunteers from Somerset County in the army which marched to western Pennsylvania to suppress the Whiskey Insurrection, although college graduates were more likely to be officers. See N.J. Adjutant General's Office, *Records of Officers & Men of N.J. in Wars 1791-1815* (1909), separately numbered section on 1794 Pa. insurrection, 3-6, 8. Leonard's letter in the alumni file, which is generally reliable, asserts that Stelle spent some time in Cuba. Although this claim has not been verified, perhaps he was involved in the Cuba-Louisiana slave trade, which flourished for a time even after being outlawed in 1808.

MANUSCRIPTS: Alexander Hamilton Papers, DLC; Winthrop Sargent Papers, MHi

JJL

Alexander Stewart

ALEXANDER STEWART, A.B., A.M. 1803, planter and public official, was born on September 30, 1773, the only son of John and Elizabeth Dashiell Stewart of Nanticoke Hundred, Somerset (now Wicomico) County, Maryland. The father served in the Revolution as a lieutenant colonel in the militia, represented Somerset County in the lower house of the state legislature several times, and also sat in the constitutional ratification convention in 1788. He was a merchant who belonged to a partnership trading under the name of Gale, Jackson, and Stewart. His partner Levin Gale fathered George Gale (Class of 1774) and Robert Gale (A.B. 1791). The firm must have prospered, for John Stewart bought himself 1,623 acres of land in Somerset County between 1784 and 1792. He was an Anglican and belonged to the Stepney Parish congregation. His wife Elizabeth died on February 2, 1774. She was his first cousin and the daughter of William and Sarah Murray Dashiell.

Alexander Stewart was named for his paternal grandfather. Like some of his near contemporaries at the College, he may have studied at the Washington Academy near Princess Anne, Somerset County. Stewart entered the College as a sophomore in November 1790. On the 29th of that month the steward complained that he was "boarding out of the College" along with five members of the class of 1791, including Robert Gale. The faculty ordered the students to "perform what the law requires." Stewart joined the Cliosophic Society sometime in 1790, taking the pseudonym Periander, for the despotic ruler of ancient Corinth who is usually reckoned one of the seven sages of Greece. Stewart was active in the society, serving terms as first assistant and president and receiving its diploma. The faculty did not assign him a speech or disputation topic for his commencement exercises, which were canceled anyway because of a Philadelphia yellow fever epidemic.

Stewart's father John died around July 1794. He left about 1,768 acres of land in Somerset County, 400 acres in Allegany County on Maryland's western frontier, and a personal estate valued at £1,027 and including fifty-two slaves. Since John was a widower whose only daughter died young, Alexander presumably inherited the bulk of the estate. On October 15, 1795 he was appointed an ensign in a Somerset County militia regiment. He gained promotion to lieutenant on July 11, 1797 and to captain on June 9, 1809. In 1799 he represented Somerset County in the lower house of the state legislature. Since Somerset was solidly Federalist around this time, Stewart probably belonged to that party.

The 1800 census indicates that Stewart owned seventy-five slaves but was otherwise alone. He seems never to have married. On July 22, 1810 he died intestate and was buried on the second terrace at "Long Hill," on Wetipquin Creek, Somerset (now Wicomico) County. After the payment of his debts he left a personal estate valued at $61,255. The inventory included eighty-six slaves, much livestock and crops, at least fifty-three books, a flute, and a tame doe. His heirs were the children of his deceased uncle William Stewart.

SOURCES: A. W. Burns, *Stepney Parish Reg., Births, Marriages & Deaths Somerset Cnty. Md.* (undated typescript in DLC), I, 99, 123. 136-37; letters, Md. Leg. Hist. Proj., 19 Nov. 1985, 21 Jan. 1986, PUA; *Biog. Dict. Md. Leg.*, I, 336-38; II, 778-79; B. J. Dashiell, *Dashiell Family Records* (1928-32), III, 710, 716; Min. Fac., 29 Nov. 1790, 15 July 1793 (quotes); Clio. Min., 1 Aug. 1792, 3 Apr. & 17 July 1793; Clio. lists; Min. Trustees, 25 Sept. 1793, 27 Sept. 1803; Md. Geneal. Soc., *Bull.*, 15 no.4 (1974), 257 (1800 census). The Dashiell genealogy indicates that Stewart had a wife named Elizabeth, who died in 1811: see the letter from the Maryland Legislative History Project for evidence that this is incorrect.

The Cliosophic Society *Catalogue* of 1837 lists Stewart as a resident of New Jersey, but this appears to be a transcription error. Extant MS Clio. membership lists call Stewart a Marylander, and a search of New Jersey sources turned up no Alexander

Stewart likely to be the Princetonian. The identification of the Princetonian with the Somerset County resident is based on his date of birth, his wealth, and his father's business connection with Levin Gale. However, other Marylanders shared the name. The 1800 census listed a second Alexander Stewart in Somerset County, but he owned only two slaves. An Alexander Stewart is mentioned in Frederick County in 1796, another died in Kent County in 1807, and the name also appears in Baltimore. See G. M. Brumbaugh, *Md. Records* (1967), I, 286; J. Hume, *Md.: Index to Wills of Howard Cnty. 1840-1950; Kent Cnty. 1642-1960* (1970), 178; Balt. city directories, 1810, 1814/15, 1816; *MHM*, 42 (1947), 44.

JJL

Bennett Taylor

BENNETT TAYLOR, A.B., attorney, was the son of John Taylor, one of the tax commissioners for Southampton County, Virginia, and a captain in the local militia. There is some confusion about whether John Taylor married once or twice. One source names only Hannah Tompkins Taylor, who died circa 1775. However, at the time of his death Taylor was survived by the former Sarah Ruffin, widowed daughter of Col. Thomas Williamson of Southampton. In different sources both women are named as the mother of Bennett Taylor. Since the date of Hannah's death is uncertain and the date of John's marriage to Sarah has not been found, it is impossible to determine who was Bennett's mother. The average age of his College classmates in 1793 was nineteen, making it most likely that he was Hannah's child and that she died at the time of his birth or later.

On January 12, 1792 Thomas Jefferson (LL.D. 1791) wrote from Philadelphia to President John Witherspoon, introducing Taylor as the bearer of the letter who had been recommended to Jefferson by a "good friend." Jefferson must have talked to the young man about his previous preparation and his aims, for the letter adds: "His principal objects will be mathematics and Natural philosophy. Rhetoric also, I presume is taught with you, and will be proper for him as destined for the bar. As he has no time to spare, I have mentioned to him that I thought he might undertake the subject of Moral philosophy in his chamber, at leisure hours, and from books, without attending lectures or exercises in that branch." Whether or not Witherspoon excused Taylor from attending the moral philosophy lectures, he did consider him well enough qualified to enter the junior class in the middle of the winter session. Taylor joined the Cliosophic Society on February 7, 1792, adopting the name of Theopompus, the Greek historian and rhetorician. He became active in the society, serving variously as president, censor, corrector of composition, clerk, and treasurer, and receiving its diploma. His oratorical skills were recognized by his choice as one of the society speakers on the evening before the 1792 commencement. On September 25, 1792 in a competition among undergraduates on English grammar, reading, and orthography, John Henry Hobart, Robert Hunt, and Bennett Taylor, all of the junior class, were declared victors. Taylor also delivered the Cliosophic Society's traditional exhortatory oration at the start of the summer term of 1793.

There seems to have been an intense rivalry between Taylor and Hobart for first place among their classmates. Added to the academic rivalry was the fact that Taylor was a Cliosophian and Hobart a member of the American Whig Society. Both were excellent students and both coveted the honor of delivering the Latin salutatory address at commencement. When the faculty met on July 15, 1793, they considered the achievements and merits of the two young men equal. Each is said to have received half of the faculty votes for the best scholar, although five members of the faculty were present: President John Witherspoon, Vice President Samuel Stanhope Smith (A.B. 1769), Professor Walter Minto, and tutors John Nelson Abeel (A.B. 1787) and Robert Finley (A.B. 1787). Smith believed that Hobart deserved the honor of being the most distinguished scholar in the class, while Minto supported Taylor. Perhaps this disagreement reflected different academic interests and talents; Smith taught moral philosophy and theology, while Minto taught mathematics and natural philosophy. The tie vote suggests either that one member of the faculty abstained from voting because he thought the two candidates equal, or that the votes of the two tutors did not receive as much weight as did those of the more experienced faculty members. In any event, Minto took a coin from his pocket and tossed it; it is controversial whether he first exclaimed, "Tails for Taylor," or Smith's cry of, "Heads for Hobart," rang out first. Hobart won the toss, leaving Taylor with the second honor of English salutatorian. He was also assigned to act as respondent to the question, "Can the fine arts more than philosophy flourish under arbitrary governments?" Still, the loss of the first honor rankled and Taylor brought his case before Vice President Smith, who in turn appealed to Hobart to relinquish the Latin salutatory voluntarily. The latter claimed that he might have done so for a fellow-Whig, but never for a Clio. All the arguments made little difference since the yellow fever epidemic in Philadelphia caused the cancellation of the public ceremonies, and degrees were awarded privately. Besides the commencement assignments, the Cliosophic Society chose Taylor to give the "congratulatory address to our absent brothers on the day of commencement," but it also had to be called off. When he resigned as treasurer of the society shortly before graduation, the committee appointed to inspect his accounts reported that he had kept them "very accurately."

An 1855 catalogue of the College of William and Mary lists a Bennett Taylor of Isle of Wight County among students who were enrolled there between 1790 and 1795, but who did not receive degrees. Taylor may have studied there during his freshman and sophomore years before transferring to the College of New Jersey, or he may have been in residence at William and Mary to study law after receiving his A.B. His Princeton classmate Abraham Skinner corresponded with Taylor in September 1794 and wrote to Hobart of Taylor's plans to begin the study of law that fall. No record has been found to indicate when he became a member of the bar; however, he practiced law in Richmond for the remainder of his life and is described as an eminent member of the Richmond bar. He settled first in the neighborhood of Berryville, Clarke County, and later moved to his plantation, "Avon Hill," reportedly located in Jefferson County, Virginia—a jurisdiction created in 1801 and forming part of the state of West Virginia since its secession from Virginia during the Civil War.

Taylor was named as executor in his father's will, which was dated January 7, 1805 and proved March 11, 1806. After bequests to his wife Sarah and his daughters Charlotte and Sarah, John Taylor left to his son Bennett "debts due me from Benj. Edwards Browne, or under the deed from Etheldred Taylor." Taylor's share of the estate apparently included considerable property, and he was also the beneficiary of a deceased brother, Charles. In February 1810 Taylor conveyed 130 acres called "Seacock," on Seacock Swamp, Southampton County, to Robert Adams. On May 10, 1811 he deeded 230 acres called "Howells" to John C. Gray.

Taylor married Susan Beverly Randolph, daughter of Governor Edmund Randolph. They had two children, a daughter Charlotte who married Moncure Robinson, a well-known civil engineer; and a son, John Charles Randolph Taylor, who married Martha Jefferson Randolph, daughter of Thomas Jefferson Randolph. Taylor died at "Avon Hill" in 1816.

SOURCES: Clio. lists; Clio. Min., 7 Aug. 1792–25 Sept. 1793 *passim* ("congratulatory address," 10 July 1793; "very accurately," 24 July 1793); Hobart, *Corres.*, I, cviii-cix, 82; J. McVickar, *Early Years of the late Bishop Hobart* (2d ed., 1836), 63-64; J. F. Schroeder, *Memorial of Bishop Hobart* (1831), xxii-xxiii; Min. Fac., class list ca. May 1792, 26 Sept. 1792, 15 July 1793; *Jefferson Papers*, XXIII, 40; H. E. Hayden, *Va. Genealogies* (1931), 584; *Genealogies of Va. Families* (1981), V, 21, 394, 398; *WMQ*, 2d ser., 1 (1921), 237, 259; 8 (1928), 71; College of William & Mary, *Cat.* (1855), 36. The *Catalogue* of the College of William and Mary lists Taylor among those who attended the college sometime between 1790 and 1795. Several sources have misinterpreted this entry and incorrectly state that he attended William and Mary throughout the period from 1790 to 1795.

RLW

Charles Tennent

CHARLES TENNENT, A.B., A.M. 1796, planter, was the fifth and youngest child of William Tennent III (A.B. 1758), trustee of the College, and his wife Susanne Vergereau. The father's brother was John Van Brugh Tennent (A.B. 1758). Tennent was christened John Charles, presumably after his recently deceased uncle. However his father's 1777 will is the last source in which this form of the name has been found; he apparently was known simply as Charles for the rest of his life. He was born in Charleston, South Carolina, on November 20, 1774, where his father was pastor of the Independent Congregational (Circular) Church, to which he had been called from the First Congregational Church in Norwalk, Connecticut. William Tennent died in August 1777, and the following month his mother-in-law Susannah Boudinot Vergereau also died in Charleston where she was evidently staying with her widowed daughter and young grandchildren. During the siege of Charleston, Susanne Tennent and her children were among the noncombatants evacuated from their home on Tradd Street. In 1783 Charles Tennent's cousin John Vergereau (Class of 1786) was lost at sea while traveling from South Carolina to New York after a visit with his southern relatives. The tone of a letter written in 1815 to Susannah Rodgers Tennent, widow of William Mackay Tennent (A.B. 1763), suggests that Charles spent some part of his youth with these childless cousins of his father.

Tennent, who entered the College in May 1790 as a freshman, joined the Cliosophic Society the same year, assuming the name of Clearchus, the Spartan general. Although he served a term as second assistant and received its diploma, he was not especially active in the society. The faculty assigned him no part in the planned commencement exercises for his class, which may suggest that he was not a particularly gifted orator.

Tennent became a rice planter, eventually acquiring "Parnassus," a large plantation in St. James, Goose Creek. In partnership with his neighbor, Peter Gaillard Stoney, Tennent continued the operation of a brick manufacturing business on the premises. On November 1, 1801 he married Ann Martha Smith of Charleston, daughter of Josiah Smith, Jr., a deacon of the Independent Congregational Church and a partner in the mercantile firm of Smiths, DeSaussure and Darrell. Ann Tennent's brothers included William Stevens Smith (A.B. 1789) and Edward Darrell Smith (A.B. 1795); a third Smith brother, Samuel, married Tennent's sister Catherine Caroline. Tennent's marriage produced ten children, eight sons and two daughters; three of the boys died as infants and a daughter died in early childhood. The household also included Ann Edmonds, a "maiden relative" of Mrs. Tennent. According to family tradition Ann Martha Tennent was exceedingly plain in appearance, a characteristic which she passed on to each of her children. However, her husband asserted that she possessed "a most heavenly temper" and declared her to be "one of the best of God's last best gifts to man," surely more than adequate compensation.

Tennent died on January 29, 1838 and was buried in the churchyard of the Independent Church. His wife was buried beside him after her death on October 31, 1859.

Sources: Alumni files, PUA; M. Tennent, *Light in Darkness* (1971), 141, 149, 179, 180, 182, 188, 190-93 (quotes re wife); *Princetonians, 1748-1768*, 247-51; Clio. lists; Clio. Min., 12 Dec. 1792, 9 Jan., 20 Mar., 17 July 1793; Min. Fac., 10 Nov. 1789, 15 July 1793; *SCHGM*, 29 (1928), 325; 33 (1932), 1-2; 61 (1960), 130; C. T. Moore, *Abstracts of Wills of ... S.C. 1760-84* (1969), 263; *Biog. Dir. S.C. House Rep.*, III, 704-06.

Manuscripts: CT, comp., "Wm. Tennent III Album," ScU, contains copies of letters of CT's father

RLW

John Terhune

John Terhune, A.B., entered the College as a junior in the fall of 1791 and joined the American Whig Society. On July 15, 1793 he was ranked eighth in his class and selected to deliver one of the honorary orations at his commencement. At that time he was listed as a resident of New York. Commencement exercises, however, were canceled that year.

Terhune planned to remain at Princeton during the winter following his graduation, presumably to continue his studies. For some reason he changed his mind, and Joseph Warren Scott (A.B. 1795) passed on news of Terhune to John Henry Hobart (A.B. 1793) in a letter dated November 27, 1794. Terhune had written that he was at Gravesend, in modern Brooklyn, reading geography and history, and he would "alternately stay at New-York and Long Island." It may be that he was also the John Terhune who, for a brief time, was an assistant teacher at Erasmus Hall Academy in nearby Flatbush. For some reason Terhune's course of study did not prove successful, for by August Hobart heard from Abraham Skinner (A.B. 1793) at Jamaica, Long Island, that Skinner had seen one of Terhune's brothers, "who tells me that Terhune confines himself continually at home." On September 15 Skinner wrote that he had seen Terhune himself, who remained at home "disengaged."

It is not known when this period of seclusion and perhaps depression ended, nor has anything further been discovered about Terhune. A John Terhune, grocer, is listed in New York City directories from 1795 through 1797, and it is possible, although unlikely, that he was the Princetonian. Terhune is first listed as deceased in the 1869 catalogues of the College, which is probably an indication that he had not kept in touch with anyone associated with the institution.

SOURCES: Alumni file, PUA; Min. Fac., Nov. 1791 class list, 15 July 1793; Amer. Whig Soc., Cat. (1840), 7; NYGBR, 11 (1880), 166; Hobart, Corres., I, 26-27, 68-69, 82, 106-07 (quotes); J. M. Van Valen, Hist. of Bergen Cnty., N.J. (1900), 165; T. M. Strong, Hist. of the Town of Flatbush (1842), 128; N.Y. City directories, 1795-98.

Information in Terhune's alumni file, a Bergen genealogy in NYGBR, and the Hobart Correspondence all incorrectly identify Terhune as the son of Stephen and Letitia Bergen Terhune of Brooklyn, New York and Bergen County, New Jersey. On April 8, 1792 this John Terhune married Elizabeth Zabriskie of Paramus, and their first child was born while Terhune was still attending classes in Princeton. Moreover, the Terhune from Brooklyn became a shoemaker, not a likely career for a college graduate. See G. O. Zabriskie, The Zabriskie Family (1963), 72.

Numerous Terhunes lived in both Brooklyn and Bergen County, and both Stephen and John were common names in the family. The subject of this sketch could have been the John S. Terhune, christened on August 27, 1777, who was the son of Stephen D. Terhune of New Barbadoes Township, Bergen County, and his wife Janet (Jannetje) Zabriskie. The wife of this John Terhune was named Antje and they had one son and one daughter. See Zabriskie Family, 69, 159.

RLW

Isaac Van Doren

ISAAC VAN DOREN, A.B., A.M. 1797, Presbyterian clergyman and women's educator, was born on July 9, 1773, the third of the ten or eleven children of Abraham and Anne Van Doren of Griggstown, Somerset County, New Jersey. The father was a wealthy miller and farmer whose complex on the Millstone River included a saw mill, separate mills for grinding flour and livestock feed, a cider mill and distillery, a carding mill and powerloom, a store, a cooperage, and smithies. He served terms as deacon and as elder of the Millstone Dutch Reformed Church. His wife Anne was the daughter of Francis Van Dyke of Amwell, Hunterdon County, New Jersey. Her granddaughter Elizabeth Honeyman recalled that she was "very strict," opposed to mirth in children, and "forever scolding me and cross to me." Other sources agree that she was "very positive" and "spirited." "She regulated everything like clock-work" and was quite pious. Peter Van Doren (A.B. 1795) was probably Isaac's first cousin.

Isaac Van Doren, A.B. 1793, and wife Abigail

George Washington and his army passed through Griggstown while making their escape from the British after the Battle of Princeton in January 1777, and they were accorded bountiful hospitality by the Van Dorens. Abraham marched off with the army, and some days after his departure his family, fearing British reprisals, packed what it could and headed for the American lines. Their slaves purposely slowed up when British troops came into view, and they were overtaken. However, the formidable Mrs. Van Doren waved her safe-conduct from Washington and so loudly refused to be plundered that she was taken to the British commander, Charles, Earl Cornwallis, who gave her family protection and a safe-conduct of his own after verifying her claim to having cared for wounded British as well as American troops. Anne and her family returned to Griggstown, where they apparently got through the rest of the war without incident.

Isaac Van Doren entered the College as a junior in November 1791. He joined the Cliosophic Society on December 27 of that year under the sobriquet Arion, for Arion of Methymna, on Lesbos, the Greek poet and musician who lived around 625 B.C. The society's minutes show that Van Doren was an active member who served as president, second assistant, censor, corrector of speaking, and clerk, and received the society's diploma. Sometime between May 15 and July 15, 1793, Van Doren somehow managed to enrage Horatio Dayton (Class of 1794), whom the faculty convicted of "threatening with a pistol in his hand the life and abusing the person of Mr. Isaac Van Doren one of the most peaceable of its members." For this "assault" they suspended Dayton and rejected his subsequent written apology because it still contained "repeated reflections on the person so maltreated." Dayton apparently refused to comply with their demand that he apologize to Van Doren and did not return to the College. Van Doren was assigned a disputation topic when his commencement exercises were planned, but the commencement was subsequently canceled during the panic created by the Philadelphia yellow fever epidemic, with the degrees awarded privately instead.

After graduating Van Doren read for the Dutch Reformed ministry under Theodore (Dirck) Romeyn (A.B. 1765) at Schenectady, New York and subsequently under John Henry Livingston at Flatbush, New York. He probably met Abigail Foster Halsey while at Schenectady. Only she reached adulthood among the several children of Luther Halsey (Class of 1777), a schoolmaster, and his first wife Sarah Foster. Van Doren married Abigail on February 10, 1800. During a happy marriage of sixty-four years they had six sons and eight daughters, including Luther Halsey Van Doren (A.B. 1831).

The Classis of New York licensed Van Doren in 1798. His whereabouts for the next five years have not been discovered. Perhaps he had trouble obtaining a call from a suitable Dutch Reformed congregation, for on June 29, 1803 he was ordained and installed as minister of the Presbyterian church at Hopewell, Orange County, New York. He spent the rest of his life in the Presbyterian ministry. For more than two decades he remained at Hopewell, presiding over a revival in 1820 during which 152 new members entered the church's communion, and enjoying good relations with his parishioners throughout his stay.

On April 20, 1825 the Presbytery of Hudson, which he had served for some time as stated clerk, dissolved Van Doren's pastoral relation with Hopewell at his own request. Probably his motive was financial. The salary his small rural congregation could offer must have been increasingly inadequate as his family became very large. Van Doren moved to Newark, New Jersey, where he and his eldest son John Livingston Van Doren opened the Newark Institute for Young Ladies. Their stay there was short. In May 1828 their Brooklyn Collegiate Institute for Young Ladies opened in rented quarters at the corner of Hicks and Clark Streets in Brooklyn, New York. The school was intended to "afford young ladies the same advantages in acquiring an education that are enjoyed by the other sex in our colleges." A prospectus promised that the curriculum would include "the highest branches of literature and all that is requisite of general science" as well as "all the elegant accomplishments."

If Van Doren's school really offered women a college-level education it was the first in the nation to do so. The cornerstone of Mount Holyoke Academy was laid in 1836, the same year that the Georgia Female College in Macon, Georgia, was established, and in 1837 Ohio's Oberlin College became coeducational. Yet the neglect historians of women's education have accorded Van Doren's institution may be justifiable. No evidence that it required its students to learn Greek or pursue a four-year course of study, the commonest criteria for collegiate status, has come to light. The promise to instill "the elegant accomplishments" is telling, as is the speech of Rev. Charles P. McIlvaine (later Episcopal bishop of Ohio) at the Brooklyn Institute's ground-breaking ceremony in October 1829, which asserted that while women should be taught "as carefully, as substantially, and as liberally" as men, they need not study exactly the same subjects. On the other hand, the school's prospectus outlined an ambitious curriculum. It featured a great deal of Latin, especially Virgil, Livy, Horace, and Tacitus, as well as algebra and geometry, political economy and geography. Scientific topics included astronomy, chemistry, geology, acoustics, and pneumatics. Students would also wrestle with logic, moral philosophy, "Intellectual Philosophy," "Evidences of Christianity," and natural theology. Greek and modern Romance languages were available as electives, while dancing and needlework seem not to have been on the curriculum. The students were required to keep a daily journal, and on the Sabbath no pupil was "to *receive* or *pay* visits," "to engage in any diversions," or to "amuse herself with unsuitable reading." While Van Doren's school may best be described as a seminary rather than a college, to the extent that it lived up to its prospectus it offered an education as demanding as that offered by the best men's secondary schools.

Initially the school flourished. The local elite subscribed $30,000 to the venture, a sum used to buy twelve lots in a scenic location at Hicks Street on Brooklyn Heights and build there a four-story structure which when completed in May 1830 was the most imposing edifice in town. In 1830 Van Doren and his son claimed to have an enrollment of 100 students and a staff of "five professors, and seven instructresses" besides themselves. However in about a year the Van Dorens left. The reasons do not appear. The institute may have encountered financial difficulties, although it subsequently flourished for some years under new management.

Van Doren proceeded to Lexington, Kentucky, and there, probably in July 1831, opened Van Doren's Collegiate Institute for Young Ladies. A contemporary in Lexington recalled Van Doren as "the esteemed principal of a respectable female academy." His two eldest sons, John L. and Luther H., taught with him. By 1838 this school had closed. From 1838 or 1839 to 1840 Van Doren operated an academy at Warsaw, Gallatin County, Kentucky. Van Doren's failure to establish himself at one place for very long does not point to extraordinary success as a pedagogue. In 1838 he had sided with the so-called Old School, which opposed cooperation with the Congregationalists, in the dispute which led to a schism within Presbyterianism. In 1840 he returned to ministerial work, opening a mission church at Iron Mountain, a mining community in St. Francois County, Missouri. His son John had become involved in 1836 in efforts to exploit the iron ore there. Van Doren continued his services at Iron Mountain until 1844, when he retired to Perth Amboy, New Jersey, and there spent the rest of his life. He died on August 12, 1864.

All sources agree that, while not brilliant, Van Doren was kindly, hospitable, and of unquestioned piety and integrity. His daughter Adelaide (or Adaline), the wife of the Reverend Robert Davidson, recalled her childhood in Hopewell with such affection that in 1863 she wrote a Sunday-School tract called *The Old Parsonage, or Recollections of a Minister's Daughter*, which memorialized her parents' virtues.

SOURCES: A. V. D. Honeyman, *Van Doorn Family* (1909), 93-95 ("very strict," "forever scolding," "very positive," "spirited," "She regulated"), 116, 318-19, 701-08; A. V. D. Honeyman, ed., *Our Home*, I (1873), 233, 337-40, 571; *NJHSP*, n.s., 12 (1927), 232; L. P. Terhune, *Episodes in the Hist. of Griggstown* (1976), 34, 140, 168-69; J. P. Snell, *Hist. of Hunterdon & Somerset Cnties.* (1881), 628; *N.J. Wills*, XI, 347; Min. Fac., Nov. 1791 class list, undated entry between 15 May & 15 July 1793 ("threatening," "repeated reflections"), 15 July 1793; Clio lists; Clio. Min., 12 July 1792–17 July 1793 *passim*, 3 Sept. 1794, 28 Sept. 1796; Alexander, *Princeton*, 269-70; Min. Trustees, 25 Sept. 1793; Trenton *State Gazette & N.J. Advt.*, 17 Oct. 1797; J. H. Raven, *Biog. Record: Theol. Sem. New Brunswick 1784-1911* (1912), 30, 60; *Princetonians, 1748-1768*, 521-25; *Princetonians, 1776-1783*, 172-74; J. L. Halsey & E. D. Halsey, *Thomas Halsey ... with his Amer. Descendants* (1895), 62, 97-102, 179-81; E. M. Ruttenber & L. H. Clark, *Hist. of Orange Cnty., N.Y.* (1881), 418, 420-21; H. A. Harlow, *Hist. of the Presby. of Hudson 1681-1888* (1888), 45, 99, 245; R. F. Weld, *Brooklyn Village 1816-34* (1938 repr. 1970), 24, 210-13, 322 ("afford young," "the highest," "as carefully," "five professors"); F. Trollope, *Domestic Manners of the Americans* (1832, ed. D. Smalley 1949), 340-42 ("Intellectual Philosophy," "to receive"); R. M. Pierson, *Preliminary Checklist of Lexington, Ky., Imprints 1821-50* (1953), 80, 85; R. Davidson, *Hist. of the Pres. Church in the State of Ky.* (1847),

370; *KSHS Reg.*, 41 (1943), 45, 346 ("the esteemed"); J. P. B. MacCabe, *Dir. of the City of Lexington* ... (1838); W. J. Beecher & M. A. Beecher, *Index of Pres. Ministers ... 1706-1881* (1883), 547; *Missouri Hist. Rev.*, 33 (1938/39), 466-67. *The Old Parsonage* is anonymous, and the minister is given the pseudonym "Mr. Thorn." Honeyman identifies the author and her subjects in *Our Home*, I, 233 & 340, and in his *Van Doorn Family*, 116, and internal evidence supports his attributions. However the copy at the Princeton Theological Seminary has a penciled note attributing authorship to one Eliza Maria Judkins. Van Doren's date of death is given as 1863 in Snell and in *Our Home*, I, 340; and as 1865 in the University's *General Catalogue* (1908), but the 1864 date given in the Van Doorn and Halsey genealogies is more convincing.

PUBLICATION: Alexander credits Van Doren with a tract entitled "'A Summary of Christian Duty,' compiled from the Douay Bible," but no copy has been located. Since the Douai Bible was a Roman Catholic translation, the compilation of such a work by a Presbyterian clergyman seems odd.

JJL

Joshua Maddox Wallace, Jr.

JOSHUA MADDOX WALLACE, JR., A.B., A.M. 1796, merchant, was born in Philadelphia on September 4, 1776, the elder of two sons of Joshua Maddox Wallace (A.B. College of Philadelphia 1767, A.M. College of Philadelphia and College of New Jersey 1770), and his wife Tace Bradford Wallace. John Bradford Wallace (A.B. 1794) was Joshua Jr.'s brother, and they had several sisters. William Bradford, Jr. (A.B. 1772) was an uncle. The father, who was named for his maternal grandfather, was the son of John Wallace, a Scottish immigrant who prospered as a merchant in Philadelphia.

Just before Philadelphia fell to the British in 1777, the Wallaces moved to a farm on the Raritan River in Bridgewater Township, Somerset County, New Jersey. They called their house there "Ellerslie," after the ancient ancestral home of the Scottish Wallaces. At the time of the move Joshua Sr. was in his mid-twenties. He had been trained as a merchant but had not yet established himself, and he now gave up active trading and became a gentleman farmer. His friends included New Jersey Governor William Livingston, who wrote him in November 1779 that he hoped to visit soon, and asked him to "Tell Master Joshua, that I intend to kill a squirrel for him" while at "Ellerslie."

In 1784 the Wallaces moved from "Ellerslie" to Burlington, New Jersey, where the senior Joshua spent the rest of his life and became a leading citizen. He was a member of the New Jersey convention that ratified the United States Constitution in 1787 and served in the New Jersey general assembly in 1791. An active Episcopalian, he was for many years a warden of St. Mary's Church, Burlington, and a member of the New Jersey diocese's standing committee. In 1795

Joshua Maddox Wallace, Jr., A.B. 1793

he helped found the Burlington Academy, and from 1798 to 1819 he was a College trustee. He served as president of the New Jersey Society for the Suppression of Vice and Immorality, and in 1816 he chaired the convention in New York which founded the American Bible Society.

Joshua Wallace, Jr., received his early education from his father, who had served briefly as a tutor at the College of Philadelphia. The son then lived with Rev. William Frazer, Episcopal minister at Amwell, Hunterdon County, New Jersey, who prepared him for the College, which he entered as a sophomore in November 1790. Vice President Samuel Stanhope Smith (A.B. 1769) wrote Joshua Sr. on March 27, 1792 that "the good morals, diligence and talents" of Joshua Jr. and his younger brother John were "every thing that the fondest and worthiest parents can wish." Joshua joined the American Whig Society. He stood seventh in a class of twenty-one and was assigned one of the intermediate honors orations for the aborted 1793 commencement. He became friendly enough with his classmate Abraham Skinner to visit him in August 1794 at Jamaica, Long Island.

A letter from John Witherspoon indicates that Wallace was in Princeton on March 27, 1794. Perhaps he pursued further studies there after his graduation. Subsequently he returned to Philadelphia and was placed in the counting house of William Crammond (or Cramond), a merchant trading to Europe. After several years with Crammond, Wallace went abroad, visiting Madeira, Britain, Ireland, and parts of continental Europe. This mercantile version of the grand tour was designed to provide business contacts and commercial know-how as much as to give a final polish to a young man's education. Wallace then settled in England, presumably as a factor for Crammond or other Philadelphia acquaintances or relatives. By early 1803 Wallace had returned to Philadelphia and set up as a merchant. At first he lived with his brother John at Mrs. Cornelia Smith's boarding house at the corner of Dock and Walnut streets. Benjamin Silliman, a fellow resident, named the Wallace brothers among eight gentlemen he fondly recalled as having

> formed a brilliant circle of high conversational powers.... Rarely in my progress in life have I met with a circle of gentlemen who surpassed them in courteous manners, in brilliant intelligence, sparkling sallies of wit and pleasantry, and cordial greeting.

The Wallace brothers subsequently shared accommodations at 96 South Third Street from at least 1804 until 1806. Thereafter Joshua had his own home and place of business, which were generally distinct, and both of which changed several times in the next fifteen years.

On November 26, 1805 Wallace married Rebecca McIlvaine at St. Mary's Church, Burlington. Rebecca was the half-sister of William McIlvaine (A.B. 1802). Her parents were William McIlvaine, a physician who moved from Philadelphia to Burlington in 1793, and his first wife Margaret Rodman. The Wallaces had at least three sons and one daughter, including Joshua Maddox Wallace (A.B. 1833) and Ellerslie Wallace, both of whom became prominent Philadelphia physicians.

Wallace appears to have prospered as a merchant in the European trade until the depression of 1819 found him overextended and ruined him. He died at Burlington on January 7, 1821 with his finances still in disarray and was buried at St. Mary's three days later. His brother John had agreed to guarantee some of Joshua's obligations, and despite valiant efforts to develop the family's remaining resources, Joshua's losses ultimately contributed to John's own bankruptcy, although the latter eventually managed to rebuild his fortunes to some extent.

SOURCES: Alexander, *Princeton*, 270-71 ("the good"); [S. B. Wallace], *Memoir* [of John Bradford Wallace] (1848), 3-6, 9, 12-13; *PMHB*, 8 (1884), xiii-xv, xliii-xliv; 40 (1916),

335-43; E. M. Woodward & J. F. Hageman, *Hist. of Burlington & Mercer Cnties, N.J.* (1883), 67; G. M. Hills, *Hist. of the Church in Burlington, N.J.* (2d ed., 1885), 324, 332, 335, 377, 382, 385, 787; *PGM*, 5 (1914), 281 (father's will); J. F. Lewis, *Hist. of an Old Phila. Land Title: 208 South 4th Street* (1934), 150-52; als, W. Livingston to JMW, Sr., 9 Nov. 1779, Wallace Family Papers, PHi, VI, 19 ("Tell Master"; a draft of this letter at NN is published in C. E. Prince et al., eds., *Papers of William Livingston* [1979-88], III, 204); G. A. Boyd, *Elias Boudinot* (1952), 259; Wallace Family Papers, PHi, VI, 13, 26, 91; Min. Fac., 29 Nov. 1790, 15 July 1793; Amer. Whig Soc., *Cat.* (1840), 7; Hobart, *Corres.*, I, 30-31, 66-68; Min. Trustees, 25 Sept. 1793; als, John Witherspoon to JMW, Sr., 27 Mar. 1794, Wallace Family Papers, PHi; *Greenleaf's N.Y. Jour., & Patriotic Reg.*, 7 Oct. 1796; "Reg. of St. Mary's Church, Burlington, N.J.," *PGM*, 2 (1903), 285-94; G. P. Fisher, *Life of Benjamin Silliman, M.D., LL.D.* (1866), I, 97-100 ("formed a brilliant"); Phila. city directories, 1804-22; Wickes, *Hist. of Medicine N.J.*, 326-29; *Hist. Cat. of the St. Andrew's Soc. of Phila. ... 1749-1907* (1907), 423, 432 (JMW a member, 1804).

JJL

Richard Willing

RICHARD WILLING, merchant and insurance company executive, a brother of George Willing (A.B.1792) and William Shippen Willing (Class of 1796), was born on Christmas Day 1775. He was the tenth child of the highly successful Philadelphia merchant, Thomas Willing, and his wife Anne McCall. The elder Willing was a partner in Willing and Morris, probably the largest mercantile establishment in the city. Educated for the law in Bath, England, Thomas Willing was active in Philadelphia as mayor of the city in 1763 and as a justice, by turn, in the city court, the court of common pleas, and the supreme court of Pennsylvania. As a member of the Continental Congress he was one of the Pennsylvania delegates who refused to sign the Declaration of Independence because he doubted that he had the authority to do so. Personally believing that the colonies were not yet ready for independence, he nevertheless gave his wholehearted support to their cause once there was no possibility of reversing their decision. He made a contribution of £5,000 to help provision the Continental Army. He was the first president of the Bank of North America, a position which he held for ten years before assuming the same role for the Bank of United States. An active member of Christ Church and a trustee of the College of Philadelphia and the University of the State of Pennsylvania, he built a large home for his family at 106 South Third Street.

Richard followed his three elder brothers to the preparatory school at the University of the State of Pennsylvania when he was only six years old. Enrolled in the English school on April 30, 1781, he dropped out by May 30. His name reappears as a student for the quarter term that began July 1, 1781, and again from 1783 through the last quarter of that year. He probably then transferred to the

Richard Willing, Class of 1793
BY GEORGE P. A. HEALY

grammar school at Nassau Hall along with his brother George. He entered the College as a freshman on November 10, 1788. For some reason he repeated his freshman year but progressed normally thereafter until 1792, when he appeared on a class list as a junior at the start of the summer session but was not included on a November roster. While George was still at the College completing his senior year, Richard was already working for the family mercantile firm of Willing and Francis. Considered "prudent" by his wealthy brother-in-law William Bingham, Richard sailed to Canton, China, in 1799 in charge of a cargo in which Bingham, as well as Willing and Francis, had an interest. The following year he was in charge of *The Canton* which sailed for Bengal along with the British Calcutta fleet, as a protection against the danger of possible French attacks. Willing made four voyages to India and also traveled to Europe supervising family cargoes. When Willing and Francis went out of business, probably about 1815, Richard Willing took an active part in winding up its affairs. Thereafter he and his brother Thomas Mayne Willing were partners in mercantile pursuits.

On February 1, 1804 Willing married Eliza, daughter of Thomas

Lloyd Moore and Sarah Stamper Moore of Philadelphia, at Christ Church. She bore seven children before her death on May 21, 1823. The eldest son was Thomas Moore Willing (Class of 1823, A.B. Union 1823). Another family connection with the College was through the marriage of Willing's sister Mary to Henry Clymer (A.B. 1786).

Several sources mention Willing's reluctance to accept any official or public offices, which suggests that a number must have been urged upon him. Elected a trustee of the Mutual Assurance Company in 1834, he was persuaded to accept the chairmanship, or presidency, in January 1841, after the position was refused by Robert Lewis, whose brother Lawrence was treasurer of the company. Willing's tenure was a time of steady growth for the company, in spite of the loss incurred because of the fire that spread along Delaware Avenue in 1850, at the time the city's worst recorded fire. Willing resigned in December 1855 in his eightieth year because of failing health, but he continued as a trustee until his death. In 1845 the Mutual Assurance Company arranged to have his portrait painted by Thomas Sully. However, in 1856 a new and "more suitable" portrait by George P. A. Healy was commissioned. Completed by April 1857, Healy's treatment was judged more successful in depicting Willing as a businessman. The Healy portrait still hangs in the insurance company offices.

From 1794 until 1810 Willing belonged to the First Troop Philadelphia City Cavalry, and he was one of the original members of the Second Company of Washington Guards which was organized on May 26, 1813 for the defense of Philadelphia and the harbor and ports of the Delaware River, but which did not see service. In 1814 Willing was elected captain of the State Fencibles, who were ordered to Camp Dupont in New Castle County, Delaware, in anticipation of a British invasion, but he refused this honor. Elected a member of the Schuylkill Fishing Company in October 1817, he resigned a year and a half later. In September 1830 he acted as secretary for a body of Philadelphians sympathetic to the three-day revolution in France which resulted in expulsion of the Bourbons. The group met to express their accord with "the enemies of tyranny." On March 7, 1848 Willing was one of the pallbearers for the coffin of John Quincy Adams (LL.D. 1806) during the interim when it was in Philadelphia, en route to Quincy, Massachusetts, from Washington.

Willing died on May 17, 1858 at his residence on Third Street, Philadelphia. Extremely wealthy, among other bequests from his father he had inherited a house in Philadelphia and all of the family lands in Warwick, England. The Mutual Assurance Company noted in its minutes of June 9, 1858 its appreciation of "his qualities of energy and frankness, of high toned honour, and of polished Courtesy, and kindness, Which render'd his Presidency most useful and ageeable."

SOURCES: C. R. Keith, *Provincial Councillors of Pa.* (1883), 89-93, 103-04; *PMHB*, 5 (1881), 452-55; 61 (1937), 401-02; MS tuition books, Univ. of the State of Pa., UPenn-Ar; J. W. Jordan, *Colonial Families of Phila.* (1911), I, 127-28; Min. Fac., 10 Nov. 1789, class list ca. May 1792; Phila. city directories; H. Simpson, *Lives of Eminent Philadelphians* (1859), 962; T. W. Balch, *Willing Letters & Papers* (1922), 173-214; J. T. Scharf & T. Westcott, *Hist. of Phila.* (1884), I, 563-64, 625, 688; B. A. Konkle, *Thomas Willing* (1937), 137, 165; Schuylkill Fishing Co., *Hist. of Schuylkill Fishing Company* (1889), 378; Hist. brochure (1984) and Min. 9 June 1858 ("his qualities"), Mutual Assurance Co. of Phila.; A. N. B. Garvan & C. A. Woftowicz, *Cat. of The Green Tree Collection* (1977), 62-63.

RLW

CLASS OF 1794

William Bay

Thomas Monteagle Bayly, A.B.

James Madison Broom, A.B.

Andrew Caldwell

George Washington Campbell, A.B.

James Revell Corbin

James Cresap, A.B.

Horatio Rolfe (Roff) Dayton

John M. Dickson, A.B.

Edmund Elmendorf, A.B.

Nicholas C. Everett, A.B.

William Belford Ewing, A.B.

James Gildersleeve Force, A.B.

John White Furman, A.B.

Moore Furman, Jr., A.B.

Isaac Gibbs

Stephen Gibbs

Andrew Gibson

Richard Montgomery Green, A.B.

James Henry

John Sylvanus Hiester, A.B.

Thomas Yardley How, A.B.

Benjamin Van Cleve Hunt

Holloway Whitefield Hunt, A.B.

Andrew Stockton Hunter

Titus Hutchinson, A.B.

Hugh Ker

Henry Knox Kollock, A.B.

William Ludwell Lee

Reuben Leigh

James Hude Neilson, A.B.

Paul Paulison, A.B.

Henry Polhemus, A.B.

Edwin Tasker Reese, A.B.

John Rush

John Neely Simpson, A.B.

—— Sitler

John Brown Slemons, A.B.

William Tennent Snowden

Samuel Voorhees

John Bradford Wallace, A.B.

James Carra Williamson, A.B.

William Rickets Williamson, A.B.

John Ramsey Witherspoon, A.B.

(Commencement took place on Wednesday, September 24, 1794)

William Bay

WILLIAM BAY, M.D. Columbia 1797, physician, was born on October 14, 1773 in Albany, New York, the second of six children of John Bay (A.B. 1765) and his wife Ann Williams Bay. Of Huguenot ancestry, the father was a prosperous lawyer who supported the Revolution and later was active politically as an Antifederalist and Republican. By 1781 he had moved his family to a large estate at Claverack, a community that was set off from Albany to Columbia County in 1786. Probably he had already moved there by June 1779 when his daughter Maria became one of the charter students of the Washington Seminary in Claverack.

Around 1780 William Bay joined his sister at the seminary, which offered classical secondary as well as grammar school instruction. Under the guidance of Andrew Mayfield Carshore, a British soldier in Gen. John Burgoyne's army who turned teacher, the school attained regional renown. Bay may have remained at the seminary until he entered the College as a junior in October 1792. The faculty minutes show that he was dining off campus in January 1794 when he was "ordered immediately to return to the dining room." He was still listed as a student when the summer session of his senior year began on May 10, 1794, but sometime thereafter ill health obliged him to withdraw.

Later in 1794 Bay went to New York City to study medicine. He became a private student of William Pitt Smith, the professor of materia medica and the clinical lecturer at Columbia College. Smith was also health officer to the port of New York, and after he died on the night of February 11-12, 1796, Bay filled this office until a permanent successor was found four months later. After Smith's death Bay became a student of Samuel Latham Mitchill, Columbia's professor of natural history. He also attended medical lectures at Columbia and in May 1797 received his M.D. His 109-page dissertation on dysentery, published the same year, argued that that disease was caused by nitric acid in the intestines. After obtaining his degree, Bay returned to Claverack and began a practice. On November 25, 1797 he married Catharine Van Ness at the Claverack Dutch Reformed Church. She was the daughter of William Van Ness and the sister of William W. Van Ness, a lawyer who was trained in John Bay's office and subsequently sat on the state supreme court. William and Catharine had three daughters and a son. On April 7, 1798 Bay was appointed a surgeon's mate in a Columbia County militia light infantry regiment. He was a founding member and first secretary of the Columbia County Medical Society, organized in June 1806.

Bay's clientele grew rapidly, but apparently he found a country practice tiring. He moved to Albany in 1810. The first relevant city directory, that for 1813, has him living at 65 North Pearl Street. He resided on this street for the rest of his life. Around 1840 the directories change his address to 32 North Pearl, where he was listed therafter. From around 1823 to 1833 he kept an office at 74 North Pearl, but otherwise he practiced out of his home.

On October 14, 1810 Bay entered a partnership with John Stearns, who had also recently moved to Albany. The partnership proved short-lived. Stearns became distraught and temporarily abandoned the profession after losing several patients to puerperal fever and observing that within the city only his patients seemed to be contracting the disease. It was not then known to be contagious, and he may have been communicating it himself. Bay subsequently became the partner of William McClelland, an Edinburgh-trained Scot and first president of the Medical Society of the State of New-York. This alliance also ended quickly with McClelland's death on January 29, 1812.

Bay soon gained a place among Albany's leading physicians. After his retirement a colleague, Sylvester Willard, recalled that he had been particularly skillful in obstetrics, and that "his medical brethren frequently sought his counsel in difficult cases." He was remembered as cheerful, with an encouraging, empathetic bedside manner. Throughout his career he reputedly never failed to respond to a call for his services.

Bay joined the Albany County Medical Society on October 9, 1810 and presented a paper on the medical properties of carbon at its meeting on April 9, 1811. A dispute whose grounds are somewhat obscure provoked Bay to resign in July 1812. He became active again around 1818 and subsequently saw service as a censor, vice president and, from 1823 to 1826, president. In 1816 he was among those who persuaded the Albany city government to change its poor relief system by dividing Albany into districts and appointing a physician to each, with an annual salary of $200. Bay was the first doctor chosen for the first district. Around the same time he was one of four "Physicians to the Vaccine Institution." On July 8, 1819 he became hospital surgeon to the New York militia's Ninth Infantry Division. During the 1832 cholera epidemic he was part of a nine-man medical staff that aided the board of health. From at least 1832 to around 1850 he was a district censor of the state medical society, an office which may have been largely honorific since the county societies were the main watchdogs of the credentials of physicians. The state society also selected Bay as vice president of its apparently short-lived New York State Vaccine Institution in February 1832

Bay's fellow physicians of Albany showed their esteem for him on March 30, 1847 when they held a "jubilee dinner" at Congress Hall to celebrate his fiftieth year in the profession. Thereafter he withdrew more and more from practice and retired in 1860. His son John W. Bay (M.D. College of Physicians and Surgeons 1823) had moved in with him in 1839 and probably took over his patients in the ensuing years. About 1830 William's brother John also joined him and remained in the household until his death in 1864.

Bay's social activity apparently centered upon a local Masonic organization, the "Master's Lodge," which he served as senior warden for at least ten years around 1840. In his retirement he remained lucid and in good health until a few days before his demise and followed with great interest the news relating to the Civil War. His wife died on January 24, 1864, and he followed her on September 7, 1865. He had been Albany's senior physician for seventeen years. His minister, Rufus W. Clark of the North Reformed Protestant Dutch Church of Albany, gave a eulogy attesting to Bay's deep piety. At a memorial meeting a colleague, Dr. B. P. Staats, observed that during "forty-five years in this city, I have never heard a word of reproach against him, but on the contrary have heard hundreds bless him, for his kindness and good treatment towards them."

SOURCES: S. D. Willard, *Annals of the Med. Soc. of the Cnty. of Albany 1806-51* (1864), 21-29, 49-73 *passim*, 88, 97-101, 107-08, 110, 190-91, 193, 213-17 (sketch of WB; "his medical," 216); S. O. Vanderpoel, sketch of WB in *N.Y. State Med. Soc. Trans.* (1866), 317-21 ("forty-five years," 320-21); *Princetonians, 1748-1768*, 27, 482-83; P. F. Miller, *Group of Great Lawyers in Columbia Cnty., N.Y.* (1904), 58-60, 138-43; E. L. Gebhard, *Parsonage Between Two Manors: Annals of Clover-Reach* (1909), 35-47; F. N. Zabriskie et al., *Hist. of the Reformed P. D. Church of Claverack* (1867), 25, 54; Min. Fac., 10 Oct. 1792, 6 & 8 Jan. ("ordered immediately"), 10 May 1794; Thomas, *Columbia*, 178, 198, 200; *N.Y. Weekly Museum*, 13 Feb. 1796; N.Y. *Amer. Minerva*, 12 Feb. 1796; *NYGBR*, 55 (1924), 110-11; 83 (1952), 204, 217; 89 (1958), 30, 33; *Military Minutes of the Council of Appointment of the State of N.Y. 1783-1821* (1901), I, 437; III, 2079; F. Ellis, *Hist. of Columbia Cnty.* (1878), 90-91, 114-15; Albany city directories, 1813-60, alphabetical listings and: (1818), 6 ("Physicians to the Vaccine"); (1832/33), 50; (1833/34), 49-50; (1834/35), 162; (1835/36), 25-26 ("Master's Lodge"); (1844/45), 96; (1845/46), 43, 48; (1848/49), [101]; (1850/51), 28; J. Munsell, *Annals of Albany* (10 vols., 1850-59), VI, 116; IX, 93, 100-01, 114-15; X, 377 ("festival"); MS will of WB, 14 Jan. 1864, proved 20 Nov. 1865, Albany Cnty. Surrogate's Court (photocopy in PUA).

PUBLICATION: STE # 31780. See also the review of this work in *The Medical Repository*, 1 (1797), 236-41.

JJL

Thomas Monteagle Bayly

THOMAS MONTEAGLE BAYLY, A.B., A.M. 1798, lawyer, planter, public official and soldier, was born on March 26, 1775 at "Hills Farm," Accomack County, on Virginia's Eastern Shore, the third son of Thomas and Ann Drummond Bayly. Richard Drummond Bayly (A.B. 1800) was a younger brother and Thomas Bayly (A.B. 1797) was a second cousin. Their father was a planter who achieved some renown during a smallpox epidemic by arranging to have almost 1,000 people vaccinated. The mother, Ann, was the daughter of Richard and Catharine Harmanson Shepherd Drummond and the widow of William Justice. She was the half-sister of the mother of Hugh Ker (Class of 1794).

Bayly probably received his preliminary education at Washington Academy in nearby Somerset County, Maryland. He and his cousin Hugh Ker were admitted to the sophomore class of the College in July 1792. Bayly and his classmate and fellow Virginian James R. Corbin were described as "formerly members of the American Whig Society" when they were admitted into the Cliosophic Society on August 28, 1793. Bayly took the pseudonym "Neckar," probably for Jacques Necker (LL.D. 1790), the finance minister of Louis XVI during much of the American Revolution. Bayly was fairly active in the Cliosophic Society, serving one term as president and obtaining its diploma, and he managed to avoid incurring any of the society's many fines. Apparently the food served at Nassau Hall did not please him, for Bayly was cited for boarding out on January 6, 1794. After producing a physician's certification of his "ill state of health" he was permitted to "diet in the town," but when the new term began in May, he lacked an excuse and was accordingly ordered "to repair to the Stewards table." At his commencement on September 24, 1794, Bayly seems not to have spoken, although he was assigned a topic. The disputation in question did not take place for some unknown reason.

In his will Bayly styled himself "attorney at law." Where he received his training has not been discovered, but reputedly he was admitted to the bar about 1796 and practiced in Accomack County. He obtained the assistance of John Marshall (LL.D. 1802) on a case in 1799. Bayly must have prospered; the Accomack County real estate records show that he steadily built an estate through purchase, inheritance, and marriage. He lived on his plantation, called "Marino," immediately after his return from College. John Cropper, whose first marriage produced Bayly's first wife and whose second was to Bayly's sister, later sold him "Mount Custis," presumably on easy terms. Bayly lived there most of his adult life. In 1830 he bought his birthplace, "Hills Farm," apparently from a nephew who inherited it and then experienced financial embarrassments. Bayly's will shows that he also possessed more than 10,000 acres of land in Ohio, including some property in Chillicothe, and that he owned property in Illinois as well.

Bayly was active politically for much of his life. He served in the state assembly from 1798 to 1801 and in the Virginia senate from 1801 to 1809. He was a Federalist for most of his career, although he apparently flirted with Republicanism in 1801. That March a friend wrote him a letter bemoaning the election of Thomas Jefferson (LL.D. 1791), whom she feared might usher in another reign of terror, but added "let me not forget that I am writing in this strain to a *Jacobin*." In November 1801 Bayly thought his Republican credentials were strong enough to warrant his applying to Daniel Brent and James Madison (A.B. 1771) for the post of customs collector at Folly Landing in Accomack County. However Jefferson noted on Brent's copy that "I understand that the writer is a tory," and Bayly seems not to have gotten the job.

During the War of 1812 Bayly's public service intensified. Beginning in 1813 he served one term in the United States House of Representatives after winning an extremely close election battle. He originally won by fifty-seven votes. When the loser, Burwell Bassett, appealed the outcome, the House confirmed Bayly's election but reduced his margin of victory to just five votes. At this time Bayly was definitely a Federalist, as is shown by his one major congressional speech on October 22, 1814 during a debate on a proposed increase in taxes on distilled spirits. He asserted that provided they were equitable, "excise and direct taxes," including the one on whiskey, were preferable to such indirect taxes as the tariff. Since the people knew they could not evade the direct taxes and thus would have "to pay for the support of their Government, [they] would examine into all extravagant expenditures." Indeed, had such taxes been relied upon, the country might have avoided ravages to its commerce, an empty treasury, and a ruinous war. Still, although Bayly conceded that he had opposed both the administration and the war, now that the country was at war he argued that it had better be won and would vote for whatever taxes were necessary, even if the administration should thereby come to "possess all the honors gained." Finally, he disagreed with those pressing to have "Federal men" taken into the administration. Coalitions were always a mistake, especially during this crisis, but "when a complete change is made in the public sentiment, then, and not till then, do I wish to see a Federal Administration."

Bayly participated in a little less than half of the roll call votes taken during his term in Congress. This poor record was not entirely his fault because he was also obliged to devote much of his time to his duties as a militia officer. He was active in the militia as early as 1803, and in 1813 he was lieutenant colonel commanding the Second Virginia Regiment, composed of Accomack County men. In April 1814 the British landed on nearby Watt's and Tangier islands. On May 30 Bayly commanded the American forces at the Battle of Pungoteague, the biggest action of the war on Virginia's Eastern Shore. Despite its name, it was merely a confused little skirmish, in which the British landed in overwhelming force and the Americans could only harass them by sniping away from too great a distance to do much damage. Throughout the summer Bayly energetically patrolled his posts, tried to procure adequate supplies of ammunition and pay for his men, and sought to prevent communication and trading with the enemy.

Bayly declined to run for a second term in Congress in 1815. He served again in the house of delegates from 1819 to 1820 and from 1828 to 1831. As a delegate to the state constitutional convention of 1829-30, from which the constitution of 1830 emerged, he was active in an attempt to give the legislature authority over the county courts rather than embedding the existing powers of the latter in the new constitution. Bayly cited a letter by Jefferson complaining that as self-perpetuating bodies, the county courts had a disturbing potential for thwarting the people's will. Governor William B. Giles (A.B. 1781) responded that Jefferson was being quoted from a strange quarter, since "Mr. Bayly had seldom agreed with Mr. Jefferson, Bayly being a Federalist." In the event, Bayly's party lost, although their viewpoint prevailed in the constitution of 1852.

Bayly wed twice. In March 1802 he married Margaret Pettit Cropper, the daughter of John and Margaret Pettit Cropper. John Cropper was an officer in the Revolution and later president of the Virginia branch of the Society of the Cincinnati. Cropper's second wife Catherine was Bayly's sister. George Corbin (A.B. 1765) was Cropper's uncle, and James R. Corbin (Class of 1794) was his first cousin. Bayly had four daughters and a son by this marriage; the son, Thomas Henry Bayly, also became a member of Congress. Bayly must have been a widower by December 21, 1826, when he married Jane O. Addison, the widow of Col. Kendall Addison and the daughter of Samuel Coward. At least two daughters and a son Samuel were born of this marriage. It seems to have been a happy match. Bayly wrote his wife from Washington in 1831 that "I think I can never leave you again for you are not out of my mind five minutes in the day. I cannot be happy 200 miles from you." In addition to his wife and children, his will mentions "The Boy William P. Bayly," who received nothing but was to be educated until he turned twelve years of age and then apprenticed to "a Mechanical or Manufacturing trade in the State of Massachusetts." William was in the junior class of the College of William and Mary in December 1836, when a register of students described him as Thomas's son. Perhaps he was illegitimate.

Bayly died on January 7, 1834 and was buried at "Hills Farm." His will suggests that he had large debts; the profits of some of his lands were to be dedicated for five years to paying them, and other properties were to be sold for the same purpose.

SOURCES: R. T. Whitelaw, *Va.'s Eastern Shore* (1951), I, 621, 664; II, 815-17, 969, 978-84, 1003, 1044, 1058, 1061-64, 1071, 1076-78, 1080; *WMQ*, 1st ser., 7 (1899), 106-08; 2d ser., 11 (1931), 108; *VMHB*, 39 (1931), 56; *BDUSC*, 592-93; Min. Fac., 20 July 1792, 6 & 8 Jan. ("ill state," "diet in"), 13 May ("to repair"), 22 Aug. 1794; Clio. Min., 14 & 28 Aug. 1793, 8 Jan. & 22 Aug. 1794 ("formerly members"); Clio. lists; *Dunlap & Claypoole's Amer. Daily Advt.*, 7 Oct. 1794; *N.Y. Daily Advt.*, 4 Oct. 1798; MS will of TMB, 9 Mar. 1828, proved 27 Jan. 1834, David Higginbotham Papers, VHi ("attorney," "The Boy," "a Mechanical"); H. A. Johnson et al., eds., *Papers of John Marshall* (1974-), IV, 17-18; *A/C*, 13th Cong., 1st sess., 131-32, 479-81, 486; 13th Cong., 2d sess., 896-97, 1202-03, 1333-34; 13th Cong., 3d sess., 438-41 ("excise and," "to pay," "to possess," "Federal men," "when a"); als, Eliz. W. Gamble (Wirt) to TMB, 11 Mar. 1801, VHi ("let me not"); als, TMB to Daniel C. Brent, 27 Nov. 1801 ("I understand"), NHi (and in Microfilm Ed. of the Papers of Albert Gallatin, 1970, C. E. Prince, ed.); *Cal. Va. St. Papers*, IX, 342, 351; X, 257, 319-21, 334-36, 339-44, 346-48, 374-75, 388; L. C. Bell, *Old Free State* (1927), 306, 309-17, 320, 338 ("Mr. Bayly had"); *Princetonians, 1748-1768*, 488-89; S. Nottingham, *Marriage License Bonds of Accomack Cnty. Va. from 1774 to 1806* (1927), 3; S. Nottingham, *Marriage License Bonds of Northampton Cnty. Va. from 1706 to 1854* (1929 rep. 1974), 5; als, TMB to wife Jane, 7 May 1831, David Higginbotham Papers, VHi ("I think"); *WMQ*, 2d ser., 3 (1923), 281. See Whitelaw, II, 983, 1063, 1078 for photographs of "Hills Farm," "Mount Custis," and "Marino."

PUBLICATION: *The substance of several speeches of Thomas M. Bayly, delivered in the Convention of Virginia* (1830, R-B # 418).

MANUSCRIPTS: Vi; VHi; Preston Family Papers, ViU; NjP; Albert Gallatin Papers, NHi; John Tyler Papers, DLC

JJL

James Madison Broom

JAMES MADISON BROOM, A.B., attorney and public official, was born around 1776, one of three sons and six daughters of Jacob and Rachel Pierce Broom of Wilmington, Delaware. The mother was

James Madison Broom, A.B. 1794
BY CHARLES B. J. FEVRET DE SAINT MEMIN

the daughter of Robert Pierce, a tanner from Greenville, Christiana Hundred, near Wilmington, and of his wife Elizabeth. Jacob Broom was a merchant, surveyor, and manufacturer who was involved in schemes to build turnpikes and canals, tried unsuccessfully to mine bog iron, and served as first chairman of the Bank of Delaware's board of directors. He also built Wilmington's first cotton mill, but after it burned he sold the site to Eleuthère Irénée du Pont, who erected his first chemical factory there. Jacob Broom was also active politically. He served several terms as Wilmington's mayor, represented New Castle County in the state legislature, and was a Signer of the United States Constitution. He had Quaker ancestors but was himself an Episcopalian by 1773, and on July 2, 1784 he had James and three of his sisters baptized at Holy Trinity (Old Swedes) Episcopal Church. Jacob P. Broom (A.B. 1807) was James's brother.

In 1785 the elder Jacob Broom became a trustee of the Wilmington Public Grammar School, better known as the Wilmington Academy or the Old Academy. Perhaps James Broom received his preparatory training there. Sometime between November 29, 1790 and May 1791 Broom entered the College's sophomore class. At some point he joined the American Whig Society. He did not do well in his first two years at the College. In winter 1791 the faculty caught him and his classmate Moore Furman playing cards and made them promise to refrain in future. However, in September 1792 Broom and Furman were in a group of seven students swept up in another gambling crackdown. This time their crime was doubly heinous, for they were caught playing cards on the Sabbath. Of the seven involved, Broom and Furman received the harshest sentence, which obliged them to read from the stage of the Prayer Hall before the assembled student body a particularly abject confession that concluded with their promise "to renounce that pernicious practice which has rendered us negligent in our studies & brought us to this public disgrace."

Whether obsessive cardplaying or some other factor was to blame, Broom really had fallen behind in his studies. Twelve days later he failed to gain promotion to the next class after the examinations concluding the academic year. The faculty postponed a decision on his fate until classes resumed, when he and other deficient students were "to be examined on particular branches of their studies." The faculty minutes do not record a final decision with respect to Broom, whose name does not appear on the class list of October 10, 1792. Either he returned to classes late and then repeated his junior year, or he spent the year somewhere else. Whatever the case, his class standing improved dramatically after his next appearance in the College records, as a senior on November 11, 1793. His father may have been referring to academic improvement when he wrote his son on February 24, 1794: "Do not be so much flattered as to relax in your application; do not forget to be a Christian." At his commencement Broom stood sixth in a class of twenty-seven and gave one of the intermediate honors orations, a speech "on the just ideas of Liberty and Equality."

After his graduation Broom studied law. He was admitted to the bar of Sussex County, Delaware, on October 10, 1797 and to that of New Castle County in April 1801. He also became a solicitor of the chancery court of Kent County, Delaware, apparently before 1803. Perhaps the delay in joining the bar of New Castle, his home county, indicates that Broom received his training in Sussex County. He is said to have moved to the town of New Castle and begun a legal practice there at the time that he joined the New Castle county bar. A reference to him in a July 1803 letter as "Broom of New Castle" confirms this claim, as does the fact that in 1810 he still owned, but did not then occupy, a three-story brick house there, which he insured against fire for $2,000. He seems, however, to have stayed in New Castle only briefly before moving back to Wilmington. Letters from Broom dated November 10, 1803 and October 21, 1806 give his address as Wilmington, where he launched his political career.

When he was still quite young, Broom became a leader of Delaware Federalism. He belonged to a new breed of Federalists interested in emulating the improvements in political organization adopted by the Jeffersonians. Broom was accordingly involved in the creation of a statewide party organization. In August 1804 a meeting held at his residence in Wilmington established a party apparatus for Kent County.

James Ashton Bayard (A.B. 1784) won election to Delaware's sole seat in the United States House of Representatives in 1804, but shortly thereafter he was elected to the Senate and therefore resigned his House seat. Broom won the special election in October 1805. Since the first session of the Ninth Congress did not convene until December 2, Broom's was essentially an election to a full term. His maiden speech in a contested election dispute on December 24 favorably impressed Samuel Taggart, a colleague from Massachusetts and a fellow Federalist. Taggart wrote that Broom

> offers fair to be no unworthy successor to Bayard. He is a young man, said to be hardly thirty, altho from his appearance I should suppose him thirty five. He has the advantage of prepossessing exterior. I think he offers fair to prove one of the first orators I have heard in the House of Representatives. He is said to be a very powerful pleader at the bar.

Taggart had also heard from a Pennsylvania clergyman that Broom "is a man of unblemished morals, and strictly a religious character."

Broom spoke regularly and took part in most roll call votes while he was present during his term in the House, but for unknown reasons he seems to have absented himself during the last, busiest month of both sessions. On January 21, 1806 he favored a bill to tax imported slaves, the most extreme antislavery measure constitutionally available to Congress before 1808. Broom forcefully answered the objections of critics of the measure, including Peter Early (A.B. 1792). He dismissed as frivolous their contentions that the tax would bring tainted money into the Treasury and give the trade respectability and some right to claim protection. Taxing luxuries of dubious value had always been viewed as a means of expressing governmental disapproval, and the tainted money argument he saw as logically equivalent to saying that by the use of convict labor a government immorally profited from and sponsored crime. The important thing, in his estimation, was to tax the trade to the full extent permitted by law until it could be banned, especially since the near certain passage of a ban on the slave trade as soon as the constitutional deadline expired was likely to lead to an influx of imports in the ensuing months. Nonetheless, the measure did not pass.

Broom's opposition to slavery had found expression earlier when he worked from 1801 to 1807 as an attorney of the Delaware Society for Promoting the Abolition of Slavery. He received a small retainer but his services, which involved securing the release of illegally held blacks and prosecuting white kidnappers, clearly were motivated by philosophical rather than financial considerations. On July 28, 1804 the society sponsored a lecture in Wilmington by Broom on the "injustice and impolicy of Slavery." When Broom's father Jacob died some years later, he willed $500 to a school for blacks.

On January 13, 1807 Broom spoke in favor of abolishing the so-called "Mediterranean fund" as well as the salt tax. He thought neither duty was necessary, since the budget would show a healthy surplus without them and too much money would only enable the government to get into mischief. The high point in Broom's political career came in February 1807 when he proposed an innocuous-sounding resolution urging better protection of federal prisoners' rights to the writ of *habeas corpus*. The measure actually was a transparent Federalist attempt to make political capital out of the Burr Conspiracy furor. Dr. Justus Erich Bollmann and Samuel Swartwout, the couriers of Aaron Burr (A.B. 1772), were arrested in New Orleans by order of Gen. James Wilkinson when confusion and concern over Burr's intentions peaked. Wilkinson ignored a *habeas corpus* for their release and sent them in irons to President Thomas Jefferson (LL.D. 1791) at Washington. Broom argued that this action showed that existing laws were insufficient and that constitutionally guaranteed liberties were in danger of military usurpation. Broom's motion was defeated in the House, but the United States Supreme Court later granted the writ and released the two men.

Broom was elected without opposition to a second term in 1806, but he resigned in August 1807 before the new Congress convened because he had moved to Baltimore. Nicholas Van Dyke (A.B. 1788) succeeded him. In Baltimore Broom lived at 20 North Calvert Street and continued to practice law. His move to Maryland may have been prompted by a need to protect the interests of his second wife or a desire to be near her relatives.

Broom had married and become a widower by the summer of 1803, as evidenced by letters to Ann Ridgely of Dover from her daughter and namesake, a friend of Broom's. Even though he had just become engaged to Ann Driver, at that time he was still grieving for his first wife, of whom all that has been discovered is that she had relatives in England. The younger Ann Ridgely commented that after taking her for an evening spin in his "four wheeled Gigg," Broom had

> begged me to come down and set with him, for that he was lonesome and disgusted at the idea of dissipation. I never saw any man so agitated and distressed as he was.

He had just been reminded of his first wife, and

> he spoke in the most affectionate and exalted terms of her.... I think I never met with any man possess't of so much sensibility, tho' at the same time I think him imprudent to express himself as he does when he is engaged to be married so soon. Ann Driver is a sweet engaging Girl but too gay for him. He says he cannot bear it.

It is only fair to add that Ann Ridgely's mother responded acidly that those who talked most about sensibility usually had the least, that Broom was a "male coquette," and that she did not like her daughter "flirting round N. Castle 'till 10 o'clock at night in a gay gig."

Ann Driver was the daughter of Matthew Driver, a planter and public official of Caroline County, Maryland, probably by his second wife Esther, the daughter of Henry and Esther Baynard Casson. Broom married her sometime before August 15, 1806. His letter to her of that date mentions their daughter Rachel. This marriage too seems to have been of short duration. Broom next wed a daughter of Daniel Lowber, a Wilmington tanner. The three unions produced at least four children, including Matthew D. Broom (Class of 1828) and Jacob Broom, presidential candidate of the Native American Party in 1852 and United States congressman from Pennsylvania, 1855-57.

Broom resided in Baltimore only briefly. He moved back to Wilmington around 1810, probably as a result of the death of his father in March of that year. He replaced his father on the board of directors of the Bank of Delaware and continued practicing law. Late in 1812 he formed a law partnership with John Davis. After its dissolution in 1815 he entered into partnership with John Wales (A.B. Yale 1801). Broom kept law offices in town but resided on a suburban estate located at present-day Broom and Chestnut streets, where he built a mansion he called "Tusculum," possibly recalling John Witherspoon's country home as well as Cicero's villa. At the second meeting of the Delaware Bible Society, on December 21, 1813, Broom joined and was elected a director. In April 1815 he was involved in an effort, which eventually failed because of insufficient funds, to build a new Episcopal church to replace or supplement the inconveniently located Holy Trinity Church.

Broom moved to Philadelphia in spring 1818. He was admitted to the city's bar on March 16, and an 1819 city directory gives his residence as 95-97 Walnut Street. He lived in Philadelphia the rest of his life and continued practicing law until within a year of his death. During their years in Philadelphia, both Broom and his third wife became "very stout." He is said to have weighed almost 400 pounds.

Broom joined the Philadelphia Society for Promoting Agriculture and gave the annual address at its meeting on January 16, 1821. In this talk he blamed the depression of 1819 on the peace in Europe ending an American commercial boom which had engendered unrealistic expectations and luxurious tastes. He prescribed a return to traditional frugality coupled with migration from cities to the land. He also urged the society to promote research on labor-saving machinery, soil chemistry and fertilizers, and crop rotation, and to encourage the founding of agricultural schools. From 1821-22 he served a term in the Pennsylvania House of Representatives, during which he reversed his position against foreign luxuries by attacking the state tax on retailers of foreign merchandise as "unconstitutional, unnecessary, unjust, oppressive and vexatious." Around 1828 he moved from Walnut to South 6th Street, and remained there until 1841. Between 1842 and 1850 Broom moved several times, which might point to financial problems in his old age but could easily be explained in other ways as well. He died on January 15, 1850 and was interred in St. Mary's Churchyard in Hamilton Village, now part of Philadelphia.

SOURCES: J. H. Martin, *Chester (& its Vicinity), Del. Cnty. in Pa.* (1877), 276-77, 281-85 ("very stout"); H. Burr, *Records of Holy Trinity (Old Swedes) Church, Wilmington, Del.* (1890, Papers of the Hist. Soc. of Del., IX), 505-06, 539, 543, 655, 668-69, 740; J. T. Scharf, *Hist. of Del.* (1888), I, 564-66, 572, 574; II, 651, 653, 708, 733-34, 828; W. W. Campbell, *Life & Character of Jacob Broom* (1909, Papers of the Hist. Soc. of Del., LI), *passim* ("Do not," 27); C. E. Hoffecker, *Del.: A Bicentennial Hist.* (1977), 34, 36; *Del. Hist.*, 3 (1948/49), 55, 181, 211-26; 4 (1951), 215-16; 8 (1958), 58, 69; 10 (1963), 300, 302, 306-07 ("injustice and impolicy"); 12 (1966/67), 144 ("unconstitutional"); 14 (1970), 79; 16 (1974/75), 6; Min. Fac., class list ca. May 1791, 10-11 Sept. ("to renounce") & 22 Sept. 1792 ("to be examined"), 11 Nov. 1793, 22 Aug. 1794; Amer. Whig Soc., *Cat.* (1840), 7; Williams, *Academic Honors*, 14; *Dunlap & Claypoole's Amer. Daily Advt.*, 7 Oct. 1794 ("on the just"); M. L. Ridgely, *Ridgelys of Del. & Their Circle* (1949), 260-63, 265-68 ("Broom of New Castle," "four wheeled," "begged me," "male coquette," "flirting round"); L. de Valinger & V. E. Shaw, *Calendar of Ridgely Family Letters 1742-1899* (1948-61), I, 236-37, 257, 265, 268; II, 103, 106, 108, 112, 118, 120, 147, 166, 181, 195, 211, 256, 278-79, 282; III, 79; D. H. Fischer, *Revolution of Amer. Conservatism* (1965), 59, 63, 107, 355 ("young Federalists"); Del. Public Archives Commission, *Governor's Register State of Del. ... 1674-1851* (1926), 56-58, 61, 63; "Letters of Samuel Taggart, Representative in Congress, 1803-14," *AASP*, n.s., 33 (1923), 167 ("offers fair," "is a man"); *A/C*, 9th Cong., 1st sess., 254, 282, 365-71, 373; 9th Cong., 2d sess., 308-12, 502-08, 520-26, 589; A. J. Beveridge, *Life of John Marshall* (1929), III, 357; city directories: Balt., 1810; Wilmington, 1814; Phila., 1818-50; *Biog. Dict. Md. Leg.*, I, 282-83; als, JMB to "My Dear Ann," 15 Aug. 1806, NjP; nongraduate file, alumni file, PUA; E. Montgomery, *Wilmington* (1851 repr. 1971),

75; J. A. Munroe, *Federalist Del. 1775-1815* (1954), 250, 253; *Martin's Bench & Bar*, 252; D. P. Brown, *Forum* (1856), II, 340; letter from Pa. Hist. & Museum Commission, 11 Apr. 1985, PUA; J. M. Broom, *Address Delivered Before the Phila. Soc. for Promoting Agriculture* (1821, Sh-C # 4844), *passim*; *BDUSC*, 677-78.

Broom used the middle initial M. at least as early as 1797. Why he or his father chose to honor James Madison (A.B 1771) in naming Broom is far from clear, unless Jacob Broom became friendly with Madison at the Constitutional Convention. No evidence to support such a connection has been found. Broom could also have been named for another James Madison, the Episcopal bishop of Virginia from 1790 to 1812, but here too no evidence of such a connection has come to light.

Around 1835 Broom's Philadelphia address changed from 56 to 79 S. 6th Street, but whether he had moved or the street's numbering had simply been changed is unclear. The Princetonian should not be confused with James M. Broom, his first cousin, a first lieutenant of marines who was killed on board the *U.S.S. Chesapeake* on June 1, 1813.

PUBLICATIONS: Sh-C # 4844; R-B # 23570; & joint author, Horace Binney et al., *Opinion ... on the Several Acts of Assembly Relating to the Lehigh Coal & Navigation Co.* (1835).

MANUSCRIPTS: NjP; NjP-SSP; Public Archives Commission of Del; Hist. Soc. of Del; Eleutherian Mills Hist. Lib., Greenville, Del.; Pa. Hist. & Museum Commission, Phila.

JJL

Andrew Caldwell

ANDREW CALDWELL entered the College as a freshman sometime between November 1790 and the end of the calendar year. His name was not on the College steward's list for the earlier date, and the Cliosophic Society includes him as one of the last to join in 1790, where he used the name Honorius. Only in the Cliosophic records is he identified as being from Pennsylvania. These same records also place him with the Class of 1793 and indicate that at one point the society suspended him for four weeks. By May 1791 he was listed with the freshman class, indicating either that the Cliosophic records are mistaken in identifying him as a sophomore or that he had failed his examinations and been reduced to a freshman.

Caldwell did not return in the fall of 1791. He may have been the Andrew Caldwell of Pennsylvania, "Further record unknown," who became a nongraduate member of the Class of 1794 at Dickinson College.

Intact Cliosophic Society records are copies of the original. Although the copies are undated they were made at a time when roughly only one-third of the members of the classes in the 1790s were deceased. Caldwell's inclusion in this group suggests a youthful demise.

SOURCES: Clio. lists; Min. Fac., class list ca. May 1791; G. L. Reed, *Alumni Record Dickinson College* (1905), 44.

E. S. Arnett, in *David Caldwell* (1976), 73, claims that Samuel, Alexander, and Andrew, the three eldest sons of David Caldwell (A.B. 1761) of North Carolina, all attended the College of New Jersey. There is no record of Samuel and Alexander ever having matriculated. Andrew could be considered for the subject of this sketch only if he was staying with his father's relatives in Lancaster County, Pennsylvania, and could therefore claim that state as his residence.

A more likely candidate for the Princeton student is the Andrew Caldwell, born July 29, 1777, who was the son of James and Sarah Mitchell Caldwell. The son was baptised in the First Presbyterian Church of Philadelphia on August 23, 1779. In the same church on December 27, 1798 Caldwell married Bathsheba Kille, daughter of Mary Kille and the late John Kille, with the Reverend Dr. John Ewing (A.B. 1754) officiating. The Killes were Quakers of Woolwich Township, Gloucester County, New Jersey. When John Kille died in 1793 he left an estate valued at £5,265.10.12, with Bathsheba receiving £500 and fifty-six acres of meadowland.

It is not known when the Caldwells moved to Haddonfield, New Jersey, also in Gloucester County. Andrew died there on July 10, 1806 and was interred in the burial ground of the Philadelphia First Presbyterian Church. His will identifies him as being of Waterford Township, which encompassed the town of Haddonfield. Bathsheba Caldwell died in Haddonfield in 1843. Neither of their wills mentions children. Andrew left an estate worth $3,028.00, including four shares in the Haddonfield Library Company. See T. Cushing & C. E. Sheppard, *Hist. of the Cnties. of Gloucester, Salem & Cumberland, N.J.* (1883), 297; records of First Pres. Church of Phila.; Phila. *True Amer. & Commercial Advt.*, 29 Dec. 1798, 11 July 1806; *N.J. Wills*, xi, 55; will & estate inv. of John Kille, estate inv. of Andrew Caldwell, will & estate inv. of Bathsheba Caldwell, Nj.

RLW

George Washington Campbell

GEORGE WASHINGTON CAMPBELL, A.B., teacher, lawyer, public official, judge, and diplomat, was born on February 8, 1769, in the parish of Tongue, Sutherlandshire, Scotland, the youngest of the ten children of Archibald and Elizabeth Mackay Matheson Campbell. The mother was a resident of Tongue before her marriage and the widow of Duncan Matheson. The father was a physician who moved his family in 1772 to Mecklenburg County, North Carolina, near or at the site of present-day Charlotte. There he worked a farm and apparently earned a middling income until his death in 1782. Three of his sons died fighting the British in the Revolution, and family tradition maintains that young George showed his patriotic zeal during the war by adopting Washington as his middle name.

Campbell's relatively advanced age at the time of his entrance to the College may have been dictated by financial constraints. He taught school, probably in or near Mecklenburg County, for a time before November 1793 when he entered the College's senior class. During his year on campus he joined the American Whig Society, and at his commencement he gave "an oration on the importance of the Mathematical sciences." The order in which the faculty listed the various

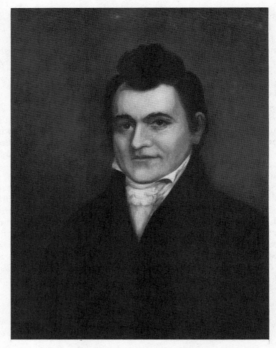

George Washington Campbell, A.B. 1794

speakers in their minutes suggests that Campbell stood fourth in his class. John Henry Hobart (A.B. 1793) wrote on August 26, 1794 that "[Thomas Yardley] How and Campbell were competitors for the Latin Salutatory." The statement could imply that Campbell ranked as high as second, but it was probably colored by Hobart's Whig loyalties.

After graduation, Campbell probably taught at a school in Trenton, New Jersey, while he began reading law. He continued his studies upon returning to North Carolina. Shortly after being admitted to the bar there, he moved to Knoxville, Tennessee, and on March 15, 1798 he was licensed to practice law in that state. Campbell immediately achieved great success as a lawyer. Along with virtually all other frontier lawyers, the bulk of his work involved disputed titles to land. This work yielded specialized knowledge both of what claims would hold up in court and of which were the choicest lands, information that served him well when he began speculating in real estate himself.

In October 1801 Campbell and three opponents sought to fill Tennessee's single seat in the House of Representatives, made vacant when William C. C. Claiborne resigned to become governor of Mississippi Territory. Campbell lost but gained publicity which helped him in 1803, when he won election to one of the three seats Tennessee held after reapportionment. The three seats were contested at large, and Campbell came in second. In 1805 the at-large system was scrapped in favor of election from districts, and in that year and again in 1807 he was returned without opposition from the Hamilton district in East Tennessee, which included Knoxville. Congressional elections in Tennessee at this time were held during odd-numbered years, after the old Congress expired but before the new one convened.

Campbell was a Jeffersonian whose abilities as a speaker earned him recognition as one of the leaders of the House during his six years of service. He first spoke on October 24, 1803 in the debate on the constitutional amendment to clarify the procedure for electing presidents so as to prevent a repeat of the Jefferson/Burr crisis of 1800-01. Campbell argued that elections thrown into the House should be restricted to the top two, rather than the three leading candidates, in order better to reflect the people's will. He voted to fund the Louisiana Purchase but objected violently to the Breckenridge bill creating a government for the new territory, because it provided for an appointive rather than an elective legislature. Rhetorically he asked those who "talk of the abuse of the elective franchise, to point out a solitary instance where the people have abused the rights they acquired under it? They will find it hard to point out one." Despotism, on the other hand, was always abused. Campbell and his backers succeeded in limiting the authorization for the appointed council to one year.

In January 1804 Campbell was chosen one of eleven House managers of the Senate trial of United States District Judge John Pickering of New Hampshire, who was impeached and removed from office for alcoholism and misconduct despite his insanity defense. In December the House also chose him to help conduct the Senate trial of Supreme Court Justice Samuel Chase, impeached in what amounted to an effort to see if the Federalist judiciary could be brought to book for its partisan behavior following the passage of the Alien and Sedition Acts. Campbell became one of the seven managers by a narrow margin, being the only one not chosen on the first ballot. At the trial he spoke immediately after Peter Early (A.B. 1792) on February 20-21, 1805. Several contemporaries agree that his speech was tedious. Federalist Senator William Plumer, admittedly a hostile witness, went into the most detail:

The speech of Mr. Campbell was feeble indeed—his law was incorrect—his statements confused—& his concessions fatal to

his cause. He was much embarrassed—He had copious notes—
they confused him—He is a disagreeable speaker—Most of the
Members of the other House left the Chamber, & a large portion
of the spectators, long before he sat down.

Representative Samuel Taggart observed that Campbell's presentation "was as usual for him, a very dull one."

In substance as well as style, Campbell's performance in the Chase
trial has not been well received, with one historian arguing that it was
"a disaster for the prosecution." Campbell maintained that Chase's
malicious intent could be inferred from his actions. He postulated
"as a settled rule of decision, that when a man violates a law, or com-
mits a manifest breach of his duty, an evil intent or corrupt motive
must be presumed to have actuated his conduct." Thus, he argued,
a defendant maintaining that his misconduct had been unintentional
or done with good motives must offer supporting proof. Had this
assertion held up it would have shifted to the defense the burden of
proving that Chase had acted in good faith, but the defense quickly
and effectually discredited it. Campbell also held that impeachment is
"a kind of inquest into the conduct of an officer, merely as it regards
his office," something "more in the nature of a civil investigation,
than of a criminal prosecution," with conviction amounting not to a
criminal punishment, but simply to "a deprivation of rights, a declaration that the person is not properly qualified to serve his country."
This attempt to divorce impeachment from private wrongdoing and
equate it with a political no-confidence motion was in keeping with
the English tradition. It did not, however, consort well with the actual
language of the Constitution, as Chase's defenders demonstrated to
the satisfaction not only of the Senate, which acquitted Chase, but of
Campbell's colleagues, who had abandoned the argument before the
trial closed.

Early in 1807 a new seat on the Supreme Court was created. The
new justice was to preside over a circuit encompassing Kentucky,
Ohio, and Tennessee. Since some familiarity with their laws would
be essential, the act provided that the justice be a resident of one of
these states. President Thomas Jefferson (LL.D. 1791) asked a caucus
of their congressmen to recommend a candidate, and Campbell was
chosen. Since, however, choice of a sitting congressman would violate
the constitutional provision against appointing a congressman to a
position he had voted to create, and since, moreover, Jefferson was
not enthusiastic about the selection of Campbell, he chose instead
Thomas Todd of Kentucky. John Randolph (Class of 1791) reported
disgustedly that before this outcome Campbell, "that Prince of Prigs
and Puppies," and his supporters had unsuccessfully tried to get

around the constitutional ban by the subterfuge of amending the bill creating the judgeship so that it would take effect after Campbell's term ended on March 3.

Jefferson may have thought Campbell lacked the stature to sit on the Supreme Court, but his loyalty to the administration soon earned him other rewards. Campbell replaced the erratic Randolph as chairman of the House Ways and Means Committee in the 1807-08 session, and in the 1808-09 session his position as administration floor leader was enhanced when he took the chair both of Ways and Means and of the Select Committee on Foreign Relations. The dominant concerns at this time were neutral rights and the impressment of American seamen, and Campbell consistently took a strong line, backing the Embargo and, despite his distrust on principle of standing armies, supporting defense appropriations. When Congressman Barent Gardenier of New York accused the majority in February 1808 of acting under the influence of France rather than out of zeal for the interests of the United States, Campbell was among the enraged Embargo supporters who responded on the floor of the House by saying the nastiest things about Gardenier that came to mind. The object of the exercise seems to have been to see who could provoke Gardenier into a challenge, and Campbell, who had accused him of displaying "the basest malignity of heart" and of speaking "in the frantic strains of a raving maniac," won. In the ensuing duel outside Washington on March 2 Campbell shot Gardenier in the chest. Gardenier survived, and Campbell is said to have met his future wife, Harriet Stoddert, the daughter of Rebecca Lowndes Stoddert and Benjamin Stoddert, secretary of the navy under John Adams, when he visited the convalescing Gardenier. If so, the courtship was a long one, for Campbell did not marry her until July 1812.

On November 28, 1808 Campbell submitted to the House a report summarizing British and French naval depredations and arguing that war or a continuation of the Embargo were America's only alternatives. Although probably written by Albert Gallatin and James Madison (A.B. 1771), the document came to be known as Campbell's Report, and he continued to accept its logic even after public opinion and the majority in Congress turned against it. In his last speech in the House, on February 20-21, 1809, he argued vehemently that the projected repeal of the Embargo would "degrade the nation" unless coupled with a vote for war.

Campbell announced in April 1809 that he would not seek another term in Congress, citing poor health and a desire to concentrate on his private interests as reasons. Disgust at the repeal of the Embargo may also have been a factor, but illness plagued Campbell throughout his public career and explains his missing much of the 1808-09 session. On November 24, 1809 he became a judge of the newly created Tennessee Supreme Court of Errors and Appeals. The act which created the court also divided the state into five districts, each with a circuit judge. The supreme court's two judges were to travel in sequence to each of the districts where, in combination with the circuit judge there, they would sit as Tennessee's highest court. Campbell served only briefly and seems to have been completely overshadowed by his colleague, Hugh Lawson White. His interests remained focused on the national political scene, and he eagerly traded his judgeship for a seat in the United States Senate when he was elected to complete Jenkins Whiteside's unfinished term on October 1, 1811.

In the Senate Campbell sided with the congressional war hawks, voting for all measures to build up the military and writing home that in the likely event that Britain did not back down, the United States must retrieve "its lost character by washing off the stains on its honor in the blood of its enemies." He soon got his war and quickly became a leader of the administration party in the Senate. He served as chairman of the Committee on Military Affairs in the 1812-13 and 1813-14 sessions but not in the special session of May to August 1813, when he chaired the Foreign Relations Committee instead.

On February 8, 1814 President Madison chose Campbell to succeed Gallatin as secretary of the treasury, and Campbell accordingly resigned from the Senate. Daniel Webster (LL.D. 1818) observed that the choice of Campbell "is very unfavorable to Peace. He is the mere creature of [Secretary of War John] Armstrong, Jr. [Class of 1776], & is a great zealot for the War, & the conquest of Canada." Wags were soon commenting that Campbell's initials also stood for "Government Wants Cash."

Campbell's brief tenure at the Treasury was unfortunate. The government's finances were bad when he arrived but far worse when he left some eight months later. His final report to Congress predicted a shortfall of $50 million through the ensuing fiscal year and offered no guidance as to how the deficit might be made up, a conclusion Henry Adams later condemned as "an admission of incompetence." Most of the situation, however, was beyond Campbell's control. Congress refused to vote heavy taxes. Disaffection with the war was so great in New England that those with capital there would not lend to the government no matter how favorable the terms. This situation goes far to explain the dubious success of the ten million dollar bond issue Campbell floated in May and the total failure of the six million dollar loan he tried to raise in the summer, although his handling of the two loans was not very astute. The government's fiscal position did not become really desperate until the British capture of Washington in August sparked a fiscal collapse in which virtually every bank in the nation outside of New England suspended specie payments. Without the leverage a national bank might have provided, the ensuing loss of any national circulating medium of exchange was inevitable. The best verdict on Campbell's tenure at the Treasury may be that while intractable realities made a financial crisis unavoidable no matter who headed the Treasury, he lacked both the imagination and the background in finance which might have enabled him to ameliorate the state of affairs.

Campbell attended the cabinet meeting on the morning of the fall of Washington, August 24, 1814, but was too ill to proceed to the site of the battle of Bladensburg. Before leaving the presidential party, he advised Madison that Armstrong was sulking about not being field commander and intended to play no role at all in the upcoming battle. This revelation prompted Madison to command Armstrong to offer such advice as occurred to him to Gen. William Henry Winder. The order only led to even more of the meddling by politicians that contributed to the ensuing fiasco. Although Campbell missed the battle, his duelling pistols did not. He loaned them to Madison, who lost them in the hectic retreat which followed, much to the delight of Federalist newswriters. Some historians assert that Campbell's departure from the Treasury was prompted either by humiliation at the capture of Washington or by his own recognition that he had failed as secretary. The disgrace of his ally Armstrong could also have played a role. Nonetheless, "the very impaired state of my health" he cited in his letter of resignation on September 26, 1814 seems to have been genuine enough. The day before, Secretary of the Navy William Jones said Campbell was so ill that "to continue would destroy him." On his way home to Tennessee Campbell spent some time recuperating at mineral springs in Virginia.

Campbell told his friends he intended to stay in private life for several years. He did refuse to run for a United States Senate seat made vacant by a resignation in March 1815, but as his health improved so did his interest in politics. On October 15, 1815 he accepted election to the Senate, which recognized his experience by making him chairman of the Finance Committee. As such he reported to the Senate in March 1816 the bill creating the Second Bank of the United States. After urging some amendment, he voted for the bill in its final form. During this term Campbell's main accomplishment was obtaining passage in March 1818, after repeated efforts, of a bill opening to settlement federal lands in the so-called Congressional Reservation, which included much of western Tennessee. He was also involved in efforts by Tennessee to negotiate land purchases from the Indians.

Campbell remained an administration loyalist and was rewarded by President James Monroe (LL.D. 1822) with appointment on April 13, 1818 as envoy extraordinary and minister plenipotentiary to Russia. After a trip home to settle his affairs, Campbell left Washington on July 3 and sailed from Boston for his new post on the naval frigate *Guerriere* on July 22. He stopped in Copenhagen on his way and had an interview with the Danish foreign minister in which he obtained permission for the United States to send a consul unofficially to St. Thomas in the Danish West Indies. He arrived in St. Petersburg on September 7 and was formally presented to Tsar Alexander I, who had been out of the country when he arrived, on February 7, 1819.

Campbell seems to have been a reasonably effective diplomat. His main task was to find out what he could about Russia's intentions regarding Spain, which was seeking support from the Holy Alliance in efforts to suppress the revolutions in its Latin American possessions, and also to find a way to avoid relinquishing Florida to the United States. Campbell's initial dispatches maintained that Russia would support Spain strongly as part of its policy of defending legitimacy, although its backing might fall short of military intervention. However, he eventually sent word that Russian ardor for Spain had cooled as a result of Spain's refusal to accept British mediation of its conflict with its Latin American colonies.

Campbell's stay in Russia was marred by tragedy in April 1819, when his three eldest children died of typhus in a single week. Grief at this disaster and concern for the health of what was left of his family prompted him to request his recall, though he agreed to serve for one more winter in order to permit a successor to be chosen and prevent too rapid a turnover at the posting. He left St. Petersburg on July 8, 1820, and after a stopover in London and a brief visit to Paris, he reached New York City on October 29 and Tennessee on January 7, 1821.

In January 1810 Campbell had moved from Knoxville to Nashville, apparently in order to facilitate looking after his sizable and growing landholdings, which were increasingly located in middle Tennessee. After his Russian mission ended, he went back to Nashville and announced the resumption of his legal practice in January 1822. His return to private life may not have been entirely welcome to him. He told Monroe when he resigned his diplomatic post that he would consider accepting one in a warmer climate, but the hint was ignored. While abroad, he seems to have lost touch with his power base in Tennessee, for in 1845 a Tennessean discussing possible cabinet appointments observed that a Virginian who had served in an embassy "has no hold on the popular affection of Virginia—He stands there pretty much as G. W. Campbell stood in Tennessee after he returned from Russia."

In January 1822 Governor Joseph McMinn appointed Campbell first vice president of the Bank of the State of Tennessee, which was founded by the legislature in an effort to relieve those suffering in the wake of the panic of 1819. Campbell remained connected with the bank for some time but apparently avoided being linked to the charges of financial mismanagement and corruption which marked its closing in 1829-31. In July 1831 he became a director of the Nashville branch of the Bank of the United States, a branch founded in 1827 after he and 200 other Nashville residents petitioned for it. From 1838 to 1842 he served as a director of the Nashville branch of the Bank of Tennessee.

Campbell was one of the thirty trustees chosen on December 3, 1807 as part of the reorganization by which Blount College at Knoxville became East Tennessee College, now the University of Tennessee. After he moved to Nashville he became a trustee of Cumberland College, later renamed the University of Nashville, and may thus have had a hand in the selection as president by that institution in 1824 of Philip Lindsley (A.B. 1804), vice president of the College of New Jersey from 1817 to 1824.

Andrew Jackson was acquainted with Campbell from at least September 5, 1801, when they were involved in the opening of a Masonic lodge, and they remained friends and correspondents from then on. Campbell presided over several Nashville dinners honoring Jackson. When President Monroe offered Jackson the post of secretary of war in 1817, Campbell declined the offer on Jackson's behalf, and in March 1822 he sounded out Jackson on behalf of friends who wanted him to run for president. In the 1828 election he served on the Nashville Jackson committee. A letter Campbell wrote Jackson on January 14, 1831 gave his reaction to Jackson's recent State of the Union address. He enthusiastically supported Jackson's stance on the tariff, internal improvements, and Indian policy, although he ventured from his experience as treasury secretary to disagree with Jackson's attack on the Bank of the United States. In 1836 Campbell supported Martin Van Buren, numbering himself among the "sound Democratic Republicans of the old Jeffersonian School, ... strongly attached personally & politically" to Jackson and opposed to those who "abandoned that party, & united with the opposition composed of Federalists, nullifiers & malcontents of all discriptions."

On his deathbed in 1845, Jackson chose Campbell to help arrange his funeral.

Jackson appointed Campbell to his last public office, a seat on the French Spoliation Claims Commission, on July 14, 1832. In the Rives Treaty with France, concluded July 4, 1831, France agreed to pay the United States 25 million francs, not quite $10 million, as indemnity for its seizures of neutral American shipping during the life of Napoleon's Continental System. Congress accordingly created a three-man commission to decide which claims were valid and distribute the money. Given Campbell's experience in Congress when the seizures were in progress, his selection was justifiable whatever his connection to Jackson. His colleagues seem to have acknowledged his status and regarded him as the unofficial chairman. The commission sat in Washington off and on from September 17, 1832 to December 31, 1835. A total of 3,148 claims involving 883 attacks on American shipping were heard, of which 1,567 petitions arising from 361 attacks were ruled valid. The final payout amounted to a little more than fifty cents on the dollar for valid claims. In some instances the commission was faced with situations in which no precedent in international law existed and was obliged to offer judgments on law as well as fact.

Campbell came home to Nashville for good in 1836. In 1840 Governor James K. Polk offered to appoint him to finish the Senate term of Felix Grundy, who had died in office, but Campbell declined. On December 11, 1843 he sold to the city the site of his house on Cedars Knob, sometimes called Campbell's Hill, for $30,000. The city had promised the state legislature that it would provide the site for a new capitol building if it were made the state's permanent capital, and Campbell's land was judged most suitable. He reaped a large profit from the sale, although the story that he originally got the land for two cows is apocryphal.

Campbell died on February 17, 1848 and was buried in the Nashville City Cemetery. He was a wealthy man by the time of his death. His will shows that he owned more than 14,000 acres of land plus substantial holdings in turnpike stock and shares in a Nashville hotel. Slaves are also mentioned, and although no numbers are given, he owned about twenty earlier in his life. Two of his children, a son and a daughter, reached adulthood. The daughter, born in St. Petersburg and named Lyzinka, the Russian form of Elizabeth, was married at least twice, the second time to her cousin Richard Stoddert Ewell, lieutenant general in the Confederate Army.

SOURCES: W. T. Jordan, *George Washington Campbell of Tenn.: Western Statesman* (1955), *passim* ("that Prince," 28; "its lost character," 96, quote from *Wilson's Knoxville Gazette*,

16 Dec. 1811; "very impaired," 130); Min. Fac., 11 Nov. 1793, 22 Aug. 1794; Amer. Whig Soc., *Cat.* (1840), 7; *Dunlap & Claypoole's Amer. Daily Advt.*, 7 Oct. 1794 ("an oration"); J. McVickar, *Early Years of the late Bishop Hobart* (2d ed., 1836), 83 ("How and"); *A/C*, 8th Cong., 1st sess. to 10th Cong., 2d sess.; 12th Cong., 1st sess. to 13th Cong., 2d sess.; 14th Cong., 1st sess. to 15th Cong., 1st sess., *passim* ("talk of," 8th Cong., 1st sess., 1064; "a kind of inquest," 8th Cong., 2nd sess., 332; "as a settled," same, 341; "the basest," 10th Cong., 1st sess., 1672; "degrade the nation," 10th Cong., 2d sess., 1478); E. S. Brown, ed., *William Plumer's Memorandum of Proc. in the U.S. Senate 1803-07* (1923), 295-97 ("The speech"); "Letters of Samuel Taggart, Representative in Congress, 1803-14," *AASP*, n.s., 33 (1923), 116, 212, 309-10, 428 ("was as usual," "Government Wants Cash"); W. P. Cutler & J. P. Cutler, *Life, Journals & Corres. of Rev. Manasseh Cutler LL.D.* (1888), II, 183-84; I. Brant, *Impeachment: Trials & Errors* (1972), 66 ("a disaster"); P. C. Hoffer & N. E. H. Hull, *Impeachment in Amer. 1603-1805* (1984), 243-45; H. Adams, *Hist. of the U.S.A. during the 1st Admin. of Thomas Jefferson* (1889 repr. 1909), II, 224-31; C. F. Adams, ed., *Memoirs of John Quincy Adams* (1874-77), I, 517; IV, 72-73, 76-78; H. Adams, *Hist. of the U.S.A. during the 2d Admin. of Thomas Jefferson* (1890 repr. 1909), II, 153, 202-03, 370-72, 380-83, 426, 448; I. Brant, *James Madison: Sec. of State, 1800-09* (1953), 441, 471; *Jour. of the House of Rep. of the U.S.* (1826), VI, 12-13, 340, 348-49; R. V. Harlow, *Hist. of Legislative Methods in the Period Before 1825* (1917), 215-16; *East Tenn. Hist. Soc.'s Pubs.*, 19 (1947), 22-23; H. Adams, *Hist. of the U.S.A. during the 1st Admin. of James Madison* (1890 repr. 1909), II, 150-51; H. Adams, *Hist. of the U.S.A. during the 2d Admin. of James Madison* (1891 repr. 1911), I, 396-97; II, 17-19, 122, 137, 152, 213, 239-42 ("an admission"); C. M. Wiltse & H. D. Moser, eds., *Papers of Daniel Webster: Corres., I, 1798-1824* (1974), 163, 165 ("is very unfavorable"); I. Brant, *James Madison: Commander in Chief 1812-36* (1961), 241, 258-60, 267-72, 312, 328-30 ("to continue would"); *A/C*, 13th Cong., 3d sess., Appendix, 1479-97 (GWC's final report as Treasury Sec.); E. R. Taus, *Central Banking Functions of the U.S. Treasury 1789-1941* (1943), 24-26; W. T. Jordan, ed., "Diary of George Washington Campbell, American minister to Russia, 1818 to 1820," *THQ*, 7 (1948), 152-70, 259-80; J. C. Hildt, *Early Diplomatic Negotiations of the U.S. with Russia* (1906), 120-27, 134-36, 141-45; B. P. Thomas, *Russo-American Relations 1815-67* (1930), 25, 32; als, GWC to James Monroe, 15 May 1819, 18/30 Jan. 1820, Monroe Papers, DLC; letter from Aaron V. Brown to O. P. Nicholson, 18 Feb. 1845, *THQ*, 3 (1944), 174 ("has no hold"); J. Woolridge, ed., *Hist. of Nashville, Tenn.* (1890), 265-68, 275-77; H. Weaver & W. Cutler, eds., *Corres. of James K. Polk* (1967-), III, 671-73, 691, 695; V, 195, 208-09, 264, 618; E. T. Sanford, *Blount College & the Univ. of Tenn.* (1894), 109-12; *THQ*, 19 (1960), 13; J. S. Bassett, *Corres. of Andrew Jackson* (1926-35), I, 59, 88-89; II, 276, 282, & *passim*; J. Parton, *Life of Andrew Jackson* (1860), III, 80-81, 142-43, 629-30, 676; A. C. Buell, *Hist. of Andrew Jackson* (1904), II, 155-57; M. James, *Andrew Jackson: Portrait of a President* (1937), 18-20, 503; als, GWC to Andrew Jackson, 14 Jan. 1831, 28 May 1836, Jackson Papers, DLC ("sound Democratic Republicans"); W. T. Jordan, "George W. Campbell's Journal of the French Spoliation Claims Comm., 1832-35," *East Tenn. Hist. Soc.'s Pubs.*, 19 (1947), 98-109; *THQ*, 4 (1945), 102; J. C. Guild, *Old Times in Tenn.* (1878), 157-58, 480-81; *THQ*, 2 (1943), 35.

MANUSCRIPTS: DLC; DNA; T; THi; Knoxville-Knox Cnty. Pub. Lib.; NjP; NHi; Pierpont Morgan Lib., N.Y.; NcD

JJL

James Revell Corbin

JAMES REVELL CORBIN was the son of George Corbin (A.B. 1765), planter and public official of Accomack County on Virginia's Eastern Shore. James was born sometime before July 19, 1778, when James

Scott of Accomack County wrote a will bequeathing him his library and one slave. George's wife has not been identified, but his son's middle name may imply that she was a Revell. Scott's will, which was proved a month later, also included bequests to a number of Revells, a surname common in Accomack at this time. James Corbin was the brother of Agnes Drummond Corbin Ker, his classmate Hugh Ker's sister-in-law, and he was the first cousin of John Cropper, both brother-in-law and father-in-law of another classmate, Thomas Monteagle Bayly.

Corbin first appears on a College class list of October 10, 1792 as a junior. He joined the American Whig Society but had left it for some reason by August 28, 1793 when he and Bayly, both described as "formerly members of the American Whig Society," were admitted to the rival Cliosophic Society, in which Corbin took the pseudonym Paine. The use of Thomas Paine's name at this time, just after he published *The Rights of Man* but before *The Age of Reason* appeared, presumably implies endorsement not of his deism but of his passionate republicanism and his role in the American Revolution. Corbin did not return in November for his senior year. Perhaps he went home to avoid the yellow fever epidemic of late summer 1793 or fell victim to it himself. That he died suddenly at this time is suggested by his father's will, dated September 24 and proved October 29, 1793, which left everything to Agnes Corbin Ker and more distant relatives and friends, and did not mention James.

SOURCES: S. Nottingham, *Wills & Administrations, Accomack Cnty., Va. 1663-1800* (1931), 238, 307; *Princetonians, 1748-1768*, 488-89; R. T. Whitelaw, *Va.'s Eastern Shore* (1951), I, 662-65, 722; II, 944, 1003, 1044, 1263, 1267, 1275, 1279, 1291; Min. Fac., 10 Oct. 1792; Clio. Min., 14 & 28 Aug. 1793; Clio. lists; will of George Corbin, 1793, microfilm, Vi (photocopy in PUA). Wanda S. Gunning kindly supplied references used in this sketch.

JJL

James Cresap

JAMES CRESAP, A.B., was probably the farmer and public official who was the son of Michael and Mary Whitehead Cresap, born in 1773 in Oldtown in the part of Frederick County, Maryland, which became Washington County in 1776 and Allegany County in 1789. In 1783 his sister Maria married Luther Martin (A.B. 1766), the eminent patriot and Federalist lawyer. The Cresaps were a renowned frontier family. The grandfather, Thomas, an immigrant from Yorkshire, England, was an Indian fighter, trader, road builder, and explorer who earned himself the nickname "the Maryland Monster" while championing that colony's interests in the "Conojacular War," a border dispute with Pennsylvania.

Michael Cresap, Thomas's youngest son, was a trader, land speculator, and well-known Indian fighter. His role in triggering the 1774 war with the Shawnee Indians variously called Lord Dunmore's War, Cresap's War, and Logan's War, has been controversial ever since Thomas Jefferson (LL.D. 1791) asserted in his *Notes on the State of Virginia* that Cresap barbarously murdered the family of the Mingo Chief Logan, thus beginning the war and incidentally eliciting from Logan a speech famous for its pathos and eloquence. A considerable literature has since arisen contesting what was Cresap's part in the massacre, whether all of Logan's kin were in fact killed, whether the murders triggered the war, and even whether Logan made the speech attributed to him. The consensus at present seems to be that Cresap probably did not kill Logan's family, but that he led two earlier attacks which may in fact have triggered the war, and that in any event the focus of the controversy has been too narrow, since Cresap was the archetype of the thrusting, aggressive frontiersmen whose activities raised tensions until war was inevitable.

When war with Britain began, Cresap led a company of riflemen to Boston. He fell ill there and died in New York in October 1775 while making his way home. Mary, the mother of his son James, was the widow of James Whitehead when she married Michael Cresap. After the latter's death she married Col. David Rodgers of Ohio County, Virginia, who moved to her home in Hampshire County, Virginia, just across the Potomac River from Oldtown. Around 1779 Simon Girty led an Indian raid which killed Rodgers, who was returning to Virginia after a trip to New Orleans. James Cresap acquired a second stepfather in 1781 with Mary's fourth marriage, to John Jeremiah Jacob, former clerk of Michael Cresap who went on to become a Methodist minister. He too moved into her home.

James Cresap entered the College as a junior sometime after October 10, 1792, when he is not included on a class list, and before February 5, 1793. An undated note in the faculty minutes prior to the latter date reported that Cresap's classmate William B. Ewing had complained to the faculty after Cresap struck him. The faculty admonished both but concluded that although both were at fault, Cresap—as the aggressor—was more to blame. In March Cresap was in trouble again. The faculty found that a number of juniors and seniors had neglected their studies, gone out drinking, and displayed "very indiscreet conduct in the street & a very indecent noise and disorder in the college." They made all the students concerned, including Cresap, sign a lengthy apology. Upon reflection, however, some of the students concluded that their characters had been maligned unbearably and requested a dismission from the College. Apparently they hoped that the faculty would back down in the face of this gesture. Only Cresap and Joseph Bonney (A.B. 1793) refused to withdraw their request when the faculty remained intractable, and both were immediately expelled. They too then lost their nerve, for a day later they petitioned to be readmitted, and since their petitions were approved they must have been couched in appropriately apologetic and respectful terms. Cresap joined neither literary society. The faculty minutes show that he was assigned a role in a disputation for his commencement, but for some unspecified reason the disputation in question did not take place, and Cresap thus did not speak.

Cresap subsequently returned to Allegany County and probably lived on lands in and near Oldtown which he inherited from his father. James had been willed a tract of almost 2,000 acres near Oldtown called "Seven Springs" by Michael Cresap, and although at the time of the latter's death his finances were tangled and litigation ensued, James probably received this property while his brother Michael obtained the family's lands in Ohio. In 1798 and 1800 James Cresap represented Allegany County in the lower house of the state legislature. He married four times. His first wife was Hannah Reid, his first cousin once removed, the daughter of John Reid, a Revolutionary War officer, and Charity Cresap Reid. Hannah was followed by Sally Gazzoway, Polly Shellhorn, and Mrs. Mary Van Bibber, the widow of Abraham Van Bibber of Baltimore. One son from each of the last three marriages reached adulthood.

Even after the death in 1796 of Maria Cresap Martin, Cresap remained close to her husband Luther Martin and their children, an attachment which nearly got him into a duel in 1802. Over Martin's bitter and vociferous opposition, his law-clerk Richard Raynal Keene (A.B. 1795) succeeded in marrying Eleanor, Martin's fifteen-year-old youngest daughter. The marriage took place in New York City, whence Eleanor had been sent from Baltimore in an effort to get her beyond Keene's reach. Cresap was also in New York, though whether in connection with the disputed marriage or for some other reason is unclear. When Keene heard that Cresap and Martin's son-in-law Hector Scott were circulating "*injurious expressions* against me," he demanded explanations from each. When first approached, Cresap expressed his "readiness to fight," but the matter was patched up so well that Keene reported that their "intercourse became frequent" while he remained in New York. Despite this happy outcome and a similarly pacific settlement with Scott, Martin took the threats to his two kinsmen, "deservedly as dear to me as my life," as his pretext for publishing *Modern Gratitude*, his rambling tirade against Keene.

On November 3, 1804 Methodist Bishop Francis Asbury described in his journal a visit to "James Cresap's, near Old Town; notwithstanding what had passed at Cokesbury, he received me as a father—*that matter might have been managed better.*" Presumably Cresap joined his mother and stepfather in converting to Methodism around 1785. The cryptic reference to Cokesbury suggests the tantalizing possibility that Cresap attended Cokesbury College, the short-lived Methodist institution in Abingdon, Maryland, before enrolling at the College of New Jersey.

Cresap was described in the 1820 census as a resident of Cumberland, also in Allegany County. He died intestate sometime before February 20, 1824 when his sister Elizabeth and her husband Lenox Martin, the brother of Luther, gave bond as administrators of his estate. The inventory of his personal estate points to his having engaged in mixed farming. He grew wheat, rye, corn, and oats, and owned nine horses, twenty-nine cows, forty pigs, and six sheep. Overall Cresap's estate was valued at $6,206.48, with his eleven slaves accounting for over half of this figure.

SOURCES: J. O. Cresap & B. Cresap, *Hist. of the Cresaps* (1937), 116-18, 293-300; J. J. Jacob, *Biog. Sketch of the Late Capt. Michael Cresap* (1826 repr. 1971), 40-51, 117-20; K. P. Bailey, *Thomas Cresap: Md. Frontiersman* (1944); Cresap Society, *Bull.*, nos. 14 (1936) & 39 (1938); *West Va. Hist.*, 6 (1944/45), 214; 17 (1956), 117-37; P. S. Clarkson & R. S. Jett, *Luther Martin of Md.* (1970), 30-31, 57; Min. Fac., 5 Feb. & 14-16 Mar. 1793 ("very indiscreet"), 22 Aug. 1794; Min. Trustees, 23 Sept. 1794; *Dunlap & Claypoole's Amer. Daily Advt.*, 7 Oct. 1794; *MHM*, 34 (1939), 328-29; *Biog. Dict. Md. Leg.*, 244-45; J. W. Thomas & T. J. C. Williams, *Hist. of Allegany Cnty., Md.* (1923 repr. 1969), 436, 666; letter from Md. Leg. Hist. Proj., 4 June 1985, PUA; L. Martin, *Modern Gratitude* (1802), 2 ("deservedly"), 80-81; R. R. Keene, *Letter ... to Luther Martin ... Upon the Subject of his 'Modern Gratitude'* (1802), 43-45 ("*injurious,*" "readiness," "intercourse"); E. E. Clark et al., eds., *Jour. & Letters of Francis Asbury* (1958), II, 31, 445-46 ("James"); C. R. Teeples, *Md. 1800 Census* (1973), 123; R. V. Jackson, *Md. 1820 Census Index* (1977), 25; MS estate inv., James M. Cresap, 30 Mar. 1824, recorded 11 May 1824, Md. Hall of Records (photocopy in PUA). See Otis K. Rice's introduction to the 1971 ed. of Jacob's life of Michael Cresap for an overview of the Cresap-Logan controversy. The identification of the Princetonian as Michael's son is based on his age and on the connection of his brother-in-law with the College. However his first cousin James, the son of Daniel and Ruth Van Swearingen Cresap, cannot be entirely ruled out. He was born on October 4, 1770, which would make him an unusually but not impossibly old graduate in 1794. He lived near Rawlings in Allegany County (which is far enough from Oldtown that the Asbury reference probably is not to him) and represented the county in the state legislature several times. In 1799 he married his half-niece Abigail Cresap, who bore him nine children, and he died in 1836. Jacob described him as "rich" in 1826. The accounts of Cresap's graduation complicate matters further by crediting him with the middle initial "E." The sons of Michael and Daniel were sometimes referred to as James M. and James D., respectively, but no likely candidate or explanation of the "E" has emerged. Perhaps it was an error. In 1795 a James Cresap represented Allegany in the lower house of the legislature: whether this was James D. or James M. has not been determined.

JJL

Horatio Rolfe (Roff) Dayton

HORATIO ROLFE (ROFF) DAYTON, soldier and merchant, was born in 1773, one of the six sons and three daughters of Elias and Hannah Rolfe Dayton of Elizabethtown, Essex (now Union) County, New Jersey. The father was a well-to-do merchant and farmer who commanded the Third New Jersey Regiment in the Continental Line in the Revolutionary War, attained the rank of brigadier general at the war's close, and served as the first president of the New Jersey Society of the Cincinnati. For safety's sake his family spent part of the war at Chatham, on the border between Essex and Morris counties. After the war he served for eight years as mayor of Elizabethtown and was elected to several terms in the New Jersey legislature. Horatio's siblings included Jonathan Dayton (A.B. 1776), a Signer of the Constitution and Speaker of the United States House of Representatives; Mary, who married Horatio's classmate James C. Williamson; Hannah, the wife of Gen. Matthias Ogden and mother of George M. Ogden (A.B. 1795), Henry W. Ogden (A.B. 1796), and Peter V. Ogden (ca. Class of 1804); and Elias Bailey Dayton, the father of Aaron Ogden Dayton (A.B. 1813) and probably also of Thomas B. C. Dayton (A.B. 1806). Elias and another brother, William, married daughters of the Reverend Thomas Bradbury Chandler and thus became brothers-in-law of John Henry Hobart (A.B. 1793) and cousins of William Chetwood (A.B. 1792). E. Dayton (Class of 1796) and J. H. Dayton (Class of 1797) also may have been related.

Jonathan Dayton was a trustee of the Elizabethtown Academy, which was burned in 1779 but reopened in June 1789. Perhaps his brother received some of his preliminary education there. Early in 1792 Horatio was an original subscriber of the Elizabethtown Library Association. He entered the College as a junior in October 1792. On November 28 he joined the Cliosophic Society, taking the pseudonym Irenio, standing either for Irenæus, the eminent early Christian theologian, or simply for the Greek word for peace-maker. Dayton's months at the College were anything but peaceful. On March 27, 1793 the Cliosophic Society found him guilty of bad scholarship but concluded that the decision itself was sufficient punishment for a first offense. On May 29 he was again arraigned on the same charge. The society voted to suspend him in two weeks unless he showed improvement, whereupon "Bro. Irenio behaving disrespectfully to the society in consequence of their determination was immediately suspended" for an indefinite period. On June 12 the Clios concluded that Dayton's "bad conduct in society" had become intolerable and resolved that "the Cliosophic Society thinking Mr. Horatio R. Dayton no longer worthy of being a member of their body do dismiss him by order."

Dayton's expulsion from the Cliosophic Society may have been triggered by the incident which led to his departure from the College. According to an undated entry in the faculty minutes between entries for May 15 and July 15, 1793, the faculty met several times to consider the "flagrant breach" of College discipline Dayton committed by "threatening with a pistol in his hand the life and abusing the person of Mr. Isaac Van Doren [A.B. 1793] one of the most peaceable of its members." Dayton requested a dismission from college after the incident, which was granted "without giving him a recommendation." After he left, the faculty wrote to Dayton's father requesting that he "order his son to come and make such reparation as the faculty should deem necessary for the good order of the institution." Horatio did not come in person but sent a letter which the faculty rejected as insufficient because it combined apologies to the faculty with "repeated reflections" on Van Doren. Their demand that Dayton apologize to Van Doren apparently met with no response, and Dayton did not return to the College. How Van Doren managed to incur his wrath is not known.

On July 17, 1794 Dayton was commissioned a lieutenant in the Corps of Artillerists and Engineers, United States Army. Since army appointments at this time usually went to Federalists, Horatio probably belonged to that party, as did his relatives. The connections and military reputation of his father and eldest brother clearly counted for more than did Horatio's own qualifications in obtaining the commission. The next day Secretary of War Henry Knox mailed Jonathan Dayton "an appointment for your Brother" and commented that "you omitted a small but essential ceremony—his name— please to transmit it." The length of his service is unclear. Francis Heitman's authoritative register of United States Army officers says that Dayton was honorably discharged at his own request on November 1, 1796, but he still held the same rank and date of commission in spring 1799. From mid-March to at least May 3, 1799, Dayton was acting commandant of Fort Jay on Governors Island in New York City harbor. The commandant, Maj. Adam Hoops (Class of 1777), had left the fort on April 19 on an authorized visit to Philadelphia, and in his absence Dayton wrote Maj. Gen. Alexander Hamilton (LL.D. 1791) to ask whether he (Dayton) or Hoops was now "held accountable for this Post." Apparently Dayton and Hoops were not on good terms. Dayton wrote Hamilton that he was contacting him "to prevent as much as may be correspondence with Major Hoops as nothing satisfactory may be obtained from him." Hamilton's response ignored the complaint about Hoops but confirmed that as senior officer at the fort Dayton would be acting commandant until Hoops's return.

On April 26, 1799 Hamilton wrote Secretary of War James McHenry proposing new postings for the two artillery regiments. He suggested that Dayton be in the contingent sent to Georgia and South Carolina. Perhaps a disinclination to venture south prompted Dayton's decision to leave the service. Apparently he had resigned by January 1800, when he seems to have acted as agent to a contractor supplying beef to two army regiments stationed in Essex County. On the 28th of the same month he married his cousin Cornelia Ryes Dayton. According to Julian Ursyn Niemcewicz, a Pole who became their next-door neighbor six months later, Cornelia's

> relatives were against the marriage and, because the abduction of girls is a criminal offence according to the law of the land the lovers arranged that the young woman would abduct the young man. In fact she came for him with a horse at night. The lover sat behind her on the horse; he carried her to the first clergyman, married her and in this way he avoided the penalty, for she, not he, was the abductor.

The marriage was performed by Menzies Rayner, rector of Elizabethtown's Episcopal church, although Elias and Jonathan Dayton were prominent Presbyterians. After the marriage the couple took up residence on Elizabethtown's main street in a house and garden which were Cornelia's dowry. In August 1800 Dayton placed a newspaper advertisement warning that he had set wolf traps in his garden in an attempt to keep out two- as well as four-legged marauders.

Dayton subsequently moved to New York City. An 1803 directory described him as a grocer at 46 Partition Street. In 1804 he was at 32 Washington Street, and later that year he was identified as a merchant at 142 Washington Street, where he remained for two more years. He made his last appearance in the 1806 directory, which still called him a merchant, but with 2 Carlisle Street as his home address and 9 South Street as his place of employment.

Eventually Dayton returned to Elizabethtown. Perhaps he retired there with the aid of his inheritance from his father, who died in October 1807. Horatio Dayton died on September 13, 1813.

SOURCES: J. U. Niemcewicz, *Under Their Vine & Fig Tree* (1965), 20-21, 270, 273, 299-300, 340 ("relatives were"); genealogical data supplied by Cornelia H. Dayton, 1983, alumni file, PUA; Phila. *True Amer. & Commericial Advt.*, 7 Sept. 1804; W. W. Clayton, *Hist. of Union & Middlesex Cnties., N.J.* (1882), 240-41; Union Cnty. Hist. Soc., *Proc.*, 2 (1923-34), 42-43, 204-11; E. F. Hatfield, *Hist. of Elizabeth, N.J.* (1868), 410, 414, 439-40, 517, 519, 550, 558-60, 603-04, 651-52; A. E. Vanderpoel, *Hist. of Chatham, N.J.* (1959),

1, 69-70, 72; alumni files, PUA; Dayton family papers filed under Jonathan Dayton, A.B. 1776 (father's will; als, Jonathan to E. B. Dayton, 14 Mar. 1803), NjP; Min. Fac., 10 Oct. 1792 & undated entry between 15 May & 15 July 1793 ("flagrant breach," "threatening," "order," "repeated"); Clio. Min., 21 Nov. 1792, 27 Mar., 29 May & 12 June 1793 ("Bro. Irenio," "bad conduct"); Clio. lists; Heitman, *U.S. Army*, I, 50-51, 362; als, Henry Knox to Jonathan Dayton, 18 July 1794 (Microfilms of the Henry Knox Papers ... [at] MHi, xxxv, 171) ("an appointment"); *Hamilton Papers*, xxiii, 72-77, 120; als, HRD to Hamilton, 20 Mar., 1 Apr. ("held accountable," "to prevent"), 4 Apr. & 3 May 1799, Hamilton to HRD, 20 Mar. & 2 Apr. 1799, HRD to W. S. Smith, 20 Jan. 1800, H. Ludlow to Smith, 11 Jan. 1800, DLC (& on microfilm ed. of DLC's Hamilton Papers); *GMNJ*, 9 (1934), 74; *N.J. Wills*, x, 207; T. Thayer, *As We Were: The Story of Old Elizabethtown* (1964), 90, 127, 153, 161, 197; N.Y. City directories, 1804-07; *N.J. Journal*, 21 Sept. 1813. The sources frequently refer to Horatio as Horace Dayton.

MANUSCRIPTS: Alexander Hamilton Papers, DLC

JJL

John M. Dickson

JOHN M. DICKSON, A.B., probably entered the College as a sophomore after the summer session of 1792 began. He joined the American Whig Society during his student days, and at his commencement he participated as respondent in a dispute on the question "Is the institution of voluntary popular societies, to watch the motions of government in the present[state of this country wise or useful[?]"

A newspaper account of his commencement and the Whig catalogue agree that Dickson was a resident of North Carolina. The 1800 census lists eleven individuals named John Dickson from eight counties. The likeliest location for the Princetonian appears to be Lincoln County in southwestern North Carolina. The census counted four men named John Dickson there, and on September 11, 1816 a John M. Dickson received a license to marry Juliet West in Lincoln County. The same or a different John M. Dickson was living in Davidson County, Tennessee, at the time of the 1820 census. Nothing permitting positive identification of the Princetonian has come to light.

SOURCES: Min. Fac., class list ca. May 1792 ("Dixion" apparently added to list late), 10 Oct. 1792, 2 Jan., 26 May, 22 Aug. 1794; Amer. Whig Soc., *Cat.* (1840), 7; *Dunlap & Claypoole's Amer. Daily Advt.*, 7 Oct. 1794 ("Is the"); E. P. Bentley, *Index to the 1800 Census of N.C.* (1977), 65; C. Bynum, *Marriage Bonds of Tryon & Lincoln Cnties.*, N.C. (1929 repr. 1962), 39. Gen. Joseph Dickson, a planter who fought at King's Mountain and represented Lincoln County in the state legislature and the United States Congress, had a son John who was twenty-two years old in 1794. However this John Dickson is said to have married in 1792 and served as Lincoln County clerk from 1788 to 1804, circumstances which would rule out his attendance at the College at this time. He was not the man who married Juliet West in 1816. Perhaps the Princetonian was the son of one of the general's brothers Robert and John, both of whom migrated with him from Pennsylvania to North Carolina. The latter, whose wife was named Agness, mentioned a son John among his five children when he made his will in Lincoln County on May 24, 1793. Joseph and many of his relatives subsequently moved to Rutherford County, Tennessee. The family was of Scots-Irish, Presbyterian stock. See A. W. Smith, *Dickson-McEwen & Allied Families Genealogy* (2d ed., 1975), 5-6, 17-19, 300, 309, 312-13, 315, 326, 371-72; suppl., 11-17; W. L. Sherrill, *Annals of Lincoln Cnty, N.C.* (1937), 29, 44, 92; *North Carolinian*, 4 (1958), 471. See W. S. Ray, *Mecklenburg Signers & Their Neighbors* (1946), 494, for a Lincoln County James Dickson possibly old enough to be the Princetonian's father. Col. John Dickson of Cumberland County, in the center of the state, could also be the Princetonian or his father. John Robinson ordained the colonel elder of the Fayetteville Presbyterian Church in 1800, and he represented the county in the state assembly from 1800 to 1802 and in the state senate in 1803, 1808, 1811 and 1815. However, inconclusive evidence suggests that he may have been the son of Robert Dickson of Duplin County, in which case he was twenty-eight in 1794, a bit old to be graduating from the College at that time. See Foote, *Sketches, N.C.*, 489; *Legislative Manual & Political Reg. of the State of N.C.* (1874), 210; A. B. Keith & D. T. Morgan, *John Gray Blount Papers* (1982), IV, 310; J. O. Carr, *Dickson Letters* (1901), esp. 5-9, 21-22. A Rev. John Dickson served as professor of languages and of moral philosophy at the College of Charleston, South Carolina and as Greek master of its grammar school from 1822 until his retirement in 1828. He has not been otherwise identified. See als, John Dickson to Samuel L. Southard (A.B. 1804), 19 Mar. 1827, NjP-SSP; letter from archivist, College of Charleston, 3 June 1985, PUA.

JJL

Edmund Elmendorf

EDMUND ELMENDORF, A.B., attorney, was born July 7, 1777, in Somerset County, New Jersey, either in or near the town of Somerville, which was located within Bridgewater Township. His parents were John Elmendorf and Margaret Zabriskie (Margritie Sabriskie) Elmendorf, who were both descended from Dutch families which had settled in the area of Kingston, New York. They were married in Kingston but moved to New Jersey, living first in Hackensack and settling later in Bridgewater Township on land near the junction of the main course of the Raritan River and the North Branch. The family belonged to the Raritan Reformed Church where John Elmendorf was a trustee.

Family connections with the College included the father's brother Peter Edmund Elmendorf (A.B. 1782) and his cousin Lucas Conrad Elmendorf (A.B. 1782). Cousins of Elmendorf's own generation were John Rutger Bleecker (A.B. 1791), Peter Bleecker (A.B. 1792), Edmund Bruyn (A.B. 1801), and Severyn Bruyn (A.B. 1803). His younger brothers William Crooke Elmendorf (A.B. 1807) and James Bruyn Elmendorf (A.B. 1807) also received their education at the College.

Elmendorf's name first appears in the College records as a sophomore in the winter session of 1791. On December 27, 1791 he joined the Cliosophic Society, as his Bleecker cousins had done. He took the name Aristomenes, the semilegendary leader of Messenia's revolt against Sparta in the seventh century B.C. Very active in the society, Elmendorf at various times served as president, first assistant, twice as second assistant, corrector of speaking, and clerk. He was also fined a number of times for such offences as not showing his composition to the "corrector" and having three books out of the society's library at the same time. He received the society's diploma and attended one of its meetings in February 1799. His skill as an orator is indicated by his role as one of the Fourth of July speakers, representing Clio in both 1793 and 1794. On January 6, 1794 his name was included on a list of students presented to the faculty by the steward because they were boarding out of the College dining room. When these students were called before the faculty on January 8 to explain their reasons for absenting themselves from the steward's table, Elmendorf pleaded temporary illness. He was ordered to return to the campus dining room as soon as he recovered. For his commencement ceremonies he stood ninth in his class and was assigned the fifth intermediate oration, for which he chose the subject of history.

Elmendorf's activities for the next few years have not been discovered, although he was studying law for at least part of that time. Perhaps he wanted to try another profession before completely committing himself to the practice of law, for on January 21, 1797 the faculty of the College appointed him a tutor to replace Robert Marshall Forsyth (A.B. 1796). Apparently he remained at the College only several months, but the date of his departure is not on record. He must have continued his legal studies with one of the lawyers residing in Princeton, for on February 4, 1798 he delivered a letter from John Henry Hobart (A.B. 1793), a tutor at the College, to Robert Smith in Philadelphia. Smith, in his return letter, which was probably also carried by Elmendorf, described him as an agreeable young gentleman. His admission as attorney to the New Jersey bar during the September 1799 term indicates that he probably spent about two years in legal studies before his brief stint as a tutor. During the September 1802 term he was admitted as a counsellor to the New Jersey bar, and one source claims that he had already become a counsellor in New York in the May 1800 term. However, he was still living in New Jersey in July 1801, when he joined his father as a signatory to a constitution providing for the establishment of a classical preparatory school to be called the Somerville Academy. Most of the other men were interested in having their sons educated in the proposed school; Elmendorf's interest may have been in the education of his two younger brothers. His father served as a trustee of the academy for a number of years.

Around 1802 or 1803 Elmendorf moved to New York City and

established his legal practice there. His name first appears in the city directories in 1803 as attorney and counsellor with an office at 16 Nassau Street. On September 3, 1803 he married Elizabeth Corre, daughter of Joseph and Barbara Corre, in the Dutch Church of New York City. The directory of the following year shows his office at 63 Pine Street with a residence at 60 Broadway. He continued to be listed as an attorney and counsellor through 1835, with offices at various locations, but most frequently at Pine Street addresses. In 1813 a residence is again listed, when he had an office at 18 Pine and a home at 9 Fair, but presumably he often practiced from an office in his home. In 1830 he moved his office to 48 Lispenard Street, and in that year his residence is first listed as "Red-hook landing."

The town of Red Hook had been formed from Rhinebeck in Dutchess County in 1812, and Elmendorf actually lived at Upper Red Hook Landing or Tivoli. An expatriate Frenchman named Peter Delabegarre (De Labigarre) bought land along the Hudson in the 1790s, where he hoped to develop an ideal community. His plans for the village, more suitable for flat terrain, never materialized, but he did construct the "Chateau de Tivoli," an enwalled, octagonal-shaped chateau, which sat on a high bluff overlooking the Hudson. When Delabegarre went bankrupt the property was sold at auction and eventually purchased by Elmendorf, who thoroughly enjoyed residing in his baronial estate while commuting to his office in the city by ferry.

Elmendorf acquired and maintained a good practice in New York City. From 1818 through 1820 he served as clerk in chancery. He invested in considerable real estate, both in New York City and in Tivoli. When his father died in 1812 he received a seventh part of the estate, which was inventoried at $51,688.54. Elmendorf probably retired, or at least practiced only in Tivoli, after 1835 when he no longer maintained an office in the city. He died on October 8, 1856, outliving his two sons, and was buried in Greenwood Cemetery in Brooklyn. His widow remained at the chateau in Tivoli until her death in 1861. His nephew, John Crook Elmendorf (Class of 1834, A.B. Rutgers 1834), became one of the leading New Jersey lawyers of his time.

Sources: Alumni file & Elmendorf family file, PUA; *Princetonians, 1776-1783*, 356-63; Alexander, *Princeton*, 272; Clio. lists; Clio. Min., 23 Jan. 1793–10 Sept. 1794 *passim*, 13 Feb. 1799; Min. Fac., Nov. 1791 class list, 6 & 8 Jan., 22 Aug. 1794, 21 Jan. 1797; *Dunlap & Claypoole's Amer. Daily Advt.*, 7 Oct. 1794; *Som. Cnty. Hist. Quart.*, 3 (1914), 186; 6 (1917), 31-32, 194-99; J. McVickar, *Early Life & Professional Years of Bishop Hobart* (1838), 34; J. P. Snell, *Hist. of Hunterdon & Somerset Cnties., N.J.* (1881), 667; Hobart, *Corres.*, I, 328; II, 14; N.Y. City directories, 1802-36; F. Hasbrouck, *Hist. of Dutchess Cnty.* (1909), 426, 428, 432; R. C. Wiles, *Tivoli Revisited: A Social Hist.* (1981),

5-6; *N.J. Wills*, XII, 125; W. W. Clayton, *Hist. of Union & Middlesex Cnties.* (1882), 510; Riker, 52.

RLW

Nicholas C. Everett

NICHOLAS C. EVERETT, A.B., A.M. 1798, merchant, justice, and possibly a lawyer, was probably born sometime in 1778 in Princeton, New Jersey. His father Israel Everett, a local school teacher, married the twice-widowed Mary Gapen Pierson Mershon on May 8, 1777. The Everetts were communicants of the Princeton Presbyterian Church, occupying pew thirty-nine. A family history says that Israel Everett suffered an accident that necessitated the amputation of an arm. The fact that young Nicholas attended the Nassau Hall grammar school suggests that the father probably taught there. The last reference to Israel Everett's presence in Princeton that has been found is for 1792. It is not known when Mary Everett was widowed for the third time, but at a date when Nicholas's sister Mary Amelia was probably in her teens, she accompanied their mother to Canonsburg, Pennsylvania, to live with her half-sister Jane Mershon Hartifell.

Everett entered the freshman class of the College in 1790 after performing best in his grammar school class of eight in an extemporaneous exercise in Latin. While a college student he joined the American Whig Society. On January 2, 1793 Everett was called before the faculty for "bringing Spirituous Liquors into the College and becoming intoxicated." Because of his usual good conduct, his admission of guilt, and "there appearing circumstances to palliate it," the faculty considered it sufficient punishment to admonish him before his class and to mention his offense before the assembled student body. At his commencement ceremonies Everett served as replicator of the question, "Are mankind in general, in their intercourse with each other, more defective in the virtue of beneficence or of gratitude?"

Princeton tradition claims that Everett studied law and practiced in New York City, where he served as a justice of one of the city courts. Since only the last part of this statement can be verified, it is difficult to know whether to give credence to the further statement by Samuel Davies Alexander (A.B. 1838) in his brief sketch of Everett in *Princeton College During the Eighteenth Century*, that the latter was "a laborious active man, but not at all brilliant." A letter from David English (A.B. 1789), dated December 16, 1797, to John Henry Hobart (A.B. 1793), who was then tutoring at the College, suggests that Everett was indeed a plodder. English, who had himself been a tutor at the College from 1794 to 1796, wrote, "It would be well for you to advise

Everet to enter upon some employ without delay. It would be better to engage to teach even an English School than to remain at Princeton under the pretence of reading for improvement." English wrote again on April 6, 1798, "I wish Mr. Everet may attend diligently to his business & his professional studies he is still young & much may be done by application, do not fail to give him some valedictory advice." Several months later Everett became master of the Nassau Hall grammar school, a position which he held until the following year. Sometime during his postgraduate residence in Princeton he joined the local fire company, which he served as clerk.

According to family tradition Everett studied law during this time and practiced for a short while in Princeton. On November 3, 1800 he married Eliza Faitoute, daughter of Euphemia and the Reverend George Faitoute (A.B. 1774), who in 1789 had moved from New Jersey to Jamaica, Long Island. Apparently the marriage took place in Princeton and the couple then moved to New York. Everett's name as a lawyer does not appear in that city's directories until almost half a century later. Instead, beginning in 1804 he is listed as "tobacco manufacturer." In 1807 this entry changed to a designation of "grocer," operating at 47 Elm Street on the corner of Anthony, a location which he maintained for over twenty years. He appeared before the common council of New York City on May 11, 1816, petitioning for remission of a penalty incurred because he had purchased butter to resell before the hour prescribed by law. However, he alleged ignorance of this law. In the winter of 1817 he was one of a group appearing before the council to complain about water thrown in the streets by the local brewers. The water froze during the night, thereby creating a hazard. The street commissioner found the complaint well founded but could propose no solution to the problem.

On April 6, 1815 Everett joined the Seventy-fifth Regiment of Infantry of New York County as an ensign. He received a promotion to lieutenant on June 21, and he resigned his post on July 8, 1816, probably without seeing active service. Everett was appointed inspector of elections for the sixth ward for the November election of 1822, a position he again held in 1823, 1829, and 1830. Apparently he encountered trouble only in 1823, for on January 6, 1824 he testified in an investigation of election disorders. In May 1827 he was appointed one of the collectors of assessments. At council meetings each collector was assigned specific improvements, such as the paving of a street, for which he assumed responsibility.

Beginning with the city directory for 1825/26 there is an entry for a "George Everitt, teacher," possibly Everett's son George Faitoute Everett. The 1835/36 directory discontinues both the listing for

George as a teacher and Nicholas as a merchant, and instead names Nicholas C. Everett as a justice for the fourth and sixth wards, residing at 125 White Street. Another new listing for "Everett & Battelle, merchants," suggests that the father may have decided to devote less time to business in order to perform his duties as justice and that the son may have been included in the new partnership. Everett continued as a justice until 1843/44, when he is listed as an assistant justice, a position which he held through the publication of the 1848/49 directory. He then lived at 117 White Street. That year the partnership also changed, to Everett and Brown. In 1849 there is a listing for "Nicholas C. Everett, lawyer," at the White Street address, which continued until the 1857/58 directory, just a few years before his death.

Everett's services as a lawyer may have been confined to obtaining land warrants for veterans of the War of 1812. Sometime after his term as justice he joined Nicholas Haight, founder and colonel of the Veterans of 1812, in securing grants of 160 acres of land each for surviving veterans. The two worked together from an office in the Chatham Bank Building on the corner of Chatham and Duane Streets. During this period Everett also presented a claim to Congress on behalf of the firm of Everett & Battelle for "reimbursement of certain moneys," which that body referred to the Commerce Committee for payment.

Everett eventually retired and moved across the Hudson River to Bergen Township, Hudson County, New Jersey, where he died in the spring of 1861. His will, which was proved on May 22, left bequests to his son George Faitoute Everett and seven daughters. His success in business is reflected by the inventory of his property. His home was a large one, with five bedrooms on the second floor and an extra bedroom on the first floor, which also contained both front and back parlors. The front parlor was large enough to hold a mahogany sofa and ten mahogany chairs, while the dining room, among other items of furniture, had twenty chairs and two spittoons.

SOURCES: Alumni file & Minto file, PUA; MS genealogical material on NCE at NjP; G. L. O. Mershon, *Peter Mershon & His Descendants* (1949), 28-30; *NJA*, XXII (1900), 127; Alexander, *Princeton*, 273; Hageman, *History*, II, 17, 83, 92; *N.J. Jour., & Polit. Intelligencer*, 29 Oct. 1788; *Pa. Packet, & Daily Advt.*, 7 Oct. 1790; Min. Fac., 29 Nov. 1790, 2 Jan. 1793, 22 Aug. 1794; Amer. Whig Soc., *Cat.* (1840), 7; *Dunlap & Claypoole's Amer. Daily Advt.*, 7 Oct. 1794; Hobart, *Corres.*, I, 332-33, 338; II, 36-38; *Princetonians, 1776-1783*, 44-46; B. F. Thompson, *Hist. of Long Island* (3d ed., 3 vols., 1918), II, 610; N.Y. City directories, 1804-61; MCCCNY, VIII, 445, 779; IX, 8, 23; XII, 169, 317, 532; XIII, 319, 463-64; XVI, 279, 308, 349-50, 363, 423; XVIII, 288; XIX, 262; *Military Minutes of the Council of Appointment of the State of N.Y., 1783-1821* (1901), II, 1539, 1643, 1730; J. A. Scoville, *Old Merchants of N.Y. City*, 3d ser. (1865), 194; 31st Cong., *Digested Summary & Alphabetical List of Private Claims ... Presented to House of Rep. from 1st to 31st Cong.* (1853), I, 601; will of NCE, 26 Apr. 1860, Nj.

The N.Y. State Court of Appeals files the registrations of members of the N.Y. bar, but their records go back only to 1898. Prior to that date no central registration agency for the state existed.

Several local historians refer to Everett as the nephew of Mary Skelton, wife of Walter Minto, who was professor of mathematics and natural philosophy at the College from 1787 until his death in 1796, but no substantiation has been found. Hageman (p. 263) refers to Walter Minto Skelton (A.B. 1825) as the nephew of Mary Skelton Minto who studied law. The will of Mary Minto, 8 Jan. 1817, Nj, leaves bequests only to two of her sisters and to Walter Minto Skelton. The alumni file of the latter gives Ennion William Skelton as a first cousin but contains no reference to Everett.

RLW

William Belford Ewing

WILLIAM BELFORD EWING, A.B., physician, justice and legislator, was born in Greenwich, Cumberland County, New Jersey, on December 12, 1776. He was the son of Dr. Thomas Ewing and his wife Sarah Fithian, the daughter of Samuel and Abigail Maskell Fithian who brought a large estate to her marriage with Ewing. Clerk of the county freeholders and an avid patriot, Ewing took part in the Greenwich tea burning in 1774 and served as surgeon with the New Jersey militia, achieving the rank of major with Gen. Nathaniel Heard's brigade and narrowly escaping capture at the Battle of Long Island. When Ewing died of consumption on October 1, 1782 at the age of 36, his older son Samuel was already deceased and William was bequeathed his father's wearing apparel, his library and pocket instruments, his sword, six silver teaspoons and six tablespoons, and two-thirds of the remaining personal estate, as well as all "land and marsh with appurtenances" upon the death of his mother, which occurred on April 1, 1806.

William Ewing received his early education at the academy at Bridgeton operated by Andrew Hunter, Jr. (A.B. 1772), who had served as chaplain with his father's brigade during the Revolution. Ewing matriculated at the College as a junior in October 1792. On February 5, 1793 he complained to the faculty of being struck by his classmate James Cresap. The faculty decided that both students were at fault and both received an admonition, even though Cresap had been the aggressor and was therefore judged more culpable. Catalogues of the American Whig Society list Ewing as a member, but minutes of the Cliosophic Society show that on July 17, 1794 "Mr. Belford Ewing of the senior class" was proposed for admission. When his candidacy was discussed on July 23, some objections were expressed which "rendered his admission doubtful." A final decision was deferred until "after the examination," which could have been either the examination of the class at the end of the summer session, or the society's examination of Ewing. In any case, on August 22 his application for membership was rejected. At his commencement Ewing took the part of replicator on the question, "Are Liberty and Equality calculated to promote the happiness and improvement of mankind?"

After graduation Ewing studied medicine with Dr. Nicholas Bellville of Trenton, a surgeon who had emigrated from France with Count Casimir Pulaski. Bellville was highly regarded in his profession, and he attracted numerous students. Ewing's uncle Maskell Ewing was practicing law in Trenton at the time, and his nephew may have been invited to share his home. Ewing also attended lectures at the University of Pennsylvania Medical School, although he did not receive the M.D. degree. There he came to the attention of Dr. Benjamin Rush (A.B. 1760), who recommended him to a physician on the island of St. Croix who was seeking a partner. From 1797 to 1799 Ewing practiced at St. Croix and St. Thomas and also served as a surgeon on a British warship, perhaps working his passage home. He then returned to Greenwich to practice both medicine and local politics. In June 1808 he married Harriet Seeley, daughter of Rebecca Gibbon and Josiah Seeley, who was also a member of the Greenwich tea-burning party. Harriet died in 1812 leaving one son, James Josiah Ewing.

Ewing apparently practiced alone until June 1, 1817 when he entered into partnership with Dr. Enoch Fithian, a distant cousin. The following year both men were present at the organizational meeting of the District Medical Society of Cumberland County, when Ewing was elected vice president and Fithian secretary. Ewing was also a member of the committee appointed to draw up the by-laws and regulations of the new society. The county group continued in existence until April 27, 1830, when it disbanded because of poor attendance and lack of interest. On several occasions Ewing served as a delegate from the Cumberland Society to the parent Medical Society of New Jersey, but in many years no Cumberland representative attended the state meetings. In November 1821 he was elected second vice president of the New Jersey medical society and on May 13, 1823 he was chosen president. For some reason he was not present at either the annual or semiannual meeting held during his term of office, and so he never presided at a general meeting of the society. In the same year, 1824, he retired from medicine and dissolved his business partnership. When the county society was revived in 1848, Ewing attended meetings, even though he had been retired from medicine for more than twenty years.

Ewing was involved in politics long before he gave up medicine.

He was a member of the Cumberland County Board of Chosen Freeholders from 1809 through 1829, serving an additional year in 1833. He was a Republican member of the New Jersey assembly from 1819 to 1823, from 1825 to 1828, and again in 1830, serving as speaker in 1827-28. During his tenure he was active in securing the abolition of imprisonment for debt in the state of New Jersey, declaring the reform "highly expedient, necessary and consistent with our free constitution."

In the winter of 1828-29 New Jersey politicians became aware that they would have the opportunity to fill two seats in the United States Senate, one because of the expiration of the term of Mahlon Dickerson (A.B. 1789), a Jeffersonian in the process of becoming a Jacksonian, and the second because of the serious illness of Ephraim Bateman, an Adams Republican from West Jersey. The anti-Jacksonians planned to support Samuel L. Southard (A.B. 1804), also an Adams Republican but from East Jersey, for Bateman's unexpired term. They backed Theodore Frelinghuysen (A.B. 1804), another future Whig, for Dickerson's East Jersey seat. However, their strategy failed to take into account that Ewing and Lucius Q. C. Elmer (A.M. 1824, LL.D. 1865), the state's district attorney, both coveted a Senate seat. Anti-Southard pamphlets and handbills, written by Ewing but signed "A West Jersey Member," soon appeared throughout the state. In them Ewing claimed that since Southard had been living in Washington as secretary of the navy in the cabinet of John Quincy Adams (LL.D. 1806), he was not a resident of the state as required by the Constitution. Ewing also reminded Southard supporters that they were violating the established practice in New Jersey politics of choosing one of the state's senators from West Jersey and the other from East Jersey, since both Southard from Somerset County and Frelinghuysen from Essex County were residents of East Jersey. Ewing was thus arguing that Southard was both a nonresident and an East Jerseyite. A Trenton caucus of nineteen West Jersey legislators supported Ewing by a vote of ten to nine, but some of his supporters were alienated when they learned that the deciding vote had been Ewing's own.

Jacksonians within the legislature were divided between Dickerson and former Federalist Garret D. Wall, and in the early balloting for Bateman's seat Southard and Dickerson had strong leads. However, neither achieved the necessary majority in succeeding ballots, and Ewing and Wall began to gain support. After the tenth ballot the Jacksonians, the Federalists, and Ewing's supporters united to pass a resolution eliminating Southard as a nonresident. Most of the ex-Federalists had no intention of supporting Ewing and joined the temporary coalition only as a means of eliminating Southard. A number of the Adams Republicans were so angered at Ewing's maneuvers that they threw their support to Dickerson. The twelfth ballot gave Bateman's unexpired seat to Dickerson with twenty-eight votes to twenty-two for Ewing and two for Wall. The Republicans then united to elect Frelinghuysen to the second Senate seat, thereby selecting two East Jersey men. The Republican caucus planned to offer Southard the post of state attorney general as a sop, but Ewing fought this strategy by throwing his support to Wall. Although his efforts failed, Southard won the position by only a small margin, and the divisiveness and rancour that Ewing created within the party contributed substantially to the spread of Jacksonianism in New Jersey.

In 1833 Ewing became a justice of the peace and in 1843 was appointed a judge of the court of common pleas. Under the constitution of 1776 judges had been selected by the legislature with no restriction on the number for each county. However, the new constitution of 1844 limited the number of appointments to not more than five in each county. Ewing was a member of the constitutional convention that set up these new regulations. In 1843 Cumberland, in an obvious move to stack the benches before the new rules went into effect, appointed twenty-five justices, Ewing among them.

As early as 1801 Ewing was an active member of Brearley Lodge, the Cumberland County Masonic lodge. Another of his interests was the Cumberland County Agricultural Society, organized in January 1823 "to promote agricultural improvements and to encourage family manufactures," with Ewing as its first president. The society's first exhibition was in November 1823; at the second one the following fall Ewing delivered an address "on an appropriate subject."

For several years prior to his death Ewing was extremely feeble, and he became gradually blinded by cataracts. He died at Greenwich on April 23, 1866, almost ninety years old.

SOURCES: Alumni file, PUA; T. Cushing & C. E. Sheppard, *Hist. of Cnties. of Gloucester, Salem & Cumberland, N.J.* (1883), 40-41, 49, 525, 533-34, 557, 565, 568, 571, 574, 580-81, 619, 681, 685; Wickes, *Hist. of Medicine N.J.*, 259; will of Thomas Ewing, Nj; A. M. Heston, ed., *South Jersey, A Hist.* (1924-[27?]), v, 72-74; Min. Fac., 10 Oct. 1792, 5 Feb. 1793, 22 Aug. 1794; Amer. Whig Soc., *Cat.* (1840), 7; Clio. Min., 17 & 23 July, 22 Aug. 1794; *Dunlap & Claypoole's Amer. Daily Advt.*, 7 Oct. 1794; *Rise, Minutes & Proc. of the N.J. Med. Soc.* (1875), 178, 185, 193, 196, 198, 222-23, 225; H. Ershkowitz, *Origin of the Whig & Democratic Parties: N.J. Politics, 1820-37* (1982), 66, 93-94; W. R. Fallaw, Jr., "The Rise of the Whig Party in N.J." (Ph.D. diss.: Princeton Univ., 1967), 52-59; W. R. Fee, *Transition from Aristocracy to Democracy in N.J.* (1933), 229-30; Trenton Hist. Soc., *Hist. of Trenton* (1929), II, 607, 641; J. H. Hough, *Origin of Masonry in N.J.* (1870), 88.

RLW

James Gildersleeve Force

JAMES GILDERSLEEVE FORCE, A.B., A.M. 1797, Presbyterian and Dutch Reformed clergyman, was born on May 8, 1766 in Jefferson Village in the part of Newark Township which eventually became Maplewood Township in Essex County, New Jersey. He was one of three sons and a daughter of James and Phebe Gildersleeve Force. Phebe's brother was Cyrus Gildersleeve (A.M. 1792). Cyrus Gildersleeve, Jr. (A.B. 1812), and Ezra S. Gildersleeve (A.B. 1827) were her nephews. Her husband died in late November or early December 1770. His will specified that his sons be put to trade when old enough. Phebe and her children apparently lived with her father, John Gildersleeve of Newark, who died in 1790.

James G. Force was probably the last incoming College undergraduate who could claim to have seen service in the Revolutionary War. His obituary asserts that "although a youth, [he] ... participated in the battle of Springfield, New Jersey." The extent of this "participation" is not entirely clear. Force was fourteen at the time of the actions fought at Springfield in June 1780, not impossibly young given the big militia turnout and the large stakes involved for Essex County residents. His granddaughter Louisa Wood Force later recalled the family tradition that Force had been ordered to drive his grandfather's cattle to safety, but that after doing so he ventured to the battlefield and took part until his two elder brothers discovered him and sent him home. In addition to this irregular service, a James Force is listed in William Stryker's register of New Jersey veterans as having served as a private in the Essex County militia at some point during the Revolution. If he was the Princetonian, this official enrollment presumably came a year or two after the battle of Springfield, when the war was essentially over.

Nothing else of Force's early activities has come to light. Apparently at some point he began studying for the ministry under the supervision of the Presbytery of New York, in the bounds of which Essex County fell. By April 10, 1793 he or his patrons had inquired about the possibility of his entering the College, for on that date the trustees voted to consider supporting him during his studies using the funds recently bequeathed by James Lesley (A.B. 1759) "for the support of poor & pious youth in the study of divinity." The faculty were ordered to examine him if he came, to use their discretion about whether to admit him, and to decide in which class he should enter.

The date of Force's matriculation is not known, but it was no later than November 20, 1793, when he was a senior. On December 18 the trustees voted to award him £20 from the Lesley Fund over the next six months in light of his having been recommended by the Presbytery of New York. He was progressing satisfactorily on April 4, 1794, and accordingly was voted £25 for the next half year. On December 3, 1793 Force had joined the Cliosophic Society, taking the pseudonym Hermes. The society fined him 6d. on January 29, 1794 for "wearing his surtoute in the society hall." He served a one-month term as the society's second assistant in February and another as president in July, but he seems not to have applied for a Clio diploma. At his commencement Force acted as respondent in a dispute on: "Are mankind in general, in their intercourse with each other, more defective in the virtue of beneficence or of gratitude?" His participation in the commencement exercises and receipt of an ordinary rather than an honorary A.B. suggest that Force was regarded as a regular student, apparently unlike his classmate and fellow charity recipient, Holloway Hunt.

At the trustees' meeting on September 23, 1794, the day before his commencement, Force was still listed among those "present in the College engaged in the study of divinity" and was voted £4. He seems to have left shortly thereafter, presumably to conclude his ministerial studies in Essex County. The Presbytery of New York ordained and installed him at New Providence, near Elizabethtown, on November 30, 1796. On September 11, 1796 or 1797 he married Sarah Hatfield, the daughter of Isaac and Damaris Noe Hatfield of Elizabethtown. Sarah was the niece of Abraham Clark, a prominent New Jersey politician and Signer of the Declaration of Independence. The Forces had five daughters and a son.

New Providence was a weak and divided congregation, having not yet recovered from a very bitter three-year controversy which culminated in 1793 in the ouster of Rev. Jonathan Elmer (A.B. Yale 1747, trustee of College of New Jersey 1782-95), who had served there since 1757. The quarrel began over an unsubstantiated charge of intemperance but soon broadened when a minority party supported Elmer in litigation and appeals to the presbytery and synod. By the time Elmer was forced out, attendance at the church was said to have dropped from 700 to 20. He retired but remained within the bounds of his former charge until his death in 1807. His continuing presence and the lingering animosities associated with his removal must have made Force's job difficult. A church manual published by the pastor in 1834 observed that "in the early part of the ministry of Mr. Force, appearances were flattering, but they soon became more gloomy than ever." He was dismissed on October 6, 1802, possibly because the church could no longer afford a full-time minister. During 1803-04 it endured a fiscal crisis in which it almost lost its lands.

Force seems to have spent the next six years without a settled charge. On November 15, 1808 he became the stated supply at Walpack Dutch Reformed Church, and on November 17, 1811 he was installed as pastor by Rev. John M. Van Harlingen. Walpack was a corporation which included four congregations: Bushkill and Dingman's Ferry in Pike County, Pennsylvania, and Peter's Valley in Sandyston Township and Flatbrookville in Walpack Township, Sussex County, New Jersey. From 1811 until 1816 he also ministered to the Dutch Reformed Congregation of Stillwater, Sussex County, but in the latter year the congregation voted to dissolve its tie with Force because of the church's "embarressed situation," which was probably financial. In 1823 Stillwater was reorganized as a Presbyterian congregation.

Walpack proved to be the most secure post in Force's otherwise marginal career as a minister. He served there for almost twenty years. When his ministry began only twenty-six people were in the church's communion. Between 1812 and 1827, sixty-two new members were received. Around 1818 the congregation at Peter's Valley replaced its wooden church building with a stone edifice which doubled as a schoolhouse. A year later the Flatbrookville congregation abandoned its old church and purchased a half interest in a building recently completed by a German Reformed congregation. The Dutch and German congregations occupied the church on alternate Sundays until the former group absorbed the latter after 1840.

In an 1874 historical sermon Samuel Mills, then the minister at Walpack, observed that Force was remembered as having been friendly, intelligent, kindhearted, and an edifying preacher. However, "he had one quite serious failing in connection with his public services," namely "a want of punctuality in commencing his services. He was seldom at the place of worship in time. His habit in this regard was a matter of general complaint." Force's immediate successor, Isaac S. Demund, recalled Force as "conspicuous for his great humility" and an able minister "who labored with acceptance and success until a few years before he gave up his call."

Force's departure from Walpack was apparently attended with controversy. Mills was purposely vague in his sermon, observing that Force resigned in 1827 and later recounting that in the same year "serious divisions arose in the Church, growing out of some cases of discipline." The struggle became so bitter that the Classis of New Brunswick agreed to the organization of a second congregation, the Lower Dutch Reformed Church of Walpack, which was set off in June 1827. The rupture was quickly healed. In August the new church's minister, Isaac Demund, got the two parties to agree to merge under his care, a decision aided by the reconsideration of "the action respecting the discipline of certain members." Perhaps the rupture had been between pro- and anti-Force factions, triggered by an attempt on Force's part to discipline some of his enemies and healed by his departure and his successor's move for reconciliation.

Force subsequently reentered the Presbyterian ministry. He was received from the Classis of New Brunswick into the Presbytery of Newton on October 7, 1828, but the presbytery had already appointed him stated supply of the congregation at Smithfield, in Pike and Northampton counties, Pennsylvania, on April 23, 1828. He served there for one year. Poverty and sickness clouded his last years. After leaving Smithfield he was a minister without charge, preaching when health permitted but sometimes too infirm to do so for years at a time. An 1868 history of the Presbytery of Newton asserts that in 1833 Force was a missionary at Tranquillity, in Green Township, Sussex County, New Jersey, where a Presbyterian congregation shared a church building with a group of Methodists from 1828 until 1866, and that subsequently he "went to Amwell," though apparently he did not serve as minister to either Presbyterian church in Amwell, Hunterdon County, New Jersey. The presbytery, including Force, adhered to the Old Side in the doctrinal disputes of 1834-38.

In 1810 Force bought a house near present-day Hainesville in Sandyston Township, and he continued to live there after his ministry at Walpack ended. After his wife's death on October 10, 1841 his eldest daughter Eliza and her husband Jacob S. Wintermute moved in with him. Force died on July 3, 1849. An obituary in *The Presbyterian* editorialized that in his last years Force had been poor enough to merit charity, had a fund for aged ministers existed in his denomination. The inventory of his personal estate bears out this point. His personal effects were appraised at less than $35, not counting a note for $182 against Jacob Wintermute. Force was buried in the cemetery of his old congregation at Peter's Valley. If a tombstone was erected, it was gone by 1874.

SOURCES: Alumni file, PUA (esp. data supplied by Donald Watt, the husband of JGF's great-great-granddaughter Audrey C. Watt); *N.J. Wills*, IV, 147; *Presbyterian*, 4 Aug. 1849 ("although a youth"); Stryker, *Off. Reg.*, 595; Min. Trustees, 10 Apr. ("for the support") & 18 Dec. 1793, 4 Apr. & 23-25 Sept. 1794 ("present in the College"); Min. Fac., 11 Nov. 1793, 22 Aug. 1794; Clio. Min., 20 Nov. 1793–6 Aug. 1794, *passim* ("wearing," 29 Jan. 1794); Clio. lists; *Dunlap & Claypoole's Amer. Daily Advt.*, 7 Oct. 1794 ("A dispute"); *State Gazette & N.J. Advt.*, 17 Oct. 1797; W. H. Burroughs, *Church Manual for the Members of the Pres. Church, New-Providence, N.J.* (1834), 6, 9 ("in the early"); Dexter, *Yale Biographies*, II, 112-13; E. F. Hatfield, *Hist. of Elizabeth, N.J.* (1868), 578-79, 588, 633; S. D. Alexander, *Presby. of N.Y. 1738-1888* (1887?), 28, 157; S. W. Mills, *Reformed (Dutch) Church of Walpack. Hist. Discourse Preached ... 13 Jan. 1874* (1874), 11-15, 21-26 ("he had one," "who labored," "serious divisions," "the action"); *GMNJ*, 42 (1967), 33 ("embarrassed"); C. E. Corwin, *Manual of the Reformed Church in Amer.* ... *1628-1922* (5th ed., 1922), 331, 715; J. P. Snell & W. W. Clayton, *Hist. of Sussex & Warren Cnties., N.J.* (1881), 227 (JGF active in 1826 in Sussex County Auxiliary Bible Society), 385-86, 430; Presby. of Newton, *Proc. of the Convention at Washington, N.J.*, Nov. 20th, 1867 ... (1868), 19-20, 66-68, 75, 87-88 ("went to Amwell"); W. J. Beecher & M. A. Beecher, *Index of Pres. Ministers* ... *1706-1881* (1883), 185; MS estate inv. of JGF, 8 Sept. 1849, recorded 26 Feb. 1850, Nj (photocopy in PUA).

JJL

John White Furman

JOHN WHITE FURMAN, A.B., businessman, was born in March 1778, the youngest son of Moore Furman and his wife, Sarah White. He was the brother of Moore Furman, Jr. (A.B. 1794). The father had been a prominent merchant and the postmaster in Trenton, New Jersey. In 1762 he moved to Philadelphia, where he married the daughter of Townsend White and Ann Renaudet. He became a partner in the importing firm of Coxe, Furman & Coxe, and the mercantile firm of Reed & Furman. It is uncertain whether John Furman was born in Philadelphia or in Pittstown, Hunterdon County, New Jersey, where the family moved in the year of his birth. The elder Furman had established the village of Pittstown, on the south branch of the Raritan, about thirty-one miles northwest of Trenton, and he maintained a home there, along with a nail factory, a distillery, flour mills, a general store, and a hotel. Furman seems to have divided his time between Pittstown, where he could look after his business interests; Lamberton, where he had a summer home; and Trenton, where he was active in civic affairs. During the Revolution he served as deputy quartermaster general of New Jersey. He became the first mayor of Trenton when it was incorporated in 1792. In 1788 he was elected a trustee of the Presbyterian Church of Trenton and remained active in its affairs, although he did not become a communicant until 1806, two years before his death.

The Furman boys would surely have received their early education at the Trenton Academy, which opened in 1782 with their father among the original proprietors and serving on the first board of trustees. The brothers enrolled at the College as sophomores in the fall of 1791. Both joined the American Whig Society, and both were among a group of students called before the faculty on September 10, 1792 to answer a charge of playing cards on campus during the Sabbath. While part of the group was accused of playing cards on Sunday evening, John Furman and two others were found guilty of "the same practice during the session." These three were required to confess that they had broken the laws of the College, promise never to do so again, and return any winnings they had realized from their games. For his commencement exercises Furman was assigned by the faculty to argue the opposition side of the question, "Ceteris paribus. Does the world pay more respect to one born of honorable and reputable parents or to the son of a rascal." A newspaper account of the commencement reported the dispute somewhat differently, "Does the world pay more respect to one born of knowledge[able] and reputable parents than to the son of parents who have been contemptible and worthless?"

Moore Furman, Sr., carried on a steady correspondence with William Edgar, a New York City merchant who was the husband of his wife's sister Isabella White. Through these letters we catch unique glimpses of John Furman's life after graduation. John was living at home in September 1795, but the following May he and his sister Maria made a trip to New York to visit relatives. Maria anticipated an extended visit, but John, "being now a man of business," could afford to be away for only a few days. In June 1797 when the father spoke of Moore Jr. voyaging to Madeira, he added, "but John holds himself in readiness to Esquire the Ladies at a minutes warning." In November Furman wrote of his three children being with him for the winter, adding, "in the Spring we begin to part for I wish to see them in a way of getting a living for themselves as soon as possible."

The father trained John to manage the Furman mills at Pittstown and on February 25, 1798 reported to his relatives in New York:

John the youngest will be twenty next month, he is now at Pitts Town where he is now employing himself in the Mills, etc. in order to get a knowledge of them and the other works there sufficient to prevent his being imposed upon by those he employs in repairing, and after they fall into his hands which I mean they shall do when convenient to me.

There is no further news of John until January 1801, when his father boasted of his being a staunch Republican, "active in the Cause." On August 6, 1801 Furman declined an invitation for a week's visit because, "I have been engaged to fix John and his partner at Pittstown for two or three months, and must be with them there some time before cold weather." On April 28, 1802, at Pittstown, John Furman fell from a horse and died.

SOURCES: Alumni file, PUA; J. Hall, *Hist. of the Pres. Church in Trenton, N.J.* (1912), 66, 188-89, 220, 353; Trenton Hist. Soc., *Hist. of Trenton 1679-1929* (1929), I, 137-38; II, 710-11; Min Fac., Nov. 1791 class list, 10 Sept. 1792; Amer. Whig Soc., *Cat.* (1840), 7; *Dunlap & Claypoole's Amer. Daily Advt.*, 7 Oct. 1794; N.J. Soc. of Colonial Dames, *Letters of Moore Furman* (1912), *passim* ("man of business," 97; "Esquire the Ladies," 104; "in the Spring," 106; "John the youngest," 107; "active in the Cause," 118; "engaged to fix John," 120); Trenton *Federalist & N.J. State Gazette*, 4 May 1802.

RLW

Moore Furman, Jr.

MOORE FURMAN, JR., A.B., import and export merchant, elder brother of John White Furman (A.B. 1794), and son of Moore Furman and Sarah White, was born in Philadelphia. His father had moved there from Trenton, New Jersey, where he had served as postmaster and managed a prosperous mercantile business. During the decade and a half that he remained in Philadelphia, the elder Furman was a partner in the firms of Coxe, Furman & Coxe and of Reed & Furman. After the family returned to New Jersey in 1778, Furman served as deputy quartermaster general of New Jersey for the Continental Army. The family's main residence was in Trenton, where the father held a number of public positions, including that of the first mayor of the city when it was incorporated in 1792. There was also a summer home in Lamberton and a residence in Pittstown, New Jersey, about thirty-one miles northwest of Trenton, where Furman had established a nail factory, several flour mills, a distillery, a hotel and a general store. Active in the affairs of the Presbyterian Church of Trenton for many years, he did not become a member of the church until 1806.

Furman would undoubtedly have sent his sons to the Trenton Academy, which was conveniently close to their Trenton home. He was one of the original proprietors when the academy opened in 1782, and he was a member of its first board of trustees. The two Furman boys entered the College as sophomores in the fall of 1791, and both joined the American Whig Society. Called before the faculty on September 10, 1792, Moore was found guilty of playing cards on the Sabbath. He and James Broom (A.B. 1794) were given the harshest punishment of the students involved, because both had been found guilty of the same infraction during the previous winter, and both had promised not to repeat the performance. While first offenders were allowed to make a confession from their seats, these two were obliged to stand on the stage and confess to the assembled College that they had "flagrantly" broken both the laws of the College and of Christian morality, "especially the flagrant violation of the sabbath by this vice." They promised "to renounce this pernicious practice which has rendered us negligent in our studies and brought us to this public disgrace." Whether or not they continued to play cards, the two were undoubtedly negligent in their studies, for on September 22 they were not passed but declared subject to reexamination "on particular branches of their studies at the commencement of the next session." Again on February 5, 1793 at the close of the quarterly examination, Furman was scheduled to be reexamined within the space of a month, after which the faculty advised him to leave the College. However, he must have persuaded the faculty to reverse its decision, since he managed to graduate with his class. For the commencement exercises he argued the negative side of the question, "Are mankind in general, in their intercourse with each other, more defective in the virtue of beneficence or of gratitude?"

The main source of information about Furman's further activities is the correspondence of Moore Furman, Sr., with his brother-in-law William Edgar of New York City, who married his wife's sister. In September 1795 John Furman and his sister Maria were living at Trenton with their father, while "Moore [is] at Philadelphia preparing for his Journey thro' Life." Apparently Furman became bored with the calmness of the journey, for on June 5, 1797 his father wrote to White: "Moore was out of his Apprenticeship in March, and not being engaged in business, and very desirous of rambling a little, steped on board of the Lamberton Brig *Fame* and is gone for Madeira." In the middle of July Furman wrote, "Moore may be for anything I know in a warm Goal, the Brig sailed 10th May, she was met about the 20th all well, since which have not heard of her, I see there is trouble for the Americans in those Seas as well as in the West Indias." By the following winter Moore was back with his family in Trenton. However he still had a yen to roam, for on February 25, 1798 Furman Sr. wrote to his brother-in-law:

> Moore seems rather inclined to make another voyage in the Brig than set down to anything on shore, when he is tired of roving then he must choose a place for himself where to rest, it is not determined yet where she will go, I rather think at present to Madeira again.

The owner and captain of the *Fame* was James Hunt, a business associate of Moore Furman, Sr. The adventures of the brig and its crew were described by Furman in a letter dated January 14, 1799:

> where or in what condition poor Moore and Capt. Hunt is in we know not, they were first taken by the French near Madeira, retaken by the British and carried to Lisbon, there ransomed and sailed again for Madeira, then taken again by the French and carried into Spain, from whence we received letters from them dated the latter end of September, since which have no

account from or of them so that I fear they are bad enough off, they did not complain of any personal bad treatment, they was in hopes of saving the Brig in which they could get freight for America, but I fear for them.

By January 21 Furman had received letters from both his son and Hunt advising that they were safe. However, "the Cargo is condemned, but the freight ordered to be paid, that they mean to lay it out in Salt sufficient for ballast, and Wines, and take in freight to fill up (which is offered) and take another chance for Philadelphia or N. York, in the run she will stand the greatest fear of the British our Offensive and Defensive Ally." By February 12, 1799 Furman was able to report jubilantly that the brig was in a home port, "and if she can square the yards the owners may think themselves well off, I expect she will be sold, it is too difficult times for those that don't live at the fountain head to own vessels at present."

The sale of the ship apparently put an end to the younger Furman's adventures at sea. No information is available about how he spent the next few years of his life, but he probably became involved in one of the many businesses in which his father had an interest. Predeceased by his older brother Adrian in 1794, and his younger brother John in 1802, Furman died in Hopewell Township, New Jersey, on April 18, 1804. The father sadly reported to William Edgar, "it has pleased God to bereave me of all my children but one."

SOURCES: Alumni file, PUA; J. Hall, *Hist. of the Pres. Church in Trenton, N.J.* (1912), 66, 188-89, 220, 353; Trenton Hist. Soc., *Hist. of Trenton 1679-1929* (1929), I, 137-38; II, 710-11; Min. Fac., Nov. 1791 class list, 10 & 22 Sept. 1792, 5 Feb. 1793; Amer. Whig Soc., *Cat.* (1840), 7; *Dunlap & Claypoole's Amer. Daily Advt.*, 7 Oct. 1794; Alexander, *Princeton*, 273; N.J. Soc. of Colonial Dames, *Letters of Moore Furman* (1912), *passim* ("Journey thro' Life," 96; "desirous of rambling," 104; "in a warm Goal," 106; "seems rather inclined," 107; "poor Moore and Capt. Hunt" & "Cargo is condemned," 113; "square the yards," 114; "pleased God," 128); *Trenton Federalist*, 23 Apr. 1804; Phila. *True Amer. & Commercial Advt.*, 30 Apr. 1804.

RLW

Isaac Gibbs

ISAAC GIBBS first appears on College records as a freshman on the steward's list of May 1791. Stephen Gibbs of the same class may have been a relative. On June 25, 1792 Isaac Gibbs, along with James and William Ross (both A.B. 1792), was called before the faculty because he had been involved in a violent quarrel and had "grossly violated" the laws of the College. All three were publicly censured before their respective classes, were required to sign a statement admitting their guilt, and had to ask the pardon of the faculty and promise not to renew the quarrel in the College "or anywhere else." Gibbs did not return for the next academic session.

Violent quarrels are not usually associated with anyone of the Quaker faith; however the Isaac Gibbs whose family were members of the Haddonfield [New Jersey] Monthly Meeting is a likely candidate for the Princeton student. This Isaac was born in 1774, the fifth of the seven children of Joshua and Hannah Borroughs Gibbs of New Hanover Township, Burlington County, New Jersey. The father died in 1787, leaving his estate to his wife "to support and educate my children that are in their minority." An inventory suggests that he was the proprietor of a yard goods store. His wife died intestate the following year. Their son Isaac died on May 21, 1802.

SOURCES: Min. Fac., class list ca. May 1791, 25 June 1792; W. Jordan, ed., *Colonial & Revolutionary Families of Pa.* (1950), 518; *GMNJ*, 3 (1927-28), 31, 114; will & estate inv. of Joshua Gibbs, will of Hannah Gibbs, and accounting of estates of "Josiah" & Hannah Gibbs, Nj.

The College had students named Gibbs or Gibbes from both Philadelphia and Charleston, but no connection to an Isaac has been found. Del. Public Archives Commission, *Governor's Register State of Del. ... 1674-1851* (1926), 64, 109, 110, shows that a Capt. Isaac Gibbs of New Castle County served in the Delaware militia during the War of 1812.

RLW

Stephen Gibbs

STEPHEN GIBBS entered the College as a freshman in or before May 1791. On March 12, 1792 he was called before the faculty for "indiscreetly discharging a gun loaded with a bullet toward the college." For this behavior he was given an admonition before his class. He did not return to the College for the summer session of 1792, and it has been impossible to determine whether or not he was related to his classmate Isaac Gibbs.

SOURCES: Min. Fac., class list ca. May 1791, 12 Mar. 1792.

In August 1798 a Stephen S. Gibbs was recommended for an army commission by William Rawle, United States attorney for the District of Pennsylvania, which suggests that this Gibbs had strong Philadelphia ties. Alexander Hamilton (LL.D. 1791) approved the recommendation and suggested that Gibbs be attached to the Third Regiment of Infantry as a second lieutenant. The appointment to this position finally came on April 24, 1800, but Gibbs's army career was brief. He was honorably discharged on June 15, 1800, the date that the new regiments, authorized by Congress when war with France seemed imminent, were paid off and disbanded. Gibbs was probably a Federalist, because the officers chosen were all considered "politically trustworthy" men. See *Hamilton Papers*, XXII, 141; XXIII, 580, 586; XXIV, 247; Heitman, *U.S. Army*, I, 453; R. H. Kohn, *Eagle & Sword* (1975), 229, 243-44 ("politically trustworthy").

RLW

Andrew Gibson

ANDREW GIBSON was a Pennsylvanian who has not been positively identified. No relationship to James (A.B. 1787) and John Gibson (A.B. 1793) has been discovered. Among the Andrew Gibsons found in Pennsylvania, the most likely to have been the Princetonian was the son of Thomas Gibson and the grandson of Andrew Gibson, both members of the Fagg's Manor Presbyterian Church. The grandfather died on October 25, 1803, leaving a will which specifically mentions his grandson Andrew, son of Thomas. The elder Andrew lived in Westfallowfield Township, Chester County, and may have been the fuller working there in 1783. Thomas Gibson died in 1834, aged 87, also leaving a will which mentions his son Andrew.

Gibson matriculated at the College in the fall of 1792 and on January 16, 1793 was proposed for admission to the Cliosophic Society. At that society's next meeting he was rejected. Whether or not this disappointment was cause enough for him to leave the College, there is no further evidence of his presence in Princeton.

An Andrew Gibson served on the Westfallowfield Democratic committee in 1814. However, this man may have been a cousin, since the elder Andrew Gibson had two other grandsons named for him. One was already married in 1792 and the other was probably too young to have been the Princetonian.

SOURCES: Min. Fac., 10 Oct. 1792; Clio. Min., 16 & 23 Jan. 1793; will of Andrew Gibson, 4 Apr. 1799, proved 7 Nov. 1803, & will of Thomas Gibson, 16 Dec. 1834, proved 16 Dec. 1834, Chester Cnty. Hist. Soc.; index of Chester Cnty. Hist. Soc.; Phila. *Poulson's Amer. Daily Advt.*, 2 Feb. 1804; *Lancaster Free Press*, 31 Jan. 1804.

RLW

Richard Montgomery Green

RICHARD MONTGOMERY GREEN, A.B., A.M. 1803, merchant and farmer, was born on November 6, 1775, the youngest of four sons of George and Anna Smith Green of "Cherry Grove," a farm a mile outside Maidenhead (renamed Lawrenceville in 1816), Hunterdon (now Mercer) County, New Jersey. Richard was probably named after the American general Richard Montgomery, who died attacking Quebec on December 31, 1775. Charles Dickinson Green (A.B. 1787) was his brother, and his nephews included Henry Woodhull Green (A.B. 1820), Caleb Smith Green (A.B. 1837), and George S. Green, the father of Edward T. Green (A.B. 1854). Richard's father George purchased "Cherry Grove" in 1770 from his uncle Jonathan Sergeant, treasurer of the College from 1750 to 1766. He saw service in the

Revolution as a captain in the First Regiment, Hunterdon County militia, but died in August 1777. His wife Anna, the daughter of Rev. Caleb Smith, a trustee of the College from 1750 to 1762, was obliged to move her family to Bucks County, Pennsylvania, after the British occupied "Cherry Grove" in the winter of 1776-77, but she was soon able to return. On September 20, 1786 she married Benjamin Vancleve, father by an earlier marriage of John Wright Vancleve (A.B. 1786). The elder Vancleve moved into "Cherry Grove" with his new wife. She died on March 30, 1789 and on November 11 of that year Richard, now over fourteen years old and thus legally capable of choosing his guardians, successfully petitioned that his mother's first cousin John Woodhull (A.B. 1766) of Freehold, Monmouth County, New Jersey, and Jonathan Phillips of Maidenhead be appointed. At Freehold Woodhull both ministered to the Presbyterian church and taught a classical academy, where Green received his early education.

In November 1791 Green entered the College as a sophomore. He joined the Cliosophic Society on December 27, 1791, taking the name Padilla, for Juan Lopez de Padilla, who led an unsuccessful insurrection by the commoners of Castile against Charles I and V in 1521. Green was an active Clio, serving terms as president, first assistant (i.e., first vice president), second assistant, censor, corrector of composition, and treasurer. Unlike most of the officers the treasurer was elected to an indefinite rather than a monthly term, with Green serving from June 19, 1793 to July 9, 1794. On August 22, 1794 he was granted a Clio diploma. Green finished fifth in his class, and the faculty assigned him the first intermediate honorary oration, but he seems not to have spoken at commencement.

Within two months of his graduation Green had departed on a trip to explore western business opportunities, and he soon converted his inheritance to cash and set up as a merchant with his brother James in Canandaigua, Ontario County, in western New York. Ontario County, which had only recently been opened to settlement, experienced massive population growth in the late 1790s. Canandaigua merchants earned their living by trading for furs with the Iroquois and selling supplies to new settlers and travelers, apparently at exorbitant rates. James Green died in 1801 but Richard prospered and was able to return to Maidenhead in 1806, buy a 185-acre farm on Main Street from Aaron Van Cleve, and spend the rest of his life there as a gentleman farmer. In 1815 he built a stone house on the property and named it "Harmony Hall." This building has served as a faculty residence since its purchase by the Lawrenceville School in 1953.

On May 6, 1806 Green married Mary, the eldest of the seven daughters of Rachel Burrowes Henderson, the second wife of Thomas

Henderson (A.B. 1761) of Freehold, who was a physician, Revolutionary War officer, and United States congressman. The Greens' six sons included Thomas Henderson Green (A.B. 1827) and Charles Gustavus Green (A.B. 1831). Matilda Margaretta, their sole daughter, was the wife of Samuel McClintock Hamill, longtime principal of the Lawrenceville Classical and Commercial High School, and the mother of Hugh Henderson Hamill (A.B. 1871) and Samuel McClintock Hamill (A.B. 1880).

Green participated in politics only at the local level, serving from 1813-29 on the township committee. The New Jersey Colonization Society elected him one its twelve managers at its founding meeting in Princeton on July 14, 1824. Green had manumitted two of his own slaves two years previously. He devoted his leisure to study and the encouragement of education and religion. Throughout his life he read and quoted from Greek and Latin poets, as well as from William Cowper and John Milton. He also enjoyed reminiscing about "his experiences among the Indian Tribes."

When in 1808 Rev. Isaac Van Arsdale Brown (A.B. 1802) founded the Union School, or Academy of Maidenhead, the predecessor of the Lawrenceville School, Green was a trustee and continued to support the institution thereafter. He founded and acted as treasurer of a village library. On November 2, 1811 he joined the Presbyterian Church of Maidenhead and became an elder on June 9, 1817. An obituary asserted that he regularly provided financial aid to students for the Presbyterian ministry. When the Hunderdon County Bible Society was founded at Amwell on October 16, 1816, he was elected one of its twenty-five managers.

Green is said to have been a nature-lover and "a great pedestrian frequently walking to Princeton" who also drove "all about the Country." His wife died on January 13, 1849. During the month of October 1853 he began to decline and was found dead in his bed the morning of November 1. He left a personal estate valued at $17,668, almost all of which consisted of notes for money he had loaned out.

SOURCES: Unsigned, undated MS biographical sketch of RMG ("his experiences," "a great," "all about"), & letters of RMG's granddaughter Louisa Green Peasley, 15 May 1912, & of archivist, Lawrenceville School, 9 Jan. 1986, alumni file, PUA; MS paper on members of Green family, NjPHi; E. F. Cooley, *Genealogy of Early Settlers in Trenton & Ewing* (1883 repr. 1976), 82, 85-86; D. H. Tyler, *Old Lawrenceville* (1965), 11, 56-58, 82; *Princeton Herald*, 8 Nov. 1946; H. J. Podmore, *Pres. Church of Lawrenceville, N.J.* (1948), 54; Stryker, *Off. Reg.*, 392; als, Anna Smith Green Van Cleve to Charles D. Green, 14 Mar. 1788, NjP; petition of RMG, 11 Nov. 1789, Surrogate's Court records, Nj; Min. Fac., 11 Nov. 1791, 22 Aug. 1794; Clio. lists; Clio. Min., 6 Feb. 1793–22 Aug. 1794, *passim*; *Dunlap & Claypoole's Amer. Daily Advt.*, 7 Oct. 1794; *Trenton Federalist*, 17 Oct. 1803; als, David English to Charles D. Green, 17 Nov. 1794, NjP; als, RMG to Charles D. Green, 17 Apr., no year given, NjP; W. H. McIntosh, *Hist. of Ontario Cnty.*,

N.Y. (1876), 102-03; C. F. Milliken, *Hist. of Ontario Cnty. N.Y.* (1911), I, 3, 36, 38, 41, 271; *Grosvenor Library Bull.*, 21 (1939), 62-63; J. U. Niemcewicz, *Under Their Vine and Fig Tree* (1965), 250; als, David English to RMG, 6 Nov. 1809, NjP; E. M. Woodward & J. F. Hageman, *Hist. of Burlington & Mercer Cnties., N.J.* (1883), 560-61, 566, 568, 571, 630, 849-51; Hageman, *Princeton*, I, 236; P. B. D'Autrechy, *Some Records of Old Hunterdon Cnty. 1701-1838* (1979), 19, 171, 185, 186; *NJHSP*, 2d ser., 11 (1890), 35; R. J. Mulford, *Hist. of the Lawrenceville School 1810-1935* (1935), 9, 11-12, 41, 87; *NJHSP*, 78 (1960), 234-35, 240; L. C. Gedney, *Church Records of the Pres. Church of Lawrenceville* (1941), 10, 26-28; J. P. Snell, *Hist. of Hunterdon & Somerset Cnties., N.J.* (1881), 245; RMG's will, 20 Mar. 1850, & estate inv., 15 Nov. 1853, both proved 19 Nov. 1853, MSS in Nj (photocopies in PUA). See Tyler, 11 & 56, for photographs of "Harmony Hall" and "Cherry Grove." The authority for RMG's election as elder is the anonymous biographical sketch in PUA, which is generally reliable. However the list in Podmore, 115, does not confirm RMG's service.

MANUSCRIPTS: NjP

JJL

James Henry

JAMES HENRY was the son of Robert Henry, Jr., and Elizabeth Vernor Henry of Albany, New York. The father was a large landholder in upstate New York who also owned a mercantile establishment in Albany. The family worshiped in the First Presbyterian Church in that city. John Vernor Henry (A.B. 1785) was an older brother.

James Henry's name appears on College records only as a sophomore during the 1791-92 academic year. On December 27, 1791 he joined the Cliosophic Society, where he was known as Brother Camillus. The following August he served a one-month term as second assistant, the equivalent of a second vice president. On November 2, 1792 John V. Henry wrote to John Abeel (A.B. 1787), then a tutor at the College, that James was too ill to attend classes at the beginning of the fall session. His physician forbade him to return to the College "until his disorder is in some measure removed. His being in a stage of life in which diseases are in general critical makes us acquiesce in this injunction." John's letter suggests that it would be at least a month or two before his brother would be able to return to Nassau Hall. John Henry and Abeel would have known each other as fellow-Whigs, and John apologized for not having introduced his brother earlier, being unaware that Abeel was one of the tutors. He closed with the hope that his brother "has not proved unworthy of your attention. You will do me a favor by candidly informing me what standing he maintains in his class." Since Robert Henry had died the previous summer, John may have been acting as guardian for his younger brother.

The absence of James Henry's name from a genealogy which credits Robert and Elizabeth Henry with a large family suggests a youthful demise. The inclusion of his name in the 1800 New York census shows that he survived his 1792 illness, but his death may have occurred soon after that date. His name does not appear in the many Albany sources where his brother, as a prominent lawyer, is frequently mentioned. James Vernor Henry (A.B. 1815) was a nephew and namesake.

SOURCES: Clio. lists; Clio. Min., 1 & 29 Aug. 1792; Min. Fac., class lists ca. Nov. 1791 & May 1792; als, John Vernor Henry to John N. Abeel, 2 Nov. 1792, NjP; W. H. Eldridge, *Henry Gen.* (1915), 103; 1800 N.Y. Census (Albany); N.Y. Surrogate's Court, Albany Cnty., *Index to Wills* (1895), 85. An unidentified E. Henry of the Class of 1796 may have been a relative (Min. Fac., 10 & 14 Dec. 1795, 7 Jan. 1796).

RLW

John Sylvanus Hiester

JOHN SYLVANUS HIESTER, A.B., lawyer, public official, and banker, was born on July 28, 1774, one of the two sons and four daughters of Joseph and Elizabeth Witman Hiester of Reading, Berks County, Pennsylvania. The father, son of an immigrant from Westphalia, Germany, became a clerk at Adam Witman's store in Reading, married his employer's daughter, eventually took over the firm, and prospered. He is said to have been the richest man in Berks, leaving at his death in 1832 an estate worth $468,000. In the Revolution he was a zealous whig, was captured at the Battle of Long Island, and held the rank of colonel at the war's end. Thereafter he moved from local to statewide political prominence in a career which included service in the United States House of Representatives from 1797 to 1805 and from 1815 to 1820. Politically he was a rather conservative Republican. He opposed the Federal Constitution but supported the conservative Pennsylvania Constitution of 1790. In 1805 he was among the Quids, or Constitutional Republicans, who joined the Federalists in support of the successful bid for reelection of conservative Republican governor Thomas McKean (LL.D. 1781). The Quids returned to the Republican fold in 1808, but when schism split the party in 1817, Joseph Hiester sided with the moderate wing, the Independent Republicans who formed an alliance with the Federalists which narrowly failed to elect him governor in 1817 and as narrowly succeeded in 1820.

Joseph belonged to Reading's German Reformed church, and so his son John may have received his early education in the school operated by that congregation. Like his father and most of his fellow Reading citizens, John probably spoke German as his first language.

He matriculated at the College as a freshman in November 1790. He joined the American Whig Society but left it and entered the Cliosophic Society on September 4, 1793, taking the pseudonym Aristarchus, for the ancient Greek astronomer or grammarian and critic. His Cliosophic brethren appreciated Hiester's rhetorical skills. They immediately chose him to join those representing them at the undergraduate competitions to be held at the subsequently canceled 1793 commencement. In 1794 he gave the annual oration commemorating the society's institution on June 8, and participated in the Fourth of July rhetorical competition. He also served one-month terms as president, first assistant, second assistant, and one of three "correctors of speaking," and he received the society's diploma on September 17, 1794. The faculty cited Hiester for eating off-campus on January 8, 1794 and ordered him "immediately to return to the dining room." At his commencement he stood seventh in a class of twenty-seven and gave one of the intermediate honors addresses, "An Oration on the past and present situation of America."

After graduating Hiester read law in Philadelphia. He is said to have begun his studies under United States Attorney General William Bradford, Jr. (A.B. 1772), which would have made him a fellow student of his classmate John Bradford Wallace. Bradford, who was a Federalist, died on August 23, 1795. Hiester concluded his studies in the office of Jared Ingersoll, Jr. (LL.D. 1821, A.B. Yale 1766), and was admitted to the Philadelphia bar on March 6, 1798. He then returned to Reading and was called to the Berks County bar on August 6, 1798. Perhaps Hiester met Margaretta Fries of Philadelphia during his professional training. He married her on May 14, 1801.

Apparently Hiester never practiced law, but he soon put his legal education to use. Governor McKean appointed him clerk of quarter sessions of Berks County in 1800 and the county's prothonotary in 1801. He held both posts until McKean left office in 1808. In 1809 Hiester ran successfully for a four-year term in the state senate, and in 1811 he won election to one term on the annually elected three-man board of county auditors. He seems to have held no elective office thereafter.

Hiester apparently shared his father's political views. In September 1807 Joseph vouched for John's Republican principles in unsuccessfully urging President Thomas Jefferson (LL.D. 1791) to appoint him collector of customs at Philadelphia in the place of the dying John Peter Gabriel Muhlenberg. In the 1808 gubernatorial election, the Quids initially nominated John Spayd, John Hiester's brother-in-law, but later decided to back Simon Snyder, the Republican candidate.

After this rapprochement Spayd was pressured to withdraw. A committee headed by John Hiester visited Spayd and called upon him to state whether or not he was still a candidate. He refused to do so, upon which Hiester announced that in his view Spayd should no longer be considered a candidate. This conclusion was disputed, but Spayd received only token support in the election, which Snyder won easily. In September 1824 Hiester was one of four men sent by the Independent Republicans of Berks to a meeting to select congressional candidates for their district, which comprised three counties and elected two congressman. Both of their candidates lost. The Hiesters seem to have been increasingly more conservative than their fellow Berks residents. The father nonetheless maintained his personal popularity, but it probably did not transfer to his son, whose failure to hold elective office after 1811 thus may not have been voluntary.

Hiester was involved in the founding of the Farmer's Bank of Reading, the city's second bank. This institution was organized on June 14, 1814, and on June 22 the directors elected William Witman president and Hiester cashier. Hiester served until 1816 and again from 1819 to 1827. The bank prospered, retaining the same name and address for more than a century. Hiester's other activities have not come to light. His only brother died in infancy, and possibly he devoted more and more time to managing his father's business interests.

Sources conflict on whether Hiester's wife Margaretta died on December 16, 1801 or on November 27, 1803. They had no children. On February 20, 1806 Hiester married Mary Catharine Muhlenberg, the daughter of Frederick Augustus Conrad Muhlenberg, the first Speaker of the United States House of Representatives, who had died in 1801, and his wife Catharine Schaeffer. The Hiesters had two sons and three daughters, including Joseph Muhlenberg Hiester (A.B. 1825), Frederick Augustus Muhlenberg Hiester (A.B. 1826), Catharine Elizabeth Hiester, the second wife of John Pringle Jones (A.B. 1831), and Eugenia Frances Hiester, whose second husband was James Murray Rush (A.B. 1831). The latter marriage improved social ties between the Hiesters and James's father Richard Rush (A.B. 1797), the statesman and diplomat. In April 1847, just before Richard departed for France, Hiester and his family visited the Rushes at "Sydenham," their estate near Philadelphia. Hiester seems to have been close to his children and grandchildren, whom he regularly visited and to whom he sent letters containing health tips and exhortations to industry.

Hiester's wife died on November 28, 1846, and he followed her on

March 7, 1849. They were probably buried in the recently established Charles Evans Cemetery in Reading, of which Hiester was a trustee, in which he owned a plot, and in which his parents were reinterred, possibly before his death. He bequeathed his children equal shares of his estate, which seems to have been large. The will asserted that he left "few if any" debts. He specifically disposed of his house on Penn Street near Fourth Street in Reading, some bank stock, and farms of 300 acres on the outskirts of Reading, of more than 400 acres in Bern township, Berks County, and of 500 acres in Dauphin County, Pennsylvania. The will implied that the estate contained much else besides and referred to a farm and mill in Franklin County, Pennsylvania, which Hiester had already deeded over to his son Joseph.

SOURCES: H. M. M. Richards, "Gov. Joseph Hiester," *Proc. & Addresses of the Pa.-German Soc.*, 16 (1907), separately paginated, *passim*, esp. 50-51; H. M. M. Richards, "Hiester Family," *Proc. & Addresses of the Pa.-German Soc.*, 16 (1907), separately paginated, 6-16; V. E. C. Hill, *Geneal. of the Hiester Family* (1941), 30-31 (1803 date of death for JSH's first wife); D. M. Gregg, "Gov. Joseph Hiester," *Hist. Rev. of Berks Cnty.*, 1 (1936), 98-107, esp. 106 (1801 date of death for JSH's first wife); Min. Fac., 29 Nov. 1790, 6 & 8 Jan. ("immediately") & 22 Aug. 1794; Amer. Whig Soc., *Cat.* (1837), 5; Clio. Min.; 28 Aug. 1793–24 Sept. 1794, *passim* ("correctors," 20 May 1794); Clio. lists; *Dunlap & Claypoole's Amer. Daily Advt.*, 7 Oct. 1794 ("An Oration"); Alexander, *Princeton*, 18; *Martin's Bench & Bar*, 278; A. K. Strunck, *Officers of Berks Cnty. ... 1752-1860* (1859), 59-71, 120-21; M. L. Montgomery, *Political Hand-Book of Berks Cnty., Pa. 1752-1883* (1883), 26, 28; als, Joseph Hiester to Thomas Jefferson, 24 Sept. 1807, DNA: Record Group 59, Letters of Application & Recommendation; S. W. Higginbotham, *Keystone in the Democratic Arch: Pa. Politics, 1800-16* (1952), 87-88, 97-98, 154-55, 173-75; B. A. Fryer, *Congressional Hist. of Berks (Pa.) Dist. 1789-1939* (1939), 14-24, 50-58, 77; R. W. Albright, *Two Centuries of Reading Pa. 1748-1948* (1948), 11, 47, 121-22, 130-31, 138-39; J. B. Nolan, *Annals of the Penn Square, Reading* (1933), 57, 59, 76; *PMHB*, 13 (1889), 204, 206; als, JSH to Richard Rush, 27 Apr. 1847, Rush Family Papers, NjP; als, JSH to Joseph M. Hiester (A.B. 1825), 12 July 1825, & JSH to Maria C. M. Hiester, 4 Feb. 1849, H. M. Hiester papers, NcD; *Hist. Rev. of Berks Cnty.*, 6 (1941), 102 (JSH a charter subscriber to Reading English Library, 1808); J. E. Livingood, "Charles Evans Cemetery," *Hist. Rev. of Berks Cnty*, 23 (1958), 119-25; will of JSH, 23 Dec. 1842, proved 13 Mar. 1849, H. M. Hiester Papers, NcD ("few if any").

MANUSCRIPTS: Rush Family Papers, NjP; Henry Muhlenberg Hiester Papers, NcD

JJL

Thomas Yardley How

THOMAS YARDLEY HOW, A.B., A.M. 1798, lawyer, secretary, merchant, Episcopal clergyman and controversial writer, and lecturer, was born around 1777, the son of Micajah and Sarah Field How of King Street, Trenton, New Jersey, in which town the father owned a tanyard in 1779. Although not a member of the bar, Micajah saw service as judge of the court of common pleas of Hunterdon County and as county sheriff. When Congress met in Trenton in autumn 1784,

Richard Henry Lee of Virginia roomed with the Hows for a month before his election as president earned him an official residence. Micajah named his son for Thomas Yardley of Trenton, his wife's brother-in-law. Yardley described Thomas as his "adopted child" in his will in 1800, even though Micajah had died only a year previously. When Yardley died in 1803 he left his namesake £1,000 and a house and lot in Trenton, with the stipulation that he support his mother during her life. Sarah Field How was the aunt of Robert Field IV (A.B. 1793).

Micajah How was an original proprietor of the Trenton Academy, which opened in 1782, and so his son may have studied there. The teachers between 1782 and 1791 were George Merchant (A.B. 1779) and James F. Armstrong (A.B. 1773). In October 1792 How entered the College as a junior. He roomed with John Henry Hobart (A.B. 1793) in his first year, thus beginning a close friendship which greatly influenced his adult life. Hobart described How on August 26, 1794, as "a fine little fellow from Trenton, ... not more than seventeen years of age." How joined the American Whig Society and soon distinguished himself as a student, standing at the head of his class at the end of his junior year. He retained this position at his graduation and accordingly gave the Latin salutatory oration at commencement.

How remained in Princeton for the next few years and read law in the office of Richard Stockton (A.B. 1779). Stockton later recalled that How "lived with me for four years," but another source suggests that during at least part of his postgraduate stay How lived at the boarding house of Mrs. Knox. During these years he became friendly with Joseph Caldwell (A.B. 1791), Frederick Beasley (A.B. 1797), and Charles Fenton Mercer (A.B. 1797). He remained active in the Whig Society and also participated in the Belles Lettres Society, a literary and debating club for College graduates and faculty. Hobart wrote Caldwell on March 3, 1798 that "our graduate society has been very lively," with one of the "foremost members" being "our old friend How as good at speaking and as fond of it as ever." He illuminated a different aspect of How's personality on July 24, 1798 in a letter to Mercer. After describing a romance of his own, Hobart remarked that "as I know Tom is pretty much in the loving stile I have given him a pretty high colored account of my love adventure."

In May 1799 How was called to the New Jersey bar. Alexander Hamilton (LL.D. 1791), inspector general of the United States Army, was looking for a secretary at this time, and both Stockton and Aaron Ogden (A.B. 1773) strongly recommended How. Stockton described him as "a young man of first rate talents and pure morality and integrity," both diligent and possessed of good handwriting. Admittedly he had "not seen much of the world, having been a student all his life, and having gone very little into company," but this simply offered Hamilton greater scope for molding him. Certainly How's politics were sound. He had made a Federalist speech at a debating club in New York a year previously that had attracted enough notice for Stockton to assume in his letter that Hamilton must know of it, and "he is almost frantic upon the subject of French Affairs." A letter How wrote Caldwell on December 27, 1796 confirms this frenzy; he worried that the French were sending agents to America "for the express purpose of converting th[e pe]ople to Deism," in the hope thus "by intrigue and bribery to govern our politics" after subverting the nation's "republican virtue."

Hamilton heeded Stockton and Ogden, and on July 11, 1799 How became his secretary, an official post carrying the salary but not the rank of captain. Shortly afterwards, in order to augment How's income and enhance his prospects for a military career, Hamilton also procured him a nominal appointment as second lieutenant in the Eleventh Regiment of Infantry, United States Army, under Ogden's command. The two positions yielded a combined income of $73 a month plus rations.

How's secretarial and military career ended abruptly in less than a year, on June 15, 1800. A congressional act which took effect that day eliminated Hamilton's office as inspector general and its subordinate positions. On the same date the Eleventh Regiment was paid off and disbanded, along with the rest of the "Additional Army" created in 1798 as a preparation for war with France. In his last act as aide to Hamilton, How accompanied him on a trip through New England from June 7 to June 30, 1800. Ostensibly Hamilton was reviewing and overseeing the discharge of his troops, but his actual purpose was to lobby against the reelection of President John Adams and instead promote the candidacy of Charles Cotesworth Pinckney. How actively seconded these efforts. Abigail Adams wrote that he had privately blamed the reduction of the army entirely on her husband. She also credited How with writing a series of sixteen newspaper essays called "The Jeffersoniad" which appeared in the Boston *Columbian Centinel* between June 25 and September 20, 1800, under the pseudonym "Decius." The series "vilified and abused" Thomas Jefferson (LL.D. 1791) and sought to prove him an atheist.

How returned from New England jobless. Possibly he began to practice law in New York or New Jersey, but he soon became involved in the frontier development schemes of Jacob Brown. How may have made the acquaintance of Brown, a Pennsylvania Quaker, when the latter attended the Trenton Academy. In 1799 Brown had founded

Brownville in northern New York at the junction of the Black River and Philomel Creek, a region so sparsely settled that when Brown arrived only three white families lived within forty-five miles. Brown and his father and brothers built a store and mills at Brownville. They also manufactured potash and farmed. Around 1802 How moved to Brownville and formed a partnership with Brown. Tradition has it that he invested $10,000 in the enterprise. The frontier village enjoyed rapid growth, from ten houses in 1803 to twenty-five in 1805, but it suffered a setback in the latter year when a bid to make it the seat of newly formed Jefferson County failed. How is said to have been the second attorney admitted to Jefferson County's bar. The extent to which he was active as an attorney at this time, as opposed to his other roles as merchant, manufacturer, and land speculator, is unclear, as is the duration of his partnership with Brown. In 1807 a short-lived Brownville Library Company was incorporated, with How as one of the trustees.

As early as July 1803 How was suffering from what Hobart termed "afflictions" which turned his mind to religion and caused him to pursue theological studies under the guidance of Beasley and Hobart and to consider taking orders. In summer 1805 William Linn (A.B. 1772), a Dutch Reformed clergyman, published a series of essays called "Miscellanies" in the *Albany Centinel*, one of which attacked episcopacy. How responded under the nom de plume "A Layman of the Episcopal Church" with a defense of the institution. Beasley, now rector of St. Peter's Church, Albany, and to a lesser extent Hobart, soon joined him in a paper war with Linn which continued until the *Centinel* refused to print any more letters on the subject. How's performance in the debate was widely remarked, and the expectation and hope that he would enter the ministry became widespread.

At the conclusion of his ninth essay defending episcopacy, How resigned his share in concluding the debate to Beasley, revealing that he expected to sail for Europe to improve his health "in a few days." Hobart and Mercer expressed concern at this time about How's "propensity to melancholy" as well as his shaky health. The wording of a letter from Mercer to How dated October 26, 1805 suggests that How's departure for Europe was then imminent, but where, when, and even whether he went has not been ascertained.

How had returned to Brownville by October 18, 1806, when Hobart congratulated him on his restored health but reproached him for his second thoughts or at least dalliance over becoming a clergyman. "The ministry is your choice; you are pledged to it by the most serious vows; you are calculated for pre-eminent usefulness in it. Why should you hesitate?" Why "hide yourself from your friend in the gloom of a wilderness?" Hobart asked. The delay may have been caused by How's efforts to wrap up his business affairs in Brownville without suffering undue monetary loss. Liquidating investments on the frontier, where cash was always in short supply, often proved a protracted, disappointing process.

When Hobart wrote How a year later, the hindrances had finally been removed, and plans for his taking orders and moving to New York City were in progress. Bishop Benjamin Moore ordained him deacon on June 15 and priest on August 5, 1808. Shortly before his ordination he published a series of *Letters Addressed to the Rev. Samuel Miller, D.D.*, defending episcopacy from a critique published in 1807 by Miller (A.M. 1792), a Presbyterian clergyman. How's book was well received and got his clerical career started with a flourish. He became an assistant minister of Trinity Parish, New York City on July 14, 1808. He may also have had the temporary charge of the newly established Grace Church. He preached its consecration sermon on December 21, 1808, but his involvement there had ended by August 8, 1809, when a rector was installed.

Trinity was the richest and perhaps the most prestigious parish in the country, with three congregations employing a staff of five clergymen headed by Bishop Moore. Beginning his ministry there spoke well for How's career prospects. Hobart, his fellow Trinity assistant minister, had become a powerful force in the parish and diocese immediately upon arriving in 1801, and How soon established himself as his able and loyal supporter. Bishop Moore suffered an attack of paralysis in 1811, necessitating election of an assistant bishop to serve as acting diocesan. How helped lead the genteel lobbying which preceded Hobart's election and consecration. When Rev. Cave Jones, another Trinity assistant minister, published an attack on Hobart's character in an effort to prevent his elevation, he also accused How of acting disrespectfully both to himself and to Rev. Abraham Beach, the senior assistant at Trinity. Most of the charges made by Jones, a reserved individual who apparently spent much of his time keeping a journal of real and imagined slights, were so petty as to border on the frivolous. They did not hinder Hobart's election, and the whole affair would have been quickly forgotten had not Hobart's partisans begun a campaign to remove Jones from his position at Trinity. This bid for vengeance succeeded only after much bitterness, controversy, and litigation. Jones credited How with leading the effort to harry him out of the diocese, describing him as "my calumniator in all companies, the universal disseminator of hatred and opposition against me, and the chief mover, planner, promoter, and executor of the whole business."

Despite this unpromising beginning, Hobart quickly established himself as an efficient and energetic diocesan, with How as his closest aide and spokesman. In 1814 at the general convention, the church's national governing body, How sat in the House of Clerical and Lay Deputies and led his diocese's delegation there in opposing plans to found a general theological seminary, since Hobart at this time preferred a diocesan seminary. By 1817 sentiment in the diocese had shifted to support of a general seminary, and the general convention elected How to a committee, consisting of three bishops, three clergymen, and three laymen, charged with establishing such an institution. In the same year How delivered an address to the Auxiliary New-York Bible and Common Prayer-Book Society in which he implicitly endorsed Hobart's opposition to the American Bible Society and other such ecumenical activities because they placed too little emphasis on important sectarian differences in church government and liturgy.

Bishop Moore died in 1816, and Hobart accordingly became bishop of New York and rector of Trinity. His first official act in the latter post, on March 11, 1816, was to appoint How the assistant rector of Trinity. As the senior assistant at Trinity and the obvious favorite of the bishop, How was now certainly in line to succeed Hobart as rector and quite possibly as bishop, too. His rise owed as much to his talents as his friendship with Hobart. He remained in the public eye as a polemical writer, publishing in 1816 a lengthy *Vindication of the Protestant Episcopal Church*, intended further to refute Samuel Miller's works. His powers as a preacher and public speaker were recognized with his appointment as chaplain of the Battalion of Governor's Guards in 1814 and as trustee of Columbia College in 1816. Rev. William Berrian, another assistant minister at Trinity, later recalled How as "a man of noble mien, of piercing eye, and commanding presence. His voice was clear and powerful, his elocution admirable, and almost perfect, his gesture natural and impressive, and his sermons were the ripe fruits of a well cultivated mind."

Everything thus bid fair for a distinguished career until March 1818, when disaster struck How's ministry. As John Pintard (A.B. 1776) reported to his daughter on March 30, How "was detected last week in attempting the seduction of a servant girl. The affair was exposed by one Dussenberry a city marshal, in whose service she was, and perhaps nothing has ever occurred in our city that has made so much noise or excited so much just resentment." The general reaction was astonishment and dismay, with "his bosom friend Bishop Hobart ... bowed down by this overwhelming calamity." How pleaded guilty to the charge and resigned his offices, after which Hobart deposed him from the ministry.

How's offense was heightened by his having a wife and children at the time. His marital history is somewhat obscure. He wed at least twice, but the date of neither marriage has been discovered. One spouse was Elizabeth Woodruff, daughter of Elias and Mary Joline Woodruff of Elizabethtown, New Jersey, and the sister of Aaron Dickinson Woodruff (A.B. 1779), George Woodruff (A.B. 1783), and Abner Woodruff (A.B. 1784). She died on July 28, 1811 in New Brunswick, New Jersey. His other wife was Angelica Van Rensselaer, youngest of the eight children of Robert and Cornelia Rutsen Van Rensselaer. The only one of How's children who has been identified is Thomas Y. How, Jr., United States congressman, 1851-53, and mayor of Auburn, New York, in 1853.

After being defrocked, How moved back to Brownville and lived there the rest of his life. At first he resumed the practice of law, but in time he decided to supplement or replace this occupation with lecturing. In December 1830 he was in Trenton, New Jersey, "delivering lectures on Political and Moral subjects, with a voluntary collection at the close." He is said to have spoken throughout northern New York and the West and to have been "well received."

How eventually managed to retrieve much of his reputation. On October 13, 1826 when St. Paul's Church, Brownville was organized, he was chosen a warden and he subsequently saw service as a vestryman there. Presumably he was present when Hobart consecrated the edifice on August 12, 1828. Berrian wrote in 1847 that How "has regained in his old age the respect which he had lost, and that he now leads a devout and exemplary life." He died on May 9, 1855.

SOURCES: Hobart, *Corres.*, I, cxc; II, 56, 64, 91 ("As I know"); III, 238-41, 332; IV, 479, 515-16, 525, 532-33; V, 40-41, 435-39 ("well received"), 473, 509; VI, 122, 398, 508; H. Schuyler, *Hist. of St. Michael's Church Trenton ... 1703-1926* (1926), 54, 76, 101, 355; *NJA*, XXII (1900), 186; *N.J. Wills*, IX, 174; X, 524 ("adopted"); J. Hall, *Hist. of the Pres. Church in Trenton, N.J.* (2d ed., 1912), 140, 146, 328-29; Trenton Hist. Soc., *Hist. of Trenton 1679-1929* (1929), I, 126, 191; II, 608, 710-11; *GMNJ*, 49 (1974), 23; Min. Fac., 10 Oct. 1792, 22 Aug. 1794; J. McVickar, *Early Years of the late Bishop Hobart* (2d ed., 1836), 62, 83 ("fine little"), 162-63, 185; J. McVickar, *Professional Years of John Henry Hobart* (1836), 107-13, 122-23, 165-69, 446-49 ("afflictions," "propensity," "the ministry," "hide yourself"); Amer. Whig Soc., *Cat.* (1840), 7; *Dunlap & Claypoole's Amer. Daily Advt.*, 7 Oct. 1794; N.Y. *Daily Advt.*, 4 Oct. 1798; R. D. W. Connor, *Doc. Hist. of the Univ. of N.C. 1776-99* (1953), II, 81, 113-16 ("for the express"), 305 ("our graduate"); W. Berrian, "Memoir of the Life of ... John Henry Hobart," vol. I of Hobart's *Posthumous Works* (1833), 64, 66; *Hamilton Papers*, XXIII, 228-29, 240-43, 245-46, 265, 271-72, 274, 281-82, 531-33, 570-71; XXIV, 574-78 ("vilified"); XXV, 3, 8, 19; als, Aaron Ogden to Alexander Hamilton, 28 June 1799, DLC, & in microfilm ed. of its Hamilton papers ("lived with," "young man," "almost frantic"; quotes taken from portion of letter in which Ogden quotes from a letter he had received from Richard Stockton favoring TYH); Riker, 58; Heitman, *U.S. Army*, I, 102, 548; F. B. Hough, *Hist. of Jefferson Cnty. in N.Y.* (1854), 106-07; J. Coughlin, *Jefferson Cnty. Centennial: 1905* (n.d.), 94, 224-25; J. A. Haddock, *Growth of a Century ... Hist. of Jefferson Cnty. ... 1793-1894* (1895), 464; J. H. Hobart, ed., *Collection of the Essays on the Subject of Episcopacy ...* (1806), *passim* ("in a few," 158); M. Dix, *Hist.*

of the Parish of Trinity Church in the City of N.Y. (1901-05), II, 184, 214; III, 19-27, 55, 159-60, 162-63, 241; IV, 566; W. R. Stewart, *Grace Church in Old N.Y.* (1924), 61-62; J. H. Hobart & T. Y. How, *Letter to the Vestry of Trinity Church* (2d. ed., 1811), *passim*; C. Jones, *Dr. Hobart's System of Intolerance ...* (1811), 9, 13-14, 59 ("my calumniator"); P. M. Dawley, *Story of the General Theol. Seminary ... 1817-1967* (1969), 31, 40; T. Y. How, *Address Delivered Before the Auxiliary N.Y. Bible & Common Prayer-Book Soc. ... 1817* (1817), *passim*; Thomas, *Columbia*, 15, 64; *Military Minutes of the Council of Appointment of the State of N.Y. 1783-1821* (1901), II, 1545; III, 2008; *Public Papers of Daniel D. Tompkins, Gov. of N.Y. 1807-17: Military* (1902), II, 67-69; III, 606; W. Berrian, *Hist. Sketch of Trinity Church N.Y.* (1847), 226-27 ("was a man," "has regained"); Pintard, *Letters*, I, 113-14 ("was detected"); II, 1-2; III, 36; N.Y. Diocese, *Jour. of Proc. of the Annual Convention*: (1818), 17-18; (1819), 19; J. A. Scoville, *Old Merchants of N.Y. City*, 3d ser. (1865), 67-68; E. F. Cooley, *Genealogy of Early Settlers in Trenton & Ewing* (1883 repr. 1976), 312; *NYGBR*, 84 (1953), 10; *BDUSC*, 1219-20; J. W. Alexander, *Forty Years' Familiar Letters* (1860), I, 155 ("delivering lectures"); alumni file, PUA. Some Columbia University sources credit TYH with an 1812 D.D. degree from that institution, but this has not been confirmed. Columbia's 1815 catalogue (Sh-Sh # 34400) lists no such award to TYH. See also letter, curator of Columbiana, Columbia University, 21 Oct. 1985, PUA, & Thomas, *Columbia*, 64, 284.

PUBLICATIONS: Sh-Sh #s 10595, 15269, 23054, 37879, 41084. How also edited the semiannual *Christian Register, and Moral and Theological Review* during its short life, from July 1816 to July 1817.

MANUSCRIPTS: NjP; Alexander Hamilton Papers, DLC; NcU

JJL

Benjamin Van Cleve Hunt

BENJAMIN VAN CLEVE HUNT, physician and merchant, was born April 14, 1773, the youngest son of Daniel and Elener Van Cleve Hunt of Hunterdon County, New Jersey. Benjamin, like his elder brother Ralph (A.B. 1786), could have been born in Hopewell Township, or possibly his birth took place after the family's move to Lebanon Township, where his father operated a gristmill in a settlement which came to be known as Hunt's Mills. During the Revolution the Hunt mill helped to supply the American army with a large quantity of flour.

Ralph Hunt prepared for college at the Nassau Hall grammar school, and Benjamin may also have received his early education there. His name first appears on College records as a freshman for the summer session of 1791. Although no records are available for nongraduate members of the American Whig Society, it seems likely that Benjamin joined the same organization with which his brother was affiliated. On September 10, 1792, when the faculty found a group of students guilty of playing cards on the Sabbath, Hunt was among a second group declared guilty "of the same practice during the session." His cardplaying companions were Whig members Manuel Eyre (A.B. 1793) and John Furman (A.B. 1794), strengthening the circumstantial evidence that Hunt was also a Whig. All were required to sign an acknowledgement that they had disobeyed the laws of the College, a pledge to return any winnings, and a promise not to indulge "in the like practice" while subject to the discipline of the College. Hunt did not return for the 1792 winter session, whether because of parental disapproval of this escapade or because he resented the strict discipline can only be conjectured. During the 1794-95 academic year he was enrolled in the medical class of Dr. Benjamin Rush (A.B. 1760) at the University of Pennsylvania, but he did not receive a medical degree. He was issued a license to practice medicine and surgery at Princeton on June 3, 1795 and became the first physician at Hunt's Mills, now part of the town of Clinton.

On January 8, 1805 Hunt married Elizabeth (Eliza) Grandin, with his classmate the Reverend Holloway Hunt, then pastor of the Kingwood and Bethlehem churches in Hunterdon County, officiating. Benjamin and Holloway were unrelated. The bride's father was Dr. John Grandin, a surgeon with the navy during the Revolution and a well-known physician in the area with a practice in Hampden, a nearby village in Lebanon Township. Although some sources claim that the Hunts remained in Hunterdon County until 1818 or 1819, there is more persuasive evidence that they left in 1806, moving to Newville, Richland County, Ohio, where Hunt entered into a partnership in a mercantile establishment with his brother-in-law Philip Grandin and Grandin's brother-in-law John Platt. The 1818 date may have been accepted in some sources because Benjamin and Elizabeth Hunt on January 15, 1818 released to Ralph Hunt all interest in the estate of Daniel Hunt. Sometime after the move to Ohio, Hunt bought land in Clark County and built a brick house on the road between Springfield and Urbana. On an unspecified date he moved to Urbana and subsequently to Cincinnati, where he died on December 31, 1848. His wife also died in Cincinnati on March 26, 1864. The couple had twelve children.

SOURCES: L. D. Cook, "Descendants of Daniel Hunt of Hunterdon Cnty., N.J.," *Natl. Gen. Soc. Quart.*, 59 (1971), 183-85; Min. Fac., class list ca. May 1791, 10 Sept. 1792 (quotes); MS class list of Benjamin Rush's medical students, UPenn-Ar; J. P. Snell, *Hist. of Hunterdon & Somerset Cnties., N.J.* (1881), 229, 266, 534, 542, 544-45, 549; D. H. Moreau, *Traditions of Hunterdon* (1957), 38, 88.

RLW

Holloway Whitefield Hunt

HOLLOWAY WHITEFIELD HUNT, A.B., A.M. 1822, clergyman and schoolmaster, was born April 9, 1769 at Hunt's Point, West Farms, Westchester County, New York. He was one of the six children of Augustine Hunt and Lydia Holloway, who was originally from Massachusetts. The Hunt family left New York to settle near Wyoming, Pennsylvania, but they sustained losses during the Indian massacres and moved to Orange County, New York. Augustine Hunt is said to have been "conversant in medicine and theology, and also often an adviser in legal affairs." Lydia Hunt is known only to have been a devoted Baptist. Whether or not her children were raised in this faith, her son Holloway first became a Methodist minister, perhaps an itinerant one.

Whatever the reason for his change of faith, on September 22, 1790 he presented himself to the New Brunswick presbytery, "renouncing the erroneous doctrines held by that Society [Methodist], and believing the doctrines taught by the Presbyterian Church to be most correspondent to the Word of God." He wished to undertake the preparation necessary to become a Presbyterian minister but stated that he was unable to bear the expense of such an education. The presbytery resolved to encourage and support him for one year "in order to discover what prospect there may be of his usefulness in the church." The ministers and elders of the presbytery were directed to raise the money for his support. John Hanna (A.B. 1755) was appointed to supervise Hunt's education, and he apparently decided that the best instructor for Hunt would be the Reverend John Woodhull (A.B. 1766) of Freehold, who was noted for his thorough training of ministerial students. For the next two years Woodhull presented accounts to the presbytery for board, lodging, and tuition for Hunt. In September 1791 that body agreed to another year of support, suggesting that he study "principally the languages intermingled with the arts and sciences."

On September 20, 1792 Hunt, while thanking the presbytery for its support during his study of "the learned languages and sciences," requested that he now be allowed to begin the study of divinity. He was advised to continue to study under Woodhull for another year, devoting half his time to the study of divinity and the other half to the study of Lucius or Xenophon and whatever other arts and sciences Woodhull might suggest. He was also urged to spend a year "at the college at Princeton, with the Senior class, devoting what time he can redeem from Collegiate exercises to the study of Divinity." The presbytery promised continued support if their recommendations were followed. On September 18, 1793 that body accepted Hunt as a probationer and resolved that "in case Mr. Holloway Hunt be permitted by the Trustees of the College to study with the senior class the ensuing year—that he also shall be under the care of Dr. Smith while he may reside at Princeton." Vice President Samuel Stanhope Smith (A.B. 1769) was then commissioned to request the trustees of the College to exempt Hunt from the rule prohibiting "persons who have not gone thro' all the previous studies and who are not full and regular members of College, from studying with any of the Classes." Smith also asked the trustees for support for Hunt from the Lesley Fund "for the education of poor and pious youth." The support was granted with the stipulation that it not exceed £40 per year. On April 4, 1794 Hunt submitted an account of his expenses while resident in Princeton amounting to £21.5.8½. Smith was reimbursed for this sum, and the treasurer of the presbytery was also authorized to give Hunt an extra pound for private expenses. During the year he studied at Princeton, Hunt also prepared discourses and submitted to examinations at the direction of the New Brunswick presbytery. Whether by chance assignment or because of his status as a charity student, he was located in one of the colder rooms in Nassau Hall. Sometime during his year's residence he joined the American Whig Society. On September 23, 1794 the trustees resolved that since Hunt had acquitted himself well in his studies and was recommended by the faculty, he be admitted to the honorary degree of Bachelor of Arts. A newspaper account of the commencement reads, "The degree of Bachelor of Arts was also conferred on Mr. Holloway Hunt, Student of Divinity in the College." College catalogues include Hunt as a member of the Class of 1794.

On December 2, 1794 Hunt was licensed to preach as a probationer and ordered to supply the church at Basking Ridge the first and second Sabbaths in January, and at Greenwich and Knowlton "at discretion," with permission to travel out of the bounds of the presbytery. The distance between these charges was rather formidable as a regular commute, and Hunt fortunately received a call by April 28, 1795 to minister to the congregations at Newton and Hardiston, both in Sussex County. Although Hardiston was under the jurisdiction of the Presbytery of New York, it readily agreed to be placed under the care of the New Brunswick presbytery. Hunt accepted the call and was ordained on June 17, 1795. His predecessor at Newton was Ira Condict (A.B. 1784), who had accepted a call from the Dutch Reformed Church in New Brunswick two years earlier. At that time the Newton church had been so deeply in debt that the building was sold by the sheriff and purchased by Daniel Stewart for the congregation. Even though Condict had donated a fifth of his time to the church, it owed him money when he left. It was said that only a few members of the congregation were "aristocratic" enough to have their pews painted. Hunt agreed to accept an assignment of the seats of the church, "together with what he can get subscribed," with the trustees bearing no accountability for any deficiencies in his yearly income. Since the church's indebtedness was not completely liquidated until 1818, Hunt did not prosper from this charge.

He applied for dismission in 1802 and in 1804 accepted a call to the united churches of Kingwood, Bethlehem, and Alexandria in Hunterdon County, following the Reverend John Hanna (A.B. 1755). In 1817 these churches came under the jurisdiction of the newly formed Presbytery of Newton. Hunt's brother Gardiner A. Hunt, pastor of the Harmony church and also a member of the Newton presbytery, is described as "a less mature scholar than his brother." Hunt soon started a school in Bethlehem, advertising for "twelve select young gentlemen, who are designed for public characters." His course offerings included Latin and Greek, English grammar, geography, history, rhetoric, philosophy, and composition. For the sum of $100 a year the youths were to receive board and tuition, together with fuel and candles, and training in "science and virtue."

In 1837 during a period of dissension in the church, the presbytery ordered an investigation of Hunt, who was considered to hold "New School" opinions. He responded by declaring his independence of the Newton presbytery. His Bethlehem and Alexandria congregations followed his lead in pulling away from the presbytery, and he continued to serve them, probably full time until 1842, and perhaps in a part-time capacity until his death in 1858. In 1838 he also became a justice of Hunterdon County. He was described as a man of fair abilities and a popular preacher while "in his prime," and his congregations were apparently devoted to him. Physically he was tall and rather portly with a fair complexion.

On June 24, 1795, exactly one week after his ordination, Hunt had married Susan Willis of Newton, daughter of Hannah Reading and Judge Jonathan Willis. They had three sons and one daughter. His second wife was Maria Hann. In a will executed on April 11, 1854 Hunt was either trying to make matters expedient for his executors or displaying the wisdom of a Solomon. He directed that if he died at his present residence in Hunterdon County, he should be buried beside his first wife in the Bethlehem graveyard. If his death occurred in Morris County, where he may have planned to retire, he was to be interred in the Pleasant Grove graveyard where his second wife was to be buried. He died in Hunterdon County on January 11, 1858 at the age of eighty-eight and was buried in the Bethlehem churchyard.

Hunt's eldest son was Holloway Whitfield Hunt, Jr. (A.B. 1819), also a Presbyterian minister. Holloway Whitfield Hunt (A.B. 1818), Presbyterian minister, and David Page Hunt (A.B. 1818), physician, were sons of Hunt's brother Gardiner. Holloway Hunt (A.B. 1818) was followed at the College by three sons, three grandsons, and one great grandson. One of the sons, Theodore W. Hunt (A.B. 1865) became a professor of rhetoric and English language at the College.

SOURCES: Alumni files (for all Hunt family alumni), PUA; Alexander, *Princeton* ("in his prime"); J. H. Nunn, *People of Hackettstown, N.J.* (1956), 18-19 (quote re father); New Brunswick Presby. Min., 22 Sept. 1790–28 Apr. 1795 *passim*; Min. Fac., 11 Nov. 1793, 10 May 1794; Amer. Whig Soc., *Cat.* (1840), 7; Hobart, *Corres.*, I, 92, 97; *Dunlap & Claypoole's Amer. Daily Advt.*, 7 Oct. 1794; Min. Trustees, 23 Sept. 1794; Presby. of Newton, *Proc. of the convention at Washington, N.J., Nov. 20, 1867 …* (1868), 14, 32, 38, 40-41; *Trenton Federalist*, 25 Sept. 1809 (adv. for HWH school); J. P. Snell, *Hist. of Hunterdon & Somerset Cnties, N.J.* (1881), 259, 399; HWH will, Nj; *Princeton Press*, 25 June 1858 (obit.).

RLW

Andrew Stockton Hunter

ANDREW STOCKTON HUNTER, honorary A.M. 1802, attorney, the son of the Reverend Andrew Hunter, Jr. (A.B. 1772), and his first wife, Ann Riddell, was born on July 24, 1776 in Greenwich, Cumberland County, New Jersey while his father was still a chaplain with the Continental army. Upon his discharge from the army the elder Hunter opened an academy first in Bridgeton, Cumberland County, and later in Woodbury, Gloucester County, where he also filled the pulpit of the local Presbyterian church. From 1788 until 1804 he was a trustee of the College.

Young Andrew was undoubtedly instructed at his father's Bridgeton academy before entering the College as a sophomore in November 1789. He appeared on a summer 1790 class list but must have then dropped out for a period, since he is not listed as a junior until October 1792. A letter from Alexander White (A.B. 1792) to John Henry Hobart (A.B. 1793), dated May 8, 1793, is presumptive evidence that Hunter joined the American Whig Society, since all of the other friends to whom White wished to be remembered were part of a Whig clique. On June 29, 1793 John Conrad Otto (A.B. 1792), who was closely associated with the Hunter family, wrote to Hobart, "I received a letter a few days ago from Andrew Hunter, in which he requests the loan of my conic sections. You will please to let him have them upon these conditions, that you are not using them, that he will return them to you whenever you want the book and that he will give them to you to transmit them to me in the fall, for he is so negligent that he will forget them."

Hunter's mother died on April 14, 1793; a Quaker neighbor described her funeral two days later as "Much useless parade" with "A pall over ye coffin, crapes on hats, arms, etc." One can only conjecture whether his mother's death or his father's subsequent courtship of Mary Stockton, sister of Richard (A.B. 1779) and Lucius Horatio Stockton (A.B. 1787), which must have taken place in Princeton, contributed to Andrew's behavior becoming erratic as well as negligent. On June 11, 1794, a senior, he was suspended from the College for "having absented himself ... without leave, and having been greatly negligent in his studies." The next day Vice President Samuel Stanhope Smith (A.B. 1769) wrote to trustee Andrew Hunter, Jr.:

> Your son left the college a few days after the session began & is just returned. But not attending properly to the duties of his class, the faculty last evening made an order that I should give you this information—& farther to say that they think your presence here, if you can by any means attend with convenience, very necessary for his interest. They have resolved not to pass any public reprehension on his conduct till they see you or at least receive an answer from you to this letter.

The letter was an unusual concession, probably to the father's position with the College, since most students received public reprimands for even minor infractions of the rules. Usually the more serious the misbehavior, the more public the reprimand. Whether or not his father was able to come and counsel him, on June 20 Hunter "produced a paper in his own hand writing, professing penitence for his past misconduct, and promising amendment and diligence in his studies for time to come." The faculty accepted this statement as partial reparation, along with a reprimand and admonishment in their presence, and readmitted Hunter on six weeks' trial. However, by July 16 he was again before the faculty, accused of having "been extremely negligent in his duty; after repeated trials and reproofs." He was therefore thought to be incorrigible and expelled from the College.

Nothing is known about Hunter during the next several years, but he probably spent part of them continuing to sow his wild oats. In August 1798 when Alexander Hamilton (LL.D. 1791) sought recommendations for possible army appointments, Federalists Jonathan Dayton (A.B. 1776) and Richard Stockton recommended Hunter for an ensign's rating, while John Rutherford (A.B. 1776) gave fuller information: "genteel manners & education[;] has been dissipated now reformed." However, there is no indication that Hunter ever received a military commission. His father, on October 13, 1794, had married Mary Stockton, and in 1797 he had resigned from his academy and church because of poor health and retired to a farm just outside of Trenton on the banks of the Delaware.

Happily, when the elder Hunter wrote to his brother David in Martinsburgh, Virginia, on February 24, 1801, he was able to report that his son Andrew was now studying law with Trenton attorney Samuel Leake, who like Hunter was originally from Cumberland County. Andrew Stockton Hunter was admitted to the bar as an attorney in 1802. No doubt in recognition of his professional status, the College awarded him the A.M. degree. Three years later he was admitted as a counsellor. He first practiced in Flemington, New Jersey, and was still living in that Hunterdon County community on September 5, 1803 when he married Sarah, the daughter of Ann Brittain and Dr. Nicholas Bellville of Trenton. Born in Metz, France, de Belleville came to America as the physician of Count Casimir Pulaski. Urged to set up practice in Trenton, he did so in 1778, anglicized his name, and became a prominent member of the community. By October 31, 1806 the elder Andrew Hunter, in another letter to his brother David, was able to report, "My Son is likely to make a handsome figure at the Bar."

It is not known just when Hunter moved his home and his practice to Trenton, but there he became prominent in masonic circles, active in both the local Trenton lodge and the New Jersey Grand Lodge. In 1811 and 1812 he served as grand marshal for the state organization, and he was appointed grand secretary in November 1812. He died on August 29, 1814 before his term in that office had expired. A newspaper obituary eulogized him as "a man of rare endowments and distinguished as an able and eloquent lawyer."

Hunter's father was now living in Washington, D.C., teaching midshipmen at the Navy Yard, and serving as a naval chaplain. Lucius Horatio Stockton, who resided in Trenton, wrote to his brother-in-law to apprise him of his son's death, but the letter never reached its destination. On October 4 Mary Stockton Hunter wrote to her sister Susan Stockton Cuthbert: "Brother Richard was here several days before he spoke to Mr. Hunter of Andrew's death, thinking he had heard of it, poor unfortunate young man the last time I saw him he was the picture of health, and humanly speaking was as fair for long life as any of our mortal race—it was a great shock to his father and all the family." The Hunters had experienced the danger and upheaval caused by the British occupation of Washington. They were worried about their son Richard and two nephews who were in military service, and it seemed "almost too much before this last stroke, his poor father indeavors to bear it with resignation but looks broken hearted."

Lewis Boudinot Hunter (A.B. 1824) was one of the half brothers of Andrew Stockton Hunter. The second husband of his half sister Mary was Charles Hodge (A.B. 1815).

SOURCES: *Princetonians, 1769-1775*, 225-29; *DAB* (father); Min. Fac., 10 Nov. 1789, summer session 1790 class list, 10 Oct. 1792, 11 June ("having absented"), 20 June ("produced a paper"), 16 July 1794 ("been extremely negligent"); F. H. Steward, *Notes on Old Gloucester Cnty., N.J.* (1934), II, 113; J. McVickar, *Early Years of the Late Bishop Hobart* (2d ed., 1836), 75; Hobart, *Corres.*, I, 28; als, S. S. Smith to A. Hunter, Jr., 12 June 1794, NjP; *Hamilton Papers*, XXII, 120; als, Andrew Hunter, Jr. to David Hunter, 24 Feb. 1801, 31 Oct. 1806, NjP; Trenton Hist. Soc., *Hist. of Trenton 1679-1929* (1929), II, 604-05; *Trenton Federalist*, 5 Sept. 1803; Wickes, *Hist. of Medicine N.J.*, 142-45; J. W. Hall, *Hist. of Pres. Church in Trenton, N.J.* (1912), 260-62; J. H. Hough, *Origin of Masonry in N.J.* (1870), 127, 135, 137, 140, 149, 150; Trenton *True American*, 6 Sept. 1814 ("a man of rare"); als, Mary Hunter to Susan Cuthbert, 4 Oct. 1814, and transcript of Hunter-Riddell Bible, NjPHi.

RLW

Titus Hutchinson

TITUS HUTCHINSON, A.B., A.M. 1797, A.M. University of Vermont 1811, lawyer and justice, was born in Grafton, Massachusetts on April 29, 1771, the youngest of the ten children of the Reverend Aaron Hutchinson (A.B. Yale 1747) and Margery Carter Hutchinson. The Hutchinson family resided in Grafton for almost twenty years, where the father was the pastor of the First Congregational Church. On November 18, 1772 he requested and was granted his dismission. He remained in Grafton for several years, preaching in neighboring towns until he received a call in 1774 to preach at the churches in Woodstock, Pomfret, and Hartford, Vermont. There were no church buildings in these towns, only congregations meeting in homes or barns. A town meeting in Pomfret granted Hutchinson the privilege of purchasing individual grants from proprietors of the New Hampshire grants, and by 1786 he had acquired forty-one of these small rights, for a total of 423 acres. On July 4, 1776 the family left Grafton to journey to Pomfret, where their first home was a rude log cabin; in 1784 they built one of the first frame houses in Vermont. The elder Hutchinson was noted for his prodigious memory and his proficiency as a classical scholar. The only person in the area to subscribe to a newspaper, he read accounts of the progress of the Revolution to

Titus Hutchinson, A.B. 1794

his congregations between services. He was equally opposed to Great Britain's control of the American colonies and to New York's control of the territory of Vermont.

In 1848, when seventy-seven years old, Titus Hutchinson wrote to his son Titus giving an intimate and detailed description of his preparation for college and his journey to Princeton. His early training in reading came from his sister Susa (Susannah), twelve years his senior. He also had "three months writing at a man's school at 3d house South of us, and three weeks where Judge Dana lately died; and cyphering at home, under the instruction of your Uncle Alexander, and any one who coud help me out of the mire, while I was digging out the use of figures myself, as well as I coud." Aaron Hutchinson had prepared a number of youths for college, including at least one of his own sons and was noted in the neighborhood for his eccentric manner of instructing his students. They recited their Latin exercises as they followed him about while he plowed his fields and milked his cows. His son did not receive similar instruction, either because of the father's advanced years or because Titus was expected to become a farmer. Whatever the case, on the first

Saturday in November 1790, when he was past nineteen, an age at which many of his contemporaries had already graduated from college, Titus Hutchinson abruptly ceased farming and began to prepare for college.

Hutchinson walked from Pomfret to Woodstock on Monday, Tuesday, and Wednesday the next week to listen to court proceedings and then on Thursday began the serious study of Latin. If Hutchinson's account can be trusted, in four weeks he had memorized all irregular Latin verbs, with the help of his older brother William Samuel, and his father when the latter was at home. Titus continued his study of Latin and Greek with the aim of admittance to the junior class at Dartmouth. The rules of that institution stipulated that anyone admitted with advanced standing must pay tuition for a full four years. Hutchinson's oldest brother Aaron Jr. (A.B. Harvard 1770, A.M. Dartmouth 1790) felt that because of his liberality to the school the trustees might waive this requirement for his younger brother. In the autumn of 1792, when Titus was considered adequately prepared, Aaron approached the trustees of the college, only to receive a firm refusal. Angered at what he considered an injustice, and "knowing the celebrity of the College of Princeton, New Jersey in point of giving a thorough education," Aaron suggested that his brother proceed there. His father wrote to President John Witherspoon inquiring about "the various circumstances of the College, the expenses of tuition, board, etc." With no post office or mail route nearby, it took three months to receive an answer, but the information contained was apparently satisfactory since Hutchinson soon set out on his horseback journey from Vermont to New Jersey. With the various delays it must have been March when he started; fortunately there was less snow upon the ground than usual at that time of the year.

His brother Oliver, who was delivering a sleighload of wheat, accompanied him on the first leg of the journey. The rest of the trip included such perils and discomforts as an attempted robbery, damp bedclothes, the necessity of crossing the ice-filled Hudson River in an open scow, then a path on the further side so steep and narrow that the riders proceeded single file, each holding the tail of the horse ahead. Somewhere along the way Hutchinson spent two nights at the home of an unidentified couple whose son, now deceased, had attended the College. They refused any payment from Hutchinson, telling him that before he was finished with college he would need more money than he could imagine.

Arriving in Princeton on a Saturday, Hutchinson found a room at the College Inn and the next morning attended the Presbyterian church, where the sermon was delivered by Vice President Samuel

Stanhope Smith (A.B. 1769). On Monday morning he rode out to the Witherspoon home, "Tusculum," arriving at sunrise while breakfast was still cooking. After delivering a letter from his father, who probably knew Witherspoon, Hutchinson joined the family for breakfast and was then quizzed exhaustively by the nearly blind Witherspoon to determine his proficiency in Latin and Greek and finally instructed to return to the inn to await the Witherspoons' carriage. The president then accompanied the would-be matriculate to the vice president's home, where the two administrators decided his fate. Witherspoon, noting that Hutchinson was behind the junior class, nevertheless suggested admitting him because "he has come not to spend his time, but to get an education," and Smith agreed, "just as you think best." Since the four-week break between semesters was imminent, Hutchinson was instructed to spend five weeks cramming the geometry and algebra that the juniors had been studying for four and a half months. At the beginning of the summer session he was ready to start trigonometry with the other members of the class who had, he proudly noted, begun their freshman year on November 10, 1790, the same day that he commenced his studies in rural Vermont.

Hutchinson's letter gives no further details of his college life but implies that he did not return home again until after his graduation. Almost immediately, on May 15, 1793, he was proposed for membership in the Cliosophic Society and admitted as Andronicus on May 29, 1793. He was active in the society, serving monthly terms as first assistant (equivalent to first vice president), president, and second assistant, delivering the customary exhortatory oration at the start of the winter semester, and receiving the society's diploma. September 24, 1794 was an important day for the Hutchinson family. Although he had been given to understand that the highest commencement honors were never accorded to students who had spent less than two full years at the College, Hutchinson, as the second ranking student in his class, was given the honor of delivering the English salutatory address. At the same ceremony both his father and his brother Aaron Jr. were awarded honorary A.M. degrees and admitted as *ad eundem* members of the College.

Hutchinson returned to New England to study law under the tutelage of his brother Aaron, who practiced in West Lebanon, New Hampshire. Admitted to the Orange County, Vermont, bar in 1798, Hutchinson moved to Woodstock, the county seat of neighboring Windsor County, and set up practice. On February 16, 1800 he married Clarissa Sage, who was to bear him five sons.

As an avid Jeffersonian Republican, Hutchinson soon became involved in state politics. From 1804 to 1812 and again in 1824 and

1825, he represented Woodstock in the state legislature, while at the same time acting as state's attorney from 1804 to 1812 and as United States district attorney from 1813 to 1823, a position which forced him to give up his private practice. When a state bank was established on November 10, 1806, Hutchinson, as one of the directors chosen by the legislature, was elected president by his peers, a position which he held until the bank closed in 1814. The new bank experienced difficulties almost from the start, even though the legislature passed an act directing the state treasurer to use it as a repository for all state revenues. With the embargo and nonintercourse acts impeding business and war seemingly imminent, it was not a propitious time to organize a bank. By November 1812 the directors were already winding down its affairs and the legislature introduced an act to expedite its closing. Although the state suffered losses, the bank made a positive contribution since the citizens of the state experienced much smaller losses than they would have in private banks, and the bank notes had provided the state with a currency that depreciated less than the paper of some neighboring states.

While in the legislature Hutchinson sat on a committee which met in October 1812 to recommend an answer to a memorial sent to the governor and council by the chiefs of the Iroquois and Cognahwaghah nations, asking for an annual compensation for lands that they had lost. The recommendation of the committee was the payment of a paltry $100, stipulated as a gift to the chiefs, and an additional $100 to cover the expenses of their trip to the capitol. The general assembly duly appropriated these sums, and the Indians accepted them and withdrew. On several occasions Hutchinson was a member of the committee to count the votes for the governor and his councillors, and in November 1824 he was chosen a presidential elector.

In 1825 Hutchinson was elected one of the justices of the state supreme court and became the presiding judge of the Windsor County Court. Reelected each year, in 1830 he was elevated to chief justice, a prestigious position and a remunerative one, with a salary on a level with the governor's. It was customary for the justice with the most seniority to receive this coveted post without regard to political affiliations. However, Hutchinson's 1830 elevation ignored the tenure of Charles K. Williams, and the appointment aroused charges of political favoritism toward Hutchinson. It is impossible to determine whether he was actually affiliated with the Anti-Mason Party at this time, or whether he simply had strong anti-Masonic sentiments. In October 1833, after Hutchinson had held the position for three years, Williams won the balloting for chief justice by the narrow margin of 118 to 113 votes. Edward D. Barber, a friend of Hutchinson's and a leader of the anti-Masonic faction, instigated an investigation of the justices. It was customary to have the chief justice deliver the opinion of the court and report to the legislature on the first case each year, with the other justices taking cases in turn. An examination showed that of the cases decided between 1828 and 1832, Hutchinson reported on a total of 168, three times as many as any other single judge, while the justices reporting fewer cases received equal remuneration. However, nothing came of a proposed reform of the system. In 1834 Williams was again elected chief justice, this time by a margin of 144 to 69. This was Hutchinson's last term as a justice, although it is impossible to determine whether he was passed over for the position the following year or whether at the age of sixty-three he simply decided to retire.

While involved in state politics, Hutchinson was also constantly busy with local affairs. On at least two occasions he delivered the Fourth of July oration at Woodstock, and in July 1817 he welcomed President James Monroe (LL.D. 1822) to the town on his tour through Vermont. In 1825 when the Marquis de Lafayette (LL.D. 1790) and his entourage passed through the village of Windsor, Hutchinson, as chairman of the committee of arrangements, gave the speech welcoming the general. During the War of 1812 he was the captain of the Washington Patriot Company, Woodstock's local militia, whose activities consisted of forming for parade days and musters, but no active service. When the Woodstock Fire Society was formed in 1820, Hutchinson was among its members. The Agricultural Society for the County of Windsor was organized the same year with Hutchinson as one of its vice presidents. For at least several years he also served as the postmaster of Woodstock, and from 1810 to 1825 he sat on the board of trustees of the University of Vermont, a troubled period for the university, since classes were suspended during the war years while the buildings were used to house the military. Three of Hutchinson's sons attended the University of Vermont.

An outspoken advocate of abolition, Hutchinson joined the Liberty Party, formed in 1840 by abolitionists who called for outright abolition and who split with William Lloyd Garrison over the question of the necessity for political action. In 1841 Hutchinson, as the new party's candidate for governor of Vermont, polled over 3,000 votes, a not inconsequential total since the party had received only 7,000 votes in the national election the previous year. The ballots cast for Hutchinson deprived both major party candidates of a majority, and the election was therefore thrown to the legislature, which chose the Whig candidate Charles Paine. By 1847 the Liberty Party had been absorbed by the Free Soil Party, and presumably Hutchinson's sympathies were transferred to the Free Soilers.

During his retirement years the former justice wrote his *Jurisdiction of Courts, That of State Courts Original; that of United States Courts Derivative,* which was published in 1855. He died on August 24, 1857 after a year and a half of a prolonged illness. An obituary described him as having had a life of continual activity and industry and, until a few years prior to his death, an iron constitution.

SOURCES: Alumni file, PUA; R. C. Hawkins, *Rev. Aaron Hutchinson of Pomfret, Vt.* (1838), 1-13, 28, 31-32; J. H. Vail, *Pomfret, Vt.* (1930), 65, 107-09, 151, 212, 332, 336, 352-57; Dexter, *Yale Biographies,* II, 121-24; M. B. Jones, *Vt. in the Making* (1939), 386-87; *Sibley's Harvard Graduates,* XII, 172-81 (father); XVII, 397-98 (brother); C. F. Emerson, *Gen. Cat. of Dartmouth College* (1911), 572, 574 (father & brother); letter of Titus Hutchinson to son Titus, 20 Sept. 1848, copy in NjP; Clio. Min., 15 May 1793–22 Sept. 1794 *passim;* Clio. lists; Min. Fac., 11 Nov. 1793, 22 Aug. 1794; Min. Trustees, 23 Sept. 1794; *Dunlap & Claypoole's Amer. Daily Advt.,* 7 Oct. 1794; L. C. Aldrich & F. R. Holmes, *Hist. of Windsor Cnty., Vt.* (1891), 100, 183, 241-42, 264, 271, 274; E. P. Walton, ed., *Records of the Governor & Council of the State of Vt.* (1873-80 repr. 1973), V, 3, 148, 241, 393, 402, 414, 444, 446, 448; VI, 276; VII, 138, 174, 185, 214, 264, 304, 357, 410, 491; VIII, 13, 75, 121, 171, 213, 291-95, 324, 441; A. E. & E. W. Nuquist, *Vt. State Govt. & Adm.* (1966), 225-26; *Vt. Hist.,* 19 (1951), 230; P. C. Dodge, *Encyc. Vt. Biog.* (1912), 84; A. M. Hemenway, *Vt. Hist. Gazetteer* (5 vols., 1868-91), I, 522; *Cat. of the Univ. of Vt.* (1856), 5, 23; D. M. Ludlum, *Social Ferment in Vt. 1791-1850* (1939), 172, 181-82, 195; *Princeton Press,* 25 June 1858 (obit.).

PUBLICATIONS: See M. A. McCorison, *Vt. Imprints* (1963) & M. D. Gilman, *Bibl. of Vt.* (1893).

RLW

Hugh Ker

HUGH KER was one of the four sons and six daughters of Edward and Margaret Shepherd Ker. The father was a planter at "Shepherd's Plain," Accomack County, on Virginia's Eastern Shore. The mother was the half-sister of Ann Drummond Bayly, the mother of Ker's classmate Thomas M. Bayly. Hugh's brother John Shepherd Ker married Agnes Drummond Corbin, the daughter of George Corbin (A.B. 1765) and the sister of James Revell Corbin (Class of 1794).

Like his cousin Thomas M. Bayly, Ker may have been educated at Washington Academy in nearby Somerset County, Maryland. They were admitted to the sophomore class of the College together in July 1792 and both joined the American Whig Society. In January 1794 Ker was cited by the steward for "boarding out of the dining room" but was permitted to continue to "diet in the Town" when he produced a doctor's certificate attesting to his "ill state of health." He last appears in the college records on the class list of May 10,

1794, just a few months from graduation. Perhaps his health took a turn for the worse shortly thereafter. John Henry Hobart (A.B. 1793) wrote a friend just before the 1794 commencement that while the graduating Whigs had won more than their share of academic honors, they would have done even better "if Ker, one of the first in the class, had not gone home last spring."

What little is known of Ker's later life suggests that it was unfortunate. His father had died in 1790 and left him a tract of land of unstated size in and near Drummondtown, now Accomack, the county seat. A document referring to a legal transaction dated July 29, 1800, refers to Hugh Ker as "an insane person" whose affairs were being handled by a committee consisting of David Bowman and William Seymour, two of his brothers-in-law.

SOURCES: R. T. Whitelaw, *Va.'s Eastern Shore* (1951), I, 523, 608, 662-65, 675, 722; II, 981-82, 1003; MS will of Edward Ker, Accomack County, probated 18 Oct. 1790, Vi (photocopy in PUA); S. Nottingham, *Land Causes Accomack Cnty. Va. 1727-1826* (n.d.), 37-38 ("an insane"); *Princetonians, 1748-1768*, 488-89; Min. Fac., 20 July 1792, 6 & 8 Jan. ("boarding," "diet," "ill state"), 10 May 1794; J. McVickar, *Early Years of the late Bishop Hobart* (2d ed., 1836), 62 ("if Ker"). Some connection between Ker and Jacob Ker (A.B. 1758), who lived for many years in adjacent Somerset County, Maryland, is possible but unlikely, since Jacob Ker was born in New Jersey and only came south in 1764. Hugh Ker's one-fourth share in the 250-acre tract of land, the partition of which was litigated in 1800, was only part of his inheritance and not the whole, as one might infer from Whitelaw. See Nottingham, and Edward Ker's will.

JJL

Henry Knox Kollock

HENRY KNOX KOLLOCK, A.B., A.M. 1797, D.D. Harvard and Union, 1806, was the oldest of the twelve children of Shepard and Susan Arnett Kollock. The son was born in New Providence, New Jersey, on December 14, 1778 while his father was still serving as a lieutenant under Gen. Henry Knox. Shepard Kollock resigned the following year in order to return to his trade as printer and to publish a newspaper supporting the Revolution. The first issue of the *New-Jersey Journal* appeared on February 16, 1779 in Chatham, New Jersey. The family remained in that community for three years, later removing to New Brunswick for two more before settling in Elizabethtown, New Jersey. During the war the elder Kollock was so identified with the American cause that when he encountered paper shortages he was sometimes supplied by the Continental quartermaster. He later became an enthusiastic Jeffersonian Republican and supported all Jeffersonian candidates. Besides publishing his paper, Kollock printed books, mainly religious works; however, his first edition of

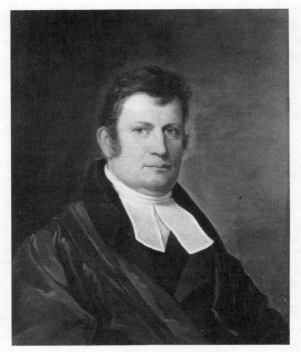

Henry Knox Kollock, A.B. 1794

The American Geography by Jedidiah Morse (A.M. 1787) was one of the best known publications of his day, and Kollock's annual almanac was a popular success. He served as a lay judge of the court of common pleas of Essex County for thirty-five years, and after selling his printing business in 1818 he became postmaster of Elizabethtown.

Henry Kollock's mother was a cousin of Isaac Blanchard (Class of 1787) and a sister of Hannah Arnett, who married Robert Hett Chapman (A.B. 1789). The Kollocks' younger son, Shepard Kosciusko Kollock (A.B. 1812), was named after another of the father's Revolutionary heroes. All of the Kollock daughters had ties with the College. With her brother Henry officiating, Mary married Frederick Nash (A.B. 1799), who became chief justice of the supreme court of North Carolina. Nash was the son of North Carolina Governor Abner Nash and the stepson of David Witherspoon (A.B. 1774). Sarah's first marriage was to Edward Harris, cousin of Samuel Harris (A.B. 1787) and Charles Wilson Harris (A.B. 1792); her second husband was Samuel King, brother of Richard Hugg King (A.B. 1786). Henrietta married the Reverend John McDowell (A.B. 1801), trustee of the College and of Princeton Theological Seminary. Jane married John McDowell's brother, the Reverend William A. McDowell (A.B. 1809), also a trustee of the College. Susan married John Nash Witherspoon (A.M. 1815, D.D. 1836, A.B. University of North Carolina 1810), the son of David Witherspoon (A.B. 1774) and the grandson of President John Witherspoon. Lydia's first husband was Asa R. Hillyer (A.B. 1812); her second husband was the Reverend Joseph Holdich (A.M. 1828). The first wife of their brother Shepard was Sarah Blount Littlejohn, sister of Thomas M. Littlejohn (A.B. 1822) and William Littlejohn (A.B. 1822), and niece of Joseph B. Littlejohn (A.B. 1796).

Henry Kollock was known as an unusually bright youth who immersed himself in books more than was considered healthy. He received his early training at the Elizabethtown Academy and entered the College as a junior in the fall of 1792. He was proposed for membership in the Cliosophic Society on November 21 and admitted on December 5, assuming the name Gama. He subsequently served the society as second assistant, first assistant (twice), corrector of composition, corrector of speaking, and president. Minutes of the society record a number of occasions when he was fined small sums for laughing or for improper conduct during a meeting, and on January 29, 1794 he and George Morton (A.B. 1795) were "arraigned before the society for insulting the same," and at a later meeting given a public admonition for their behavior. In spite of these lapses Kollock must have shown promise of the oratorical eloquence for which he was noted in later life. He was one of the speakers chosen to represent the society on the evening before commencement in 1793, and on November 20 of that year he gave a memorial oration in honor of Frederick Stone (A.B. 1791) after the latter's death of yellow fever. In 1794 he delivered a Washington's birthday address "to the great satisfaction of all present." He was one of the special speakers on the afternoon of July 4, and he was chosen to give the congratulatory address on the evening of his graduation. At his commencement he was ranked tenth in his class and delivered an oration on the passions of men. John MacPherson Berrien (A.B. 1796) remembered him as active and lively in his participation in college pastimes but with enough time to be kind to the younger student, with whom he developed a brotherly relationship. Kollock received a Clio diploma and attended the society's annual meetings from 1798 to 1800.

Kollock spent the next three years in Elizabethtown assisting his father in the printing and publishing business and continuing to read omnivorously. During this period he became "hopefully pious," and sometime in the early months of 1796 he joined the Presbyterian Church of Elizabethtown and began theological studies under the direction of its pastor, the radical millennialist and Jeffersonian, David Austin. On May 4, 1797 Kollock was accepted as a candidate for the ministry by the Presbytery of New York, and the following fall he was appointed a tutor in the College, joining the group of ministerial students who were studying under President Samuel Stanhope Smith (A.B. 1769).

Although the two had been acquainted previously, Kollock and his fellow tutor, John Henry Hobart (A.B. 1793), established a lifelong friendship during this period that persisted in spite of their religious and political differences. Both roomed at the boarding house of Mrs. Knox, and both were members of the Belles Lettres Society, an organization made up of the College faculty and graduate alumni residing in the town. This group met biweekly in the library on Saturday afternoons for discussions or debates on topics of interest. The occasion when Kollock and Hobart debated the exclusive right of Episcopal bishops to ordain to the ministry became a legend on the campus. Undergraduates, learning that these two eloquent orators were to face each other, listened to the debate through the open windows. Each speaker so persuasively defended his side of the question that the subject was continued for two successive meetings. During his tenure as tutor, Kollock studied Hebrew, Chaldean, and Arabic, and read both English and French theologians. Although he did not speak French well, he read it easily and became something of an authority on French theology. In May 1798 Kollock accepted the additional duties of clerk of the faculty. His minutes appear in a neat and distinctive handwriting, and his lists of students contain more information than is usually available, including the reasons why nongraduates left the College.

Kollock was licensed to preach by the Presbytery of New York on May 7, 1800, but he continued in his position as tutor until the fall commencement. At the request of the ailing Samuel Snowden (A.B. 1786), pastor of the Princeton Presbyterian Church, Kollock preached there on Sunday afternoons. The popularity of his sermons was a portent of the eminence he was to achieve as a preacher. People from neighboring towns drove into Princeton to hear Kollock, and the College students who were required to attend Sunday morning services began returning voluntarily for Kollock's afternoon service. Early in his career he wrote out his sermons in full, placing them in the pulpit Bible; however as he gained self-confidence and control he was able to preach without notes. Surprisingly, Kollock had a slight speech impediment that developed into a stammer when he became excited. This drawback must have been insignificant compared to the power of his oratory and a style which employed language easily understood by even his illiterate listeners, while it also incorporated a beauty and richness of imagery that appealed to the more sophisticated in his audiences. His discourses were always highly evangelical and delivered with a "glowing earnestness."

Kollock expected to be sent to assist the elderly Reverend Alexander MacWhorter (A.B. 1757) at the First Presbyterian Church in Newark. However, in October 1800 John Giles requested a dismission from his pastoral duties in the Elizabethtown Presbyterian church because of ill health, and Kollock was chosen as his successor. Ordained and installed on December 10, 1800, Kollock seems to have performed his duties adequately and added a number of communicants to the Elizabethtown church, including his own mother, but there is no indication that he achieved the extravagant popularity that came so quickly in Princeton. However, during the summer of 1801 he made a trip to New England, producing a "great sensation wherever he preached." That fall he wrote the four-page valedictory oration delivered at the College commencement by Nicholas Biddle (A.B. 1801). It was an established custom for the graduates to ask more experienced speakers among their acquaintance to provide them with a speech. Kollock apparently acceded to Biddle's request reluctantly, and the oration on the lamentable literary taste of the time was accompanied by a note saying, "I like neither the subject nor the execution. Such as it is, it is all yours."

During his Elizabethtown pastorate Kollack frequently joined other Presbyterian ministers who worked in pairs holding week-long revival meetings in the rural areas of Morris and Sussex counties that were without churches. In September 1802 when the trustees of the College appointed President Stanhope Smith (A.B. 1769) to tour the southern states soliciting donations for the College, Kollock was invited to accompany him at the expense of the board of trustees, but Smith seems to have made the trip alone. At the request of the standing committee of missions, Kollock on May 23, 1803 delivered a missionary sermon before the general assembly in Philadelphia. His preaching on this occasion was at his charismatic best, moving the assemblage to applause and the missions committee to publication of the sermon. As his reputation spread, Kollock apparently received a number of calls, all of which he refused, including one from the Reformed Dutch Church of Albany, New York. From Princeton came a dual offer that he finally accepted, preaching his last sermon in Elizabethtown on December 21, 1803.

Kollock returned to Princeton in January 1804 as professor of theology in the College and pastor of the Presbyterian church. Samuel Snowden had left the Princeton church in 1801 because of failing health, and President Smith had filled the pulpit in the interim. The trustees of the College voted in September 1803 to institute a professorship of theology, which Ashbel Green (A.B. 1783) was unanimously invited to fill. At his refusal the trustees on December 8, 1803 unanimously voted to elect Kollock to fill this position and "to request him to take measures to remove to Princeton as soon as possible." He was offered a salary of $800 a year, "instead of $1,000 heretofore appropriated, $200 being the considered equivalent to the rent of a house." For this sum he was expected to hold classes in both Hebrew and theology three days a week. Of the theology classes, one would be devoted to Biblical criticism and two to ecclesiastical history. In addition he was required to lecture to the junior class on the Scriptures every Sunday, to attend two-hour sessions of the theological society every Monday evening, and to assist the other professors in governing the College and keeping order in the refectory. In 1804 he took on the additional duties of librarian.

Kollock was installed in the Princeton church on June 12, 1804 with the Reverend James Armstrong (A.B. 1773) preaching and the Reverend Joseph Clark (A.B. 1781) giving the charges to pastor and congregation. The $500 per annum salary offered by the church was considered a means for him to augment his income as a professor, but ironically Kollock proved to be much more effective as a preacher than as a teacher. From the pulpit, "The weighty truths of the Gospel were set forth in a lucid and forcible manner, so that sinners were made to tremble, and saints were directed, strengthened, and comforted." Kollock also provided religious instruction for the children and cared for all parochial duties required of the congregation's pastor. He became so popular that the front gallery of the church, normally allocated to the student body, became too small to hold the increasing numbers who attended services. The trustees of the church then gave the students the entire west gallery, and the College released a part of the front gallery for the congregation. A pew was also reserved for Kollock's family, which consisted of his bride, Mehetable Hylton Campbell of Richmond, Virginia, and her young daughter, Mary Johnson Campbell. The Kollocks were married on June 1, 1804 at Elizabethtown, where the bride's grandmother resided, with the groom's friend John Henry Hobart officiating. The couple had no children, but Kollock and his stepdaughter were apparently devoted to each other.

In the fall of 1806 Kollock resigned both of his Princeton positions to accept the pastorate of the Independent Presbyterian Church of Savannah, Georgia, one of the wealthiest and most influential churches in the South. That year he was honored by receiving D.D.

degrees from both Harvard and Union College at an exceptionally young age. On behalf of the congregation, the trustees of the
Princeton church expressed their deep regret at losing his services
and the great satisfaction they had felt during his pastorate. Kollock is said to have based his decision to move on a concern for
his wife's health; having been raised on the island of Jamaica, she
may have found northern winters difficult to endure. However, the
climate of Savannah was so unwholesome during the late summer
and early fall that for several years Kollock's congregation insisted
that he leave the city during this period. He usually traveled in the
North, visiting his parents and preaching wherever he happened to
be staying. One summer he made a preaching tour of New England
which attracted so much favorable attention that he received a call
from the influential Park Street Church of Boston. In 1810 he was
invited to become the president of the University of Georgia, and at
some time was offered the headmastership of Savannah's Chatham
Academy. Kollock refused all of these offers, yet his renown as an
eloquent preacher continued to grow, along with his reputation for
kindness and concern for all to whom he ministered. When Savannah
suffered from earthquakes during the winter of 1811, he conducted
several "preaching exercises" and spent a great deal of time counsel-
ing frightened citizens. He was instrumental in starting the Savannah
Public Library and made the selection of the first books purchased
by that institution.

Only one incident in Kollock's distinguished career seems to have
aroused disapprobation from either colleagues or parishioners. The
Independent Presbyterian Church of Savannah was truly independent of any presbyterial jurisdiction. It had been established in 1765
by freeholders who described themselves as "Dissenters from the
Church of England and Professors of the Doctrines of the Church
of Scotland," in short, Presbyterians. However, no presbytery had
as yet been formed. The congregation later chose not to give up its
independence by coming under the authority of a presbytery. When
Kollock came to their pulpit they granted him permission to join
the Presbytery of Harmony, which in 1812 urged the Independent
Church to follow the example of its pastor. After the congregation
rejected this proposal, Kollock felt that he should present a united
front with them, and he tendered his own resignation to the presbytery in July 1813. Although the actions of the presbytery a few
months later may have been motivated by annoyance at Kollock's
withdrawal, there must have been some facts, however exaggerated, upon which to base their disapproval. Probably motives were
mixed when Kollock was summoned to appear before an extra meet-

ing of the Presbytery of Harmony to answer a charge of habitual intemperance. He refused to attend on the grounds that since his resignation the presbytery held no authority over him. That body, however, assumed the right to censure him and reported its action to the general assembly. As a result the censure was recorded in the minutes of the highest governing body of the Presbyterian church in the country.

This was no deterrent to Kollock's popularity, and in 1815 his congregation built him a new manse at a cost of $8,000. In 1817 they laid the cornerstone for a new church building to be erected on the corner of South Broad and Bull Streets. New York architect John N. Green was invited to design an edifice which was described as one of the handsomest in the country, "a poem in architecture, a dream in stone, and a petrified religion." The building, excluding land, cost $96,108.67$\frac{1}{2}$ It was so spacious that the middle aisle was eleven feet wide and the sanctuary could accommodate 1,350 people, sometimes not sufficient space when Kollock was preaching. On May 11, 1818 pews on the ground floor were auctioned for a total of $60,000.

During the midst of the building campaign the congregation sent Kollock and his wife on a trip to Europe. After his first few years in Savannah he had refused to leave his duties during the period when the climate was most insalubrious. His own parish obligations, plus work among the poor of the city which he undertook on his own, had taken a toll on his health. The trustees of the church increased his salary and advanced him half of his annual salary to make the trip possible. Sailing in March 1817, he visited the major cities in England, Scotland, Ireland, and France. He preached to overflow crowds and received enthusiastic demonstrations wherever he went. He returned in November after what hardly sounds like a restful vacation.

The new church building was dedicated with great ceremony on May 9, 1819 with President James Monroe (LL.D. 1822) in attendance. In 1813 Kollock's stepdaughter had married James Moore Wayne (A.B. 1808), and the young couple made their home with the Kollocks. Wayne was elected mayor of Savannah on September 8, 1818 and so became official host to the president. Another highlight of the latter's visit to the city was a cruise on the new steamship *Savannah*, with Kollock as one of the distinguished guests.

Kollock preached his last sermon on Sunday, December 13, 1819 in the magnificent edifice that was dedicated to the glory of God but erected on the strength of Kollock's eloquence. A "pestilence" had spread through Savannah during the latter part of the year, and ministering to the ailing and dying severely taxed Kollock's strength. Although he felt ill before mounting the pulpit, he could not be dissuaded from delivering a sermon on the Good Samaritan and soliciting funds for the Union Society, which supported orphans in the community. Immediately after the service he had two slight strokes, and a week later he lapsed into a coma. News of his illness sent shock waves through the city, and groups gathered each day to offer prayers for his recovery. He was also remembered in the services of all of the Savannah churches the following Sunday. Kollock died on December 29, after reviving briefly to suggest the hymns to be sung at his funeral and to bid goodbye to family and friends. A postmortem examination showed that his heart was severely enlarged.

The mayor ordered the suspension of business within the city on the day following Kollock's death and ordered all public buildings and all ships in the harbor to fly their colors at half-mast. All of the Protestant clergy of Savannah were represented at the funeral, with Kollock's friend, the Reverend William Capers, pastor of the Methodist church, delivering the sermon. "At the death of this great man the city was draped in mourning, the stores were closed, and universal grief expressed. All the city officers, members of the bar, societies, judges, children of the schools, and citizens generally attended his funeral." The church trustees requested that he be buried in the church's South Broad Street Cemetery, and his widow agreed with the stipulation that she could be buried beside him at her own death, which occurred in 1833.

In 1850 Shepard Kollock obtained permission from President James Carnahan (A.B. 1800), who had once been a pupil of Henry Kollock's, to erect a monument to the latter in the area of the Princeton Cemetery where professors of the College are buried. Shepard Kollock contacted former friends of his brother to help defray the expense of a cenotaph "of Italian marble, neat, and in every respect appropriate," bearing a Latin inscription that was "chaste and simple, concise and forcible." In 1854 Kollock's son-in-law James Wayne, by then a justice of the United States Supreme Court, received the permission of the Independent Church trustees to move the remains of the Kollocks, as well as their monument, to his own plot at the new Laurel Grove Cemetery. For some reason this reinterment did not take place until 1886.

Kollock's will left his entire estate to his wife and also appointed her executrix. His sermons were published posthumously in four volumes in 1822, with a memoir by his brother. Kollock's impression upon those who heard him preach was so great that it is said that many kept treasured copies of his sermons beside their Bibles. One eulogist described him as "the indefatigable student, the universal, accurate, and polished scholar, the thorough divine, the eloquent writer and preacher, and the laborious pastor."

SOURCES: Alumni files (inc. letter of S. Kollock to J. M. Berrien, 9 Dec. 1850, "of Italian marble" & "chaste & simple"), PUA; *GMNJ*, 55 (1980), 97-104; 56 (1981), 31-36, 72-78, 92-96; *DAB* (father); *Biog. Encyc. of N.J. of the 19th Cent.* (1877), 296; T. Thayer, *As We Were, The Story of Old Elizabethtown* (1964), 154-57, 190, 193-94, 198; Min. Fac., 10 Oct. 1792, 22 Aug. 1794; Clio. lists; Clio. Min., 21 Nov. 1792–22 Aug. 1794 *passim* ("arraigned," 29 Jan. 1794; "great satisfaction," 22 Feb. 1794), 26 Sept. 1798, 25 Sept. 1799, 24 Sept. 1800; *Dunlap & Claypoole's Amer. Daily Advt.*, 7 Oct. 1794; Sprague, *Annals*, IV, 263-74 ("hopefully pious"); J. F. Schroeder, *Memorial of Bishop Hobart* (1831), xxvi; H. L. Savage, MS sketch of HKK (n.d.), PUA; N. M. Butler, *Notes on Elizabeth-Town* (1941), 128-31; E. Hatfield, *Hist. of Elizabeth, N.J.* (1868), 607-09 ("great sensation"); J. McVickar, *Early Life & Professional Years of Bishop Hobart* (1838), I, 45, 112-13; II, 316-19; T. P. Govan, *Nicholas Biddle* (1959), 8 ("I like"); Maclean, *History*, II, 55; Hageman, *History*, I, 209; II, 54-55, 97; *Amer. Missionary Register*, 1 (1821), 377-80 ("indefatigable student"); H. G. Hinsdale, *First Pres. Church, Princeton, N.J.* (1888), 34-35; R. R. Cawley, *Brief Hist. of the First Pres. Church of Princeton* (1954), n.p. ("The weighty truths"); A. S. Link, *First Pres. Church of Princeton* (1967), 56-58 ("glowing earnestness"); Min. Trustees, Sept. 1802–Apr. 1804 ("instead of $1,000"); W. W. Clayton, *Hist. of Union & Middlesex Cnties., N.J.* (1882), 215-16; C. C. Jones, *Hist. of Savannah, Ga.* (1890), 500-02, 513 ("a poem," "At the death"); S. K. Kollock, *Sermons on Various Subjects by the Late Henry Kollock, D.D. with a Memoir of the Life of the Author* (1822), xiii-xlviii; G. White, *Hist. Collections of Ga.* (3d. ed., 1855), 369-70; T. Gamble, *Savannah Duels & Duellists* (1923), 69-70; F. D. Lee & J. L. Agnew, *Hist. Reg. of City of Savannah* (1869), 175; A. A. Laurence, *James Moore Wayne* (1943), 19-20; M. Bell, Jr., *Savannah, Ahoy!* (1959), 4-5, 12, 36-37; E. D. Barrow & L. P. Bell, *Anchored Yesterdays* (1923), 117.

PUBLICATIONS: Sh-Sh #s 4489, 23169 & 9219. *National Union Catalog: Pre-1956 Imprints* also credits him with *Course of 14 theological lectures in the College of New Jersey* (Princeton, 1806-07) and gives NjP as the only repository. No such copy has been found.

RLW

William Ludwell Lee

WILLIAM LUDWELL LEE, planter, was born January 23 or 25, 1775 in London, the son of William and Hannah Philippa Ludwell Lee. His twin brother was stillborn, but he had two sisters who reached adulthood. The father had come to London from Virginia in 1768 as a merchant in the Virginia trade. He was also active in Wilkesite radical politics, which led to his election as sheriff of London in 1773 with his partner Stephen Sayre (A.B. 1757), and to Lee's election as an alderman in 1775, the only American ever to hold that office. The mother was the eldest daughter and coheiress of Philip Ludwell, and brought as her dowry "Greenspring," the large estate near Jamestown in James City County, Virginia, which had been the seat of Governor Sir William Berkeley in the seventeenth century.

In 1777 William Lee was appointed American commercial agent in Nantes, France, and later that year he became commissioner to the courts of Vienna and Berlin. His career as a diplomat was largely a failure, thanks to the difficulty of his task, his own personality, and his becoming entangled in the dispute between his brother Arthur Lee and the other two commissioners to France, Benjamin Franklin and Silas Deane. In June 1779 he was recalled, but he remained in Brussels for four more years. William Ludwell Lee's earliest memories would thus have been of the assorted European cities to which his father moved his family.

In September 1783 Lee sailed for Virginia with his father, who retired to "Greenspring." The females planned to follow shortly thereafter, but the mother died, and Lee's sisters, Portia and Cornelia, were cared for by relatives in London until their return to Virginia in November 1785. In January 1786 they went to live with their uncle and aunt, Francis Lightfoot Lee and Rebecca Tayloe Lee, at "Menokin," Richmond County, and shortly afterwards young William was placed in the school of Walker Maury (William and Mary 1771) in Williamsburg. The elder William Lee, now in poor health and almost blind, apparently lacked the vigor to raise his own children.

Lee did not remain under Maury's tutelage long. Sometime in 1786 Maury moved his school to Norfolk, Virginia, and Lee did not follow him there. By 1790 Lee was a student in the grammar school at Princeton, for on September 30 he gave the valedictory when a number of "the grammar scholars delivered orations in the college hall." In November he entered the College as a freshman. The decision to educate him in Princeton is not surprising. His aunt Alice Lee had married Dr. William Shippen, Jr. (A.B. 1754), and Henry Lee (A.B. 1773), Charles Lee (A.B. 1775), Richard Bland Lee (Class of 1779), and Edmund Jennings Lee (A.B. 1792) were first cousins once removed through their mothers and second cousins through their fathers. Cassius Lee (Class of 1798) was a first cousin and Francis Lightfoot Lee (Class of 1820) a first cousin once removed.

Lee's stay at the College was short. He joined the Cliosophic Society, taking Orchomenius as his pseudonym. Two towns of ancient Greece were named Orchomenus, but the reason for Lee's choice seems obscure, unless a clue is provided by the renowned temple to the Graces in Orchomenus of Boeotia, after the building of which they became known as the Orchomenian goddesses. Sometime before March 3, 1791 Lee fell seriously ill, for in a letter on that date from his uncle Richard Henry Lee to his cousin and fellow student, Edmund Jennings Lee, the former noted that, although William was now recovering, every precaution should be taken to avoid a relapse. One such precaution apparently was sending him home to recuperate, for he did not return to the College for the spring semester.

Lee's father died in 1795 and left him approximately 8,000 acres, the bulk of his estate. In the will he asked his son to drop the surname

Lee and become William Ludwell only, in order to revive the name of his maternal ancestors, a request to which his son did not adhere. Lee embarked on his career as a landed gentleman with some vigor. In July 1796 the architect Benjamin Henry Latrobe visited "Greenspring," charged with the task of designing a new house. Lee had decided to raze the rambling old mansion, which dated back to the seventeenth century, though possibly not to Berkeley's tenure, and "erect a modest Gentleman's house" in its stead. Latrobe observed that Lee "seems activated by the spirit of improvement, and indeed the Estate wants it in every respect." Latrobe abandoned the project a year later. The old house was now gone, but Latrobe and Lee could not agree on a plan for its replacement, although Latrobe submitted a new design three times. Latrobe complained that as Lee's

> meanness seemed to grow upon him daily, I found it impossible for me to bend my ideas, to a compliance with his mode of procedure with his workmen. I therefore declined any further connection with him.

After the death of their uncle and aunt in January 1797, Lee sent a carriage to bring his two sisters to "Greenspring" to live with him, but they chose instead to move in with their cousin Richard Bland Lee. In 1798 Lee commanded a company of militia. That July, when fears of war with France were at their peak, he asked the governor to equip his men with firelocks. In 1800 he was named a visitor of the College of William and Mary.

Lee's health seems always to have been frail, and he died unmarried on January 24, 1803. He was buried near his father in the church yard at Jamestown. His sisters became his coheiresses, and a friend reported that at his death their "rich Brother" had had "an unencumbered fortune of at least fifty thousand pounds, half of which is in money in England." Not everything went to them, however. Lee manumitted and made some provision for all of his slaves, probably numbering around one hundred, a move which is said to have cost the estate $30,000. He left his library to the College of William and Mary and also tried to endow a free school in James City County "for the benefit of such persons whose indigent situation forbids their acquiring even the rudiments of an education." This wish was frustrated, because the tract he had allotted for the purpose was inadequate, because of technical flaws in the language of the will, and because none of the heirs or executors lived nearby, which turned the settling of the estate into a protracted and probably a badly managed business.

SOURCES: E. J. Lee, *Lee of Va.* (1895), 235-53; C. G. Lee, Jr., *Lee Chronicle* (1957), 79, 117, 204-05, 236-41; "William Lee," *DAB*; *VMHB*, 38 (1930), 50; *WMQ*, 1st ser., 24 (1915), 1-2; 2d ser., 14 (1934), 170; 3d ser., 11 (1954), 378; *Pa. Packet, & Daily Advt.*, 7 Oct. 1790 ("the grammar"); Min. Fac., 29 Nov. 1790; Clio. lists; alumni file of Edmund J. Lee (A.B. 1817), PUA (for transcript of 1791 R. H. Lee letter); E. C. Carter II et al., eds., *Va. Journals of Benjamin Henry Latrobe* (1977), I, 181-82 ("erect," "seems activated"), 247 ("meanness seemed"); L. R. Caywood, "Green Spring Plantation," *VMHB*, 65 (1957), 67-83; *VMHB*, 85 (1977), 390; L. L. Montague, "Cornelia Lee's Wedding," *VMHB*, 80 (1972), 453-55 ("an unencumbered"); *Cal. Val. St. Papers*, VIII, 497-98; College of William & Mary, *Cat.* (1859), 22; letter from archivist, William & Mary, 25 Jan. 1983, PUA; E. G. Swem, "The Lee Free School & the College of William & Mary," *WMQ*, 3d ser., 16 (1959), 207-13 ("for the benefit").

JJL

Reuben Leigh

REUBEN LEIGH was born on January 25, 1776, the eldest child among three sons and five daughters of Joseph and Jerusha Evans Leigh of Princeton. The father was a tailor who lived on the east side of what is now Witherspoon Street. He helped found a company of firefighters in Princeton in 1788, and contributed to the town's Presbyterian church in 1784 and 1804 and to the founding of a Princton academy in 1790. Subsequently he moved to nearby Hopewell, joined its Old School Baptist Church, and died in that town in 1823. Jerusha Evans Leigh was the daughter of Richard Evans of Hopewell and his second wife, Elizabeth.

Leigh was a student at the Nassau Hall grammar school in September 1788, when he was ranked first in the second class at the school's examination. He continued to excel as a student in September 1790, when he was among the grammar school students who entered the College. He was one of three winners of a competition in Latin extemporizing, and delivered a salutatory oration in Latin at a series of orations by the grammar scholars held in Nassau Hall. Leigh remained at the College through his sophomore year but did not return in November 1792.

Leigh's subsequent activities have not been traced. He died on February 16, 1811.

SOURCES: Transcript made in 1938 of Joseph Leigh's family Bible (given him in 1770), Leigh family folder, Hopewell Museum, Hopewell, N.J.; MS bill, Joseph Leigh to John H. Hobart (A.B. 1793), Nov. 1791–Mar. 1792 (father's occupation), Hobart Papers, TxAuCH (photocopy in Hobart file, PUA); Hageman, *Princeton*, I, 72, 212; II, 18, 88, 99, 219; Phila. *Independent Gazetteer*, 3 Oct. 1788; *Pa. Packet, & Daily Advt.*, 7 Oct. 1790; Min. Fac., 29 Nov. 1790, undated class list ca. May 1792. College sources describe Leigh as a resident of Princeton, and Joseph was the only Leigh who owned property in Princeton at the time of Reuben's matriculation (information supplied by Wanda S. Gunning). Reuben Lee of Alexandria Township, Hunterdon County, who was a trustee in 1825 of the Alexandria Methodist Meeting (now Everittstown United Methodist Church), was a bit too young to have attended the College in 1790 (P. B. D'Autrechy, *Some Records of Old Hunterdon Cnty. 1701-1838* [1979], 35; MS 1830 Federal census schedules for Hunterdon Cnty., microfilm in NjP). The 1790 newspaper account refers to "Heuben Leight," an apparent misprint. Wanda S. Gunning kindly supplied references used in this sketch.

JJL

James Hude Neilson

JAMES HUDE NEILSON, A.B., merchant, was the second son of William Neilson and Susan Hude Neilson of New York City. William Neilson was a nephew of John and James Neilson, the grandfather and great uncle of John Neilson (A.B. 1793). Orphaned at eighteen, he was brought from Ireland by James Neilson, who trained his nephew in his prosperous mercantile establishment in New Brunswick. As early as 1768 William Neilson was already well established in his own business in New York City. He owned a number of ships that traded with Ireland, from where he imported Irish clover seed, Hibernian pig metal, Irish beef, and indentured servants. After the Revolution he opened a freight and passenger service to Bordeaux. Sometime about 1773, he married the daughter of James Hude, who had served several terms as the mayor of New Brunswick and who was a trustee of the College from 1748 to 1762. Susan Hude Neilson may have been deceased by the time her son began his college education, for her father's will of 1791 mentions only a niece and nephew as his heirs.

Neilson matriculated at the College as a freshman in November 1790. Like his cousin John Neilson he joined the American Whig Society. At his commencement ceremonies he took the part of the opponent on the question, "Is the institution of voluntary popular societies, to watch the motions of government in the present state of this country wise or useful[?]"

Neilson may have served his mercantile apprenticeship under Col. John Neilson of New Brunswick, father of John Neilson, the Nassau Hall graduate, in reciprocation for two of the colonel's sons who received their business training in New York under William Neilson's tutelage. In 1797 William Neilson made his older son, William Neilson, Jr., a partner, changing the firm name to William Neilson & Co. At this time James Neilson was serving as head clerk. At the turn of the century the Neilson firm was considered one of the most extensive commercial establishments in the city. William Neilson's position among the leading families of New York is amply demonstrated by his marriage on September 19, 1801 to Lady Catherine Duer, widow of William Duer, and daughter of William Alexander, Lord Stirling. On July 25, 1804 James Neilson married Sarah Coles, daughter of Gen. Nathaniel Coles of Dosoris, Long Island (present-day Oyster Bay), with the Reverend Dr. John Rodgers (D.D. 1760), pastor of the First Presbyterian Church of New York City, officiating. William Neilson, Jr., married a daughter of John B. Coles, a wealthy New York merchant who was a city alderman and became the president of the American Insurance Company. The two Coles/Neilson marriages have caused some confusion in several sources; the brides may have been cousins, but no relationship has been established.

No further information about James Neilson has been found. He did not continue with the Neilson business, probably leaving some time before 1807, when the firm name was changed to William Neilson & Son. The only thing known is that he left New York; there is no indication that he either returned to New Brunswick or settled near his wife's former home on Long Island. He is reputed to have had a son who became known as "Captain Bill" Neilson. He is first listed as deceased in the 1827 College catalogue.

SOURCES: Alumni file, PUA; H. W. Lanier, *Century of Banking in N.Y., 1822-1922* (1922), 124; W. W. Clayton, *Hist. of Union and Middlesex Cnties.* (1882), 501; W. H. Benedict, *New Brunswick in Hist.* (1925), 48; Min. Fac., 29 Nov. 1790, 22 Aug. 1794; Amer. Whig Soc., *Cat.* (1840), 7; *Dunlap & Claypoole's Amer. Daily Advt.*, 7 Oct. 1794; J. A. Scoville, *Old Merchants of N.Y. City*, 2d ser. (1864), 45, 224; 4th ser. (1866), 142-46; 5th ser. (1870), 84, 169-70; M. Armstrong, *Five Generations: Life & Letters of an Amer. Family* (1930), 143-44; W. H. Benedict, *Neilsons of the 18th Century* (1924), 24-25; MS will of James Hude, Nj.

Neilson may have moved south to establish his own mercantile business. A James C. Neilson was in Baltimore, Maryland in 1818 when he sat for a portrait by Thomas Sully. In 1814 Sully had done a portrait of Miss Eliza Neilson of Ireland. By 1818 she was deceased and Sully made two copies of her likeness. In 1820 the painter William Dunlap, visiting Norfolk, Virginia, was engaged to make yet another copy of Miss Neilson's portrait and also to do an original of James Neilson, then of that city. Neilson's cousin James was actively involved in the family business in New Brunswick. The man in Baltimore could have been either the subject of this sketch, with an incorrect middle initial added, or a nephew of that name. See E. Biddle & M. Fielding, *Life & Works of Thomas Sully* (1969), 239; *Diary of William Dunlap* (1929-31), II, 504-81.

RLW

Paul Paulison

PAUL PAULISON, A.B., teacher and surveyor, was born January 31, 1770, the son of John and Gertrude Terhune Paulison of Hackensack, Bergen County, New Jersey. The Paulison family traced its ancestry to a Paulus Pieterse who was one of Peter Stuyvesant's commissioners for fortifying Bergen, New Jersey, and one of the founders of the Reformed Dutch Church in that area. For several generations the sons followed the Dutch tradition of adopting a surname meaning "son of." Paul Paulison was the first to use the same surname as his father. The elder Paulison was one of the liberal contributors when a new building was erected for the Reformed Dutch Church of Hackensack between 1790 and 1792 and accordingly had his name cut in the stone of the front of the church.

Paulison was probably related though his mother to John Terhune (A.B. 1793), and on June 3, 1793 he wrote to Terhune inquiring about the requirements for entering the College as a senior. The letter was sent from Flatbush, Long Island, where Paulison may have been studying at the Erasmus Hall Academy. Wherever he received his preparation, he evidently qualified as a senior, for he matriculated as a member of that class in November 1793. He was proposed for membership in the Cliosophic Society on November 20, 1793, but on November 27, "some objections appearing," his proposal was withdrawn. There is no way of knowing whether he had any personal characteristics to which the society members objected or whether the fact that his father was a loyalist, who in 1777 had been ordered arrested for his political leanings, made Paulison unacceptable as a Cliosophian. If the latter was the case, the question which he was chosen to replicate at commencement was particularly pertinent: "Ceteris paribus. Does the world pay more respect to one born of honorable and reputable parents or to the son of a rascal."

Paulison is said to have studied theology after graduation, with the intent of entering the ministry of the Reformed Dutch Church. He was, however, never ordained. A family genealogy claims that ill health prevented him from preaching. One source states that he remained in Princeton as a teacher of languages. He was never so employed by the College, but it is possible that he taught at the Nassau Hall grammar school and that he was one of the theology students who studied privately under Samuel Stanhope Smith (A.B. 1769), although no confirmation of this conjecture has been found. Another source claims that Paulison obtained a teaching post at the New Bern Academy headed by Thomas P. Irving (A.B. 1789) in New Bern, Craven County, North Carolina, and later taught at Erasmus Hall Academy.

Paulison eventually returned to Hackensack where he became a surveyor and was responsible for drawing up many local maps and land records. On October 3, 1813, at the age of forty-three, he married twenty-year-old Mary Cleveland, the daughter of Ichabod Cleveland of Hackensack. The marriage produced nine children, eight of whom reached adulthood. In 1830 or 1831 Paulison retired to a farm at Old Hackensack (Ridgefield Park), where he died on January 6, 1832, leaving his personal estate to be divided among his offspring. His real estate was to be split among his four sons, each of whom was assigned to give $400 to a specific sister. Paulison's will showed that he owned pews in both the English Neighborhood and Hackensack Dutch Reformed churches. Soon after his death his widow moved to New York City with her children.

Christian Zabriskie Paulison (A.B. 1822) and Richard R. Paulison (A.B. 1834) were nephews, sons of Paulison's brother Richard, and John C. Paulison (A.B. 1866) was a great nephew.

SOURCES: Alumni files, PUA; Min. Fac., 11 Nov. 1793, 22 Aug. 1794; Clio. Min., 20 & 27 Nov. 1793; E. Alfred Jones, "Loyalists of N.J.," N.J. Hist. Soc. Colls., 10 (1926/27), 298; A. C. Leiby, Revolutionary War in the Hackensack Valley (1962), 108, 123-24, 213-14; B. C. Taylor, Annals of the Classis of Bergen (1857), 192-94; Alexander, Princeton, 277; W. W. Clayton, Hist. of Bergen & Passaic Cnties. (1882), 293-94; E. J. Cleveland, Gen. of the Cleveland & Cleaveland Families (1899), 456-57; Paulison will, dated 29 Dec. 1831, Nj; N.Y. City directories, 1834-38.

RLW

Henry Polhemus

HENRY POLHEMUS, A.B., Reformed Dutch minister, the son of Daniel and Cornelia Polhemus, was born in Harlingen, Somerset County, New Jersey, on May 31, 1772 and baptized in the Dutch church there on August 2, 1772. Members of the Polhemus family in New Jersey claimed descent from Johannes Theodorus Polhemus, a minister of the Reformed Church in the Netherlands.

Henry Polhemus matriculated at the College as a sophomore at the start of the 1792 summer session and joined the Cliosophic Society on June 6 of that year with the pseudonym Androcles. Minutes of the society show that he was an active member, serving as corrector of speaking, corrector of composition, censor, two terms as second assistant, and one as president. At the end of his senior year Polhemus ranked eighth in his class as one of the intermediate honorees. At the commencement exercises he gave an oration on the gratitude due to those who have established the independence and freedom of the United States.

The next three years were spent in theological studies under the Reverend Theodore (Dirck) Romeyn (A.B. 1765), pastor of the Schenectady, New York, Dutch Reformed Church. Licensed by the Classis of New York in April 1798, Polhemus on February 7, 1799 received a call from the united Dutch churches of Harlingen and Neshanic, where he was to preach two sabbaths at his home church of Harlingen and one sabbath at Neshanic, alternating with the Reverend William Richmond Smith (A.B. 1773). For his labors Polhemus received from the Harlingen church the use of its parsonage, rated as worth £27.10, and £72.10 in two half-yearly payments. From Neshanic, still sometimes referred to as "Shannick," he received £50 proclamation money in half-yearly payments. The first consistory meeting recorded in Polhemus's handwriting was July 22, 1799, when the chief business discussed was the application for dismission from membership submitted by John Staats. His request was denied, and it was agreed that "if the Consistory would not suffer the new repeating tunes to be sung as often as they had been latterly, he would be satisfied, and would again unite in harmony and brotherly love." At the same meeting Polhemus requested that a "waggon house" be erected on the parsonage property; the consistory agreed and empowered the managers to proceed with the construction.

On March 13, 1799, almost immediately after his pastoral appointment, Polhemus married Mary, daughter of Henry and Catharine Van Marter Disbrough. Before her death on July 18, 1807 the couple had two sons and two daughters, including Henry Disbrough Polhemus (A.B. 1818) and Catherine, who married James Schureman Nevius (A.B. 1816). Polhemus's second marriage was to Lucretia, daughter of Martin and Altje Van Dyke Hageman, on March 3, 1808, at the Kingston Presbyterian Church, with the Reverend David Comfort (A.B. 1795) officiating. The couple had one son.

Polhemus had a reputation at the Harlingen church for being earnest and acceptable in his preaching and laborious and conscientious in the performance of his duties. In 1800 he took on the added duties of trustee of Queen's College in New Brunswick, a position which he held until his death. In 1809 he accepted a call from the English Neighborhood Church, present Ridgefield, in Bergen County, New Jersey. He moved again in June 1813, accepting a call to the Shawangunk Church, now Wallkill, in Ulster County, New York. His death occurred on November 2, 1815, with accounts differing as to whether he was returning from a visit to New Jersey or to New York City when he was stricken with typhoid fever. He was buried beneath the pulpit of the Shawangunk Church in accordance with the custom of the congregation. He was described as a man of fine appearance and manners who was thoroughly devoted to his work. It is said that his parishioners frequently referred to him as "that dear dominie Polhemus."

Sources: Alumni file, PUA; *NYGBR*, 92 (1961), 163-65; *GMNJ*, 15 (1940), 25-26; 29 (1954), 61; 32 (1957), 33; 41 (1966), 12; Min. Fac., class list ca. May 1792, 22 Aug. 1794; Clio. lists; Clio. Min., 9 Jan. 1793–9 July 1794 *passim*; *Dunlap & Claypoole's Amer.*

Daily Advt., 7 Oct. 1794; *Princetonians, 1748-1768*, 521-25; A. Messler, *Forty Years at Raritan* (1873), 261-63; C. C. Hoagland, *Hist. of Prot. Reformed Church of Harlingen* (1847), 10; C. E. Corwin, *Manual of the Reformed Church in Amer. ... 1628-1922* (5th ed., 1922), 454, 727; *Cat. of the Officers & Alumni of Rutgers College* (1909), 8; *Trenton Federalist*, 21 Mar. 1808; P. H. Smith, *Legends of the Shawangunk* (1965), 201.

RLW

Edwin Tasker Reese

EDWIN TASKER REESE, A.B., educator, was born May 24, 1774, probably at Salem, Sumter District, South Carolina, where his father, the Reverend Thomas Reese (A.B. 1768, D.D. 1794), had accepted a call during the previous year to serve the local Presbyterian church. His mother was Jane Harris Reese, daughter of Charles Harris and his first wife Jane McIlhenny. Samuel Harris (A.B. 1787) was her half-brother by her father's second wife Elizabeth Thomson Baker, daughter of the Reverend John Thomson. Charles Wilson Harris (A.B. 1792) was the son of Jane's elder brother Robert Harris. Both families came from the Mecklenburg District of North Carolina, and both of Edwin Reese's grandfathers as well as his uncle Robert Harris were signers of the Mecklenburg Declaration.

When the British invaded South Carolina, Thomas Reese and his family fled to Mecklenburg for safety, where he continued to preach as much, it appears, against the British as on the Gospels. In 1782 the family returned to Salem where Reese along with his pastoral duties conducted a Latin grammar school that included John R. Witherspoon (A.B. 1794) among its pupils and would certainly have included the master's own son. In 1792 Reese moved to the Pendleton District of South Carolina to minister to the Hopewell and Carmel churches.

At about this time Edwin Reese entered the College. His name first appears in the faculty minutes at the start of the 1792 summer session as a sophomore. On December 5 Reese and his classmate John R. Witherspoon were proposed for admission into the Cliosophic Society. The next week, however, they withdrew their names from consideration. Sometime before the following spring they joined the American Whig Society. A letter from his cousin Charles Wilson Harris to their uncle Dr. Charles Harris, dated July 30, 1793, indicates Reese's satisfaction with college life.

> Since I wrote to you, a letter from Cousin Edwin dated about May 1st came to hand by post. He was well, had become a whig, and is very much attached to the place, a sure sign of diligence.

Reese was not one of the speakers at his commencement ceremonies, at which his father was awarded the D.D. However, John Henry Hobart (A.B. 1793) wrote to a friend (presumably another Whig) extolling the superiority of the Whigs, suggesting that their honors would have been greater if Reese, whom he described as a valuable member, had not been ill when commencement assignments were made in July.

Reese reportedly read medicine for a time after graduation. He may have studied under his half-uncle Dr. Charles Harris of Cabarrus, North Carolina, as Charles Wilson Harris had also briefly done. Abandoning medicine, Reese turned to teaching as a profession and was appointed rector, or principal, of the Hopewell Academy, conducted at the Presbyterian church in Hopewell, South Carolina. Because the church building was erected in 1797, it is not certain whether Reese had already accepted a position there when, on August 26, 1797, Charles Wilson Harris wrote to him about a teaching vacancy at the University of North Carolina. Harris, who had taught there for a time, was now studying law but still retained an interest in the university and its affairs. Nothing has been found to indicate that Reese was at all interested in pursuing this vacancy. Rather than remain at the Hopewell Academy, he gave up this position to travel from home to home to teach. This rather ambiguous description of his teaching does not indicate whether he worked as an itinerant, teaching in turn at various sections of the district, or whether he lived with different families in succession, tutoring their sons for college. Neither pattern of life would have been conducive to a happy married life, and apparently Reese did not try to combine the two. He is described as tall and handsome, always dressed in a dignified manner with a black silk stock collar. He lived to "a grand old age" and was buried in the Hopewell Cemetery at the Old Stone Church in an unmarked grave.

SOURCES: *Princetonians, 1748-1768*, 651-53; Sprague, *Annals*, III, 331-32 (father); alumni file, PUA (quote re age at death from family letter); Min. Fac., class list ca. May 1792, 10 May 1794; Clio. Min., 5 & 12 Dec. 1792; Amer. Whig Soc., *Cat.* (1840), 7; D. A. Tompkins, *Hist. of Mecklenburg Cnty. & the city of Charlotte* (1903), 29; W. S. Ray, *Mecklenburg Signers & Their Neighbors* (1946), 347, 416, 421, 444; H. M. Wagstaff, "The Harris Letters," *James Sprunt Hist. Publications*, 14 (1916), 6, 10, 12, 49, 60, 88; *Dunlap & Claypoole's Amer. Daily Advt.*, 7 Oct. 1794; J. McVickar, *Early Life & Professional Years of Bishop Hobart* (1838), 34; B. A. Kosky, *Pendleton Legacy* (1971), 25-26.

RLW

John Rush

JOHN RUSH, M.D. Pennsylvania 1804, physician and naval officer, was the oldest of the thirteen children of Dr. Benjamin Rush (A.B. 1760) and Julia Stockton, daughter of Richard Stockton (A.B. 1748). The father was a brother of Jacob Rush (A.B. 1765) and the mother a sister of Richard (A.B. 1779) and Lucius Horatio Stockton (A.B. 1787). The proud father recorded the birth as follows: "John Rush, son of the above, born July 17, 1777, between the hours of 12 and 1 in the morning, at Elihu Hall's Esq., at Mount Welcome, Cecil County, Mary[lan]d and baptised July 20th following by the Revd Dr. John Ewing [(A.B. 1754)]." Rush later noted that John "stood alone at 6 months supported by a wall." He described the infant in a letter to a friend as so good tempered that he seldom cried, but spent his time sleeping, eating, "and pulling his mama's caps and handkerchiefs to pieces." The Rush home and Benjamin Rush's medical office were on Fourth Street in Philadelphia, but at the time of John's birth Julia Rush was staying with relatives in Maryland because of the danger of a British occupation of the city.

The elder Rush was a prominent physician, who lectured at the College of Philadelphia, and later at the University of Pennsylvania through its various changes of name. He served on the staff of the Pennsylvania Hospital and was one of the founders of the Philadelphia College of Physicians. An ardent supporter of the American cause, he served a term in the Continental Congress and was, like his father-in-law, a Signer of the Declaration of Independence. For seven months he held the appointment of physician general of the Middle Department of the army's medical services. Rush was always an ardent supporter of whatever causes attracted his attention. In the newspapers and in a large and active correspondence he aired his views on such diverse topics as slavery, spirituous liquors, female education, crime and punishment, and the state of the new republic. It is not surprising that he also had firm opinions about child rearing or that John, as the eldest, probably suffered most because of his father's strong convictions.

Both loving and stern, Rush had great expectations for his son. He was to write, "Where the eldest son or daughter is honored and preferred by parents a family is never without government in the absence of the parents from home, and when these parents are removed by death there is a foundation laid in the habits of the younger children for a continuance of subordination in a family." Julia Rush generally left the city for most of the summer months, staying with her family at "Morven" in Princeton, and John spent most of his youthful summers there.

In a letter to his mother written "Monday [June] 19, 1786," James Gibson (A.B. 1787), a junior at the College, informed her that Dr. Rush had delivered not only her letter but advice regarding his health as well. Rush told Gibson that his son John had gone to Lewistown, Pennsylvania, which probably meant that he was attending the academy there and was thus unable to accompany his mother to Princeton that summer. In late August he was with his father in Philadelphia, and Rush wrote to his wife that John, who had just turned nine, had accompanied him three times on his hospital rounds, in the course of which he had witnessed an operation and asked questions about a patient's madness. "I will be nothing but a doctor," his father quoted him as saying. John visited "Morven" "during holidays" the following July. In July 1788 Rush wrote a friend describing John's part in Philadelphia's Fourth of July procession "in honor of the establishment of the new government," where he was to portray a midshipman on board the "Union."

A letter written to Enos Hitchcock on April 24, 1789 reveals the stern and unyielding side of Rush as a parent. Discussing the discipline of children, he pontificated that solitude was the most effective form of discipline.

> My eldest son, who is now near 12 years old, has more than once begged me to flog him in preference to confining him....I have in one instance confined my two eldest sons in separate rooms for two days. The impression which this punishment has left upon them I believe will never wear away, nor do I think it will ever require to be repeated.

To a cousin Rush wrote, "Our eldest son is a promising boy and bids fair to make a scholar," but in a letter to his wife at "Morven," July 31, 1791, he was again the autocrat. "I objected chiefly to John's using a gun *contrary* to *my* orders. His offense arises from an act of disobedience to my authority. This must be supported in trifles or no government will long be maintained over him."

John may have matriculated as a freshman at the College for the winter term beginning in November 1790, since Cliosophic Society records indicate that he joined the society as Brother Octavius sometime before the end of the calendar year. He is listed as a freshman in College records for the 1791 summer session, but he did not attend the winter session of 1791-92. Some incident or incidents had taken place that were deeply disturbing to his father, and the illicit use of the gun may have been part of the problem.

By the following spring the elder Rush had decided to give his son another opportunity in the College, but under much more protective conditions. He wrote to Walter Minto, professor of mathematics and natural philosophy, on March 24, 1792:

I wish to send my son John to the Jersey College, provided he can be boarded and *study* in a private family. My respect for you, and the high character I have heard of your amiable lady, have induced me to solicit a place for my son in your home. He will rejoin the sophomore class and of course become your pupil in mathematics. You will oblige me by taking charge of him and superintending his morals as well as his studies. I shall expect that he will *study* constantly in your house and never enter the College except when he goes to say his lessons or perform some academical exercise. On no other condition can I consent to sending him to Princeton, for I consider a *college life* and *college society* to boys of his age as alike fatal to morals and manners.

When Minto agreed to take John as a boarder, Rush wrote that he and his wife were very happy about the arrangements, but added further restrictions:

I shall expect you to know where he spends all his time in the interval of college hours, and by no means ever to pass an evening out of your house without your consent. He is a lad of promising talents and has of late become more inquisitive and studious than formerly. His temper, though a little quick, is not violent, and soon gives way to a firm spirit of government in his superiors. As yet his morals are pure, and I hope they derive that purity from good religious principles. He has a taste for music. I have indulged him with a flute, but upon two conditions—that he give up his gun, and that he never touch his flute except in the evening or in the interval of college hours.

Rather wistfully Rush added that since John was their first-born he was "spes gregis," a quotation from Virgil which translates as the "hope of the flock."

When John arrived at the Mintos' on May 9, he carried a letter from his father again urging Minto to pay strict attention to his new boarder's morals and manners. "He is at present innocent. His temper is a little irritable, but he is as easily governed as a child when he sees a degree of authority over him. He inclines to be idle, but by a little attention he can be made to spend whole days in study." John dutifully wrote to his father that he was pleased with his situation at the Mintos', and Rush relayed this information to his younger son

Richard (A.B. 1797) who was enrolled at the Woodbury academy of Andrew Hunter, Jr. (A.B. 1772).

In spite of all these precautions John Rush managed to compromise both his manners and morals. Fines for small infractions of the Cliosophic Society's rules were quite common, and Rush received his share of them. However, on July 8 he was also "called up for his irregularity" and on August 5 for "his bad scholarship," when he was given an indefinite suspension. On September 12, "The Society taking into consideration the ungentleman-like conduct of Bro. Octavius" expelled him. Two days earlier Rush had been found guilty by the faculty of playing cards on the sabbath. The four culprits were required to make a confession before the College, assembled for evening prayers, with the two repeat offenders making their confession from the stage. Rush and John Jordan as first offenders were able to make their confession from their seats. All promised to return any goods and money that they had won and "never to indulge ourselves in the like practice while subject to the discipline of the college."

It must have taken more than a week for the news to reach Philadelphia, because it is impossible to imagine the elder Rush wasting any time before dashing off his September 19 letter to Minto.

> I have heard with great distress of the offense and of the public disgrace of my son in your College. As I conceive, after what has past, he can never recover his character so as to appear to advantage either with his masters or among his fellow students, I have concluded to take him home. I lament the occasion of it, and shall always ascribe it not less to the depravity of his mind than to the temptations and opportunities of vice which are inseparably connected with a number of boys herding together under one roof without the restraints which arise from female and family society.

Mrs. Minto was asked to help John pack his belongings, Professor Minto was to send a bill for board and tuition, and nothing was to prevent John from taking the sophomore examination before leaving. On September 22 the faculty announced that all classes had finished their examinations, and presumably John Rush left for Philadelphia.

It is not clear how he occupied himself the next year, but he may have enrolled in another school since, on August 21, 1793, Benjamin Rush wrote to Julia who was at "Morven," reminding her that John "should come home as soon as his vacation expires." A few days later John and Richard were at home, the yellow fever epidemic had begun, and the father was anxious to get the boys out of the city. Julia Rush was now at Trenton visiting her uncle Samuel Witham Stockton

(A.B. 1767), and on August 27 Rush sent his sons by night coach to join her. He worried about their traveling at night but believed no time should be lost in removing them from the infected city. Mrs. Rush and her children returned to "Morven" and remained there until mid-November when cooler weather ended the danger of contracting yellow fever. In September 1794 John became a medical apprentice under his father. On December 8, 1795 the elder Rush was able to write to his friend Dr. John Redman Coxe, "My son John is becoming enthusiastic in medicine."

By May 1796 John Rush had acquired enough medical knowledge to secure a position on the ship *Calcutta*, an "Indiaman." He apparently had a chronic low-grade fever which his father felt might develop into consumption without the bracing effects of a sea voyage. The young man's ever solicitous parents gave the ship captain a letter to be delivered to John a week after setting sail. Here he found advice on his conduct while away from home, carefully divided into sections on morals, knowledge, health, and business. The closing exhortation read, "Whenever you are tempted to do an improper thing, fancy that you see your father and mother kneeling before you and imploring you with tears in their eyes to refrain from yielding to the temptation, and assuring you at the same time that your yielding to it will be the means of hurrying them to a premature grave."

By September 1797 John Rush had returned to Philadelphia, where he was employed as his father's "principal assistant." He also became the defender of his father's name when, on October 6, the *Gazette of the United States* printed an anonymous newspaper article scathingly criticizing the elder Rush's methods of treating his yellow fever patients. Medical opinion was sharply divided about Rush's copious bleeding and purging of fever victims, and although the article was actually written by Dr. William Currie, John for some reason thought it came from the pen of Dr. Andrew Ross. Accosted by the young man, Ross declared him an "impudent puppy," and the two engaged in a street brawl. Ross blamed the father for instigating the son and challenged Benjamin Rush to a duel, which the latter refused on the grounds that he wanted neither to commit murder nor to place anyone else in the position of being a murderer.

Whether because of patriotism or merely the constant restlessness which seemed to drive him, John Rush was soon back at sea, this time serving with the United States Navy in the Quasi-War with France. He was appointed a surgeon in the navy on May 11, 1798 and a lieutenant on March 5, 1799. While on leave in March 1800 he read a copy of the first issue of *Rush-Light*, a series of pamphlets written and published by the political journalist William Cobbett for the sole purpose of attacking Dr. Rush, who had recently won a libel suit against him in Pennsylvania. Now in New York City, Cobbett renewed the attack, including a biased account of the affair with Dr. Ross and stating, "I affirm this John Rush to be an *impertinent puppy*, a *waylaying coward*, a *liar*, and a *rascal*." John reacted by rushing from the house, still in naval uniform, to catch the stage to New York in order to demand satisfaction from Cobbett. His distraught father wrote to Brockholst Livingston (A.B. 1774) on March 5, urging him to use "persuasion or the force of law" to stop John from committing any rash actions.

The stage ride to New York probably cooled John's temper, since Livingston found him at a theater and extracted a promise from the young man that he would not seek out Cobbett. However, on March 8 James T. Stelle (A.B. 1793) attempted to deliver a challenge to Cobbett on Rush's behalf. Whether Stelle simply carried a dress cane or was armed with a "bludgeon cane" as Cobbett declared, Stelle left Cobbett's shop when the latter began to brandish an iron poker while refusing the invitation to a duel. Rush justified his actions in a long article printed in the *Commercial Advertiser* on March 11, while Cobbett published an open letter to Secretary of War James McHenry, protesting Stelle's conduct and suggesting that the Federal government keep its soldiers under control. Stelle, who was stationed at Fort Jay, had been a student at the College during Rush's short stay there. The two were "brothers" in the Cliosophic Society and may have become reacquainted the previous summer when Stelle married Lydia Field Hubley, sister-in-law of Rush's uncle Richard Stockton of "Morven."

Rush presumably returned to his naval duties after this incident, but by January 1802 he was anxious for another change of career. He left the Navy, he explained, because of its limited prospects of providing for old age and sickness. On January 25 his father wrote to Secretary of the Navy Robert Smith (A.B. 1781) requesting permission for John to resign in order to accept a berth on another Indiaman. John submitted his resignation on January 29, 1802 with expectations of sailing to the East Indies in March. The voyage must have been extraordinarily unpleasant. On December 11, 1802 Benjamin Rush wrote in his commonplace book: "This day my son John resumed the study of medicine. So anxious was he to return to my house and business that he said 'he would supply the place of one of my men servants, and even clean my stable rather than continue to follow a sea life.' "

John was enrolled in the medical department of the University of Pennsylvania, and despite a bout with jaundice the next November, he was able to complete the work for his M.D. in 1804. His doctoral thesis, entitled "An Essay on the Causes of Sudden Death and the Means of Preventing It," was dedicated to his father. That summer he read a paper before the Philadelphia Medical Society. Entitled "Elements of Life, or the Laws of Vital Matters," it was considered bold in its hypothesis that all of nature had a material basis. It supported his father's theory that insanity depended upon malfunctions of the cerebral blood vessels. The same summer Dr. John Redman Coxe began publication of the quarterly *Philadelphia Medical Museum*, and John Rush contributed to the first volume.

Rush was offered an appointment on the medical board of the Philadelphia Almshouse but, with the excuse that he had "lost his health," he left for South Carolina on October 16, 1804 with his father's friend Maj. Pierce Butler, who was returning home after having resigned from Congress. Presumably Rush was to locate some place in which to settle that would be both more beneficial to his health than Philadelphia and more suitable for setting up a new practice. Perhaps he was actually offered a position as physician on a plantation of Butler's, since a letter to his brother Richard, written May 28, 1805 from Charleston, expressed his gratitude to Butler, adding that Butler had repaid him for his services. The main purpose of the letter to Richard was to announce that John did not intend to settle in Prince William Parish, but rather had decided to move to Havana, Cuba, where he hoped to make enough money to pay his debts. Richard was asked to forward his bills and if possible to sell a tract of land owned by John "at almost any price, for the sake of my creditors." The letter also mentioned a "mutual attachment" between John and an unnamed lady. However, her "father in law & guardian it seems, were miffed at my not consulting them," and managed to keep the pair separated. Unable to see her before he sailed, John had sent her a letter declaring his "unaltered affections." There is no further record of this romantic interest.

By September 1805 Rush had reentered the navy as a sailing master, taking a demotion upon returning to the service. He was assigned to duty in Boston and from there a new friend, William Minot, wrote to Richard Rush on July 28, 1806 asking him to act as mediator between his father and John. Minot described John as a skillful seaman who had the respect and esteem of his fellow officers but who was nonetheless deeply melancholy because of an estrangement from his family. Although eager for a reconciliation, John sounded anything but submissive as described by Minot, claiming that he had been treated with undue severity and that his family regarded him "as the degenerate son of an eminent and respectable father, as a foil

to the fair reputation of his brothers & in short ... as a blackguard."
Minot recounted that when John had arrived in Boston, due to an
error in accounting he was thought to be in arrears to the Navy for
more than $1,000. His salary was held back and before the error
was discovered he fell ill and stayed at a tavern where he could not
afford proper care. Richard was apparently able to effect at least a
temporary reconciliation between his father and his oldest brother,
but it is impossible to tell whether his "opening again ... the door
of his father's house" is simply a figure of speech or whether John
indeed visited the family home while en route to his next assignment
in Washington.

By early 1807 he was commanding Gunboat No. 18 at New
Orleans, with the rank of acting lieutenant. The skipper of Gunboat
No. 15 was Lt. Benjamin Turner. Whether they had known each
other before or became acquainted only in New Orleans, Turner
and Rush were apparently close friends; however, a slight disagreement between the two ended in a duel on October 1, 1807 in which
Turner was killed. Dr. Samuel Heap of New Orleans, a friend of
Benjamin Rush who later treated John, gave a sympathetic account
of the affair. John had fully intended to waste his fire, but acted to
defend himself upon being told that his opponent intended to kill or
be killed.

After an investigation of the affair, Rush was returned to duty
within a few weeks. A letter to Richard written June 25, 1808 shows
him more deeply estranged from his father and extremely bitter.
It is impossible to ascertain whether he had requested funds from
his father and been refused or whether he had attempted to draw
upon one of his father's accounts without permission. In any case,
his resentment is clear:

> Beg my father to give himself no concern about my drawing
> money on him, or trouble himself further concerning me, and
> as it will favor the setting up of his son Ben as a merchant (forty
> times the *draw* I wanted) and enable him to afford assistance
> to a Son in *law* request him further to alter his will (if he hath
> not done so already) and strike me out.... Beg my father not to
> assume my debts I would rather answer for them in jail.

Another letter to Richard on July 29 reaffirmed John's position but
expressed the hope that the previous letter had not been shown to
his father.

By September 1808 Rush was again in trouble because of a quarrel
and what was termed "gunplay" aboard his vessel. Whether or not
the gunplay was an actual duel, Rush was relieved of naval duty and

ordered to Washington, perhaps to be hospitalized. He was troubled enough to attempt suicide on March 7, 1809, which was reported to the family by Capt. David Porter. By August a letter of his father's included the news that John was recovered and again on active duty, even though a gloom still pervaded his spirit. However, no naval records have been found that confirm this return to duty. By February 1810 Rush's melancholia had increased to a point where it was necessary for his brother Benjamin and "black William" to escort him home. He arrived in a deep depression, with a thoroughly unkempt appearance, and refused to communicate with any members of his family. After three days he was taken to the Pennsylvania Hospital where he remained until his death on August 9, 1837.

His father was initially very hopeful: "I do not despair, with the medical resources of the Hospital, of his recovery." John did improve to some extent. His father eventually was able to report that he was more attentive to his dress, occasionally opened a book, and sometimes conversed lucidly. But he continued to be deeply melancholy and quite deranged on any subject that reminded him of the duel in which his friend had died. He spent most of his days walking to and fro in the ward or on the boardwalk in the yard, so much so that he wore grooves in the walk from his constant pacing and the section where he trod became known as "Rush's Walk." The proud and frequently demanding Benjamin Rush handled this tragedy with restraint and dignity. He described the situation frankly in letters to friends, never with the sense of shame that frequently accompanied a family member's mental derangement, always blaming the evils of duelling, and probably never suspecting the part that his own high expectations and rigid standards may have played. The hopefulness of his early letters gradually changed to an acceptance that "there is too much reason to believe he will end his days" in the Pennsylvania Hospital. On September 24, 1810, in a statement to the managers of the hospital urging reforms in the care and housing of the insane patients, Dr. Rush's closing sentence read:

> I shall conclude this letter by an appeal to several members of your board to vouch for my having more than once suggested most of the above means for the recovery and comfort of the deranged persons under your care long before it pleased God to interest me in their adoption by rendering one of my family an object of them.

In 1812 when Richard Rush was residing in Washington as comptroller of the treasury for President James Madison (A.B. 1771), his father repeatedly requested him to check with the Navy Department in regard to John's account. Apparently John's half-pay naval pension had been discontinued upon an erroneous report of his death. Then the Navy Department began questioning his qualifications as a pensioner since he had not been disabled in the line of duty, and there was no reasonable expectation that he might be able to return to active service. Richard felt that his involvement would present a conflict of interest with his position in the Treasury Department and requested his father to deal directly with naval authorities. However, after the father's death the following year, Richard tried to help his mother straighten out John's "unsettled and confused" accounts. Their father had provided John's support during his lifetime, Richard wrote, and a portion of his estate provided for John's maintenance, with their mother as executrix. Finally, on July 6, 1815 Secretary of the Treasury Alexander J. Dallas, in a review of John Rush's case, put an end to Mrs. Rush's hopes for compensation by stating that "feelings of humanity must be controuled by the obligation of duty."

Sources: *Princetonians, 1748-1768*, 318-25; *PMHB*, 17 (1893), 334; 27 (1903), 150n ("John Rush, son of the above," "stood alone"); D. F. Hawke, *Benjamin Rush, Revolutionary Gadfly* (1971), 202, 398 ("Where the eldest"); Butterfield, *Rush Letters, passim* ("pulling his mama's caps," 178; "nothing but a doctor," 395; "in honor of," 469; "My eldest son," 511-12; "Our eldest son," 519; "I objected chiefly," 601; "I wish," 613; "I shall expect," "spes gregis," 615-616; "at present innocent," 618-19; "I have heard," 622; "should come home," 638; "My son John," 766; "whenever you are tempted," 777; "persuasion or the force," 817; "I affirm," 818n; "I do not despair," 1036; "I shall conclude," 1066; "there is too much reason," 1074); alumni file of James Gibson (copy of letter from JG to his mother), PUA; Clio. lists; Clio. Min., 6 & 18 July, 5 Aug., 12 Sept. 1792, 23 Sept. & 19 Nov. 1795, 29 Aug. 1798; Min. Fac., class lists ca. May 1791 & May 1792, 10 & 11 Sept. 1792 ("never to indulge"); Rush, *Autobiography, passim*, esp. 369-71 ("This day my son John," 261); *Gen. Alumni Cat. of Univ. of Pa.* (1922), 483; E. W. Callahan, *List of Officers of the Navy of the U.S.* (1901), 477; *Jour. of the Exec. Proc. of the U.S. Senate* (1828), I, 274-75, 334; F. P. Henry, ed., *Standard Hist. of Medical Profession of Phila.* (1897), 141; T. G. Morton, *Hist. of the Pa. Hospital* (1895), 148, 150, 152; W. F. Neilson, *Verdict for the Doctor* (1958), 35, 38, 56, 129, 136, 209-15; M. E. Clark, *Peter Porcupine in Amer.: The Career of William Cobbett* (1937 repr. 1974), 162-66; G. D. H. Cole, ed., *Letters from William Cobbett to Edward Thornton* (1937), 19, 72-73; M. L. Pearl, *William Cobbett* (1953), 50-51; A. M. Brescia, ed., *Letters & Papers of Richard Rush* (1980 microfilm), items 33 ("as the degenerate"), 1205, 1211, 1789 ("feelings of humanity"); 1793, 12446 ("mutual attachment"), 12447 ("Beg my father"), 12448. JR's letter to RR, 25 June 1808 (item 12447) is incorrectly dated 1805 in the microfilm edition. A. M. Brescia has acknowledged 1808 as the proper date for this letter.

The *Letters & Papers of Richard Rush* show that Benjamin Rush was just as compulsively autocratic and authorative in his relationship with Richard as he had been with John. Richard, however, was able to tell his father quite firmly that, although he still respected him as a parent, he was prepared to live his own life and no longer welcomed suggestions on his behavior, proper social contacts, or politics.

The literature on Benjamin Rush contains some harsh evaluations of his psychiatric practices, one of the most negative being that of T. S. Szaz in *The Manufacture of Madness* (1970).

Publications: Sh-Sh #s 7215 & 7216

MANUSCRIPTS: Rush-Williams-Biddle Archive, Rosenbach Foundation, Phila.; Benjamin Rush Papers, Library Company of Phila.; letters of naval officers, DNA

RLW

John Neely Simpson

JOHN NEELY SIMPSON, A.B., A.M. 1798, merchant, banker, distiller, transportation entrepreneur, and public official, was born on April 6, 1770, one of the three sons and six daughters of William and Isabella Wilson Simpson of Makefield Township, Bucks County, Pennsylvania. The father was a Scots-Irish immigrant from County Antrim, Ireland. Josiah Simpson (A.B. 1803) was John's brother.

John entered the College as a junior in October 1792. He joined the Cliosophic Society on March 6, 1793, taking as his society name Pindar, for the ancient Greek poet. He was active in the society, serving as clerk, as one of the "correctors of speaking," twice as first assistant (i.e., first vice president), and as president. He was one of six underclassmen the society chose to participate in the debating competition scheduled for the night before the canceled 1793 commencement, and on August 22, 1794 he received a Clio diploma. Simpson was eating off campus as of January 8, 1794, when the faculty ordered that he and two other students "return to the dining room ... as soon as they should recover from a temporary illness." During the second semester of Simpson's senior year, Joseph Caldwell (A.B. 1791), later president of the University of North Carolina, returned to Nassau Hall to study divinity. In his memoirs he recalled becoming friendly with a student named Simpson, almost certainly John, whom he described as "a young man fully grown, ... larger than the ordinary size in bone and muscle" and having "the appearance of unusual strength." On one occasion they went swimming together and Simpson, who "could swim but little," ventured out too far and nearly drowned both himself and Caldwell before the latter succeeded in rescuing him. Simpson took part as opponent in a disputation at his commencement on the question, "Are Liberty and Equality calculated to promote the happiness and improvement of mankind?"

After graduating Simpson seems to have stayed on in Princeton, where he became a merchant. The date of his marriage to Mary Brunson has not been discovered, but their first child was born on June 24, 1796. Mary was the daughter of John Brunson and his wife, whose maiden name was Arrowsmith. The Brunson homestead was a mile from the College. John and Mary Simpson had at least five daughters and four sons, including Josiah Simpson (A.B. 1833,

M.D. University of Pennsylvania 1836); Gen. James Hervey Simpson (U.S. Military Academy 1834, A.M. College of New Jersey 1848); and Eleanor, the wife of Peter O. Studdiford (hon. A.B. 1817, D.D. 1844) and mother of Peter A. Studdiford (A.B. 1849), James H. Studdiford (A.B. 1852), and Samuel M. Studdiford (A.B. 1856).

On August 31, 1801 Simpson purchased a tract of almost 250 acres of land called "Mansgrove Farm" from David Walker and his wife Anne Marshall Dill Witherspoon Walker, who had inherited the land from her second husband John Witherspoon, the College president. Simpson subsequently lived on this farm. The house called "Mansgrove," which still stands, contains a large addition which may have been built during Simpson's tenure, as well as a wing dating from the mid-eighteenth century. An 1803 lawsuit shows that Simpson was engaged in the sale of corn meal at that time. If the reminiscences of one Henry Clow in 1850 can be trusted, around 1804 "Simpson & Wilson's store" was on the north side of Main (now Nassau) Street, the third building from African Lane (now Witherspoon Street) in the direction of the house of College faculty member John Maclean. Wilson has not been further identified; perhaps he was related to Simpson's mother.

In 1803 Simpson became a judge of the Somerset County court of quarter sessions, a post which required neither specialized training nor full-time commitment. At some point during his residence in Princeton he also served as clerk of a fire company which was active from 1788 to at least 1817. In March 1804 he subscribed $15 to the salary of Henry Kollock (A.B. 1794), the new pastor of the Princeton Presbyterian Church. Later that year Dr. Thomas Wiggins (A.B. Yale 1752, A.M. College of New Jersey 1758, treasurer College of New Jersey 1786-87) died without issue and left the bulk of his estate to the church. Wiggins's siblings and their heirs detected legal flaws and challenged the will. Simpson, who was interested because his wife was Wiggins's niece, was nonetheless chosen by the church to negotiate with the heirs and mediated a compromise under which the church obtained the property in exchange for a cash settlement.

Simpson probably moved to Basking Ridge, in Bernard Township, Somerset County, New Jersey, around January 1806, when he sold "Mansgrove." He was certainly in Basking Ridge by November 1807, when three of his children were baptized in its Presbyterian church. On March 13, 1809 he became one of five charter trustees of the apparently short-lived Basking Ridge Library Company. From 1809-11 he represented Somerset County in the general assembly.

Simpson next moved to New Brunswick, Middlesex County, New Jersey, where he engaged in a wide range of commercial activities.

He is said to have owned a bookstore in 1811. When the local grain trade collapsed during and after the War of 1812, he was among the New Brunswick residents who started distilleries and breweries. His distillery on Little Burnet Street was sufficiently well-known that in 1825 a New York dealer asked a New Brunswick middleman to secure all of Simpson's output.

By 1817 Simpson was one of the directors of the Bank of New Brunswick. In a six-to-five vote that summer he helped authorize the bank to accept from its debtors its own stock at par as repayment. The minority on the board saw this move, which led to a drastic reduction in the bank's capital and probably to its eventual bankruptcy, as an unethical maneuver by the majority to pay their debts to the bank with stock purchased at depreciated rates. Simpson became cashier of the bank in 1821 and served until 1830, when its growing fiscal decline forced a reorganization. On March 23, 1822 Simpson and twelve other "Associators" opened the New Jersey Bank for Savings at his countinghouse in Burnet Street. The venture was not a rival of the Bank of New Brunswick but an attempt to encourage thrift among workers, as illustrated by its paying interest on a minimum of $5 and its being open on Saturday nights, when most employees were paid. The institution aroused little interest and closed in less than a year. Around 1823 Simpson promoted a new steelmaking process devised by one of his associates. The two obtained a patent and sought a government contract which they hoped would overcome "old and deep-rooted prejudices" against domestic steel. In 1828 Simpson was a shareholder in the short-lived New Brunswick Coal Association, which incorporated as the Raritan Coal Mining Company but went out of business after exploratory searches using artesian well machinery found no coal in the vicinity.

Simpson did not prosper, in spite of his multifarious activities. Between February 1819 and June 1828 he regularly wrote his friend Samuel Lewis Southard (A.B. 1804), United States senator (1821-23) and secretary of the navy (1823-29), requesting help in obtaining government jobs for himself and commissions in the navy or appointments to West Point for his sons. He complained in 1821 that "I have by the operation of the times, & a series of adverse providences lost the principal part of my property, & have a large and helpless family to provide for." He did not retrieve his lost wealth thereafter. At his death his personal estate was valued at only $155.

Simpson was active in New Brunswick public life. Politically he was a Federalist in 1814. In late 1823 he supported the presidential candidacy of John C. Calhoun and opposed that of William H. Crawford. He seems to have favored Andrew Jackson when Calhoun dropped out of the race. In 1814 and 1815 Simpson was elected to represent Middlesex County in the general assembly, and in 1818 he served a term on the council, the legislature's upper house. In 1819 he became a justice of the peace and a judge of the Middlesex County court of common pleas. In April of the same year he helped found and became the president of the New Brunswick Association for Encouraging Domestic Manufactures, which hoped by promoting industrial growth to find a way out of the depression then raging. The society set up a factory and began producing cotton cloth. It was incorporated on November 22, 1821 and added a dyeing plant a few months later, but the venture went under shortly thereafter.

In October 1819 Simpson helped found the Association for the Protection of Property in and around New Brunswick and later served as its president. The organization attempted to promote law and order by detecting and prosecuting thieves, suppressing ale-houses, and "removing persons of loose and disorderly habits ... to their proper townships." Contemporary newspapers credited the association with some success, but it had ceased to exist by the end of 1827. Simpson was active in the New Brunswick Presbyterian Church, of which he became a trustee in 1813 and a ruling elder on April 14, 1822.

An active supporter of education, Simpson is said to have started a subscription for rebuilding Nassau Hall while it was burning down on March 6, 1802, and to have obtained pledges of $5,000, headed by his own of $500, before the flames were extinguished. In April 1814 he was serving as a trustee of the female academy in New Brunswick run by Joseph Hanson. He became involved in the massive lobbying campaign of 1828 which led to the Common School Act of 1829. Mass meetings and petitions calling for public support of education led to state conventions at Princeton in September and Trenton in November, the latter purposely timed to permit lobbying the legislature. At the latter meeting Simpson, Charles Ewing (A.B. 1798), and Theodore Frelinghuysen (A.B. 1804) were appointed a committee to obtain and disseminate data about "the state of the common schools in New Jersey." Subcommittees from all over the state sent in information, and the forty-six page pamphlet which the committee produced shocked the public with its assertion that almost 12,000 children were receiving no education whatever. The resulting act of 1829 provided for the licensing of teachers and for expenditure of some state money on public education. The act was weakened in 1830 and repealed in 1831. Although many of its goals were not achieved for decades, the agitation of 1828 was significant for having set a precedent and provided tactical training for supporters of publicly supported education who obtained more enduring successes in the late 1830s and 1840s.

Simpson's commercial and public service activities merged in the time and energy he lavished on attempts to promote improved transportation in New Jersey. He was active in the New Jersey Turnpike Company, chartered in 1806 to operate a road between New Brunswick and Easton, Pennsylvania. On December 1, 1804, March 2, 1820, and December 30, 1824, he was named an incorporator in the charters of the first three companies authorized to build a canal linking the Delaware and Raritan rivers. Simpson's son James later recalled that this canal was "the great project of my father's life and ambition." None of the three companies managed to begin construction. Neither the 1804 New Jersey Navigation Company nor the 1820 New Jersey Delaware and Raritan Canal Company sold enough stock to make the scheme viable. In between, the legislature appointed Simpson on February 13, 1816 to a three-man commission to consider the feasibility of the canal project and survey a route. Both it and a second commission in 1823 reported favorably, and the 1824 Delaware and Raritan Canal Company seemed to have a good chance to succeed, especially after the sale of stock in May 1825 was heavily oversubscribed.

This company organized itself on July 6, 1825, when Simpson was elected president by the shareholders. Two major problems remained. One was the charter's requirement that Pennsylvania's consent be obtained, since water from the Delaware River would be diverted to the canal. The Pennsylvania legislature's enabling act of April 6, 1825 was so restrictive as to be useless, but after intense lobbying a second act was obtained on March 28, 1826, which appeared to be workable despite some irritating restrictions. The second problem, however, turned out to be fatal. The great majority of the stock had been subscribed by New York and New England speculators who hoped to sell it for a quick profit and had no intention of sinking large sums into actual construction. They removed Simpson as president on April 4, 1826 and immediately took steps to wind up the company's affairs, claiming that the remaining restrictions imposed by Pennsylvania amounted to a rejection by that state which voided the charter. Even the demise of this third effort seems not to have discouraged Simpson and his allies, the most important of whom was James Neilson, the brother of John Neilson (A.B. 1793). On September 25, 1827 a state convention on internal improvements met at Princeton, with Simpson among the sixty-one delegates. They voted to send two delegates from each county to Trenton in November to lobby the legislature and there to organize a permanent New

Jersey society for encouraging internal improvements. In late 1828 Governor Isaac H. Williamson (LL.D. 1839) commissioned Simpson to report on the probable tonnage the proposed canal would generate and came out in favor of a state-funded canal after Simpson estimated that it would earn $233,200 annually. However, Simpson seems to have played little or no role in the Delaware and Raritan Canal Company of 1830, which finally succeeded in opening the canal in July 1834.

Simpson also participated in an early effort to start a steamboat line between New Brunswick and New York. The monopoly granted Robert Fulton and Robert R. Livingston by the New York legislature in 1803 kept competing steamboats out of New York waters, and New Jersey responded in November 1813 by awarding a monopoly in that state to Daniel Dod and Aaron Ogden (A.B. 1773). It thus became illegal to travel by steamboat from New York to New Jersey nonstop. Simpson became president in June 1814 of a company which sought to get around this problem by operating both a steamboat on the Raritan River, and a horse-drawn teamboat to which passengers would be transferred for the trip into New York waters and on to the city. The twelve associates, initially known as John N. Simpson & Co., included Ogden and thus the protection of his monopoly. Construction of the horse-drawn teamboat, called the *Retaliation*, was nearing completion and a contract for a steamboat had been signed when on February 3, 1815, the New Jersey legislature pulled the rug from under the enterprise by repealing Ogden's monopoly. With Livingston steamboats able to travel up the Raritan, a system based on transferring to slower horse-drawn boats obviously became impractical. After a final effort to persuade the New York legislature to retract the Livingston company's monopoly narrowly failed, Simpson's company, which had been chartered on February 15 as the New Brunswick Steam-boat Ferry Company, voted to disband on March 15, 1815.

Simpson seems to have moved back to Princeton shortly before September 27, 1831, when he served as a secretary at a meeting there of eighty-three New Jersey Revolutionary War veterans calling for more pension money. On October 13 he chaired a meeting of "the inhabitants of Princeton and its vicinity, friendly to the protection of American Industry." They resolved that the "extraordinary and dangerous doctrine" that protective tariffs are unconstitutional must be opposed and voted to send a seven-man slate of delegates headed by Simpson to a convention in New York City on October 26.

Simpson died on May 13, 1832. His wife survived him. He was buried in the Princeton Cemetery, near the grave of his wife's uncle Thomas Wiggins.

SOURCES: Alumni file of JNS, PUA (esp. letters from S. M. Studdiford, 26 Oct. 1896, & "S. A. W.," 26 Mar. 1916); D. Murray, *Hist. of Education in N.J.* (1899), 151-64 ("the state"); Min. Fac., 10 Oct. 1792, 6 & 8 Jan., 22 Aug. 1794; Clio. Min., 16 Jan. 1793–22 Aug. 1794 *passim* ("correctors," 20 May 1794), & 28 Sept. 1803; Clio. lists; J. Caldwell, "Autobiography," *N.C. Univ. Magazine*, 9 (1859), 85-87 ("a young man," "could swim"); *Dunlap & Claypoole's Amer. Daily Advt.*, 7 Oct. 1794 ("Are Liberty"); N.Y. *Daily Advt.*, 4 Oct. 1798; typescript of pre-1900 Princeton Cemetery inscriptions, NjPHi; *Som. Cnty. Hist. Quart.*, 3 (1914), 289; indentures for purchase of "Mansgrove" from David & Ann Walker, 31 Aug. 1801, & its sale to Benjamin Clarke, 31 Jan. 1806, NjP; C. M. Greiff, M. W. Gibbons & E. G. C. Menzies, *Princeton Architecture* (1967), 29, 35 fig. 24 (photo of "Mansgrove"); Hageman, *History*, I, 74, 209-12 ("Simpson & Wilson's"), 236 (JNS a founder of the N.J. Colonization Society, 1824); II, 17-21, 98-101, 179-81; R. T. Thompson, *Col. James Neilson ... 1784-1862* (1940), 23, 30-31, 38-40, 42, 88-89, 115-26, 157-86, 219-22, 224, 293-95, 297; *N.J. Wills*, x, 498-99; XI, 213; J. P. Snell, *Hist. of Hunterdon & Somerset Cnties. N.J.* (1881), 313, 643-44; *GMNJ*, 7 (1932), 79; *NJHSP*, 2d ser., 4 (1875-77), 58-62 ("the great"); n.s., 15 (1930), 437; *NJHSP*, 53 (1935), 174-76, 178-79; 67 (1949), 170-71; 68 (1950), 93, 101-02, 322; W. H. Benedict, *New Brunswick in Hist.* (1925), 162-64, 175, 176 ("Associators"), 178-79, 181, 212-21, 340, 359; nine als, JNS to Samuel L. Southard, 23 Feb. 1819–16 June 1828, NjP-SSP ("I have by," 9 Feb. 1821; "old and deep-rooted," 17 Feb. 1824); MS estate inv. of JNS, recorded 19 June 1833, Nj (photocopy in PUA); *Votes & Proc. of the 39th Gen. Assembly of ... N.J.* (1814-15), 7, 104-16 (JNS a Federalist), 224; W. W. Clayton, *Hist. of Union & Middlesex Cnties., N.J.* (1882), 532-35, 710; Alexander, *Princeton*, 277-78; N. R. Burr, *Education in N.J.: 1630-1871* (1942), 246-60; D. C. Skemer, *Guide to the MS Collections of the N.J. Hist. Soc.* (1979), 3, 173; C. C. Madeira, *Del. & Raritan Canal: A Hist.* (1941), 11-12, 22-23; *Princeton Courier*, 8 & 22 Oct. 1831 ("the inhabitants"). Alexander asserts that JNS edited the *Princeton Courier* "a few years before his death," but this seems unlikely. The paper does not mention JNS on the title page, it did not begin publication until March 5, 1831, only 14 months before his death, and its politics (opposed to Henry Clay and favorable to modifying the tariff) do not seem to match those of JNS. Alexander also asserts that while a merchant in New Brunswick, JNS had "a partner in a large house in New York." Possibly this was a Beekman, for in 1814 both JNS in his own right and "Simpson, Beekman and Co." held shares in the teamboat and steamboat company (Thompson, 121). If so, however, it seems odd that JNS should not be in the index of P. L. White, *Beekmans of N.Y. in Politics & Commerce (1647-1877)* (1956).

PUBLICATION: Joint compiler, Sh-C # 35003

MANUSCRIPTS: NjP; NjP-SSP; Neilson Papers, NjR; NjHi

JJL

—— Sitler

—— SITLER entered the College as a freshman in or before May 1791. He remained a student through the summer of 1792 but did not return for his junior year. All three of the class lists on which he appears give only his surname, and he is not otherwise mentioned in the College sources.

The Sitler (Sittler, Sidler) family in America was founded by two brothers, Mathias and Dietrich, who migrated in 1736 from the vicinity of Elsoff, a village in Westphalia, Germany, to Pennsylvania. Both brothers were Lutheran. Mathias moved from York County, Pennsylvania, to Baltimore, Maryland. Dietrich settled in Richmond Township, Berks County, Pennsylvania. The 1790 census counted two families of Sitlers in Baltimore, one in the town of York, Pennsylvania, and six in Berks County. Perhaps Sitler was a friend or distant relation of his classmate John S. Hiester, who was from Reading, Berks County. Hiester's grandfather moved to Pennsylvania from Elsoff, the same village as the Sitlers, in 1732. Sitler and Hiester both entered the College as freshmen. Apparently they did not matriculate at the same time, for Hiester's name first appears on an earlier class list than does Sitler's.

Efforts to identify Sitler further have been unsuccessful.

SOURCES: Min. Fac., undated class lists ca. May & Nov. 1791 & May 1792; *Schuylkill Cnty. Pa.: Geneal.—Fam. Hist.—Biog.* (1916), I, 361-67; *First Census, Pa.*, 34, 40, 282; *First Census, Md.*, 32, 35; genealogical data supplied by W. K. Schweitzer, 12 Dec. 1985, alumni file, PUA (for Jacob, George & John Sitler, born in 1767, 1771 & 1773, respectively, sons of Philip & Catherine Magdalena Sitler of Berks County); *PGM*, 26 (1970), 140; 31 (1980), 262 (for a Martin Sitler, born in Berks County in 1775); 32 (1981), 89. See T. Cushing & C. E. Sheppard, *Hist. of the Cnties. of Gloucester, Salem, & Cumberland, N.J.* (1883 repr. 1974), 248-49, for a Peter Sitley, a sheepshearer who lived in Gloucester County, New Jersey around 1780. Wanda S. Gunning kindly supplied references used in this sketch.

JJL

John Brown Slemons

JOHN BROWN SLEMONS, A.B., A.M. 1800, Presbyterian clergyman, was born on August 11, 1771 in Pequea, Lancaster County, Pennsylvania, probably the son of Thomas and Margaret Slemons and the nephew of John Slemmons (A.B. 1760). Thomas Slemons was assessed in 1780 for 122 acres valued at £6,100. He was a trustee of the Pequea Presbyterian Church.

John Slemons probably received his early education at the classical school taught by the pastor of the Pequea church, Robert Smith (A.M. 1760, D.D. 1786, College trustee, 1772-93). He entered the College as a junior in October 1792. On December 12 of that year he joined the Cliosophic Society with the name Alcæus, a reference to the ancient Greek poet, contemporary of Sappho and fellow resident of Lesbos. The society's minutes show that Slemons was active until August 14, 1793, when the members resolved that his "scholarship & character as a student in college, were such as to render him unworthy of a seat in this society." He was therefore asked to resign and did so. Apparently Slemons showed improvement in the ensuing months. On December 18, 1793 he was readmitted to the society, and on August 27, 1794 he received its diploma. The faculty minutes do not show whether he experienced similar difficulties in his coursework. At his commencement he was respondent in "A dispute on this question, Ceteris peribus [sic]—Does the world pay more respect to one born of knowledge[able] and reputable parents, than to the son of parents who have been contemptible and worthless?"

Slemons then returned to Lancaster County and studied for the Presbyterian ministry under the guidance of Rev. Nathaniel Welshard Semple (A.B. 1776) at Strasburg. In 1797 he was licensed by New Castle presbytery, and the churches of Manokin and Wicomico, Somerset County, Maryland, in Lewes presbytery, sent him a call on April 15, 1799. They guaranteed him a total of £180 a year and promised to try to raise a further £20 by subscription. Slemons accepted and was ordained and installed on June 27, 1799. He served the two congregations until 1821.

Slemons is said to have written excellent sermons but to have been less successful in his delivery of them. Nonetheless, his was a popular pastorate. His services must have been well attended, for in 1801 the Manokin session had to repair "a late break having happened from a crowded gallery," and in 1813 it discussed building an addition to the church. His success is especially notable since Presbyterianism on the Eastern Shore was in decline during his ministry. In 1810 the Presbytery of Lewes, which consisted of most of the Delmarva Peninsula, was dissolved and merged with New Castle presbytery and not reorganized as a separate entity until 1824. The session records also show that under Slemons "the discipline of the church was, in a most commendable degree, enforced, and that public scandals and unworthy members were faithfully removed."

Slemons had three wives. On June 22, 1801 he married Leah Murray McBride, daughter of a Scots immigrant, who apparently brought Slemons a plantation on the Wicomico River as a dowry or inheritance. He subsequently married a Miss Wilson of Somerset County and a Miss Wise of Virginia. Miss Wilson may be the "Polly Slemmons" who was alive in 1810, when her father David Wilson of neighboring Worcester County bequeathed her one slave and a piece of land in Somerset County. Polly was the sister of Ephraim K. Wilson (A.B. 1789). Slemons may have died a widower, since his will mentions no living wife. It does refer to an unspecified number of deceased wives and children, near whom he wished to be buried, and five surviving sons.

After his resignation in 1821 Slemons retired to his farm called "Slemons Experiment." It was within the bounds of his erstwhile pastoral charge, where he continued to officiate from time to time. His ministry ended on a sour note. In the years after Slemons became a clergyman, temperance advocates became increasingly strong among the Presbyterian clergy, until in 1829 Lewes presbytery unanimously resolved to abstain wholly from all "ardent spirits" except when medically prescribed. In 1831 Slemons, still subject to the presbytery's discipline as a minister without a charge, transgressed and was made an example of. After he was convicted of intemperance, "not only was he deposed from his ministerial office, but he was also excommunicated from the Christian Church." Whether either punishment was lifted before his death, which followed shortly thereafter, has not been ascertained.

Slemons died between March 3, 1832, when he wrote his will, and September 25, 1832, when it was proved. The will showed a strong sense of family pride. Each son received several specified heirlooms, including his gold watch, a gold locket, his walking cane, his diplomas, and his manuscript sermons, frequently with the stipulation that they were "to be for ever kept in the name." Several books were disposed of by title, including John Witherspoon's *Works*, three copies of the *Comprehensive View of the ... Principles of Natural and Revealed Religion*, by Samuel Stanhope Smith (A.B. 1769), and one copy of Smith's *Lectures*. Slemons willed his soul to God and asked to be buried on his farm in a plain black coffin, with "not a word of Funeral Services [to] be spoken" at his interment.

SOURCES: Alumni files of JBS & John Slemmons (A.B. 1760), PUA; F. Ellis & S. Evans, *Hist. of Lancaster Cnty., Pa.* (1883), 1042-43, 1049; *LCHSPA*, 15 (1911), 15, 17; 25 (1921), 139-40; Min. Fac., 10 Oct. 1792, 22 Aug. 1794; Clio. Min., 28 Nov. 1792–27 Aug. 1794 *passim* ("scholarship," 14 Aug. 1793); Clio. lists; *Dunlap & Claypoole's Amer. Daily Advt.*, 7 Oct. 1794 ("A dispute"); *Federalist & N.J. Gazette*, 14 Oct. 1800 (confirms middle name); Alexander, *Princeton*, 278-79; H. P. Ford, *Hist. of the Manokin Pres. Church, Princess Anne, Md.* (1910), 19-20, 36-37, 53-58, 70 ("a late," "the discipline"); J. L. Vallandigham & S. A. Gayley, *Hist. of the Presby. of New Castle from ... 1717 to 1888* (n.d.), 18; A. W. B. Bell, *Marriage Licenses of Somerset Cnty. Md., 1796-1831* (typescript in DLC, 1939), 83, 88; MS will of David Wilson, 14 Apr. 1810, proved 30 Oct. 1810, photocopy in alumni file of Ephraim K. Wilson (A.B. 1789), of original in Md. Hall of Records, Annapolis; J. H. Lappen, *Presbyterians on Delmarva: The Hist. of New Castle Presby.* (1972), 26-27, 29-30 ("ardent spirits," "not only"); MS will of JBS, 3 Mar. 1832, proved 25 Sept. 1832, Somerset Cnty. Court House, Princess Anne, Md. ("to be for ever," "not a word").

JJL

William Tennent Snowden

WILLIAM TENNENT SNOWDEN was born on August 24, 1776, the youngest son of Isaac Snowden, Sr., and his second wife, Mary Coxe McCall. The father was a Philadelphia merchant, a prominent public official, an active Presbyterian, and a trustee of the College from 1782 until 1809. A half-brother, Benjamin Parker Snowden (A.B. 1776), graduated from the College the year that William was born. Five other brothers also attended the College: Gilbert Tennent (A.B. 1783); Isaac Jr. (Class of 1785), who served as treasurer of the institution between 1788 and 1791; Samuel Finley (A.B. 1786); Nathaniel Randolph (A.B. 1787); and Charles Jeffry (A.B. 1789).

When Nathaniel Snowden accepted a teaching position at the grammar school run by Andrew Hunter, Jr. (A.B. 1772), in Woodbury, New Jersey, early in January of 1788, "Billy" was there as a student. The entry in Nathaniel's diary for January 14, "Billy cried in school," would seem to indicate that the younger brother had just been enrolled in the school and was probably homesick. The brothers often took long walks together, but Nathaniel was so unhappy with his brief teaching career that he was probably not much comfort to the younger boy. By June, when pleasant weather probably made the walks more frequent, Hunter's wife Ann Riddell Hunter had to remind Nathaniel that he should not be more familiar with his brother than with the other students. By late summer Nathaniel had left the school to pursue theological studies, but the two brothers were together again in the family home in Philadelphia in October, probably during the school break before the beginning of the winter session. On October 10 Nathaniel accompanied Billy to Woodbury to return him to Hunter's school.

William Snowden must have enrolled at the College for the summer session of 1789, for on June 10, 1789 he joined the Cliosophic Society under the pseudonym of Sydenham, for the renowned English physician. His name first appears on College records on November 10, 1789, when he is listed as a sophomore, and he returned for the 1790 summer session. However, his name then disappears from the College lists until the summer session of 1792, when he is again on the rolls as a sophomore. This unaccounted absence from the school may possibly have occurred during a period of stress, a preliminary manifestation of his later severe mental instability. On his return to the College he immediately became active in the Cliosophic Society. In August he was chosen as one of the six representatives of the society to speak on the evening before commencement. On that occasion he was one of the four victors in the competition on pronouncing an English oration, and he moved on to the junior class with other members of the Class of 1794. Meanwhile his record at Clio shows a series of small fines for offenses such as interrupting a meeting, being out of a meeting too long, and leaving without permission. On February 5, 1793 the faculty ordered Snowden, who had for some reason been exempted from the last quarterly examination, to take the test within a month. He did well enough to be permitted to go on with his class. His skill at oratory must have been valued in spite of his erratic behavior, since his Cliosophic brothers chose him to represent them as one of the speakers on July 4 and again on the evening before the commencement of 1793. His scholarship, however, must have been less than satisfactory; in November 1793 he was again listed in College records as a junior. The Cliosophic Society chose him first assistant on November 13, but a few weeks later, on December 3, no address was delivered on its meeting night because Snowden was unprepared. In February he was fined two shillings for reading a composition before the society that he had already read in class. In spite of these irregularities, on March 19, 1794 he was again chosen to represent the society on July 4.

At about this time Snowden's mental turmoil became critical. His name is no longer included on the May 10, 1794 list of students enrolled in the College, and on May 20 he declined the honor of speaking at the annual Fourth of July celebration. On June 20, 1794 David English (A.B. 1789), who had recently been appointed a tutor at the College and who should have been more discreet about divulging confidential information, wrote to his friend Charles Dickinson Green (A.B. 1787):

A very extraordinary circumstance has taken place in the Snowdon family it is yet a kind of secret but will not long remain so it was communicated confidentially to me but I have learned it from an other source since. While the Old gentleman & Lady were here Billy left home & two lette[rs] were afterwards found for his papa and mamma [info]rming them of his departure & requesting them [not] to be distressed on his account he was going to embark for Europe as a voyage to sea was necessary for his health—that they need not attempt to stop him for he had taken measures so as to prevent their finding him out before he should sail—he did not take many clothes with him—It is doubtless very distressing to the family—you need not mention it to any one until you hear more on the subject—

Whether or not Billy actually managed to sail to Europe, he was home by July of the following year, when his father wrote to

Nathaniel urging him to come home (which was now in Princeton) to discuss his brother's condition. Nathaniel's diary entry of July 5, 1795 says of Billy, "He [is] a very great trouble to us and exercises my mind very much." Later that month, when Charles Snowden visited Nathaniel, who was living in Carlisle, Pennsylvania, they spent much of the visit discussing Billy's condition. At a family conference held in Princeton on September 8, Billy was the only member not present; however, he did attend a family dinner on February 24, 1796. At another family gathering in late October, Gilbert, who had come from nearby Cranbury, grew "very violent" when discussing Billy. The climax came early in November when Mrs. Snowden wrote that Billy had run away from home. Apparently he did not get far; on December 28 the other Snowden brothers, who all lived in or near Princeton, summoned Nathaniel from Pennsylvania for another family meeting because Billy was "very much out of order." On December 30 the distraught Snowdens consulted with "Dr. Smith [Samuel Stanhope Smith (A.B.1769), president of the College], Dr. McLane [John Maclean, professor at the College and a practicing physician], Dr. Stockton [Ebenezer Stockton (A.B. 1780), Princeton's leading physician and Maclean's medical partner] & they advised & we put Billy to the hospital, he very outrageous before."

1797 dawned as a bad year for the Snowdens. Charles was not adapting to the ministry, Nathaniel was in debt, repeatedly asking his father for help, and Gilbert died suddenly on February 20. With all of these distractions Nathaniel still noted in his diary on March 25, "Billy is quite ill." Through the spring he prayed for "poor brother William in particular." On a visit to Princeton in August he found the family in good health, "only Billy who was at a Dr. Mount." Ten days later Nathaniel and Isaac visited their brother at a Dr. Montgomery's and found him "pretty well in body but not quite so in mind." This physician may have been Dr. Thomas West Montgomery, who had a practice first in Allentown, New Jersey, and later in Princeton.

Sometime during the next year Snowden was hospitalized in Philadelphia, where Nathaniel visited him on June 22 and noted that, "He seemed well in body & tolerably so in mind. He took a walk with me into ye garden & picked currants, raspberries." By February 1, 1799 Billy had returned to his parents' home, which was now in Gilbert's house in Cranbury. He was apparently well enough to remain at home, at least until May 30, 1801, when on a visit to Cranbury Nathaniel found "Momma pretty well & Billy better in body but still deranged." Although Nathaniel continued his diaries until 1839, this is the last mention of his youngest brother. A genealogy of the Snowden family says only that William died young.

SOURCES: Snowden family folder, PUA; Min. Fac., 10 Nov. 1789, class lists 1790 & 1792 summer sessions, 5 Feb. & 11 Nov. 1793; N. R. Snowden, MS Diaries, 1788-89 & 1795-1801, PHi; Clio. lists; Clio. Min., 7 [i.e., 8] Aug. 1792–20 May 1794 *passim*; als, David English to Charles D. Green, 20 June 1794, PPPrHi; Wickes, *Hist. of Medicine N.J.*, 317-19, 334-35, 409. William's name is not included in many of the Snowden family genealogies at PHi. See also sketches for the six other Snowden brothers in *Princetonians*.

LKS & RLW

Samuel Voorhees

SAMUEL VOORHEES entered the College as a sophomore in November 1791. He must have been a poor student, for on September 22, 1792 the faculty decided against promoting him. He was among four students "to be examined on particular branches of their studies at the commencement of the next session." Apparently he declined to face this ordeal, for his name makes no further appearance in the College sources.

Samuel Voorhees may have been the man of that name who was born on September 7, 1777, one of four sons and six daughters of James and Anna Harris Voorhees of Bound Brook, Somerset County, New Jersey. He married Agnes (or Agness) Tunison on September 23, 1802. Their daughter and three of their four sons were baptized at the Raritan Dutch Reformed Church in Somerville, Somerset County. In 1814 and 1816 Voorhees served as coroner of Somerset County. He died in early January 1820, and was buried at the Raritan Cemetery on Bridge Street in Somerville. He left his wife the bulk of his estate during her widowhood, after which it was to go to their children in equal shares. She survived him by eighteen years. His personal estate had an appraised value of $1,817.34, more than half of it in cash and promissory notes. The inventory, which included a slave, two horses, five cows, two ploughs, and $35 worth of "Blacksmiths tools," points to his having farmed only on a small scale, perhaps not as his primary occupation.

The College records do not give Voorhees's place of origin, and as the surname is common, positive identification is difficult. A search through the sources for New Jersey, Pennsylvania, and New York turned up two viable alternatives to the Somerset County man. Coincidentally, both were sometime residents of Fishkill, Dutchess County, New York. Samuel Newton Van Voorhis (or Van Voorhees) was born on July 10, 1774, the eldest of five sons and three daughters of Daniel Van Voorhis. The father lived at Fishkill until about 1780, when he moved to Rancocas Creek, Burlington County, New Jersey.

In 1785 he moved to Pigeon Creek, Washington County, Pennsylvania. He married thrice. His first wife, the mother of Samuel and his sister Sarah, was the widow of Francis Brett and the daughter of Coert Van Voorhis of Fishkill. The latter bequeathed Samuel and Sarah some money and a 150-acre farm in Charlotte Precinct of Dutchess County at his death in 1785. Samuel lived in or near Fishkill. He married Sarah Myers at the Fishkill Dutch Reformed Church on June 22, 1800. They had four sons and three daughters. Later he is said to have settled in or near Bucyrus, the seat of Crawford County, Ohio.

Samuel N. Van Voorhis's first cousin Samuel Lawrence Van Voorhis (or Van Voorhees) was born on December 26, 1772, the eldest of two sons and three daughters of Zacharia Van Voorhis and his first wife, Anna Lawrence. Samuel L. married Sarah Cooper at the Dutch Reformed Church of Fishkill on December 6, 1797. They had six sons and two daughters. Van Voorhis became an ensign in the Dutchess County militia in 1806 and rose to lieutenant in 1810 and captain in April 1812. By this time he was living in the part of Dutchess which was set off to Putnam County later that year. He resigned his commission sometime before March 18, 1816, and his subsequent activities have not been traced, unless he was the Samuel L. Voorhees who became a lieutenant of a militia regiment in Onondaga County, New York, on July 8, 1816. He died on September 28, 1848, and his wife followed on August 9, 1859.

The Van Voorhis cousins have ages closer to the norm for College students at this time. However, Samuel Voorhees was not impossibly young, and the "Van" is not included in any of the three references to Voorhees in the faculty minutes which are the only evidence of his stay at the College. Without further evidence a positive identification is impossible.

SOURCES: Min. Fac., 11 Nov. 1791 & ca. May 1792 class lists, 22 Sept. 1792 ("to be examined"); E. W. Van Voorhis, *Geneal. of the Van Voorhees Fam. in Amer.* (1888), 201-22, 255-58, 276-80, 530-34; J. P. Snell & F. Ellis, *Hist. of Hunterdon & Somerset Cnties., N.J.* (1881), 646; *GMNJ*, 4 (1928), 62; *Som. Cnty. Hist. Quart.*, 4 (1914), 296-97; 5 (1916), 66, 69; 8 (1919), 306; *N.J. Wills*, x, 108; xi, 84, 159, 384; xii, 406; Samuel Voorhees's will, dated 12 Oct. 1819, proved 8 Jan. 1820, & estate inv., dated 14 Jan. 1820, recorded 27 Mar. 1820 ("Blacksmiths"), MSS in Nj (photocopies in PUA); *NYGBR*, 61 (1930), 386; 65 (1934), 357 (1800 Census); 70 (1939), 82; 83 (1952), 159, 161; *Military Minutes of the Council of Appointment of the State of N.Y. 1783-1821* (1901), i, 861; ii, 1116, 1354, 1690, 1728. The transcription of the Raritan Cemetery's gravestone inscriptions in *GMNJ*, 4 (1928), 62, gives SV's date of death as 23 Jan. 1820. The day given must be a misreading, for his will was proved and his estate inventoried earlier in the month. See *GMNJ*, 46 (1971), 2, for the marriage on 31 Jan. 1811 of a Samuel Voorhees and Elizabeth Brown in Monmouth County, New Jersey.

Samuel Stockton Voorhees (1775-1819), soldier, Philadelphia merchant, and luckless settler of Alabama, the son of John and Ruth Stockton Voorhees, would have been the prime candidate to have been the Princetonian because of his strong links with the College. He was the nephew of Stephen Voorhees (A.B. 1765) and of Andrew Hunter, Jr. (A.B. 1772), a number of his Stockton cousins were Princetonians, his first cousin Andrew Stockton Hunter was his classmate, and John Hunn Voorhees (A.B. 1841) was his son. Inconveniently, an extant ledger of Andrew Hunter, Jr., seems to rule out Samuel S. Voorhees's attendance at the College. The ledger contains what are presumably accounts of the expenses of several students during their attendance at Hunter's academy in Woodbury, Gloucester County, New Jersey, and there are entries both for Samuel and for his brother Hunter Voorhees. The entry for Samuel begins on March 12, 1792 and runs through 1795. Admittedly Andrew Hunter could have been handling his nephew's expenses at the College, of which he was a trustee, but since Voorhees's father was alive such an arrangement seems implausible. More likely Voorhees attended the Woodbury academy instead of the College. The ledger was reused by Hunter's second wife in the 1820s, and the entries respecting the Voorhees boys are to be found in the first few pages behind bills she then pasted over them. See Mary Stockton Hunter Record Book (1827-43), Stockton Family Papers, NjPHi. For more on Samuel Stockton Voorhees, see E. W. Van Voorhis, *Genealogy of the Van Voorhees Fam. in Amer.* (1888), 357-58; T. C. Stockton, *Stockton Family of N.J. & Other Stocktons* (1911), 22 & *passim*; *N.J. Wills*, IX, 194; *Hamilton Papers*, XXII, 87-88, 122, 130-31; Heitman, *U.S. Army*, I, 990; Phila. city directories, 1811-18; *PMHB*, 11 (1887), 218-19; 39 (1915), 322; 91 (1967), 301, 319-20, 323; C. E. Carter, ed., *Territorial Papers of the U.S.* (26 vols., 1934-62), XVIII, *Territory of Alabama 1817-19*, 389-90; W. Smith, *Days of Exile: The Story of the Vine & Olive Colony in Alabama* (1967), 46, 50, 56, 94-96. Wanda S. Gunning kindly supplied references used in this sketch.

JJL

John Bradford Wallace

JOHN BRADFORD WALLACE, A.B., A.M. 1797, lawyer, public official, and land speculator, was born on August 17, 1778 at "Ellerslie," an estate on the Raritan River in Bridgewater Township, Somerset County, New Jersey, the son of Joshua Maddox Wallace (A.B. College of Philadelphia 1767, A.M. College of Philadelphia and College of New Jersey 1770) and Tace Bradford Wallace. The mother was the daughter of William and Rachel Budd Bradford and the sister of William Bradford, Jr. (A.B. 1772). Joshua Wallace was the son of a prosperous Philadelphia merchant and received training in a countinghouse, but he declined a career in trade and "lived upon the income of a liberal inherited fortune," a decision possibly aided by the onset of the Revolution. Just before Philadelphia fell to the British in 1777, he moved his family to "Ellerslie" and remained there for the duration of the war. Joshua Maddox Wallace, Jr. (A.B. 1793), was John's elder brother.

In 1784 the Wallaces moved to Burlington, New Jersey, where Joshua Sr. resided until his death in 1819. He served a term in the New Jersey general assembly in 1791 and was a leading Episcopalian, serving as a warden of St. Mary's Church, Burlington and as a mem-

John Bradford Wallace, A.B. 1794

ber of the New Jersey diocese's standing committee. He aided his friend Elias Boudinot in the efforts leading to the organization of the American Bible Society and in 1816 chaired the convention which founded it when Boudinot was too ill to attend. From 1798 until his death, Wallace also joined Boudinot in serving as a College trustee. John Wallace and his brother Joshua Jr. were initially taught by their father, who had been a tutor at the College of Philadelphia for a short time. They were then sent to the boarding school of Rev. William Frazer, the Episcopal minister at Amwell, Hunterdon County, New Jersey.

Wallace entered the College as a freshman in November 1790 and joined the American Whig Society. He was a particular favorite both of Vice President Samuel Stanhope Smith (A.B. 1769), who is said to have praised his recitations, and of President John Witherspoon, who wrote Wallace's father on March 27, 1794 that "John who is in the Senior class maintains a very good character & is reckoned one among the best scholars in the class." At the undergraduate competitions held the day before the September 1792 commencement, Wallace was one of four victors in "Pronouncing English Orations."

During his years at the College he spoke frequently at such exercises on topics ranging from "The Genius of Love," "Public Gratitude," and "Enthusiasm" to panegyrics to Christopher Columbus and the Marquis de Lafayette (LL.D. 1790) and a defense of women's right to participate in politics.

As a senior Wallace stood third in a class of twenty-seven. He gave the valedictory orations both at his commencement and at the annual meeting of the American Whig Society held about the same time. An anonymous relative, probably his son John, had the former printed in 1874. This address called for the abolition of slavery and raised an exuberant paean to America as the haven of liberty and to the American Revolution which had in France now

> kindled a blaze which promises to pervade & purify the world. Behold the despots of Europe making a last struggle to support their tottering thrones—See the proselytes of Roman superstition, with all their host of vices & prejudices, scattered & consumed by the rising splendors of reason & liberty—See, too, the oppressed vassals of Europe, ready to resume their long lost rights & to avenge their accumulated wrongs.... See too the mighty people of France—those pioneers of universal liberty, with principles more formidable to despotism than their arms, advance in support of European freedom.

Apparently even Maximilien Robespierre's Terror did not give Wallace pause in 1794. Commencement orators at this time frequently used pieces written for them by others, but presumably Wallace's address reflected his own sentiments, especially since some of his undergraduate orations had a similar theme. In an address on "Arbitrary Imprisonment" delivered in March 1792, Wallace called the French Revolution "perhaps the most astounding" event since the Creation, to which it was similar, for "from the political chaos of a corrupted and senile Government, has arisen a fair creation of constitutional liberty." Given his subsequent political convictions, Wallace may have recalled these youthful effusions with embarrassment.

After graduation Wallace read law with his uncle William Bradford, then attorney general of the United States, until the latter's untimely death in August 1795. Wallace is said to have added his middle name after he graduated, and the death of his uncle and mentor quite likely prompted the change. When Bradford died he was living at "Rose Hill," the estate of his father-in-law Elias Boudinot located two miles from Philadelphia. Wallace was still studying law there in January 1796, presumably now under Boudinot's tutelage. According to a letter of that date from Wallace's aunt Rachel Bradford, John was also teaching geography to "Hetty and Mary," who were probably his sisters.

On December 9, 1799 Wallace was admitted to the Philadelphia bar, and in 1800 his name first appeared in a city directory as an attorney at 28 North Fifth Street. Until 1822 he practiced in Philadelphia, with his address changing several times from Walnut to South Second, South Third, South Fourth, and finally back to Walnut Street. He first called himself a "councellor at law" in the 1810 directory. His legal career prospered. He was appointed court reporter of the Third Circuit Court of the United States in 1801 and served until at least 1816. His manuscript notes until the latter year survive, but he published only one volume, covering the May 1801 session. In 1802 he was an incorporator and the first secretary and treasurer of the Law Library Company of Philadelphia, which merged with a bar association in 1827 to form the Law Association of Philadelphia.

Wallace became an avid Federalist. He helped lead a group of "young Gentlemen of Philadelphia" who offered to give a dinner in honor of Timothy Pickering (LL.D. 1798) in January 1801. One historian has described Wallace's association of Philadelphia Federalists as "an organized group of men who served first as an auxiliary to the party committees, and gradually took them over." Wallace served on Federalist committees of correspondence and attended the national meeting in New York in 1812. At this meeting the Federalists decided to back DeWitt Clinton for the presidency instead of running a candidate of their own, on the theory that no Federalist was electable and anyone was to be preferred to James Madison (A.B. 1771). Also in 1812 Wallace and twelve other self-styled "friends and companions" of Joseph Dennie contributed $15 each to build a monument over his grave. Dennie founded and edited *The Port Folio* and served as arbiter of literary taste for a generation of conservative Philadelphians. In 1815 Wallace belonged to the select council, the upper house of the city's legislative body. Service in 1807 as one of the managers of the fashionable Philadelphia Assembly demonstrated his good standing in Philadelphia society. He was also one of the seventy-one founders of the Pennsylvania Academy of the Fine Arts, and in 1804 he joined the St. Andrew's Society of Philadelphia, of which his grandfather John Wallace, the Scottish immigrant, had been a founder.

On April 2, 1805 Wallace married Susan Binney, the daughter of Dr. Barnabas and Mary Woodrow Binney and the sister of Horace Binney, who became an eminent lawyer. The Wallaces had four sons and two daughters. Their son John William Wallace (A.B. University of Pennsylvania 1833) became a legal scholar of some renown and from 1864 to 1875 was reporter of the United States Supreme Court. He served as president of the Historical Society of Pennsylvania for fifteen years. His wife Dorothea Francis Willing was the daughter of George Willing (A.B. 1792). Another son, Horace Binney Wallace (A.B. 1835), also wrote on jurisprudence but became better known as a novelist and writer on European art, travel, and literature.

As early as 1807 Wallace was serving as an agent for western land sales, and he soon began speculating on a very large scale himself. On February 1, 1810 Wallace and federal judge William Griffith of Burlington agreed to pay $180,000 for the entire interest of the Holland Land Company in property and mortgages west of the Allegheny River. The first $20,000 was due in five years, with the balance then beginning to accrue six per cent interest and final payment to be made within twenty years. Griffith and Wallace thereby acquired almost 350,000 acres of unsold real estate in northwestern Pennsylvania, plus $100,000 in promissory notes and interest that settlers owed for land purchases already made. In 1811 another group of Dutch investors sold Wallace and Griffith 1,014 shares in the Pennsylvania Population Company, a land company similar to the Holland Company in its holdings and history. The price was $60,000. This purchase gave them a little under half of that company's stock and thus of its assets, which consisted of lands valued at $344,855 and of securities and mortgages which were auctioned for $70,739 when the company was dissolved in 1812.

Wallace and Griffith thus found themselves in 1812 in possession of substantial pieces of Erie, Crawford, Warren, and Venango counties. What concerned them now was converting it into cash in time to pay off debts of almost a quarter of a million dollars. Their hopes of making a fortune proved illusory. Both the Holland and the Population companies had initially had great difficulty evicting squatters, but by the time Griffith and Wallace took possession this problem had been largely resolved and the major headache was obtaining payment from purchasers. Sales were generally made on a long-term contract, with little or no money down, either to settlers who hoped to earn the purchase price by working the land or to middlemen who anticipated paying their debt by finding purchasers of their own. Both expectations proved wildly optimistic. Griffith and Wallace must have realized the dimensions of their plight after their experience with William S. Hart and Augustus Sacket, who served as their land agents from 1812 to 1815. Hart and Sacket "sold" more than $330,000 worth of land in just one year, but after almost none of the sales proved collectable, Griffith and Wallace became aware that their agents were unreliable and fired them. In 1816 Griffith became alarmed at his mounting debts and sold his interest in the western lands to the Messrs. Wurtz. Two years later, Wallace ended the partnership by deeding to the Wurtzes mortgages and lands with a book value of $310,000. Wallace retained both the partnership's liabilities and the bulk of its assets.

The panic of 1819 ruined Wallace's brother Joshua, a merchant who died early in 1821 leaving John responsible for many of his debts. This blow precipitated a financial crisis for John, who was already badly overextended by land speculations which the depression would now make that much harder to turn into cash. Persuaded by his bitter experience with agents that only his own supervision could retrieve the situation, Wallace moved in 1822 to Meadville, Crawford County, in the center of his landholdings in northwestern Pennsylvania. Here his energetic efforts to recoup his losses failed, and in 1828 or 1829 he conceded defeat and made a general assignment of his assets to his creditors. He had paid only $1,600 on the principal due the Holland Company and $4,000 on that owed for the Population Company stock. Wallace remained in Meadville and eventually seems to have put his financial house in order.

Wallace was elected to the Pennsylvania assembly from Crawford County in 1831, 1832, and 1833. In a broadside published during one of these elections, he disclaimed any party connection, since the Federalist party no longer existed and "until I find another as pure, patriotic, honest, and disinterested as it was (and this I shall never do), I shall not connect myself with any." He supported the Second Bank of the United States when it was attacked by President Andrew Jackson, and he was a friend and political backer of Daniel Webster (LL.D. 1818). Apparently because of his pro-Bank stance, Wallace lost his bid for reelection in 1834.

Even before he moved to Meadville, Wallace made one of the largest contributions, $500, to the subscription in 1815 which led to the founding of Allegheny College. Its act of incorporation of March 1817 named him a trustee. He was instrumental in founding Christ Episcopal Church, Meadville, which was organized in January 1825. The building was consecrated on his fiftieth birthday.

Wallace had moved back to Philadelphia by April 1835 and in his last years lived at 7 Portico Square. He died suddenly in his sleep at 11 p.m. on January 7, 1837 and was buried in the churchyard of St. Peter's Church, the parent parish of which he had served as warden and vestryman during his earlier years in Philadelphia. In 1848 his widow wrote a memoir recalling his piety, unostentatious charity and public service, courtesy, energy, and integrity.

SOURCES: [S. B. Wallace], *Memoir* [of John Bradford Wallace] (1848), *passim* ("lived upon," 5; "until I find," 16); *PMHB*, 8 (1884), xiii-xliv; 11 (1887), 360; 49 (1925), 86-87; 75 (1951), 36-38; G. M. Hills, *Hist. of the Church in Burlington, N.J.* (2nd. ed., 1885), 324, 382-83, 385, 495; E. M. Woodward & J. F. Hageman, *Hist. of Burlington & Mercer Cnties., N.J.* (1883), 67; *PGM*, 5 (1914), 281 (father's will); 29 (1975), 4; G. A. Boyd, *Elias Boudinot* (1952), 188, 227, 259; Alexander, *Princeton*, 270-71 ("the good"), 279; Min. Fac., 29 Nov. 1790, 26 Sept. 1792 ("Pronouncing"), 22 Aug. 1794; Amer. Whig Soc., *Cat.* (1840), 7; "Orations Delivered at Nassau Hall, Princeton, N.J., A.D. 1791-94, by JBW" ("perhaps the most," "from the political," speech topics), als, John Witherspoon to Joshua M. Wallace, Sr., 27 Mar. 1794 ("John who is"), & "Valedictory Oration pronounced at CNJ, Princeton, by JBW, 1 Oct. 1794" ("kindled"), MSS in Wallace Family Papers, PHi (microfilm at PUA); Hobart, *Corres.*, I, 30, 232-33; *Dunlap & Claypoole's Amer. Daily Advt.*, 7 Oct. 1794; *State Gazette & N.J. Advt.*, 17 Oct. 1797; J. J. Boudinot, *Life, Public Services, Addresses & Letters of Elias Boudinot* (1896), II, 116-18 ("Hetty"); *Martin's Bench & Bar*, 191-92, 219, 243, 320; Phila. city directories, 1800-22, 1835-39; G. P. Fisher, *Life of Benjamin Silliman, M.D., LL.D.* (1866), I, 97-100; als, Richard Peters & JBW to Timothy Pickering, 5 Jan. 1801, Pickering Papers, MHi ("young Gentlemen"); D. H. Fischer, *Revolution of Amer. Conservatism* (1965), 352 ("an organized"); S. W. Higginbotham, *Keystone in the Democratic Arch: Pa. Politics 1800-16* (1952), 260-61, 371; J. F. Lewis, *Hist. of an Old Phila. Land Title: 208 South Fourth Street* (1934), 121, 142-52 (see p. 152 for a different silhouette profile of JBW); *Hist. Cat. of the St. Andrew's Soc. of Phila. ... 1749-1907* (1907), 33, 90, 349, 423; P. D. Evans, *Holland Land Co.* (1924, in Buffalo Hist. Soc., *Pubs.*, vol. 28), 168-69, 171-76; N. M. Tiffany & F. Tiffany, *Harm Jan Huidekoper* (1904), 127-31; R. N. Hale, "Pa. Population Co.," *Pa. Hist.*, 16 (1949), 122-30; R. D. Ilisevich, "Early Land Barons in French Creek Valley," *Pa. Hist.*, 48 (1981), 291; alumni file, PUA; E. A. Smith, *Allegheny—A Century of Education 1815-1915* (1916), 16, 22-23, 43; J. E. Reynolds, *In French Creek Valley* (1938), 241-42; C. M. Wiltse & H. D. Moser, eds., *Papers of Daniel Webster, Corres., III, 1830-34* (1977), 317-18, 320, 351, 493; letter from R. D. Ilisevich, 21 May 1985, PUA; W. W. Bronson, *Inscriptions in St. Peter's Church Yard, Phila.* (1879), 22-24, 70, 521. PHi owns a photograph of a badly cracked oil portrait of JBW as a young man.

PUBLICATIONS: *Reports of Cases Adjudged in the Circuit Court of the U.S. for the Third Circuit* (1st ed. 1801, Sh-Sh # 1600; 2d ed. 1838; reprint of 2d ed. 1871); *Remarks upon the Law of Bailment* (1840); *Valedictory Oration Pronounced at CNJ on the Graduation of the Class of 1794* (1874). JBW is also credited with editing the American edition of Charles Abbot, First Baron Tenterden, *Treatise on the Law Relative to Merchant Ships* (1802, Sh-Sh # 3152, see J. T. Scharf & T. Westcott, *Hist. of Phila. 1609-1884* [1884], II, 1154).

MANUSCRIPTS: Wallace Family Papers, PHi; PPL; Timothy Pickering Papers, MHi; Harm Jan Huidekoper Collection, Crawford Ctny. Hist. Soc., Public Lib., Meadville; DLC. PHi owns JBW's MS of his valedictory oration, which appears to be the earliest extant College valedictory. The same repository possesses a MS copy made in 1877 of eight orations JBW gave at various College competitions and functions during his undergraduate years. Only three have been definitely dated, the earliest being that of March 1792. While earlier examples of commencement orations by graduating seniors have been identified, these speeches, and the almost contemporary but slightly later orations of John Henry Hobart, A.B. 1793 (Hobart Papers, TxAuCH), are among the earliest known examples of such preparatory forensic exercises by CNJ undergraduates. PUA has photocopies of JBW's & Hobart's speeches.

JJL

James Carra Williamson

JAMES CARRA WILLIAMSON, A.B., A.M. 1798, merchant, was one of the four children of William and Lydia Hampton Williamson of Elizabethtown, Essex (now Union) County, New Jersey. William Rickets Williamson (A.B. 1794) was his brother, and he was the nephew of Matthias Williamson, Jr. (A.B. 1770), Jacob Williamson (A.B. 1771), and Susannah Williamson, who married Jonathan Dayton (A.B. 1776). William Chetwood (A.B. 1792) and Benjamin Williamson (A.B. 1827) were cousins, and E. Dayton (Class of 1796) and J. H. Dayton (Class of 1797) may also have been related. Lydia was probably the daughter of Jonathan Hampton of Elizabethtown. The Williamsons were a prominent Elizabethtown family. Matthias, William Williamson's father, served as a general in the state militia in the Revolutionary War. William, however, achieved little fame. The tax lists of 1778 and 1780 point to his having farmed, but agriculture need not have been his primary occupation. Like his father, he served on the vestry of St. John's Anglican Church, Elizabethtown. He died in 1785.

James Williamson entered the College as a junior in October 1792. He joined the American Whig Society, but his brother became a Clio. At his commencement he was replicator in "A dispute on this question, Is the institution of voluntary popular societies, to watch the motions of government in the present state of this country wise or useful[?]"

Williamson subsequently became a merchant and immigrated to Louisiana before its cession to the United States. In a letter to Chandler Price at the United States Department of State dated August 18, 1803, Benjamin Morgan of New Orleans named Williamson in a list of men born in the United States and now resident in New Orleans whom he thought worthy of consideration for office. On September 1, 1804 Williamson married Mary Dayton in Elizabethtown, with Presbyterian clergyman Azel Roe (A.B. 1756) officiating. Mary was one of nine children of Elias and Hannah Rolfe Dayton of Elizabethtown. Jonathan Dayton (A.B. 1776) and Horatio Dayton (Class of 1794) were her brothers, and she was the aunt of several other Princetonians.

Williamson was back in New Orleans by June 2, 1805. On that date subscribers to a plan to found a Protestant church in that city placed him on a four-man committee to correspond with, among other individuals, the presidents of the College of New Jersey, Yale, Columbia, William and Mary, and the University of Pennsylvania in order to identify a suitable clergyman. The subscribers voted on

June 16 that the new church be Episcopal. They ultimately lured Philander Chase (A.B. Dartmouth 1795) to New Orleans and installed him as rector of Christ Church. Chase later became bishop of Ohio. Williamson served as a vestryman of the new church in 1806 and 1807.

An 1805 census of New Orleans listed no Williamsons, but "James C. Williams" at 25 Rue Royale South should probably be read as Williamson. "Williams" had a household comprising three adult white males, one adult white female, and two slaves. Williamson's name did not appear in the two New Orleans directories of 1807, but he was definitely in that city on March 21, 1811, when he asked Henry Clay to obtain payment on some notes for him. He died sometime between then and March 24, 1814, when Lydia Hampton Williamson bequeathed part of her estate to Henry, Lydia, and Dayton, children "of my late son, James C. Williamson."

SOURCES: *NYGBR*, 75 (1944), 156-57; *GMNJ*, 5 (1929), 38; 43 (1968), 36; alumni files, PUA; E. F. Hatfield, *Hist. of Elizabeth, N.J.* (1868), 212, 448, 542, 545, 664; T. Thayer, *As We Were: The Story of Old Elizabethtown* (1964), 102, 105, 123-24; Min. Fac., 10 Oct. 1792, 22 Aug. 1794; Amer. Whig Soc., *Cat.* (1837), 5; *Dunlap & Claypoole's Amer. Daily Advt.*, 7 Oct. 1794 ("A dispute"); N.Y. *Daily Advt.*, 4 Oct. 1798; C. E. Carter, ed., *Territorial Papers of the U.S.* (26 vols., 1934-62), IX (*Territory of Orleans 1803-12*), 8-10; Phila. *True Amer. & Commercial Advt.*, 7 Sept. 1804; H. Carter & B. W. Carter, *So Great a Good* (1955), 4, 6-8, 410; H. C. Duncan, *Diocese of Louisiana ... 1805-88* (1888), 48; *Louisiana Hist. Quart.*, 22 (1939), 431-34, 436, 439; Hobart, *Corres.*, IV, 527-28; *New Orleans in 1805* (1936), 74; *Clay Papers*, I, 549-50; *N.J. Wills*, XI, 376-77; XIII, 480-81 ("of my late"). Williamson's middle name is given in the 1797 College catalogue. The name James Carra, sometimes spelled Cara or Curra, recurs frequently in the Williamson family. See *GMNJ*, 6 (1930-31), 5, 113, 114, 116. James C. Williamson of New Orleans was not the Williamson in the mercantile firm of Meeker, Williamson & Patton, whose first name was John. See als, John Williamson to Andrew Jackson, 12 Dec. 1805, Andrew Jackson Papers, Presidential Papers Microfilm, DLC. Wanda S. Gunning kindly supplied references used in this sketch.

JJL

William Rickets Williamson

WILLIAM RICKETS WILLIAMSON, A.B., A.M. 1798, attorney and soldier, was the brother of his classmate James C. Williamson and the son of William and Lydia Hampton Williamson of Elizabethtown, Essex (now Union) County, New Jersey. The father left little trace in the records and died aged thirty-seven on July 29, 1785. However the Williamsons were a prominent family politically. The elder William's siblings included Isaac Halsted Williamson (LL.D. 1839), later governor of New Jersey, and Susannah, the wife of the nationally eminent Jonathan Dayton (A.B. 1776), as well as Matthias Williamson, Jr. (A.B. 1770), and Jacob Williamson (A.B. 1771). Their father was Matthias Williamson, a Revolutionary War general.

In October 1792 the younger William entered the College's junior class. Although his brother became a Whig, William joined the Cliosophic Society on December 5 of that year, taking the pseudonym Sempronius, a name too common among the ancient Romans to permit exact identification. The society's minutes suggest that Williamson was a poor student. He was cited for bad scholarship three times between March and May 1793. On the third occasion the Clios threatened him with suspension, upon which he "amended considerably." The society convicted him and George M. Ogden (A.B. 1795) on February 12, 1794 of "playing at cards and keeping bad company" and suspended them for four weeks. On March 4 the Clios readmitted Williamson early because he was among the seniors who were to speak publicly at the close of the semester and wanted the suspension lifted so that he could "appear on the stage with a distinction." The entry is puzzling. Although the literary societies coached and sometimes chose those who participated in such exercises, they almost certainly lacked enough recognition from the faculty to bar members not in good standing from College exercises, as this phrasing seems to imply. Perhaps Williamson was sensitive about making a public appearance while under censure, albeit censure not officially sanctioned.

On July 2, 1794 the Clios elected Williamson to a one-month term as second assistant. He held no other society position, an unusually limited record of officeholding and a final proof of his shaky standing in the society. However he applied for and received its diploma on August 22, 1794 and remained interested enough in its affairs to attend the annual meeting on September 28, 1796. This continuous involvement in the Cliosophic Society makes Williamson's appearance in the catalogues of the American Whig Society difficult to explain. Perhaps a mistake involving his brother's name crept in at some point.

At his commencement on September 24, 1794, Williamson was respondent in a dispute with the topic "Are Liberty and Equality calculated to promote the happiness and improvement of mankind?" The New Jersey supreme court called him to the bar as an attorney in May 1799. He settled in Elizabethtown and on June 1, 1812 was one of five depositors who started accounts when the State Bank at Elizabeth first opened its doors. On November 8, 1813 he married Joanna B. Shute, the daughter of William Shute, at St. John's Episcopal Church, Elizabethtown. They seem to have had no children. Williamson served as the quartermaster of Col. John Dod's Regiment of Infantry, New Jersey Detailed Militia, while it was stationed at the Highlands, near Sandy Hook, Monmouth County, New Jersey, from September 1 to November 28, 1814.

Williamson died shortly before October 20, 1818, when he was buried from St. John's Church. In his will he left everything to his wife. His personal estate, valued at $912.75, consisted mostly of furniture and furnishings but also included a female slave and five shares of stock in the State Bank at Elizabeth.

SOURCES: *N.J. Wills*, IX, 368; X, 272; XI, 376-77; XII, 376; XIII, 480-81; *NYGBR*, 75 (1944), 156-57; *GMNJ*, 5 (1929), 38; 43 (1968), 36; alumni files, PUA; E. F. Hatfield, *Hist. of Elizabeth, N.J.* (1868), 212, 448, 542, 545, 664; T. Thayer, *As We Were: The Story of Old Elizabethtown* (1964), 102, 105, 123-24; Min. Fac., 10 Oct. 1792, 22 Aug. 1794; Clio. lists; Clio. Min., 21 Nov. 1792–22 Aug. 1794 *passim* ("amended," "playing at," "appear on"), 28 Sept. 1796; Amer. Whig Soc., *Cat.* (1837), 5; *Dunlap & Claypoole's Amer. Daily Advt.*, 7 Oct. 1794 ("Are Liberty"); N.Y. *Daily Advt.*, 4 Oct. 1798; Riker, 79; P. L. Kleinhans, *Down Through the Years: The Story of the National State Bank of Elizabeth, N.J.* (1937), 43-44; Trenton *True American*, 22 Nov. 1813; letter from Rev. David R. King, 18 Oct. 1985, PUA; N.J. Adjutant General's Office, *Records of Officers & Men of N.J. in Wars 1791-1815* (1909), separately numbered section on War of 1812, 61; will of WRW, 20 Feb. 1818, & estate inv. of WRW, 26 Oct. 1818, both proved 28 Oct. 1818, MSS in Nj (photocopies in PUA). On May 24, 1807 a William Williamson married Margaret Cadmus at the Second River (now Belleville) Dutch Reformed Church, and the couple's son was baptized there in 1812 (see *NJHSP*, 3d ser., 2 [1897], 69, 135). Belleville was in Essex County, but as the Princetonian certainly was in Elizabethtown in 1812 and was an Episcopalian, there is probably no connection. The name was common in New Jersey at the time.

JJL

John Ramsey Witherspoon

JOHN RAMSEY WITHERSPOON, A.B., A.M. 1814, M.D. Transylvania University 1823, physician and public official, was born March 17, 1774, near Kingstree, later Williamsburg, on the Black River in Prince Frederick County, South Carolina. His grandfather James, one of the original Scots-Irish settlers in the area, was said to be a triple second cousin of President John Witherspoon. James taught his trade of weaving to his son Robert who, after his marriage to Elizabeth Heathly, supported his family by weaving, reed making, and farming. John Ramsey Witherspoon was the eighth of their nine children. Robert Witherspoon was a dedicated Presbyterian and a ruling elder in the Williamsburg Church. He died in 1788 before his son reached college age.

John R. Witherspoon received his preparatory schooling at the Latin grammar school conducted by the Reverend Thomas Reese (A.B. 1768) at Salem, South Carolina, and matriculated at the College in the fall of 1792 as a member of the junior class. On December 5 Witherspoon and Edwin Reese (A.B. 1794), his former schoolmaster's son, were proposed for membership in the Cliosophic Society. However, they withdrew their names the following week and both joined the American Whig Society, whose records incorrectly list Witherspoon as John Rodgers Witherspoon. In later life Witherspoon was such a close friend of William Johnson, Jr. (A.B. 1790), that the two exchanged portraits. Johnson had graduated from the College before Witherspoon arrived, but they probably already knew each other, and perhaps Johnson persuaded Witherspoon to affiliate with the Whigs.

During his two years at the College Witherspoon acted as secretary for the aging president, who by this time was completely blind. The student went to the president's home, "Tusculum," at least once a week, sometimes more frequently, to care for the elder Witherspoon's correspondence. Dr. Witherspoon still preached at the Princeton Presbyterian Church every third Sunday. On Saturday afternoons he would prepare for such occasions by having John Ramsey read aloud one of his earlier sermons, deciphering the notoriously difficult handwriting. Witherspoon would then repeat the address verbatim from the pulpit the next morning.

It would be interesting to know whether arrangements were made prior to the younger Witherspoon's matriculation for him to serve as amanuensis as a means of helping to pay his tuition at the College. The only record of payment found is a $3.00 fee which he received for copying the College laws in April 1794. Professor Walter Minto was reimbursed forty-five cents for taking the copy to Trenton, probably to a printer in that city. Whether or not any money regularly changed hands, the relationship between the two Witherspoons seems to have been warm and affectionate. Following his commencement, at which he was not one of the public speakers, the new graduate went to "Tusculum" to say goodbye and to give the customary fee of a gold English sovereign to the president, who refused it, and with tears in his eyes gave the young man his blessing. In later years John Ramsey Witherspoon referred to President Witherspoon as his "venerated friend and preceptor" and expressed his appreciation of the informal, intimate, and instructive conversations he had had with the older man.

Witherspoon returned to South Carolina where he studied medicine and began his practice in Christ Church Parish, the district which he represented in the South Carolina general assembly from November 28, 1803 through December 19, 1809. On December 21, 1802, at Pine Grove, in Christ Church Parish, he married Jane Harrison McCalla, the daughter of the Reverend Daniel (A.B. 1766) and Eliza Todd McCalla, with the Reverend William Hollinshead (D.D. 1793) of Charleston, uncle of the bride, officiating. Jane McCalla Witherspoon died on February 23, 1808, leaving one son, Daniel McCalla Witherspoon (A.B. 1825).

Sometime in 1810 Witherspoon moved to Kentucky where, on November 13 at Wappetaw near Lexington, he married Mary Ann Todd, his first wife's cousin. The daughter of Gen. Robert Todd, she was also a first cousin of Robert Smith Todd, father of Mary Todd Lincoln. Mary Ann Witherspoon was only eighteen when she died childless on August 25, 1812. Witherspoon's first two wives were both granddaughters of the Reverend John Todd (A.B. 1749), who died leaving over 20,000 acres of land in Kentucky. Witherspoon or his young son may have inherited some of this acreage when his McCalla in-laws both died the year after their only child, Jane. John Todd had also been instrumental in helping to obtain a charter for Transylvania Seminary, later incorporated into Transylvania University, an institution to which he contributed a portion of his library and scientific equipment, the beginning of its medical library. Witherspoon reportedly studied medicine at Transylvania and received the M.D. degree on March 19, 1823. The degree was probably an honorary one. A catalogue of the school does not list him as having earned a degree, and it is rather unlikely that he would have attended classes after more than twenty years of practice. He had, moreover, become a member of the board of trustees of Transylvania in April 1815. He also represented Fayette County in the Kentucky house of representatives for 1821-22. On December 18, 1821 he was listed as a member of a committee appointed to confer with eminent educators, collect information, and prepare a plan for common schools in the state. The committee presented an elaborate report to the general assembly the following year.

On June 2, 1815 Witherspoon married Sophia Graham, eldest daughter of the thirteen children of Gen. Joseph Graham of Lincoln County, North Carolina, and his late wife, Isabella Davidson Graham. At the death of her mother, Sophia had taken over the care of her younger siblings and was responsible for raising her youngest brother, William A. Graham, governor of North Carolina from 1845 to 1849 and vice presidential candidate on the Whig ticket in 1852. John Ramsey Witherspoon, in his retirement, brought up to 1840 a family genealogy begun by his father, the original of which was destroyed by a fire in the home of John's eldest daughter in 1879. In this family history Witherspoon described his first two wives as possessed of "youth, beauty, innocence, virtue, all combined to render them lovely." Sophia Witherspoon, however, was remembered only for her "faithfulness, consideration and affection." She bore nine children, including John James Witherspoon (A.B. 1839) and John Graham Witherspoon (A.B. 1841). Sometime before their matriculation at the College the family moved to "Brookland" plantation in Hale County near Greensboro, Alabama. Witherspoon's brother Thomas had moved to Green County outside of Greensboro in 1825. John Ramsey Witherspoon died on May 9, 1852 and was buried in the Stokes Cemetery north of Greensboro, with a monument bearing the inscription, "Honored, Loved and Mourned." He was considered a "fine physician, quite literary, ... and greatly respected for his learning and integrity."

Destroyed in the same fire as the family genealogy was a manuscript "History of the Presbyterian Church at Williamsburg" by Witherspoon who, like his father, had served as a ruling elder of the church. In 1810 he edited two volumes containing the sermons of his first father-in-law Daniel McCalla, which he published for a list of private subscribers. Passed down from Daniel McCalla to Daniel McCalla Witherspoon and to succeeding eldest sons was a manuscript Latin Vulgate Bible, handwritten in German script about 1330, probably in a monastery in Cornwall, England. John Ramsey Witherspoon may have published a description of this Bible, also by subscription.

Henry Goldthwaite (A.M. 1839) married Witherspoon's eldest daughter Elizabeth (Eliza) Isabella, and their descendants included William H. Goldthwaite (A.B. 1854), Thomas Goldthwaite (A.B. 1859), Henry Goldthwaite (A.B. 1860), John Witherspoon Goldthwaite and Joseph Graham Goldthwaite (Class of 1864), Alfred Goldthwaite (Class of 1868), Charles Goldthwaite (Class of 1894), Joseph G. Goldthwaite (Class of 1899), and Beverly Goldthwaite (A.B. 1931).

SOURCES: Alumni files & Witherspoon genealogy file, PUA; Giger, Memoirs; V. L. Collins, *Pres. Witherspoon: A Biog.* (1925), 230-34; M. L. L. Stohlman, *John Witherspoon: Parson, Politician, Patriot* (1976), 166; J. G. Wardlaw, *Gen. of the Witherspoon Family* (1910), 7, 16-19, 37, 59-60, 146-47; J. B. Witherspoon, *Hist. & Gen. of the Witherspoon Family* (1973), 47-51, 93-95, 137-42; Min. Fac., 10 Oct. 1792, 22 Aug. 1794; Clio. Min., 5 & 12 Dec. 1792; Amer. Whig Soc., *Cat.* (1840), 7; CNJ Treasurer's Report, Apr. 1794, PUA; W. W. Boddie, *Hist. of Williamsburg* (1923), 8-9, 236; *Biog. Dir. S.C. House Rep.*, I, 259, 264, 268, 273; III, 785; *SCHGM*, 25 (1924), 140; 33 (1932), 41; 35 (1934), 171; 37 (1936), 162; 40 (1939), 102; 58 (1957), 85-86; Federal Writers' Project, Ky., *Lexington & the Bluegrass Country* (1938), 9; C. A. Vance, "Transylvania Medical Library," *Annals of Surgery*, 123 (1946), 483; R. Sobel & J. Raimo, *Biog. Dir. of the Governors of the U.S., 1789-1978* (1978), III, 1131 (Wm. Graham biog.); *KSHS Reg.*, 39 (1941), 68; 45 (1947), 197; *Southern Pres. Review*, 6 (1853), 116-20; M. J. Witherspoon, *Hist. of the Witherspoon Manuscript Bible* (1975), 11-13, 17, 44-47, 55-56. The Witherspoon Bible is now in the Rare Books Room of Washington Univ. Lib., St. Louis, Mo., along with a brief history of the Bible written by JRW circa 1809.

PUBLICATIONS: See text.

RLW

APPENDIX A

EVIDENCE that the subjects of the following biographies attended the College came to light after publication of earlier volumes of *Princetonians*. Since the present volume concludes this series, the lives are included here as addenda.

Matthias Pierson

MATTHIAS PIERSON, Class of 1764, physician, was born at Newark Mountains, New Jersey, on June 20, 1734, the third son among the nine children of Samuel Pierson II, a farmer, and his wife, the former Mary Sargeant. The Piersons were a strongly Presbyterian family, as befitted descendants of Thomas Pierson, the brother of and fellow settler with Rev. Abraham Pierson (A.B. Trinity College, Cambridge, 1632), the minister who had led his ardent Puritans out of Branford to found Newark in 1666 rather than submit to what they regarded as the excessively lenient government of Connecticut then being imposed on severely orthodox New Haven Colony.

Matthias began his formal education quite late, a pattern that often indicated someone who had decided to become a minister, although it was occasionally also pursued by some men who needed to acquire sufficient classical learning to practice medicine. At the age of twenty-five he enrolled in the grammar school of Rev. Caleb Smith (A.B. Yale 1743 and the first tutor at the College of New Jersey), where he studied for two years. Smith's account book for October 26, 1761 contains the only hard evidence for Pierson's presence at Nassau Hall. It says, "Then Received of you [Pierson] £2,0,0. It being in full for your Schooling until you entered the college." For a Presbyterian in 1761, "the college" had to mean Princeton, as against Anglican King's in nearby New York City. The past tense of the verb "entered" indicates that Pierson, who had studied with Smith at least into January 1761, must have matriculated at the College of New Jersey for the summer term of 1761, quite possibly entering as a second-semester freshman just as Samuel Finley replaced the deceased Samuel Davies as president. Thus Pierson has been tentatively assigned to the Class of 1764. According to family tradition he remained in Princeton for only a year. If he ever had ambitions of becoming a preacher, he probably abandoned them when he left the College.

Instead, perhaps after an apprenticeship with Dr. Ichabod Burnet of nearby Elizabethtown, he returned to Newark Mountains and began practicing medicine around 1764 at about age thirty, thereby inaugurating a tradition that would continue through three more generations of his descendants. He had clearly spent time in Elizabethtown, for in 1764 he married twenty-two year old Phebe, one of the three children of blacksmith Isaac Nuttman (Nutman) and his wife Joanna of that community. Isaac died in 1749 while the children were still young, and on May 19, 1760 Morris Bloomfield became the guardian of Phebe and her sister Sarah. Matthias and Phebe had at least five daughters and three sons, including Isaac Pierson (A.B. 1789).

Even before Newark Mountains became the town of Orange in Essex County in 1780, Pierson assumed a prominent role there as its only physician until joined in the 1780s by future Congressman John Condit, by distant relative Cyrus Pierson (A.B. 1776) who married his daughter Nancy, and by Matthias's son Isaac in the 1790s. Pierson's practice extended to nearby communities, and he visited his patients on horseback. He may have been one of the first physicians to accept obstetrics cases, which might have meant, in effect, taking business away from experienced and probably better qualified midwives. Or perhaps he entered a dangerous case only when summoned by the midwife herself. The warm testimonial that he wrote for midwife Martha Dod when she moved to New York City in 1784 does suggest an amicable relationship. Throughout his long career he never joined the Medical Society of New Jersey, which was organized in 1766.

Pierson supported the Revolution and paid for his loyalties when the British looted his house of nearly everything but his medicines during the 1776 invasion of New Jersey. He also played a major role in encouraging education in the community both before and after the war. In January 1773 he joined other local notables to support the school just opened by Caleb Cooper (hon. A.B. 1769, A.M. 1771, A.B. King's 1769) "at Newark Mountains, for the instruction of youth in the Latin and Greek languages and other branches of literature, necessary for their entering any class in college." The organizers promised to "take particular care respecting the morals" of the boys.

With the return of peace the community took decisive action to support education. On April 21, 1785 a public meeting unanimously decided to erect a schoolhouse and chose five trustees, including Pierson, to oversee the construction of what quickly became a handsome two-story building across from the meetinghouse. Soon after it opened it was being called "the Academy of Orange-Dale." Pierson probably had a hand in engaging a succession of graduates of the College to staff the school. Beginning in November 1785 James McCoy (A.B. 1785) taught for two years and was joined in 1786-87 by classmate Matthias Cazier. Samuel Harris and George Crow (both A.B. 1787) replaced them for the 1787-88 academic year but then moved on, Harris to study for the ministry while serving as a Princeton tutor, Crow to open his own academy in Morristown. Their impending departure may have prompted several prominent Morris County men to secure incorporation of the Society for the Promotion of Learning and Religion in early 1788, designed "to support the education of youths, particularly for the ministry." Pierson's pastor, Rev. Jedediah Chapman (A.M. 1765, A.B. Yale 1762), probably set the tone for the society which, the *New-Jersey Journal, and Political Intelligencer* declared, "has a school at present at Orange Dale where the Rev. Mr. Chapman preaches."

Pierson, an Essex County resident, was not a trustee of this Morris County society, but he undoubtedly supported its activities, especially the academy. He became one of the organizers of a lottery to benefit the institution in 1794. How much was raised for the school is unknown, but over $4,000 in prizes were distributed to lucky winners. Not surprisingly, Pierson was also one of the first trustees of the local Presbyterian church from its incorporation in 1783, although for some reason it did not adopt the name of Orange but instead called itself the Second Presbyterian Church of Newark three years after Orange had become a distinct community.

Pierson was clearly a prosperous man by the 1790s when he accepted Isaac into his practice. In the will that he drafted on April 9, 1799, he promised his widow £200, £170 to each daughter, and £50 plus real and personal estate to each son. He died on May 9, 1809 at age seventy-four, and the will was proved on September 13. His wife survived him by seventeen years, finally dying in 1826. Both were buried in the parish grounds, but their remains were later removed to the family vault in Rosedale Cemetery.

SOURCES: L. B. Pierson, *Pierson Genealogical Records* (1878), 37, 39-40; S. Wickes, *Hist. of the Oranges in Essex Cnty., N.J., from 1606 to 1806* (1892), 133 ("Then Received of you"), 229-30, 290-98; Wickes, *Hist. of Medicine N.J*, 363-64; *N.J. Wills*, II, 357 (Nuttman's will); III, 238 (Bloomfield as guardian); XI, 264 (MP's will); D. L. Pierson, *Hist. of the Oranges to 1921*, ... (3 vols, 1922), I, 175-77; *N.Y. Independent Jour.*, 10 Jan. 1784 (Dod testimonial); *N.J. Archives*, XXVIII, 380-81 ("at Newark Mountains"); *N.Y. Gazetteer*, 1 Nov. 1785 (Orange-Dale Academy opens); Elizabethtown *N.J. Jour., & Polit. Intelligencer*, 4 Oct. 1786, 17 Oct. 1787 ("Academy of Orange-Dale"), 27 Feb. 1788 ("to support the education"; "has a school").
Wanda S. Gunning provided important sources for this biography.

JMM

Samuel Greville (Graville)

SAMUEL GREVILLE (GRAVILLE), actor and physician, was probably a member of the Class of 1766, although he may have enrolled with either the preceding or following class. Records for this period are sketchy at best, especially for nongraduates, and extant faculty minutes do not begin until two decades later. Contemporary College records do not mention Greville, but other sources show that a student of this name was at Princeton sometime in the 1760s. However, the classes to which his college friends belonged and the date at which he was pursuing a career indicate that he must have been a student in the middle of the decade.

Samuel Greville was the stepson of Edward Dempsey of Berkeley County, South Carolina, who was probably a merchant or possibly a slave trader. Dempsey married Jane Graveell, widow, on August 2, 1756 at St. Philip's Church, Charleston. A Frederick Greville who was granted a mortgage in 1736 in St. John's Parish, Berkeley County, may have been Samuel's father, but no further information about him has been found. No dates for Greville's arrival at or departure from Nassau Hall are known, but he apparently left after a short stay because he considered college life too strict. He next tried the College of Philadelphia with the same result, and then began an apprenticeship in the Philadelphia law offices of Joseph Galloway (LL.D. 1769), speaker of the Pennsylvania assembly. Sometime in 1766 Greville severed his connection with Galloway and the legal profession to join "The American Company" of actors headed by David Douglass.

Douglass, who had earlier built a theatre in New York City, had recently returned from several years in England hoping to break down Philadelphia's prejudice against public drama, which many of that city's residents considered a "dangerous School of Vice." Douglass built a brick and wood building in the Southwark section of the city, on South Street above Fourth, which became the first permanent theatre in America, remaining in use until the beginning of the nineteenth century. It opened on November 12, 1766, but Greville probably first appeared on the stage on January 2, 1767. *The Pennsylvania Journal; and the Weekly Advertiser* listed the cast of Nicholas Rowe's *Tamerlane* to be performed on that date, including "a young man his first appearance on any stage," performing the part of Moneses. On January 9 the anonymous young man played the role of Horatio in William Shakespeare's *Hamlet*. This occasion probably marked Greville's try-out, which evidently was satisfactory, since he continued with the company for the remainder of the season.

Edward Burd, a student at the College of Philadelphia, was given a ticket to the performance of *Hamlet* by his uncle Joseph Shippen. On January 14, 1767 Burd wrote to his sister Sarah, first giving his opinion of the main actors, and then noting:

A young Gentleman by Name Mr. Gravel has commenced an Actor on Account of his Debts, for He is accounted an extravagant Young Fellow. He was of a good Family in South Carolina. And was sent to Prince Town College with a view of qualifying him for the Gown—But disliking the strict Rules of that Seminary He came to our College, & shortly after he left it too & commenced a Student of the Law under Mr. Galloway, but his Mother having married again, She refused to supply his Extravagance upon which he now takes to the Stage for his Support, notwithstanding the kind Offers of Mrs. Galloway to maintain him till he is settled in the World, if he will quit his Designs. He is a very handsome young Fellow & has a clear Voice—He has acted twice but has no action which is the very Soul of good Playing. The People in general here rather pity than condemn him: this is the Consequence of loose Morals & may serve as a Lesson to others.

Greville continued in small roles in the group's repertoire of over twenty dramas, usually playing characters that were at least dignified by a proper name. However, he also appeared in such bit parts as a servant, a coachman, a committeeman, and the second citizen. Greville had the role of Phraates in the April 24 performance of Thomas Godfrey's *The Prince of Parthia*, a particularly significant occasion because it was the first play written by an American to be produced upon an American stage by a company of professional actors.

William Paterson (A.B. 1763) and John MacPherson (A.B. 1766) also discussed Greville's career as an actor after MacPherson graduated from the College and left Princeton. Paterson had remained in the community after his own graduation, studying law under Richard Stockton (A.B. 1748). His family home and his father's store were close to Nassau Hall, enabling him to keep in close touch with the students and affairs on the campus. His friend MacPherson was a native of Philadelphia, and when he returned there to study law, he and Paterson began a correspondence which included news and gossip about mutual college acquaintances.

On January 17, 1767 MacPherson wrote the probably titillating news: "I suppose you have heard ere this, that Sam Greville has forsaken the dull profundity of the Law for the more lively profession of a Stage-player, in which, ut ante in aliis, he scarcely will shine. We have now no fewer than two who studied law on our stage at present, so that the Bar is fruitful in forming actors."

Answering on January 26, Paterson made it clear that he considered a decision to desert the law for the stage to be at least rash, if not actually scandalous.

> Poor Grevill! [sic] w^t. a noble subject is he to moralise upon, were I in a moralising mood.
>> "I swear, in truth, 'tis strange, 'tis passing strange!
>> 'Tis pitiful, 'tis wond'rous pitiful"—
> Sam's fate reach'd Princeton long ago, even before he appeared on the stage—Methinks you might have been more particular about him. I shou'd be glad to be informed, w^t. induced him to take the unhappy course. Was it because his finance was reduced to a low ebb, or was it because he was smit wth. the charms of one of the actresses; the latter has been a rock on wch. many have split—I was indeed informed that he made poverty the plea, but that some gentlemen, in order to obviate this objection, promised to maintain him during his continuance with Galloway—Such a proposal wou'd entirely remove that plea. Perhaps his high spirit cou'd not brook it—But enough's said about Sam.

On May 12 MacPherson mentioned Sam again:

> Greville is going to leave the Stage when he has his benefit night which will be in a few weeks now. Perhaps you may have heard of the Treaty on foot between his Mother and him, which, from what I have said above, you will perceive, is to be finished soon. Well, I wish Greville more Stability and less Pride, more real honour and less false, more religion and less Stiffness, and more Ease in behaviour and less foppery.

Benefit performances were common to promote charitable causes and also to augment the incomes of both dramatists and actors. According to custom all the actors in a troupe were assigned benefits as part of their compensation, usually late in the season to guarantee that the actors would remain with the company. Playbills advertised these occasions and might request that "all Gentlemen and Ladies and others, who are his Well-Wishers," favor with their attendance the one to be benefited. Actors and actresses sometimes went from house to house soliciting patronage. Greville's pact with his mother was probably a promise to quit the stage after he had received the rewards of his benefit night.

Paterson answered on May 21: "[Burt] lodged with me while he was in town, and as he told me he had been in Philad^a., I was very inquisitive, & almost stunned him with questions. He very particularly informed me, among other things, concerning Sam. Grevill's circumstances, & gave me a more adequate idea of the merit of the respective actors, than I ever had before been favored with." Paterson's visitor could have been Joseph Burt (A.B. 1766), or may have been Edward Burd, who had viewed at least one of Greville's performances.

Susannah Centlivre's *The Wonder! A Woman Keeps A Secret* was performed on June 25 as Greville's benefit play. The cast for that evening is not available, but in later presentations of the same comedy he appeared as Lissardo. On July 22 MacPherson informed Paterson: "Greville made £25 Clear Cash: his mother is dead." A South Carolina newspaper confirms that on June 11 "Mrs. Dimpsey, wife of Mr. Edward Dimpsey," died in Charleston.

On August 5, a month after Philadelphia's theatrical season ended, Paterson wrote, "W^t. is Grevill going to do? Pray tell me all about him." Unfortunately, MacPherson's answer is not available. Perhaps after the death of his mother, Greville felt released from any promises he had made to her.

During the remainder of the summer and autumn of 1767 Douglass oversaw the construction of a new theatre for the American Company on John Street in New York City. When this building was not ready for a fall opening, the company performed at the Southwark theatre in Philadelphia for a short season, lasting from September 24 to November 23. Greville's name occasionally appears on the rare cast lists that have survived. Obviously he was still in Philadelphia and still associated with the American Company.

The new John Street Theatre in New York opened on December 7, 1767. Greville was not listed among the actors in the first two plays, but on December 14 he took the part of Blunt in Shakespeare's *Richard III* in a command performance for a group of Indian chiefs visiting from South Carolina. Greville continued in his usual small roles, which this season included a haymaker, a "spouter" (amateur actor), and a watchman. The company's final presentation took place on June 28, but Greville probably last trod the boards on May 19. Evidently he was given no benefit performance, either because he left the company before that event was scheduled or because the manager had decided not to assign him one. His continued appearances mostly in bit parts probably indicates that he never acquired a talent for "action," and better and more experienced actors in the company precluded his advancement to leading roles. Douglass may have fired him because he showed little improvement as a thespian, or Greville may have found his lack of progress so discouraging that he decided to switch careers and look for a better way to reduce his debts. In any case, his minor parts could not have been especially remunerative. However, in spite of his small roles, the custom of the time insured that Greville's name did not appear at the bottom of the cast list in local newspapers. Although he was the last of the eight males in the company, his name preceded those of the four actresses.

Greville's name next appears as a Charleston physician in the October 25, 1771 will of his stepfather, who was nearly seventy years old. While the missing period in Greville's life may seem a very short span in which to obtain medical training, many practicing physicians at that time devoted even less than two and a half years to learning the skills of their profession. Greville was still practicing in Charleston in Feburary 1773 when he conveyed part of a Union Street lot to a Margaret Stewart, spinster. In August he married Elizabeth Mary Pendarvis, daughter of James Pendarvis and Catherine Rumph Pendarvis of St. Paul's Parish. Greville's bride was an octoroon, a fact that she may not have realized. Her father was a prosperous planter who owned more than a hundred slaves, her mother was white, and both her brother and sister were married to whites. It may have been at the time of the marriage that Greville moved to St. Paul's Parish. The couple had only a short time together, since Greville died intestate sometime between the 19th and 25th of November 1774.

The Dempsey-Greville estate instantly became a subject of bitter litigation. Dempsey's 1771 will had conveyed all of his property to Greville except for half of his slaves. They were to be sold and the proceeds divided equally among the testator's three sisters. On November 5, just ten days after writing the will, Dempsey conveyed to Greville all of his estate, real and personal—a legal arrangement that threatened to disinherit Dempsey's sisters. After Dempsey died on March 4, 1772, Greville became administrator of the estate. Probably in an effort to satisfy his step-aunts, he inventoried the personal property already conveyed to him—the most valuable portion of it apparently was the slaves—as still a part of Dempsey's estate. This arrangement probably gave Greville maximum flexibility in paying off his own debts, and it produced no litigation while he lived. But when he died in November 1774 and his principal creditor James Fallows promptly obtained a court appointment to administer his estate, Dempsey's sister Rose objected through her husband Walter Fitzgerald. In December Fitzgerald denounced Greville as the "pretended Executor" of Dempsey's estate and asked the court to void the will, presumably in favor of an earlier one, because the 1771 document had been "obtained by fraud, circumvention & imposition upon the said Edward Dempsey when not in his proper senses" and had been, in any case, effectively revoked by the deed. By April 1775 Fitzgerald had softened his charge. He accused Greville of acting "through Ignorance and for want of proper advice," and he persuaded the court of chancery to revoke Fallows's letters of administration. By then each party had gained possession of some of Dempsey's slaves. The litigants probably worked out an adequate settlement between them, for on July 28 the court again recognized Fallows as administrator, the Fitzgeralds accepted the arrangement, and the litigation ceased. When the Greville estate was appraised, his personal property was valued at £2,860 and included a dozen slaves.

SOURCES: R. H. Ball, "Samuel Greville, First Player," *Princeton Alumni Weekly*, 30 (1929-30), 117-24; non-graduate file, PUA; B. H. Holcomb, *S.C. Marriages, 1688-1799* (1980), 62; *Princetonians, 1748-1768*, 437-40, 574-78; J. MacPherson to W. Paterson, 17 Jan. ("I suppose"), 12 May ("Greville is going"), 22 July 1767 ("Greville made £25"), transcripts by William Paterson (A.B. 1835), Paterson Family Papers, NjP; Paterson to MacPherson, 26 Jan. ("Poor Grevill!"), 21 May ("[Burt] lodged"), 5 Aug. 1767 ("W^r. is Grevill"), disassembled letterbook in author's hand, Paterson Family Papers, NjP; V. L. Collins, "Princeton Dramatics in the 18th Cent.," *Princeton Alumni Weekly*, 17 (1916-17), 228-29; A. H. Quinn, *Hist. of the Amer. Drama* (1923), 15-17; *SCHGM*, 10 (1909), 168, 221; 43 (1942), 135; W. Dunlap, *Hist. of the Amer. Theatre* (1832), 25-27; H. F. Rankin, *Theatre in Colonial Amer.* (1965), 33-34, 111-113, 173, 199; L. B. Walker, ed., *Selections from Letters written by Edward Burd 1763-1828* (1899), 13-14 ("A young gentleman"); C. A. Langley, *S.C. Deed Abstracts 1719-72* (4 vols., 1983-84), IV, 303; B. H. Holcomb, *Probate Records of S.C.* (ca. 1979-   ), II, 39, 135, 138 ("pretended Executor"), 160-62 ("through Ignorance," 161), 170, 171, 188; C. T. Moore, *Abstracts of the Wills of the State of S.C., 1760-84* (1969), 178.

On 2 May 1767 Chief Justice Charles Shinner of South Carolina addressed a memorial to Gov. Charles Greville Montague, of South Carolina, and Charles Garth, Esq., agent for the province in London. Shinner accused an Edward Dempsey of being a "Crimp," i.e., "a Decoyer of Negroes, white Servants and Sailors in Order to make Advantage of them." It is unclear whether this Edward Dempsey was Greville's stepfather or whether the middle name of the British governor indicated some relationship. See *SCHGM*, 30 (1929), 27-49 ("a Decoyer," 39).

RLW

Robert Yancey

ROBERT YANCEY, Class of 1767, Church of England clergyman, was born on a plantation at Little River in St. Martin's Parish, Louisa County, Virginia, in 1744 or earlier, but presumably after the creation of Louisa County out of Hanover County in 1740. He was the youngest of the four sons of Charles Yancey and the grandson of Robert Yancey, an early settler in Louisa who died in 1745. Robert's mother was a "Mlle. Dumas," almost certainly a daughter of Jeremiah Dumas who obtained adjacent 400-acre patents of land on Little Creek in 1725 and 1728. Jeremiah in turn was the son of Dr. Jeremiah Jerome Dumas, a prominent Huguenot refugee who

reached Virginia from London in 1700. Charles Yancey probably
died while Robert was quite young but sometime after April 20, 1745
when the father gave "my loving son, Robert" a slave girl Nanow
and her increase. Robert's older brother Archelaus died in 1764 or
1765, leaving behind an adult son, which suggests a considerable
age gap between the two siblings. The Yancey family, according to
Samuel Gist of London in 1768, "were Posses'd of Sufficient Estate
to live decently." John Norton, a London merchant well known in
the tobacco trade, agreed that the Yanceys were "a reputable family
in good circumstances."

Robert's youth, as recounted in family tradition, "was characterized by precociousness of his mental development and amiability of
character." After receiving his early education near home, Yancey
entered the junior class of the College in November 1765, somewhat older than most of his classmates. Nothing indicates whether
the massive intercolonial nullification of the Stamp Act, which took
full effect in that month, had any impact on his studies. On June
24, 1766, about three weeks before the July 17 death in Philadelphia
of Samuel Finley, President of the College, Yancey withdrew from
Nassau Hall. His "infirm state of Health ... obliged [him] to intermit
his Studies for some Time," explained Jeremiah Halsey (A.B. 1752)
and Joseph Periam (A.B. 1762), who certified that Yancey "has pros-
ecuted his Studies" for eight months "with Diligence and Success and
has constantly maintained an unspotted moral Character." Halsey
and Periam were both tutors at the College in 1765-66, and as senior
tutor Halsey was probably in charge during that phase of Finley's
terminal illness when Yancey withdrew.

Yancey was the only native-born Virginian before the American
Revolution who entered the Anglican priesthood after studying at
a colonial college other than William and Mary. In April 1768 he
collected affadavits in Virginia that testified to his suitability for
ordination. Three inhabitants of St. Martin's Parish affirmed that he
was more than twenty-four years old, the minimum canonical age for
ordination. Rev. Ichabod Camp (A.B. Yale 1743) of Amherst Parish
in Amherst County described him as "a Youth of Sound & Strict
Morals, Integrity of Life & of an Unblemished Reputation" who had
made "more than Common Progress" in his studies for the ministry.
Joseph Tickell, rector of Trinity Parish, Louisa County, affirmed that
he would pay Yancey £30 sterling per year once the young man had
received an appointment as curate of the parish, which had been
created in 1762. Robert Barrett (A.B. William and Mary ca. 1732),
rector of Yancey's home parish of St. Martin's, also endorsed Yancey,
who stopped in Williamsburg long enough to get the approval of

the very aged acting governor John Blair (William and Mary ca. 1705) before sailing for London. Yancey's petition for ordination won instant approval, for after the family's London acquaintances authenticated the handwriting of his clerical supporters on July 13, he was ordained in the chapel of Fulham Palace by Richard Terrick, bishop of London, in a special ceremony on Monday, July 25. Nineteenth-century family lore claims that Yancey preached before the royal family on the next day. He probably returned to Virginia with the fall tobacco fleet, for he was installed in his parish before the end of 1768, just in time to replace rather than assist Tickell, who died before December 1. Serving in Trinity and neighboring Tillotson parishes, he won a reputation for generosity to the poor. He also presided over a working farm with considerable livestock that produced sixty barrels of corn plus other crops in 1774.

Not long after he took charge of his parish, Yancey married Ann, the daughter of David and Ann Anderson Crawford of Amherst County, for the young couple's first child was born on March 22, 1770. No doubt Robert already knew the Crawfords well because his brother Charles had married Anne's sister Mary. Anne and Mary soon became the aunts of William H. Crawford, one of Georgia's most prominent politicians in the early republic, who was born in Amherst County in 1772. The rector may have been the Robert Yancey (there were several in Louisa County) who sold land to Jeremiah Yancey, probably his brother, for £100 about that time. He definitely bought a slave girl named Unity, aged fourteen, in 1771, and by 1774 he also owned Nick (an adult male), a boy named Jacob, and three other women—Betty, Venus, and Rachel. He or another Robert Yancey was assessed for a plantation of 396 acres and three slaves as early as 1770. Yancey's library contained Samuel Johnson's *A Dictionary of the English Language*, a four-volume edition of the works of John Locke, and three volumes of Archbishop John Tillotson's writings, which together suggest that a year at the College of New Jersey had not prevented him from absorbing latitudianarian principles.

Increasingly uncomfortable with the doctrine of eternal damnation, Yancey first tried out his ideas quietly with a few gentlemen, only one of whom refused to yield to his logic. As rumors of his heterodox convictions spread through neighboring counties, they occasioned "some rash and uncharitable speeches ... concerning my sentiments, which I thought did not deserve such treatment." Yancey thus went public with his principles and in the process became the first minister "who preached in that section of the country the doctrine of universal redemption." According to family tradition, hundreds of people came from considerable distances to hear and challenge a sermon that he apparently gave in early 1774. In response to the obvious criticism that his doctrine would destroy conventional Christian morality, he announced that he was prepared to believe that the torments of hell might endure for "ten thousand millions of ages"— but not forever. Even Satan would eventually be saved. Yancey had almost no time to enjoy what was apparently a striking oratorical success. In the spring of 1774 he died "after many years laboring under a tedious Illness [probably consumption]," reported the *Virginia Gazette* (Purdie and Dixon) on May 5, 1774. "His Candour, and exemplary Piety, render his Loss much regretted by all who had the Pleasure of his Acquaintance."

Yancey was survived by his mother, two brothers, his wife Ann who at the time was expecting their second child, Betsy, and by a son Charles. His will of March 16, 1774, written while "in my usual health," made careful provision for his widow and prescribed that each child should receive three years' education, that sons should share equally in land, and that any daughter should get half a son's portion of land. An inventory several months later valued his personal property at £630, which shrunk to about £467 by the time the estate was settled in 1784. Ann later moved the family to Buckingham County where, on New Year's Day in 1815, Episcopal Bishop Richard Channing Moore preached her funeral sermon. As an adult Betsy frequently graced the levees of James Madison (A.B. 1771) and Thomas Jefferson (LL.D. 1791). Yancey's son Charles served many terms in the state legislature, where he won a reputation as the "Wheel Horse of Democracy" and the "Duke of Buckingham." As a delegate for a county adjacent to Jefferson's district in the lower house, he corresponded frequently with the former president.

SOURCES: J. R. Gunderson, *The Anglican Ministry in Va., 1723-66: A Study of a Social Class* (1989), 287; M. H. Harris, *Hist. of Louisa Cnty., Va.* (1936), 174 (mistakenly identifies the father as Col. Stephen Yancey); R. L. Yancey, *Ancestors & Descendants of Capt. William Layton Yancey & his Wife Frances Lynn Lewis, 1600-1900* (1977), 4-5; W. H. Norwood et al., *Geneal. of Yancey-Medearis & Related Lines* (1958), 113, 116; R. F. Yancey, *Lynchburg & its Neighbors* (1935), 440-41; M. K. Mulkey, *Kimbrough, Dumas, & Related Southern Families* (1977), 100; Va. Land Office card file under Jeremias Dumas, Vi; Louisa Cnty., Va., Wills No. 1: 1746-61, pp. 62-63, Vi (Archelaus Yancey's will); R. E. Davis, *Louisa Cnty., Va., Deed Books A & B, 1742-59* (1976), 20 ("my beloved son, Robert"); *A Sermon Preached by the Rev. Robert Yancey ...* (1853), 3-4 ("characterized by precociousness" & ordination certificate, incl. date), 9 ("ten thousand millions of ages"), 33 ("some rash and uncharitable speeches"); Min. Trustees, 26 Sept. 1759 (Halsey as senior tutor), 25 June & 24 Sept. 1766 (Finley illness & death); RY's ordination file, Fulham Papers (Lambeth Palace), xxv: Va. Ordination Papers, 1765-70, ff. 156-65, esp. 156 ("infirm state of Health" at CNJ), 157 (Camp quote), 158 (age in 1768), 159 (agreement with Tickell), 160 (Barrett testimonial), 161 (Blair testimonial), 163 (Gist quote), & 165 (Norton quote), DLC microfilm, reel 9; J. B. Bell, "Anglican Clergy in Colonial Amer. Ordained by the Bishop of London," *AASP*, n.s., 83 (1973), 103-60 at 159 (which gives the date of ordination incorrectly as 17 July 1768); R. E. Davis, ed., *Louisa Cnty., Va., Tithables & Census, 1743-85* (1981), 27, 36, 42, 50; R. E. Davis, ed., *Louisa Cnty., Va., Deed Books C, C½, D & D½, 1759-74* (1977), 85, 118; R. T. Green, *Geneal. & Hist. Notes on Culpeper Cnty., Va., Embracing a Rev. & Enlarged Ed. of Dr. Philip Slaughter's Hist. of St. Mark's Parish* (2 vols., 1900), II, 81 ("preached ... universal redemption," "Wheel Horse" & "Duke of Buckingham"); Williamsburg *Va. Gazette* (Purdie & Dixon), 5 May 1774 (obit.); Louisa Cnty., Va., Will Book No. 2, 1767-83, pp. 193-96 (RY will; "in my usual health," p. 193), 227-29 (estate inv., incl. names of slaves, value of farm products, titles in library), Vi; N. Chappelear & K. B. Hatch, *Abstracts of Louisa Cnty., Va., Will Books, 1743-1801* (1964), 74-75 (1784 settlement of estate). The Stephen Yancey who was executed for murder in Virginia in 1783 was a nephew of RY, not a son as is sometimes claimed.

PUBLICATION: *A Sermon Preached by the Rev. Robert Yancey, of Louisa County, who was Ordained as an Episcopal Minister under the Colonial Government of the State of Virginia, in the Year 1768* (1853), which is incomplete. According to a note on p. 34, an earlier and complete edition of the manuscript was published about twenty years earlier, but no copy of it has been found.

JMM

Joseph Gaston Chambers

JOSEPH GASTON CHAMBERS, Class of 1778, farmer, teacher, inventor, and linguistic reformer, was born in 1756 or 1759 in Allen Township, Northampton County, Pennsylvania, the eldest of three sons of David Chambers by his first wife Ann Gaston. The mother was the child of Joseph Gaston of what later became Bernard Township, Somerset County, New Jersey. Sometime after Joseph's birth, David Chambers moved his family to a 380-acre farm in Amwell Township, Hunterdon County, New Jersey. He apparently belonged to Amwell's Presbyterian church. After the Revolution he moved to a farm named "Violet Bank" in Hopewell Township, Washington County, Pennsylvania. Later still he moved to nearby Ohio County in present-day West Virginia, where he operated a farm, mill, and store at or near the mouth of Short Creek. Joseph was a second cousin of Joseph Logan (A.B. 1792).

Presbyterian clergyman Samuel Kennedy (A.B. 1754), who sometimes preached at Amwell, kept an academy on his farm near Basking Ridge, Somerset County, at which he could have taught Chambers. Since Chambers's name does not appear on the seemingly complete steward's account for the semester which ended on April 10, 1775, he presumably matriculated at the College at some point after that date and before the near approach of the British forced it to close on November 29, 1776. His attendance is established by family tradition and by his own comment in 1792 that "I was a Student at New Jersey Colege which was broken up by the irruption of the Brittish in '76." The silence of extant College sources on his attendance renders arbitrary even his placement in the Class of 1778.

In the exciting period leading up to and following the abrupt closing of the College, Chambers occupied himself with the planning of several military inventions. He "conceived a project of constructing a Vessel in the nature of a Row Galley which should be sufficient to combat and destroy a whole Fleet," but failed to obtain backing, for "I underwent the usual fate of projectors my Friends concluded the Boy was mad and thus refused me every assistance to the Design."

In an even more novel project directed against British naval might, Chambers attempted to develop a very early version of scuba gear that would enable divers to attach explosives to the hulls of enemy vessels and escape undetected. He went so far as to construct a prototype suit and air tank and tried it out "in a Pond formed for the purpose upon a small stream (no larger being in convenient vicinity)." The initial test failed because the linseed oil and paint with which he had waterproofed some of the internal parts produced "noxious exhalations" which hindered breathing. Before he could complete and test an improved model, both limited means and the British army's "sudden irruption through Jersey (which was the place of my residence)" forced him to abandon the project. The evidence points to the intriguing possibility that Chambers conducted his diving experiments while he was a student at the College, though he could equally well have done so at his father's farm during the autumn vacation. The main drawback of the plan as he described it years later was his apparent failure to discern the need for pressurizing the air supply.

Chambers later recalled that for some time after the College shut down he "followed our Army," where he unsuccessfully attempted to interest Gen. George Washington in his diving invention. The nature of Chambers's military service is unclear. The register of Continental Army officers does not list him, and neither does that of New Jersey's Revolutionary War militia and Continental Army soldiers. Several men named Joseph Chambers served as privates in Pennsylvania units. Men with the wherewithal to attend the College generally achieved more exalted ranks. Perhaps Joseph served as a commissary, like his uncle Alexander Chambers. In November 1777 at the Continental Army camp at Whitemarsh, Montgomery County, Pennsylvania, "Mr. Joseph Chambers late Commissary to Genl. Greens Division" was whipped by a sergeant and his men on the orders of Col. Josiah Parker of the Fifth Virginia Regiment. Chambers complained, and the subsequent court of inquiry reprimanded Parker, finding "that how[ever] Negligent the Commissary might have been in the Discharge of the Duty of his Department," Parker still had no right "to Inflict Private Punishment upon him." On August 20, 1780, the same or a different Joseph Chambers was involved in "forwarding flour from West-Point to Head Quarters."

For a lengthy interval after he left the College, the movements of Chambers are difficult to determine. He seems to have spent some time at his birthplace in Northampton County, Pennsylvania, where his father could possibly have retained some lands. In 1779 or 1780 he married Mary, the daughter of Jeremiah and Elizabeth Hart Woolsey, and the eldest of their four sons and three daughters was born in Northampton County in November 1780. Their second son was born around 1782 in York County, Pennsylvania, and Chambers was definitely living in Hunterstown in York (later Adams) County around July 1791. Perhaps he was the Joseph Chambers who was elected one of six assessors of York County on October 15, 1777, and was himself assessed for ownership of more than 400 acres in Tyrone Township and of a house and lot and from one to three slaves in York Town during the years 1779-83. He gave his return address as Mercersburg, Franklin County, Pennsylvania during the period August-November 1792.

In the early 1790s Chambers began work on two projects which exercised him for many years thereafter. The first was improvement of the English language. He devised a new, much more phonetic alphabet and new rules of spelling which he calculated would save printers a fortune by rendering one-sixteenth of the letters in any text superfluous. He maintained that once his system was adopted mothers would be able to teach their children to read and write with less effort than they were currently expending preparing lunches for them to take to school. The first version of Chambers's plan came out in a serialized article which appeared between July and October 1791 in the *Universal Asylum and Columbian Magazine*. In 1811 he had the proposal printed in the form of a pamphlet entitled *Elements of Orthography; or, An Attempt to Form a Complete System of Letters*. He reissued it with slight revisions in 1812 and 1817, and prepared an abridgement which came out in 1824. His enthusiasm for this scheme may have prompted his decision to place his son David, who later became a United States congressman from Ohio, in a Philadelphia printing shop in 1796. Chambers was at some pains and expense to have special types cast so that samples using his new system could be printed, and in 1817 he even proposed to start a monthly magazine called the *English Orthoepist or Correct Pronouncing Register*. All his efforts were to no avail. The public failed to show any enthusiasm for his plan, and lack of subscriptions seems to have kept the monthly magazine from beginning publication.

Chambers introduced his plans for linguistic reform with an attack on contemporary educational practice which suggests that he was unimpressed by his stay at the College. He argued that much time was wasted teaching students to write and speak Latin and Greek. Pronunciation, he maintained, was almost impossible to recover from the past, yet

> in public seminaries ... students, with a very superficial knowledge of the written system, are required also to speak the dead languages. Here are pompous harangues delivered in Latin, if we may so call that, of which probably not a single sentence would have been intelligible to a Roman assembly.

A reading knowledge could be acquired in half the time spent learning to speak and write, he claimed, and the time saved should be used acquiring a good grounding in classical literature or in learning a modern language. He also argued that "a large proportion" of "logic, and the various fluctuating opinions and conjectures of philosophy," were "rather probable than certain, and more curious than useful," and "cannot with propriety be considered as necessary objects of public instruction," however entertaining they might be "for private leisure."

By 1792 Chambers had also begun work on another invention, a repeating firearm. The plan, which had originally occurred to him during the Revolution as a way of defending his row-galley, involved placing a number of charges and bullets one on top of the next in the barrel of a musket or rifle. He experimented and found that ten or more charges, with four balls per charge, could be loaded into "a common Musquet." With specially reinforced barrels even more might be crammed in. Depending on the size and nature of the charge and wadding, the gun would fire at intervals of from one to eight seconds, with each discharge setting off the next shot in turn "without any further attention." The invention would be of no use at long range, but if sprung on an unsuspecting enemy during a charge would produce "incredible sudden havoc."

Chambers attempted to enlist President George Washington and Secretary of War Henry Knox as patrons of his weapon, and eventually aroused enough interest that on a trip to Philadelphia early in May 1792 he was issued several muskets and some powder and shot from government stores and allowed to give a demonstration. The initial response must have been noncommittal, for in August 1792

Chambers broached his idea to Secretary of State Thomas Jefferson (LL.D. 1791). Since "I feel myself highly interested for the Friends of Liberty and the Rights of men in Europe and throughout the world," Chambers wanted to know the best way to convey his findings secretly "to France or rather to Poland." He was prepared to go to Europe himself but thought his prospects might be improved if he could "procure the Attention of some Notable Character at home."

Jefferson proved slow to respond, and on November 20 Chambers wrote him that

> I begin to be anxious lest the Tyrants of Europe should complete their Triumphs before you will suffer me to bring my Guns to bear upon them. Poland has bowed the neck to the yoke of Despotism; and France with Difficulty maintains the Conflict.... [Therefore,] ought not such to be encouraged who are willing to risk somewhat for the honor of our Country and the interests of humanity[?]

Jefferson evinced little interest in the scheme, although Chambers apparently persuaded him to watch a firing of the "Gun of seven shots" at Jefferson's "seat near Schuylkill in the Spring of '93." The demonstration probably took place during a journey of "several hundred miles" Chambers undertook for the express purpose of interesting the new French minister to the United States, Edmond Charles Genet, in his invention. Upon discovering that Genet had yet to arrive at Philadelphia, Chambers proceeded to Maryland and intercepted him at Harford County, where he showed him his gun between May 10 and 15, 1793. Although Genet's reception was sufficiently encouraging that Chambers sent him "some further hints," Chambers's offer to journey to France with the invention, which he lamented that lack of resources had prevented his making on his own and for which he asked in return only indemnification for his time and expenses, was evidently ignored by Genet. An earlier application to Genet's predecessor Jean Baptiste Ternant had met with a similar fate. As late as August 5, 1793, Chambers wrote Washington to say that he had still further improvements to report. No evidence that his invention either attracted a government contract at this time or led to a trip overseas has come to light.

Chambers's strongly republican politics apparently extended to involvement in the Whiskey Insurrection. His father is said to have chaired a meeting in Ohio County protesting the excise on whiskey. Chambers himself was one of about 150 western Pennsylvanians who were arrested on the night of November 13, 1794 by the federal army dispatched to restore order. Chambers's role could have ranged from active rioting to vocal opposition to the whiskey excise, or even to complete neutrality on the subject, given the wide net cast by the army on this occasion. Of the hundreds of prisoners brought to Pittsburgh for interrogation, only twenty were sent to Philadelphia for trial. Chambers was not among them.

By 1796 Chambers had moved to a farm in West Middleton, Hopewell Township, Washington County, Pennsylvania, and he spent the rest of his life there. He probably received some or all of his father's holdings in the area, perhaps at the latter's death in 1795. On May 20, 1801 Chambers momentarily took his hand "from the Plow" to write Jefferson a letter enthusiastically congratulating him on his election to the presidency and predicting for the nation an end to "the progress of Political Degeneracy" now that "Jefferson, the Friend of Farmers, the Patron of the Republican Virtues of Agricultural life," was in charge. In 1807 Chambers heard that Robert Fulton was working on a submarine, and he sent Jefferson a detailed description of his earlier experiments on diving in the apparently fruitless hope that it might contribute "some shade or Suggestion of improvement" to Fulton's scheme.

Chambers "adopted teaching as a pursuit," according to one of his sons, but nothing else of his career as a pedagogue has come to light. He educated his children himself and taught them Greek, Latin, and German. He also knew French, and his publications on orthography imply some acquaintance with Spanish, Teutonic, and Gallic or Norman as well. A year before his death his was said to be one of four log schoolhouses in Hopewell Township.

During the War of 1812 Chambers resumed work on his repeating firearms, and at last succeeded in obtaining backing for his invention. He secured a patent for his repeater in March 1813. In an apparent improvement on the 1792 model, in which the first shot triggered the rest at regular intervals, his invention now used multiple touchholes and a movable lock in such a way that each shot could be fired separately. Philadelphia arms manufacturers George W. Tryon and John Joseph Henry agreed to produce the guns for Chambers, and on February 16, 1814 the partnership contracted to supply the United States Navy with 200 muskets at $23 each and twenty swivels at $100 apiece. Each swivel gun consisted of seven multishot musket barrels collectively capable of firing 224 rounds with each loading. They were intended for placement in the tops of ships and designed to sweep the decks of enemy vessels. The navy is said to have appointed Chambers a sailing master and two of his sons gunners to supervise the manufacture of these weapons and offer instruction in their use.

In April 1814 fifteen Chambers swivels and fifty each of his repeating muskets and pistols were ordered sent to Commodore Isaac Chauncey on the Great Lakes, but although he armed a ship with them the war ended without their having been used. On January 2, 1815 Chambers agreed to sell the state of Pennsylvania twenty-five swivel guns and to alter 500 of its muskets into twelve-shot repeaters, and this contract was declared to have been fulfilled on March 4, 1816. A different manufacturer, Lewis Ghriskey of Philadelphia, sold 100 Chambers repeating rifles to the United States Army under a contract dated January 31, 1815. The interest in Chambers's weapons seems to have come too late in the war to secure them a test in battle, and their quick disappearance from the record thereafter raises doubt about their practicality under most conditions.

Nothing of Chambers's activities after the war has come to light. He died on June 1, 1829 and is said to have been buried in Buffalo Cemetery, Buffalo, Washington County, Pennsylvania. Tileston Fracker Chambers (A.B. 1890) and David Laurance Chambers (A.B. 1900) were his great-great-grandsons.

SOURCES: F. G. Griffin, *Tales From the Past: Our Family in Amer.* (1975), 74-90; W. D. Chambers, *Chambers Hist.* (1925), 31-37, 41, 44 ("adopted teaching"); alumni file of JGC, PUA; *Som. Cnty. Hist. Quart.*, 5 (1916), 34-37, 40-43; *N.J. Wills*, v, 87-88, 201; vi, 40; East Amwell Bicentennial Committee, *Hist. of East Amwell, 1700-1800* (2d ed., 1979), 122, 212-14; als, JGC to Thomas Jefferson, 13 Aug. 1792, DNA ("I was," "I underwent," "followed our Army," "a common," "without any," "I feel"; published in *Jefferson Papers*, xxiv, 290-93); als, JGC to Jefferson, 17 Nov. 1807, DLC ("conceived a project," "in a Pond," "noxious exhalations," "sudden irruption," "some shade"); letter from Alex Roland, 31 July 1985, PUA; *Pa. Arch.*, 3d ser., xxi, 4, 42, 170, 328, 339, 553, 611, 645, 663, 814; xxiii, 228, 297, 319, 658; 5th ser., ii, 209; iii, 221; iv, 282, 432; vi, 77, 640; vii, 198, 1075; 6th ser., ii, 54, 65, 344; iii, 414; iv, 796; xi, 207-08, 419-21; *PMHB*, 35 (1911), 174, 178-79 ("Mr. Joseph," "that how Negligent"); als, [Joseph] Chambers to Benedict Arnold, 30 Aug. 1780, George Washington Papers, DLC ("forwarding flour"); *BDUSC*, 761; *PGM*, 6 (1916), 176; 12 (1935), 75; *Universal Asylum & Columbian Magazine*, 2 (1791), 33-38 ("in public," 34; "large proportion," 36), 113-17, 175-78, 225-28; J. G. Chambers, *Elements of Orthography* (1817), *passim* ("English Orthoepist"); als, JGC to Jefferson, 10 Oct. 179[2], DNA ("to France," "procure the attention"; published in *Jefferson Papers*, xxiv, 459-60); als, Jefferson to JGC, 5 Nov. 1792, DLC, published in *Jefferson Papers*, xxiv, 580; als, JGC to Jefferson, 20 Nov. 1792, DNA ("I begin"; published in *Jefferson Papers*, xxiv, 644-45); ms testimonial for JGC's gun signed by Robert Parker and seven others, 20 Nov. 1792, DNA; 2 als, JGC to Henry Knox, 3 & 4 May 1792, MHi; als, JGC to Jefferson, 20 May 1801, DLC ("Gun of seven," "from the Plow," "the progress," "Jefferson, the friend"); 2 als, JGC to E. C. Genet, 10 May ("several hundred") & 15 May 1793 ("some further hints"), DLC; H. M. Brackenridge, *Hist. of the Western Insurrection in Western Pa., commonly called the Whiskey Insurrection 1794* (1859), 329-330; T. P. Slaughter, *Whiskey Rebellion* (1986), 217-18; B. Crumrine, *Hist. of Wash. Cnty. Pa.* (1882), 815, 820; A. Creigh, *Hist. of Wash. Cnty.* (2d ed., 1871), 357; B. R. Lewis, "The First U.S. Repeaters," *Amer. Rifleman*, 97 (Dec. 1949), 38-42; *List of Patents Granted by the U.S. ... 1790-1836* (1872), 124. The last two sources conflict on whether JGC's 1813 patent was dated March 13 or 23. See Lewis for photographs of a Chambers rifle and pistol. JGC's father is sometimes identified as the colonel of that name who served in the Hunterdon County militia from 1776-1779, but this claim is disputed in "Chambers of West Va.," MS in Mary O. Steinmetz Collection, Collections of Geneal. Soc. of Pa. at PHi. Wanda S. Gunning kindly supplied references used in this sketch.

PUBLICATIONS: *Universal Asylum & Columbian Magazine*, 2 (1791), 33-38, 113-17, 175-78, 225-28; *Elements of Orthography; or, An Attempt to Form A Complete System of Letters* (eds. in 1811, 1812 [Sh-Sh # 25047], & 1817 [Sh-Sh # 40438]); *A Critical Orthography, & Easy Guide to Pronunciation of the English Language. Extracted from "Elements of Orthography" With Improvements* (1824, Sh-C # 15710).

MANUSCRIPTS: Thomas Jefferson, George Washington, and Edmond Charles Genet papers, DLC; Misc. Letters Received, Record Group 59, DNA; Henry Knox Papers, on deposit at MHi.

JJL

APPENDIX B

THE MASTER'S DEGREE:
A NOTE TO READERS, BY
J. JEFFERSON LOONEY

ON September 24, 1760 the trustees of the College ruled that candidates for the degree of master of arts must take up residence in or near Nassau Hall a week before commencement, submit to the College's discipline, present two letters attesting to their good behavior, and pass an examination on "such Branches of Literature as have a more direct Connection with that Profession of Life which they have entered upon or have in View, whether Divinity, Law, or Physick" (Maclean, *History*, 1, 210). During the preparation of these volumes, these requirements were initially taken at face value. Thus an early draft of the sketch of John Baldwin (A.B. 1784) argued that "the fact that he received the master's degree three years after graduation tends to support the family tradition that he became a lawyer." Further research has suggested that such inferences cannot be adequately defended. Perhaps almost immediately after 1760 and certainly once normal activities resumed at the end of the Revolution, the requiring of residency and an examination seems to have been abandoned. By the late 1780s an A.B. recipient apparently had to do no more than wait three years, pay the relevant fees, and show up at a commencement (or, like Alexander White [A.B. 1792], obtain it through the mail) to get his A.M. No evidence that they were screened in any way has emerged. Plenty of examples of men who received an A.M. without professional training can be cited, such as John N. Simpson (A.B. 1794, A.M. 1798), merchant; Richard M. Green (A.B. 1794, A.M. 1803), farmer, retired merchant; Robert Field IV (A.B. 1793, A.M. 1797), farmer; and Joshua M. Wallace (A.B. 1793, A.M. 1796), merchant. For purposes of prestige professional men were perhaps rather more likely to go to the trouble of obtaining an A.M. than others. However, if one can infer from possession of the higher degree only that an otherwise unknown Princetonian probably became a lawyer, physician, or minister, the conclusion is too vague to be useful, especially since that is what the majority of A.B.s did anyway.

The resolution in 1760 argued that degrees "promiscuously distributed as cursory Formalities after the usual Intervals of Time, without any previous evidence of suitable Qualifications, ... sink into Contempt as insignificant Ceremonies" (Maclean, *History*, I, 210). The fear was well founded. By 1816 William Williamson (A.B. 1813) seems to have met the requirements for the A.M. simply by writing President Ashbel Green (A.B. 1783) as follows:

> Dear Sir, In the year 1813 I recieved the degree of Bachelor of Arts from the College over which you preside, since which time I have attended to the study of Medicine of which I am now a practitioner. Not being able to attend at the commencement I request the degree of Master of Arts to be confered on me— Yours &c with due respect, William Williamson
>
> P.S. I was formerly a resident in Elizabeth Town New Jersey.

(als, 19 Sept. 1816, in Williamson's alumni file, PUA). John Maclean (A.B. 1816) conceded in 1877 that testing candidates for the A.M. would be a logistical impossibility, and that all that was then demanded was "evidence that the candidate has been engaged in professional or other studies, and that he is a person of correct deportment" (Maclean, *History*, I, 211-12). However, the same year a new era for postgraduate studies began with the offering of a schedule of graduate courses, for which forty-two students enrolled (T. J. Wertenbaker, *Princeton, 1746-1896* [1946], 301-03).

The situation for the period covered by this volume is rendered murkier by the fact that compilers of the early College catalogues, and of the Cliosophic and American Whig Society catalogues which were partly based on them, frequently credited graduates with A.M.s after three years, whether they were awarded one by the trustees or not. In the 1797 catalogue fifteen of the twenty-seven who received the A.B. in 1794 are credited with the A.M. Yet the trustees awarded only four of them A.M.s that year. In 1798 the trustees gave six more of them A.M.s, while three got theirs even later. In other words, the compiler(s) of the early catalogues had some criteria other than award of the A.M. by the trustees for referring to alumni as "Mr." What these criteria were is obscure. Perhaps an alumnus who was called "Mr." in a College catalog was so designated because he was known to be or thought to be studying a profession. Unfortunately, no proof of this hypothesis has emerged, and even if it is correct the compiler seems to have been in error too often to warrant inferences about the careers of individual graduates where other evidence is lacking. Therefore, no effort has been made to note such discrepancies in the sketches in these volumes.

APPENDIX C
GEOGRAPHICAL AND OCCUPATIONAL LISTINGS

═══════════

PLACE OF ORIGIN

Canada

John Jordan '93

Connecticut

John Staples '93

Delaware

James Madison Broom '94

Maryland

James P. Bayley '92
William Bordley '91
Thomas Contee Bowie '91
Robins Chamberlaine '93
James Cresap '94
John Dennis '91
John Dickinson '91
Samuel Sharp Dickinson '91
Allen Bowie Duckett '91
John Edmondson '91
Robert H. Gale '91

Richard Hall Harwood '91
Thomas Robins Hayward '91
Henry Hollyday '91
Samuel Hughes '92
James Witter Nicholson '91
Henry Steele '92
Alexander Stewart '93
Frederick A. Stone '91
John Sullivan '91
Thomas Wright '91

Massachusetts

Benjamin Hodgdon '92

Titus Hutchinson '94

New Jersey

David Barclay '91
Joseph Bonney '93
George Whitefield Burnet '92
Jacob Burnet '91
Joseph Caldwell '91
William Chetwood '92
Horatio Rolfe Dayton '94
Edmund Elmendorf '94
Nicholas C. Everett '94
William Belford Ewing '94
Robert Field IV '93
James Gildersleeve Force '94
Jacob Ford '92
John White Furman '94
Moore Furman, Jr. '94
Richard Montgomery Green '94

George Henry '91
Samuel Henry III '91
Thomas Yardley How '94
Benjamin Van Cleve Hunt '94
Nathaniel Hunt '93
Robert Hunt '93
Andrew Stockton Hunter '94
Henry Knox Kollock '94
Reuben Leigh '94
Stevens Johnes Lewis '91
Joseph Logan '92
George Clifford Maxwell '92
John Berrien Maxwell '91
Joseph Kirkbride Milnor II '92
John Neilson '93
Robert Ogden IV '93

John Conrad Otto '92
Paul Paulison '94
Ebenezer Howell Pierson '91
Henry Polhemus '94
William Roat '93
John Johnson Sayrs '92
John Sloan '92
William B. Sloan '92
Enoch Smith '93
James T. Stelle '93

Job Stockton '92
Jacob Stern Thomson '92
Elias Van Arsdale '91
Isaac Van Doren '93
John Bradford Wallace '94
Joshua Maddox Wallace, Jr. '93
Peter Wikoff '91
James Carra Williamson '94
William Rickets Williamson '94
Henry Veghte Wyckoff '92

New York

William Bay '94
John Rutger Bleecker '91
Peter Edmund Bleecker '92
Dow Ditmars '93
Maltby Gelston '91
James Henry '94
William Arden Hosack '92
Holloway Whitefield Hunt '94

George Washington Morton '92
James Hude Neilson '94
Lewis Searle Pintard '92
James Christopher Roosevelt '91
John Pelion Ryers '92
Abraham Skinner '93
Jacob Ten Eyck '92
John Terhune '93

North Carolina

Joseph McKnitt Alexander '92
George Washington Campbell '94
John M. Dickson '94
Charles Wilson Harris '92

George Merrick Leech '92
J. J. Long '92
David McRee '92

Pennsylvania

Nicholas Bayard '92
Andrew Caldwell '94
Manuel Eyre '93
Andrew Gibson '94
John Gibson '93
John Sylvanus Hiester '94
John Henry Hobart '93
Joseph Reed, Jr. '92
Ebenezer Rhea '91

Charles Ross '91
John Rush '94
Robert Russel '92
John Neely Simpson '94
John Brown Slemons '94
William Tennent Snowden '94
Isaac Wayne '91
George Willing '92
Richard Willing '93

South Carolina

James Chesnut '92
Robert Deas '92
William Cattell Ferguson '91
Robert Heriot '92
Jacob Motte Huger '93
John McCrady '91
Peter Timothy Marchant '91

John Noble '91
Henry Purcell '91
Edwin Tasker Reese '94
Jesse Taylor '91
Charles Tennent '93
Stephen Wayne '91
John Ramsey Witherspoon '94

Virginia

Thomas Monteagle Bayly '94
George Minos Bibb '92
Henry Tate Callaway '91
Robert J. Callaway '91

James Campbell '91
William Campbell '91
Walter Coles '93
Edward F. Conrad '93

James Revell Corbin '94
Peter Early '92
Hugh Ker '94
Edmund Jennings Lee '92
William Ludwell Lee '94
Boyd Mercer '91
John Randolph '91

Theodorick Bland Randolph '91
James D. Ross '92
William Ross '92
Bennett Taylor '93
William Morton Watkins '92
Alexander White '92

West Indies

Francis Markoe '91
Peter Markoe '91

James Ruan '92

Unknown

—— Archer '93
Isaac Gibbs '94
Stephen Gibbs '94
Alexander Johnes '91

Stephen Maxwell '93
—— Sitler '94
Samuel Voorhees '94

PLACE OF PRIMARY RESIDENCE AFTER COLLEGE

Delaware

James Madison Broom '94

District of Columbia

Edmund Jennings Lee '92

Georgia

Nicholas Bayard '92

Peter Early '92

Kentucky

George Minos Bibb '92

John Ramsey Witherspoon '94

Louisiana

Robert Ogden IV '93
James T. Stelle '93

James Carra Williamson '94

Maryland

William Bordley '91
Thomas Contee Bowie '91
Robins Chamberlaine '93
James Cresap '94
John Dennis '91
John Dickinson '91
Samuel Sharp Dickinson '91
Allen Bowie Duckett '91
John Edmondson '91

Robert H. Gale '91
Richard Hall Harwood '91
Thomas Robins Hayward '91
Henry Hollyday '91
Samuel Hughes '92
John Johnson Sayrs '92
John Brown Slemons '94
Alexander Stewart '93
Thomas Wright '91

Massachusetts

Benjamin Hodgdon '92

New Jersey

Joseph Bonney '93
William Chetwood '92
Horatio Rolfe Dayton '94
William Belford Ewing '94
Robert Field IV '93
James Gildersleeve Force '94
John White Furman '94
Richard Montgomery Green '94
George Henry '91
Samuel Henry III '91
Holloway Whitefield Hunt '94
Nathaniel Hunt '93
Robert Hunt '93

Andrew Stockton Hunter '94
George Clifford Maxwell '92
Paul Paulison '94
Ebenezer Howell Pierson '91
Henry Polhemus '94
William Roat '93
John Neely Simpson '94
William B. Sloan '92
William Tennent Snowden '94
Job Stockton '92
Jacob Stern Thomson '92
Elias Van Arsdale '91
William Rickets Williamson '94

New York

William Bay '94
John Rutger Bleecker '91
Peter Edmund Bleecker '92
Dow Ditmars '93
Edmund Elmendorf '94
Nicholas C. Everett '94
Maltby Gelston '91
James Henry '94
John Henry Hobart '93
William Arden Hosack '92
Thomas Yardley How '94
Stevens Johnes Lewis '91

Francis Markoe '91
Joseph Kirkbride Milnor II '92
George Washington Morton '92
John Neilson '93
Lewis Searle Pintard '92
James Christopher Roosevelt '91
John Pelion Ryers '92
Abraham Skinner '93
Jacob Ten Eyck '92
Isaac Van Doren '93
Henry Veghte Wyckoff '92

North Carolina

Joseph McKnitt Alexander '92
Joseph Caldwell '91
Charles Wilson Harris '92

George Merrick Leech '92
John Sloan '92

Ohio

George Whitefield Burnet '92
Jacob Burnet '91

Benjamin Van Cleve Hunt '94

Pennsylvania

David Barclay '91
Manuel Eyre '93
John Gibson '93
John Sylvanus Hiester '94
Boyd Mercer '91
James Witter Nicholson '91
John Conrad Otto '92
Joseph Reed, Jr. '92
Charles Ross '91

John Rush '94
Robert Russel '92
Enoch Smith '93
Frederick A. Stone '91
John Bradford Wallace '94
Joshua Maddox Wallace, Jr. '93
Isaac Wayne '91
George Willing '92
Richard Willing '93

South Carolina

James Chesnut '92
Robert Deas '92
William Cattell Ferguson '91
Jacob Ford '92
Robert Heriot '92
Henry Knox Kollock '94
John McCrady '91

Peter Timothy Marchant '91
John Noble '91
Henry Purcell '91
Edwin Tasker Reese '94
Jesse Taylor '91
Charles Tennent '93

Tennessee

George Washington Campbell '94

J. J. Long '92

Vermont

Titus Hutchinson '94

Virginia

Thomas Monteagle Bayly '94
Henry Tate Callaway '91
Walter Coles '93
Edward F. Conrad '93
Hugh Ker '94
William Ludwell Lee '94
John Randolph '91

Theodorick Bland Randolph '91
James D. Ross '92
William Ross '92
Bennett Taylor '93
William Morton Watkins '92
Alexander White '92

West Indies

Peter Markoe '91

Ebenezer Rhea '91

Unknown

—— Archer '93
James P. Bayley '92
Andrew Caldwell '94
Robert J. Callaway '91
James Campbell '91
William Campbell '91
John M. Dickson '94
Moore Furman, Jr. '94
Isaac Gibbs '94
Stephen Gibbs '94
Andrew Gibson '94
Jacob Motte Huger '93
Alexander Johnes '91
John Jordan '93
Reuben Leigh '94

Joseph Logan '92
John Berrien Maxwell '91
Stephen Maxwell '93
David McRee '92
James Hude Neilson '94
James Ruan '92
—— Sitler '94
John Staples '93
Henry Steele '92
John Sullivan '91
John Terhune '93
Samuel Voorhees '94
Stephen Wayne '91
Peter Wikoff '91

OCCUPATION OR PROFESSION
(Some men are listed under more than one category)

Business (Banking, Commerce, Land Development, etc.)

John Rutger Bleecker '91
Jacob Burnet '91
William Chetwood '92
Horatio Rolfe Dayton '94
Nicholas C. Everett '94
Manuel Eyre '93
John White Furman '94
Moore Furman, Jr. '94
Maltby Gelston '91
John Gibson '93
Richard Montgomery Green '94
George Henry '91
John Sylvanus Hiester '94
Benjamin Hodgdon '92
Thomas Yardley How '94

Benjamin Van Cleve Hunt '94
Francis Markoe '91
Peter Markoe '91
Joseph Kirkbride Milnor II '92
James Hude Neilson '94
James Witter Nicholson '91
James Christopher Roosevelt '91
Charles Ross '91
John Neely Simpson '94
John Bradford Wallace '94
Joshua Maddox Wallace, Jr. '93
James Carra Williamson '94
George Willing '92
Richard Willing '93

Education

Joseph Caldwell '91
George Washington Campbell '94
Dow Ditmars '93
Charles Wilson Harris '92
Nathaniel Hunt '93

Henry Knox Kollock '94
Edwin Tasker Reese '94
John Johnson Sayrs '92
Isaac Van Doren '93

Law

Thomas Monteagle Bayly '94
George Minos Bibb '92
James Madison Broom '94
George Whitefield Burnet '92
Jacob Burnet '91
Henry Tate Callaway '91
George Washington Campbell '94
William Chetwood '92
John Dennis '91
Allen Bowie Duckett '91
Peter Early '92
Edmund Elmendorf '94
Nicholas C. Everett '94
William Cattell Ferguson '91
Jacob Ford '92
Maltby Gelston '91
Charles Wilson Harris '92
Robert Heriot '92
John Sylvanus Hiester '94*
Henry Hollyday '91
William Arden Hosack '92
Thomas Yardley How '94
Samuel Hughes '92

Nathaniel Hunt '93*
Robert Hunt '93
Andrew Stockton Hunter '94
Titus Hutchinson '94
Edmund Jennings Lee '92
J. J. Long '92
John McCrady '91
George Clifford Maxwell '92
George Washington Morton '92
Robert Ogden IV '93
Joseph Reed, Jr. '92
Edwin Tasker Reese '94*
Abraham Skinner '93*
Enoch Smith '93
James T. Stelle '93*
Frederick A. Stone '91*
Jesse Taylor '91*
Bennett Taylor '93
Jacob Ten Eyck '92
Jacob Stern Thomson '92
Elias Van Arsdale '91
John Bradford Wallace '94
William Morton Watkins '92

The symbol * indicates that the Princetonian named studied for the profession in question but seems never to have practiced.

Isaac Wayne '91
Alexander White '92

William Rickets Williamson '94

Medicine

Joseph McKnitt Alexander '92
Nicholas Bayard '92
William Bay '94
Joseph Bonney '93
Edward F. Conrad '93
Robert Deas '92
Samuel Sharp Dickinson '91*
Dow Ditmars '93
William Belford Ewing '94
Charles Wilson Harris '92*

Benjamin Van Cleve Hunt '94
Stevens Johnes Lewis '91
John Neilson '93
John Noble '91
John Conrad Otto '92
Ebenezer Howell Pierson '91
Ebenezer Rhea '91*
John Rush '94
John Sloan '92
John Ramsey Witherspoon '94

Ministry, Dutch Reformed

James Gildersleeve Force '94
Paul Paulison '94*
Henry Polhemus '94

Isaac Van Doren '93*
Henry Veghte Wyckoff '92

Ministry, Episcopalian

John Henry Hobart '93
Thomas Yardley How '94

John Johnson Sayrs '92

Ministry, Methodist

Holloway Whitefield Hunt '94

Ministry, Presbyterian

David Barclay '91
Joseph Caldwell '91
James Gildersleeve Force '94
Holloway Whitefield Hunt '94
Henry Knox Kollock '94

Boyd Mercer '91
Robert Russel '92
John Brown Slemons '94
William B. Sloan '92
Isaac Van Doren '93

Planters and Farmers

Thomas Contee Bowie '91
Robins Chamberlaine '93
James Chesnut '92
Walter Coles '93
James Cresap '94
Samuel Sharp Dickinson '91
Dow Ditmars '93
John Edmondson '91
Robert Field IV '93
Thomas Robins Hayward '91
Henry Hollyday '91
Nathaniel Hunt '93

William Ludwell Lee '94
Peter Timothy Marchant '91
Peter Markoe '91
John Randolph '91
James D. Ross '92
James T. Stelle '93
Alexander Stewart '93
Job Stockton '92
Charles Tennent '93
William Morton Watkins '92
George Willing '92
Thomas Wright '91

Professional Military and Naval Officers

Robins Chamberlaine '93
Edward F. Conrad '93

Horatio Rolfe Dayton '94
William Arden Hosack '92

Thomas Yardley How '94   John Rush '94
Jacob Motte Huger '93   James T. Stelle '93
Robert Hunt '93

Publishing

Peter Timothy Marchant '91

Surveyor

Paul Paulison '94

Unknown

—— Archer '93   Reuben Leigh '94
James P. Bayley '92   Joseph Logan '92
William Bordley '91   John Berrien Maxwell '91
Andrew Caldwell '94   Stephen Maxwell '93
Robert J. Callaway '91   David McRee '92
James Campbell '91   Lewis Searle Pintard '92
William Campbell '91   Henry Purcell '91
John Dickinson '91   William Roat '93
John M. Dickson '94   William Ross '92
Robert H. Gale '91   James Ruan '92
Isaac Gibbs '94   John Pelion Ryers '92
Stephen Gibbs '94   —— Sitler '94
Andrew Gibson '94   John Staples '93
Richard Hall Harwood '91   Henry Steele '92
Samuel Henry III '91   John Sullivan '91
Alexander Johnes '91   John Terhune '93
John Jordan '93   Samuel Voorhees '94
Hugh Ker '94   Stephen Wayne '91
George Merrick Leech '92   Peter Wikoff '91

HOLDERS OF MAJOR PUBLIC OFFICES

Important City and County Offices

George Minos Bibb '92   John Sylvanus Hiester '94
James Chesnut '92   Edmund Jennings Lee '92
William Chetwood '92   Joseph Reed, Jr. '92
William Belford Ewing '94   James T. Stelle '93
Robert Heriot '92   Jacob Stern Thomson '92

Members of State Constitutional Conventions

Thomas Monteagle Bayly '94   John Randolph '91
William Belford Ewing '94   Elias Van Arsdale '91

Members of State Legislatures

Thomas Monteagle Bayly '94   William Chetwood '92
George Minos Bibb '92   James Cresap '94
James Madison Broom '94   John Dennis '91
Jacob Burnet '91   Allen Bowie Duckett '91
Henry Tate Callaway '91   Peter Early '92
James Chesnut '92   John Edmondson '91

William Belford Ewing '94
Robert H. Gale '91
Richard Hall Harwood '91
John Sylvanus Hiester '94
Henry Hollyday '91
Titus Hutchinson '94
John Pelion Ryers '92
John Neely Simpson '94

Alexander Stewart '93
Jacob Ten Eyck '92
Jacob Stern Thomson '92
John Bradford Wallace '94
William Morton Watkins '92
Isaac Wayne '91
John Ramsey Witherspoon '94

State Governor

Peter Early '92

State Judges

George Minos Bibb '92
Jacob Burnet '91
George Washington Campbell '94
Peter Early '92

William Belford Ewing '94
Richard Hall Harwood '91
Titus Hutchinson '94
Robert Ogden IV '93

State Attorneys-General

Titus Hutchinson '94

Joseph Reed, Jr. '92

Other High State Offices

Allen Bowie Duckett '91

Joseph Reed, Jr. '92

Members of U.S. House of Representatives

Thomas Monteagle Bayly '94
James Madison Broom '94
George Washington Campbell '94
William Chetwood '92
John Dennis '91

Peter Early '92
George Clifford Maxwell '92
John Randolph '91
Isaac Wayne '91

Members of U.S. Senate

George Minos Bibb '92
Jacob Burnet '91

George Washington Campbell '94
John Randolph '91

U.S. Secretaries of the Treasury

George Minos Bibb '92

George Washington Campbell '94

U.S. Diplomatic Service

George Washington Campbell '94
Maltby Gelston '91

John Randolph '91

U.S. District Attorneys

George Minos Bibb '92

Titus Hutchinson '94

U.S. District Judges

Allen Bowie Duckett '91

George Clifford Maxwell '92

Presidential Elector

Titus Hutchinson '94

THOSE PERFORMING SOME FORM OF MILITARY SERVICE DURING:

Revolutionary War

James Gildersleeve Force '94

Whiskey Rebellion

William Chetwood '92   Charles Ross '91

Quasi-War with France

Edward F. Conrad '93   William Ludwell Lee '94
Horatio Rolfe Dayton '94   George Washington Morton '92
Henry Hollyday '91   James T. Stelle '93
William Arden Hosack '92   Alexander Stewart '93
Thomas Yardley How '94   Job Stockton '92
Robert Hunt '93

War of 1812

Thomas Monteagle Bayly '94   Jacob Stern Thomson '92
Nicholas C. Everett '94   Isaac Wayne '91
Henry Hollyday '91   William Rickets Williamson '94
John Neilson '93   George Willing '92
Charles Ross '91   Richard Willing '93
James T. Stelle '93

APPENDIX D

ERRATA AND ADDITIONS
FOR FIRST THREE VOLUMES,
COMPILED BY
RUTH L. WOODWARD

===

PRINCETONIANS: 1748-1768

p. xvi—In the second new paragraph change "William A. Dix" to "William S. Dix.'

p. xxvii—Under *Presbyterian Encyclopaedia* correct the name of the editor of *Encyclopaedia of the Presbyterian Church in the United States of America* to "Alfred Nevin."

p. 70—Add to the third sentence of the last paragraph of Browne sketch, "... and on February 21 of that year he was commissioned justice of the peace for Annapolis County." Change the last sentence of the sketch to read: "He died on February 24, 1799 with an Anna Browne named as his executrix. It is not known whether she was his wife or another relative. In 1800 Browne's Annapolis County lands reverted to the crown by escheat." Add to sources: "Public Archives of Nova Scotia, Halifax: N.S. Commission Book, 1781-1783 [sic], 70; Paymaster General's Records, Half-Pay Ledgers, 4th Ser., vol. 62, p. 182."

p. 114—Change the last two sentences of Ramsey sketch to read: "Three of the boys were raised by their uncle in Charleston, South Carolina, and John attended the College as a member of the class of 1787 but did not graduate. Ramsay's widow married the Reverend Robert Smith of Pequea, Pennsylvania, the father of Samuel Stanhope Smith (A.B. 1769), John Blair Smith (A.B. 1773), and William Richmond Smith (A.B. 1773)."

p. 133—Reference in sources to *Fithian Journal* should be changed from "133-34" to "33-34."

p. 195—In two sentences in the first complete paragraph delete "s" from "Cummings" to read "Cumming."

p. 231—Add to the last sentence of P. R. Livingston sketch: "eleven children, including Peter William Livingston (A.B. 1786)."

p. 244—Change the first sentence of Smith sketch to read: "... was born in 1737 at Maidenhead ..."

p. 245—Add to sources: "*GMNJ*, 46 (1971), 54-55."

p. 273—In the second sentence of the second paragraph change date to "August 1, 1762."

p. 274—Add to sources: "E. Wheelock, *Continuation of the Narrative of the State, & of the Indian Charity-School, at Lebanon, in Conn., from Nov. 27, 1762 to Nov. 27, 1765* (1765)."

p. 300—Add to the second paragraph of Alexander sketch: "Alexander was also an uncle of Joseph McKnitt Alexander, Jr. (A.B. 1792)."

p. 326—In J. B. Smith sketch delete the last sentence of the second paragraph and substitute: "The Smiths had two daughters and two sons: Samuel Harrison Smith, who became editor of the Washington *National Intelligencer*, and John Rhea Smith (A.B. 1787), who practiced law in Philadelphia. Smith also had a son and daughter by a second wife whose identity has not been discovered."

p. 328—Add to sources: "Jonathan Bayard Smith Collection, Peter Force MSS Collection, DLC."

p. 350—In second paragraph change Oliver Livermore Ker degree to "A.B. 1785."

p. 351—In John Lefferty sketch change the second sentence of the second paragraph to read: "On May 6, 1766 Lefferty married Elizabeth Johnes, daughter of Timothy Johnes, ..."

p. 373—Insert at the end of the second sentence of the last paragraph: "although she died later the same year." Change the fifth sentence to begin: "On April 1, 1773 Bainbridge moved ..."

p. 374—Insert at the beginning of the fifth paragraph: "Bainbridge enlisted in the British forces the first week of December 1776."

p. 413—In sources delete "GMNJ, 85 (1954), 85-88."

p. 482—In John Bay sketch delete "A.M. 1765" in first sentence.

p. 489—In the first paragraph change the sentence beginning: "His standing" to read: "... for support of Washington College in Chestertown, Kent County, on Maryland's Eastern Shore, a project ..." Add to sources: L. W. Barroll, "Washington College, 1783," MHM, 6 (1911), 164-79."

p. 525—In sixth sentence of second paragraph, after "Schranenburgh," insert "Bergen County, New Jersey."

p. 531—In John Staples sketch, add to the third full sentence of the lead paragraph: "sister of Nathan Perkins (A.B. 1770) and Matthew Perkins (Class of 1777)."

p. 533—In the last sentence of the first paragraph of Van Arsdale sketch, after "five children" insert "including Elias Van Arsdale (A.B. 1791)."

p. 550—Add to sources of Burt sketch: "The diary of the Reverend Samuel Jones, 1757, reprinted in the 1882 Hopewell Herald as 'Old School Days at Hopewell Academy' lists one of the students at the academy in 1757 as 'Burt,' with no first name given. He was in the '1st class' with James Manning (A.B. 1762)." This reference courtesy of Virginia Creesy.

pp. 552-53—The third from last sentence of the Clymer sketch should read: "A candidate for Congress on the Federalist ticket in 1798, he was defeated (3,356 votes to 797) by a Democratic-Republican, Joseph Hiester, who later became governor of Pennsylvania and was also the father of John Sylvanus Hiester (A.B. 1794)."

p. 553—Add to sources of Clymer sketch: "H. M. Tincom, Republicans & Federalists in Pa., 1790-1801 (1950), 189."

p. 597—Add to last paragraph of Benjamin Stelle sketch: Cousins of different degrees were James T. Stelle (A.B. 1793), Stelle Fitz Randolph (A.B. 1802), and Ephraim Fitz Randolph Smith (A.B. 1804).

p. 633—In the last sentence of the opening paragraph after "George Willing" insert "(A.B. 1792)."

p. 638—In the listing of children near the end of the second paragraph, change the sentence to read, "among them John Stark Edwards (A.B. 1796), Henry Waggaman Edwards (A.B. 1797) who became a governor of Connecticut, and Moses Ogden Edwards (Class of 1800)."

p. 689—"Hanna, William (1789)," should be changed to "Hanna, William (1790)." Delete "Heister, Joseph, 553."

p. 690—Add "Hiester, Joseph, 553."

p. 691—Insert "Johnes" as preferred spelling for "Johns, Elizabeth, 351" and "Johns, Timothy, 351."

PRINCETONIANS: 1769-1775

p. xxxiv—*MHSP* is abbreviation for *Massachusetts Historical Society Proceedings*, not *Publications*.

p. 118—In the first sentence of the second paragraph change "Botecourt" to "Botetourt."

p. 177—Change the genealogical information in the first paragraph to read: "Information pieced together from documents and genealogical lists reproduced in W. S. Ray, *Mecklenburg Signers & Their Neighbors* (1946), shows that Isaac Alexander's mother was Dorcas Alexander. Evan Alexander (A.B. 1787) was a first cousin. Joseph Alexander (A.B. 1760) and Joseph McKnitt Alexander, Jr. (A.B. 1792) were sons of two first cousins of his father. Nathaniel Alexander (A.B. 1776) was probably a distant cousin, but the relationship cannot be definitely traced."

p. 236—Change the third sentence of the first paragraph to read: "Livingston was the older brother of Peter R. (A.B. 1784) and Maturin (A.B. 1786) and of Susannah Livingston, who became the wife of James Francis Armstrong (A.B. 1773) and the mother of Robert Livingston Armstrong (A.B. 1802). He was also the cousin, uncle, or nephew of several Livingstons and Smiths who were fellow alumni."

p. 352—Change the first paragraph of Lewis Feuilleteau Wilson sketch to read: "Lewis Feuilleteau Wilson, A.B., physician and Presbyterian clergyman, was born on St. Christopher in the British West Indies in June 1752. He was the son of Mary Feuilleteau and Richard Wilson, a wealthy sugar planter, and the grandson of Richard Wilson, chief justice of St. Christopher. The father moved to London about 1758, and Lewis was educated in England until 'about the 17th year of his age,' when he came to America with an uncle who settled in New Jersey."

p. 354—Add to sources—"Genealogical information supplied by Robert G. Harper, Washington, D.C."

p. 369—In the third sentence of the second complete paragraph, after "Jacob Read," insert "brother of James Bond Read (Class of 1787)."

PRINCETONIANS: 1776-1783

p. xxxviii—*MHSP* is abbreviation for *Massachusetts Historical Society Proceedings*, not *Publications*.

p. 16—The last paragraph of Beekman sketch should be changed to read: "At Trinity Church, New York City, on June 17, 1800, Beekman married Lydia Watkins Drew, widow of Capt. James Drew and daughter of John Watkins and Lydia Stillwell. They had no children. Beekman died on April 8, 1837 and his estate went to a nephew." Add to sources: G. E. McCracken, *The Commodore's Kinsmen* (1984), sec. 1817.

p. 56—Add to Johnes sketch: "Johnes was followed at the College by several nephews—Timothy Ford (A.B. 1783), Gabriel Ford (A.B. 1784), Jacob Ford (A.B. 1792), and Stevens Johnes Lewis (A.B. 1791)."

p. 88—In the second line of the third full paragraph "Dr. Samuel Hays" should be changed to "Dr. Samuel Hayes (A.B. 1795)."

p. 118—Add "William Snowden (Class of 1794)" to the list of brothers in the first paragraph of the Benjamin P. Snowden sketch, and change "five sons" to "six sons."

p. 286—In the middle of the page, after "on January 1, 1777," insert "with the pseudonym Rollin, for the French educator and historian of antiquity, Charles Rollin (1661-1741)."

p. 288—Add to sources: "Cliosophic Society membership lists, PUA."

pp. 293-96—John Rhea (A.B. 1780) is here identified as probably being the son of Jonathan Rhea of Freehold, New Jersey, who was a brother of John Rhea, the Philadelphia merchant. But the College's Rhea was "of Pennsylvania," and there is no reason to believe that this information is incorrect. Additional research has persuaded the editors that a much more likely identification of the Princetonian is John Rhea of Philadelphia, older brother of Ebenezer Rhea (A.B. 1791). Records of the Second Presbyterian Church of Philadelphia show that John and Mary Smith Rhea also had a son John, born on June 30, 1762, and baptized in the Presbyterian Church in September of that year, making him the same age as the John Rhea of Freehold. Genealogical records indicate that the John Rhea born in Philadelphia was the third child and eldest son of his parents. He enrolled in the preparatory school of the College of Philadelphia during 1771 and 1772. His withdrawal at that point may have been due to the death of his father in March 1773.

Second Presbyterian Church records also show that on December 1, 1780 a John Rhea married Hulda Montgomery of Bucks County. Hulda was a widow, the daughter of Henry and Mary Wilkinson Huddleston of Bucks County. A Huddleston family genealogy says that "Huldah Huddleston" moved with her brothers to Bedford County, presumably after her widowhood, and there married "John Ray," with whom she settled in the Chester District of South Carolina. Supporting the removal to this location is a power of attorney (date illegible) executed by Nathan Huddleston, as surviving executor of the will of his father Henry Huddleston. This document authorized John Ray to sell the thirty-three acres "devised to my sister Hulday [sic] Ray formerly Huldah Montgomery." The will was dated February 21, 1780 and proved March 14, 1780.

This John Ray was still listed in Bedford County, Pennsylvania, in the 1790 census. His household also contained one male under sixteen and two females. By 1798 he had moved south, for on April 16 he was among a group of men assigned the unglamorous task of keeping "Loves old road" repaired in Chester County, South Carolina. J. Ray in Chester District was included in each decennial census from 1800 through 1830. The last enumeration places him next door to his son-in-law Joseph Shaddinger. Ray did not achieve prominence, for he is mentioned in no other public records. If this John Ray was the Princetonian, he must have died after the 1830 census was compiled but before the College's 1830 catalogue was published.

A family history written by Lewis Krumbhaar, the grandson of Mary Rhea Turnbull, elder sister of John and Ebenezer Rhea, has John migrating further west. If so, he must have been a different person from the South Carolinian, or—more likely—his descendants moved further west after his death in 1830. Shaddinger was not listed in South Carolina censuses after that year. Krumbhaar's account is describing the same family, even though it includes the unlikely claim that "John Rhea settled in the West in Kentucky, I think, or Tennessee, never returning to this City not even for a visit, thus was separated from the family and as travelling in those days was attended with difficulties, intercourse with him was cut off and little was known of him."

The Huddleston family genealogy lists five children of Huldah, with the comment that it was not known which were Montgomerys and which

"Rays." Sarah, the third child, was born in 1788, and so it is possible that all of the children were born of the Rhea marriage, especially since the two eldest were given the names of John Rhea's parents, Mary and John. Hulda Shaddinger Oberst of Somerville, Tennessee, traced her descent for admission to the Daughters of the American Revolution through Sarah to John Ray and Hulda Huddleston. She claimed that her great-grandfather was born in Philadelphia County in 1760 and served as a sergeant in the Tenth Pennsylvania Regiment in 1778. The two-year discrepancy in the birth date can easily be explained by a boy's falsifying his age to qualify for enlistment. Since his commencement in 1780 is the only recorded occasion when Rhea was at the College, it is quite possible that he either matriculated in the fall of 1778 for his junior year, or enrolled earlier and absented himself for a year of military service. Neither would have been unusual at the time.

College catalogues first list Rhea as deceased in 1830. See records of the 2nd Pres. Church of Phila., PHi; L. Krumbhaar, notebook entitled "Frege & Early Krumbhaar also Rheas & some Trumbull," part of MS on "Krumbhaar-Frege Families," Collections of Geneal. Soc. of Pa. at PHi; MS College of Philadelphia tuition book, UPenn-Ar; G. Huddleston, *Huddleston Family Tables* (1933), 56-58; "Bucks Cnty., Pa. Abstracts of Wills, 1685-1795," book no. 4: 69, bound MS in collection of Geneal. Soc. of Pa. at PHi; Daughters of the Amer. Rev., *D.A.R. Patriot Index* (1966), 558; Daughters of the Amer. Rev., *Lineage Book*, 104 (1913 pub. 1928), 145 (D.A.R. no. 103478); *First Census, Pa.*, 21; B. H. Holcomb & E. O. Parker, *Chester Cnty., S.C. Minutes of the Cnty. Court 1785-99* (1979), 388 ("Loves old road"); R. V. Jackson & G. R. Teeples, *S.C. 1800 Census* (2d ed., 1975); same, *S.C. 1810 Census Index*

(1976); same, *S.C. 1820 Census Index* (1976); same, *S.C. 1830 Census Index* (1976); microfilm of Huddleston family records, Warren S. Ely Collection, PHi.

p. 294—In the sources, change the sentence in the middle of the second paragraph to read: "John, son of Jonathan Rhea of Freehold, appears to have been the brother of one graduate and the cousin of two."

p. 303—Insert after the first sentence of Stockton sketch: "His brother Job was a nongraduating member of the Class of 1792."

p. 306—Add to the second sentence of the Abraham Bedford Venable sketch: "and a cousin of Henry Edward Watkins (A.B. 1801)."

p. 310—Add to the first sentence of the Samuel Woodson Venable sketch: "and cousin of Henry Edward Watkins (A.B. 1801)."

p. 331—The opening sentence of the second paragraph of the James sketch should read: "James was married to Nancy Stockton, daughter of Maj. Robert Stockton of Princeton and sister of Ebenezer Stockton (A.B. 1780) and Job Stockton (Class of 1792), at a time ..."

p. 332, line 5—Insert after "Peter R. Livingston (A.B. 1784)": "and Maturin Livingston (A.B. 1786). Edward's sister-in-law Susannah became the wife of James Francis Armstrong (A.B. 1773) and the mother of Robert Livingston Armstrong (A.B. 1802). Edward was also the cousin, uncle, or nephew of several Livingstons and Smiths who were fellow alumni."

p. 388—Add to the second sentence of Richard N. Venable sketch: "as well as a cousin of Henry Edward Watkins (A.B. 1801)."

p. 401—Add at the end of the first paragraph of the Ford sketch: "William Johnes (Class of 1776) was his uncle, and Stevens Johnes Lewis (A.B. 1791) was a cousin."

p. 402—Add at the end of the third complete paragraph: "The following

year he visited his family in Morristown, returning to Charleston in early
November."

p. 403—In the first complete paragraph
change the third sentence to read:
"Sarah died in May 1799, and on
November 18, 1800 Ford married
Mary Magdalen Prioleau, ..."

p. 404—Add to sources: "*NJHSP*, 61
(1943), 197."

p. 430—Near the end of the second
paragraph change sentence to read:
"Perhaps their meetings were only
incidental, since LeRoy's daughter
Maria Anna (Mary Ann) had, in May
1775, married John Livingston, son of
Robert, third Lord of the Manor, and
apparently Smith ..."

p. 443—Change the third sentence of the
second paragraph to read: "He was
soon admitted to the rival Cliosophic
Society, where he assumed the name
of Swift, no doubt for the satirist
Jonathan Swift. This action led to ..."

p. 445—Add at the end of the first
complete paragraph: "A diary of his
brother Nathaniel places Gilbert in
Maryland in March 1788." The last
sentence of the second complete paragraph should read: "Earlier he had
married Ruth Lott of Princeton, sister
of Ralph Lott (Class of 1790), and by
1794 they had two daughters."

p. 446—After the second full sentence
of the last paragraph in the Snowden
sketch, copy should read: "Dissatisfied with the parsonage allotted

to him, Snowden had had an 'elegant' house built for his family in
1794 at a cost of $3,500. In addi-
tion to all its furnishings, his possessions at the time of his death included
surveying instruments, two spy glasses, books valued at £500, and three
slaves. He may have overextended
himself financially, since correspondence between two of his brothers
indicates that their father was embarrassed by the state of Gilbert's affairs.
On August 23, 1797 the elder Snowden bought the Cranbury house for
his own occupancy at the bargain
price of $1,600. Nathaniel Snowden
thought for a time that he might
take over his brother's congregation,
but Gilbert's pulpit at the Cranbury
church went instead to George Spafford Woodhull (A.B. 1790). On April
30, 1801 Snowden's widow married
the Reverend Andrew King (A.B.
1773)." Add to sources: "Clio. Soc.
Min., 25 Sept. 1792, 30 Sept. 1795,
28 Sept. 1796 (Clio. pseudonym and
attendance at three annual meetings,
that of 1792 in the office of second
assistant), PUA; N. R. Snowden, MS
Diary, 1788-89, PHi."

p. 455—Add at the end of the lead
paragraph: "Patrick Houstoun (A.B.
1795) was Jean Woodruff's younger
brother."

p. 465—Delete "John Armstrong, Jr. '76"
from the list of "Members of the Constitutional Convention of 1787."

INDEX

This index is alphabetized by letter, not by word. All women are cross-referenced by maiden name and by all married names included within an individual biography. A single date within parentheses following a male name indicates a Princetonian and the class to which he belonged. The name of every matriculate for whom a biography appears in this volume is listed in italic type, as is the location of the sketch, which follows immediately after the class identification. In the case of identical family names the relationship to the College of New Jersey student is indicated in parentheses as, for example, father or son. Non-family members with identical names are identified by profession or place of residence. Place names are made specific by including the colony or state, and occasionally the county. Abbreviations for states follow standard postal usage.

Badollet, John, 81
Bahama Islands, 172
Bailey, Aeltje Van Wyck, 9
Bailey, Esther. *See* Bleecker, Esther Bailey Linn
Bailey, James. P. *See* Bayley (Bayly, Bailey), James P. (1792)
Bailey, Col. John, 9
Bainbridge, Abigail White, 502
Bainbridge, Absalom (1762), 502
Baker, Bryant, xi, 159
Baker, Elizabeth Thomson. *See* Harris, Elizabeth Thomson Baker
Baker, Frances Stelle, 304
Baker, Joshua, 304
Baldwin, John (1784), 489
balls. *See* dancing
Baltimore, MD: defense of in 1814, 110; Episcopal church, 187; married at, 113, 251n; merchants, 255; musical instrument repair at, 255; physicians, 251n; portraiture at, 423n; practiced law at, 337; residents of, 307n, 338, 446; wife from, 255, 354
Baltimore City Hospital, MD, 251n
Bancroft, George, 216
Bane, Jane. *See* Alexander, Jane Bane
Bank of Delaware, 334, 338
Bank of New Brunswick, NJ, 441
Bank of North America, Philadelphia, PA, 243, 320
Bank of Tennessee: Nashville branch, 349
Bank of the Commonwealth, KY, 140, 141
Bank of the Manhattan Company, NY, 56
Bank of the State of Tennessee, 349
Bank of the United States, First, 243, 320
Bank of the United States, Second: Baltimore, MD, branch, 18; Cincinnati, OH, branch, 17-18; created (1816), 347; directors, 263, 264; Nashville, TN, branch, 349; opponent, 98; and Panic of 1837, 56-57; supporters, 155, 347, 349, 459; supporters, ambivalent, 142-43
bankruptcy, 74, 459
banks and banking: and Embargo, 406; land banks, 140, 141; national bank attacked, 98; national bank defended, 142, 155, 347, 349, 459; and Panic of 1819, 17-18, 349; and Panic of 1837, 56-57; and War of 1812, 347
by location: in DE, 334, 338; in KY, 140, 141; in MD, 18, 49, 65; in NJ, 86, 116, 154, 284, 441, 463, 464; in NY,

56-57, 144; in OH, 17-18; in PA, 223, 238, 243, 245, 263, 264, 320, 386; in SC, 150; in TN, 349; in VT, 406
officers and investors: cashiers, 386, 441; commissioner, 86; depositor, 463; directors, 49, 65, 150, 154, 263, 264, 284, 338, 349, 406, 441; directors, chairman of the board of, 334; presidents, 17-18, 56-57, 116, 154, 243, 320, 386, 406; stockholders, 49, 65, 238, 245, 464; vice president, 349
Baptist Church, U.S.A.: and CNJ alumni, xxxv
Barber, Anne Ogden, 154
Barber, Edward D., 407
Barber, Francis (1767), 154, 156n, 292
Barber, George Clinton (1796), 154, 292
Barber, Mary. *See* Chetwood, Mary Barber
Barber, Mary Ogden, 292
Barbour, James, 98
Barclay, Catherine Gordon, 3
Barclay, Charles, 3
Barclay, Charles Ray (Ried) (1816), 6
Barclay, David (1791), *3-7*, lvi
Barclay, David (cousin), 7n
Barclay, Mrs. Francis, 187
Barclay, Rev. Francis, 187
Barclay, John, 3, 7n
Barclay, Mary Dey (Dye), 3, 5
Barclay, Robert (cousin of David), 7n
Barclay, Robert (pedestrian). *See* Allardice, Robert Barclay
Barclay, Robert (Quaker apologist), 3
Barclay Square, Punxsutawney, PA, 6
Bardstown, KY, 138
Barrett, Robert, 478
Barry, William T., 143
Bartas, Guillaume du, 3
Basking Ridge, NJ, 66, 199, 200, 229, 230, 440, 481; Presbyterian church, 3, 397, 440
Basking Ridge Library Company, NJ, 440
Bassett, Burwell, 331
"baste ball," xix
Bastille Day: celebrated at CNJ, xviii-xix
Bateman, Ephraim, 368, 369
Bath, England, 320
Bath, PA, 223
Bath Co., VA, 218
battledores, xix
Baumholder, Germany, 258
Bay, Ann Williams, 327
Bay, Catharine Van Ness, 327
Bay, John, 329
Bay, John (1765), 327, 502

Homer: works read at CNJ, xxiv
Honeyman, Elizabeth, 312
Honorius: Cliosophic Society
    pseudonym, 340
Hooper, Helen Hogg. See Caldwell,
    Helen Hogg Hooper
Hooper, Thomas Clark, 32
Hooper, William, 32
Hoops, Adam (1777), 301, 357-58
Hope, Henry, 216
Hope Lodge (estate), PA, 216
Hopewell, NJ, 421; Old School Baptist
    Church, 421
Hopewell, NY, 314, 316
Hopewell, SC: Old Stone Church, 428;
    Presbyterian church, 427, 428
Hopewell Academy, NJ, 502
Hopewell Academy, SC, 428
Hopewell Cemetery, SC, 428
Hopewell Presbyterian Church, NC, 131,
    132, 133
Hopewell Township, NJ, 378, 394
Hopewell Township, PA, 481, 486
Hopkins, Samuel, l-li
Hopper, Mary Anne. See Bordley, Mary
    Anne Hopper Blake
Hopper, Mary Anne Wright, 10
Hopper, William, 10
Horace: works read at CNJ, xxiv; works
    read by women, 315
Horatio: Cliosophic Society pseudonym,
    40
Horatio (character in play), 472-73
Horseshoe, PA, 79
Horsfall, Mary. See Wikoff, Mary Hors-
    fall
Hosack, Alexander, 178, 181
Hosack, Alexander, Jr., 182
Hosack, David (1789), xxi, xli, xlii, 178-
    82, 290
Hosack, Jane Arden, 178
Hosack, W. E. See Hossack (Hosack), W.
    E.
Hosack, William Arden (1792), *178-83*, xxi,
    xlii, 265
hospitals, 108, 205, 206, 251n, 429, 435,
    437-38, 451
Hossack (Hosack), W. E., 183n
Houston, William Churchill (1768), xxvii
Houstoun, Jean (Jane). See Woodruff,
    Jean (Jane) Houstoun
Houstoun, Patrick (1795), 506
How, Angelica Van Rensselaer, 393
How, Elizabeth Woodruff, 393
How, Micajah, 387, 388, 390
How, Sarah Field, 265, 387, 388
How, Thomas Y., Jr., 393

How, Thomas Yardley (1794), *387-94*, lvi,
    29, 265, 269, 342
Howard, Joseph, 48
Howard, Margaret. See Duckett, Mar-
    garet Howard
Howard, Margaret Hall, 48
Howard, Samuel Harvey, 49
Howard, Susanna. See Edmondson,
    Susanna Howard
Howe, Nathaniel (1786), xliii, lvi
Howell, David (1766), xx
Howell, Mary. See Pierson, Mary Howell
Howell, Richard, 238
Howells (estate), VA, 309
Howells Point (estate), MD, 45
Hubley, Adam, 301
Hubley, Lydia Field. See Stelle, Lydia
    Field Hubley
Huddleston, Henry, 504
Huddleston, Hulda. See Rhea, Hulda
    (Huldah, Hulday) Huddleston Mont-
    gomery
Huddleston, Mary Wilkinson, 504
Huddleston, Nathan, 504
Hude, James, 422
Hude, Susan. See Neilson, Susan Hude
Hudson, Presbytery of, 314
Hudson Co., NJ, 365
Huger, Ann Broun Cusack, 281
Huger, Benjamin J. (1850), 282
Huger, Charlotte Motte, 280
Huger, Daniel, 281, 282n
Huger, Daniel Elliott (1798), 282
Huger, Daniel Lionel (1789), 282
Huger, Jacob Motte (1793), *280-82*, 287
Huger, John, 280, 281
Huger (Hugher), Samuel. See Hughes,
    Samuel (1792)
Hughes, Ball, 279
Hughes, Daniel, 183, 184
Hughes, Mrs. —— Holker, 184
Hughes, John, 183
Hughes, Margaret Chamberlaine, 183,
    254
Hughes, Marie Antoinette, 184
Hughes, Napoleon B., 184
Hughes, Rebecca Lux, 183
Hughes, Robert (1787), 183, 254
Hughes, Samuel, 183
Hughes, Samuel (1792), *183-84*, 254
Huguenot ancestry, 208, 300, 327, 477-
    78
Hume, David: Cliosophic Society
    pseudonym, 150; Walter Minto stud-
    ies with, xxvii; works owned or read by
    alumni, 26, 60
Hunt, Abraham, 62, 63, 282, 283